Senior

Biology 1

2004

Student Resource and Activity Manual

BIOZONE

Senior Biology 1 2004

Student Resource and Activity Manual

Previous annual editions 2002-2003
Third Edition 2004

ISBN 1-877329-09-6

Copyright © **2003** Richard Allan
Published by **BIOZONE International Ltd**
Printed in New Zealand using paper from
sustainably managed forests

About the Writing Team

Tracey Greenwood joined the staff of BIOZONE at the beginning of 1993. She has a Ph.D. in biology, specialising in lake ecology, and taught undergraduate and graduate biology at the University of Waikato for four years.

Richard Allan has had 11 years experience teaching senior biology at Hillcrest High School in Hamilton, New Zealand. He attained a Masters degree in biology at Waikato University, New Zealand.

The authors acknowledge and thank our graphic artist **Daniel Butler** for his tireless pursuit of the perfect 3-D image.

Purchases of this manual may be made direct from the publisher:

BIOZONE   **www.thebiozone.com**

EUROPE & MIDDLE EAST:
BIOZONE Learning Media (UK) Ltd.
P.O. Box 16710, Glasgow G12 9WS
United Kingdom
Telephone: +44 (141) 337 3355
FAX: +44 (141) 337 2266
E-mail: info@biozone.co.uk

ASIA & AUSTRALIA:
BIOZONE Learning Media Australia
P.O. Box 7523, GCMC 4217 QLD
Australia
Telephone: +61 (7) 5575 4615
FAX: +61 (7) 5572 0161
E-mail: info@biozone.com.au

NORTH & SOUTH AMERICA, AFRICA:
BIOZONE International Ltd.
P.O. Box 13-034, Hamilton
New Zealand
Telephone: +64 (7) 856 8104
FAX: +64 (7) 856 9243
E-mail: sales@biozone.co.nz

Preface to the Year 2004 Edition

This is the third edition of **Senior Biology 1**. It is designed to meet the needs of students undertaking biology at grades 11 and 12 or equivalent. It is particularly well suited to students taking **Advanced Placement** (AP), **Honors Biology**, or **International Baccalaureate** courses. Our Senior Biology 1 and 2 manuals cater for a wide audience, and may contain more material than is required by any one particular biology course. Due to the large amount of material covered, and the inconvenience that one large write-on resource would create, we have produced two smaller manuals. Note that the order in which topics are taught is usually at the discretion of each school; we therefore recommend purchasing both manuals at the commencement of the course. Previous editions have received very favorable reviews; see our web site: **www.the biozone.com** for details. This year we have continued to refine the stimulus material in the manual to improve its accessibility and interest level. In response to input from users, we have also removed the video and software listings from each topic and have included them in a supplementary product, the **Teacher Resource Handbook** (on CD-ROM), which is available free of charge with the first order of five or more manuals. This handbook also contains a detailed account of changes in the manual since the previous edition (previously provided as a looseleaf handout) and expanded and updated information on the suppliers of scientific equipment and the publishers of all listed software and video resources. Because supplier information is more appropriate to teachers, this information has also been removed from the introductory section in the manual. As in previous years, we have updated all our lists of resources: comprehensive and supplementary textbooks, video documentaries, computer software, periodicals, and internet sites. Most topics this year contain upgraded material, and there are a number of new activities. Check the contents pages for information on these. These annual upgrades are in keeping with our ongoing commitment to providing up-to-date, relevant, interesting, and accurate information to students and teachers.

A Note to the Teacher

This manual has been produced as a student-centered resource, aimed at facilitating independent learning. By providing a highly visual format, a clear map through the course, and a synopsis of available supplemental resources, these manuals will motivate and challenge a wide range of students. Today, many teachers are finding that a single textbook does not provide all of the information they need. This manual is **not a textbook**. It is a generic resource and, to this end, we have made a point of referencing texts from other publishers. Above all, we are committed to continually revising and improving this resource **each and every year**. The price, at only US$17 for student purchase, is a reflection of our commitment to providing high-quality, cost effective resources for biology. Please do not treat this resource as a *photocopy master* for your own handouts. We simply cannot afford to supply single copies of manuals to schools and continue to provide annual updates as we intend. Please **do not photocopy** from this manual. If you think it is worth using, then we recommend that the students themselves own this resource and keep it for their own use. A free model answer book is supplied, with the Teacher Resource Handbook, with your **first order** of 5 or more manuals.

How Teachers May Use This Manual

This manual may be used in the classroom to guide students through each topic. Some activities may be used to introduce topics while others may be used to consolidate and test concepts already covered by other means. The manual may be used as the primary tool in teaching some topics, but it should not be at the expense of good, 'hands-on' biology. Students may attempt the activities on their own or in groups. The latter provides opportunities for healthy discussion and peer-to-peer learning. Many of the activities may be set as homework exercises. Each page is perforated, allowing for easy removal of pages that must be submitted for formal marking. Teachers may prescribe the specific activities to be attempted by the students (using the check boxes next to the objectives for each topic), or they may allow students a degree of freedom with respect to the activities they attempt. The objectives for each topic will allow students to keep up to date even if they miss lessons. Teachers who are away from class may set work easily in their absence.

I thank you for your support.

Richard Allan

Acknowledgements

We would like to thank the people who have contributed to this edition:
• Dan Butler for his cheerful attack on graphics • Stacey Farmer and Greg Baillie, Waikato DNA Sequencing Facility, University of Waikato, for their assistance with material on PCR, DNA sequencing, and genetic profiling • Jan Morrison for her diagrams • Nathalie Loussert for proofreading • Mary McDougall and Sue FitzGerald for their efficient handling of the office • TechPool Studios, for their clipart collection of human anatomy: Copyright ©1994, TechPool Studios Corp. USA (some of these images were modified by R. Allan and T. Greenwood) • Totem Graphics, for their clipart collection • Corel Corporation, for use of their eps clipart of plants and animals from the Corel MEGAGALLERY collection

Photo Credits

Royalty free images, purchased by Biozone International Ltd, are used throughout this manual and have been obtained from the following sources: **Corel** Corporation from various titles in their Professional Photos CD-ROM collection; **IMSI** (International Microcomputer Software Inc.) images from IMSI's MasterClips® and MasterPhotosTM Collection, 1895 Francisco Blvd. East, San Rafael, CA 94901-5506, USA; ©1996 **Digital Stock**, Medicine and Health Care collection; ©**Hemera** Technologies Inc, 1997-2001; ArtToday ©1999-2001 www.arttoday.com; ©Click Art, ©T/Maker Company; ©1994., ©**Digital Vision**; Gazelle Technologies Inc.; **PhotoDisc**®, Inc. USA, www.photodisc.com • 3D modeling software, Poser IV (Curious Labs) and Bryce.

We would like to thank the following individuals and institutions who kindly provided photographs: • Dena Borchardt at HGSI for photos of large scale DNA sequencing • Campus Photography at the Uni. of Waikato (NZ) for photographs of monitoring equipment • Genesis Research and Development Corp. Auckland (NZ), for the photo used on the HGP activity • Kurchatov Inst., for the photo of Chornobyl • Stephen Moore, for his photos of stream invertebrates • PASCO for their photographs of probeware (available for students of biology in the USA) • Pharmacia (Aust) Ltd. for providing the photographs of DNA gel sequencing • The Roslin Institute, for their photographs of Dolly • Dr. Nita Scobie, Cytogenetics Department, Waikato Hospital (NZ) for chromosome photographs • Jane Ussher, for her photo of the albatross bycatch • Dr. David Wells, Agresearch, NZ, for his photos on cattle cloning.

Contributors identified by coded credits are as follows: **AT**: ArtToday ©1999-2001 www.arttoday.com, **BF**: Brian Finerran (Uni. of Canterbury), **BH**: Brendan Hicks (Uni. of Waikato), **BOB**: Barry O'Brien (Uni. of Waikato), **CDC**: Centers for Disease Control and Prevention, Atlanta, USA, **COD**: Colin O'Donnell, **DEQ**: Dept of Environment Queensland Ltd., **DOC**: Dept of Conservation (NZ), **EII**: Education Interactive Imaging, **EW**: Environment Waikato, **FRI**: Forest Research Institute, **GT**: ©1994 Gazelle Technologies Inc., **GW**: Graham Walker, **HGSI**: Human Genome Sciences Inc., **JDG**: John Green (Uni. of Waikato), **MPI**: Max Planck Institute for Developmental Biology, Germany; **NASA**: National Aeronautics and Space Administration, **NOAA**: National Oceanic and Atmospheric Administration www.photolib.noaa.gov **RA**: Richard Allan, **RCN**: Ralph Cocklin, **TG**: Tracey Greenwood, **VM**: Villa Maria Wines, **WBS**: Warwick Silvester (Uni. of Waikato), **WMU**: Waikato Microscope Unit.

Special thanks to all the partners of the Biozone team for their support.

Cover Photographs

Main photograph: The distinctive warning coloration of the painted mantella (*Mantella baroni*) advertises its highly poisonous nature. Although still relatively abundant in its range in eastern Madagascar, a large number are captured for the pet trade. PHOTO: FPG/Imagesource.
Background photograph: SEM of the inside of the atrium of a human heart. PHOTO: © 1996 Digital Stock Corporation, Medicine and Healthcare collection.

Contents

CODES: Δ **Upgraded** this edition   ☆ **New** this edition   **Activity** is marked: • to be done; ✓ when completed

CONTENTS *(continued)*

CODES: Δ **Upgraded** this edition   ☆ **New** this edition   **Activity** is marked: • to be done;   ✔ when completed

CONTENTS *(continued)*

CODES: Δ **Upgraded** this edition ☆ **New** this edition Activity is marked: • to be done; ✓ when completed

How to Use this Manual

This manual is designed to provide you with a resource that will make the subject of biology more enjoyable and fun to study. The manual addresses the requirements of the **International Baccalaureate** (IB) and **Advanced Placement** (AP) courses. Consult the Syllabus Guides on pages 12-14 of this manual to establish where material for

your syllabus is covered. It is hoped that this manual will reinforce and extend the ideas developed by your teacher. It must be emphasized that this manual is **not a textbook**. It is designed to complement the biology textbooks provided for your course. The manual provides the following useful resources for each topic:

Guidance Provided for Each Topic

Learning objectives:

These provide you with a map of the topic content. Completing the relevant learning objectives will help you to satisfy the knowledge requirements of your course. Your teacher may decide to leave out points or add to this list.

Topic outcomes:

This panel provides details of the learning objectives that need to be completed to satisfy requirements relevant to that topic for each designated course. Attempt to meet the objectives relating to your course only. See pages 12-14 for a listing of your syllabus requirements.

Key words:

Key words are displayed in **bold** type in the learning objectives and should be used to create a glossary as you study each topic. From your own reading and your teacher's descriptions, write your own definition for each word.

Note: Only the terms relevant to your learning objectives should be used to create your glossary. Free glossary worksheets are also available from our web site.

Textbook references:

Provides a list of current texts appropriate for your course. Go to the *Textbook Reference Grid* on page 8 to see the comprehensive textbooks listed (these are texts providing coverage of the majority of course topics at least). The grid provides the page numbers from each text relevant to each topic in the manual. Page numbers for supplementary texts, which have only a restricted topic coverage, are provided as appropriate in each topic.

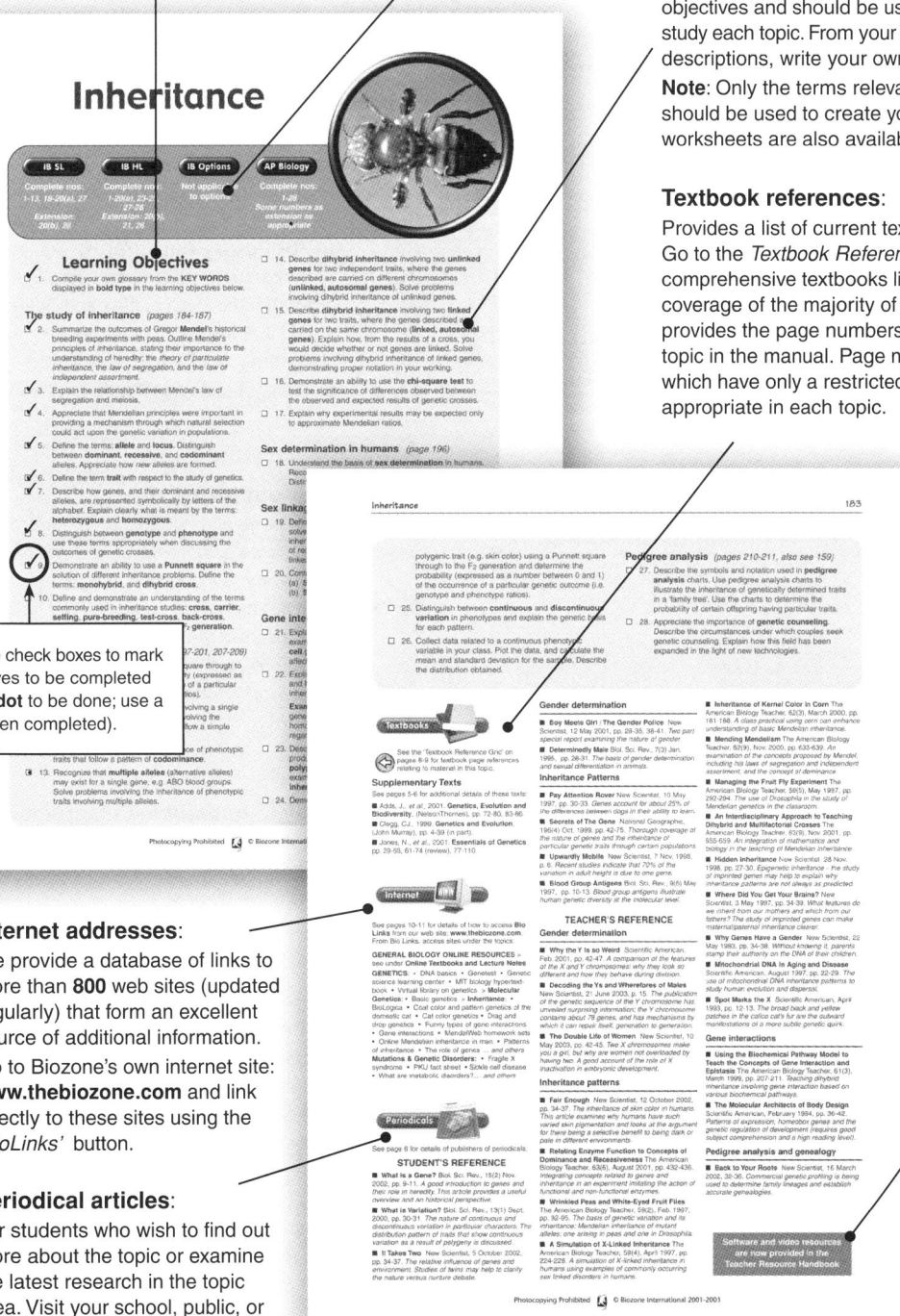

Use the check boxes to mark objectives to be completed (use a **dot** to be done; use a **tick** when completed).

Internet addresses:

We provide a database of links to more than **800** web sites (updated regularly) that form an excellent source of additional information.

Go to Biozone's own internet site: **www.thebiozone.com** and link directly to these sites using the *'BioLinks'* button.

Periodical articles:

For students who wish to find out more about the topic or examine the latest research in the topic area. Visit your school, public, or university library for these articles.

Video documentaries and computer software:

Listings of computer software and videos relevant to each topic in the manual are now provided in the "Teacher Resource Handbook", which is provided free of charge with your first order of five or more manuals.

Some of the titles listed may already be available in your school collections. If not, and you are interested in purchasing them, full supplier details are provided via the resource hub at Biozone's website.

Activity Pages

The activities and exercises make up most of the content of this book. They are designed to reinforce the concepts you have learned about in the topic. Your teacher may use the activity pages to introduce a topic for the first time, or you may use them to revise ideas already covered. They are excellent for use in the classroom, and as homework exercises and revision. In most cases, the activities should not be attempted until you have carried out the necessary background reading from your textbook. Your teacher should have a model answer book with the answers to each activity. This manual caters for more than one exam board, and you will find some activities and even whole topics that may not be relevant to your course. Although you will miss out these pages, our manuals still represent exceptional value.

Activity code:
To assist you in identifying the type of activities in this manual and the skills they require, activities are coded. Note that most activities will require some knowledge recall. Unless this is all that is required, this code is excluded from the coding list.

```
66
```

R D A 2

Activity Level

1 = Simple questions not requiring complex reasoning
2 = Some complex reasoning may be required
3 = More challenging, requiring integration of concepts

Type of Activity

D = Data handling and/or interpretation
P = Paper practical
R = Research outside the information on the page*
A = Application of knowledge to solve a problem
K = Knowledge recall from information on the page
E = Extension material

* Material to assist with the activity may be found on other pages of the manual or in textbooks.

Introductory paragraph:
The introductory paragraph sets the 'scene' for the focus of the page. Note any words that appear in **bold**, as they are 'key words' worthy of including in a glossary of biological terms for the topic.

```
138                                                    The Genetic Code
```

A 2

Transcription

Transcription is the process by which the code contained in the DNA molecule is transcribed (rewritten) into a **mRNA** molecule. Transcription is under the control of the cell's metabolic processes which must activate a gene before this process can begin. The enzyme that directly controls the process is RNA polymerase, which makes a strand of mRNA using the single antisense (template) strand of DNA as a template. The enzyme transcribes only a gene length of DNA at a time and therefore recognises start and stop signals (codes) at the beginning and end of the gene. Only RNA polymerase is involved in mRNA synthesis; it causes the unwinding of the DNA as well. It is common to find several RNA polymerase enzyme molecules on the same gene at any one time; allowing a high rate of mRNA synthesis to occur.

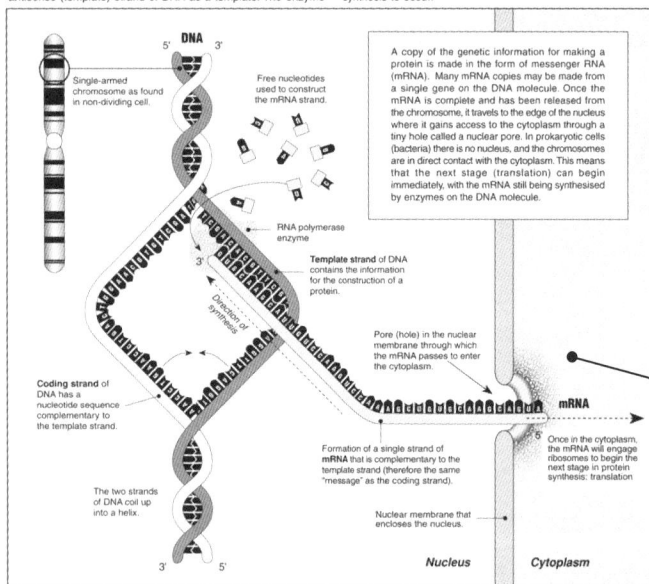

1. Explain the role of messenger RNA (mRNA) in protein synthesis: _____
_____

2. The genetic code contains punctuation codons to mark the starting and finishing points of the code for synthesis of polypeptide chains and proteins. Consult the *mRNA–Amino Acid Table* earlier in this manual and state the codes for:

(a) Start codon: _____ (b) Stop (termination) codons: _____

3. For the following triplets on the DNA, determine the **codon** sequence for the mRNA that would be synthesised:

(a) Triplets on the DNA: T A C   T A G   C C G   C G A   T T T

Codons on the mRNA: _____

(b) Triplets on the DNA: T A C   A A G   C C T   A T A   A A A

Codons on the mRNA: _____

Photocopying Prohibited   © Biozone International 1998-2002

Tear-out pages:
Each page of the book has a perforation that allows easy removal. Your teacher may ask you to remove activity pages from this manual for marking. Your teacher may also ask you to tear out the pages and place them in a ring-binder folder with other work on the topic.

Easy to understand diagrams:
The main ideas of the topic are represented and explained by clear, informative diagrams.

Write-on format:
Your understanding of the main ideas of the topic are tested by asking you questions and providing spaces for your answers. Your answers should be concise (brief) and even a list of descriptive terms may be adequate to convey the answer. Writing your answers in pencil will allow you to easily make corrections.
Take care that you answer the questions adequately (see the facing page that explains the questioning terms used).

Explanation of Terms

Questions come in a variety of forms. Whether you are studying for an exam, or writing an essay, it is important to understand exactly what the question is asking. A question has two parts to it: one part of the question will provide you with information, the second part of the question will provide you with instructions as to how to answer the question. Following these instructions is most important. Often students in examinations know the material but fail to follow instructions and, as a consequence, do not answer the question appropriately. Examiners often use certain key words to introduce questions. Look out for them and be absolutely clear as to what they mean. Below is a list of commonly used terms that you will come across and a brief explanation of each.

Commonly used Terms in Biology

The following terms are frequently used when asking questions in examinations and assessments. Most of these are listed in the IB syllabus document as action verbs indicating the depth of treatment required for a given statement. Students should have a clear understanding of each of the following terms and use this understanding to answer questions appropriately.

Analyze: Interpret data to reach stated conclusions.

Annotate: Add **brief** notes to a diagram, drawing or graph.

Apply: Use an idea, equation, principle, theory, or law in a new situation.

Appreciate: To understand the meaning or relevance of a particular situation.

Calculate: Find an answer using mathematical methods. Show the working unless instructed not to.

Compare: Give an account of similarities and differences between two or more items, referring to both (or all) of them throughout. Comparisons can be given using a table. Comparisons generally ask for similarities more than differences (see contrast).

Construct: Represent or develop in graphical form.

Contrast: Show differences. Set in opposition.

Deduce: Reach a conclusion from information given.

Define: Give the precise meaning of a word or phrase as concisely as possible.

Derive: Manipulate a mathematical equation to give a new equation or result.

Describe: Give a detailed account, including all the relevant information.

Design: Produce a plan, object, simulation or model.

Determine: Find the only possible answer.

Discuss: Give an account including, where possible, a range of arguments, assessments of the relative importance of various factors, or comparison of alternative hypotheses.

Distinguish: Give the difference(s) between two or more different items.

Draw: Represent by means of pencil lines. Add labels unless told not to do so.

Estimate: Find an approximate value for an unknown quantity, based on the information provided and application of scientific knowledge.

Evaluate: Assess the implications and limitations.

Explain: Give a clear account including causes, reasons, or mechanisms.

Identify: Find an answer from a number of possibilities.

Illustrate: Give concrete examples. Explain clearly by using comparisons or examples.

Interpret: Comment upon, give examples, describe relationships. Describe, then evaluate.

List: Give a sequence of names or other brief answers with no elaboration. Each one should be clearly distinguishable from the others.

Measure: Find a value for a quantity.

Outline: Give a brief account or summary. Include essential information only.

Predict: Give an expected result.

Solve: Obtain an answer using algebraic and/or numerical methods.

State: Give a specific name, value, or other answer. No supporting argument or calculation is necessary.

Suggest: Propose a hypothesis or other possible explanation.

Summarize: Give a brief, condensed account. Include conclusions and avoid unnecessary details.

In Conclusion

Students should familiarize themselves with this list of terms and, where necessary throughout the course, they should refer back to them when answering questions. The list of terms mentioned above is not exhaustive and students should compare this list with past examination papers and essays etc. and add any new terms (and their meaning) to the list above. The aim is to become familiar with interpreting the question and answering it appropriately.

Resources Information

Your set textbook should always be a starting point for information. There are also many other resources available, including scientific journals, magazine and newspaper articles, supplementary texts covering restricted topic areas, dictionaries, computer software and videos, and the internet.

A synopsis of currently available resources is provided below. Access to the publishers of these resources can be made directly from Biozone's web site through our resources hub: **www.thebiozonecom/resource-hub.html**, or by typing in the relevant addresses provided below. Most titles are also available through www.amazon.com. Please note that our listing any product in this manual does not, in any way, denote Biozone's endorsement of that product.

Comprehensive Biology Texts Referenced

Appropriate texts for this course are referenced in this manual. Page or chapter references for each text are provided in the text reference grid on page 8. These will enable you to identify the relevant reading as you progress through the activities in this manual. Publication details of texts referenced in the grid are provided below and opposite. For further details of text content, or to make purchases, link to the relevant publisher via Biozone's resources hub or by typing:
www.thebiozone.com/resources/us-comprehensive-pg1.html

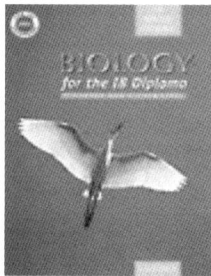

Allott, Andrew, 2001
Biology for the IB Diploma - Standard and Higher Level
Publisher: Oxford University Press
Pages: 192
ISBN: 0-19-914818-X
Comments: *Book structure mirrors that of the new IB program. Includes core and option material.*

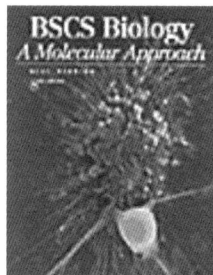

Bloom, M. and J. Greenberg, 2001
Biological Science: A Molecular Approach, (BSCS Blue Version), 8/edn
Publisher: Glencoe/McGraw Hill
Pages: 821 including glossary
ISBN: 0-538-69039-9 (student edition)
Comments: *A teacher's annotated edition, resource book, and overhead transparency booklet are also available.*

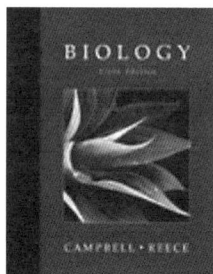

Campbell, N. A. and J.B. Reece, 2002
Biology , 6/edn
Publisher: Benjamin Cummings
Pages: 1175
ISBN: 0-8053-6624-5
Comments: *Comes with CD-ROM. A wide range of supplemental material is available. Also available in softback. The 5th edition is still in print and available.*

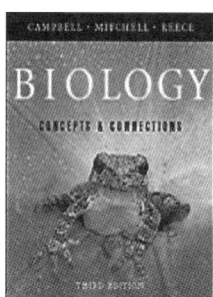

Campbell, N. A., L.G. Mitchell, and J.B. Reece, 2000
Biology; Concepts and Connections, 3/edn
Publisher: Benjamin Cummings
Pages: 807 plus appendices
ISBN: 0-8053-6625-3
Comments: *Set at a more introductory level than Campbell and Reece. Comes with an interactive study partner on CD-ROM. A CourseCompass version and an unbound flextext version are also available.*

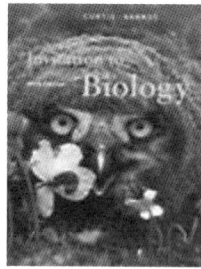

Curtis, H. and N. Sue Barnes, 1994
Invitation to Biology, 5 edn
Publisher: W.H. Freeman
Pages: 862
ISBN: 0-87901-679-5
Comments: *A well illustrated introduction to biology at this level. Evolution as a theme is integrated throughout. Also available as a split edition in two volumes.*

Freeman, S., 2002
Biological Science
Publisher: Prentice Hall
Pages: 1017 plus appendices and index
ISBN: 0-13-081923-9
Comments: *Aimed at the Advanced Placement audience, this book provides an introductory chapter, followed by nine units covering core themes. Each chapter concludes with a review, questions, and ideas for resources and additional reading.*

Ghalayini, 2000
Higher level Biology
Publisher: purchase directly from the author:
www.biology-books.com
P.O. Box 922333, Amman, Jordan
Pages: approx 450
ISBN: not available at the time of printing
Comments: *Written for both core and options for the IB course (higher level). A text for standard level is also available.*

Gould, J.L. and W.T. Keeton, 1996
Biological Science, 6 edn
Publisher: W.W. Norton
Pages: 1206
ISBN: 0-393-96920-7
Comments: *Also available as a two volume set in softback.*

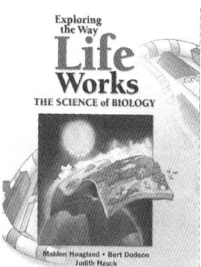

Hoagland, M., B. Dodson, & J. Hauck, 2001
Exploring the Way Life Works
Publisher: Jones & Bartlett Publishers, Inc.
Pages: 353 plus glossary and answers
ISBN: 0-7637-1688-X
Comments: *Ideal for those looking for a new approach. This text combines an innovative, student-friendly format with accurate information and clear presentation of ideas. Includes suggested web site links.*

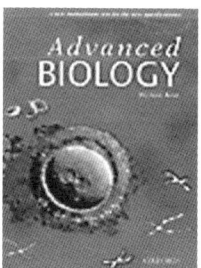

Kent, N. A. 2000
Advanced Biology
Publisher: Oxford University Press
Pages: 624
ISBN: 0-19-914195-9
Comments: *Each book comes with a free CD-ROM to help with specification planning. Book is formatted as a series of two page concept spreads.*

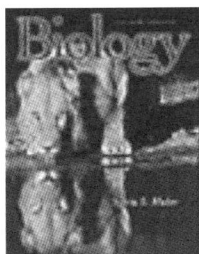

Mader, Sylvia, 2001
Biology, 7 edn
Publisher: McGraw Hill
Pages: 939 plus appendices
ISBN: 0-07-250819-1
Comments: *Comes with CD-ROM and OLC passcard. Also available as "Biology with study partner".*

Miller, R. and J. Levine, 2000
Biology, 5 edn
Publisher: Prentice-Hall
Pages: 1114 plus references
ISBN: 0134362659
Comments: *This edition also available on CD-ROM at slightly less cost.*

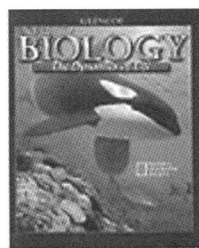

National Geographic Society, 2002
Biology: The Dynamics of Life
Publisher: Glencoe/McGraw-Hill
Pages: 1089 plus appendices
ISBN: 0-07-825925-8
Comments: *Highly colorful text, which uses a fairly large, easy-to-read format. A number of supplementary resources are also available to complement this text.*

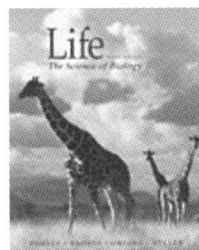

Purves, W.K., D. Sadava, G.H. Orians, and H.C. Heller, 2000
Life: The Science of Biology, 6/edn
Publisher: W.H. Freeman/Sinauer
Pages: 1100
ISBN: 0-7167-3873-2
Comments: *Available as a three volume set maintaining original pagination.*

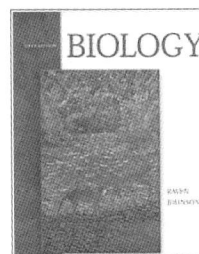

Raven, P.H. and G.B. Johnson, 2002
Biology , 6 edn
Publisher: McGraw-Hill
Pages: 1238 plus appendices
ISBN: 0-07-249937-0
Comments: *Comes with OLC and biocourse.com password card. 5th edition (1999) is also available.*

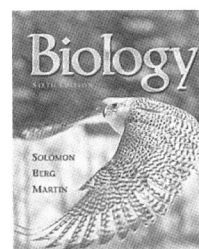

Solomon, E., L. Berg, and D.W. Martin, 2002
Biology , 6 edn
Publisher: Brooks/Cole
Pages: 1368
ISBN: 0-03-033503-5
Comments: *Significantly revised and updated. This edition is also available with CD-ROM & InfoTrac on-line library access.*

Starr, C. and R. Taggart, 2001
Biology: The Unity & Diversity of Life, 9 edn
Publisher: Brooks/Cole
Pages: 942
ISBN: 0-534-37795-5
Comments: *Comes with CD-ROM. Includes web links. Book is formatted as a series of two page concept spreads.*

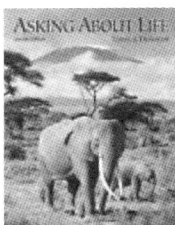

Tobin, A.J. and J. Dusheck, 2001
Asking About Life, 2 edn
Publisher: Brooks/Cole
Pages: 960
ISBN: 0-03-027044-8
Comments: *Revision to make the writing style more concise and accessible.*

Towle, Albert, 2002
Modern Biology, 10/edn
Publisher: Holt, Rinehart, and Winston
Pages: 53 chapters
ISBN: 0030565413
Comments: *Annotated teacher's edition is also available. A wide range of resources complementary to this text is available. The earlier edition (2000) is also available.*

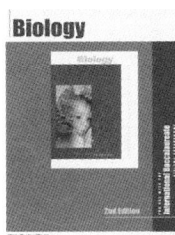

Weem, M.P., 2001
Biology, 2 edn
Publisher: IBID Press
Pages: 494
ISBN: 1-876659-47-5
Comments: *Written specifically to support the revised IB course, which began in September 2001. Contains theory and worked examples.*

Supplementary Texts

For further details of text content, or to make purchases, link to the relevant publisher via Biozone's resources hub or by typing:
www.thebiozone.com/resources/us-supplementary-pg1.html

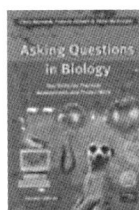

Barnard, C., F. Gilbert, F., and P. McGregor, 2001
Asking Questions in Biology: Key Skills for Practical Assessments & Project Work, 208 pp.
Publisher: Prentice Hall
ISBN: 0130-90370-1
Comments: *Covers many aspects of design, analysis and presentation of practical work in senior level biology.*

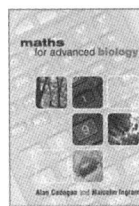

Cadogan, A. and Ingram, M., 2002
Maths for Advanced Biology
Publisher: NelsonThornes
ISBN: 0-7487-6506-9
Comments: *Provides coverage of basic mathematics requirements for biology at grades 11 and 12 (UK AS/A2). Includes worked examples.*

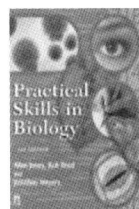

Jones, A., R. Reed, and J. Weyers, 1994
Practical Skills in Biology, 292 pp.
Publisher: Longman
ISBN: 0-582-06699-9
Comments: *Provides information on all aspects of experimental and field design, implementation, and data analysis. Available directly from www.amazon.com*

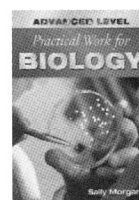

Morgan, S., 2002
Advanced Level Practical Work for Biology, 128 pp.
Publisher: Hodder and Stoughton
ISBN: 0-340-84712-3
Comments: *Caters for the practical and investigative requirements of biology at this level: experimental design, technique, observations and measurement, and interpretation and analysis.*

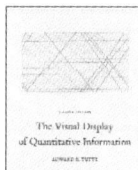

Tufte, E., 2001
The Visual Display of Quantitative Information
Publisher: Graphics Press
ISBN: 0961392142
Comments: *A highly respected text covering all aspects of the display and presentation of various types of data. Available from www.amazon.com*

Advanced Biology Readers (John Murray Publishers)
Two texts in a series designed as supplemental texts supporting a range of specific topics in biology. They are also useful as teacher reference and student extension reading.

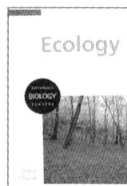

Chenn, P., 1999.
Ecology, 224 pp.
ISBN: 0-7195-7510-9
A useful, well organized supplemental resource covering ecological principles, energy flow and geochemical cycles, distribution and abundance, ecological interactions, communities and succession, practical ecology, and human impact.

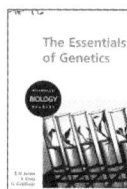

Jones, N., A. Karp., & G. Giddings, 2001.
Essentials of Genetics, 224 pp.
ISBN: 0-7195-8611-9
Thorough supplemental for genetics and evolution. Comprehensive coverage of cell division, molecular genetics, and genetic engineering is provided, and the application of new gene technologies to humans is discussed in a concluding chapter.

Collins Advanced Modular Sciences (HarperCollins)
Modular-style texts covering material related to specific topic options in the UK, but suitable as teacher reference and student extension reading for specific topic areas.

Allen, D, M. Jones, and G. Williams, 2001.
Applied Ecology, 104 pp.
ISBN: 0-00-327741-0
Includes coverage of methods in practical ecology, the effects of pollution on diversity, adaptations, agricultural ecosystems and harvesting (including fisheries), and conservation issues. Local (UK) examples are emphasized throughout.

Illustrated Advanced Biology (John Murray Publishers)
One title in a modular-style series aimed as supplemental resources for biology students at grades 11 and 12.

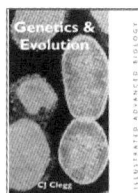

Clegg, C.J., 1999.
Genetics and Evolution, 96 pp.
ISBN: 0-7195-7552-4
Concise but thorough coverage of molecular genetics, genetic engineering, inheritance, and evolution. An historical perspective is included by way of introduction, and a glossary and a list of abbreviations used are included.

Nelson Advanced Sciences (NelsonThornes)
Modular-style texts suitable as teacher reference and student extension reading for specific topics in grades 11 and 12 biology.

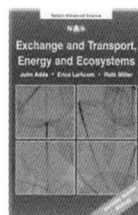

Adds, J., E. Larkcom & R. Miller, 2000.
Exchange and Transport, Energy and Ecosystems, 216 pp.
ISBN: 0-17-448294-9
Includes exchange processes (gas exchanges, digestion, absorption), transport systems, adaptation, sexual reproduction, energy and the environment, and human impact. Practical activities are included in several of the chapters.

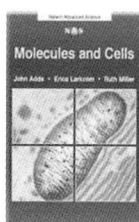

Adds, J., E. Larkcom & R. Miller, 2000.
Molecules and Cells, 112 pp.
ISBN: 0-17-448293-0
Includes coverage of the basic types of biological molecules, with extra detail on the structure and function of nucleic acids and enzymes, cellular organization, and cell division. Practical activities are provided for most chapters.

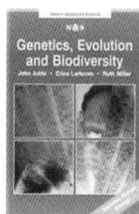

Adds, J., E. Larkcom & R. Miller, 2001.
Genetics, Evolution, and Biodiversity, 200 pp.
ISBN: 0-17-448296-5
A range of topics including photosynthesis and the control of growth in plants, classification and quantitative field ecology, populations and pest control, conservation, Mendelian genetics and evolution, gene technology and human evolution. Practical activities are included in many chapters.

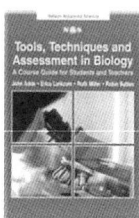

Adds, J., E. Larkcom, R. Miller, & R. Sutton, 1999.
Tools, Techniques and Assessment in Biology, 160 pp.
ISBN: 0-17-448273-6
A course guide covering basic lab protocols, microscopy, quantitative techniques in the lab and field, advanced DNA techniques and tissue culture, data handling and statistical tests, and exam preparation. Includes several useful appendices.

Periodicals, Magazines, and Journals

Articles in *Biological Sciences Review (Biol. Sci. Rev.)*, *New Scientist*, and *Scientific American* can be of great value in providing current information on specific topics. Periodicals may be accessed in your school, local, public, and university libraries. Listed below are the periodicals referenced in this manual. For general enquiries and further details regarding subscriptions, link to the relevant publisher via Biozone's resources hub or type:
www.thebiozone.com/resources/resource-journal.html

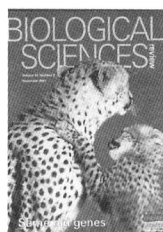

Biological Sciences Review: *An excellent quarterly publication for all teachers and students of biology. The content is current and the language is accessible.* Subscriptions available from Philip Allan Publishers, Market Place, Deddington, Oxfordshire OX 15 OSE.
Tel. 01869 338652
Fax: 01869 338803
E-mail: sales@philipallan.co.uk

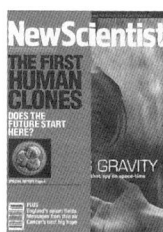

New Scientist: *Published weekly and found in many libraries. It often summarizes the findings published in other journals. Articles range from news releases to features.*
Subscription enquiries:
Tel. (UK and international): +44 (0)1444 475636. (US & Canada) 1 888 822 3242.
E-mail: ns.subs@qss-uk.com

Scientific American: *A monthly magazine containing mostly specialist feature articles. Articles range in level of reading difficulty and assumed knowledge.*
Subscription enquiries:
Tel. (US & Canada) 800-333-1199.
Tel. (outside North America) 515-247-7631
Web: www.sciam.com

The American Biology Teacher: *The official, peer-reviewed journal of the National Association of Biology Teachers. Published nine times a year and containing information and activities relevant to the teaching of biology in the US and elsewhere.*
Subscription enquiries:
NABT, 12030 Sunrise Valley Drive, #110, Reston, VA 20191-3409
Web: www.nabt.org

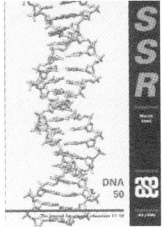

School Science Review: *A quarterly journal published by the ASE for science teachers in 11-19 education. SSR includes articles, reviews, and news on current research and curriculum development. Free to all Ordinary Members of the ASE or available on subscription.*
Subscription enquiries:
Tel: 01707 28300
Email: info@ase.org.uk *or visit their web site.*

Biology Dictionaries

Access to a good biology dictionary is of great value when dealing with the technical terms used in biology. Below are some biology dictionaries that you may wish to locate or purchase. They can usually be sourced directly from the publisher or they are all available (at the time of printing) from www.amazon.com. For further details of text content, or to make purchases, link to the relevant publisher via Biozone's resources hub or by typing:
www.thebiozone.com/resources/dictionaries-pg1.html

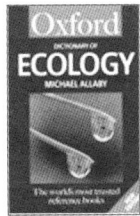

Allaby, M. (ed)
A Dictionary of Ecology 2 ed., 1999, 448 pp. Oxford University Press
ISBN: 0192800787
A revised edition, with 5000 entries fully updated to incorporate developments in this rapidly evolving field. Covers plant and animal physiology, behaviour, evolution, and all aspects of ecology and conservation biology.

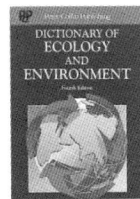

Collin, P.H.
A Dictionary of Ecology and Environment 4 ed., 2001, 560 pp. Peter Collin Publishers Ltd
ISBN: 1901659615
A revised edition, with 8500 entries. All main entries include pronunciation guides. A special feature is the frequent concise comment or quotation at the end of each entry.

Hale, W.G. and J.P. Margham
HarperCollins: Dictionary of Biology, reprint ed., 1991, 576 pp. HarperCollins
ISBN: 0064610152
More than 5600 entries and nearly 300 diagrams. Entries go beyond basic definitions to provide in-depth explanations and examples. There are no pronunciation guidelines provided.

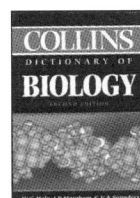

Hale, W.G., J.P. Margham, and V.A. Saunders
Collins: Dictionary of Biology, 2 ed., 1995, 656 pp. HarperCollins
ISBN: 0004708059
6500 entries covering all major fields within biology, and recently expanded to reflect recent developments in the science. There are no pronunciation guidelines provided.

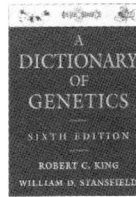

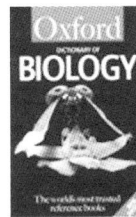

King, R.C. and W.D. Stansfield
A Dictionary of Genetics, 6 ed., 2002, 544 pp. Oxford University Press.
ISBN: 0195143256
A good source for the specialized terminology associated with genetics and related disciplines. Genera and species important to genetics are included, cross linked to an appendix.

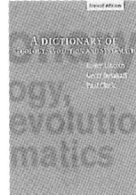

Lincoln, R.J., G.A. Boxshall, & P.F. Clark. **A Dictionary of Ecology, Evolution, and Systematics**, 2 ed., 1998, 371 pp. Cambridge Uni. Press.
ISBN: 052143842X
6500 entries covering all major fields within biology, and recently expanded to reflect recent developments in the science. There are no pronunciation guidelines provided.

Market House Books (compiled by).
Oxford Dictionary of Biology 4 ed., 2000, 648 pp. Oxford University Press.
ISBN: 0192801023. Includes biographical entries on key scientists.
Fully revised and updated, with many new entries. This edition contains biographical entries on key scientists and comprehensive coverage of terms in biology, biophysics, and biochemistry.

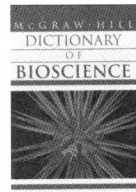

Parker, S. (ed).
McGraw-Hill Dictionary of Bioscience, International edn, 1996, 448 pp. McGraw-Hill.
ISBN: 0070524300
Provides explanatory detail of 16 000 essential terms in the biosciences. Contains a number of appendices and cross references. Pronunciation guidelines are also provided.

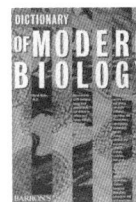

Rudin, N.
Dictionary of Modern Biology (1997), 504 pp. Barron's Educational Series Inc
ISBN: 0812095162.
More than 6000 terms in biosciences defined for college level students. Includes extensive cross referencing and several useful appendices.

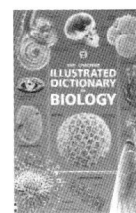

Stockley, C., 2000.
The Usborne Illustrated Dictionary of Biology 2nd ed., 128 pp. Usborne Publishing Ltd.
ISBN: 0746037929
Topics are arranged thematically so that words are explained in context. Includes cross referencing and a comprehensive index. Definitions are supported by detailed pictures and diagrams. Ideal for the visual learner.

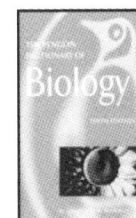

Thain, M. and M. Hickman.
Penguin Dictionary of Biology 10/e (2000), 704 pp. Penguin (USA).
ISBN: 0140513590
Pocket sized reference with definitions to more than 7500 terms, including more than 400 new entries. It includes explanations of fundamental concepts ad explorations of some of the more recent discoveries and developments in biology.

Internet Resources

The internet is a powerful tool for locating information. See pages 10-11 for details of how to access internet resources.

Textbook Reference Grid

Guide to use: Page numbers given in the grid refer to the material provided in each text relevant to the stated topic in the manual.

TOPIC IN MANUAL	Allott 2001	Bloom & Greenberg 2001	Campbell & Reece 2001	Campbell *et al.* 2000	
Skills in Biology	N/A	p. 4	Appendices 1 & 2	N/A	
The Chemistry of Life	11-15	Chpt. 1-2	Chpt. 4-6 as required	32-45, 76-79	
Cell Structure	1-7	Chpt. 6	Chpt. 7, 12, pp. 368-373	50-69	
Cell Membranes and Transport	8	Chpt. 3	Chpt. 8	78-85	
Cellular Energetics	16-17	Chpt. 4-5	Chpt. 9-10	72-75, 88-122	
Molecular Genetics	18-19	Chpt. 1, 8-9	Chpt. 16-17 to p. 321, pp. 87, 347-351, 362-67	46-47, 182-200, 209-219	
Genes and Chromosomes	21-22, 28, 131	Chpt. 13 & 15	234-42, 264-66, 269-75, 279-83, 322-24, 354-61	138-51, 173-76, 201, 273	
Inheritance	23-27	Chpt. 13-14	247-263, 269-278	154-172, 177-179	
Aspects of Biotechnology	28-31, 150	Chpt. 15	Chpt. 20 as required	230-252, 722	
Ecosystems	155-56	Chpt. 24-25 (in part)	Chpt. 50, 53 (in part)	678-697	
Energy Flow and Nutrient Cycles	40-43, 154, 160	Chpt. 2 & 24	1198-1213	724-731	
The Dynamics of Populations	35-37	Chpt. 24	Chpt. 52 (in part)	698-721	
Practical Ecology	157	N/A	N/A	N/A	
Classification	33-34	Chpt. 18	Chpt. 25, other chpts as required	282, 312-313	
Human Impact and Conservation	44-45, 159, 161-162	Chpt. 25 (in part)	1214-1237	733-734, 772-775	

	Mader 2001	Miller & Levine 2000	National Geo. Soc. 2002	Purves *et al.* 2000	
Skills in Biology	9-12	7-11	Chpt. 1 & selected biolabs and minilabs	10-14	
The Chemistry of Life	Chpt. 3 & 6	70-77	Chpt. 6-7 (in part)	Chpt. 3	
Cell Structure	Chpt. 4	86-99	Chpt. 7	Chpt. 4	
Cell Membranes and Transport	Chpt. 5	99-104	Chpt. 6 (in part) & 8	Chpt. 5	
Cellular Energetics	Chpt. 7-8	112-133	Chpt. 9	Chpt. 7-8	
Molecular Genetics	Chpt. 14-16	136-55	Chpt. 11 (in part)	pp. 47-49, Chpt. 11-14	
Genes and Chromosomes	Chpt. 10,12, & 13 (in part)	193-96, 204-209, 212-13, 231-33, 239-41, 248-49	Chpt. 10-11 (in part)	Chpt. 9	
Inheritance	Chpt. 11, 13, & 16 (in part)	180-92, 197-99, 209-11, 215-16, 230-31, 234-38	Chpt. 10 (in part) & 12	Chpt. 10	
Aspects of Biotechnology	Chpt. 17	250-265	Chpt. 13	Chpt. 17-18	
Ecosystems	Chpt. 24 (in part), 26	304-305, 1006-1020	Chpt. 2 (in part) & 3	Chpt. 57	
Energy Flow and Nutrient Cycles	Chpt. 24 (in part), 25	1021-1027	Chpt. 2	Chpt. 55-56	
The Dynamics of Populations	Chpt. 23	1032-1043	Chpt. 4	Chpt. 54	
Practical Ecology	N/A	N/A	N/A	N/A	
Classification	Chpt. 28	318-333	Chpt. 17	Chpt. 23	
Human Impact and Conservation	Chpt. 25 & 27	301-302, 318-333, 1048-1075	Chpt. 5	Chpt. 58	

Figures refer to page numbers unless indicated otherwise

Curtis & Barnes 1994	Freeman 2002	Ghalayini 2000	Gould & Keeton 1996	Hoagland et al 2001	Kent 2000
12-15	see CD-ROM	N/A	Chpt. 1	15, and 59 and other "Doing Science" pages	16-35, 40-53
Chpt. 3, pp. 133-137	44-47, 56, 70-72	Chpt. 2-3	Chpt. 3	40-43, 52-57, 88-91, 102, 118-21, 184-85, 216-17	16-35, 40-53
Chpt. 4 & 5	70, 80, chpt. 5, 8, 20	Chpt. 4	Chpt. 5	2-28, 254-276	56-65, 77, 80-81
Chpt. 6	72-82, chpt. 5 as reqd	Chpt. 5	Chpt. 4	32-34 and ideas integrated throughout	66-73
Chpt. 7-9	Chpt 6-7	Chpt. 7-8	Chpt. 6-7	92-118, 122-135	86-110
pp. 65-67, Chpt. 14-16	47, chpt. 11-15 as reqd	Chpt. 9	Chpt. 3, 8, 9, & 11	138-61, 170-71, 174-77, 190-205, 210-23, 264-65	390-405
Chpt. 11	Chpt. 9, 16	Chpt. 10	Chpt. 12	162-163, 172-173, 178-179, 320-321	78-79, 414-415, 424-425, 430-431
Chpt. 12 & 13	Chpt. 10	Chpt. 11	Chpt. 16	144-145 (historical)	416-431
Chpt. 18	Chpt. 17	N/A	Chpt. 10	164-69, 276-77, 324-25	113-125
pp. 809-811, Chpt. 46	Chpt. 50	Chpt. 25	Chpt. 2, 39-40	Integrated as part of a whole	506, 512, 522-525, 530-535, 554-555
pp. 45-46, 173, Chpt. 45	Chpt. 51	Chpt. 21 & 25 (in part)	Chpt. 40	92-95, 104-105	506-513, 526-29
Chpt. 43-44	Chpt. 48-49	Chpt. 21	Chpt. 39	N/A	514-521
N/A	942, 984	N/A	N/A	N/A	570-572
Chpt. 23	484-86, 503, 520-22, 540, 561, 577-83, 1004	Chpt. 22	Chpt. 18-19	Integrated as part of a whole	464-489, 494-501
843, 859	Chpt. 52	Chpt. 21 & 25 (in part)	N/A	N/A	538-561

Raven & Johnson 2002	Solomon et al. 2002	Starr & Taggart 2001	Tobin & Dusheck 2001	Towle 2002	Weem 2001
6-9	15-20	12-15	N/A	Chpt. 1	452-457
Chpt. 3, pp. 149-153	48-69, 143-150	38-47, 104-107	Chpt. 2-3	Chpt. 2-3	33-38, 294-298
Chpt. 5	Chpt. 4	Chpt. 4	Chpt. 4	Chpt. 4	2-12
Chpt. 6	Chpt. 5	Chpt. 5	Chpt. 5	Chpt. 5	13-17
Chpt. 8-10	Chpt. 6-8	pp. 94-103, Chpt. 7-8	Chpt. 6-7	Chpt. 6-7	pp. 47-52, Chpt. 7, pp. 299-311
pp. 46-49,155-56, Chpt. 14-16	Chpt. 11, 12, & 13	pp. 48-49, Chpt. 13-15	Chpt. 10-11	Chpt. 10-11	pp. 39-46, Chpt. 6
Chpt. 12-13, & 18	Chpt. 9, 11, 12, & 15 as reqd	Chpt. 10-12, 14	Chpt. 9 (in part)	Chpt. 9	58-64, 190-192
Chpt. 13	Chpt. 10	Chpt. 11-12	Chpt. 9 (in part)	Chpt. 12	64-69, 193-200
Chpt. 19	Chpt. 14-16 as reqd	Chpt. 16	Chpt. 13-14	Chpt. 13	70-77
pp. 516-518, 530-531, Chpt. 29	Chpt. 52 & 54	pp. 864-865, Chpt. 50	Chpt. 25-26	Chpt. 19 & 22	82
Chpt. 28	Chpt. 53	Chpt. 49	Chpt. 27 (in part)	Chpt. 21	83-89
Chpt. 24, pp. 519-529	Chpt. 51 & 52	Chpt. 48	Chpt. 27-28	Chpt. 20	90-93
N/A	N/A	N/A	N/A	N/A	93-97
Chpt. 32	pp. 10-12, 407-408, Chpt. 22	298-299, 320-327	Chpt. 19	Chpt. 18	101-103
Chpt. 30-31	Chpt. 55	Chpt. 51	N/A	Chpt. 23	pp. 104-108, Chpt. 20

Using the Internet

The internet is a vast, global network of computers connected by a system that allows information to be passed through telephone connections. When people talk about the internet they usually mean the **World Wide Web** (WWW). The WWW is a service that has made the internet so simple to use that virtually anyone can find their way around, exchange messages, search libraries and perform all manner of tasks. The internet is a powerful resource for locating information. Listed below are two useful articles giving information on use of the internet, together with examples of useful web sites.

- **Click Here: Biology on the Internet** Biol. Sci. Rev., 10(2) November 1997, pp. 26-29.
- **Using the Internet as a Supplemental Instructional Tool for Biology Teachers** The American Biology Teacher 62(3), March 2000, pp. 171-176.

Using the Biozone Website: www.thebiozone.com

The **Back** and **Forward** buttons allow you to navigate between pages displayed on a WWW site

The current **internet address (URL)** for the web site is displayed here. You can type in a new address directly into this space.

Tool bar provides a row of buttons with shortcuts for some commonly performed tasks, such as printing a page or 'refreshing' the page (i.e. making the page load again).

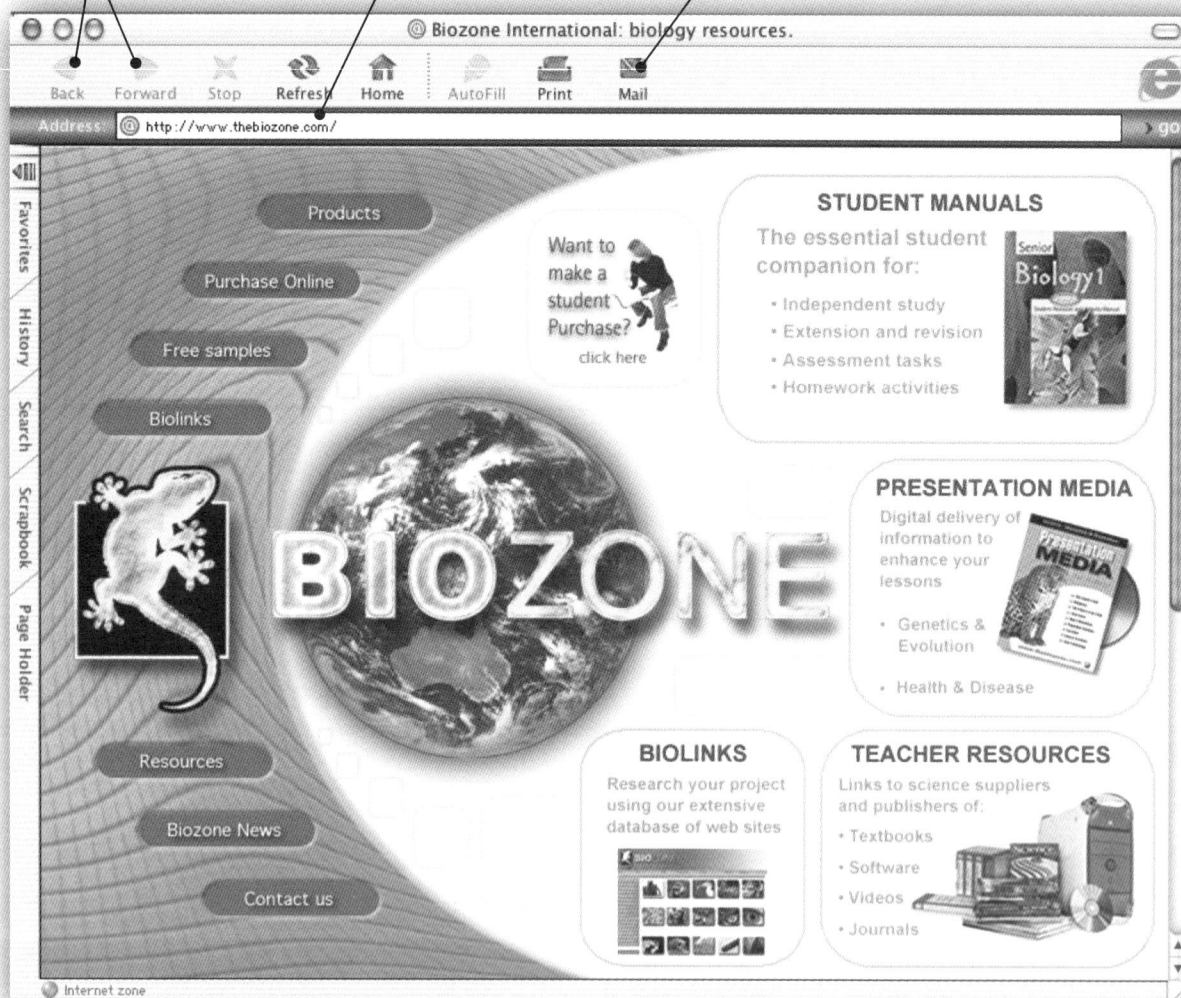

@ Biozone International: biology resources.

Back   Forward   Stop   Refresh   Home   AutoFill   Print   Mail

Address: @ http://www.thebiozone.com/   > go

Favorites | History | Search | Scrapbook | Page Holder

Products
Purchase Online
Free samples
Biolinks

Want to make a student Purchase? click here

STUDENT MANUALS

The essential student companion for:
- Independent study
- Extension and revision
- Assessment tasks
- Homework activities

Senior Biology 1

Resources
Biozone News
Contact us

BIOZONE

PRESENTATION MEDIA

Digital delivery of information to enhance your lessons
- Genetics & Evolution
- Health & Disease

BIOLINKS

Research your project using our extensive database of web sites

TEACHER RESOURCES

Links to science suppliers and publishers of:
- Textbooks
- Software
- Videos
- Journals

Internet zone

Searching the Net

The WWW addresses listed throughout the manual have been selected for their relevance to the topic in which they are listed. We believe they are good sites. Don't just rely on the sites that we have listed. Use the powerful 'search engines', which can scan the millions of sites for useful information. Here are some good ones to try:

Alta Vista:	**www.altavista.com**
Ask Jeeves:	**www.ask.com**
Excite:	**www.excite.com/search**
Google:	**www.google.com**
Go.com:	**www.go.com**
Lycos:	**www.lycos.com**
Metacrawler:	**www.metacrawler.com**
Yahoo:	**www.yahoo.com**

Biozone International provides a service on its web site that links to all internet sites listed in this manual. Our web site also provides regular updates with new sites listed as they come to our notice and defunct sites deleted. Our **BIO LINKS** page, shown below, will take you to a database of regularly updated links to more than 800 other quality biology web sites.

The **Resource Hub**, accessed via the homepage or publishers online, provides links to the supporting resources referenced in the manual and the *Teacher Resource Handbook*. These resources include *comprehensive* and *supplementary texts, biology dictionaries, computer software, videos*, and *science supplies*. These can be used to supplement and enhance your learning experience.

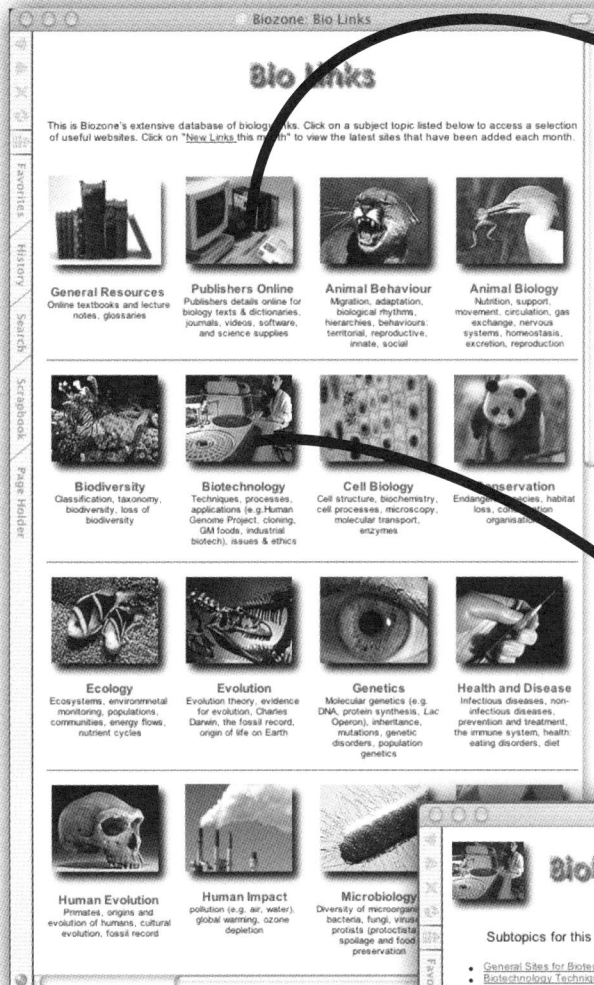

Click on each topic to see a list of all related biology links. Each topic has relevant subtopics to make searching easier and each link has a brief description.

Index of sub-topics on this page. Click on these to jump down to the desired section.

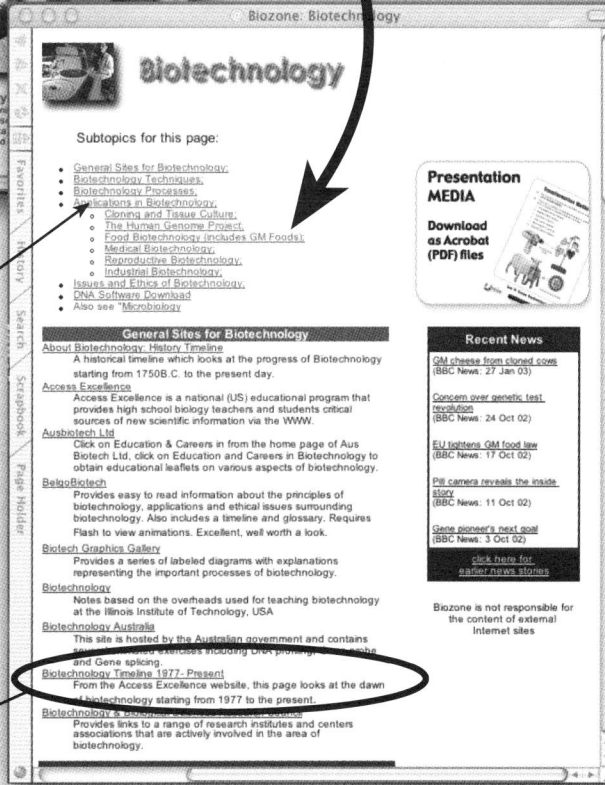

Click on the link to access the named site. The brief description tells you how the site may be of interest, as well as any country specific bias, if this is relevant.

International Baccalaureate Course

The IB biology course is divided into three sections: core, additional higher level material, and option material. All **IB candidates** must complete the **core** topics. Higher level students are also required to undertake Additional HL **(AHL)** material as part of the core. Options fall into three categories: those specific to standard level students **(OPT-SL)**, those specific to higher level students **(OPT-HL)** and those offered to both **(OPT-SL/HL)**. All candidates are required to study two options. All candidates must also carry out **practical work** and must participate in **the group 4 project**. In the guide below, we have indicated where the relevant material can be found: SB1 for Senior Biology 1 and SB2 for Senior Biology 2.

Topic	See manual	Topic	See manual
CORE: *(All Students)*		systems in homeostasis. Role of the kidney in excretion and water balance.	
1 Cells		5.7 Human reproduction: urinogenital systems. Role of hormones in birth and sexual development. Fertilization and embryonic development. The placenta. Contraception. Reproductive technologies and ethical issues.	SB2 Reproduction and Development
1.1 Cell theory. Viral structure. Cell sizes. Light and electron microscopy. SA:Volume ratio. Cell specialization.	SB1 Cell Structure, Cell Membranes and Transport		
1.2 Prokaryotic cells: structure and function.	SB1 Cell Structure		
1.3 Cell organelles. Plant vs animal cells. Prokaryotic vs eukaryotic cells.	SB1 Cell Structure	**COMPULSORY: AHL Topics** *(HL students only)*	
1.4 Membrane structure. Active and passive transport. Diffusion and osmosis.	SB1 Cell Membranes and Transport	**6 Nucleic acids and proteins**	
1.5 Cell division and the origins of cancer.	SB1 Cell Structure	6.1 DNA structure: nucleosomes, purines, pyrimidines.	SB1 Molecular Genetics
2 The chemistry of life		6.2 DNA replication including the role of enzymes and Okazaki fragments.	SB1 Molecular Genetics
2.1 Elements of life. The properties and importance of water.	SB1 The Chemistry of Life	6.3 Transcription and its control. Reverse transcriptase and its applications.	SB1 Molecular Genetics
2.2 Structure and function of carbohydrates, lipids, and proteins.	SB1 The Chemistry of Life	6.4 The structure of tRNA and ribosomes. The process of translation.	SB1 Molecular Genetics
2.3 Enzyme structure and function.	SB1 The Chemistry of Life	6.5 Protein structure and function. Fibrous and globular proteins.	SB1 The Chemistry of Life
2.4 Nucleotides and the structure of DNA.	SB1 Molecular Genetics	6.6 Enzymes: induced fit model. Inhibition. Allostery in the control of metabolism.	SB1 The Chemistry of Life
2.5 Semi-conservative DNA replication.	SB1 Molecular Genetics		
2.6 RNA and DNA structure. The genetic code. Transcription. Translation.	SB1 Molecular Genetics	**7 Cell respiration and photosynthesis**	
2.7 Cellular respiration and ATP production.	SB1 Cellular Energetics	7.1 Structure and function of mitochondria. Biochemistry of cellular respiration.	SB1 Cellular Energetics
2.8 Biochemistry of photosynthesis. Factors affecting photosynthetic rates.	SB1 Cellular Energetics	7.2 Chloroplasts, the biochemistry of photosynthesis, chemiosmosis. Action and absorption spectra. Limiting factors.	SB1 Cellular Energetics
3 Genetics		**8 Genetics**	
3.1 Eukaryote chromosomes. Karyotyping. Gene mutations and consequences.	SB1 Genes and Chromosomes	8.1 Meiosis, and the process of crossing over. Recombination. Mendel's laws.	SB1 Genes and Chromosomes
3.2 Meiosis and non-disjunction (Down syndrome). Law of segregation.	SB1 Genes and Chromosomes	8.2 Dihybrid crosses in unlinked genes. Using the chi-squared test in genetics.	SB1 Inheritance
3.3 Theoretical genetics: alleles and inheritance, sex linkage, pedigrees.	SB1 Inheritance	8.3 Autosomes and sex chromosomes. Crossing over. Dihybrid crosses involving autosomal linkage.	SB1 Inheritance
3.4 Genetic engineering and biotechnology: PCR, gel electrophoresis, DNA profiling, genetic screening. HGP. Transformation. GMOs. Gene therapy. Cloning.	SB1 Gene Technology	8.4 Polygenic inheritance.	SB1 Inheritance
4 Ecology and evolution		**9 Human reproduction**	
4.1 Ecosystems. Food chains and webs. Trophic levels. Ecological pyramids. Carbon cycle. The role of decomposers.	SB1 Ecosystems, Energy Flow and Nutrient Cycles	9.1 Testis structure and spermatogenesis. Ovarian structure and oogenesis.	SB2 Reproduction and Development
4.2 Factors influencing population size. Population growth. Random sampling. Analyzing ecological data (mean & SD).	SB1 The Dynamics of Populations, Practical Ecology	9.2 Fertilization. The role of HCG in early development. Structure and function of the placenta, including its hormonal role.	SB2 Reproduction and Development
4.3 Genetic variation. Sexual reproduction as a source of variation in species. Natural selection. Evolution in response to environmental change (e.g. antibiotic resistance in bacteria).	SB1 Genes and Chromosomes SB2 Mechanisms of Evolution	**10 Defence against infectious disease**	
		10.1 Blood clotting. Clonal selection. Acquired immunity. Antibodies. Monoclonal antibodies. Vaccination.	SB2 Defence Against Infectious Disease
4.4 The species concept. Classification of organisms. Binomial nomenclature. Five kingdom classification. Use of keys.	SB1 Classification	**11 Nerves, muscles, and movement**	
4.5 Human impact on the environment (e.g. greenhouse effect). Mitigation.	SB1 Human Impact and Conservation	11.1 Structure and function of the human nervous system. Motor neuron structure. Action potential. Synapses.	SB2 Nerve, Muscles and Movement
5 Human health and physiology		11.2 Locomotion in animals. Roles of nerves, muscles, and bones in movement. Joints. Skeletal muscle and contraction.	SB2 Nerve, Muscles and Movement
5.1 Role of enzymes in digestion. Structure and function of the digestive system.	SB2 Diet and Animal Nutrition	**12 Excretion**	
5.2 Structure and function of the heart. The control of heart activity. Blood.	SB2 Animal Transport Systems	12.1 The need for excretion. The relationship between waste products and habitat.	SB2 Homeostasis and Excretion
5.3 Pathogens and their transmission. Antimicrobial drugs. HIV/AIDS.	SB2 Pathogens and Disease	12.2 Structure and function of the human kidney. Urine production. Kidney dialysis.	SB2 Homeostasis and Excretion
5.4 Role of skin as a barrier to infection. Role of phagocytic leukocytes. Antigens. Antibody production. Effects of HIV on the immune system.	SB2 Pathogens and Disease, Defence Against Infectious Disease	**13 Plant science**	
		13.1 Plant diversity.	SB1 Classification
5.5 Ventilation systems. Control of breathing.	SB2 Gas Exchange	Structure of a dicot plant. Function and distribution of tissues in stem, root, and leaves. Xerophytes and hydrophytes.	SB2 Plant Science
5.6 Principles of homeostasis. Control of blood glucose and body temperature. Role of the nervous and endocrine	SB2 Homeostasis and Excretion		

International Baccalaureate Course *continued*

Topic		See manual
13.2	Support in terrestrial plants. Transport in angiosperms: active ion uptake by roots, transpiration, translocation. Food storage.	SB2 Plant Science
13.3	Dicot flowers. Pollination and fertilization. Seeds: structure, germination, dispersal.	SB2 Plant Science

OPTION: OPT - SL *(SL students only)*

A Diet and human nutrition

A.1	Main constituents of diet. A balanced diet. Interpretation of dietary information.	SB2 Diet and Animal Nutrition
A.2	The source and use of lipids, proteins, and carbohydrates in the diet. Energy requirements. Importance of fiber, vitamins, and minerals in the diet.	SB2 Aspects covered in Diet and Animal Nutrition
A.3	Health problems associated with high fat diets. Balanced diet. Malnutrition. Food additives. Food handling.	SB2 Aspects covered in Diet and Animal Nutrition

B Physiology of exercise

B.1	Structure and function of the human skeleton. Muscle structure and contraction.	SB2 Nerve, Muscles and Movement
B.2	Human nervous system. Sensory and motor neurons. Synaptic transmission. Control of muscle function by the brain.	SB2 Aspects covered in Nerve, Muscles and Movement
B.3	Respiration and exercise intensity. Roles of myoglobin and adrenaline. Oxygen debt and lactate in muscle fatigue.	SB2 Nerve, Muscles and Movement, Gas Exchange
B.4	Principles of training. Measuring fitness. Training and the cardiovascular system.	SB2 Nerve, Muscles and Movement
B.5	Exercise induced injuries and treatment.	*Not yet covered*

C Cells and energy

C.1	Protein structure and function. Fibrous and globular proteins.	SB1 The Chemistry of Life
C.2	Enzymes: induced fit model. Inhibition. Allostery in the control of metabolism.	SB1 The Chemistry of Life
C.3	Biochemistry of cellular respiration.	SB1 Cellular Energetics.
C.4	The biochemistry of photosynthesis including chemiosmosis. Action and absorption spectra. Limiting factors.	SB1 Cellular Energetics

OPTION: OPT - SL/HL *(SL and HL students)*

D Evolution

D.1	Prebiotic experiments. Origins of prokaryotic cells. Endosymbiotic theory.	SB2 The Origins and Evolution of Life
D.2	Lamarck's theory of evolution by inheritance of acquired characteristics. Darwin-Wallace theory of evolution by natural selection. Other theories for the origins of life.	SB2 Aspects covered in The Origins and Evolution of Life, Mechanisms of Evolution
D.3	Evidence for evolution. Fossil dating. Modern day examples of evolution.	SB2 The Origins and Evolution of Life
D.4	Primate features. Hominid features. Genetic and cultural evolution.	SB2 The Evolution of Humans
D.5	Sources of mutations. Gene and chromosomal mutations (PKU, CF, Klinefelter syndrome). Gene pools and evolution. Speciation (migration, isolating mechanisms, adaptation). Gradualism and punctuated equilibrium.	SB1 Molecular Genetics SB2 Mechanisms of Evolution, also see SB1: Classification for the species concept
D.6	The Hardy-Weinberg principle. Transient and balanced polymorphism.	SB2 Mechanisms of Evolution

E Neurobiology and behavior

E.1	Innate behavior. Behavior patterns in animals and the role of natural selection.	SB2 Animal Behavior
E.2	Sensory receptors. Structure and function of the human eye.	SB2 Nerves, Muscles and Movement
E.3	Innate behavior and its role in survival. The reflex arc: cranial & spinal reflexes. Brain structure. Taxes and kineses.	SB2 Nerves, Muscles and Movement, Animal Behavior
E.4	Types of learned behavior.	SB2 Animal Behavior
E.5	Social behavior and organization. The role of altruism in sociality.	SB2 Animal Behavior
E.6	Structure and function of the ANS. Conscious control of reflexes.	SB2 Nerves, Muscles and Movement
E.7	Neurotransmitters and synapses. Hormones as painkillers. Effects of drugs on synaptic transmission.	*Not covered* but see SB2: Nerves, Muscles and

	Behavioral effects of excitatory and inhibitory psychoactive drugs.	Movement for basic information.

F Applied plant and animal science

F.1	Plant productivity. Human control of plant growth. Farming methods and their implications. Pest control.	SB2 Applied Plant and Animal Science
F.2	Evaluation of animal rearing techniques (including misuse of growth promoters). Artificial insemination. Animal health.	SB2 Aspects covered in Applied Plant and Animal Science
F.3	Fertilization. Plant growth regulators. Auxin & plant growth. Micropropagation.	SB2 Applied Plant and Animal Science
F.4	Gene banks and genetic diversity. Production of cereal crops & livestock.	SB2 Applied Plant and Animal Science
F.5	Uses of transgenic techniques in agriculture (including ethics).	SB1 Aspects covered in Gene Technology
F.6	Monocot flowers. Wind and insect pollinated flowers. Asexual reproduction and artificial propagation. Phytochrome.	SB2 Plant Science Applied Plant and Animal Science

G Ecology and conservation

G.1	Factors affecting plant and animal distribution. Ecological niche and the competitive exclusion principle. Analysis of ecological data (student t-test).	SB1 Ecosystems, Practical Ecology
G.2	Species interactions: competition, predation, herbivory, parasitism, and mutualism. Trophic levels. Ecological pyramids. Ecological succession and climax communities.	SB1 Ecosystems, Energy Flow and Nutrient Cycles, The Dynamics of Populations
	Plant productivity (includes calculating gross and net production, and biomass).	SB2 Applied Plant and Animal Science
G.3	Conservation of biodiversity. The Simpson diversity index. Human impact on ecosystems. Conservation strategies and the role of international agencies.	SB1 Ecosystems, Human Impact and Conservation

G.4-G.5 is extension for HL only

G.4	Details of the nitrogen cycle including the role of bacteria. Use of fertilizers, crop rotation to increase nitrogen fertility of soil.	SB1 Energy Flow and Nutrient Cycles SB2 Applied Plant and Animal Science
G.5	Human impact: ozone depletion, water pollution (e.g. raw sewage, BOD), acid rain. Biomass as a source of fuel.	SB1 Human Impact and Conservation

OPTION: OPT - HL *(HL students only)*

H Further human physiology

H.1	Hormones and their modes of action. Hypothalamus and pituitary gland. Control of thyroxine and ADH secretion.	SB2 Homeostasis and Excretion
H.2	Digestion and digestive enzymes. The role of bile in lipid digestion.	SB2 Diet and Animal Nutrition
H.3	Structure of villus. Absorption of nutrients and transport of digested food.	SB2 Diet and Animal Nutrition
H.4	The structure and function of the liver (including role in nutrient processing). Production and secretion of bile.	SB2 Homeostasis and Excretion, also Diet and Animal Nutrition
H.5	The cardiac cycle and control of heart rhythm. Lymph and the transport role of lymphatic system. Atherosclerosis and coronary heart disease.	SB2 Animal Transport System
H.6	Gas exchange: oxygen dissociation curves and the Bohr shift. Ventilation rate and exercise. Effects of lung cancer and asthma. Breathing at high altitude.	SB2 Gas Exchange

Practical Work *(All students)*

Practical work consists of short and long term investigations, and an interdisciplinary project (The Group 4 project). Also see the "Guide to Practical Work" on the last page of this introductory section.

Short and long term investigations
Investigations should reflect the breadth and depth of the subjects taught at each level, and include a spread of content material from the core, options, and AHL material, where relevant.

The Group 4 project
All candidates must participate in the group 4 project. In this project it is intended that students analyze a topic or problem suitable for investigation in each of the science disciplines offered by the school (not just in biology). This project emphasizes the processes involved in scientific investigations rather than the products of an investigation.

Advanced Placement Course

The AP biology course is designed to be equivalent to a college introductory biology course. It is to be taken by students after successful completion of first courses in high school biology and chemistry. In the guide below, we have indicated where the relevant material can be found: SB1 for Senior Biology 1 and SB2 for Senior Biology 2. Because of the general nature of the AP curriculum document, the detail provided here is based on the content in the manuals.

Topic	See manual

Topic I: Molecules and Cells

A Chemistry of life

1 The chemical & physical properties of water. The importance of water to life. — SB1 The Chemistry of Life

2 The role of carbon. Structure and function of carbohydrates, lipids, nucleic acids, and proteins. The synthesis and breakdown of macromolecules. — SB1 The Chemistry of Life, Molecular Genetics, Cell membranes and Transport

3 The laws of thermodynamics and their relationship to biochemical processes. Free energy changes. — SB1 The Chemistry of Life

4 The action of enzymes and their role in the regulation of metabolism. Enzyme specificity. Factors affecting enzyme activity. Applications of enzymes. — SB1 The Chemistry of Life

B Cells

1 Comparison of prokaryotic and eukaryotic cells, including their evolutionary relationships. — SB1 Cell Structure, SB2 The Origin and Evolution of Life

2 Membrane structure: fluid mosaic model. Active and passive transport. — SB1 Cell Membranes and Transport

3 Structure and function of organelles. Organization of cell function. Comparison of plant and animal cells. Cell size and surface area: volume ratio. — SB1 Cell Structure, Cell Membranes and Transport

4 Mitosis and the cell cycle. Mechanisms of cytokinesis. Cancer (tumor formation) as the result of uncontrolled cell division. — SB1 Cell Structure

C Cellular energetics

1 Nature and role of ATP. Anabolic and catabolic processes. Chemiosmosis. — SB1 Cellular Energetics

2 Structure and function of mitochondria. Biochemistry of cellular respiration, including the role of oxygen in energy yielding pathways. Anaerobic generation of ATP. — SB1 Cellular Energetics

3 Structure and function of chloroplasts. The biochemistry of photosynthesis. Adaptations for photosynthesis in different environments. — SB1 Cellular Energetics

Topic II: Heredity and Evolution

A Heredity

1 The importance of meiosis in heredity. Gametogenesis. Similarities and differences between gametogenesis in animals and plants. — SB1 Genes and Chromosomes SB2 Reproduction, Plant Science

2 Structure of eukaryotic chromosomes. Heredity of genetic information. — SB1 Genes and Chromosomes

3 Mendel's laws. Inheritance patterns. — SB1 Inheritance

B Molecular genetics

1 RNA and DNA structure and function. Eukaryotic and prokaryotic genomes. — SB1 Molecular Genetics

2 Gene expression in prokaryotes and eukaryotes. The *Lac* operon model. — SB1 Molecular Genetics

3 Causes of mutations. Gene mutations (e.g. sickle cell disease). Chromosomal mutations (e.g. Down syndrome). — SB1 Genes and Chromosomes

4 Viral structure and replication. — SB2 Pathogens and Disease

5 Nucleic acid technology and applications. legal and ethical issues. — SB1 Gene Technology

C Evolutionary biology

1 The origins of life on Earth. Prebiotic experiments. Origins of prokaryotic cells. Endosymbiotic theory. — SB2 The Origins and Evolution of Life

2 Evidence for evolution: comparative anatomy, vestigial organs, biochemistry, biogeography. Dating of fossils. — SB2 The Origins and Evolution of Life

3 Mechanisms of evolution: natural selection, speciation, macroevolution. The species concept. — SB2 Mechanisms of Evolution SB1 Classification

Topic III: Organisms and Populations

A Diversity of organisms

1 Evolutionary patterns: major body plans of plants and animals. — SB1 Classification

2 Diversity of life: representative members from the five kingdoms Monera (=Prokaryotae), Fungi, Protista (=Protoctista), Animalia and Plantae. — SB1 Classification

3 Phylogenetic classification. Binomial nomenclature. Five kingdom classification. Use of dichotomous keys. — SB1 Classification

4 Evolutionary relationships: genetic and morphological characters. Phylogenies. — SB1 Classification SB2 The Origin and Evolution of Life

B Structure and function of plants and animals

1 Plant and animal reproduction and development (includes humans). Adaptive significance of reproductive features and their regulation. — SB2 Reproduction, Plant Science

2 Organization of cells, tissues & organs. — SB1 Cell Structure
   The structure and function of animal and plant organ systems. Adaptive features that have contributed to the success of plants and animals in occupying particular terrestrial niches. — SB2 Plant Science, Diet and Animal Nutrition, Animal Transport Systems, Homeostasis and Excretion, Gas Exchange

3 Plant and animal responses to environmental cues. The role of hormones in these responses. — SB2 Animal Behavior, Applied Plant and Animal Science

C Ecology

1 Factors influencing population size. Population growth curves. — SB1 The Dynamics of Populations

2 Abiotic and biotic factors: effects on community structure and ecosystem function. Trophic levels: energy flows through ecosystems and relationship to trophic structure. Nutrient cycles. — SB1 Ecosystems, Energy Flow and Nutrient Cycles

3 Human influence on biogeochemical cycles: (e.g. use of fertilizers). — SB1 Human Impact and Conservation

Practical Work

Integrated practicals as appropriate: see Senior Biology 1: Skills in Biology. Also see the page "Guide to Practical Work" on the last page of this introductory section.

Guide to Practical Work

A practical or laboratory component is an essential part of any biology course, especially at senior level. It is through your practical sessions that you are challenged to carry out experiments drawn from many areas within modern biology. Both AP and IB courses have a strong practical component, aimed at providing a framework for your laboratory experience. Well executed laboratory and field sessions will help you to understand problems, observe accurately, make hypotheses, design and implement controlled experiments, collect and analyze data, think analytically, and communicate your findings in an appropriate way using tables and graphs. The outline below provides some guidelines for AP and IB students undertaking their practical work. Be sure to follow required safety procedures at all times during practical work.

International Baccalaureate Practical Work

The practical work carried out by IB biology students should reflect the depth and breadth of the subject syllabus, although there may not be an investigation for every syllabus topic. All candidates must participate in the group 4 project, and the internal assessment (IA) requirements should be met via a spread of content from the core, options and, where relevant, AHL material. A wide range of IA investigations is possible: *short laboratory practicals and longer term practicals or projects, computer simulations, data gathering and analysis exercises, and general laboratory and field work.*

Suitable material, or background preparation, for this component can be found in this manual and its companion title, Senior Biology 2.

College Board's AP® Biology Lab Topics

Each of the 12 set laboratory sessions in the AP course is designed to complement a particular topic area within the course. The basic structure of the lab course is outlined below:

LAB 1: Diffusion and osmosis
Overview: To investigate diffusion and osmosis in dialysis tubing. To investigate the effect of solute concentration on water potential (ψ) in plant tissues.

Aims: An understanding of passive transport mechanisms in cells, and an understanding of the concept of water potential, solute potential, and pressure potential, and how these are measured.

LAB 2: Enzyme catalysis
Overview: To investigate the conversion of hydrogen peroxide to water and oxygen gas by catalase.

Aims: An understanding of the effects of environmental factors on the rate of enzyme catalyzed reactions.

LAB 3: Mitosis and meiosis
Overview: To use prepared slides of onion root tips to study plant mitosis. To simulate the phases of meiosis by using chromosome models.

Aims: Recognition of stages in mitosis in plant cells and calculation of relative duration of cell cycle stages. An understanding of chromosome activity during meiosis and an ability to calculate map distances for genes.

LAB 4: Plant pigments and photosynthesis
Overview: To separate plant pigments using chromatography. To measure photosynthetic rate in chloroplasts.

Aims: An understanding of Rf values. An understanding of the techniques used to determine photosynthetic rates. An ability to explain variations in photosynthetic rate under different environmental conditions.

LAB 5: Cell(ular) respiration
Overview: To investigate oxygen consumption during germination (including the effect of temperature).

Aims: An understanding of how cell respiration rates can be calculated from experimental data. An understanding of the relationship between gas production and respiration rate, and the effect of temperature on this.

LAB 6: Molecular biology
Overview: To investigate the basic principles of molecular biology through the transformation of E.coli cells. To investigate the use of restriction digestion and gel electrophoresis.

Aims: An understanding of the role of plasmids as vectors, and the use of gel electrophoresis to separate DNA fragments of varying size. An ability to design appropriate experimental procedures and use multiple experimental controls.

LAB 7: Genetics of organisms
Overview: Use Drosophila to perform genetic crosses. To collect and analyze the data from these crosses.

Aims: An understanding of the independent assortment of two genes and an ability to determine if genes are autosomal or sex linked from the analysis of the results of multigeneration genetic crosses.

LAB 8: Population genetics and evolution
Overview: To learn about the Hardy-Weinberg law of genetic equilibrium and study the relationship between evolution and changes in allele frequency.

Aims: An ability to calculate allele and genotype frequencies using the Hardy-Weinberg formula. An understanding of natural selection and other causes of microevolution.

LAB 9: Transpiration
Overview: To investigate transpiration in plants under controlled conditions. To examine the organization of plant stems and leaves as they relate to this.

Aims: An understanding of the effects of environmental variables on transpiration rates. An understanding of the relationship between the structure and function of the tissues involved.

LAB 10: Physiology of the circulatory system
Overview: To measure (human) blood pressure and pulse rate under different conditions. To analyze these variables and relate them to an index of fitness. To investigate the effect of temperature on heart rate in Daphnia.

Aims: An understanding of blood pressure and pulse rate, and their measurement and significance with respect to fitness. An understanding of the relationship between heart rate and temperature in a poikilotherm.

LAB 11: Animal behavior
Overview: To investigate responses in pillbugs (woodlice). To investigate mating behavior in fruit flies.

Aims: To understand and describe aspects of animal behavior. To understand the adaptiveness of appropriate behaviors.

LAB 12: Dissolved oxygen & aquatic primary productivity
Overview: To measure & analyze dissolved oxygen concentration in water samples. To measure and analyze the primary productivity of natural waters or lab cultures.

Aims: An understanding of primary productivity and its measurement. To use a controlled experiment to investigate the effect of changing light intensity on primary productivity.

Skills in Biology

IB SL
Complete nos:
1-28, 32

IB HL
Complete nos:
1-32

IB Options
Complete nos:
Option G: *29-31*

AP Biology
Complete nos:
1-32

Teachers may wish to make some points extension as appropriate

Learning Objectives

☐ 1. Compile your own glossary from the **KEY WORDS** displayed in **bold type** in the learning objectives below.

☐ 2. Demonstrate an understanding of the meaning of the following terms: **compare**, **contrast**, **define**, **describe**, **discuss**, **explain** (or account for), **evaluate**, **identify**, **illustrate**, **list**, **outline**, **state**, **suggest**, **summarize**. A correct understanding of these terms will enable you to answer questions appropriately *(see page 3 for help)*.

Scientific method *(pages 18-19)*

☐ 3. Explain what is meant by the **scientific method**. Understand its importance to science and the acquisition of new scientific knowledge. Understand the purpose of each of the common features of all science:
  • *Observing and measuring*
  • *Hypothesizing and predicting*
  • *Designing and planning investigations*
  • *Recording and interpreting data*
  • *Drawing conclusions and communicating findings.*

☐ 4. Recall the role of **observation** as a prelude to forming a **hypothesis**. In your research, you will make observations and use these to formulate a hypothesis, which you can then test. Your skills in planning and implementing an investigation may be required for:
  ☐ An experiment in which the effect of manipulating one variable on another is investigated (a fair test).
  ☐ A field study in which a pattern or relationship in a population or community is investigated.

☐ 5. Formulate an appropriate **hypothesis** based on your own observations or knowledge of a biological phenomenon. Make predictions about the expected outcome of your investigation.

Planning an investigation *(pages 20-25, 28)*

☐ 6. Appreciate that your study design will be determined by the nature of the investigation, e.g., a controlled experiment versus a field study. *Some of the following objectives apply specifically to controlled experiments involving the manipulation of a variable. However, they may apply, with modification, to field studies.*

☐ 7. Define and explain the purpose of each of the following variables in a controlled experiment:
  ☐ **Independent variable** (manipulated variable)
  ☐ **Dependent variable** (response variable)
  ☐ **Controlled variables** (to control nuisance factors)

☐ 8. For your own investigation distinguish clearly between:
  ☐ A **data value** for a particular **variable**, e.g., height.
  ☐ The individual sampling unit, e.g., a test-tube with an enzyme at a particular pH.
  ☐ The sample size, e.g., the number of test-tubes in each treatment.

☐ 9. Determine the amount of data that you need to collect in order to reasonably test your hypothesis.
  ☐ For lab based investigations, determine the **sample size** (e.g., the number of samples within each treatment) and the number of treatments (the range of the independent variable).
  ☐ For field based investigations, determine the size of the sampling unit (it may be an individual organism or a quadrat size) and the sample size (e.g., the number of organisms or quadrats).

☐ 10. Determine the type of data that you will collect (e.g., counts, measurements) and how you will collect it. Have a clear idea about how you are going to analyze your data before you start and appreciate why this is important. Explain why it is desirable to collect **quantitative** rather than **qualitative** data.

☐ 11. Determine whether or not any preliminary experiments are necessary and be able to incorporate changes to your proposed methods following such experiments.

☐ 12. Determine the **control** for your investigation, explaining how it acts as a reference against which the responses to treatments can be reliably interpreted.

☐ 13. Decide on the method by which you will **systematically record** the data as they are collected. Appreciate the advantages and disadvantages of different methods for systematically recording data: tables, spreadsheets, and software linked to **dataloggers**. Appreciate why a method for systematically recording data is important.

☐ 14. Identify **sources of error** in your experimental design and explain how you will minimize these.

☐ 15. Recognize that all biological investigations should be carried out with appropriate regard for safety and the well-being of living organisms and their environment.

Collecting data *(pages 24-25, 38-39)*

☐ 16. Demonstrate an ability to keep an accurate record of the progress of your investigation in a laboratory or field notebook. You should record ideas, possible future investigations, attempts, raw results, and failures.

☐ 17. Collect and record data systematically according to your plan (#13). Critically evaluate the **accuracy** of your methods for data collection, any **measurement errors**, and the repeatability (**precision**) of any measurements you make.

☐ 18. Make good **biological drawings** as a way of recording information where appropriate to your investigation.

Transforming raw data *(pages 26-27)*

☐ 19. Understand the difference between **raw data** and **transformed data**. Explain why data are often transformed before analysis. Evaluate the need for transformation with respect to the data you collect.

□ 20. Demonstrate an understanding of common data transformations and their use: *totals, percentages, rates, reciprocals, relative values*.

□ 21. If necessary, modify a table used for data collection to a formal table that can be included in the report. Include space in the table for transformed data.

Drawing graphs *(pages 29-35, 37)*

□ 22. Describe the benefits of graphing data. Recognize the **x axis** and **y axis** of graphs and identify which variable (dependent or independent) is plotted on each.

□ 23. Demonstrate an ability to present data appropriately using different types of graphs. Review the guidelines for the presentation of data in the following formats: **bar graphs, histograms, pie graphs, kite graphs, line graphs, scatter plots**.

□ 24. Explain what is meant by a '**line of best fit**' and when it is appropriate to use it. Draw 'lines of best fit' to graphs with plotted points.

Basic data analysis *(pages 28, 36, 40-41)*

□ 25. Demonstrate an ability to use **SI units** and an appropriate number of **significant figures**. Understand the relationship between the appropriate number of significant figures and the accuracy of a measurement.

□ 26. Distinguish between the terms **statistic** and **parameter**. Demonstrate an ability to use descriptive statistics to condense your data for presentation. Consider:

    (a) Sample **mean** and **standard deviation**. Identify when the use of these statistics is appropriate.

    (b) **Median** and **mode** (calculated from your own, or second hand, data). Explain what each statistic summarizes and when its use is appropriate.

□ 27. Identify trends in your data for later discussion. These could include any **positive** or **negative relationships** between variables and any lines of best fit.

□ 28. Evaluate unexpected results and outlying data points and be prepared to discuss them in your write-up.

Statistical tests *(pages 42-43, 199, 319-321)*

□ 29. Explain what is meant by **significance** and explain why significance tests are important in scientific studies.

□ 30. Understand that different statistical tests are appropriate for different types of data. Distinguish between tests for difference (chi-squared, Student's *t*) and tests for a relationship or trend (e.g., correlation).

□ 31. Examples of student's *t* test and chi-square have been provided in this topic. Use the data provided or your own data to practise the calculation of each statistic.

    Student's t-test is good for comparing two means even when sample sizes are small. The *t* test makes the assumption that the data are **normally distributed** about a central mean. However, the test is relatively unaffected by minor departures from normality.

    Chi-square (pronounced "ky" square) is also a test for difference between two groups. It is a simple test to perform but students should recognize the restrictions on the type of data appropriate to the chi-square test.

    Recognize that in a statistical analysis you will be able to calculate "a value", even if you do not satisfy the requirements of the test. However, the statistical result may not be a valid one, nor of any biological significance.

Writing a report *(pages 44-47)*

□ 32. Write up your report. Give it a concise, descriptive title, and organize it into the following sections:

    □ **Introduction**: The aim and hypothesis, and a summary of the current state of the knowledge in the topic area.

    □ **Materials and methods**: Describe your methodology in a way that allows it to be reproduced by others.

    □ **Results**: Use text, graphs, and tables to describe your results; do not discuss them at this stage.

    □ **Discussion**: Discuss your results, including unexpected results (#28), and with reference to the work of others.

    □ **Conclusion**: Summarize your findings with respect to your original hypothesis. Draw conclusions *only* about the variable that you planned to investigate.

    □ **Bibliography** or **reference list**: List all sources of information, including personal communications.

Textbooks

See the 'Textbook Reference Grid' on pages 8-9 for textbook page references relating to material in this topic.

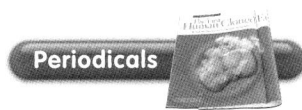

Supplementary Texts

See pages 5-6 for additional details of these texts:

■ Adds, J. *et al.*, 1999. **Tools, Techniques and Assessment in Biology** (NelsonThornes).

■ Barnard, C., *et al.*, 2001. **Asking Questions in Biology ...**, 2 edn (Prentice Hall).

■ Cadogan, A. and Sutton, R., 2002. **Maths for Advanced Biology** (NelsonThornes).

■ Morgan, S., 2002. **Advanced Level Practical Work for Biology** (Hodder and Stoughton).

Internet

See pages 10-11 for details of how to access **Bio Links** from our web site: **www.thebiozone.com**. From Bio Links, access sites under the topics:

GENERAL BIOLOGY ONLINE RESOURCES > Online Textbooks and Lecture Notes. **STUDENT PROJECTS:** • A scientific report • ActivStats • Investigation into the blowfly larva's response to light • Scientific investigation • Study skills - biology • The scientific method • Tree lupins • Woodlice online ... *and others*

Periodicals

See page 6 for details of publishers of periodicals:

STUDENT'S REFERENCE

■ **Correlation** Biol. Sci. Rev., 14(3) February 2002, pp. 38-41. *An examination of the relationship between variables. An excellent synopsis.*

■ **Experiments** Biol. Sci. Rev., 14(3) February 2002, pp. 11-13. *The basics of experimental design and execution: determining variables, measuring them, and establishing a control.*

■ **Descriptive Statistics** Biol. Sci. Rev., 13 (5) May 2001, pp. 36-37. *A synopsis of descriptive statistics. The appropriate use of standard error and standard deviation is discussed.*

■ **Testing Hypotheses** New Scientist, 4 Dec. 1993 (Inside Science). *Scientific method, statistical analyses, and hypothesis testing.*

■ **Statistical Modelling** New Scientist, 17 Sept. 1994 (Inside Science). *Useful presentation of data; distributions, normal curves, and histograms.*

■ **Statistical Sampling** New Scientist, 10 June 1995 (Inside Science). *An excellent account of hypothesis testing, sampling methodology and accuracy, significance, & the central limit theorem.*

■ **The Truth is Out There** New Scientist, 26 Feb. 2000 (Inside Science). *The philosophy of scientific method: starting with an idea, formulating a hypothesis, and following through to theory.*

■ **Describing the Normal Distribution** Biol. Sci. Rev., 13(2) November 2000, pp. 40-41. *The characteristics of the normal distribution: spread, mean, median, variance, and standard deviation.*

■ **Estimating the Mean and Standard Deviation** Biol. Sci. Rev., 13(3) January 2001, pp. 40-41. *Simple statistical analysis. Includes formulae for calculating sample mean and standard deviation.*

■ **The Variability of Samples** Biol. Sci. Rev., 13(4) March 2001, pp. 34-35. *The variability of sample data and the use of sample statistics as estimators for population parameters.*

TEACHER'S REFERENCE

■ **Biology Statistics made Simple using Excel** SSR 83(303), Dec. 2001, pp. 29. *An instructional account on the use of spreadsheets for statistics in A level science (excellent).*

■ **Biological Drawing** The American Biology Teacher, 63(4), April 2001, pp. 271-279. *Guidelines for student observation and drawing.*

■ **Teaching and Learning the Scientific Method** American Biology Teacher 63(4), April 2001, pp. 242-245. *The nature of biological investigations.*

■ **The Generality of Hypothetico-Deductive Reasoning...** The American Biology Teacher, 62(7), Sept. 2000, pp. 482-495. *The application of the hypothetico-deductive method in science.*

Software and video resources are now provided in the Teacher Resource Handbook

Forming a Hypothesis

Scientific knowledge grows through a process called the **scientific method**. This process involves observation and measurement, hypothesizing and predicting, and planning and executing investigations designed to test formulated hypotheses. Generating a hypothesis is crucial to scientific investigation. A scientific hypothesis is a possible explanation for an observation, which is capable of being tested by experimentation. Hypotheses lead to predictions about the system involved and they are accepted or rejected on the basis of findings arising from the investigation. Scientific hypotheses have specific characteristics (below) and may be modified as more information becomes available. For the purposes of investigation, hypotheses are often constructed in a form that allows them to be tested statistically. The **null hypothesis** (H_0) is the hypothesis of no difference or no effect. H_0 can be tested statistically, and may then be rejected in favor of accepting the alternative hypothesis (H_A) that is supported by the predictions. New information is generated as scientists make discoveries through testing hypotheses.

Making Observations

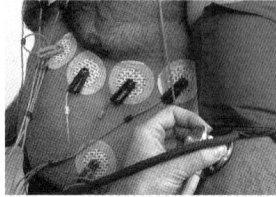

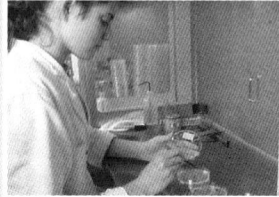

These may involve the observation of certain behaviors in wild populations, physiological measurements made during previous experiments, or 'accidental' results obtained when seeking answers to completely unrelated questions.

Testing predictions may lead to new observations

Asking Questions

The observations lead to the formation of questions about the system being studied.

Testing the Predictions

The predictions are tested out in the practical part of an investigation.

Accept or reject the hypothesis*

Forming a Hypothesis

Features of a sound hypothesis:
- It offers an explanation for an observation.
- It refers to only one independent variable.
- It is written as a definite statement and not as a question.
- It is testable by experimentation.
- It is based on observations and prior knowledge of the system.
- It leads to predictions about the system.

Designing an Investigation

Investigations are planned so that the predictions about the system made in the hypothesis can be tested. Investigations may be laboratory or field based.

* Rejection of the hypothesis may lead to new, alternative explanations (hypotheses) for the observations.

* Acceptance of the hypothesis as a valid explanation. These explanations are not necessarily permanent and may be rejected on the basis of future investigation. This process eventually leads to new knowledge (theory, laws, or models).

Useful Types of Hypotheses

- **Hypothesis involving manipulation** is used when the effect of manipulating a variable on a biological entity is being investigated. **Example**: Fertilizer concentration influences the rate of growth of plant A.

- **Hypothesis of choice** is used when species preference, e.g., for habitat, is being investigated. **Example**: Green woodpeckers show a preference for tree type when nesting.

- **Hypothesis involving observation** is used when organisms are being studied in the field where conditions cannot be changed. **Example**: Fern abundance is influenced by the degree to which the forest canopy is established.

1. A student noticed that woodlice (pillbugs) were often found in moist areas when she went looking for them. From this observation, she formulated the hypothesis stated below. Outline three features that make this a good hypothesis:

"Moisture level of the microhabitat influences woodlouse distribution"

(a) _____

(b) _____

(c) _____

2. Transform the following phrases into well written hypotheses:

(a) _"We wondered whether plants transpire faster in different weather conditions."_ _____

_____

(b) _"Does the slope of the surface affect the rate of movement of snails?"_ _____

_____

3. During the course of any investigation, new information may arise as a result of observations unrelated to the original hypothesis. This can lead to the generation of further hypotheses about the system. For each of the incidental observations described below, formulate a possible hypothesis and the outline of an investigation to test it. _Remember that the observation described in each case was not related to the hypothesis the experiment was designed to test:_

(a) **Bacterial cultures**

Hypothesis: _____

_____

Outline of the investigation: _____

_____

_____

_____

_____

_____

_____

_____

_____

_____

Bacterial Cultures

Observation: During an experiment on bacterial growth, the girls noticed that the cultures grew at different rates when the dishes were left overnight in different parts of the laboratory.

(b) **Plant cloning**

Hypothesis: _____

_____

Outline of the investigation: _____

_____

_____

_____

_____

_____

_____

_____

Plant Cloning

Observation: During an experiment on plant cloning, a scientist noticed that the root length of plant clones varied depending on the concentration of a hormone added to the agar.

Planning an Investigation

A 2

Investigations involve written stages (planning and reporting), at the start and end. The middle stage is the practical work when the data are collected. Practical work may be laboratory or field based. Typical lab based studies involve investigating how a biological response is affected by manipulating a particular **variable**, e.g., temperature. Field work often involves investigating features of a population or community. These may be interrelationships, such as competition, or patterns, such as zonation. Where quantitative information must be gathered from the population or community, particular techniques (such as quadrat sampling) and protocols (e.g., random placement of sampling units) apply. These aspects of practical work are covered in the topic *Practical Ecology*. Investigations in the field are usually more complex than those in the laboratory because natural systems have many more variables that cannot easily be controlled or accounted for.

Planning	Execution	Analysis and Reporting
		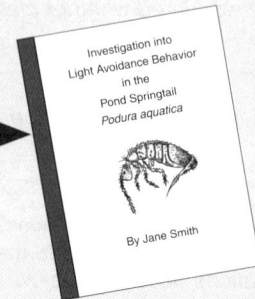

Planning
- Formulate your hypothesis from an observation.
- Use a checklist (see the next activity) or a template (above) to construct a plan.

Execution
- Spend time (as appropriate to your study) collecting the data.
- Record the data in a systematic format (e.g., a table or spreadsheet).

Analysis and Reporting
- Analyze the data using graphs, tables, or statistics to look for trends or patterns.
- Write up your report including all the necessary sections.

Identifying Variables

A variable is any characteristic or property able to take any one of a range of values. Investigations often look at the effect of changing one variable on another. It is important to identify all variables in an investigation: independent, dependent, and controlled, although there may be nuisance factors of which you are unaware. In all fair tests, only one variable is changed by the investigator.

Dependent variable
- Measured during the investigation.
- Recorded on the y axis of the graph.

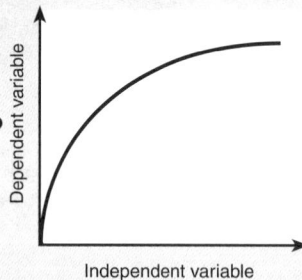

Controlled variables
- Factors that are kept the same or controlled.
- List these in the method, as appropriate to your own investigation.

Independent variable
- Set by the person carrying out the investigation.
- Recorded on the x axis of the graph.

Assumptions

In any experimental work, you will make certain assumptions about the biological system you are working with.

Assumptions are features of the system (and your experiment) that you assume to be true but do not (or cannot) test.

Examples of Investigations

Aim		Variables	
Investigate the effect of varying ...	on the following ...	Independent variable	Dependent variable
Temperature	Leaf width	Temperature	Leaf width
Light intensity	Activity of woodlice	Light intensity	Woodlice activity
Soil pH	Plant height at age 6 months	pH	Plant height

In order to write a sound method for your investigation, you need to determine how the independent, dependent, and controlled variables will be set and measured (or monitored). A good understanding of your methodology is crucial to a successful investigation. You need to be clear about how much data, and what type of data, you will collect. You should also have a good idea about how you plan to analyze those data. Use the example below to practise your skills in identifying this type of information.

Case Study: Catalase Activity

Catalase is an enzyme that converts hydrogen peroxide (H_2O_2) to oxygen and water. An experiment investigated the effect of temperature on the rate of the catalase reaction. Small (10 cm^3) test tubes were used for the reactions, each containing 0.5 cm^3 of enzyme and 4 cm^3 of hydrogen peroxide. Reaction rates were assessed at four temperatures (10°C, 20°C, 30°C, and 60°C). For each temperature, there were two reaction tubes (e.g. tubes 1 and 2 were both kept at 10°C). The height of oxygen bubbles present after one minute of reaction was used as a measure of the reaction rate; a faster reaction rate produced more bubbles. The entire experiment, involving eight tubes, was repeated on two separate days.

$$H_2O_2\ (l) \xrightarrow{\text{Catalase}} H_2O\ (l) + O_2\ (g)$$

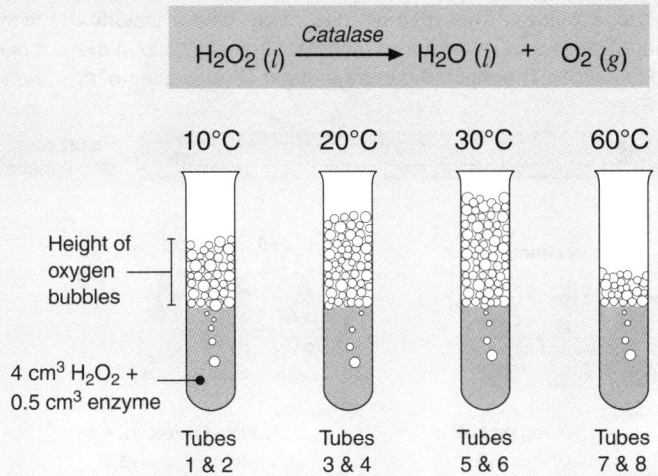

Height of oxygen bubbles

4 cm^3 H_2O_2 + 0.5 cm^3 enzyme

10°C	20°C	30°C	60°C
Tubes 1 & 2	Tubes 3 & 4	Tubes 5 & 6	Tubes 7 & 8

1. Write a suitable aim for this experiment: _____

    _____

2. Write a suitable hypothesis for this experiment: _____

    _____

3. (a) Name the **independent variable**: _____

    (b) State the range of values for the independent variable: _____

    (c) Name the unit for the independent variable: _____

    (d) List the equipment needed to set the independent variable, and describe how it was used:

    _____

4. (a) Name the **dependent variable**: _____

    (b) Name the unit for the dependent variable: _____

    (c) List the equipment needed to measure the dependent variable, and describe how it was used:

    _____

5. (a) Each temperature represents a treatment/sample/trial (circle one):

    (b) State the number of tubes at each temperature: _____

    (c) State the sample size for each treatment: _____

    (d) State how many times the whole investigation was repeated: _____

6. Explain why it would have been desirable to have included an extra tube containing no enzyme:

    _____

7. Identify three variables that might have been controlled in this experiment, and how they could have been monitored:

    (a) _____

    (b) _____

    (c) _____

8. Explain why controlled variables should be monitored carefully: _____

    _____

Experimental Method

A 3

An aim, hypothesis, and method for an experiment are described below. Explanations of the types of variables for which data are collected, and methods of recording these, are provided in the next two activities. The method described below includes numbered steps and incorporates other features identified in the previous activity. The method can be thought of as a 'statement of intent' for the practical work, and it may need slight changes during execution. The investigation described below was based on the observation that plant species 'A' was found growing in soil with a low pH (pH 4-5). The investigators wondered whether plant species 'A' was adapted to grow more vigorously under acid conditions than under alkaline or neutral conditions.

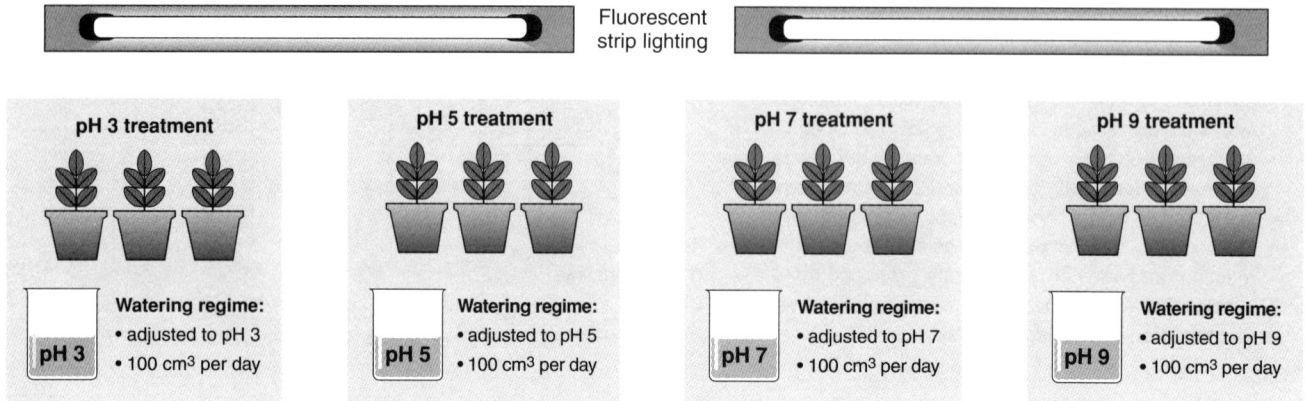

Fluorescent strip lighting

pH 3 treatment	pH 5 treatment	pH 7 treatment	pH 9 treatment

Watering regime:
- adjusted to pH 3
- 100 cm³ per day

pH 3

Watering regime:
- adjusted to pH 5
- 100 cm³ per day

pH 5

Watering regime:
- adjusted to pH 7
- 100 cm³ per day

pH 7

Watering regime:
- adjusted to pH 9
- 100 cm³ per day

pH 9

Aim: To investigate how pH affects the growth of plant species 'A'.

Hypothesis: pH has an effect on the vigour with which species A grows.

Prediction: Species 'A' will grow more vigorously at pH 5 than at pH 7 or higher.

Method

Seedling height ●

1. Germinate 20 seeds of species 'A' on damp blotting paper and choose 12 of them with equal height (12 mm).

Pot size and type ●

2. Plant the 12 seedlings into 12 test pots (all with dimensions of 5 cm tall and 2.5 cm diameter). Use the same type and quantity (80 g) of potting mix, and the same volume of water (100 cm³), for each planting.

Soil type and volume ●

The **independent variable** is soil pH.

3. Label the seedlings (on their pots) according to their treatments: pH 3, 5, 7, and 9.

4. Weigh each seedling in its pot to the nearest 0.1 g. Record their masses in the table of results in the day 0 (trial 1) column.

The **dependent variable** is plant mass.

5. Re-weigh the seedlings in their pots exactly 48 hours later. Record the new weights in a results table, in the day 2 (trial 1) column.

6. Give each plant 100 cm³ water at the appropriate pH immediately following weighing.

Watering regime ●

7. Repeat steps 5 and 6 every other day until day 10.

8. Keep the plants under fluorescent strip lighting to maintain constant light conditions.

Lighting regime ●

9. Record the temperature at regular intervals each day to monitor any variations.

Temperature ●

10. Repeat the entire procedure (steps 1-8) twice more to assess the variability between trials. Record the results in the spaces called trial 2 and trial 3 of the results table.

Controlled variables

Variable that is monitored but difficult to control

1. Explain the best way to take account of natural variability between individuals when designing an experiment:

_____

_____

_____

_____

A note about replication in experiments

Replication refers to the number of times you repeat your entire experimental design (including controls). True replication is not the same as increasing the sample size (*n*) although it is often used to mean the same thing. Replication accounts for any unusual and unforseen effects that may be operating in your set-up (e.g., field trials of plant varieties where soil type is variable).

Replication is necessary when you expect that the response of treatments will vary because of factors outside your control. It is a feature of higher level experimental designs, and complex statistics are needed to separate differences between replicate treatments. For simple experiments, it is usually more valuable to increase the sample size than to worry about replicates.

2. Explain the importance of ensuring that any influencing variables in an experiment (except the one that you are manipulating) are controlled and kept constant across all treatments:

_____

_____

3. In the experiment outlined on the previous page, explain why only single plants were grown in each pot:

_____

_____

4. Suggest why it is important to consider the physical layout of treatments in an experiment:

_____

_____

_____

YOUR CHECKLIST FOR EXPERIMENTAL DESIGN

The following provides a checklist for an experimental design. Check off the points when you are confident that you have satisfied the requirements in each case:

1. **Preliminary:**

 ☐ (a) You have determined the aim of your investigation and formulated a hypothesis based on observation(s).

 ☐ (b) The hypothesis (and its predictions) are testable using the resources you have available (the study is feasible).

 ☐ (c) The organism you have chosen is suitable for the study and you have considered the ethics involved.

2. **Assumptions and variables:**

 ☐ (a) You are aware of any assumptions that you are making in your experiment.

 ☐ (b) You have identified all the variables in the experiment (controlled, independent, dependent, uncontrollable).

 ☐ (c) You have set the range of the independent variable and established how you will fix the controlled variables.

 ☐ (d) You have considered what (if any) preliminary treatment or trials are necessary.

 ☐ (e) You have considered the layout of your treatments to account for any unforseen variability in your set-up and you have established your control(s).

3. **Data collection:**

 ☐ (a) You have identified the units for all variables and determined how you will measure or monitor each variable. You have determined how much data you will collect, e.g., the number of samples you will take. The type of data collected will be determined by how you are measuring your variables.

 ☐ (b) You have considered how you will analyze the data you collect and made sure that your experimental design allows you to answer the questions you have asked.

 ☐ (c) You have designed a method for systematically recording your results and had this checked with a teacher. The format of your results table or spreadsheet accommodates all your raw results, any transformations you intend to make, and all trials and treatments.

 ☐ (d) You have recorded data from any preliminary trials and any necessary changes to your methodology.

Recording Results

Designing a table to record your results is part of planning your investigation. Once you have collected your data, you will need to analyze and present it (see pages 29-37, 40-43). To do this, it may be necessary to transform your data first, as has been done below with the calculation of averages (also see pages 26-27). An example of a table for recording results is presented below. This particular example pertains to the investigation described in the previous activity, but it represents a relatively standardized layout. The labels on the columns and rows are chosen to represent the design features of the investigation. The first column contains the entire range chosen for the independent variable. There are spaces for multiple sampling units, repeats (trials), and averages. A more formal version of this table (neatly written and titled) should be presented in your final report.

Dependent variable and its units

Space for repeats of the experimental design (in this case, three trials).

Space for three plants at each pH

The range of values for the independent variable are in this column

All masses are in grams and to the nearest 0.1 g.

Recordings of the dependent variable

Space for averages

	Plant no.	Trial 1 (plant mass in grams)						Trial 2 (plant mass in grams)						Trial 3 (plant mass in grams)					
		Day No.						Day No.						Day No.					
		0	2	4	6	8	10	0	2	4	6	8	10	0	2	4	6	8	10
pH 3	1	0.5	1.1																
	2	0.6	1.2																
	3	0.7	1.3																
	Av.	0.6	1.2																
pH 5	1	0.6	1.4																
	2	0.8	1.7																
	3	0.5	1.9																
	Av.	0.6	1.7																
pH 7	1	0.7	1.3																
	2	0.8	1.3																
	3	0.4	1.7																
	Av.	0.6	1.4																
pH 9	1	0.5	0.6																
	2	0.9	1.1																
	3	0.8	1.0																
	Av.	0.7	0.9																

1. In the space (below, right) design a table to collect data from the case study below. Include space for individual results and averages from the three set ups (use the table above as a guide).

Case Study
Carbon dioxide levels in a respiration chamber

A datalogging system was used to monitor the concentrations of carbon dioxide (CO_2) in respiration chambers containing five green leaves from one plant species.

The entire study was done in conditions of full light (quantified) and involved three identical set-ups. The CO_2 concentrations were measured every minute, over a period of ten minutes, using a carbon dioxide sensor. An average CO_2 concentration (for the three set-ups) was calculated. The study was carried out two more times, two days apart.

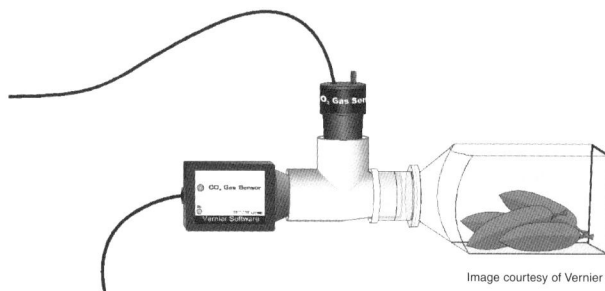

Image courtesy of Vernier

2. Next, the effect of varying the light intensity on CO_2 concentration was investigated, using a range of light values (measured values for low light, half-light, and full light). Describe how the results table for this investigation would differ from the one you have drawn opposite (which was for full light only):

Variables and Data

When planning any kind of biological investigation, it is important to consider the type of data that will be collected. It is best, whenever possible, to collect quantitative or numerical data, as these data lend themselves well to analysis and statistical testing. Recording data in a systematic way as you collect it, e.g., using a table or spreadsheet data, is important, especially if data manipulation and transformation are required. It is also useful to calculate summary, descriptive statistics (e.g., mean, median) as you proceed. These will help you to recognize important trends and features in your data as they become apparent.

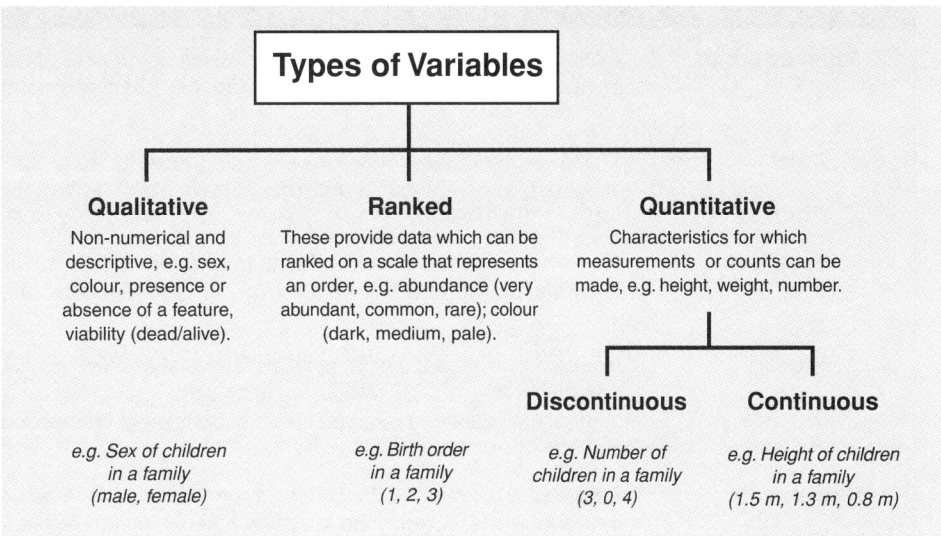

Types of Variables

Qualitative
Non-numerical and descriptive, e.g. sex, colour, presence or absence of a feature, viability (dead/alive).

Ranked
These provide data which can be ranked on a scale that represents an order, e.g. abundance (very abundant, common, rare); colour (dark, medium, pale).

Quantitative
Characteristics for which measurements or counts can be made, e.g. height, weight, number.

Discontinuous

Continuous

e.g. Sex of children in a family (male, female)

e.g. Birth order in a family (1, 2, 3)

e.g. Number of children in a family (3, 0, 4)

e.g. Height of children in a family (1.5 m, 1.3 m, 0.8 m)

The values for monitored or measured variables, collected during the course of the investigation, are called **data**. Like their corresponding variables, data may be quantitative, qualitative, or ranked.

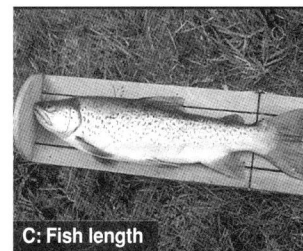

A: Leaf shape

B: Number per litter

C: Fish length

1. For each of the photographic examples (A – C above), classify the variables as quantitative, ranked, or qualitative:

    (a) Leaf shape: _____

    (b) Number per litter: _____

    (c) Fish length: _____

2. (a) Explain why it is desirable to collect quantitative data where possible in biological studies:

    _____

    _____

    (b) Give an example of data that could not be collected in a quantitative manner:

    _____

3. Sometimes, biological studies involve descriptive variables. In such cases, biologists often attempt to apply **quantitative** measures to a **qualitative variable** so that it can be objectively assessed. One example of this is the measure of *skull robustness* that changes during the course of human evolution (i.e., how ruggedly built the face and jaws are). This qualitative variable of 'robustness' can be assessed in other ways. Provide two ways in which you could assess skull robustness in a quantitative manner:

    (a) _____

    _____

    _____

    (b) _____

    _____

    _____

DA 2 Transforming Raw Data

Data often have to be transformed as a first step in the initial analysis of results. Transforming data can make them more useful by helping to highlight trends and making important features more obvious. Data transformations may be quite simple (e.g. percentages, totals, and rates) or they may be more complex transformations used before statistical procedures (e.g. log transformations). Some of the simple transformations are outlined below.

Transformation	Rationale for Transformation
Frequency table	A tally chart of the number of times a value occurs in a data set. It is a useful first step in data analysis as a neatly constructed tally chart can double as a simple histogram.
Total	The sum of all data values for a variable. Useful as an initial stage in data handling, especially in comparing replicates. Used in making other data transformations.
Percentages	Provide a clear expression of what proportion of data fall into any particular category. This relationship may not be obvious from the raw data values.
Rates	Expressed as a measure per unit time. Rates show how a variable changes over a standard time period (e.g. one second, one minute or one hour). Rates allow meaningful comparison of data that may have been recorded over different time periods.
Reciprocals	Reciprocals of time (1/data value) can provide a crude measure of rate in situations where the variable measured is the total time taken to complete a task e.g. time taken for a color change to occur in an enzyme reaction.
Relative values	These involve expression of data values relative to a standard value e.g. number of road deaths per 1000 cars or calorie consumption per gram of body weight. They allow data from different sample sizes or different organisms to be meaningfully compared. Sometimes they are expressed as a percentage (e.g. 35%) or as a proportion (e.g. 0.35).

1. (a) Explain what it means to **transform data**: ⎯⎯⎯⎯⎯⎯⎯⎯⎯⎯⎯⎯⎯⎯⎯⎯⎯⎯⎯⎯⎯⎯⎯⎯⎯⎯

⎯⎯

(b) Briefly explain the general purpose of transforming data: ⎯⎯⎯⎯⎯⎯⎯⎯⎯⎯⎯⎯⎯⎯⎯⎯⎯⎯⎯

⎯⎯

⎯⎯

⎯⎯

2. For each of the following examples, state a suitable transformation, together with a reason for your choice:
(a) Determining relative abundance from counts of four plant species in two different habitat areas:

Suitable transformation: ⎯⎯⎯⎯⎯⎯⎯⎯⎯⎯⎯⎯⎯⎯⎯⎯⎯⎯⎯⎯⎯⎯⎯⎯⎯⎯⎯⎯⎯⎯⎯⎯⎯⎯⎯⎯⎯⎯

Reason: ⎯⎯⎯

(b) Making a meaningful comparison between animals of different size in the volume of oxygen each consumed:

Suitable transformation: ⎯⎯⎯⎯⎯⎯⎯⎯⎯⎯⎯⎯⎯⎯⎯⎯⎯⎯⎯⎯⎯⎯⎯⎯⎯⎯⎯⎯⎯⎯⎯⎯⎯⎯⎯⎯⎯⎯

Reason: ⎯⎯⎯

(c) Making a meaningful comparison of the time taken for chemical precipitation to occur in a flask at different pH values:

Suitable transformation: ⎯⎯⎯⎯⎯⎯⎯⎯⎯⎯⎯⎯⎯⎯⎯⎯⎯⎯⎯⎯⎯⎯⎯⎯⎯⎯⎯⎯⎯⎯⎯⎯⎯⎯⎯⎯⎯⎯

Reason: ⎯⎯⎯

(d) Determining the effect of temperature on the production of carbon dioxide by respiring seeds:

Suitable transformation: ⎯⎯⎯⎯⎯⎯⎯⎯⎯⎯⎯⎯⎯⎯⎯⎯⎯⎯⎯⎯⎯⎯⎯⎯⎯⎯⎯⎯⎯⎯⎯⎯⎯⎯⎯⎯⎯⎯

Reason: ⎯⎯⎯

Incidence of cyanogenic clover in different areas

3. Complete the transformations for each of the tables on the right. The first value is provided in each case.

(a) TABLE: *Incidence of cyanogenic clover in different areas*

Working: 124 ÷ 159 = 0.78 = 78%

This is the number of cyanogenic clover out of the total.

Clover plant type	Frost free area		Frost prone area		Totals
	Number	%	Number	%	
Cyanogenic	124	78%	26		
Acyanogenic	35		115		
Total	159				

Plant transpiration loss using a bubble potometer

(b) TABLE: *Plant transpiration loss using a bubble potometer*

Working: (9.0 − 8.0) ÷ 5 min = 0.2

This is the distance the bubble moved over the first 5 minutes. Note that there is no data entry possible for the first reading (0 min) because no difference can be calculated.

Time (min)	Pipette arm reading (cm^3)	Plant water loss ($cm^3 min^{-1}$)
0	9.0	–
5	8.0	0.2
10	7.2	
15	6.2	
20	4.9	

(c) TABLE: *Photosynthetic rate at different light intensities*

Working: 1 ÷ 15 = 0.067

This is time taken for the leaf to float. A reciprocal gives a per minute rate (the variable measured is the time taken for an event to occur).

NOTE: In this experiment, the flotation time is used as a crude measure of photosynthetic rate. As oxygen bubbles are produced as a product of photosynthesis, they stick to the leaf disc and increase its buoyancy. The faster the rate, the sooner they come to the surface. The rates of photosynthesis should be measured over similar time intervals, so the rate is transformed to a 'per minute' basis (the reciprocal of time).

Photosynthetic rate at different light intensities

Light intensity %	Average time for leaf disc to float (min)	Reciprocal of time (min^{-1})
100	15	0.067
50	25	
25	50	
11	93	
6	187	

Frequency of size classes in a sample of eels

(d) TABLE: *Frequency of size classes in a sample of eels*

Working: (7 ÷ 270) x 100 = 2.6 %

This is the number of individuals out of the total that appear in the size class 0-50 mm. The relative frequency is rounded to one decimal place.

Size class (mm)	Frequency	Relative frequency (%)
0-50	7	2.6
50-99	23	
100-149	59	
150-199	98	
200-249	50	
250-299	30	
300-349	3	
Total	270	

Terms and Notation

The definitions for some commonly encountered terms related to making biological investigations are provided below. Use these as you would use a biology dictionary when planning your investigation and writing up your report. It is important to be consistent with the use of terms i.e use the same term for the same procedure or unit throughout your study. Be sure, when using a term with a specific statistical meaning, such as sample, that you are using the term correctly.

General Terms

Data: Facts collected for analysis.

Qualitative: Not quantitative. Described in words or terms rather than by numbers. Includes subjective descriptions in terms of variables such as color or shape.

Quantitative: Able to be expressed in numbers. Numerical values derived from counts or measurements.

The Design of Investigations

Hypothesis: A tentative explanation of an observation, capable of being tested by experimentation. Hypotheses are written as clear statements, not as questions.

Control treatment (control): A standard (reference) treatment that helps to ensure that responses to other treatments can be reliably interpreted. There may be more than one control in an investigation.

Dependent variable: A variable whose values are determined by another variable (the independent variable). In practice, the dependent variable is the variable representing the biological response.

Independent variable: A variable whose values are set, or systematically altered, by the investigator.

Controlled variables: Variables that may take on different values in different situations, but are controlled (fixed) as part of the design of the investigation.

Experiment: A contrived situation designed to test (one or more) hypotheses and their predictions. It is good practice to use sample sizes that are as large as possible for experiments.

Investigation: A very broad term applied to scientific studies; investigations may be controlled experiments or field based studies involving population sampling.

Parameter: A numerical value that describes a characteristic of a population (e.g., the mean height of all 18 year-old females).

Random sample: A method of choosing a sample from a population that avoids any subjective element. It is the equivalent to drawing numbers out of a hat, but using random number tables. For field based studies involving quadrats or transects, random numbers can be used to determine the positioning of the sampling unit.

Repeat / Trial: The entire investigation is carried out again at a different time. This ensures that the results are reproducible. Note that repeats or trials are not replicates in the true sense unless they are run at the same time.

Sample: A sub-set of a whole used to estimate the values that might have been obtained if every individual or response was measured. A sample is made up of **sampling units**, In lab based investigations, the sampling unit might be a test-tube, while in field based studies, the sampling unit might be an individual organism or a quadrat.

Sample size (n): The number of samples taken. In a field study, a typical sample size may involve 20-50 individuals or 20 quadrats. In a lab based investigation, a typical sample size may be two to three sampling units, e.g., two test-tubes held at 10°C.

Sampling unit: Sampling units make up the sample size. Examples of sampling units in different investigations are an individual organism, a test tube undergoing a particular treatment, an area (e.g., quadrat size), or a volume. The size of the sampling unit is an important consideration in most field studies where the area or volume of a habitat is being sampled.

Statistic: An estimate of a parameter obtained from a sample (e.g., the mean height of all 18 year-old females based on those in your class). *Compare this with the definition for parameter*.

Treatments: Well defined conditions applied to the sample units. The response of sample units to a treatment is intended to shed light on the hypothesis under investigation. What is often of most interest is the comparison of the responses to different treatments.

Variable: A factor in an experiment that is subject to change. Variables may be controlled (fixed), manipulated (systematically altered), or represent a biological response.

Accuracy and Significance of Data

Accuracy: The correctness of the measurement (the closeness of the measured value to the true value). Accuracy is often a function of the calibration of the instrument used for measuring.

Measurement errors: When measuring or setting the value of a variable, there may be some difference between your answer and the 'right' answer. These errors are often as a result of poor technique or poorly set up equipment.

Objective measurement: Measurement not significantly involving subjective (or personal) judgment. If a second person repeats the measurement they should get the same answer.

Precision: The repeatability of the measurement. As there is usually no reason to suspect that a piece of equipment is giving inaccurate measures, making precise measurements is usually the most important consideration. You can assess or quantify the precision of any measurement system by taking repeated measurements from individual samples.

The Expression of Units

The value of a variable must be written with its units where possible. Common ways of recording measurements in biology are: volume in liters, mass in grams, length in meters, time in seconds. The following example shows different ways to express the same term. Note that ml and cm^3 are equivalent.

Oxygen consumption (milliliters per gram per hour)

Oxygen consumption ($ml g^{-1} h^{-1}$) (or $mL g^{-1} h^{-1}$)

Oxygen consumption ($ml/g/h$) (or $mL/g/h$)

Oxygen consumption/$cm^3 g^{-1} h^{-1}$

Statistical significance: An assigned value that is used to establish the probability that an observed trend or difference represents a true difference that is not due to chance alone. If a level of significance is less than the chosen value (usually 1-10%), the difference is regarded as statistically significant. Remember that in rigorous science, it is the hypothesis of no difference or no effect (the null hypothesis, H_0) that is tested. The alternative hypothesis (your tentative explanation for an observation) can only be accepted through statistical rejection of H_0.

Validity: Whether or not you are truly measuring the right thing.

Data Presentation

Data can be presented in a number of ways. Tables provide an accurate record of numerical values and allow you to organize your data in a way that allows you to clarify the relationships and trends that are apparent. Graphical presentation provides a visual image of trends in the data in a minimum of space. The choice between graphing or tabulation depends on the type and complexity of the data and the information that you are wanting to convey. Outlined below are some of the basic rules for constructing tables and graphs. Values for standard errors are included in this example, although it is not a requirement to calculate these. In your report, always allow enough space for a graph e.g., one third to one half of a page. The examples in this manual are usually reduced for reasons of space.

Presenting Data in Tables

Tables should have an accurate, descriptive title. Number tables consecutively through the report.

Table 1: Length and growth of the third internode of bean plants receiving three different hormone treatments (data are given ± standard error).

Independent variable in left column.

Control values (if present) should be placed at the beginning of the table.

Each row should show a different experimental treatment, organism, sampling site etc.

Treatment	Sample size	Mean rate of internode growth (mm day $^{-1}$)	Mean internode length (mm)	Mean mass of tissue added (g day $^{-1}$)
Control	50	0.60 ± 0.025	32.3 ± 2.3	0.36 ± 0.025
Hormone 1	46	1.52 ± 0.030	41.6 ± 3.4	0.51 ± 0.030
Hormone 2	98	0.82 ± 0.018	38.4 ± 0.9	0.56 ± 0.028
Hormone 3	85	2.06 ± 0.019	50.2 ± 1.4	0.68 ± 0.020

Heading and subheadings identify each set of data and show units of measurement.

Tables can be used to show standard errors or standard deviations although this is optional.

Show values only to the level of significance allowable by your measuring technique.

Columns that need to be compared should be placed alongside each other.

Organize the columns so that each category of like numbers or attributes is listed vertically.

Presenting Data in Graph Format

Plot points accurately. Different responses can be distinguished using different symbols, lines or bar colors.

Label both axes (provide SI units of measurement if necessary).

Place the dependent variable e.g. biological response, on the vertical (y) axis (if you are drawing a scatter graph it does not matter).

A break in an axis allows economical use of space if there are no data in the "broken" area. A floating axis (where zero points do not meet) allows data points to be plotted away from the vertical axis.

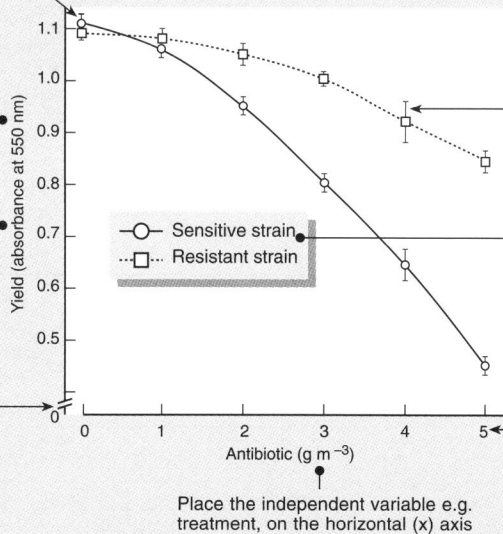

Fig. 1: Yield of two bacterial strains at different antibiotic levels. Vertical bars show standard errors ($n= 6$)

Graphs (called figures) should have a concise, explanatory title. If several graphs appear in your report they should be numbered consecutively.

If they have been calculated, graphs may show standard error or some other measure of the spread of the data around the plotted value.

A key identifies symbols. This information sometimes appears in the title.

Each axis should have an appropriate scale. Decide on the scale by finding the maximum and minimum values for each variable.

Place the independent variable e.g. treatment, on the horizontal (x) axis

1. State an advantage of using a table format for data presentation:

2. (a) Explain the importance of using an appropriate scale on a graph:

   (b) Scales on x and y axes may sometimes be "floating" (not meeting in the lower left corner), or they may be broken using a double slash and recontinued. Explain the purpose of these techniques:

DA 2 Drawing Bar Graphs

Guidelines for Bar Graphs

Bar graphs are appropriate for data that are non-numerical and **discrete** for at least one variable, i.e., they are grouped into separate categories. There are no dependent or independent variables. Important features of this type of graph include:

- Data are collected for discontinuous, non-numerical categories (e.g., place, color, and species), so the bars do not touch.

- Data values may be entered on or above the bars if you wish.

- Multiple sets of data can be displayed side by side for direct comparison (e.g., males and females in the same age group).

- Axes may be reversed so that the categories are on the x axis, i.e., the bars can be vertical or horizontal. When they are vertical, these graphs are sometimes called column graphs.

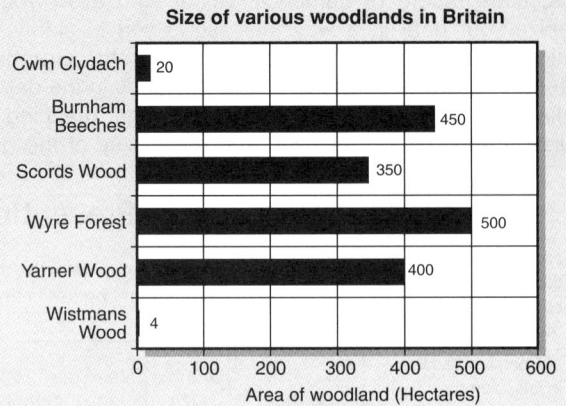

Size of various woodlands in Britain

Woodland	Area (Hectares)
Cwm Clydach	20
Burnham Beeches	450
Scords Wood	350
Wyre Forest	500
Yarner Wood	400
Wistmans Wood	4

Area of woodland (Hectares)

1. Counts of eight mollusc species were made from a series of quadrat samples at two sites on a rocky shore. The summary data are presented here.

   (a) Tabulate the mean (**average**) numbers per square meter at each site in Table 1 (below left).

   (b) Plot a **bar graph** of the tabulated data on the grid below. For each species, plot the data from both sites side by side using different colors to distinguish the sites.

Average abundance of 8 mollusc species from two sites along a rocky shore.

Species	Average (no m^{-2})	
	Site 1	Site 2

Field data notebook

Total counts at site 1 (11 quadrats) and site 2 (10 quadrats). Quadrats 1 sq. m.

Species	Site 1 Total	Site 1 Mean (No m^{-2})	Site 2 Total	Site 2 Mean (No m^{-2})
Ornate limpet	232	21	299	30
Radiate limpet	68	6	344	34
Limpet sp. A	420	38	0	0
Cats-eye	68	6	16	2
Top shell	16	2	43	4
Limpet sp. B	628	57	389	39
Limpet sp. C	0	0	22	2
Chiton	12	1	30	3

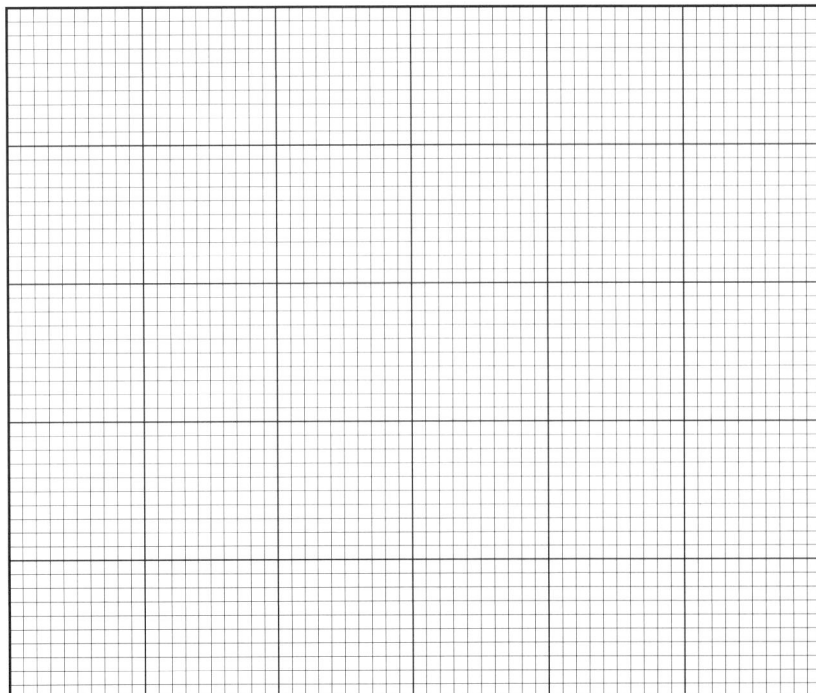

DA ② Drawing Histograms

Guidelines for Histograms

Histograms are plots of **continuous** data and are often used to represent frequency distributions, where the y-axis shows the number of times a particular measurement or value was obtained. For this reason, they are often called frequency histograms. Important features of this type of graph include:

- The data are numerical and continuous (e.g., height or weight), so the bars touch.

- The x-axis usually records the class interval. The y-axis usually records the number of individuals in each class interval (frequency).

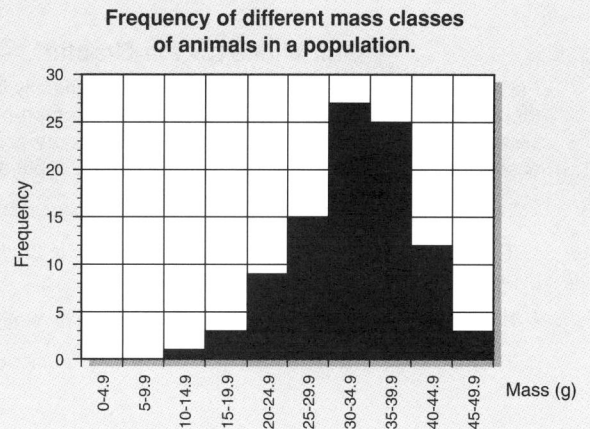

Frequency of different mass classes of animals in a population.

1. The weight data provided below were recorded from 95 individuals (male and female), older than 17 years.

    (a) Create a tally chart (frequency table) in the frame provided, organizing the weight data into a form suitable for plotting. An example of the tally for the eight grouping 55-59.9 kg has been completed for you as an example. Note that the raw data values, once they are recorded as counts on the tally chart, are crossed off the data set in the notebook. It is important to do this in order to prevent data entry errors.

    (b) Plot a **frequency histogram** of the tallied data on the grid provided below.

Weight (kg)	Tally	Total
45-49.9		
50-54.9		
55-59.9	LHt //	7
60-64.9		
65-69.9		
70-74.9		
75-79.9		
80-84.9		
85-89.9		
90-94.9		
95-99.9		
100-104.9		
105-109.9		

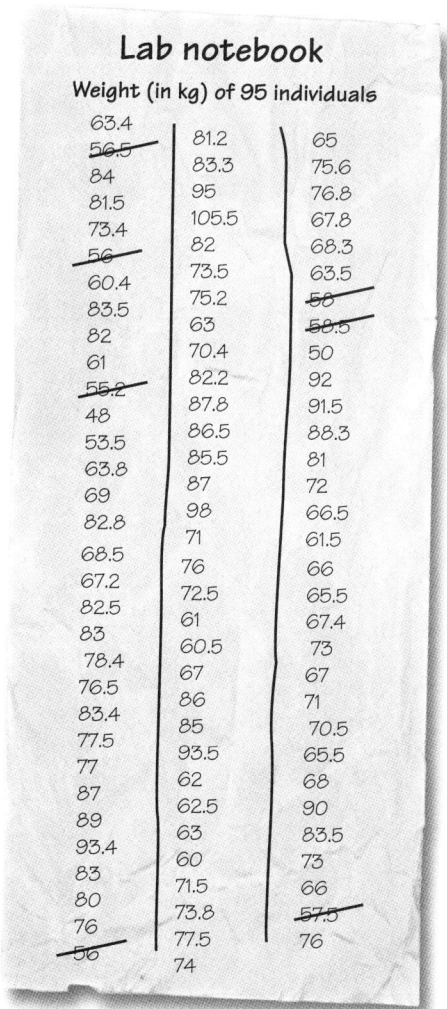

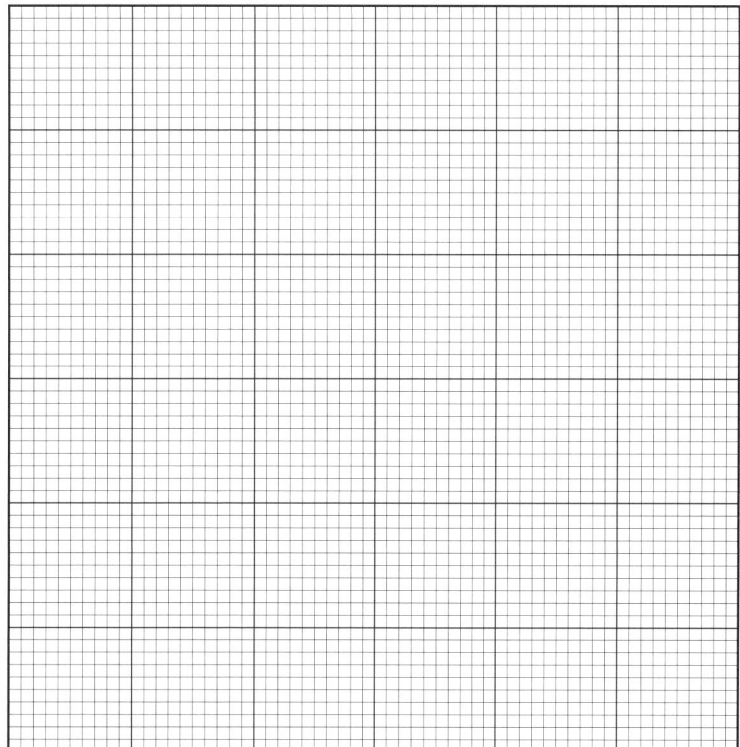

Lab notebook

Weight (in kg) of 95 individuals

63.4	81.2	65
56.5	83.3	75.6
84	95	76.8
81.5	105.5	67.8
73.4	82	68.3
56	73.5	63.5
60.4	75.2	56
83.5	63	56.5
82	70.4	50
61	82.2	92
55.2	87.8	91.5
48	86.5	88.3
53.5	85.5	81
63.8	87	72
69	98	66.5
82.8	71	61.5
68.5	76	66
67.2	72.5	65.5
82.5	61	67.4
83	60.5	73
78.4	67	67
76.5	86	71
83.4	85	70.5
77.5	93.5	65.5
77	62	68
87	62.5	90
89	63	83.5
93.4	60	73
83	71.5	66
80	73.8	57.5
76	77.5	76
56	74	

Drawing Pie Graphs

DA 2

Guidelines for Pie Graphs

Pie graphs can be used instead of bar graphs, generally in cases where there are six or fewer categories involved. A pie graph provides strong visual impact of the relative proportions in each category, particularly where one of the categories is very dominant. Features of pie graphs include:

- The data for one variable are discontinuous (non-numerical or categories).

- The data for the dependent variable are usually in the form of counts, proportions, or percentages.

- Pie graphs are good for visual impact and showing relative proportions.

- They are not suitable for data sets with a large number of categories.

Average residential water use

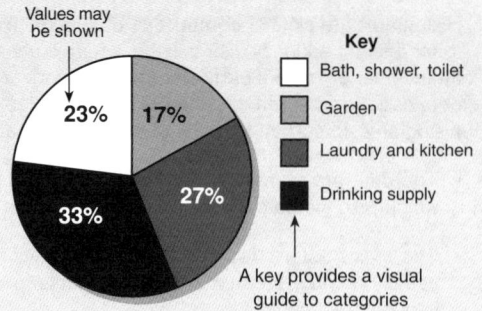

Values may be shown

23% 17% 33% 27%

Key
- Bath, shower, toilet
- Garden
- Laundry and kitchen
- Drinking supply

A key provides a visual guide to categories

1. The data provided below are from a study of the diets of three vertebrates.

   (a) Tabulate the data from the notebook in the frame provided. Calculate the angle for each percentage, given that each percentage point is equal to 3.6° (the first example is provided: 23.6 x 3.6 = 85).

   (b) Plot a pie graph for each animal in the circles provided. The circles have been marked at 5° intervals to enable you to do this exercise without a protractor. For the purposes of this exercise, begin your pie graphs at the 0° (= 360°) mark and work in a clockwise direction from the largest to the smallest percentage. Use one key for all three pie graphs.

Field data notebook

% of different food items in the diet

Food item	Ferrets	Rats	Cats
Birds	23.6	1.4	6.9
Crickets	15.3	23.6	0
Other insects (not crickets)	15.3	20.8	1.9
Voles	9.2	0	19.4
Rabbits	8.3	0	18.1
Rats	6.1	0	43.1
Mice	13.9	0	10.6
Fruits and seeds	0	40.3	0
Green leaves	0	13.9	0
Unidentified	8.3	0	0

Percentage occurrence of different foods in the diet of ferrets, rats, and cats. Graph angle representing the % is shown to assist plotting.

Food item in diet	Ferrets		Rats		Cats	
	% in diet	Angle (°)	% in diet	Angle (°)	% in diet	Angle (°)
Birds	23.6	85				

Ferrets

0°

Rats

0°

Cats

0°

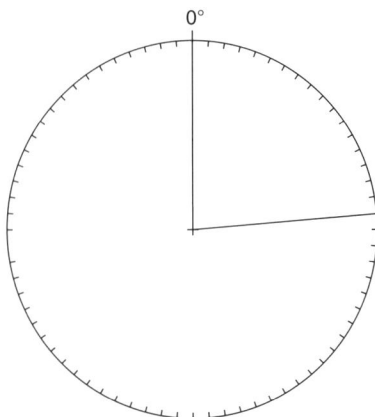

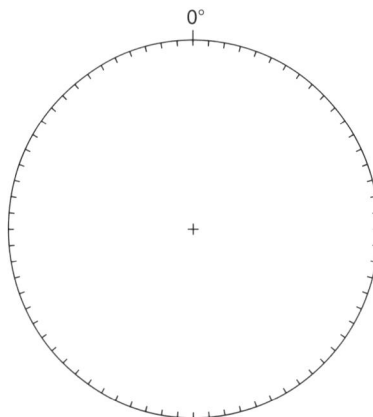

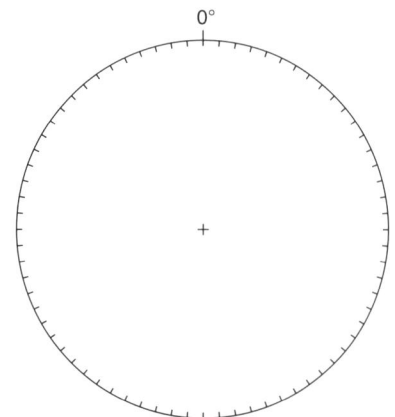

Key to food items in the diet

| Birds | Crickets | Other insects | Voles | Rabbits | Rats | Mice | Green leaves | Fruits & seeds | Unidentified |

DA 2   Drawing Kite Graphs

Guidelines for Kite Graphs

Kite graphs are ideal for representing distributional data, e.g., abundance along an environmental gradient. They are elongated figures drawn along a baseline. Important features of kite graphs include:

- Each kite represents changes in species abundance across a landscape. The abundance can be calculated from the kite width.

- They often involve plots for more than one species; this makes them good for highlighting probable differences in habitat preferences between species.

- A thin line on a kite graph represents species absence.

- The axes can be reversed depending on preference.

- Kite graphs may also be used to show changes in distribution with time, for example, with daily or seasonal cycles of movement.

Species abundance along a rocky shoreline

1. The following data were collected from three streams of different lengths and flow rates. Invertebrates were collected at 0.5 km intervals from the headwaters (0 km) to the stream mouth. Their wet weight was measured and recorded (per m^2).

   (a) Tabulate the data below for plotting.

   (b) Plot a **kite graph** of the data from all three streams on the grid provided below. Do not forget to include a scale so that the weight at each point on the kite can be calculated.

Wet mass of invertebrates along 3 different streams

Distance from mouth (km)	Wet weight (g m^{-2})		
	Stream A	Stream B	Stream C

Field data notebook

Mass per m^2 of invertebrates from 3 streams.

Stream A: Slow flowing

Km from mouth	g m^{-2}
5.0	0.3
4.5	2.5
4.0	0.2
3.5	0.7
3.0	0.1
2.5	0.6
2.0	0.3
1.5	0.3
1.0	0.4
0.5	0.5
0	0.4

Stream B: Fast, steep

Km from mouth	g m^{-2}
2.5	0.3
2.0	0.4
1.5	0.5
1.0	0.1
0.5	0.6
0	0.4

Stream C: Steep torrent

Km from mouth	g m^{-2}
1.5	0.2
1.0	0
0.5	0.5
0	0

DA 2 Drawing Line Graphs

Guidelines for Line Graphs

Line graphs are used when one variable (the independent variable) affects another, the dependent variable. Line graphs can be drawn without a measure of spread (top figure, right) or with some calculated measure of data variability (bottom figure, right). Important features of line graphs include:

• The data must be continuous for both variables.

• The dependent variable is usually the biological response.

• The independent variable is often time or the experimental treatment.

• In cases where there is an implied trend (e.g., one variable increases with the other), a line of best fit is usually plotted through the data points to show the relationship.

• If fluctuations in the data are likely to be important (e.g., with climate and other environmental data) the data points are usually connected directly (point to point).

• Line graphs may be drawn with measure of error. The data are presented as points (the calculated means), with bars above and below, indicating a measure of variability or spread in the data (e.g., standard error, standard deviation, or 95% confidence intervals).

• Where no error value has been calculated, the scatter can be shown by plotting the individual data points vertically above and below the mean. By convention, bars are not used to indicate the range of raw values in a data set.

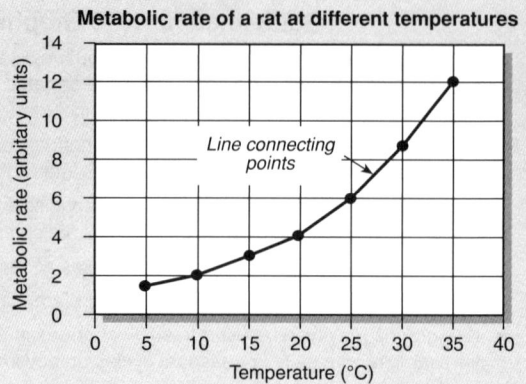

Metabolic rate of a rat at different temperatures

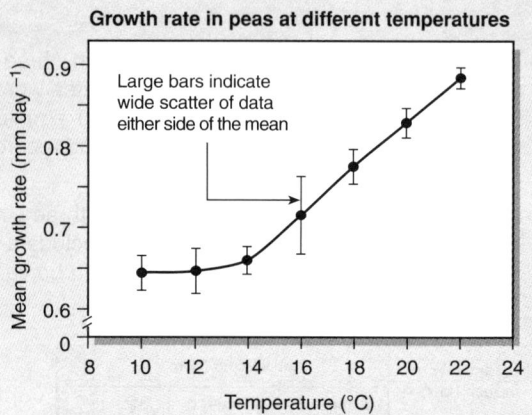

Growth rate in peas at different temperatures

1. The results (shown right) were collected in a study investigating the effect of temperature on the activity of an enzyme.

    (a) Using the results provided in the table (right), plot a line graph on the grid below (draw a line of best fit):

    (b) Estimate the rate of reaction at 15°C:

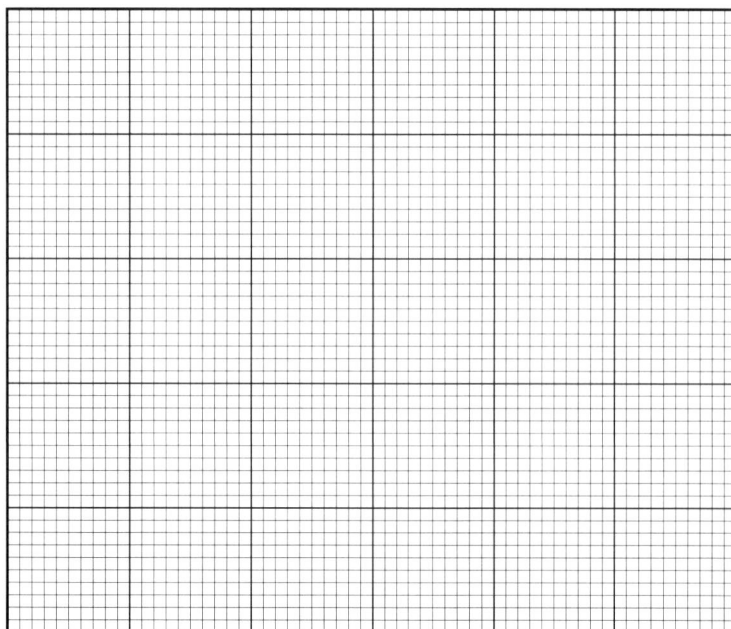

Lab Notebook

An enzyme's activity at different temperatures

Temperature (°C)	Rate of reaction (mg of product formed per minute)
10	1.0
20	2.1
30	3.2
35	3.7
40	4.1
45	3.7
50	2.7
60	0

Plotting Multiple Data Sets

A single figure can be used to show two or more data sets, i.e., more than one curve can be plotted per set of axes. This type of presentation is useful when you want to visually compare the trends for two or more treatments, or the response of one species against the response of another. Important points regarding this format are:

- If the two data sets use the same measurement units and a similar range of values for the independent variable, one scale on the y axis is used.

- If the two data sets use different units and/or have a very different range of values for the independent variable, two scales for the y axis are used (see example provided). The scales can be adjusted if necessary to avoid overlapping plots

- The two curves must be distinguished with a key.

Transpiration and root uptake rates in peas at different relative humidity

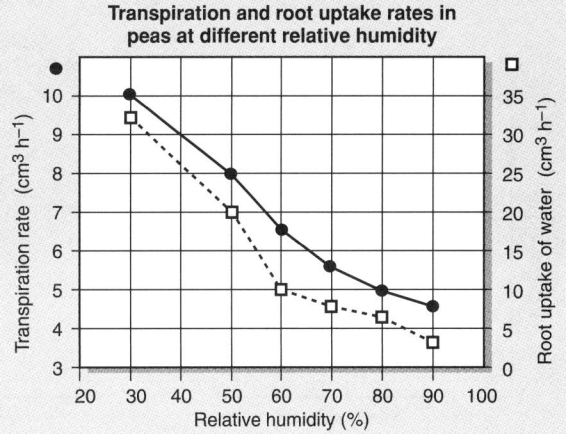

2. A census of a deer population on an island indicated a population of 2000 animals in 1960. In 1961, ten wolves (natural predators of deer) were brought to the island in an attempt to control deer numbers. Over the next nine years, the numbers of deer and wolves were monitored. The results of these population surveys are presented in the table, right.

   Plot a line graph (joining the data points) for the tabulated results. Use one scale (on the left) for numbers of deer and another scale (on the right) for the number of wolves. Use different symbols or colors to distinguish the lines and include a key.

Field data notebook
Results of a population survey on an island

Time (yr)	Wolf numbers	Deer numbers
1961	10	2000
1962	12	2300
1963	16	2500
1964	22	2360
1965	28	2244
1966	24	2094
1967	21	1968
1968	18	1916
1969	19	1952

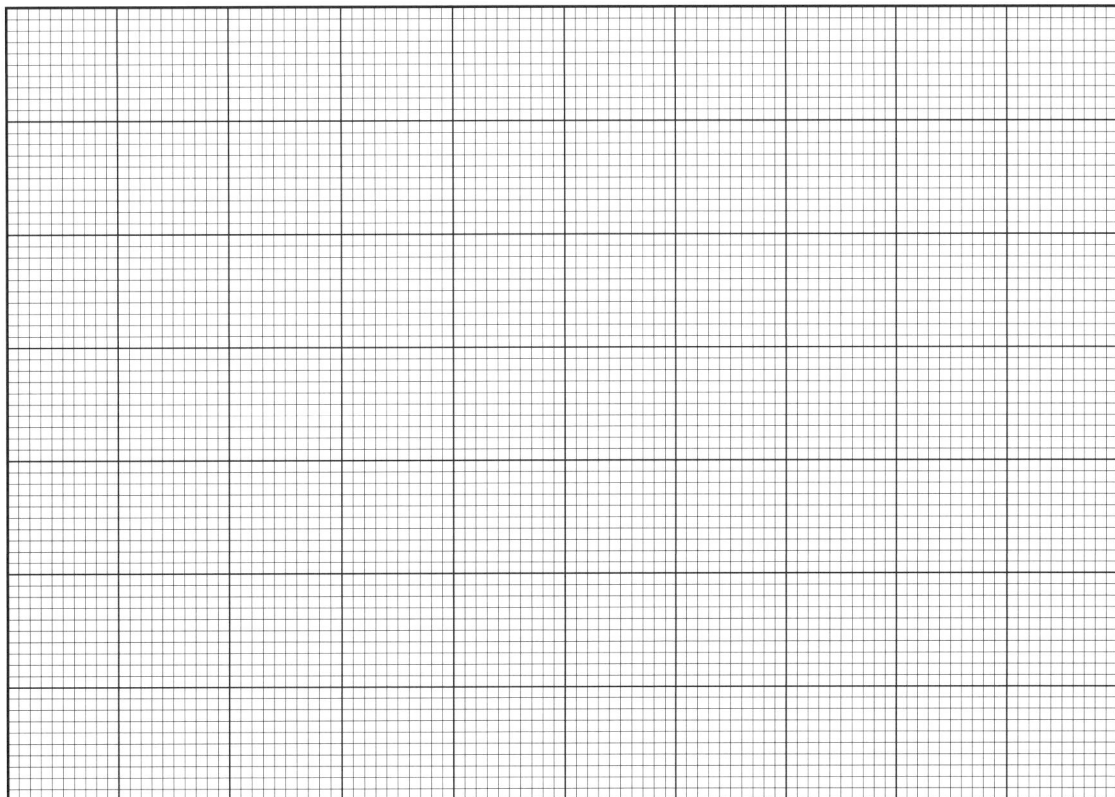

DA 2 Interpreting Line Graphs

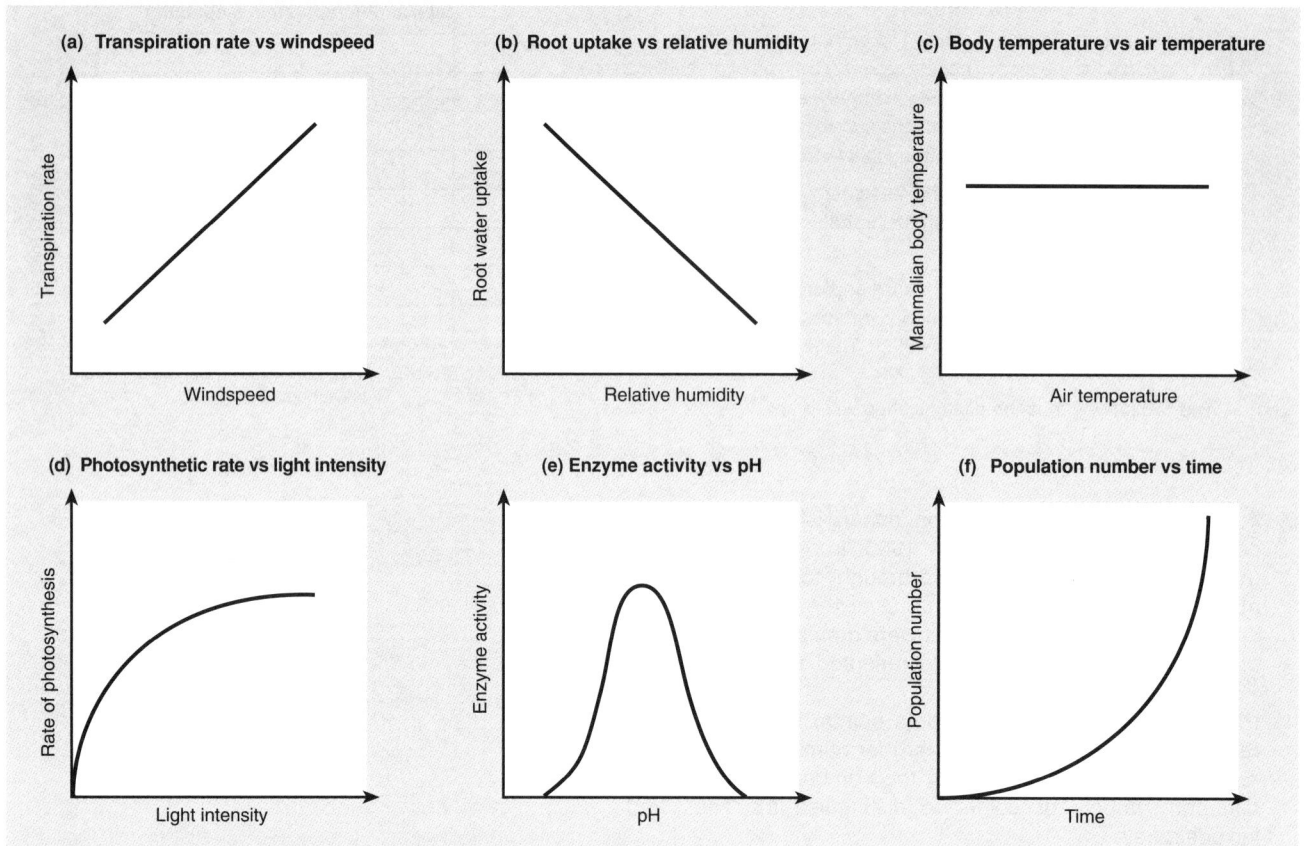

(a) Transpiration rate vs windspeed

(b) Root uptake vs relative humidity

(c) Body temperature vs air temperature

(d) Photosynthetic rate vs light intensity

(e) Enzyme activity vs pH

(f) Population number vs time

1. For each of the graphs (a-f) above, give a description of the slope and an interpretation of how one variable changes with respect to the other. For the purposes of your description, call the independent variable (horizontal or x-axis) in each example "variable X" and the dependent variable (vertical or y-axis) "variable Y". Be aware that the existence of a relationship between two variables does not necessarily mean that the relationship is causative (although it may be).

   (a) Slope: _Positive linear relationship, with constantly rising slope_ _____

   Interpretation: _Variable Y (transpiration) increases regularly with increase in variable X (windspeed)_ _____

   (b) Slope: _____

   Interpretation: _____

   (c) Slope: _____

   Interpretation: _____

   (d) Slope: _____

   Interpretation: _____

   (e) Slope: _____

   Interpretation: _____

   (f) Slope: _____

   Interpretation: _____

2. Study the line graph that you plotted for the wolf and deer census on the previous page. Provide a plausible explanation for the pattern in the data, stating the evidence available to support your reasoning:

   _____

   _____

   _____

Drawing Scatter Plots

DA 2

Guidelines for Scatter Graphs

A scatter graph is a common way to display continuous data where there is a relationship between two interdependent variables.

- The data for this graph must be continuous for both variables.
- There is no independent (manipulated) variable, but the variables are often correlated, i.e. they vary together in some predictable way.
- Scatter graphs are useful for determining the relationship between two variables.
- The points on the graph need not be connected, but a line of best fit is often drawn through the points to show the relationship between the variables (this may be drawn be eye or computer generated).

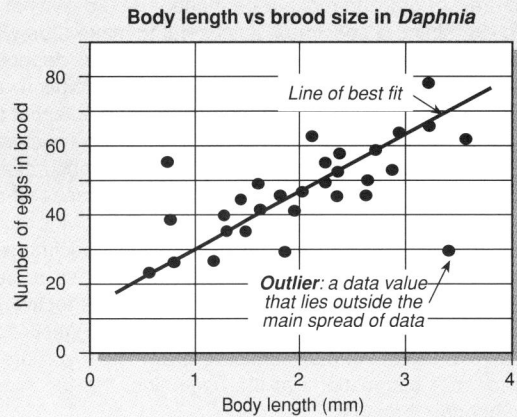

Body length vs brood size in *Daphnia*

Line of best fit

Outlier: a data value that lies outside the main spread of data

1. In the example below, metabolic measurements were taken from seven Antarctic fish *Pagothenia borchgrevinski*. The fish are affected by a gill disease, which increases the thickness of the gas exchange surfaces and affects oxygen uptake. The results of oxygen consumption of fish with varying amounts of affected gill (at rest and swimming) are tabulated below.

(a) Using **one** scale only for oxygen consumption, plot the data on the grid below to show the relationship between oxygen consumption and the amount of gill affected by disease. Use different symbols or colors for each set of data (at rest and swimming).

(b) Draw a line of best fit through each set of points.

2. Describe the relationship between the amount of gill affected and oxygen consumption in the fish:

(a) For the **at rest** data set:

_____

_____

_____

_____

_____

(b) For the **swimming** data set:

_____

_____

_____

_____

_____

_____

Oxygen consumption of fish with affected gills

Fish number	Percentage of gill affected	Oxygen consumption *(cm³ g⁻¹ h⁻¹)*	
		At rest	**Swimming**
1	0	0.05	0.29
2	95	0.04	0.11
3	60	0.04	0.14
4	30	0.05	0.22
5	90	0.05	0.08
6	65	0.04	0.18
7	45	0.04	0.20

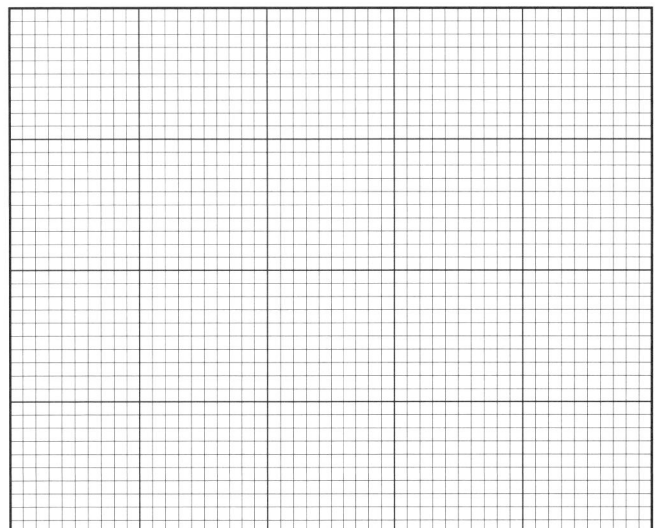

3. Describe how the gill disease affects oxygen uptake in resting fish:

_____

_____

_____

_____

Biological Drawings

A 2

Microscopes are a powerful tool for examining cells and cell structures. In order to make a permanent record of what is seen when examining a specimen, it is useful to make a drawing. It is important to draw **what is actually seen**. This will depend on the **resolution** of the microscope being used. Resolution refers to the ability of a microscope to separate small objects that are very close together. Making drawings from mounted specimens is a skill. Drawing forces you to observe closely and accurately. While photographs are limited to representing appearance at a single moment in time, drawings can be composites of the observer's cumulative experience, with many different specimens of the same material. The total picture of an object thus represented can often communicate information much more effectively than a photograph. Your attention to the outline of suggestions below will help you to make more effective drawings. If you are careful to follow the suggestions at the beginning, the techniques will soon become habitual.

1. **Drawing materials**: All drawings should be done with a clear pencil line on good quality paper. A sharp HB pencil is recommended. A soft eraser of good quality is essential. Diagrams in ballpoint or fountain pen are unacceptable because they cannot be corrected.

2. **Positioning**: Centre your diagram on the page. Do not draw it in a corner. This will leave plenty of room for the addition of labels once the diagram is completed.

3. **Size**: A drawing should be large enough to easily represent all the details you see without crowding. Rarely, if ever, are drawings too large, but they are often too small. Show only as much as is necessary for an understanding of the structure – a small section shown in detail will often suffice. It is time consuming and unnecessary, for example, to reproduce accurately the entire contents of a microscope field.

4. **Accuracy**: Your drawing should be a complete, accurate representation of the material you have observed, and should communicate your understanding of the material to anyone who looks at it. Avoid making "idealized" drawings – your drawing should be a picture of what you actually see, not what you imagine should be there. Proportions should be accurate. If necessary, measure the lengths of various parts

with a ruler. If viewing through a microscope, estimate them as a proportion of the field of view, then translate these proportions onto the page. When drawing shapes that indicate an outline, make sure the line is complete. Where two ends of a line do not meet (as in drawing a cell outline) then this would indicate that it has a hole in it - ruptured.

5. **Technique**: Use only simple, narrow lines. Represent depth by stippling (dots close together). Indicate depth only when it is essential to your drawing (usually it is not). Do not use shading. Look at the specimen while you are drawing it.

6. **Labels**: Leave a good margin for labels. All parts of your diagram must be labeled accurately. Labeling lines should be drawn with a ruler and should not cross. Where possible, keep label lines vertical or horizontal. Label the drawing with:
   - A title, which should identify the material (organism, tissues or cells).
   - Magnification under which it was observed, or a scale to indicate the size of the object.
   - Names of structures.
   - In living materials, any movements you have seen.

Remember that drawings are intended as records for you, and as a means of encouraging close observation; artistic ability is not necessary. Before you turn in a drawing, ask yourself if you know what every line represents. If you do not, look more closely at the material. *Take into account the rules for biological drawings and draw what you see, not what you think you see!*

Examples of acceptable biological drawings: The diagrams below show two examples of biological drawings that are acceptable. The example on the left is of a whole organism and its size is indicated by a scale. The example on the right is of plant tissue – a group of cells that are essentially identical in the structure. It is not necessary to show many cells even though your view through the microscope may show them. As few as 2-4 will suffice to show their structure and how they are arranged. Scale is indicated by stating how many times larger it has been drawn. Do not confuse this with what magnification it was viewed at under the microscope. The abbreviation **T.S.** indicates that the specimen was a *cross* or *transverse section*.

Cyclopoid copepod

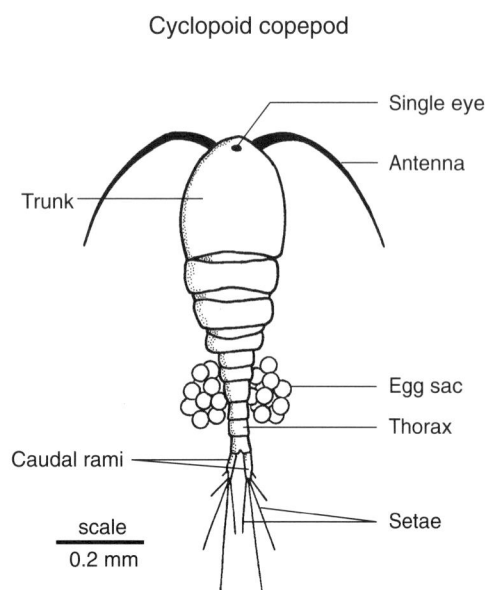

- Single eye
- Antenna
- Trunk
- Egg sac
- Thorax
- Caudal rami
- Setae

scale
0.2 mm

Collenchyma T.S. from Helianthus stem
Magnification x 450

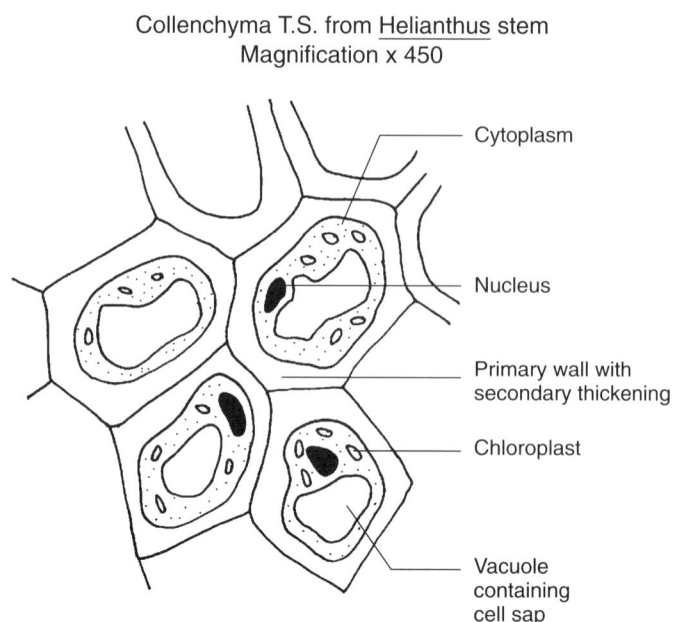

- Cytoplasm
- Nucleus
- Primary wall with secondary thickening
- Chloroplast
- Vacuole containing cell sap

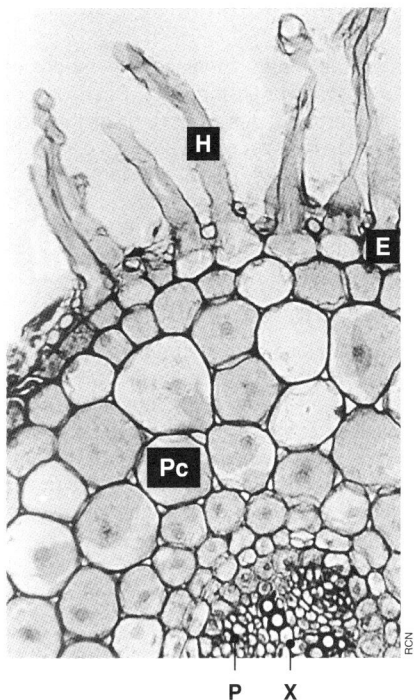

P   X

Specimen used for drawing

The photograph above is a light microscope view of a stained transverse section (cross section) of a root from a *Ranunculus* (buttercup) plant. It shows the arrangement of the different tissues in the root. The vascular bundle is at the center of the root, with the larger, central xylem vessels (**X**) and smaller phloem vessels (**P**) grouped around them. The root hair cells (**H**) are arranged on the external surface and form part of the epidermal layer (**E**). Parenchyma cells (**Pc**) make up the bulk of the root's mass. The distance from point **X** to point **E** on the photograph (above) is about 0.15mm (150μm).

An Unacceptable Biological Drawing

The diagram below is an example of how *not* to produce a biological drawing; it is based on the photograph to the left. There are many aspects of the drawing that are unacceptable. The exercise below asks you to identify the errors in this student's attempt.

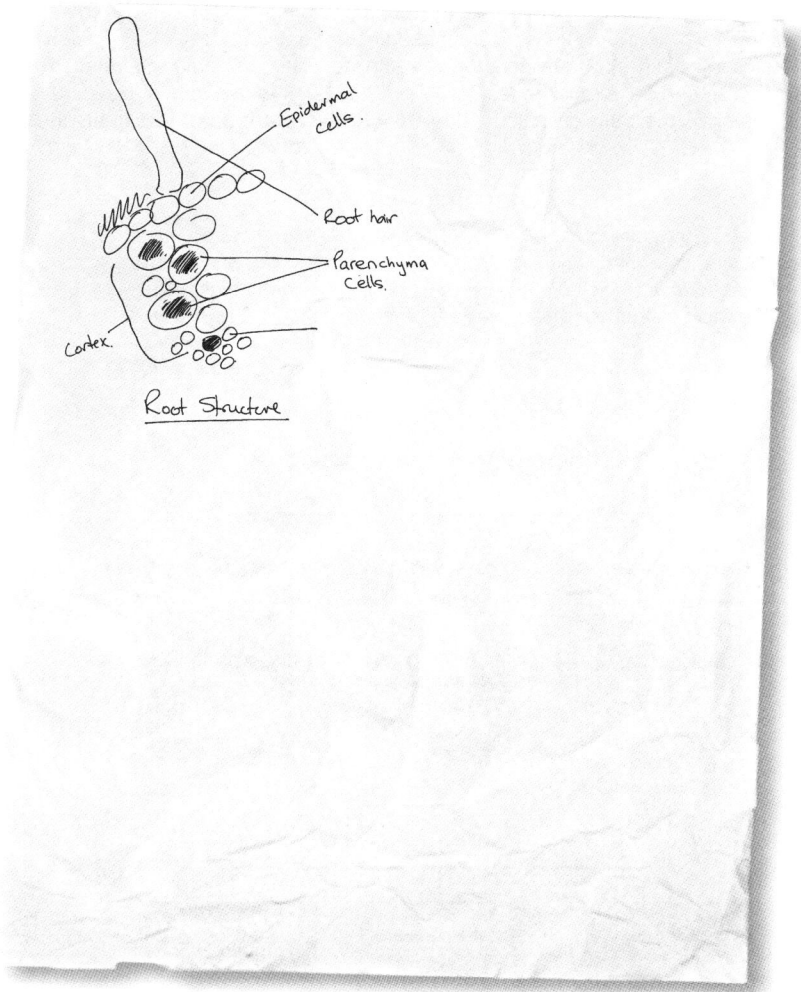

1. Identify and describe eight unacceptable features of the student's biological diagram above:

   (a) _____

   (b) _____

   (c) _____

   (d) _____

   (e) _____

   (f) _____

   (g) _____

   (h) _____

2. In the remaining space next to the 'poor example' (above) or on a blank piece of refill paper, attempt your own version of a biological drawing for the same material, based on the photograph above. Make a point of correcting all of the errors that you have identified in the sample student's attempt.

3. Explain why accurate biological drawings are more valuable to a scientific investigation than an 'artistic' approach:

   _____

   _____

   _____

Descriptive Statistics

For most investigations, measures of the biological response are made from more than one sampling unit. The sample size (the number of sampling units) will vary depending on the resources available. In lab based investigations, the sample size may be as small as two or three (e.g., two test-tubes in each treatment). In field studies, each individual may be a sampling unit, and the sample size can be very large (e.g., 100 individuals). It is useful to summarize the data collected using **descriptive statistics**.

Descriptive statistics, such as mean, median, and mode, can help to highlight trends or patterns in the data. Each of these statistics is appropriate to certain types of data or distributions, e.g., a mean is not appropriate for data with a skewed distribution (see below). Frequency graphs are useful for indicating the distribution of data. Standard deviation and standard error are statistics used to quantify the amount of spread in the data and evaluate the reliability of estimates of the true (population) mean.

Variation in Data

Whether they are obtained from observation or experiments, most biological data show variability. In a set of data values, it is useful to know the value about which most of the data are grouped; the center value. This value can be the mean, median, or mode depending on the type of variable involved (see schematic below). The main purpose of these statistics is to summarize important trends in your data and to provide the basis for statistical analyses.

Type of variable sampled

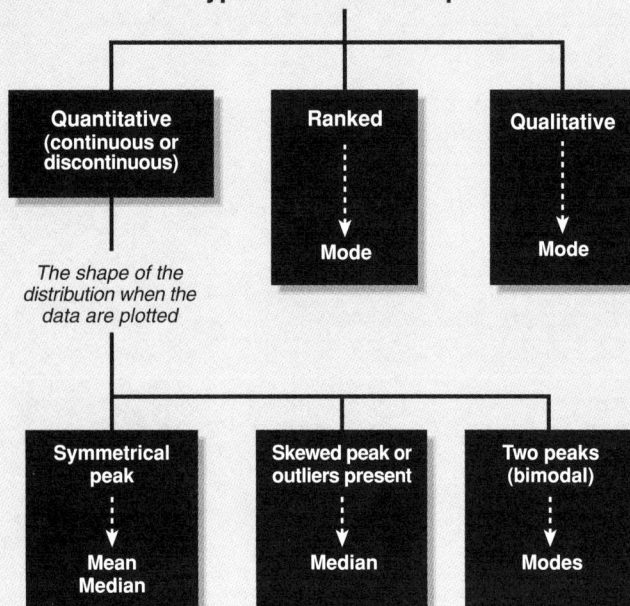

```
                    Type of variable sampled
       ┌──────────────────────┬──────────────────────┐
  Quantitative            Ranked              Qualitative
  (continuous or            ↓                     ↓
  discontinuous)          Mode                  Mode
       │
The shape of the
distribution when the
data are plotted
       │
  ┌──────────────┬──────────────────┬──────────────┐
Symmetrical    Skewed peak or      Two peaks
  peak         outliers present    (bimodal)
   ↓                 ↓                 ↓
 Mean            Median             Modes
 Median
```

Statistic	Definition and use	Method of calculation
Mean	• The average of all data entries. • Measure of central tendency for normally distributed data.	• Add up all the data entries. • Divide by the total number of data entries.
Median	• The middle value when data entries are placed in rank order. • A good measure of central tendency for skewed distributions.	• Arrange the data in increasing rank order. • Identify the middle value. • For an even number of entries, find the mid point of the two middle values.
Mode	• The most common data value. • Suitable for bimodal distributions and qualitative data.	• Identify the category with the highest number of data entries using a tally chart or a bar graph.
Range	• The difference between the smallest and largest data values. • Provides a crude indication of data spread.	• Identify the smallest and largest values and find the difference between them.

Distribution of Data

Variability in continuous data is often displayed as a **frequency distribution**. A frequency plot will indicate whether the data have a normal distribution (A), with a symmetrical spread of data about the mean, or whether the distribution is skewed (B), or bimodal (C). The shape of the distribution will determine which statistic (mean, median, or mode) best describes the central tendency of the sample data.

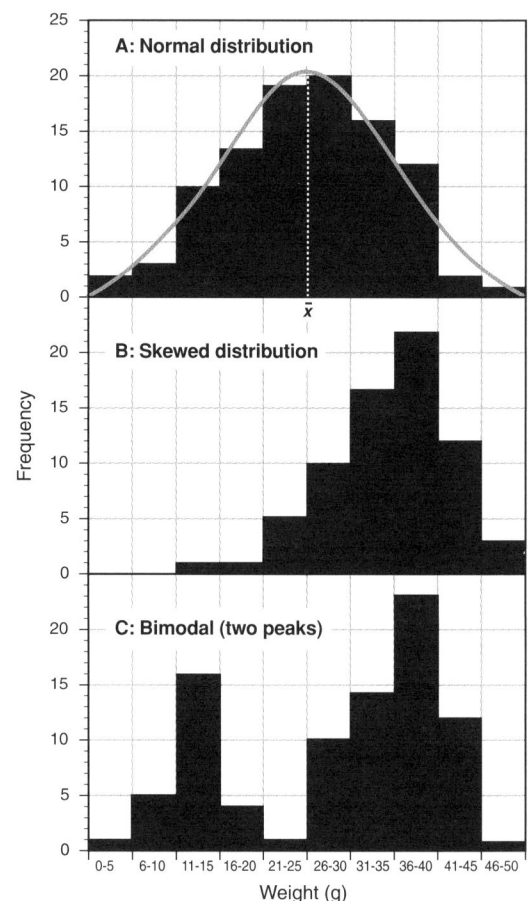

A: Normal distribution
B: Skewed distribution
C: Bimodal (two peaks)
Weight (g)
Frequency

When NOT to calculate a mean:

In certain situations, calculation of a simple arithmetic mean is inappropriate.

Remember:

• *DO NOT* calculate a mean from values that are already means (averages) themselves.

• *DO NOT* calculate a mean of ratios (e.g., percentages) for several groups of different sizes; go back to the raw values and recalculate.

• *DO NOT* calculate a mean when the measurement scale is not linear (e.g. pH units are not measured on a linear scale).

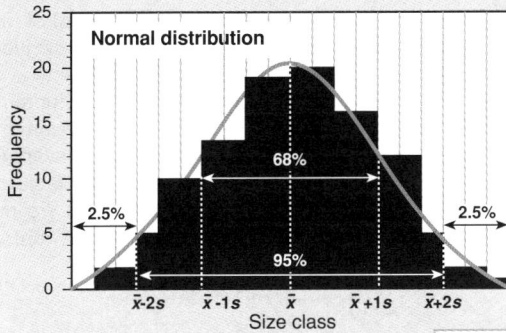

Normal distribution

68%

2.5% 2.5%

95%

$\bar{x}$-2s $\bar{x}$-1s $\bar{x}$ $\bar{x}$+1s $\bar{x}$+2s

Size class

Frequency

EXTENSION: Measuring Spread

The **standard deviation** is a frequently used measure of the variability (spread) in a set of data. It is usually presented in the form $\bar{x} \pm s$. In a normally distributed set of data, 68% of all data values will lie within one standard deviation (s) of the mean ($\bar{x}$) and 95% of all data values will lie within two standard deviations of the mean (left).

Two different sets of data can have the same mean and range, yet the distribution of data within the range can be quite different. In both the data sets pictured in the histograms below, 68% of the values lie within the range $\bar{x} \pm 1s$ and 95% of the values lie within $\bar{x} \pm 2s$. However, in B, the data values are more tightly clustered around the mean.

Histogram A has a larger standard deviation; the values are spread widely around the mean.

Both plots show a normal distribution with a symmetrical spread of values about the mean.

Histogram B has a smaller standard deviation; the values are clustered more tightly around the mean.

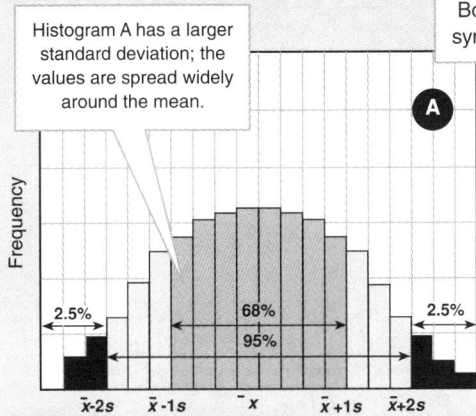

A

2.5% 68% 2.5%

95%

$\bar{x}$-2s $\bar{x}$-1s $\bar{x}$ $\bar{x}$+1s $\bar{x}$+2s

Frequency

Calculating *s*

Standard deviation is easily calculated using a spreadsheet.

$$s = \sqrt{\frac{\sum x^2 - ((\sum x)^2 / n)}{n}}$$

$(\sum x)$ = sum of value x
$\sum x^2$ = sum of value x^2
n = sample size

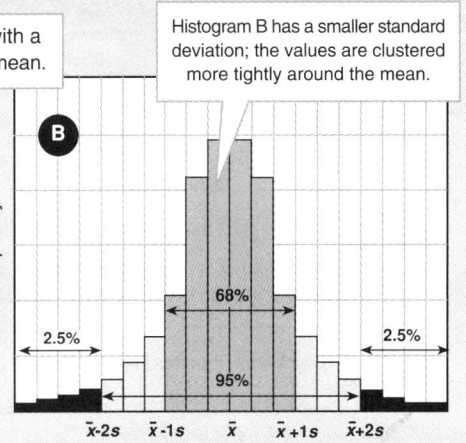

B

2.5% 68% 2.5%

95%

$\bar{x}$-2s $\bar{x}$-1s $\bar{x}$ $\bar{x}$+1s $\bar{x}$+2s

Frequency

Case Study: Fern Reproduction

Fern spores

Raw data (below) and descriptive statistics (right) from a survey of the number of spores found on the fronds of a fern plant.

Raw data: Number of spores per frond						
64	60	64	62	68	66	63
69	70	63	70	70	63	62
71	69	59	70	66	61	70
67	64	63	64			

Total of data entries = 1641 = **66** spores
Number of entries   25

Mean

Number of spores per frond (in rank order)	
59	66
60	66
61	67
62	68
62	69
63	69
63	70
63	70
63	70
64	70
64	70
64	71
64	

Median

Mode

Spores per frond	Tally	Total
59	✔	1
60	✔	1
61	✔	1
62	✔✔	2
63	✔✔✔✔	4
64	✔✔✔✔	4
65		0
66	✔✔	2
67	✔	1
68	✔	1
69	✔✔	2
70	✔✔✔✔✔	5
71	✔	1

1. Give a reason for the differences between the mean, median, and mode of the fern spore data:

_____

_____

_____

_____

2. Calculate the mean, median, and mode of the data on beetle masses below. Draw up a tally chart and show all calculations:

Beetle masses (g)		
2.2	2.1	2.6
2.5	2.4	2.8
2.5	2.7	2.5
2.6	2.6	2.5
2.2	2.8	2.4

_____

_____

_____

_____

_____

DA 3

The Student's *t* Test

The Student's *t* test is a commonly used test when comparing two sample means, e.g., means for a treatment and a control in an experiment, or the means of some measured characteristic between two animal or plant populations. The test is a powerful one, i.e., it is a good test for distinguishing real but marginal differences between samples. The *t* test is a simple test to apply, but it is only valid for certain situations. It is a two-group test and is not appropriate for multiple use, i.e., sample 1 vs 2, then sample 1 vs 3. *You must have only two sample means to compare.* You must also assume that the data have a normal (not skewed) distribution, and the scatter (standard deviations) of the data points is similar for both samples. You may wish to exclude obvious outliers from your data set for this reason. Below is a simple example outlining the general steps involved in Student *t* test. The example uses a set of data from a fictitious experiment involving a treatment and a control (the units are not relevant in this case, only the values). A portion of the Student's *t* table of critical values is provided, sufficient to carry out the test. Follow the example through, making sure that you understand what is being done at each step in the calculation.

Steps in performing a Student's *t* test	Explanatory notes
Step 1 *Calculate basic summary statistics for your two data sets* Control (A): 6.6, 5.5, 6.8, 5.8, 6.1, 5.9 $n_A = 6$, $\bar{x}_A = 6.12$, $s_A = 0.496$ Treatment (B): 6.3, 7.2, 6.5, 7.1, 7.5, 7.3 $n_B = 6$, $\bar{x}_B = 6.98$, $s_B = 0.475$	n_A and n_B are the number of values in the first and second data sets respectively (these need not be the same). $\bar{x}$ is the mean. s is the standard deviation (a measure of scatter in the data).
Step 2 *Set up and state your null hypothesis (H_0)* H_0: there is no treatment effect. The differences in the data sets are the result of chance variation only and they are not really different	The alternative hypothesis is that there is a treatment effect and the two sets of data are truly different.
Step 3 *Decide if your test is one or two tailed* This tells you what section of the *t* table to consult. Most biological tests are two-tailed. Very few are one-tailed.	A one-tailed test looks for a difference only in one particular direction. A two-tailed test looks for any difference (+ or –).
Step 4 *Calculate the t statistic* For our sample data above the calculated value of *t* is –3.09. The degrees of freedom (df) are $n_1 + n_2 - 2 = 10$. Calculation of the *t* value uses the variance which is simply the square of the standard deviation (s^2). You may compute the *t* value by entering your data onto a computer and using a simple statistical program.	It does not matter if your calculated t value is a positive or negative (the sign is irrelevant). If you do not have access to a statistical program, computation of *t* is not difficult. Step 4 (calculating *t*) is detailed in the *t* test exercise following (both manual and spreadsheet versions).
Step 5 *Consult the t table of critical values* Selected critical values for Student's *t* statistic (two-tailed test) {{TABLE}}	The absolute value of the *t* statistic (3.09) well exceeds the critical value for $P = 0.05$ at 10 degrees of freedom. *We can reject H_0 and conclude that the means are different at the 5% level of significance.* If the calculated absolute value of *t* had been less than 2.23, we would have accepted H_0.

Table inside Step 5:

Degrees of freedom	$P = 0.05$	$P = 0.01$	$P = 0.001$	
5	2.57	4.03	6.87	
10	2.23	3.17	4.59	Critical value of *t* for 10 degrees of freedom. The calculated *t* value must exceed this
15	2.13	2.95	4.07	
20	2.09	2.85	3.85	

1. (a) In an experiment, data values were obtained from 4 plants in experimental conditions and 3 plants in control conditions. The mean values for each data set (control and experimental conditions) were calculated. The *t* value was calculated to be 2.16. The null hypothesis was: "The plants in the control and experimental conditions are not different". State whether the calculated *t* value supports the null hypothesis or its alternative (consult *t* table above):

_____

   (b) The experiment was repeated, but this time using 6 control and 6 "experimental" plants. The new *t* value was 2.54. State whether the calculated *t* value supports the null hypothesis or its alternative now:

_____

2. Suggest why, in terms of applying Student's *t*, extreme data values (outliers) are often excluded from the data set(s):

_____

_____

3. Explain what you understand by statistical significance (for any statistical test): _____

_____

_____

The Chi-Square Test

The **chi-square test**, χ^2, is a test for difference between two data sets. It is a simple test to perform but the data must meet strict requirements. It can **only** be used on data that are raw counts (not measurements or derived data), it should only be used when comparing an experimental result to an expected theoretical outcome, and it is an unreliable test when sample sizes are small (less than 20). Like all statistical tests, it aims to test the null hypothesis (the hypothesis of no difference between the data sets). The following exercise describes the use of chi-square for testing the outcomes of genotype ratios in Mendelian genetics.

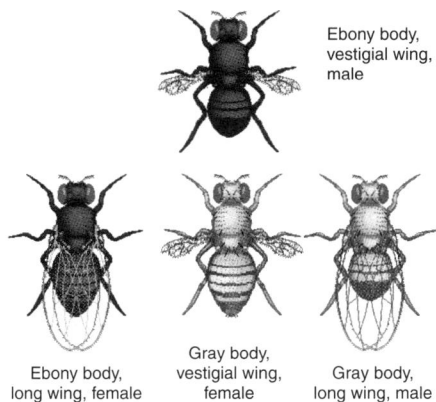

Ebony body, vestigial wing, male

Ebony body, long wing, female

Gray body, vestigial wing, female

Gray body, long wing, male

Using χ^2 in Mendelian Genetics

In a *Drosophila* genetics experiment, two individuals were crossed (the details of the cross are not relevant here). The predicted Mendelian ratios for the offspring of this cross were 1:1:1:1 for each of the four following phenotypes: gray body-long wing, gray body-vestigial wing, ebony body-long wing, ebony body-vestigial wing.

The observed results of the cross were not exactly as predicted. The following numbers for each phenotype were observed in the offspring of the cross:

Observed results of the example *Drosophila* cross

Gray body, long wing	98	Ebony body, long wing	102
Gray body, vestigial wing	88	Ebony body, vestigial wing	112

Using χ^2, the probability of this result being consistent with a 1:1:1:1 ratio could be tested. Worked example as follows:

Step 1: Calculate the expected value (E)

In this case, this is the sum of the observed values divided by the number of categories (see note below)

$$\frac{400}{4} = 100$$

Step 2: Calculate O – E

The difference between the observed and expected values is calculated as a measure of the deviation from a predicted result. Since some deviations are negative, they are all squared to give positive values. This step is usually performed as part of a tabulation (right, darker gray column).

Category	O	E	O – E	$(O-E)^2$	$\frac{(O-E)^2}{E}$
Gray, long wing	98	100	–2	4	0.04
Gray, vestigial wing	88	100	–12	144	1.44
Ebony, long wing	102	100	2	4	0.04
Ebony, vestigial wing	112	100	12	144	1.44

Total = 400

$\chi^2 \qquad \sum = 2.96$

Step 3: Calculate the value of χ^2

$$\chi^2 = \sum \frac{(O-E)^2}{E}$$

Where: O = the observed result
E = the expected result
$\sum$ = sum of

The calculated χ^2 value is given at the bottom right of the last column in the tabulation.

Step 5a: Using the χ^2 table

On the χ^2 table (part reproduced in Table 1 below) with 3 degrees of freedom, the calculated value for χ^2 of 2.96 corresponds to a probability of between 0.2 and 0.5 (see arrow). *This means that by chance alone a χ^2 value of 2.96 could be expected between 20% and 50% of the time.*

Step 4: Calculating degrees of freedom

The probability that any particular χ^2 value could be exceeded by chance depends on the number of degrees of freedom. This is simply **one less than the total number of categories** (this is the number that could vary independently without affecting the last value). **In this case: 4–1 = 3.**

Step 5b: Using the χ^2 table

The probability of between 0.2 and 0.5 is higher than the 0.05 value which is generally regarded as significant. The null hypothesis cannot be rejected and we have no reason to believe that the observed results differ significantly from the expected (at $P = 0.05$).

Footnote: Many Mendelian crosses involve ratios other than 1:1. For these, calculation of the expected values is not simply a division of the total by the number of categories. Instead, the total must be apportioned according to the ratio. For example, for a total of 400 as above, in a predicted 9:3:3:1 ratio, the total count must be divided by 16 (9+3+3+1) and the expected values will be 225: 75: 75: 25 in each category.

Table 1: Critical values of χ^2 at different levels of probability. By convention, the critical probability for rejecting the null hypothesis (H_0) is 5%. If the test statistic is less than the tabulated critical value for $P = 0.05$ we accept H_0 and the result is said to be not significant. If the test statistic is greater than the tabulated value for $P = 0.05$ we reject H_0 in favor of the alternative hypothesis.

Degrees of freedom	Level of probability (P)									
	0.98	0.95	0.80	0.50	0.20	0.10	0.05	0.02	0.01	0.001
1	0.001	0.004	0.064	0.455	1.64	2.71	3.84	5.41	6.64	10.83
2	0.040	0.103	0.466	1.386	3.22	4.61	5.99	7.82	9.21	13.82
3	0.185	0.352	1.005	2.366	4.64	6.25	7.82	9.84	11.35	16.27
4	0.429	0.711	1.649	3.357	5.99	7.78	9.49	11.67	13.28	18.47
5	0.752	0.145	2.343	4.351	7.29	9.24	11.07	13.39	15.09	20.52

χ^2 (at 0.50, row 1)

← Accept H_0 Reject H_0 →

RA② The Structure of a Report

Once you have collected your data and analyzed it, you can write your report. The structure of a scientific report is described below. The final order of the different sections of a report is not usually the order in which they are written. It is a good idea to write either the methods or the results sections first, followed by the discussion and conclusion. Although you should do some background reading in preparation, the introduction should be one of the last sections that you write. Writing the other sections first provides you with a better understanding of your investigation and enables you to be better able to make clear statements about the topic you investigated.

Section	Content	Purpose
Title	Provides a clear description of the project.	Provides the reader with a summary of the type and extent of the investigation.
Introduction	Includes the aim and hypothesis, and background information to the project.	Provides the reader with the relevant background to the topic and the rationale for the investigation.
Materials and method	A description of the materials used and the experimental procedures involved.	Important because it allows the procedures to be repeated and confirmed.
Results	A full description of the results including tables and graphs. This section should not discuss the results, but can state trends.	Provides the reader with the findings of the investigation and allows them to evaluate these for themselves.
Discussion	An interpretation of the results written in paragraph form. It includes a description of trends and a discussion of the findings in light of the biological concepts involved. It also includes comments on sources of error, limitations of the data, assumptions made by the investigator about the system, and ideas for further investigations.	Provides the reader with the investigator's evaluation of the investigation. It also informs the reader as to the limitations of the investigation, and ideas on how the design of the investigation could have been improved.
Conclusion	A clear statement describing whether or not the results of the investigation support the hypothesis.	Provides the reader with the investigator's analysis of the results.
Acknowledgements / Bibliography	A list of all sources of information and assistance. This includes citations of written material (e.g., texts, journals), web pages, and practical and advisory help.	Acknowledging sources of information and assistance is part of scientific integrity. It acknowledges the work and expertise of others and allows your work to be assessed in the light of other work in the area.

As is often the case in science, after completing your investigation and discussing your results, you may conclude that your hypothesis is not supported. This does not necessarily mean that the science was flawed or of no value. However, it does present the opportunity to propose a new, tentative explanation (hypothesis) for the observations you made. The example below describes this type of situation. Completing the questions will develop your skills in evaluating your results even if your investigations do not turn out as you might expect:

1. A student found that a herbaceous plant species was found growing around, but not right up to, a stand of rhododendrons. In a controlled experiment, she investigated the effect of soil, taken from within the rhododendron stand, on the vigour with which the soft leaved species grew. She found no effect:

   (a) Propose a suitable hypothesis and conclusion for this investigation:

      Hypothesis: _____

      _____

      Conclusion: _____

   (b) The student then measured the water content of the soil immediately around the rhododendrons, and found it to be drier than the soil in which the herbaceous plants were growing. Revise your hypothesis in the light of this information:

      _____

      _____

Writing the Methods Section

The materials and methods section of your report should be brief but informative. All essential details should be included but those not necessary for the repetition of the study should be omitted. The following diagram illustrates some of the important details that should be included in a methods section. Obviously, a complete list of all possible equipment and procedures is not possible because each experiment or study is different. However, the sort of information that is required for both lab and field based studies is provided.

Field Studies

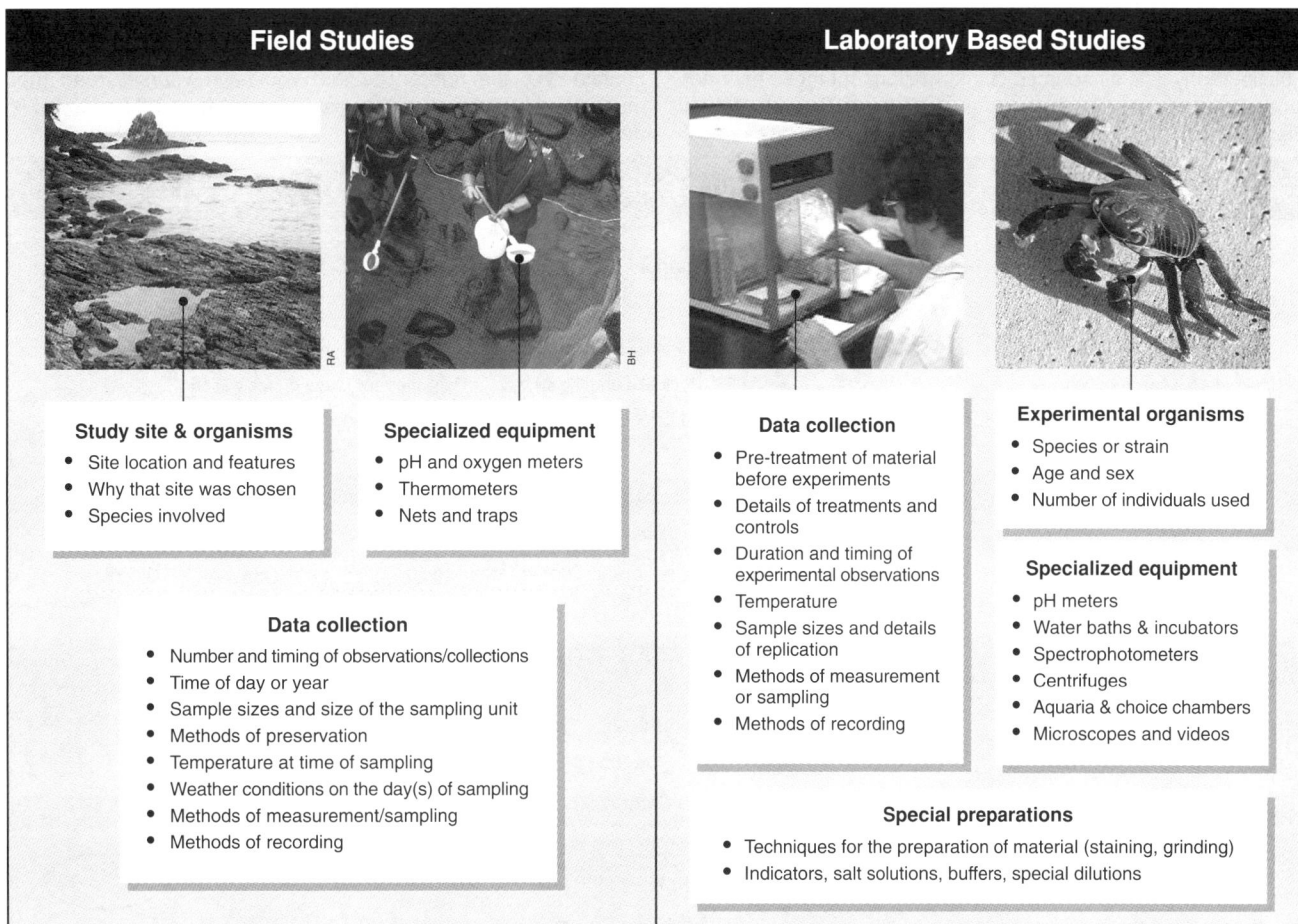

Study site & organisms
- Site location and features
- Why that site was chosen
- Species involved

Specialized equipment
- pH and oxygen meters
- Thermometers
- Nets and traps

Data collection
- Number and timing of observations/collections
- Time of day or year
- Sample sizes and size of the sampling unit
- Methods of preservation
- Temperature at time of sampling
- Weather conditions on the day(s) of sampling
- Methods of measurement/sampling
- Methods of recording

Laboratory Based Studies

Data collection
- Pre-treatment of material before experiments
- Details of treatments and controls
- Duration and timing of experimental observations
- Temperature
- Sample sizes and details of replication
- Methods of measurement or sampling
- Methods of recording

Experimental organisms
- Species or strain
- Age and sex
- Number of individuals used

Specialized equipment
- pH meters
- Water baths & incubators
- Spectrophotometers
- Centrifuges
- Aquaria & choice chambers
- Microscopes and videos

Special preparations
- Techniques for the preparation of material (staining, grinding)
- Indicators, salt solutions, buffers, special dilutions

General guidelines for writing a methods section

- Choose a suitable level of detail. *Too little detail and the study could not be repeated. Too much detail obscures important features.*
- Do NOT include the details of standard procedures (e.g., how to use a balance) or standard equipment (e.g., beakers and flasks).
- Include details of any statistical analyses and data transformations.

- Outline the reasons why procedures were done in a certain way or in a certain order, if this is not self-evident.

- If your methodology involves complicated preparations (e.g. culture media) then it is acceptable to refer just to the original information source (e.g. lab. manual) or include the information as an appendix.

1. The following text is part of the methods section from a report. Using the information above and on the checklist on the previous page, describe eight errors (there are ten) in the methods. The errors are concerned with a lack of explanation or detail that would be necessary to repeat the experiment (they are not typographical, nor are they associated with the use of the active voice, which is now considered preferable to the passive):

"We collected the worms for this study from a pond outside the school. We carried out the experiment at room temperature on April 16, 1997. First we added full strength seawater to each of three 200 cm³ glass jars; these were the controls. We filled another three jars with diluted seawater. We blotted the worms dry and weighed them to the nearest 0.1 g, then we added one worm to each jar. We reweighed the worms (after blotting) at various intervals over the next two hours."

(a) _____

(b) _____

(c) _____

(d) _____

(e) _____

(f) _____

(g) _____

(h) _____

Citing and Listing References

A 3

Proper referencing of sources of information is an important aspect of report writing. It shows that you have explored the topic and recognize and respect the work of others. There are two aspects to consider: **citing sources** within the text (making reference to other work to support a statement or compare results) and **compiling a reference list** at the end of the report. A bibliography lists all sources of information, but these may not necessarily appear as citations in the report. In contrast, a reference list should contain only those texts cited in the report.

Citations in the main body of the report should include only the authors' surnames and publication date, and the citation should be relevant to the statement it claims to support. Accepted methods for referencing vary, but your reference list should provide all the information necessary to locate the source material, it should be consistently presented, and it should contain only the references that you have *yourself* read (not those cited by others). A suggested format for a reference list is described below.

Preparing a Reference List

Lab notes can be listed according to title if the author is unknown.
→ Practical biology laboratory manual. 2000. Cell membranes. pp. 16-18. Sunhigh College.

Cooper, G.M. 1997: <u>The cell: A molecular approach</u>. ASM Press, Washington D.C., pp. 77-85.
Book title underlined   Publisher and place of publication

Internet sites change often so the full date is included. Quotation marks can be used to distinguish the title from the address.
→ Dalton, M. 12 March 2003: "Introduction to cell biology". http://www.cbc.umn.edu/~mwd/cell_intro.html

Davis, P. 1996: Cellular factories. <u>New Scientist</u> 2057: Inside science supplement.
Journal title underlined   A supplement may not need page references

References are listed alphabetically according to the author's surname.

Indge, B. 2001: Diarrhoea, digestion and dehydration <u>Biological Sciences Review</u> 14(1): 7-9.
Article title follows date

If a single author appears more than once, then list the publications from oldest to most recent.

Indge, B. 2002: Experiments <u>Biological Sciences Review</u> 14(3): 11-13.

Kingsland, J (2000.) Border control. <u>New Scientist</u> 2247: Inside science supplement.
Publication date

Laver, H. 1995: Osmosis and water retention in plants. <u>Biological Sciences Review</u> 7(3): 14-18 .

Spell out only the last name of authors. Use initials for first and middle names.
→ Steward, M. 1996: Water channels in the cell membrane <u>Biological Sciences Review</u> (9(2): 18-22.)

Volume: Issue number: Pages

1. Following are the details of references and source material used by a student in preparing a report on enzymes and their uses in biotechnology. He provided his reference list in prose. From it, compile a correctly formatted reference list:

> Pages 18-23 in the sixth edition of the textbook "Biology" by Neil Campbell. Published by Benjamin/Cummings in California (2002). New Scientist article by Peter Moore called "Fuelled for life" (January 1996, volume 2012, supplement). "Food biotechnology" published in the journal Biological Sciences Review, page 25, volume 8 (number 3) 1996, by Liam and Katherine O'Hare. An article called "Living factories" by Philip Ball in New Scientist, volume 2015 1996, pages 28-31. Pages 75-85 in the book "The cell: a molecular approach" by Geoffrey Cooper, published in 1997 by ASM Press, Washington D.C. An article called "Development of a procedure for purification of a recombinant therapeutic protein" in the journal "Australasian Biotechnology", by I Roberts and S. Taylor, pages 93-99 in volume 6, number 2, 1996.

REFERENCE LIST

_____

_____

_____

_____

_____

_____

_____

Report Checklist

A 3

A report of your findings at the completion of your investigation may take one of the following forms: a written document, seminar, poster, web page, or multimedia presentation. The following checklist identifies points to consider when writing each section of your report. Review the list before you write your report and then, on satisfactory completion of each section of your write-up, use the check boxes to tick off the points:

Title (see page 44):

☐ (a) Gives a clear indication of what the study is about.

☐ (b) Includes the species name and a common name of all organisms used.

Introduction (see pages 18-23, and 44 for examples and guidance):

☐ (a) Includes a clear aim.

☐ (b) Includes a well written hypothesis.

☐ (c) Includes a synopsis of the current state of knowledge about the topic.

Materials and methods (see pages 22, and 44-45 for guidance):

☐ (a) Written clearly. Numbered points are appropriate at this level.

☐ (b) Describes the final methods that were used.

☐ (c) Includes details of the how data for the dependent variable were collected.

☐ (d) Includes details of how all other variables were manipulated, controlled, measured, or monitored.

☐ (e) If appropriate, it includes an explanatory diagram of the design of the experimental set-up.

☐ (f) Written in the past tense, and in the active voice (We investigated ...) rather than the passive voice (An investigation was done ...).

Results (see pages 30-35, 37, 40-43, and 44 for guidance):

☐ (a) Includes the raw data (e.g., in a table).

☐ (b) Where necessary, the raw data have been averaged or transformed.

☐ (c) Includes graphs (where appropriate).

☐ (d) Each figure (table, graph, drawing, or photo) has a title and is numbered in a way that makes it possible to refer to it in the text (Fig. 1 etc.).

☐ (e) Written in the past tense and, where appropriate, in the active voice.

Discussion (see page 44)

☐ (a) Includes an analysis of the data in which the findings, including trends and patterns, are discussed in relation to the biological concepts involved.

☐ (b) Includes an evaluation of sources of error, assumptions, and possible improvements to design.

Conclusion (see page 44):

☐ (a) Written as a clear statement, which relates directly to the hypothesis.

Bibliography or References (see pages 44 and 46):

☐ (a) Lists all sources of information and assistance.

☐ (b) Does not include references that were not used.

The Chemistry of Life

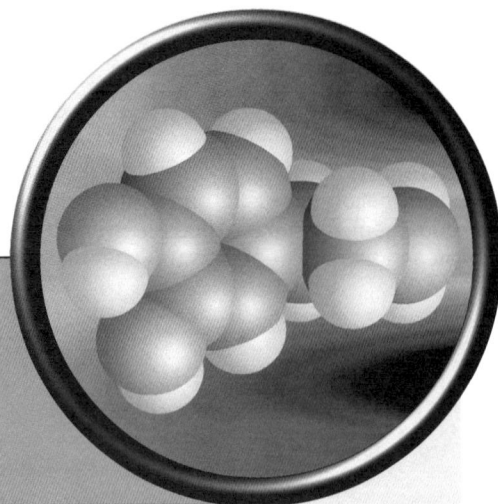

IB SL
Complete nos:
1-4, 6-10, 12-19, 22, 27, 32-33, 39-40
Extension: 5, 11, 21, 30-31, 41-42

IB HL
Complete nos:
1-4, 6-10, 12-20, 22-29, 32-40
Extension: 5, 11, 21, 30-31, 41-42

IB Options
Complete nos:
Option C: 20, 22-26, 28-29, 34-38

AP Biology
Complete nos:
1-29, 32-40
Extension 30-31, 41-42 or as appropriate

Learning Objectives

The learning objectives relating to the structure and function of ***nucleic acids*** *are provided in the topic "Molecular Genetics".*

☐ 1. Compile your own glossary from the **KEY WORDS** displayed in **bold type** in the learning objectives below.

Understanding organic chemistry *(page 50)*

☐ 2. List the four most common elements found in living things. Provide examples of where these elements occur in cells. Distinguish between an atom and an ion. Explain what is meant by **organic chemistry** and explain its importance in biology.

☐ 3. Distinguish between ionic bonds and covalent bonds and understand the importance of **covalent bonds** in carbon-based compounds.

☐ 4. Distinguish between **monomers** and **polymers** and provide examples of each type. Explain clearly what is meant by a **macromolecule** and give examples.

☐ 5. Explain how the laws of thermodynamics relate to the biochemical processes occurring in living systems. Understand the concept of **free energy** and explain how the concept of free energy helps us to determine whether or not a process will occur spontaneously. Explain the terms **endergonic** and **exergonic** in relation to their free energy changes.

Water and inorganic ions *(pages 50-51)*

☐ 6. Describe the structure of water, including reference to the polar nature of the water molecule, the nature of the bonding within the molecule, and the importance of **hydrogen bonding** *between* water molecules.

☐ 7. Identify the physical properties of water that are important in biological systems. Explain why water is termed the **universal solvent** and describe its various biological roles: *e.g. metabolic role, as a solvent, as a lubricant, as a coolant, as a transport medium, and as a fluid in hydrostatic skeletons and cell turgor.*

☐ 8. Provide a definition of an **inorganic** (mineral) **ion**. With reference to specific examples, describe the role of inorganic ions in biological systems. Examples could include: Na^+, K^+, Mg^{2+}, Cl^-, NO_3^-, and PO_4^{3-}.

Carbohydrates *(pages 52-53)*

☐ 9. Describe the basic composition and general formula of carbohydrates. Explain the main roles of carbohydrates in both plants and animals.

☐ 10. Describe what is meant by a **monosaccharide** and give its general formula. Provide examples of **triose**, **pentose**, and **hexose sugars** (including fructose and galactose). For each, identify its biological role.

☐ 11. Appreciate that monosaccharides show **isomerism**. Recognize structural isomers of glucose (α **and** β **glucose**) and understand their biological significance.

☐ 12. Describe what is meant by a **disaccharide**. Explain how disaccharides are formed by a **condensation** reaction and broken apart by **hydrolysis**. Identify the **glycosidic bond** formed and broken in each case. Give examples of disaccharides and their functions, and name the monosaccharides involved in each case.

☐ 13. Explain what is meant by a **polysaccharide** and describe how polysaccharides are formed. Describe the molecular structure of the following examples of polysaccharides: *starch, glycogen, cellulose* and relate their structure to their function in biological systems.

Lipids *(pages 54-55)*

☐ 14. Describe the general properties of lipids. Recognize the diversity of lipids in biological systems and describe their functional roles. Consider: *phospholipids*, *waxes*, *steroids*, and *fats* and *oils*.

☐ 15. Recognize that most lipids are **triglycerides** (triacyl-glycerols). Describe how triglycerides are classified as *fats* or *oils* and explain the basis of the classification.

☐ 16. Using a diagram, describe the basic structure of a triglyceride. Explain their formation by **condensation** reactions between glycerol and three fatty acids. Identify the **ester bonds** that result from this. Distinguish between **saturated** and **unsaturated fatty acids** and relate this difference to the properties of the fat or oil that results.

☐ 17. Using a diagram, describe the basic structure of a **phospholipid** and explain how it differs from the structure of a triglyceride. Explain how the structure of phospholipids is important to their role in membranes.

Amino acids and proteins *(pages 56-60)*

☐ 18. Draw or describe the general structure and formula of an **amino acid**. Explain the basis for the different properties of amino acids.

☐ 19. Recognize that, of over 170 amino acids, only 20 are commonly found in proteins. Distinguish between **essential** and **non-essential amino acids**.

☐ 20. Distinguish between **polar** and **non-polar amino acids** and explain their biological significance.

☐ 21. Appreciate the basis of **optical isomerism** in amino acids. Distinguish L- and D- forms and identify which form is active in biological systems.

☐ 22. Using a diagram, describe how amino acids are joined together in a **condensation reaction** to form **dipeptides** and **polypeptides**. Describe the nature of **peptide bonds** that result. Describe how polypeptides are broken down by **hydrolysis**.

☐ 23. Identify where (in the cell) proteins are made and recognize the ways in which they can be modified after production. Distinguish between the **primary structure** of a protein and its **secondary structure**. Recognize the two main types of secondary structure found in proteins: *alpha-helix* and *ß-pleated sheet*.

☐ 24. Explain what is meant by the **tertiary structure** of a protein and explain how it arises. Describe the relationship between the tertiary structure of a **globular protein** and its biological function.

☐ 25. With reference to examples, distinguish between **globular** and **fibrous proteins**. Consider the structure, properties, and biological functions of the protein.

☐ 26. With reference to specific examples (e.g. collagen, insulin, hemoglobin), describe the role of different types of bonds in proteins: *hydrogen bonds*, *ionic bonds*, *disulfide bonds*, *hydrophobic interactions*.

☐ 27. Explain what is meant by protein **denaturation** and explain why it destroys the activity of proteins. Describe how different agents denature proteins.

☐ 28. Explain what is meant by the **quaternary structure** of a protein. In a named example (e.g. *hemoglobin, a globular protein*) describe how the quaternary structure arises and relate it to the protein's function.

☐ 29. Recognize the ways in which proteins can be classified:
  • By their structure (e.g. *globular* or *fibrous*)
  • By their functional role: *structural, protective (role in immunity), as enzymes, as hormones, as respiratory pigments, in transport, contractile, in storage*.

Tests for organic compounds *(page 61)*

☐ 30. Explain the basis of **chromatography** as a technique for separating and identifying biological molecules. Describe the calculation and use **Rf values**.

☐ 31. In your practical work, demonstrate an understanding of some basic tests for organic compounds: the **I₂/KI** *(iodine in potassium iodide)* **test** for starch, the **Benedict's test** for **reducing** sugars, the **emulsion test** for lipids, the **biuret test** for proteins. For each, explain the basis of the test and its result.

Enzymes *(pages 62-68, also see 146-147)*

☐ 32. Define: **enzyme**, **catalyst**, **active site**, and **substrate**. Describe the general properties of enzymes and explain their role in regulating cell metabolism.

☐ 33. Using the terms: **enzyme-substrate complex** and **activation energy**, explain how enzymes work as catalysts to bring about reactions in cells. Describe the **lock and key** model of enzyme function.

☐ 34. Explain the **induced fit** model of enzyme function, contrasting it with the older lock and key model.

☐ 35. Describe ways in which the time course of an enzyme-catalyzed reaction can be followed: by measuring the rate of product formation *(e.g. catalase)* or by measuring the rate of substrate use *(e.g. amylase)*.

☐ 36. Distinguish between **coenzymes** and **cofactors**. Explain how cofactors enable an enzyme to work.

☐ 37. Distinguish **reversible** from **irreversible** inhibition. Describe the effects of **competitive** and **non-competitive inhibitors** on enzyme activity.

☐ 38. Appreciate the role of **allostery** in the control of metabolic pathways by end-product inhibition.

☐ 39. Describe the effect of the following factors on enzyme activity: *substrate concentration, enzyme concentration, pH, temperature*. Identify the **optimum conditions** for some named enzymes. Recognize that enzymes (being proteins) can be **denatured**.

☐ 40. Appreciate some of the commercial applications of microbial enzymes, e.g., *pectinases* and *rennin* in the food industry and *proteases* in biological detergents.

☐ 41. Distinguish between **intracellular** and **extracellular** enzymes and outline the basic procedure for the production of enzymes from microorganisms (including growth in culture and **downstream processing**).

☐ 42. Explain the advantages of enzyme isolation and immobilization in industry. Identify necessary properties of enzymes used in industry (e.g., thermostability).

Textbooks

See the 'Textbook Reference Grid' on pages 8-9 for textbook page references relating to material in this topic.

Supplementary Texts

See pages 5-6 for additional details of these texts:

■ Adds, J. *et al.*, 2000. **Molecules and Cells**, (NelsonThornes), pp. 1-19, 31-46.

■ Adds, J., E. Larkcom, R. Miller, & R. Sutton, 1999. **Tools, Techniques and Assessment in Biology**, (NelsonThornes), pp. 9-12, 45-47, 74-76.

Periodicals

See page 6 for details of publishers of periodicals:

STUDENT'S REFERENCE

■ **Smart Proteins** New Scientist, 17 March 2001 (Inside Science). *An excellent account of the structure of proteins and their roles in metabolism.*

■ **Universal Body Builder** New Scientist, 23 May 1998 (Inside Science). *The structural and functional role of collagen in the body.*

■ **Making Proteins Work (I)** Biol. Sci. Rev., 15(1) Sept. 2002, pp. 22-25. *A synopsis of how globular and fibrous proteins become functional.*

■ **Making Proteins Work (II)** Biol. Sci. Rev., 15(2) Nov. 2002, pp. 24-27. *How carbohydrates are added to proteins to make them functional.*

■ **Stuck with Structures?** Biol. Sci. Rev., 15(2) Nov. 2002, pp. 28-29. *A guide to interpreting the structural formulae of common organic compounds.*

■ **Fat Burns in the Flame of Carbohydrates** Biol. Sci. Rev., 15(3) Jan. 2003, pp. 37-41. *The basics of fat and carbohydrate metabolism.*

■ **Enzyme Technology** Biol. Sci. Rev., 12 (5) May 2000, pp. 26-27. *The range and importance of industrial enzymes in modern biotechnology.*

■ **Enzymes from Fungi** Biol. Sci. Rev., 13(3) Jan. 2001, pp. 19-21. *A discussion of the production and applications of fungal enzymes.*

■ **A New Look at Dietary Carbohydrates** Biol. Sci. Rev., 9(3) Jan. 1997, pp. 16-20. *Carbohydrates: their classification, role, & metabolism.*

TEACHER'S REFERENCE

■ **An Introduction to Lipid Analysis** The Am. Biology Teacher 64(2) Feb. 2002, pp. 122-129. *Thin-layer chromatography to examine lipid mixes.*

■ **Using Gel Electrophresis to Illustrate Protein Diversity and Isoelectric Point** The Am. Biology Teacher 64(7) Sept. 2002, pp. 535-537. *A how-to-do-it article looking at techniques for examining the structure and diversity of proteins.*

■ **Using Peroxidases to Demonstrate Enzyme Kinetics** The Am. Biology Teacher 65(2) Feb. 2003, pp. 116-121. *A how-to-do-it article for examining the effect of two competitive inhibitors on the rate of peroxidase activity.*

Internet

See pages 10-11 for details of how to access **Bio Links** from our web site: **www.thebiozone.com**. From Bio Links, access sites under the topics:

GENERAL BIOLOGY ONLINE RESOURCES > **Online Textbooks and Lecture Notes**.

BIOTECHNOLOGY > Applications in Biotechnology > Industrial Biotechnology: • About industrial enzymes • Biotechnology in industry • Chapter 19: industrial microbiology • Discover enzymes ... *and others*

CELL BIOLOGY AND BIOCHEMISTRY: • Cell & molecular biology online • MIT biology hypertextbook ... *and others* **Biochemistry and Metabolic Pathways:** • Enzymes • Energy and enzymes • Reactions and enzymes ... *and others*

> Software and video resources are now provided in the Teacher Resource Handbook

Biological Molecules

A 1

The molecules that make up living things can be grouped into five classes: water, carbohydrates, lipids, proteins, and nucleic acids. An understanding of the structure and function of these molecules is necessary to many branches of biology, especially biochemistry, physiology, and molecular genetics. The diagram below illustrates some of the common ways in which biological molecules are portrayed. Note that the **molecular formula** expresses the number of atoms in a molecule, but does not convey its structure; this is indicated by the **structural formula**. The role of water in biological systems is described opposite.

Portraying Biological Molecules

The numbers next to the carbon atoms are used for identification when the molecule changes shape

$C_6H_{12}O_6$
Glucose

| **Molecular formula** | **Structural formula** Glucose (straight form) | **Structural formula** α glucose (ring form) | **Ball and stick model** Glucose | **Space filling model** β-D-glucose |

Biological molecules may also include atoms other than carbon, oxygen, and hydrogen atoms. Nitrogen and sulfur are components of molecules such as amino acids and nucleotides. Some molecules contain the **C=O** (carbonyl) group. If this group is joined to at least one hydrogen atom it forms an **aldehyde**. If it is located between two carbon atoms, it forms a **ketone**.

Ketone   **Aldehyde**   **Carboxyl**

Examples of Biological Molecules

Acetate   Formaldehyde   Cysteine

$H_3C-C \begin{smallmatrix} O \\ \\ O \end{smallmatrix}$ $H_2N-C \begin{smallmatrix} H \\ \\ O \end{smallmatrix}$ $HS-C-C-C \begin{smallmatrix} OH \\ \\ O \end{smallmatrix}$

Key to Symbols

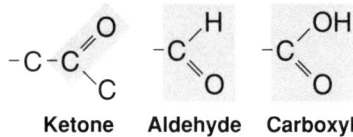

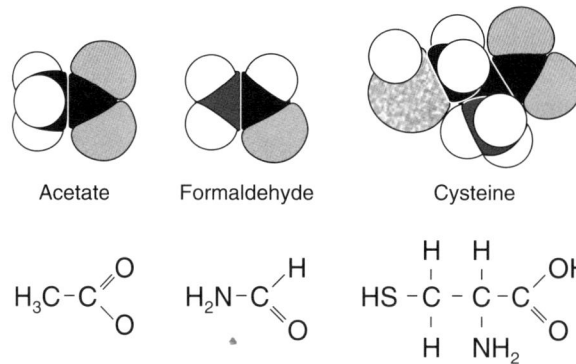

- ● Carbon
- ○ Hydrogen
- ◐ Oxygen
- ● Nitrogen
- ◌ Sulfur

Water and Inorganic Ions

Water provides an environment in which metabolic reactions can happen. Water takes part in, and is a common product of, many reactions. The most important feature of the chemical behavior of water is its **dipole** nature. It has a small positive charge on each of the two hydrogens and a small negative charge on the oxygen.

Small -ve charge
Small +ve charges

Oxygen is attracted to the Na^+

Hydrogen is attracted to the Cl^-

Water molecule
Formula: H_2O

Water surrounding a positive ion (Na^+)

Water surrounding a negative ion (Cl^-)

Inorganic ions are important for the structure and metabolism of all living organisms. An ion is simply an atom (or group of atoms) that has gained or lost one or more electrons. Many of these ions are soluble in water. Some of the inorganic ions required by organisms and their biological roles are listed in the table on the right.

Ion	Name	Biological role
Ca^{2+}	Calcium	Component of bones and teeth
Mg^{2+}	Magnesium	Component of chlorophyll
Fe^{2+}	Iron (II)	Component of hemoglobin
NO_3^-	Nitrate	Component of amino acids
PO_4^{3-}	Phosphate	Component of nucleotides
Na^+	Sodium	Involved in the transmission of nerve impulses
K^+	Potassium	Involved in controlling plant water balance
Cl^-	Chloride	Involved in the removal of water from urine

1. On the diagram above, showing a positive and a negative ion surrounded by water molecules, draw the positive and negative charges on the water molecules (as shown in the example provided in the same panel).

Biologically Important Properties of Water

Property of water	Significance for life
Ice is less dense than water.	Ice floats and also insulates the underlying water.
High surface tension.	Water forms droplets on surfaces and runs off.
Low viscosity.	Water flows through very small spaces and capillaries.
Liquid at room temperature.	Liquid medium for aquatic life and inside cells.
Colorless with a high transmission of visible light.	Light penetrates tissue and aquatic environments.
Strong cohesive properties and high tensile strength.	Water can be lifted and does not pull apart easily.
Many substances can dissolve in water (i.e. it is classified as a universal solvent).	Medium for the chemical reactions of life (metabolism). Water is the main transport medium in organisms.
Significant amounts of energy are required before water will change state (high latent heat of fusion)	Contents of cells are unlikely to freeze.
In order for water to evaporate it must absorb a large amount of energy (high latent heat of vaporization).	Heat is lost by evaporation of water. Sweating and transpiration causes rapid cooling.
Water can absorb a lot of energy for only a small rise in temperature (high specific heat capacity).	Aquatic environments are thermally stable. Organisms have stable internal temperatures when the external temperature is fluctuating.

Floating ice provides habitat for animals such as seals.

Waxes on leaf surfaces prevent water loss from plants.

Water provides habitat for aquatic plants and animals.

Oceans and large water bodies tend to be thermally stable.

Most organisms require regular water intake (active or passive).

2. Describe the importance of the **dipole nature** of water molecules to the chemistry of life:

_____

_____

3. Identify the three main elements comprising the structure of organic molecules: _____

_____

4. Name two other elements that are also frequently part of organic molecules: _____

5. State how many covalent bonds a carbon atom can form with neighboring atoms: _____

6. Classify formaldehyde according to the position of the C=O group: _____

7. For (a)-(e), state the property of water that is significant, and give one example of that property's biological importance:

(a) Property important in clarity of seawater: _____

   Biological importance: _____

(b) Property important in water travelling up the xylem tissue in plants: _____

   Biological importance: _____

(c) Property important in transport of glucose around the body: _____

   Biological importance: _____

(d) Property important in the relatively stable temperature of water bodies: _____

   Biological importance: _____

(e) Property important in the cooling effect of evaporation: _____

   Biological importance: _____

A ②

Carbohydrates

Carbohydrates are a family of organic molecules made up of carbon, hydrogen, and oxygen atoms with the general formula $(CH_2O)_x$. The most common arrangements found in sugars are hexose (6 sided) or pentose (5 sided) rings. Simple sugars, or monosaccharides, may join together to form compound sugars (disaccharides and polysaccharides), releasing water in the process (**condensation**). Compound sugars can be broken down into their constituent monosaccharides by the opposite reaction (**hydrolysis**). Sugars play a central role in cells, providing energy and, in some cells, contributing to support.

Classification of Sugars

Monosaccharides

Monosaccharides are used as a primary energy source for fuelling cell metabolism. They are **single-sugar** molecules and include glucose (grape sugar and blood sugar) and fructose (honey and fruit juices). During the fruit ripening process, starch is converted into fructose. This provides the sweetness that attracts animals that might assist in seed dispersal. All monosaccharides are classified as **reducing** sugars (i.e., they are able to participate in reduction reactions)

Single sugars (monosaccharides)

Triose
C
|
C
|
C

e.g., glyceraldehyde

Pentose
e.g., ribose, deoxyribose

Hexose
e.g., glucose, fructose, galactose

Disaccharides

Disaccharides are **double-sugar** molecules and are used as energy sources and as building blocks for larger molecules. The type of disaccharide formed depends on the monomers involved and whether they are in their α- or β- form. Only a few disaccharides (e.g., lactose) are classified as reducing sugars.

Sucrose = α-glucose + β-fructose (simple sugar found in plant sap)
Maltose = α-glucose + α-glucose (a product of starch hydrolysis)
Lactose = β-glucose + β-galactose (milk sugar)
Cellobiose = β-glucose + β-glucose (from cellulose hydrolysis)

Double sugars (disaccharides)

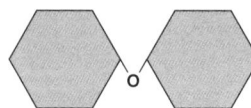

Examples
sucrose,
lactose,
maltose,
cellobiose

Polysaccharides

Cellulose

Cellulose is a structural material in plants and is made up of unbranched chains of β-**glucose** molecules held together by **1-4 glycosidic links**. As many as 10,000 glucose molecules may be linked together to form one chain.

Cellulose is a major component of plants, forming their **cell walls** and structural components. It is by far the most abundant carbohydrate.

Symbolic form: cellulose

1-4 glycosidic bonds create unbranched chains

Starch

Starch is made up of long chains of α-**glucose** molecules linked together. It contains a mixture of **amylose** (unbranched chains) and **amylopectin** (branched chains).

Starch is an energy storage molecule in plants and is found concentrated in **starch granules** in plant cells. It can be rapidly converted into glucose monomers when required.

Symbolic form: starch

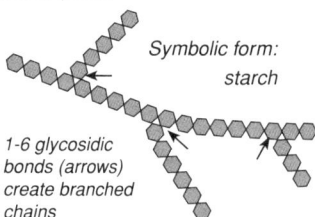

1-6 glycosidic bonds (arrows) create branched chains

Chitin

Chitin is a tough modified polysaccharide made up of chains of β-**glucose** molecules. It is chemically similar to cellulose but each glucose has an amine group ($-NH_2$) attached. After cellulose, chitin is the second most abundant carbohydrate. It is found in the cell walls of fungi and is the main component of the **exoskeleton** of insects and other arthropods.

Symbolic form: chitin

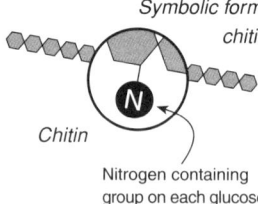

Chitin

Nitrogen containing group on each glucose

Glycogen

Glycogen, like starch, is a branched polysaccharide. It is chemically similar to starch, being composed of α-**glucose** molecules but there are more 1-6 glycosidic links mixed with 1-4 links. This makes it more highly branched and water-soluble than starch. Glycogen is a storage compound in animal tissues and is found mainly in the **liver** and **muscle** cells.

Symbolic form: glycogen

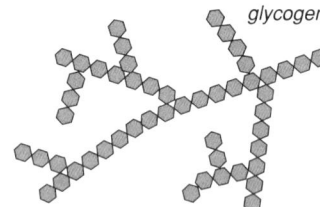

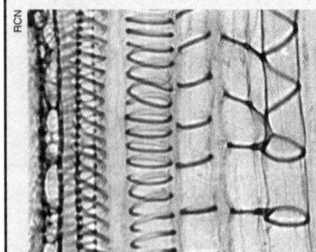

Cellulose provides strength to cell walls as in these xylem vessels.

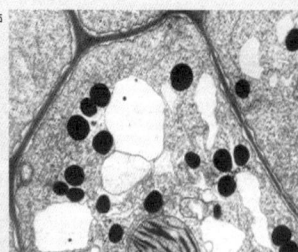

Starch granules are often visible as a storage compound in plant cells.

The exoskeleton of arthropods and the cell walls of fungi contain chitin.

Skeletal muscle tissue (above) and liver contain large stores of glycogen.

1. Describe a biological function of each of the following carbohydrates:

   (a) Cellulose: _____

   (b) Starch: _____

   (c) Glycogen: _____

Isomers of Glucose

Compounds with the same chemical formula (same types and numbers of atoms in their molecules) may differ in the arrangement of their atoms. Such variations in the arrangement of atoms in molecules are called **isomers**. In **structural isomers**, the atoms are linked in different sequences; fructose and glucose are structural isomers. **Optical isomers** are identical in every way but are mirror images of each other.

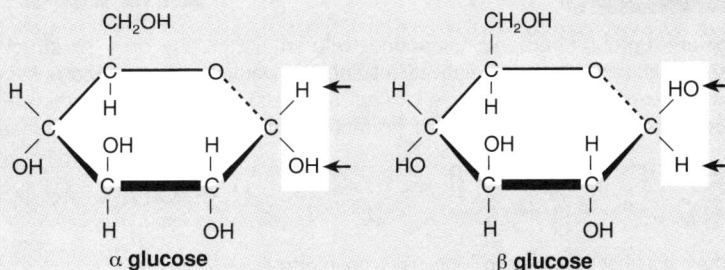

α **glucose**   β **glucose**

Condensation and Hydrolysis Reactions

Monosaccharides can combine to form compound sugars in what is called a **condensation** reaction. Compound sugars can be broken down by **hydrolysis** to simple monosaccharides.

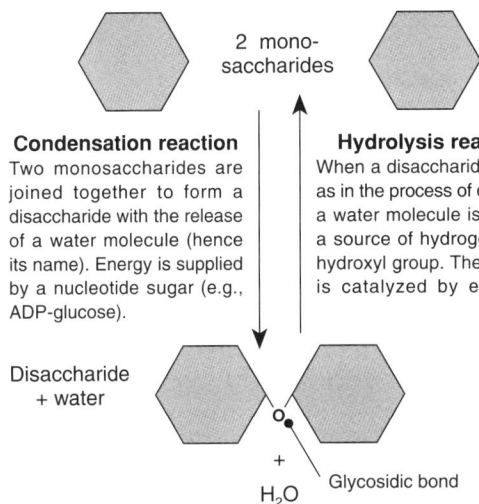

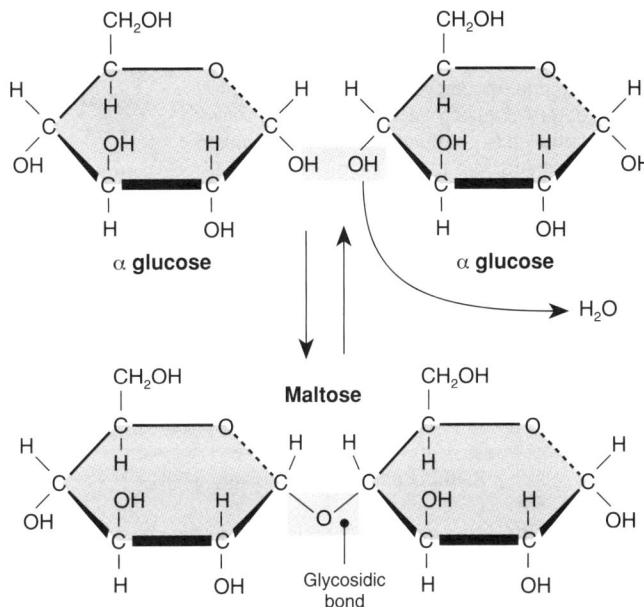

2 mono-saccharides

Condensation reaction
Two monosaccharides are joined together to form a disaccharide with the release of a water molecule (hence its name). Energy is supplied by a nucleotide sugar (e.g., ADP-glucose).

Hydrolysis reaction
When a disaccharide is split, as in the process of digestion, a water molecule is used as a source of hydrogen and a hydroxyl group. The reaction is catalyzed by enzymes.

Disaccharide + water

+
H_2O Glycosidic bond

α **glucose**   α **glucose**

H_2O

Maltose

Glycosidic bond

(d) Deoxyribose: _____

(e) Sucrose: _____

2. Distinguish between the following types of isomers:

   (a) Structural isomer: _____

   _____

   (b) Optical isomer: _____

   _____

3. Explain how the isomeric structure of a carbohydrate may affect its chemical behavior: _____

   _____

4. Study the two isomers of glucose at the top of this page. Describe how they differ from one another:

   _____

   _____

5. Describe briefly the process of the **condensation** reaction for carbohydrates: _____

   _____

   _____

6. Describe briefly the process of the **hydrolysis** reaction for carbohydrates: _____

   _____

   _____

Lipids

Lipids are a group of organic compounds with an oily, greasy, or waxy consistency. They are relatively insoluble in water and tend to be water-repelling (e.g. cuticle on leaf surfaces). Lipids are important biological fuels, some are hormones, and some serve as structural components in plasma membranes. Proteins and carbohydrates may be converted into fats by enzymes and stored within cells of adipose tissue. During times of plenty, this store is increased, to be used during times of food shortage.

Neutral Fats and Oils

The most abundant lipids in living things are **neutral fats**. They make up the fats and oils found in plants and animals. Fats are an economical way to store fuel reserves, since they yield more than twice as much energy as the same quantity of carbohydrate. Neutral fats are composed of a glycerol molecule attached to one (monoglyceride), two (diglyceride) or three (triglyceride) fatty acids. The fatty acid chains may be saturated or unsaturated (see below). **Waxes** are similar in structure to fats and oils, but they are formed with a complex alcohol instead of glycerol.

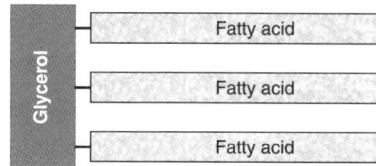

Triglyceride: an example of a neutral fat

Saturated and Unsaturated Fatty Acids

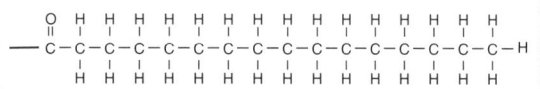

Palmitic acid (saturated fatty acid)

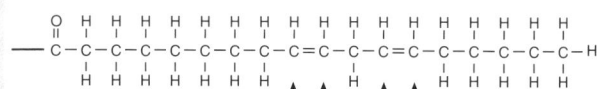

Linoleic acid (unsaturated fatty acid)

Fatty acids are a major component of neutral fats and phospholipids. About 30 different kinds are found in animal lipids. **Saturated fatty acids** contain the maximum number of hydrogen atoms. **Unsaturated fatty acids** contain some carbon atoms that are double-bonded with each other and are not fully saturated with hydrogens. Lipids containing a high proportion of saturated fatty acids tend to be solids at room temperature (e.g., butter). Lipids with a high proportion of unsaturated fatty acids are oils and tend to be liquid at room temperature. Regardless of their degree of saturation, fatty acids yield a large amount of energy when oxidized.

Condensation reactions

Three separate condensation reactions are involved in producing a triglyceride (right). Triglycerides form when glycerol bonds with three fatty acids. Glycerol is an alcohol containing three carbons. Each of these carbons is bonded to a hydroxyl (-OH) group. When glycerol bonds with the fatty acid, an **ester bond** is formed and **water is released**.

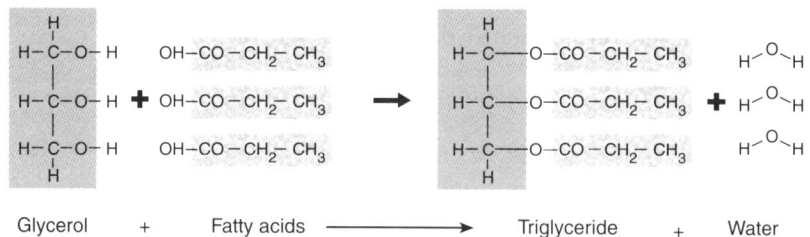

Glycerol   +   Fatty acids   ⟶   Triglyceride   +   Water

Phospholipids

Phospholipids are the main component of cellular membranes. They consist of a glycerol attached to two fatty acid chains and a phosphate (PO_4^{3-}) group. The phosphate end of the molecule is attracted to water (it is hydrophilic) while the fatty acid end is repelled (hydrophobic). The hydrophobic ends turn inwards in the membrane to form a **phospholipid bilayer**.

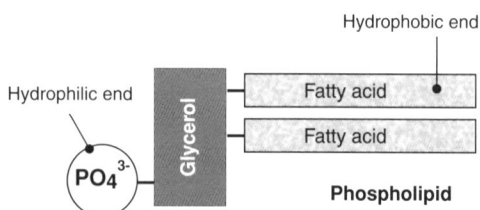

Phospholipid

Steroids

Although steroids are classified as lipids, their structure is quite different from that of other lipids. Steroids have a basic structure of three rings made of 6 carbon atoms each and a fourth ring containing 5 carbon atoms. Examples of steroids include the male and female sex hormones (testosterone and estrogen), and the hormones cortisol and aldosterone. Cholesterol, while not a steroid itself, is a sterol lipid and is a precursor to several steroid hormones.

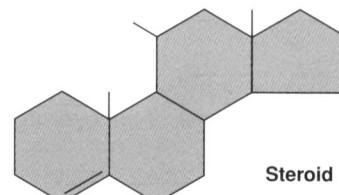

Steroid

Important Biological Functions of Lipids

Lipids are concentrated sources of energy and provide fuel for aerobic respiration.

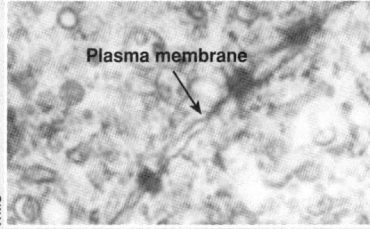

Phospholipids form the structural framework of cellular membranes.

Waxes and oils secreted on to surfaces provide waterproofing in plants and animals.

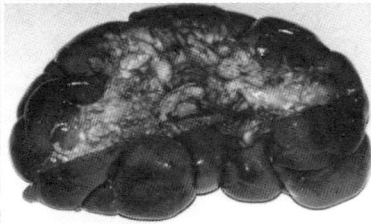

Fat absorbs shocks. Organs that are prone to bumps and shocks (e.g., kidneys) are cushioned with a relatively thick layer of fat.

Lipids are a source of metabolic water. During respiration stored lipids are metabolized for energy, producing water and carbon dioxide.

Stored lipids provide insulation. Increased body fat levels in winter reduce heat losses to the environment.

1. Define the following terms:

    (a) Hydrophilic: _____

    (b) Hydrophobic: _____

2. Name the type of fatty acids found in lipids that form the following at room temperature:

    (a) Solid fats: _____   (b) Oils: _____

3. Describe two key differences between saturated fatty acids and unsaturated fatty acids:

    (a) _____

    (b) _____

4. Explain the key difference between a neutral fat and a wax: _____

5. Outline the key **chemical** difference between a phospholipid and a triglyceride: _____

6. Name two examples of steroids. For each example, describe its physiological function:

    (a) _____

    (b) _____

7. Relate the properties of phospholipids to their role in the structure of membranes: _____

8. Explain how fats can provide an animal with the following:

    (a) Energy: _____

    (b) Water: _____

    (c) Insulation: _____

Amino Acids

A 2

Amino acids are the basic units from which proteins are made. Plants can manufacture all the amino acids they require from simpler molecules, but animals must obtain a certain number of ready-made amino acids (called **essential** amino acids) from their diet. All other amino acids can be constructed from these essential amino acids. The order in which the different amino acids are linked together to form proteins is controlled by genes on the chromosomes.

Structure of Amino Acids

There are over 150 amino acids found in cells, but only 20 occur commonly in proteins. The remaining, non-protein amino acids have specialized roles as intermediates in metabolic reactions, or as neurotransmitters and hormones. All amino acids have a common structure (see right). The only difference between the different types lies with the 'R' group in the general formula. This group is variable, which means that it is different in each kind of amino acid.

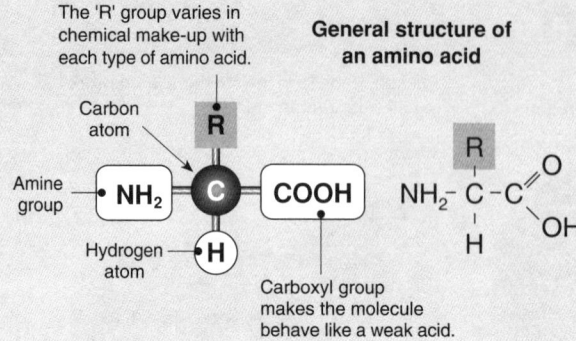

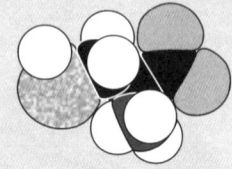

The 'R' group varies in chemical make-up with each type of amino acid.

General structure of an amino acid

Carbon atom

Amine group — NH₂

Hydrogen atom — H

Carboxyl group makes the molecule behave like a weak acid.

$NH_2 - C - C {\overset{O}{\underset{OH}{}}}$

Example of an amino acid shown as a space filling model: cysteine.

Properties of Amino Acids

Three examples of amino acids with different chemical properties are shown right, with their specific 'R' groups outlined. The 'R' groups can have quite diverse chemical properties.

This 'R' group can form **disulfide bridges** with other cysteines to create cross linkages in a polypeptide chain.

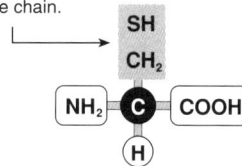

SH
CH₂

NH₂ — C — COOH
H

Cysteine

This 'R' group gives the amino acid an **alkaline** property.

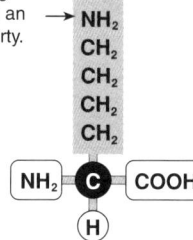

NH₂
CH₂
CH₂
CH₂
CH₂

NH₂ — C — COOH
H

Lysine

This 'R' group gives the amino acid an **acidic** property.

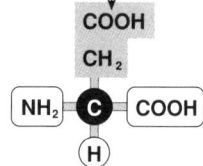

COOH
CH₂

NH₂ — C — COOH
H

Aspartic acid

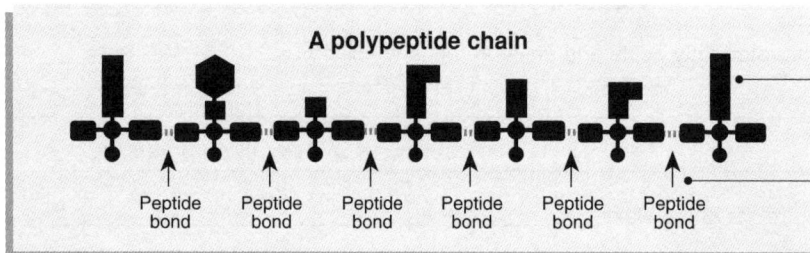

A polypeptide chain

The order of amino acids in a protein is directed by the order of nucleotides in DNA and mRNA.

Peptide bonds link amino acids together in long polymers called polypeptide chains. These may form part or all of a protein.

Peptide bond (×6)

The amino acids are linked together by peptide bonds to form long chains of up to several hundred amino acids (called polypeptide chains). These chains may be functional units (complete by themselves) or they may need to be joined to other polypeptide chains before they can carry out their function. In humans, not all amino acids can be manufactured by our body: ten must be taken in with our diet (eight in adults). These are the 'essential amino acids' (indicated by the symbol ◆ on the right).

Amino acids occurring in proteins

Alanine	Glycine	Proline
Arginine	Histidine ◆	Serine
Asparagine	Isoleucine ◆	Threonine ◆
Aspartic acid	Leucine ◆	Tryptophan ◆
Cysteine	Lysine ◆	Tyrosine ◆
Glutamine	Methionine ◆	Valine ◆
Glutamic acid	Phenylalanine ◆	

1. Describe the biological functions of amino acids:

_____

_____

2. Describe what makes each of the 20 amino acids found in proteins unique: _____

_____

_____

3. Name the type of bond that links amino acids together: _____

Optical Isomers of Amino Acids

All amino acids, apart from the simplest one (glycine) show optical isomerism. The two forms that these optical isomers can take relate to the arrangement of the four bonding sites on the carbon atom. This can result in two different arrangements as shown on the diagrams on the right. With a very few minor exceptions, only the **L-forms** are found in living organisms.

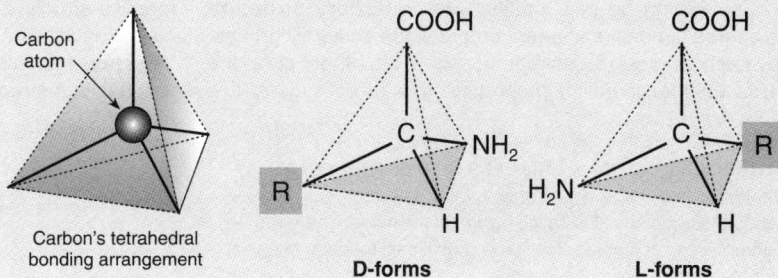

Carbon atom

Carbon's tetrahedral bonding arrangement

COOH

C — NH₂

R

H

D-forms

COOH

H₂N — C — R

H

L-forms

Condensation and Hydrolysis Reactions

Amino acids can combine to form peptide chains in what is called a **condensation** reaction. Peptide chains can be broken down by **hydrolysis** to simple amino acids.

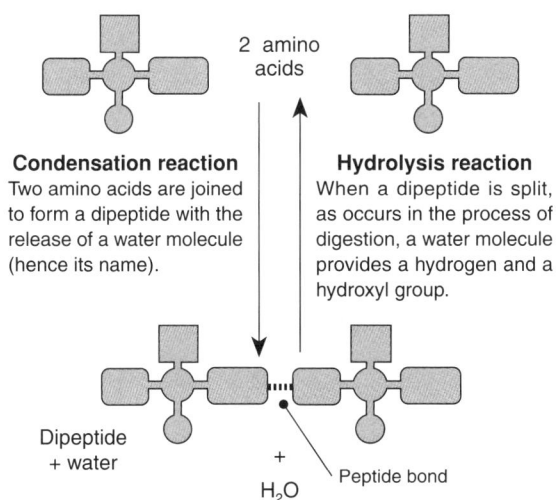

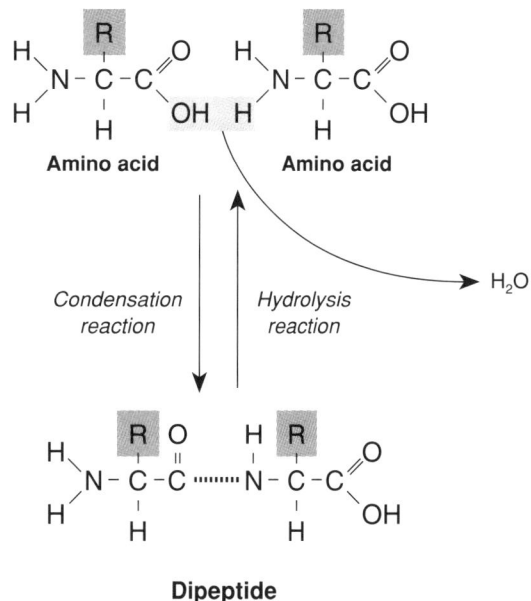

2 amino acids

Condensation reaction
Two amino acids are joined to form a dipeptide with the release of a water molecule (hence its name).

Hydrolysis reaction
When a dipeptide is split, as occurs in the process of digestion, a water molecule provides a hydrogen and a hydroxyl group.

Dipeptide + water

+

H₂O

Peptide bond

Amino acid

Amino acid

Condensation reaction

Hydrolysis reaction

H₂O

Dipeptide

4. Describe the process that determines the sequence in which amino acids are linked together to form polypeptide chains:

_____

_____

5. Explain what is meant by **essential amino acids**: _____

_____

_____

6. Describe briefly the process of the **condensation** reaction for amino acids: _____

_____

_____

_____

7. Describe briefly the process of the **hydrolysis** reaction for amino acids: _____

_____

_____

_____

8. Name the optical isomeric form that occurs in nearly all amino acids in living things: _____

Proteins

RA 2

The precise folding up of a protein into its **tertiary structure** creates a three dimensional arrangement of the active 'R' groups. The way each 'R' group faces with respect to the others gives the protein its unique chemical properties. If a protein loses this precise structure (denaturation), it is usually unable to carry out its biological function. Proteins are often classified on the basis of structure (globular vs fibrous). Some of the properties used for the basis of structural classification are outlined opposite.

Primary Structure - 1° *(amino acid sequence)*
Strings of hundreds of amino acids link together with peptide bonds to form molecules called polypeptide chains. There are 20 different kinds of amino acids that can be linked together in a vast number of different combinations. This sequence is called the **primary structure**. It is the arrangement of attraction and repulsion points in the amino acid chain that determines the higher levels of organization in the protein and its biological function.

Secondary Structure - 2° *(α-helix or ß-pleated sheet)*
Polypeptides become folded in various ways, referred to as the secondary (2°) structure. The most common types of 2° structures are a coiled α-**helix** and a β-**pleated sheet**. Secondary structures are maintained with hydrogen bonds between neighboring CO and NH groups. H-bonds, although individually weak, provide considerable strength when there are a large number of them. The example, right, shows the two main types of secondary structure. In both, the **'R' side groups** (not shown) project out from the structure. Most globular proteins contain regions of α-helices together with β-sheets. Keratin (a fibrous protein) is composed almost entirely of α-helices. Fibroin (silk protein), is another fibrous protein, almost entirely in β-sheet form.

Tertiary Structure - 3° *(folding)*
Every protein has a precise structure formed by the folding of the secondary structure into a complex shape called the **tertiary structure**. The protein folds up because various points on the secondary structure are attracted to one another. The strongest links are caused by bonding between neighboring *cysteine* amino acids which form di-sulfide bridges. Other interactions that are involved in folding include weak ionic and hydrogen bonds as well as hydrophobic interactions.

Quaternary Structure - 4°
Some proteins (such as enzymes) are complete and functional with a tertiary structure only. However, many complex proteins exist as aggregations of polypeptide chains. The arrangement of the polypeptide chains into a functional protein is termed the **quaternary structure**. The example (right) shows a molecule of hemoglobin, a globular protein composed of 4 polypeptide subunits joined together; two identical *beta chains* and two identical *alpha chains*. Each has a heme (iron containing) group at the centre of the chain, which binds oxygen. Proteins containing non-protein material are **conjugated proteins**. The non-protein part is the **prosthetic group**.

Denaturation of Proteins
Denaturation refers to the loss of the three-dimensional structure (and usually also the biological function) of a protein. Denaturation is often, although not always, permanent. It results from an alteration of the bonds that maintain the secondary and tertiary structure of the protein, even though the sequence of amino acids remains unchanged. Agents that cause denaturation are:
• **Strong acids and alkalis**: Disrupt ionic bonds and result in coagulation of the protein. Long exposure also breaks down the primary structure of the protein.
• **Heavy metals**: May disrupt ionic bonds, form strong bonds with the carboxyl groups of the R groups, and reduce protein charge. The general effect is to cause the precipitation of the protein.
• **Heat and radiation** (e.g. UV): Cause disruption of the bonds in the protein through increased energy provided to the atoms.
• **Detergents and solvents**: Form bonds with the non-polar groups, thereby disrupting hydrogen bonding.

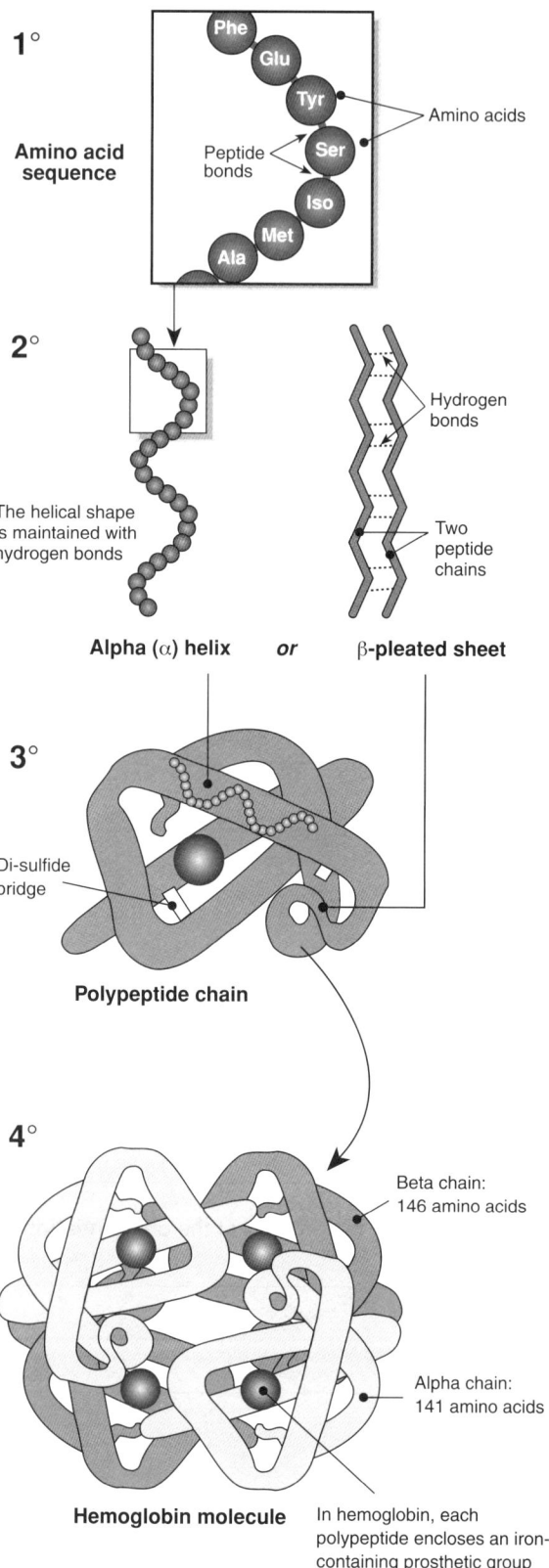

1°
Amino acid sequence

Phe / Glu / Tyr / Ser / Iso / Met / Ala — Amino acids, Peptide bonds

2°
The helical shape is maintained with hydrogen bonds

Hydrogen bonds / Two peptide chains

Alpha (α) helix *or* **β-pleated sheet**

3°
Di-sulfide bridge

Polypeptide chain

4°
Beta chain: 146 amino acids
Alpha chain: 141 amino acids

Hemoglobin molecule — In hemoglobin, each polypeptide encloses an iron-containing prosthetic group

Hemoglobin's Chemical Formula:

$$C_{3032} H_{4816} O_{872} N_{780} S_8 Fe_4$$

Structural Classification of Proteins

Fibrous Proteins

Properties
- Water insoluble
- Very tough physically; may be supple or stretchy
- Parallel polypeptide chains in long fibres or sheets

Function
- Structural role in cells and organisms *e.g. collagen found in connective tissue, cartilage, bones, tendons, and blood vessel walls.*
- Contractile *e.g. myosin, actin*

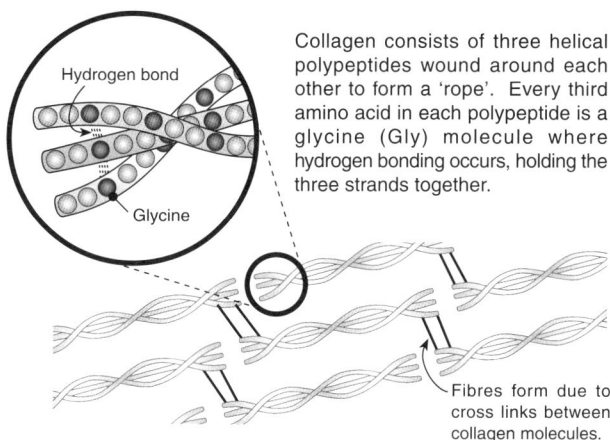

Hydrogen bond

Glycine

Collagen consists of three helical polypeptides wound around each other to form a 'rope'. Every third amino acid in each polypeptide is a glycine (Gly) molecule where hydrogen bonding occurs, holding the three strands together.

Fibres form due to cross links between collagen molecules.

Globular Proteins

Properties
- Easily water soluble
- Tertiary structure critical to function
- Polypeptide chains folded into a spherical shape

Function
- Catalytic *e.g. enzymes*
- Regulatory *e.g. hormones (insulin)*
- Transport *e.g. hemoglobin*
- Protective *e.g. antibodies*

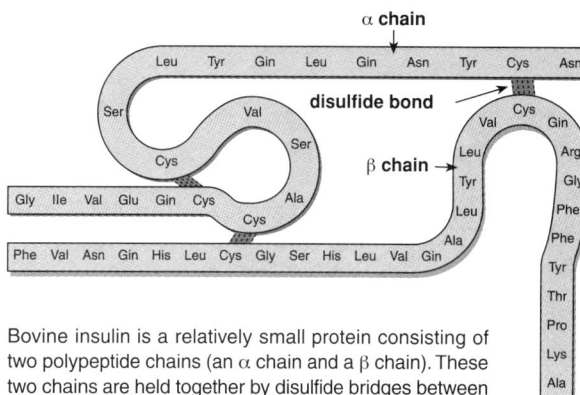

α chain

disulfide bond

β chain

Bovine insulin is a relatively small protein consisting of two polypeptide chains (an α chain and a β chain). These two chains are held together by disulfide bridges between neighboring cysteine (Cys) molecules.

---

1. Giving examples, briefly explain how proteins are involved in the following functional roles:

   (a) Structural tissues of the body: _____

   _____

   (b) Regulating body processes: _____

   _____

   (c) Contractile elements: _____

   _____

   (d) Immunological response to pathogens: _____

   _____

   (e) Transporting molecules within cells and in the bloodstream: _____

   _____

   (f) Catalyzing metabolic reactions in cells: _____

   _____

2. Explain how denaturation destroys protein function: _____

   _____

   _____

3. Describe one structural difference between globular and fibrous proteins: _____

   _____

   _____

4. Determine the total number of amino acids in the α and β chains of the insulin molecule illustrated above:

   (a) α chain: _____ (b) β chain: _____

Modification of Proteins

Proteins may be modified after they have been produced by ribosomes. After they pass into the interior of rough endoplasmic reticulum, some proteins may have carbohydrates added to them to form **glycoproteins**. Proteins may be further altered in the Golgi apparatus. The **Golgi apparatus** functions principally as a system for processing, sorting, and modifying proteins. Proteins that are to be secreted from the cell are synthesized by

ribosomes on the rough endoplasmic reticulum and transported to the Golgi apparatus. At this stage, carbohydrates may be removed or added in a step-wise process. Some of the possible functions of glycoproteins are illustrated below. Other proteins may have fatty acids added to them to form **lipoproteins**. These modified proteins transport lipids in the plasma between various organs in the body (e.g. gut, liver, and adipose tissue).

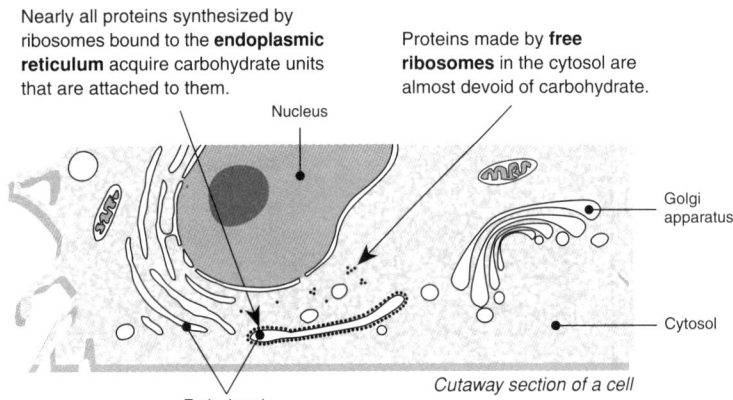

Nearly all proteins synthesized by ribosomes bound to the **endoplasmic reticulum** acquire carbohydrate units that are attached to them.

Proteins made by **free ribosomes** in the cytosol are almost devoid of carbohydrate.

Branching chains of carbohydrates are made up of different kinds of sugars linked together.

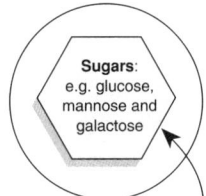

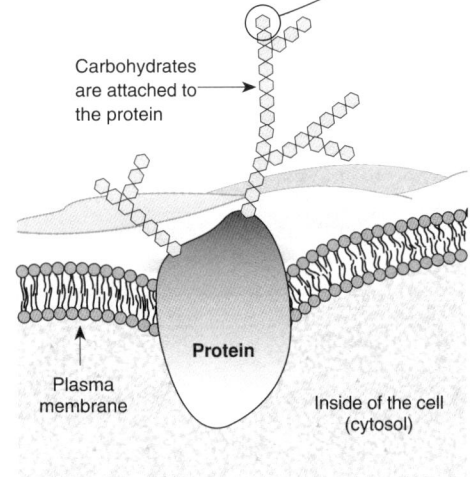

Sugars: e.g. glucose, mannose and galactose

Nucleus

Golgi apparatus

Cytosol

Cutaway section of a cell

Endoplasmic reticulum

Carbohydrate groups may act as markers that determine the **destination** of a glycoprotein within the cell or for export (the carbohydrates may be removed after the protein has reached its destination).

Carbohydrate groups may help **position** or **orientate** glycoproteins in membranes (the carbohydrate groups prevent them from rotating in the membrane).

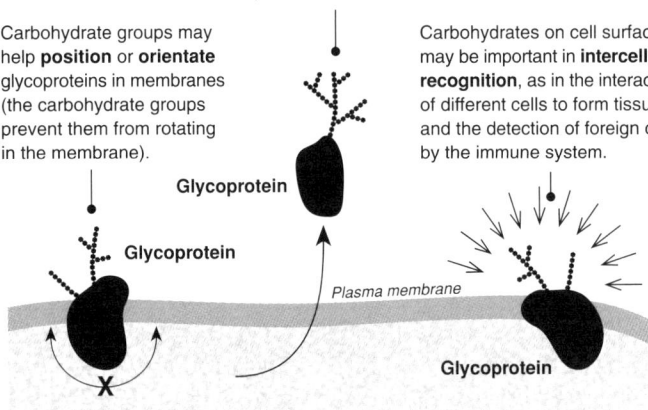

Carbohydrates on cell surfaces may be important in **intercellular recognition**, as in the interaction of different cells to form tissues and the detection of foreign cells by the immune system.

Carbohydrates are attached to the protein

Glycoprotein

Glycoprotein

Plasma membrane

Glycoprotein

X

Plasma membrane

Protein

Inside of the cell (cytosol)

Enlarged section of a plasma membrane showing a glycoprotein embedded in it.

1. (a) Explain what a **glycoprotein** is: _____

    (b) Briefly describe three **roles** of glycoproteins: _____

    _____

    _____

2. (a) Explain what a **lipoprotein** is: _____

    (b) Briefly describe the **role** of lipoproteins: _____

    _____

    _____

3. Suggest why proteins made by free ribosomes in the cytosol are usually free of carbohydrate: _____

    _____

4. Suggest why the orientation of a protein in the plasma membrane might be important: _____

    _____

    _____

Biochemical Tests

DA 1

Biochemical tests are used to detect the presence of nutrients such as lipids, proteins, and carbohydrates (sugar and starch) in various foods. These simple tests are useful for detecting nutrients when large quantities are present. A more accurate technique by which to separate a mixture of compounds involves **chromatography**. Chromatography is used when only a small sample is available or when you wish to distinguish between nutrients. Simple biochemical food tests will show whether sugar is present, whereas chromatography will distinguish between the different types of sugars (e.g. fructose or glucose).

Paper Chromatography

Set Up and Procedure

The chromatography paper is folded so it can be secured by the bung inside the test tube. The bung also prevents the solvent evaporating.

Chromatography paper may be treated with chemicals to stain normally invisible pigments.

A spot of concentrated sample is added using a pipette and suspended above the solvent. As the solvent travels up the paper it will carry the sample with it. The distance the sample travels depends on its solubility.

A pencil line is used to show the starting point.

Solvent

Determining R_f Values

To identify the substances in a mixture an Rf value is calculated using the equation:

$$R_f = \frac{\text{Distance traveled by the spot (x)}}{\text{Distance traveled by the solvent (y)}}$$

These R_f values can then be compared with R_f values from known samples or standards, for example: Glycine's R_f value = 0.50
Alanine's R_f value = 0.70
Arginine's R_f value = 0.72
Leucine's R_f value = 0.91

Simple Food Tests

Proteins: The Biuret Test

Reagent:	Biuret solution.
Procedure:	A sample is added to biuret solution and gently heated.
Positive result:	Solution turns from blue to lilac.

Starch: The Iodine Test

Reagent:	Iodine.
Procedure:	Iodine solution is added to the sample.
Positive result:	Blue-black staining occurs.

Lipids: The Emulsion Test

Reagent:	Ethanol.
Procedure:	The sample is shaken with ethanol. After settling, the liquid portion is distilled and mixed with water.
Positive result:	The solution turns into a cloudy-white emulsion of suspended lipid molecules.

Sugars: The Benedict's Test

Reagent:	Benedict's solution.
Procedure:	*Non reducing sugars*: The sample is boiled with dilute hydrochloric acid, then cooled and neutralized. A test for reducing sugars is then performed.
	Reducing sugar. Benedict's solution is added, and the sample is placed in a water bath.
Positive result:	Solution turns from blue to orange.

1. Calculate the R_f value for the example given above (show your working): _____

_____

2. Explain why the R_f value of a substance is always less than 1: _____

_____

3. Discuss when it is appropriate to use chromatography instead of a simple food test: _____

_____

_____

4. Explain what would happen if a sample was immersed in the chromatography solvent, instead of suspended above it:

_____

_____

5. With reference to their R_f values, rank the four amino acids (listed above) in terms of their solubility: _____

_____

6. Outline why lipids must be mixed in ethanol before they will form an emulsion in water: _____

_____

RA 2

Enzymes

Most enzymes are proteins and are called **biological catalysts** because they **catalyze** biochemical reactions. Enzymes act on one or more compounds (the **substrate**). They may break a substrate molecule down into simpler substances, or join two or more substrate molecules chemically together. The enzyme itself is unchanged in the reaction; its presence merely allows the reaction to take place more rapidly. Once a substrate attains the **activation energy** required to enable it to change into the product, there is a 50% chance that the reaction will proceed,

otherwise it reverts back to a stable form of the reactant again. The part of the enzyme's surface into which the substrate is bound and undergoes reaction is known as the **active site**. This is made of different parts of polypeptide chain folded in a specific shape so they are closer together. In most cases, the complexity of the binding site is such that only one type of substrate will bind. Enzymes with a lower **specificity** accept a range of substrates of the same general type because they are specific to a bond type (e.g. lipases break up any fatty acid chain length of lipid).

Enzyme Structure

The model on the right is of an enzyme called *Ribonuclease S*, that breaks up RNA molecules. It is a typical enzyme, being a globular protein and composed of up to several hundred atoms. The darkly shaded areas are called **active sites** and make up the **cleft**; the region into which the substrate molecule(s) are drawn. The correct positioning of these sites is critical for the catalytic reaction to occur. The substrate (RNA in this case) is drawn into the cleft by the active sites. By doing so, it puts the substrate molecule under stress, causing the reaction to proceed more readily.

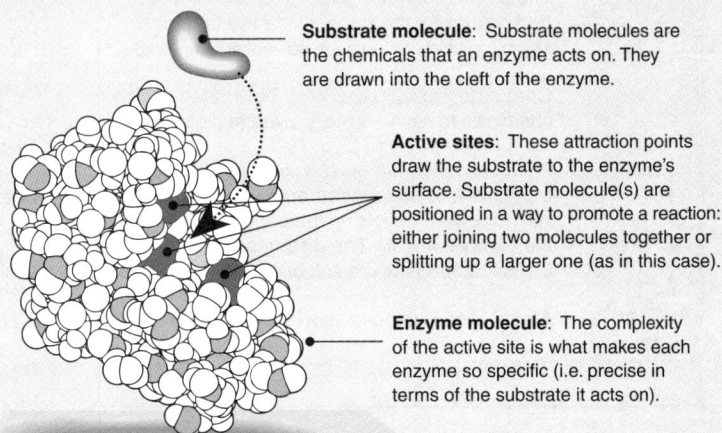

Substrate molecule: Substrate molecules are the chemicals that an enzyme acts on. They are drawn into the cleft of the enzyme.

Active sites: These attraction points draw the substrate to the enzyme's surface. Substrate molecule(s) are positioned in a way to promote a reaction: either joining two molecules together or splitting up a larger one (as in this case).

Enzyme molecule: The complexity of the active site is what makes each enzyme so specific (i.e. precise in terms of the substrate it acts on).

Source: After *Biochemistry*, (1981) by Lubert Stryer

How Enzymes Work

The **lock and key** model proposed earlier this century suggested that the substrate was simply drawn into a closely matching cleft on the enzyme molecule. More recent studies have revealed that the process more likely involves an **induced fit** (see diagram on the right), where the enzyme or the reactants change their shape slightly. The reactants become bound to enzymes by weak chemical bonds. This binding can weaken bonds within the reactants themselves, allowing the reaction to proceed more readily.

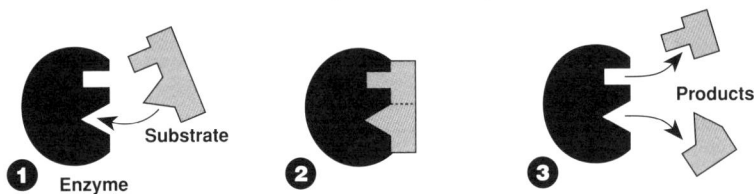

① Enzyme / Substrate

②

③ Products

The presence of an enzyme simply makes it easier for a reaction to take place. All **catalysts** speed up reactions by influencing the stability of bonds in the reactants. They may also provide an alternative reaction pathway, thus lowering the activation energy needed for a reaction to take place (see the graph below).

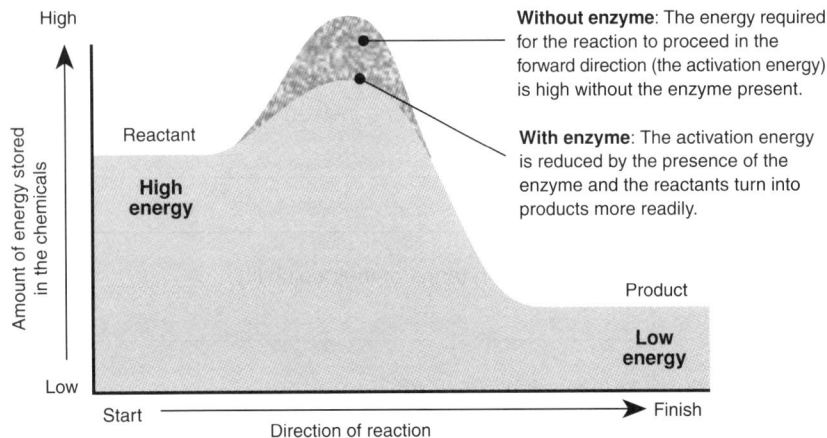

High

Reactant

High energy

Without enzyme: The energy required for the reaction to proceed in the forward direction (the activation energy) is high without the enzyme present.

With enzyme: The activation energy is reduced by the presence of the enzyme and the reactants turn into products more readily.

Amount of energy stored in the chemicals

Product

Low energy

Low

Start ──────────────────────────→ Finish

Direction of reaction

Induced Fit Model

An enzyme fits to its substrate somewhat like a lock and key. The shape of the enzyme changes when the substrate fits into the cleft (called the **induced fit**):

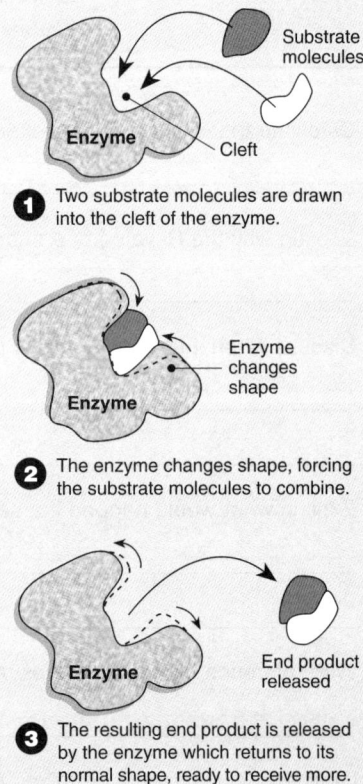

Substrate molecules

Enzyme / Cleft

① Two substrate molecules are drawn into the cleft of the enzyme.

Enzyme changes shape

Enzyme

② The enzyme changes shape, forcing the substrate molecules to combine.

Enzyme

End product released

③ The resulting end product is released by the enzyme which returns to its normal shape, ready to receive more.

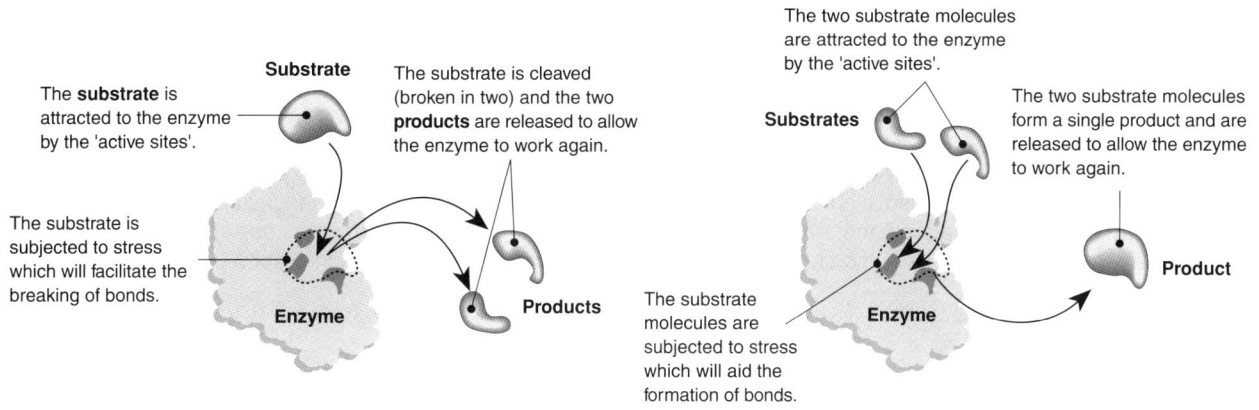

The **substrate** is attracted to the enzyme by the 'active sites'.

Substrate

The substrate is subjected to stress which will facilitate the breaking of bonds.

The substrate is cleaved (broken in two) and the two **products** are released to allow the enzyme to work again.

Enzyme

Products

The two substrate molecules are attracted to the enzyme by the 'active sites'.

Substrates

The two substrate molecules form a single product and are released to allow the enzyme to work again.

The substrate molecules are subjected to stress which will aid the formation of bonds.

Enzyme

Product

Catabolic reactions

Some enzymes can cause a single substrate molecule to be drawn into the active site. Chemical bonds are broken, causing the substrate molecule to break apart to become two separate molecules. **Examples**: *digestion, cellular respiration.*

Anabolic reactions

Some enzymes can cause two substrate molecules to be drawn into the active site. Chemical bonds are formed, causing the two substrate molecules to form bonds and become a single molecule. **Examples**: *protein synthesis, photosynthesis.*

1. Explain why an enzyme is called a biological catalyst: _____

_____

_____

2. Explain what the substrate is when considering enzyme action: _____

_____

3. Describe the role of the **active site** in enzyme function: _____

_____

_____

4. Explain what is meant by **metabolism**: _____

_____

5. Define each of the following terms, giving an example and stating whether the reaction is **endergonic** or **exergonic**:

(a) **Catabolism**: _____

_____

(b) **Anabolism**: _____

_____

6. Outline the key features of the '**lock and key**' model of enzyme action: _____

_____

_____

7. Outline the '**induced fit**' model of enzyme action, explaining how it differs from the lock and key model:

_____

_____

_____

8. Explain what might happen to the functioning of an enzyme if the gene that codes for it was altered by a mutation:

_____

_____

(RDA2) Enzyme Reaction Rates

Enzymes are sensitive molecules. They often have a narrow range of conditions under which they operate properly. At low temperatures there is little activity. As temperature is increased, so does the enzyme activity until the point is reached when the temperature is so high it damages the protein (**denaturation**). This causes the enzyme to stop working. Extremes in acidity (pH) can also cause the protein structure of enzymes to denature. Poisons often work by causing enzymes to cease functioning. Cofactors such as vitamins and trace elements are required for many enzymes to function. In the four graphs below, the *rate of reaction* or *degree of enzyme activity* is plotted against each of four factors that affect enzyme performance. Answer the questions that relate to each graph:

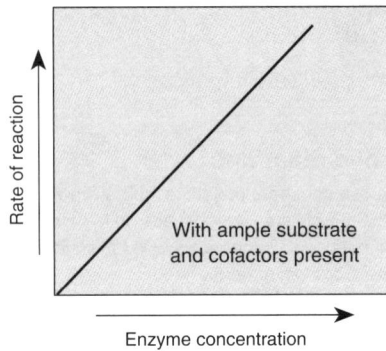

Rate of reaction / Enzyme concentration

With ample substrate and cofactors present

1. **Enzyme concentration**
   (a) Describe the change in the rate of reaction when the enzyme concentration is increased (assuming there is plenty of the substrate present):

   _____

   _____

   (b) Suggest how a cell may vary the amount of enzyme present in a cell:

   _____

   _____

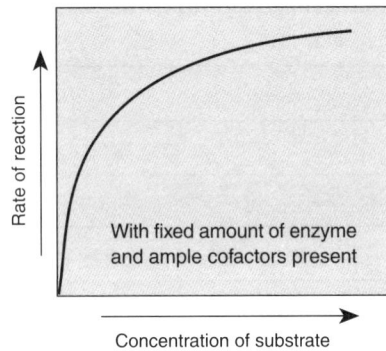

Rate of reaction / Concentration of substrate

With fixed amount of enzyme and ample cofactors present

2. **Substrate concentration**
   (a) Describe the change in the rate of reaction when the substrate concentration is **increased** (assuming a fixed amount of enzyme and ample cofactors):

   _____

   _____

   (b) Explain why the rate changes the way it does: _____

   _____

   _____

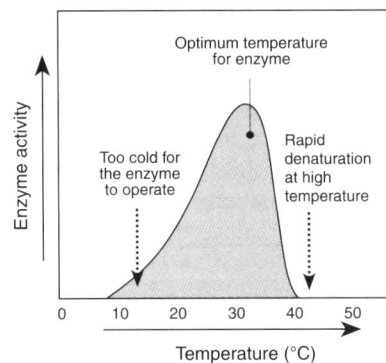

Enzyme activity / Temperature (°C)

Optimum temperature for enzyme

Too cold for the enzyme to operate

Rapid denaturation at high temperature

0   10   20   30   40   50

3. **Temperature**
   Higher temperatures speed up all reactions, but few enzymes can tolerate temperatures higher than 50–60°C. The rate at which enzymes are **denatured** (change their shape and become inactive) increases with higher temperatures.

   (a) Describe what is meant by an optimum temperature for enzyme activity:

   _____

   _____

   (b) Explain why most enzymes perform poorly at low temperatures:

   _____

   _____

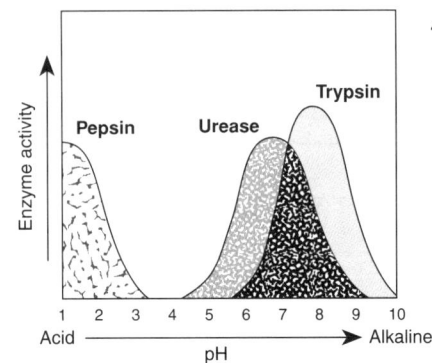

Enzyme activity / pH

Pepsin   Urease   Trypsin

1   2   3   4   5   6   7   8   9   10

Acid ——————→ Alkaline

4. **Acidity (pH)**
   Like all proteins, enzymes are **denatured** by extremes of **pH** (very acid or alkaline). Within these extremes, most enzymes are still influenced by pH. Each enzyme has a preferred pH range for optimum activity.

   (a) State the optimum pH for each of the enzymes:

   Pepsin: _____ Trypsin: _____ Urease: _____

   (b) Pepsin acts on proteins in the stomach. Explain how its optimum pH is suited to its working environment:

   _____

   _____

Enzyme Cofactors and Inhibitors

Enzyme activity is often influenced by the presence of other chemicals. Some of these may enhance an enzyme's activity. Called **cofactors**, they are a nonprotein component of an enzyme and may be organic molecules (**coenzymes**) or inorganic ions (e.g. Ca^{2+}, Zn^{2+}). Enzymes may also be deactivated, temporarily or permanently, by chemicals called enzyme **inhibitors**.

Types of Enzyme

Nearly all enzymes are made of protein, although RNA has been demonstrated to have enzymatic properties. Some enzymes consist of just protein, while others require the addition of extra components to complete their catalytic properties. These may be permanently attached parts called **prosthetic groups**, or temporarily attached pieces (**coenzymes**) that detach after a reaction, and may participate with another enzyme in other reactions.

Protein-only enzymes

Active site

— enzyme

Enzyme comprises only protein, e.g., lysozyme

Conjugated protein enzymes

Active site

Prosthetic group is more or less permanently attached

Apoenzyme

Prosthetic group required
Contains apoenzyme (protein) plus a prosthetic group, e.g., flavoprotein + FAD

Active site

Coenzyme becomes detached after the reaction

Apoenzyme

Coenzyme required
Contains apoenzyme (protein) plus a coenzyme (non-protein) e.g., dehydrogenases + NAD

Reversible Enzyme Inhibitors

Substrate

S

Good fit

Enzyme

No inhibition

Competitive inhibitor blocks the active site

S

Enzyme

Competitive inhibitor

The substrate binds to the active site but slows the speed of reaction

Enzyme

Noncompetitive inhibitor

Noncompetitive inhibitor

The substrate cannot bind to the active site

S

Active site is distorted

Enzyme

Noncompetitive inhibitor

Allosteric enzyme inhibitor

Enzyme inhibitors may be reversible or irreversible. **Reversible inhibitors** are used to control enzyme activity. There is often an interaction between the substrate or end product and the enzymes controlling the reaction. Buildup of the end product or a lack of substrate may serve to deactivate the enzyme. This deactivation may take the form of **competitive** (competes for the active site) or **noncompetitive** inhibition. While noncompetitive inhibitors have the effect of slowing down the rate of reaction, **allosteric inhibitors** block the active site altogether and prevent its functioning.

Irreversible Inhibitors (Poisons)

Substrate

Active site

Mercury acts as an inhibitor and blocks the active site

Hg

Papain enzyme

Certain **heavy metals** bind tightly and permanently to the active sites of enzymes, destroying their catalytic properties. Examples of toxic heavy metals include *cadmium* (Cd), *lead* (Pb), *mercury* (Hg), and *arsenic* (As). They are generally non-competitive inhibitors, although mercury is an exception and deactivates the enzyme papain. Heavy metals are retained in the body, and lost slowly.

1. Describe the general role of **cofactors** in enzyme activity: _____

_____

2. **Heavy metals** can be very toxic to life forms.
   (a) Name four heavy metals that are toxic to humans: _____

   (b) Explain in general terms why these heavy metals are toxic: _____

   _____

3. There are many enzyme inhibitors that are not heavy metals (e.g. those found in some pesticides).

   (a) Name a **common poison** that is an enzyme inhibitor, but not a heavy metal: _____

   (b) Try to find out how this poison interferes with enzyme function. Briefly describe its effect on a named enzyme:

   _____

   _____

4. Explain the difference between **competitive** and **noncompetitive** inhibition: _____

   _____

5. Explain how **allosteric inhibitors** differ from other noncompetitive inhibitors: _____

   _____

Industrial Production of Enzymes

Humans have used enzymes for thousands of years in food and beverage production, but the use of enzymes in industry is a comparatively recent development. Many industries now rely on the large scale production of microbial enzymes to catalyze a range of reactions. In the absence of enzymes, these reactions sometimes require high temperatures or pressures to proceed. Industrial enzymes must be relatively robust against denaturation and capable of maintaining activity over a wide temperature and pH range. Enzyme technology involves the production, isolation, purification, and application of useful enzymes. Commercial enzymes are produced from three main sources: plants, animals,

and microorganisms (mainly bacteria and fungi). Most enzymes used in industrial processes today are microbial in origin and are produced in industrial-scale microbial fermentations using liquid or semi-solid growth media. Note that the term **fermentation**, when used in reference to industrial microbiology, applies to both aerobic and anaerobic microbial growth in **bioreactors**. Generalized plans for the industrial production of both extracellular and intracellular enzymes are illustrated below. Note that the isolation of intracellular enzymes (below, right) is more complex because the cells must first be disrupted to release the enzymes within.

1 **Growth of the microorganisms**:
A closed fermenter system is an enclosed, **sterile system** containing culture broth in which the microorganisms (bacteria or fungi) are grown until the extracellular products (or the cells themselves) have accumulated for harvesting. Conditions in the fermenter vessel are closely monitored and carefully regulated so that the conditions for maximal microbial growth are optimized.

The model (right) shows a cutaway section of a cylindrical fermentation chamber, typical of that used for continuous microbial cultures.

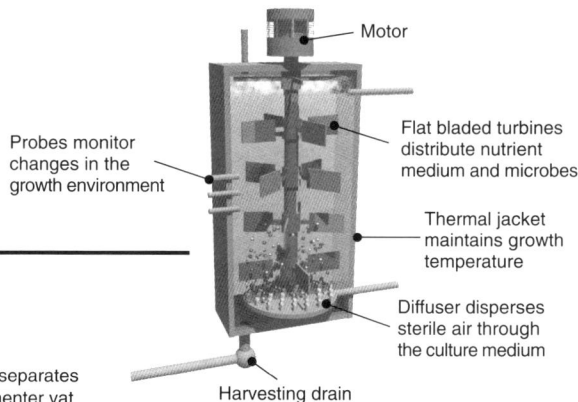

Motor

Flat bladed turbines distribute nutrient medium and microbes

Probes monitor changes in the growth environment

Thermal jacket maintains growth temperature

Diffuser disperses sterile air through the culture medium

2 **Separation**: Drum filtration separates the components of the fermenter vat

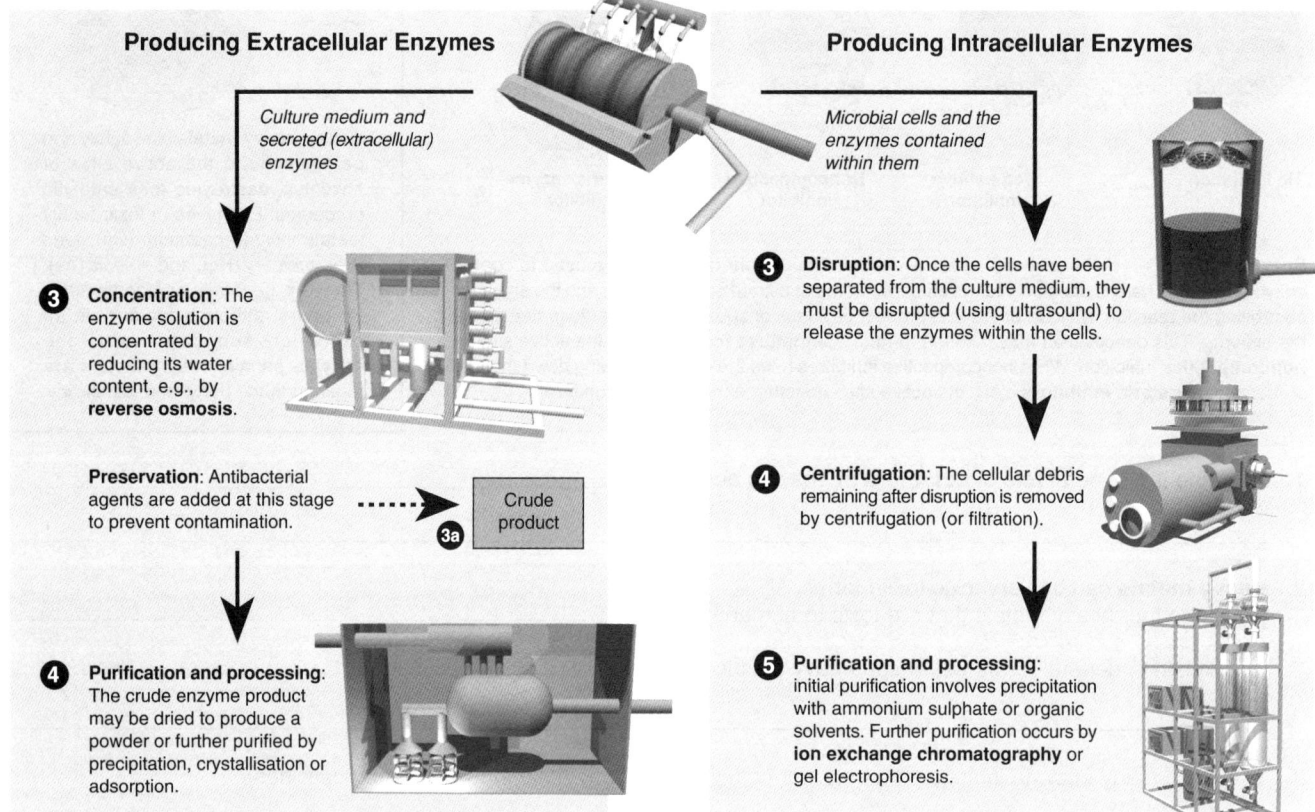

Harvesting drain

Producing Extracellular Enzymes

Culture medium and secreted (extracellular) enzymes

3 **Concentration**: The enzyme solution is concentrated by reducing its water content, e.g., by **reverse osmosis**.

Preservation: Antibacterial agents are added at this stage to prevent contamination. **(3a)** ----→ Crude product

4 **Purification and processing**: The crude enzyme product may be dried to produce a powder or further purified by precipitation, crystallisation or adsorption.

Producing Intracellular Enzymes

Microbial cells and the enzymes contained within them

3 **Disruption**: Once the cells have been separated from the culture medium, they must be disrupted (using ultrasound) to release the enzymes within the cells.

4 **Centrifugation**: The cellular debris remaining after disruption is removed by centrifugation (or filtration).

5 **Purification and processing**: initial purification involves precipitation with ammonium sulphate or organic solvents. Further purification occurs by **ion exchange chromatography** or gel electrophoresis.

1. The industrial production of microbial enzymes varies according to the enzyme involved and its desired end use. Compare the two flow diagrams, for intracellular and extracellular enzymes, above:

    (a) Explain the main way in which the two production methods differ: _____

    _____

    (b) Suggest the reason for this difference: _____

    _____

2. Enzyme solutions can be packaged and used as crude extracts without further purification (3a). State one benefit of this:

    _____

Putting Enzymes to Use

Depending on the way in which the desired end-product is produced, enzymes may be used as crude whole cell preparations or as cell-free enzyme extracts. Whole cell preparations are cost effective, and appropriate when the processes involved in production of the end product are complex, as in waste treatment and the production of semi-synthetic antibiotics. Cell free enzyme extracts are more expensive to produce, but can be a more efficient option overall. To reduce costs and improve the efficiency of product production, enzymes are sometimes immobilized within a matrix of some kind and the reactants are passed over them. The various methods by which enzymes are put to work are compared in the diagram below.

Industrial enzymes

	Advantages	Disadvantages	Methods of Enzyme Immobilization
Cell-free enzyme extract Enzyme is used in solution	There is generally a high level of enzyme activity when the enzymes are free in solution.	The enzyme may be washed away after use. The end-product is not enzyme free and may require purification.	**Micro-encapsulation** The enzyme is held within a membrane, or within alginate or polyacrylamide capsules.
Immobilized enzyme Enzyme is held in an inert material	The enzymes can be used repeatedly and recovered easily (this reduces costs). The enzyme-free end-product is easily harvested. The enzymes are more stable due to the protection of a matrix. The life of some enzymes, e.g., proteases, is extended by immobilization.	The entrapment process may reduce the enzyme activity (more enzyme will be needed). Some methods offering high stability (e.g. covalent bonding) are harder to achieve. Immobilization can be costly.	**Lattice entrapment** Enzyme is trapped in a gel lattice, e.g., silica gel. The substrate and reaction products diffuse in and out of the matrix. Enzymes trapped in a gel lattice **Covalent attachment** Enzyme is covalently bonded to a solid surface e.g. collagen or a synthetic polymer.
Whole cell preparation Whole cells may be immobilized	Useful for enzymes that are unstable or inactivated when outside the cell. Useful for complex processes utilizing more than one intracellular enzyme.	Less expensive and more rapid than first producing a pure enzyme extract. Some of the substrate is used for microbial growth, so the process is less efficient overall.	**Direct cross-linking** Glutaraldehyde is used to cross-link the enzymes. They then precipitate out and are immobilized without support.

Partially permeable membrane

Enzyme

Substrate, e.g., collagen

Glutaraldehyde

1. (a) Explain one benefits of using a cell free enzyme extract to produce a high-value end-product:

    (b) Identify one factor that might be important when deciding *not* to use a cell free extract:

2. (a) Describe two benefits of using immobilized enzymes (rather than enzymes in solution) for industrial processes:

    (b) Describe a disadvantage associated with the use of immobilized enzymes:

    (c) Describe a factor that would affect the rate of end-product harvest from immobilized enzymes:

3. The useful life of protease enzymes is extended when they are immobilized (as opposed to being in solution). Using what you know of enzyme structure, explain why immobilization has this effect in this case:

4. Suggest why immobilization would reduce the activity of certain enzymes:

Applications of Enzymes

Microbes are ideal organisms for the industrial production of enzymes because of their high productivity, ease of culture in industrial fermenters, and the ease with which they can be genetically modified to produce particular products. In addition, because there is an enormous diversity in microbial metabolism, the variety of enzymes available for exploitation is very large. Some of the microorganisms involved in industrial fermentations, and their enzymes and their applications are illustrated below.

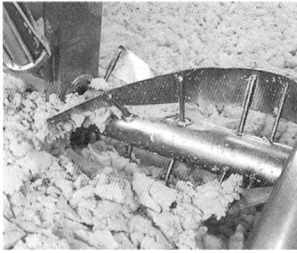

Enzymes are used in the production of both **beer** (e.g. amylase, proteases, and amyloglucosidases) and **cheese** (e.g. chymosin).

Cellulases and pectinases are used in the manufacture of packaged (as opposed to fresh) fruit juices to speed juice extraction and prevent cloudiness.

The manufacture of **jams** and candies relies on **citric acid**, which is produced by industrial fermentation of the fungus *Aspergillus niger*.

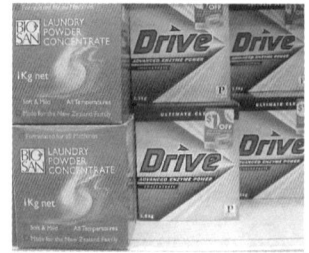

Biological detergents use **proteases**, **lipases**, and **amylases** extracted from fungi and thermophilic bacteria to break down organic material in stains.

Fungal ligninases are used in **pulp and paper industries** to remove lignin from wood pulp and treat wood waste.

Tanning industries now use proteases from *Bacillus subtilis* instead of toxic sulphide chemicals to treat hides.

Bacterial lactase converts lactose to glucose and galactose in the production of lactose free milks.

In **soft centered chocolates**, **invertase** from yeast breaks down the solid filling to produce the soft center.

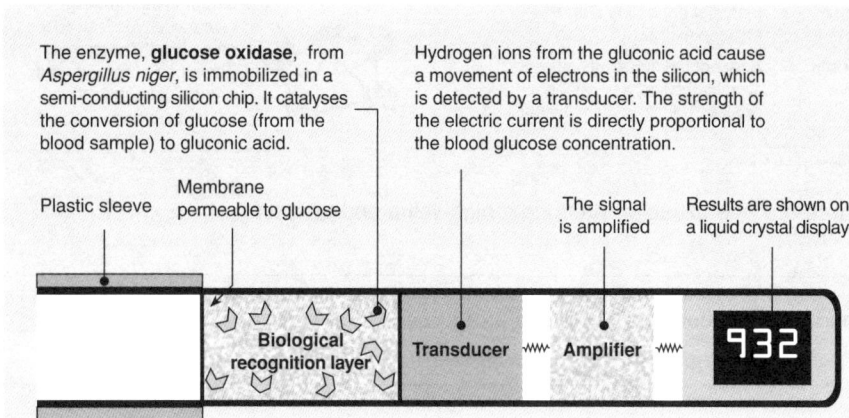

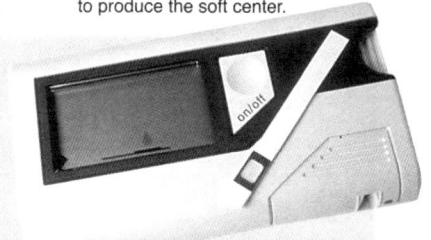

The enzyme, **glucose oxidase**, from *Aspergillus niger*, is immobilized in a semi-conducting silicon chip. It catalyses the conversion of glucose (from the blood sample) to gluconic acid.

Hydrogen ions from the gluconic acid cause a movement of electrons in the silicon, which is detected by a transducer. The strength of the electric current is directly proportional to the blood glucose concentration.

Plastic sleeve

Membrane permeable to glucose

The signal is amplified

Results are shown on a liquid crystal display

Biological recognition layer

Transducer

Amplifier

932

Biosensors are electronic monitoring devices that use biological material to detect the presence or concentration of a particular substance. Enzymes are ideally suited for use in biosensors because of their specificity and sensitivity. This example illustrates how glucose oxidase is used in a biosensor to detect blood sugar level in diabetics.

1. (a) Outline the basic principle of enzyme-based biosensors: _____

_____

(b) In general terms, explain how a biosensor could be used to monitor blood alcohol level: _____

_____

_____

2. Identify two probable consequences of the absence of enzymes from a chemical reaction that normally uses them:

(a) _____ (b) _____

3. Choose one example from those described above and, in more detail, identify:

(a) The enzyme and its specific microbial source: _____

(b) The application of the enzyme in industry and the specific reaction it catalyses: _____

_____

_____

Cell Structure

IB SL	IB HL	IB Options	AP Biology
Complete nos: 1-16, 19-26, 29	Complete nos: 1-16, 19-26, 29	Not applicable to options	Complete nos: 1-31
Extension: 17-18, 27-28, 30-31	Extension: 17-18, 27-28, 30-31		

Learning Objectives

☐ 1. Compile your own glossary from the **KEY WORDS** displayed in **bold type** in the learning objectives below.

Cell theory *(page 71)*

☐ 2. Discuss the **cell theory** with respect to the organization of living things. Recognize the contribution of microscopy to the development of cell theory and our present knowledge of cell structure.

Microscopy *(pages 76-79)*

☐ 3. Distinguish between **optical** and **electron microscopes**, outlining the structure of each. With respect to light and electron microscopy, explain and distinguish between: **magnification** and **resolution**.

☐ 4. With respect to structure, operation, and type of image produced, distinguish between TEM (**transmission electron microscopy**) and SEM (**scanning electron microscopy**). Recognize electron microscopy as an important tool in investigating cell structure.

☐ 5. Distinguish between **compound** and **stereo light microscopes**. Identify the situations in which these different microscopes would be used.

☐ 6. Demonstrate an ability to correctly use a microscope to locate material and focus images. Identify the steps required for preparing a **temporary mount** for viewing with a compound light microscope.

☐ 7. Demonstrate an ability to use simple **staining techniques** to show specific features of cells. Demonstrate a knowledge of some specific stains, identifying the purpose of each named example.

Features of cells *(pages 38-39, 72-75, 80-89, 102)*

☐ 8. Define a **cell** and recognize it as the basic unit of living things. In simple terms, describe the main features of a cell (**plasma membrane, cytoplasm, organelles**). Identify the features that characterize living things and explain why cells are considered to be living entities.

☐ 9. Appreciate the range of cell sizes and use different units of measurement (mm, μm, nm) to express cell sizes. Compare the relative sizes of molecules, plasma membrane thickness, viruses, bacteria, cell organelles, and cells using appropriate SI units. Appreciate the importance of surface area to volume ratio as a factor limiting cell size (see "*Cell Membranes and Transport*").

☐ 10. Contrast the generalised structure of **prokaryote** and **eukaryote** cells and provide examples of each type. If required, describe the specific features of protistan cells. Explain why **viruses** are regarded as non-cellular.

☐ 11. Identify specific differences between **fungal cells** and the cells of other eukaryotes. Consider fungal structure in relation to cell theory.

☐ 12. Describe the structure of a **prokaryotic** (bacterial) **cell** and its inclusions, as illustrated by a named example (e.g. *E. coli*). Identify the **cell wall** and the structures associated with it (e.g. **flagella**), **plasma membrane, cytoplasm, ribosomes**, and **mesosomes**, and the **nucleoid region, bacterial chromosome**, and **plasmids**. Identify the major functions of each of these structures. Recognize them in electron micrographs and identify which of them are unique to prokaryotes.

NOTE: Mesosomes, once thought to be structural features, are now known to be artifacts of cell preparation for electron microscopy.

☐ 13. Describe and interpret drawings and photographs of typical **plant** and **animal cells** (e.g. leaf palisade cell and liver cell) as seen using light microscopy.

☐ 14. Describe and interpret drawings and photographs of typical plant and animal cells, as seen using electron microscopy. Identify and describe the role of:
   - **nucleus, nuclear envelope, nucleolus**
   - **mitochondria, chloroplasts** (if present),
   - *rough/smooth* **endoplasmic reticulum, ribosomes**,
   - **plasma membrane, cell wall** (if present)
   - **Golgi apparatus, lysosomes, vacuoles** (if present),
   - **cytoplasm, cytoskeleton** (of **microtubules**), **centrioles, cilia** (if present).

☐ 15. Identify which of the cellular structures above would be visible under *light microscopy, transmission electron microscopy*, and *scanning electron microscopy*.

☐ 16. List the differences between plant and animal cells, noting relative size and shape, and presence or absence of particular structures and organelles.

Separating cellular components *(page 86)*

☐ 17. Describe the principles of **cell fractionation** (**differential centrifugation**) and explain how it is achieved through homogenization of a sample followed by ultracentrifugation.

☐ 18. Identify the components of the four fractions normally obtained from differential centrifugation: *the nuclear fraction, the mitochondrial fraction, the microsomal fraction, and the soluble fraction*. Explain the role of speed of centrifugation in separating these fractions.

Mitosis and cell division *(pages 90-93)*

☐ 19. Recall the structure of chromosomes. Using diagrams, describe the behavior of chromosomes during a mitotic **cell cycle** in eukaryotes. Include reference to: **mitosis, growth** (G_1 and G_2), and DNA replication (S).

☐ 20. Demonstrate appropriate staining techniques in the study of mitosis in plant material e.g. root tip squash.

☐ 21. Recognize and describe the following events in *mitosis*: **prophase, metaphase, anaphase**, and **telophase**.

☐ 22. With respect to both plant and animal cells, understand the term **cytokinesis**, and distinguish between nuclear division and division of the cytoplasm.

☐ 23. Understand the role of mitosis in growth and repair, and asexual reproduction. Recognize the importance of **daughter nuclei** with chromosomes identical in number and type. Recognize cell division as a prelude to **cellular differentiation**.

☐ 24. Explain how **carcinogens** can upset the normal controls regulating cell division. Define the terms: **cancer, tumor suppressor genes, oncogenes**. List factors that increase the chances of cancerous growth.

Cellular differentiation *(pages 94-97)*

☐ 25. Summarize how the **zygote** (fertilized egg) undergoes division to produce an adult. Define the terms: **cellular differentiation, specialized cell**. Comment on the basic similarity of cells early in development.

☐ 26. Understand that cellular differentiation occurs through the control of gene expression. Describe how the fate of cell lines is dependent on the decisions made along **developmental pathways**.

☐ 27. Identify and describe the structural adaptations and function of some specialized cells in humans, e.g. blood cells, liver cells, or intestinal epithelial cells. For each cell type, identify the tissue where it occurs.

☐ 28. Identify and describe the structural adaptations and function of some of the specialized cell types found in angiosperm plant tissues, including the leaf palisade (mesophyll) cell. Categorize these into cells associated with the stem, roots, leaves, or reproductive structures.

Tissues and organs *(pages 98-99)*

☐ 29. Recognize the hierarchy of organization in multicellular organisms: *molecular, organelle, cell, **tissue***, and ***organ***. With respect to the function of specialized cells, outline the benefits of being multicellular.

☐ 30. With reference to specific examples (e.g. epithelial tissues, blood, xylem, and/or phloem), explain *how* cells are organized into **tissues**.

☐ 31. Describe examples of tissues in plants (e.g. xylem) and animals (e.g. blood, epithelium), identifying their functional role in each case. Illustrate your examples and calculate the linear magnification of your drawings in each case.

Textbooks

See the 'Textbook Reference Grid' on pages 8-9 for textbook page references relating to material in this topic.

Supplementary Texts

See pages 5-6 for additional details of these texts:

■ Adds, J., *et al.*, 2000. **Molecules and Cells**, (NelsonThornes), pp. 48-60, 67-76.

■ Adds, J., *et al.*, 1999. **Tools, Techniques and Assessment in Biology**, (NelsonThornes), pp. 13-26.

■ Clegg, C.J., 1998. **Mammals: Structure and Function**, (John Murray), pp. 4-7, 10-11.

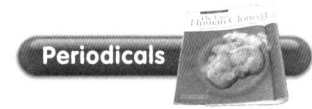

Periodicals

See page 6 for details of publishers of periodicals:

STUDENT'S REFERENCE

■ **The Living Dead** New Scientist, 13 October 2001, (Inside Science). *The non-cellular nature of viruses: what are they and how do they operate.*

Mitosis and cell differentiation

■ **The Cell Cycle and Mitosis** Biol. Sci. Rev., 14(4) April 2002, pp. 37-41. *Cell growth and division, key stages in the cell cycle, and the complex control over different stages of mitosis.*

■ **Out of Control - Unlocking the Genetic Secrets of Cancer** Biol. Sci. Rev., 11(3) Jan. 1999, pp. 36-39. *The control of cell division: oncogenes and their role in the development of cancer.*

■ **Rebels without a Cause** New Scientist, 13 July 2002, (Inside Science). *The causes of cancer: the uncontrolled division of cells that results in tumor formation. Breast cancer is a case example.*

Cell structure and organelles

■ **Control Centre** New Scientist, 17 July 1999 (Inside Science). *An excellent four page article on the role of the nucleus: its origin, the organization of DNA in eukaryotic cells, how genes code for proteins, and the function of ribosomes and RNA.*

■ **Water Channels in the Cell Membrane** Biol. Sci. Rev., 9(2) November 1996, pp. 18-22. *The role of proteins in membrane transport, including mechanisms involved in physiological processes.*

■ **Cellular Factories** New Scientist, 23 November 1996 (Inside Science). *The structure and role of organelles in plant and animal cells.*

■ **Bacteria** National Geographic, 184(2) August 1993, pp. 36-61. *The structure and diversity of bacteria: the most abundant organisms on Earth.*

■ **Secret Language of Cells** New Scientist, 16 February 2002 (Inside Science). *An account of cellular communication, including the role of gap junctions, hormones, ligands and receptors. It leads onto a discussion of how cell division is disrupted in cancer and following thalidomide use.*

Microscopy

■ **Transmission Electron Microscopy** Biol. Sci. Rev., 13(2) Nov. 2000, pp. 32-35. *An account of the techniques and applications of TEM. Includes a diagram comparing features of TEM and LM.*

■ **Scanning Electron Microscopy** Biol. Sci. Rev., 13(3) January 2001, pp. 6-9. *The techniques and applications of SEM. Includes specimen preparation and advancements in the technology.*

■ **Light Microscopy** Biol. Sci. Rev., 13(1) Sept. 2000, pp. 36-38. *An excellent account of the basis and various techniques of light microscopy.*

■ **X-Ray Microscopy** Biol. Sci. Rev., 14(2) November 2001, pp. 38-40. *A short account of the technique and application of X-ray microscopy. Its advantages over EM are explained, particularly with respect to specimen preparation.*

■ **Preparing Microscope Slides** Biol. Sci. Rev., 8(1) Sept. 1995, pp. 34-36. *Preparing & examining stained and fixed slides for light microscopy.*

TEACHER'S REFERENCE

Mitosis and cell differentiation

■ **Modeling Mitosis and Meiosis** The American Biology Teacher, 62(3), March 2000, pp. 204-206. *Promoting problem solving for students so that they better understand aspects of nuclear division.*

Cell structure and organelles

■ **Cells by Design** New Scientist, 3 June 1989, pp. 24-26. *Artificially produced cells have been made by simulating the plasma membrane and enclosing materials within.*

■ **Protein Potluck** The American Biology Teacher, 59(2), Feb 1997, pp.108-111. *An experiment on protein synthesis and the role of organelles.*

■ **Eukaryotic Cell Function** The American Biology Teacher, 61(7), Sept 1999, pp. 539-542. *An interactive exercise on eukaryotic cell structure and the function of organelles.*

■ **The Birth of Complex Cells** Scientific American, April 1996, pp. 38-45. *An excellent article covering the evolution of cell structure and the functions of various organelles.*

■ **Bacteria** National Geographic, 184(2) August 1993, pp. 36-61. *Structure and diversity of bacteria: the most abundant and useful organisms on Earth.*

■ **The Force** New Scientist, 26 February 2000, pp. 30-35. *An account of mitochondria and how they can exercise control over reproduction.*

■ **The Machinery of Cell Crawling** Scientific American, September 1994, pp. 40-49. *Excellent article covering the complex ultrastructure that allows cells to move.*

■ **The Architecture of Life** Scientific American, January 1998, pp. 30-39. *The cytoskeleton within cells and the universal patterns of design.*

■ **Budding Vesicles in Living Cells** Scientific American, March 1996, pp. 50-55. *The function of the Golgi apparatus in cell transport.*

Internet

See pages 10-11 for details of how to access **Bio Links** from our web site: **www.thebiozone.com** From Bio Links, access sites under the topics:

GENERAL BIOLOGY ONLINE RESOURCES > Online Textbooks and Lecture Notes: • S-Cool! A level biology revision guide • Learn.co.uk • Mark Rothery's biology web site ... *and others*

CELL BIOLOGY AND BIOCHEMISTRY: • Cell and molecular biology online ... *and others* > **Microscopy**: • A guide to microscopy and microanalysis • Biological applications of electron and light microscopy • Histology • Scanning Electron Microscope • Selected microscopy educational resources ... *and others* > **Cell Structure and Transport**: Animal cells • CELLS alive! • Cell breakage and fractionation - Part 1 • Nanoworld • Talksaver cell biology • The virtual cell • Techniques of cell fractionation > **Cell Division**: • Comparison of meiosis and mitosis • Cell division: binary fission and mitosis • Mitosis in the onion root tip ... *and others*

> **Software and video resources are now provided in the Teacher Resource Handbook**

The Cell Theory

The idea that all living things are composed of cells developed over many years and is strongly linked to the invention and refinement of the microscope. Early microscopes in the 1600's (such as Leeuwenhoek's below) opened up a whole new field of biology – the study of cell biology and microorganisms. The cell theory is a fundamental idea of biology.

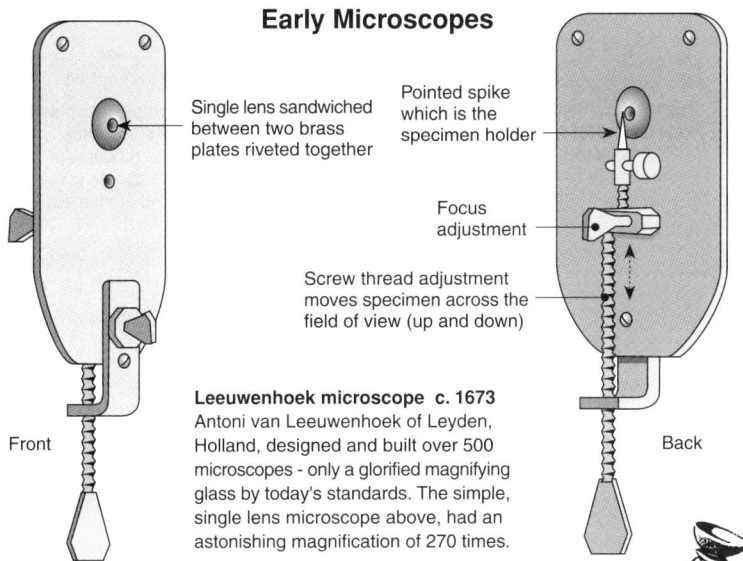

Early Microscopes

Single lens sandwiched between two brass plates riveted together

Pointed spike which is the specimen holder

Focus adjustment

Screw thread adjustment moves specimen across the field of view (up and down)

Leeuwenhoek microscope c. 1673
Antoni van Leeuwenhoek of Leyden, Holland, designed and built over 500 microscopes - only a glorified magnifying glass by today's standards. The simple, single lens microscope above, had an astonishing magnification of 270 times.

Front

Back

Microscope

Lamp

Mirror

Robert Hooke c. 1665
Hooke was fascinated by microscopy, and in his book *Micrographia* (1665) he described the use of the compound microscope that he had devised. He was the first to coin the name cell after he observed the angular spaces that he saw in a thin section of cork.

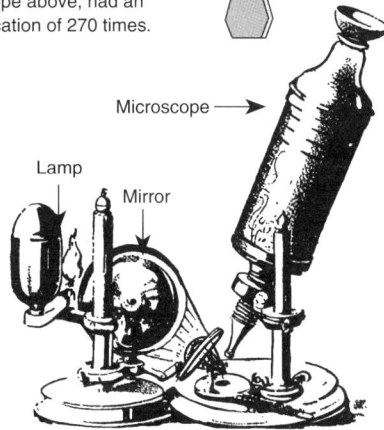

Milestones in Cell Biology

1500s	Convex lenses with a magnification greater than x5 became available.
Early 1600s	First compound microscopes used in Europe (used two convex lenses to make objects look larger). Suffered badly from color distortion; an effect called 'spherical aberration'.
1632-1723	**Antoni van Leeuwenhoek** of Leyden, Holland, produced over 500 single lens microscopes. Discovered bacteria, human blood cells, spermatozoa, and protozoa. Friend of Robert Hooke of England.
1661	**Marcello Malpighi** used lenses to study insects. Discovered capillaries and may have described cells in writing of 'globules' and 'saccules'.
1662	**Robert Hooke** introduced the term 'cell' in describing the microscopic structure of cork. He believed that the cell walls were the important part of otherwise empty structures. Published *Micrographia* in 1665.
1672	**Nehemiah Grew** wrote the first of two well-illustrated books on the microscopic anatomy of plants.
1700s	Little serious work published.
1838-1839	Botanist **Matthias Schleiden** and zoologist **Theodor Schwann** proposed the *cell theory* for plants and animals: *plants and animals are composed of groups of cells and that the cell is the basic unit of living organisms.*
1855	**Rudolph Virchow** extended the cell theory by stating that: *new cells are formed only by the division of previously existing cells.*
1880	**August Weismann** added to Virchow's idea by pointing out that: *all the cells living today can trace their ancestry back to ancient times* (the link between cell theory and evolution).

The Cell Theory

The idea that cells are fundamental units of life is part of the cell theory. These ideas were formulated by a number of early biologists (see Milestones on the right).

1. All living things are composed of cells and cell products.

2. New cells are formed only by the division of preexisting cells.

3. The cell contains inherited information (genes) that are used as instructions for growth, functioning, and development.

4. The cell is the functioning unit of life; the chemical reactions of life take place within cells.

1. Briefly describe the impact the invention of microscopes has had on biology: _____

_____

_____

2. Before the development of the cell theory, it was commonly believed that living organisms could arise by spontaneous generation. Explain what this term means and why it has been discredited as a theory:

_____

_____

_____

Characteristics of Life

A 2

Viruses and cells have some major differences in their structural features. Viruses lack many of the complex structures found in cells and do not exhibit all the characteristics of living things. The diagram below highlights some of these differences. Note that the two examples below are not to the same scale; refer to the scale bars for comparative sizes (1000 nm = 1 µm = 0.001 mm).

Metabolism: The cytoplasm of the cell carries out a vast array of chemical reactions.

Although some viruses may contain an **enzyme**, it is incapable of working until it is inside a host cell's cytoplasm.

Single or double stranded molecule of **RNA** or **DNA**.

The genetic material is composed of **chromosomes** of double-stranded DNA molecules. In eukaryotes they are enclosed in a nuclear membrane.

All cell types contain **cytoplasm**; the liquid 'soup' of nutrients, enzymes and the products of metabolism. Eukaryotes contain membrane-bound organelles.

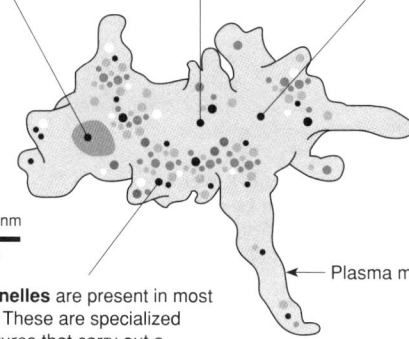

A **protein coat** surrounds the viral genetic material and enzyme (if present). There is no cellular membrane.

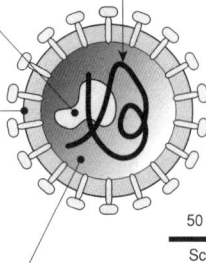

50 nm
Scale

100 000 nm
Scale

Plasma membrane

No metabolism: The absence of cytoplasm means that a virus can not carry out any chemical reactions on its own; it is dependent upon parasitizing a cell and using the cell's own machinery.

Organelles are present in most cells. These are specialized structures that carry out a specific role in the cell.

Virus
(e.g., HIV)

Viruses cannot become active outside a living host cell. They simply exist as inert virus particles called **virions**. Only when they invade a cell and take over the cell's metabolic machinery, can the virus carry out its 'living program'.

Cell
(e.g., Amoeba)

Cells remain alive so long as their metabolic reactions in the cytoplasm are maintained. With a few rare exceptions (that involve freezing certain types of cells) if metabolism is halted, the cell dies.

1. List three features that all cells have in common: _____

_____

2. Describe how viruses differ from cells in the following ways:

   (a) Size: _____

   _____

   (b) Metabolism: _____

   _____

   (c) Organelles: _____

   _____

   (d) Genetic material: _____

   _____

   (e) Life cycle: _____

   _____

3. Viruses are not considered 'living' when outside a host cell. Give the general name for this state: _____

4. Explain why many biologists do not consider viruses to be living organisms: _____

_____

_____

Types of Living Things

K 1

Living things are known as organisms. Organisms are made up of one or more cells. Under the five kingdom system, cells can be divided into two basic kinds: the **prokaryotes**, which are simple cells without a distinct, membrane-bound nucleus, and the more complex **eukaryotes**. The eukaryotes can be further organized into broad groups according to their basic cell type: the protists, fungi, plants, and animals. Viruses are non-cellular and have no cellular machinery of their own. All cells must secure a source of energy if they are to survive and carry out their metabolic processes. **Autotrophs**, are able to meet their energy requirements using light or chemical energy from the physical environment. Other types of cell, called **heterotrophs**, obtain their energy from other living organisms or their dead remains.

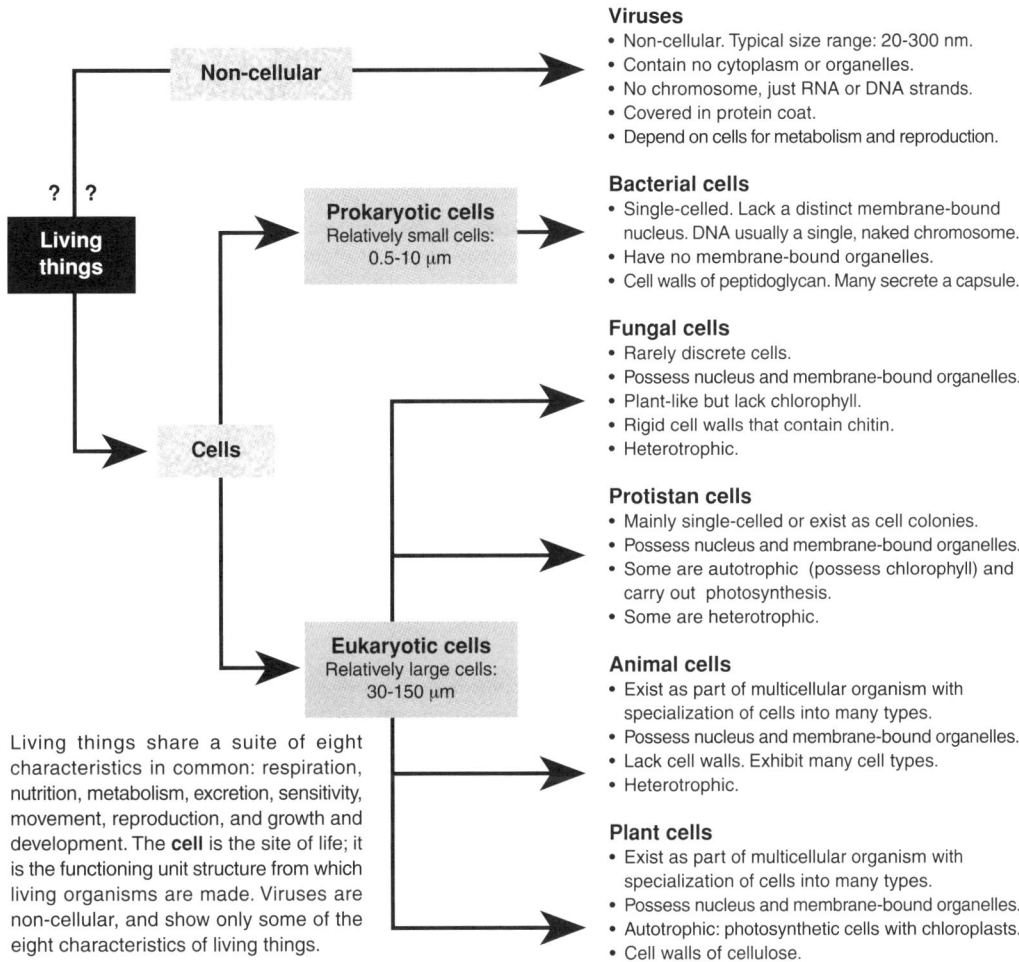

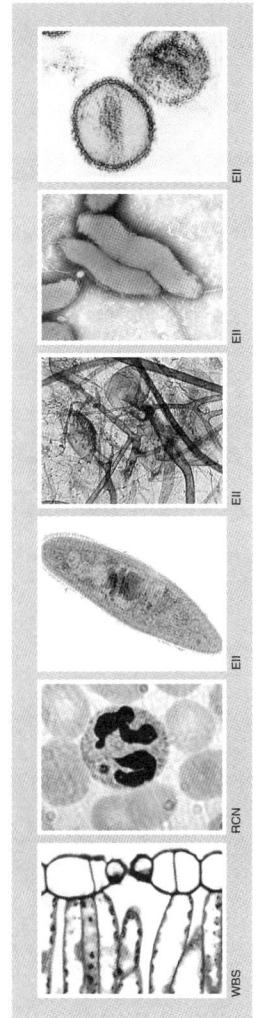

? ?

Living things

Non-cellular

Cells

Prokaryotic cells
Relatively small cells:
0.5-10 µm

Eukaryotic cells
Relatively large cells:
30-150 µm

Living things share a suite of eight characteristics in common: respiration, nutrition, metabolism, excretion, sensitivity, movement, reproduction, and growth and development. The **cell** is the site of life; it is the functioning unit structure from which living organisms are made. Viruses are non-cellular, and show only some of the eight characteristics of living things.

Viruses
• Non-cellular. Typical size range: 20-300 nm.
• Contain no cytoplasm or organelles.
• No chromosome, just RNA or DNA strands.
• Covered in protein coat.
• Depend on cells for metabolism and reproduction.

Bacterial cells
• Single-celled. Lack a distinct membrane-bound nucleus. DNA usually a single, naked chromosome.
• Have no membrane-bound organelles.
• Cell walls of peptidoglycan. Many secrete a capsule.

Fungal cells
• Rarely discrete cells.
• Possess nucleus and membrane-bound organelles.
• Plant-like but lack chlorophyll.
• Rigid cell walls that contain chitin.
• Heterotrophic.

Protistan cells
• Mainly single-celled or exist as cell colonies.
• Possess nucleus and membrane-bound organelles.
• Some are autotrophic (possess chlorophyll) and carry out photosynthesis.
• Some are heterotrophic.

Animal cells
• Exist as part of multicellular organism with specialization of cells into many types.
• Possess nucleus and membrane-bound organelles.
• Lack cell walls. Exhibit many cell types.
• Heterotrophic.

Plant cells
• Exist as part of multicellular organism with specialization of cells into many types.
• Possess nucleus and membrane-bound organelles.
• Autotrophic: photosynthetic cells with chloroplasts.
• Cell walls of cellulose.

1. List the cell types above according to the way in which they obtain their energy. Include viruses in your answer as well:

   (a) Autotrophic: _____

   (b) Heterotrophic: _____

2. Consult the diagram above and determine the **two** main features distinguishing **eukaryotic** cells from **prokaryotic** cells:

   (a) _____

   (b) _____

3. Fungi were once classified as belonging to the plant kingdom. List 3 features that set fungal cells apart from plant cells:

   (a) _____

   (b) _____

   (c) _____

4. Suggest why the Protista have traditionally been a difficult group to classify: _____

   _____

Cell Sizes

Cells are extremely small and can only be seen properly when viewed through the magnifying lenses of a microscope. The diagrams below show a variety of cell types, together with a virus and a microscopic animal for comparison. All photographs were taken using an optical microscope, except for the virus, which was photographed using a transmission electron microscope.

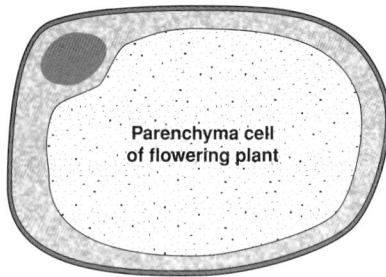

Parenchyma cell of flowering plant

Human white blood cell

Eukaryotic cells
(e.g. plant and animal cells)
Size: 10–100 μm diameter. Cellular organelles may be up to 10 μm.

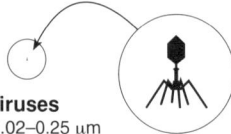

Prokaryotic cells
Size: Typically 2–10 μm length, 0.2–2 μm diameter. Upper limit, 30 μm long.

Viruses
Size: 0.02–0.25 μm (20–250 nm)

Units of length (International System)

Unit	Meters	Equivalent
1 meter (m)	1 m	= 1000 millimeters
1 millimeter (mm)	10^{-3} m	= 1000 micrometers
1 micrometer (μm)	10^{-6} m	= 1000 nanometers
1 nanometer (nm)	10^{-9} m	= 1000 pedometers

Micrometers are sometime referred to as **microns**. Smaller structures are usually measured in nanometers (nm) e.g. molecules (1 nm) and plasma membrane thickness (10 nm).

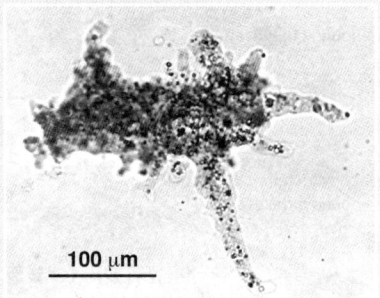

100 μm

An **Amoeba** showing extensions of the cytoplasm called pseudopodia. This protoctist changes its shape, exploring its environment.

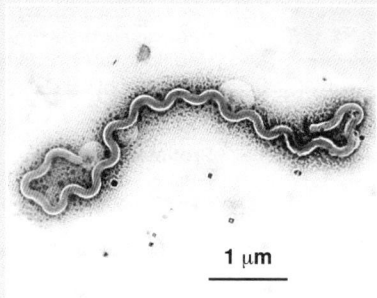

1 μm

This TEM shows a long thin cell of the spirochete bacterium **Leptospira pomona**, which causes the disease leptospirosis.

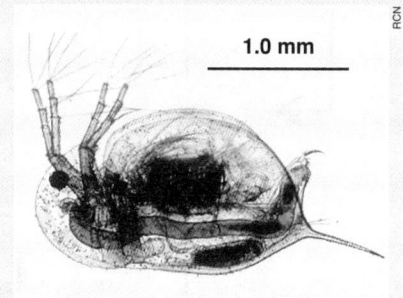

1.0 mm

Daphnia showing its internal organs. These freshwater microcrustaceans are part of the zooplankton found in lakes and ponds.

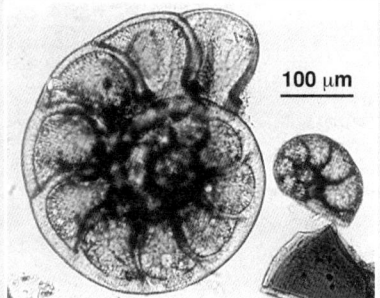

100 μm

A **foraminiferan** showing its chambered, calcified shell. These single-celled protozoans are marine planktonic amoebae.

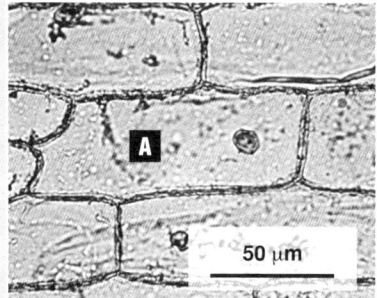

A

50 μm

Epidermal cells (skin) from an onion bulb showing the nucleus, cell walls and cytoplasm. Organelles are not visible at this resolution.

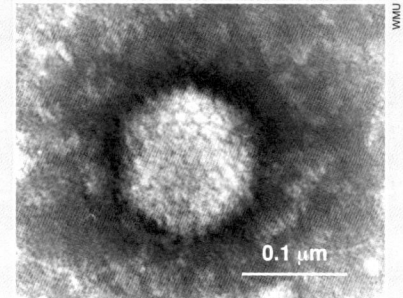

0.1 μm

Papillomavirus (human wart virus) showing its polyhedral protein coat (20 triangular faces, 12 corners) made of ball-shaped structures.

1. Using the measurement scales provided on each of the photographs above, determine the longest dimension (length or diameter) of the cell/animal/virus in μm and mm (choose the cell marked 'A' for epidermal cells):

    (a) *Amoeba*: _____ μm _____ mm   (d) Epidermis: _____ μm _____ mm

    (b) Foraminiferan: _____ μm _____ mm   (e) *Daphnia*: _____ μm _____ mm

    (c) *Leptospira*: _____ μm _____ mm   (f) *Papillomavirus*: _____ μm _____ mm

2. List these 6 organisms in order of size, from the smallest to the largest: _____

    _____

3. Study the scale of your ruler and state which of these six organisms you would be able to see with your unaided eye:

    _____

4. Calculate the equivalent length in millimeters (mm) of the following measurements:

    (a) 0.25 μm: _____   (b) 450 μm: _____   (c) 200 nm: _____

🖐 EA① Unicellular Eukaryotes

Unicellular (single-celled) **eukaryotes** comprise the majority of the diverse phylum, Protista. They are found almost anywhere there is water, including within larger organisms (as parasites or symbionts). The protists are a very diverse group, exhibiting some features typical of generalized eukaryotic cells, as well as specialized features, which may be specific to one genus. Note that even within the genera below there is considerable variation

in size and appearance. *Amoeba* and *Paramecium* are both **heterotrophic**, ingesting food, which accumulates inside a **vacuole**. *Euglena and Chlamydomonas* are autotrophic algae, although *Euglena* is heterotrophic when deprived of light. Other protists include the marine foraminiferans and radiolarians, specialized intracellular parasites such as *Plasmodium*, and zooflagellates such as the parasites *Trypanosoma* and *Giardia*.

Euglena
Size: 130 x 50 μm (varies considerably with species)
Habitat: Freshwater

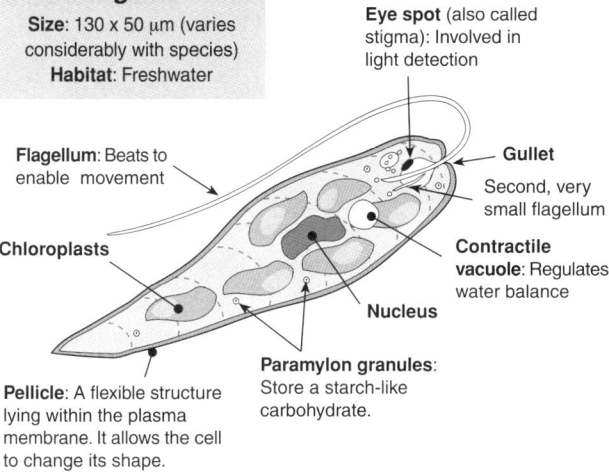

Eye spot (also called stigma): Involved in light detection

Flagellum: Beats to enable movement

Gullet
Second, very small flagellum

Chloroplasts

Contractile vacuole: Regulates water balance

Nucleus

Paramylon granules: Store a starch-like carbohydrate.

Pellicle: A flexible structure lying within the plasma membrane. It allows the cell to change its shape.

Amoeba
Size: 800 x 400 μm
Habitat: Most moist habitats, including soil

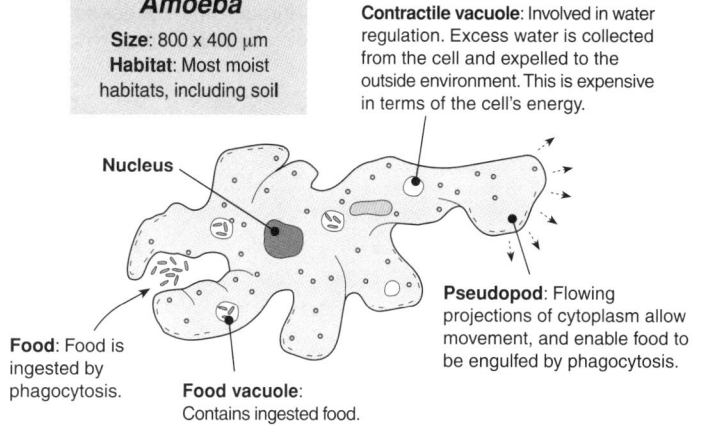

Contractile vacuole: Involved in water regulation. Excess water is collected from the cell and expelled to the outside environment. This is expensive in terms of the cell's energy.

Nucleus

Pseudopod: Flowing projections of cytoplasm allow movement, and enable food to be engulfed by phagocytosis.

Food: Food is ingested by phagocytosis.

Food vacuole: Contains ingested food.

Chlamydomonas
Size: 20 x 10 μm
Habitat: Freshwater

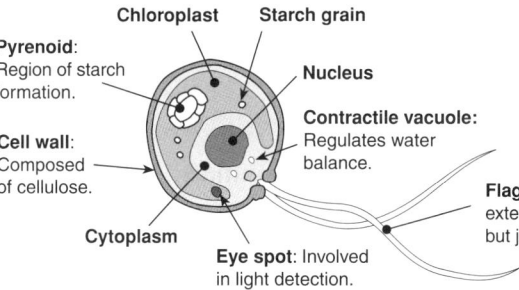

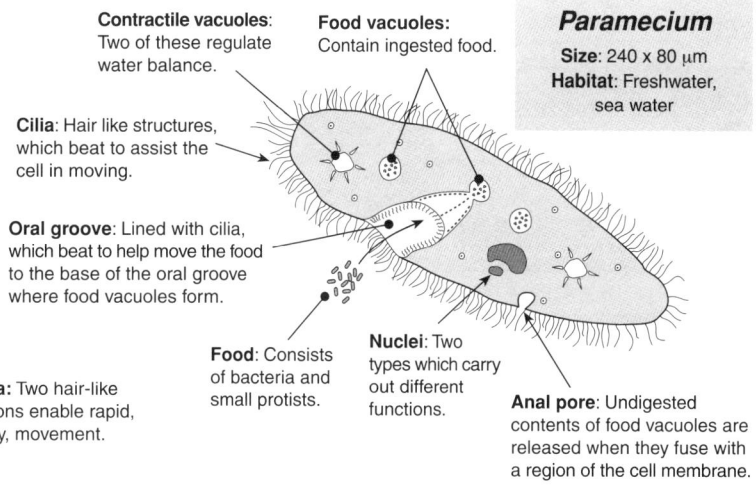

Chloroplast   **Starch grain**

Pyrenoid: Region of starch formation.

Nucleus

Cell wall: Composed of cellulose.

Contractile vacuole: Regulates water balance.

Cytoplasm

Eye spot: Involved in light detection.

Flagella: Two hair-like extensions enable rapid, but jerky, movement.

Paramecium
Size: 240 x 80 μm
Habitat: Freshwater, sea water

Contractile vacuoles: Two of these regulate water balance.

Food vacuoles: Contain ingested food.

Cilia: Hair like structures, which beat to assist the cell in moving.

Oral groove: Lined with cilia, which beat to help move the food to the base of the oral groove where food vacuoles form.

Food: Consists of bacteria and small protists.

Nuclei: Two types which carry out different functions.

Anal pore: Undigested contents of food vacuoles are released when they fuse with a region of the cell membrane.

1. Fill in the table below to summarize differences in some of the features and life functions of the protists shown above:

Organism	Nutrition	Movement	Osmoregulation	Eye spot present / absent	Cell wall present / absent
Amoeba					
Paramecium					
Euglena					
Chlamydomonas					

2. List the four organisms shown above in order of size (largest first): _____

_____

3. Suggest why an autotroph would have an eye spot: _____

_____

Optical Microscopes

RA 2

The light microscope is one of the most important instruments used in biology practicals, and its correct use is a basic and essential skill of biology. High power light microscopes use a combination of lenses to magnify objects up to several hundred times. They are called **compound microscopes** because there are two or more separate lenses involved. A typical compound light microscope (bright field) is shown below (top photograph). The specimens viewed with these microscopes must be thin and mostly transparent. Light is focused up through the condenser and specimen; if the specimen is thick or opaque, little or no detail will be visible. The microscope below has two eyepieces (**binocular**), although monocular microscopes, with a mirror rather than an internal light source, may still be encountered. Dissecting microscopes (lower photograph) are a type of binocular microscope used for observations at low total magnification (x4 to x50), where a large working distance between objectives and stage is required. A dissecting microscope has two separate lens systems, one for each eye. Such microscopes produce a 3-D view of the specimen and are sometimes called stereo microscopes for this reason.

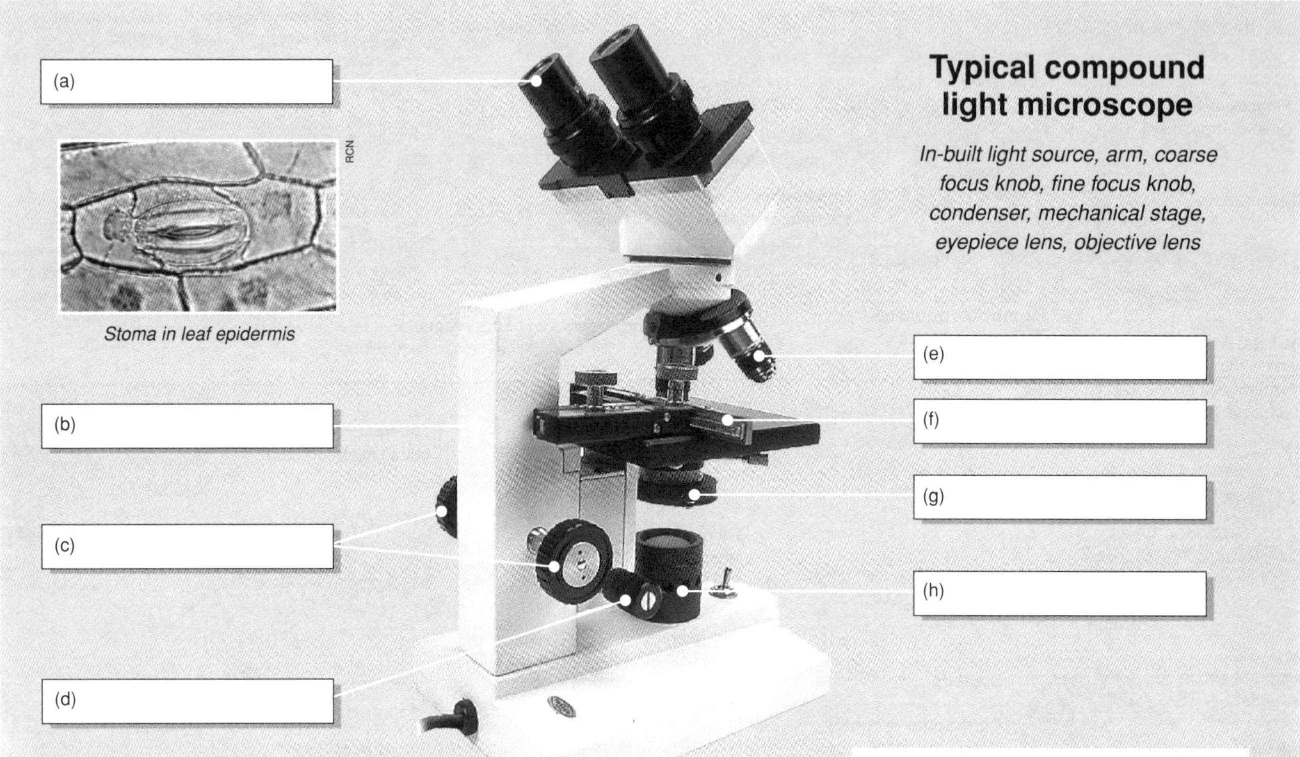

(a)

Stoma in leaf epidermis

(b)

(c)

(d)

Typical compound light microscope

In-built light source, arm, coarse focus knob, fine focus knob, condenser, mechanical stage, eyepiece lens, objective lens

(e)

(f)

(g)

(h)

Resolution

One important factor that determines the usefulness of a microscope is its **resolving power**; the ability to separate out objects that are close together and to see greater detail. Below is an example of high, medium and low resolution for separating two objects viewed under the same magnification.

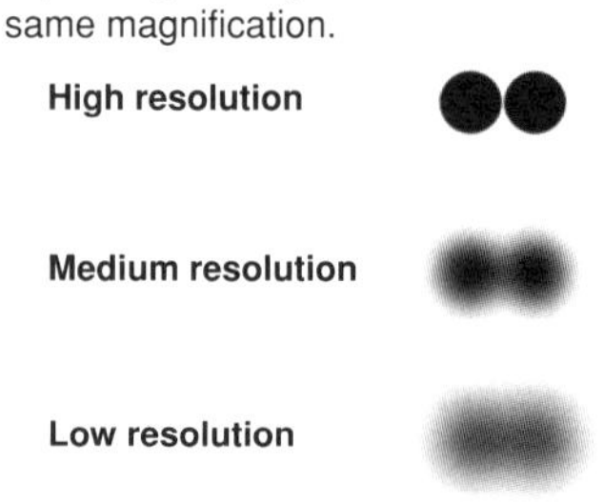

High resolution

Medium resolution

Low resolution

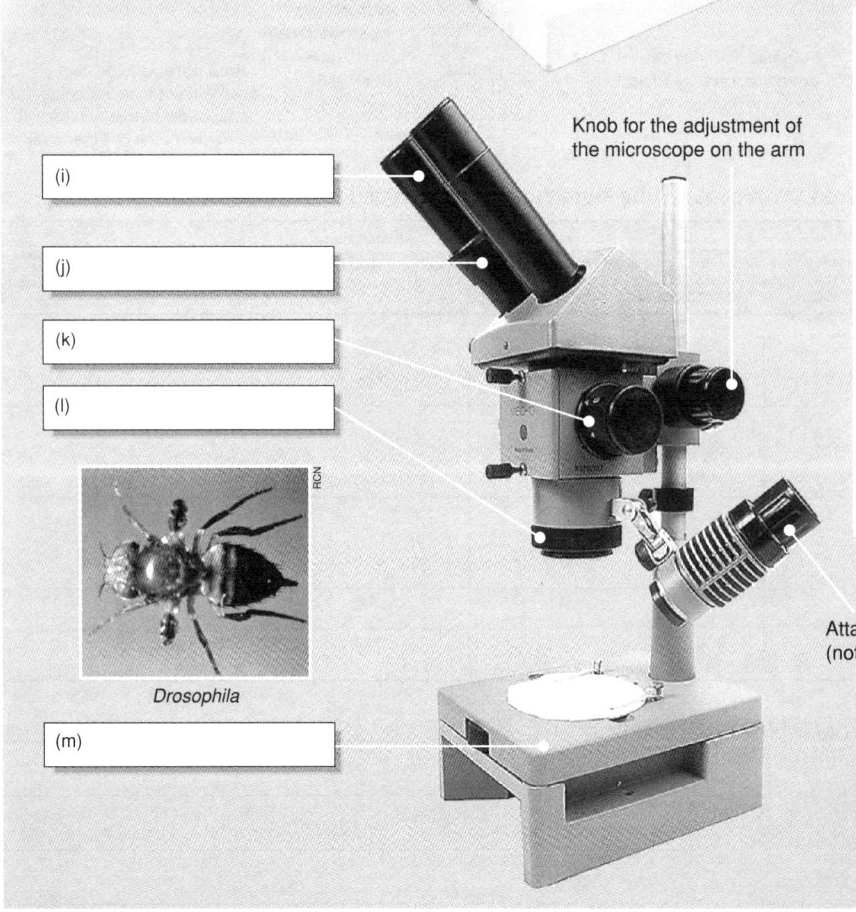

(i)

(j)

(k)

(l)

Knob for the adjustment of the microscope on the arm

Drosophila

(m)

Attached light source (not always present)

Dissecting microscope

Focus knob, stage, eyepiece lens, objective lens, eyepiece focus

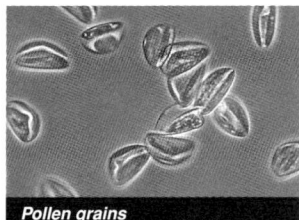

Pollen grains

Phase contrast illumination increases contrast of transparent specimens by producing interference effects.

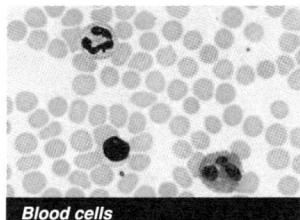

Blood cells

Leishman's stain is used to show red blood cells as red/pink, while staining the nucleus of white blood cells blue.

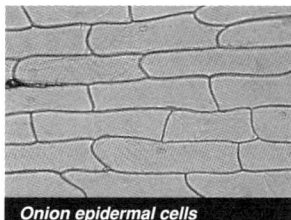

Onion epidermal cells

Standard bright field lighting shows cells with little detail; only cell walls, with the cell nuclei barely visible.

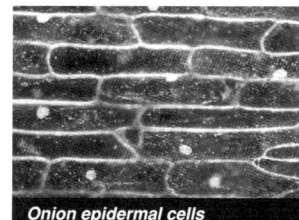

Onion epidermal cells

Dark field illumination is excellent for viewing near transparent specimens. The nucleus of each cell is visible.

Steps in preparing a permanent mount

1. **Fixation**: Preserves freshly killed tissues in a lifelike state by immersing them in a chemical (e.g. formalin) or applying heat (as in the case of microorganisms).

2. **Sectioning**: Cutting very thin sections; thin enough to let light through. May be embedded in wax or plastic and sliced with a microtome, or sectioned with a hand-held razorblade.

3. **Staining**: Dyes are applied that stain some structures while leaving others unaffected (see table on right).

4. **Dehydration**: The thin section is immersed in a series of increasing concentrations of ethanol to gradually remove water from the sample. This helps to make the tissue transparent.

5. **Clearing**: A liquid such as xylol is added to replace the ethanol (used above) and ensures the material remains transparent.

6. **Mounting**: The thin sections are mounted on a microscope slide in a medium (e.g. balsam) that excludes air and protects the sample indefinitely.

Stain	Final color	Application
Temporary stains		
Iodine solution	blue-black	Starch
Aniline sulfate or Aniline hydrochloride	yellow	Lignin
Schultz's solution	blue	Starch
	blue or violet	Cellulose
	yellow	Protein, cutin, lignin, suberin
Permanent stains		
Methylene blue	blue	Nuclei
Safranin	red	Nuclei; suberin and lignin of plants
Aniline blue	blue	Fungal spores and hyphae
Leishman's stain	red-pink blue	Red blood cells Nucleus of white blood cells
Eosin	pink/red	Cytoplasm/cellulose
Hematoxylin (NOTE: mainly used as a counterstain for eosin)	blue	Nuclei of animal cells
Feulgen's stain	red/purple	DNA (chromosomes in cell division)

1. Label the two diagrams on the left, the bright field microscope (a) to (h) and the dissecting microscope (i) to (m), using words from the lists supplied.

2. Describe a situation where phase contrast microscopy would improve image quality: _____

_____

3. List two structures that could be seen by light microscopy in:

   (a) A plant cell: _____

   (b) An animal cell: _____

4. Name one cell structure that can not be seen by light microscopy: _____

5. Name a stain that would be appropriate for improving definition of the following:

   (a) Blood cells: _____   (d) Fungal spores: _____

   (b) Starch: _____   (e) Nuclei of animal cells: _____

   (c) DNA: _____   (f) Cellulose: _____

6. Determine the magnification of a microscope using:

   (a) 15 X eyepiece and 40 X objective lens: _____   (b) 10 X eyepiece and 60 X objective lens: _____

7. Describe the main difference between a bright field light microscope and a dissecting microscope. _____

_____

_____

8. Explain the difference between magnification and resolution (resolving power) with respect to microscope use:

_____

_____

Electron Microscopes

RA 2

Electron microscopes (EMs) use a beam of electrons, instead of light, to produce an image. The higher resolution of EMs is due to the shorter wavelengths of electrons. There are two basic types of electron microscope: **scanning electron microscopes** (SEM) and **transmission electron microscopes** (TEM). In SEMs, the electrons are bounced off the surface of an object to produce detailed images of the external appearance. TEMs produce very clear images of specially prepared thin sections.

Transmission Electron Microscope (TEM)

The transmission electron microscope is used to view extremely thin sections of material. Electrons pass through the specimen and are scattered. Magnetic lenses focus the image onto a fluorescent screen or photographic plate. The sections are so thin that they have to be prepared with a special machine, called an **ultramicrotome**, that can cut wafers to just 30 thousandths of a millimeter thick. It can magnify several hundred thousand times.

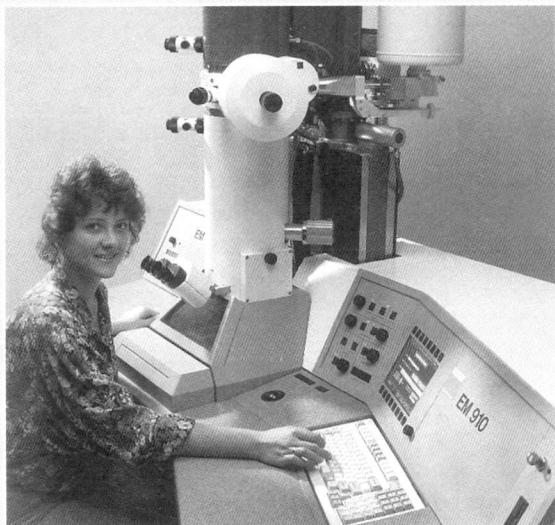

- Electron gun
- Electron beam
- Electromagnetic condenser lens
- Specimen
- Electromagnetic objective lens
- Electromagnetic projector lens
- Eyepiece
- Fluorescent screen or photographic plate

Vacuum pump

Ultrastructure of a cell showing the Golgi (**G**) and a mitochondrion (**M**).

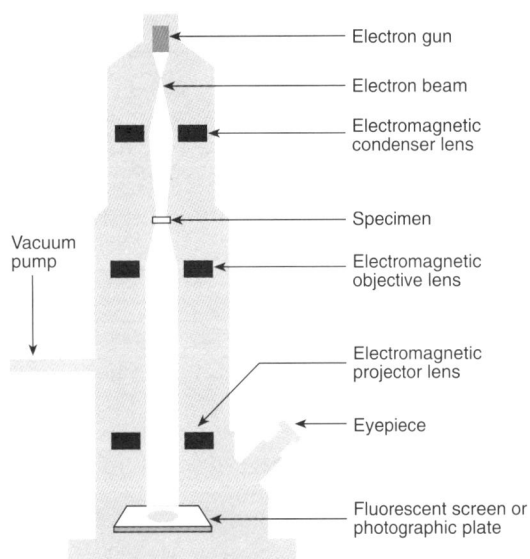

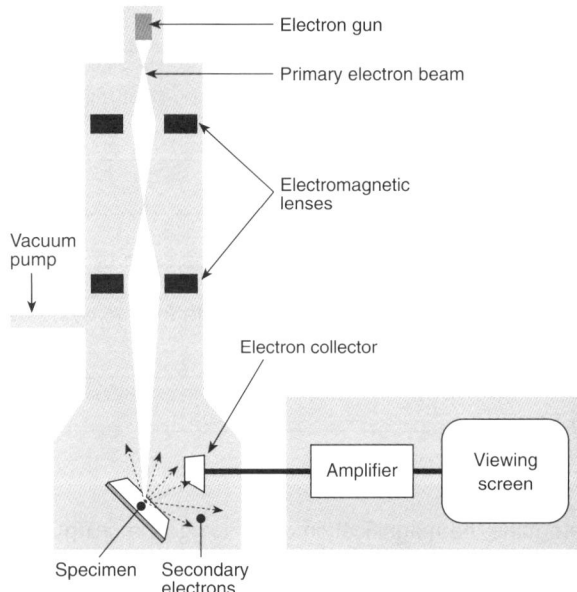

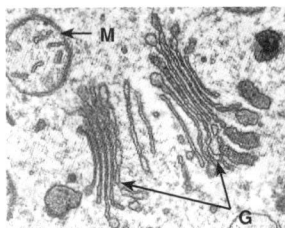

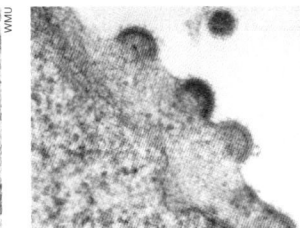

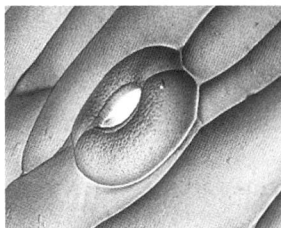

Three HIV viruses budding out of a human lymphocyte.

Scanning Electron Microscope (SEM)

The scanning electron microscope scans a sample with a beam of primary electrons that knock electrons from its surface. These secondary electrons are picked up by a collector, amplified, and transmitted onto a viewing screen or photographic plate, producing a superb 3-D image. A microscope of this power can easily obtain clear pictures of organisms as small as bacteria and viruses. The image produced is of the outside surface only.

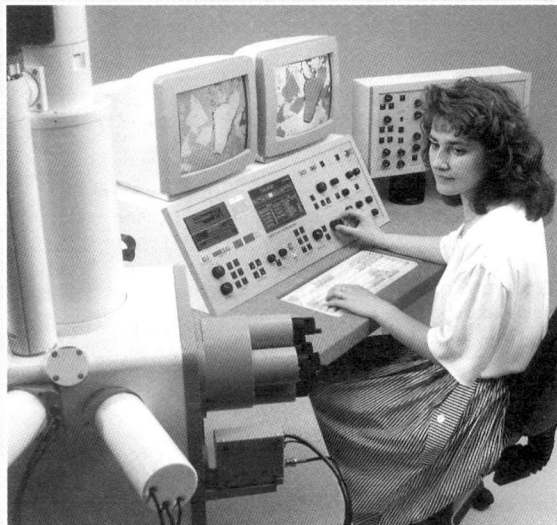

- Electron gun
- Primary electron beam
- Electromagnetic lenses
- Electron collector
- Amplifier
- Viewing screen
- Specimen
- Secondary electrons

Vacuum pump

Stoma and epidermal cells on the upper surface of a leaf.

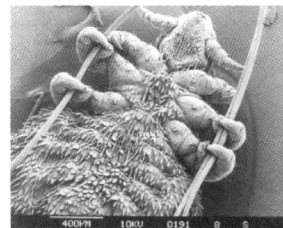

Hair louse clinging to two hairs on a Hooker's sealion.

	Light Microscope	Transmission Electron Microscope (TEM)	Scanning Electron Microscope (SEM)
Radiation source:	light	electrons	electrons
Wavelength:	400-700 nm	0.005 nm	0.005 nm
Lenses:	glass	electromagnetic	electromagnetic
Specimen:	living or non-living supported on glass slide	non-living supported on a small copper grid in a vacuum	non-living supported on a metal disc in a vacuum
Maximum resolution:	200 nm	1 nm	10 nm
Maximum magnification:	1500 x	250 000 x	100 000 x
Stains:	colored dyes	impregnated with heavy metals	coated with carbon or gold
Type of image:	colored	monochrome (black & white)	monochrome (black & white)

1. Explain why electron microscopes are able to resolve much greater detail than a light microscope:

   _____

   _____

   _____

2. List two typical applications for each of the following types of microscope:

   (a) Transmission electron microscope (TEM): _____

   _____

   (b) Scanning electron microscope (SEM): _____

   _____

   (c) Bright field microscope (thin section): _____

   _____

   (d) Dissecting microscope: _____

   _____

3. Identify which type of electron microscope (SEM or TEM) or optical microscope (compound, bright field or dissecting) was used to produce each of the images in the photos below (A-H):

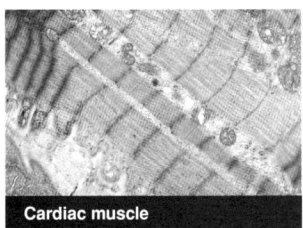
Cardiac muscle

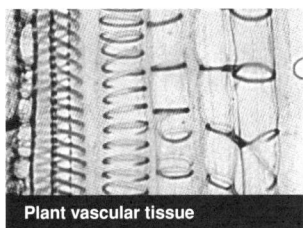
Plant vascular tissue

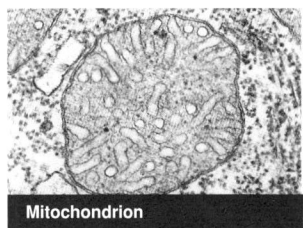
Mitochondrion

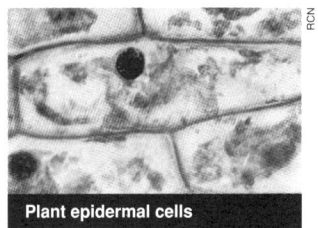
Plant epidermal cells

A _____ B _____ C _____ D _____

Head louse

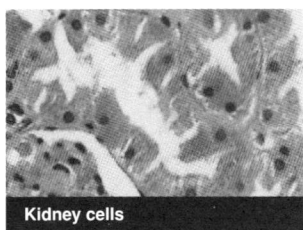
Kidney cells

Alderfly larva

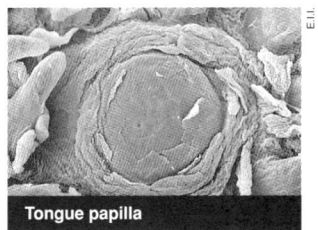
Tongue papilla

E _____ F _____ G _____ H _____

Bacterial Cells

Bacterial (prokaryotic) cells are much smaller and simpler than the cells of eukaryotes. They lack many eukaryotic features (e.g. a distinct nucleus and membrane-bound cellular organelles). The bacterial cell wall is an important feature. It is a complex, multi-layered structure and often has a role in virulence. These pages illustrate some features of bacterial structure and diversity.

Structure of a Generalized Bacterial Cell

Plasmids: Small, circular DNA molecules (accessory chromosomes) that can reproduce independently of the main chromosome. They can transfer from one cell to another, and even between species, by a process called **conjugation** (see below). This property accounts for the transmission of antibiotic resistance between bacteria. Plasmids are also used as vectors in recombinant DNA technology (genetic engineering).

Fimbriae: Hairlike structures that are shorter, straighter, and thinner than flagella. They are used for attachment, not movement.

Cell surface membrane: Similar in composition to eukaryotic membranes, although less rigid.

Glycocalyx. A general term referring to the viscous, gelatinous layer outside the cell wall. It is composed of polysaccharide and/or polypeptide. If the layer is firmly attached to the wall it is called a **capsule**. If loosely attached it is called a **slime layer**. Capsules are important in contributing to virulence in pathogenic species, e.g. by protecting the bacteria from the host's immune attack. In some species, the glycocalyx allows attachment to substrates.

Single, circular main chromosome: Makes them haploid for most genes. It is possible for some genes to be found on both the plasmid and chromosome and there may be several copies of a gene on a group of plasmids.

1 μm

The cell lacks a nuclear membrane, so there is no distinct nucleus and the chromosomes are in direct contact with the cytoplasm. It is possible for free ribosomes to attach to mRNA while the mRNA is still in the process of being transcribed from the DNA.

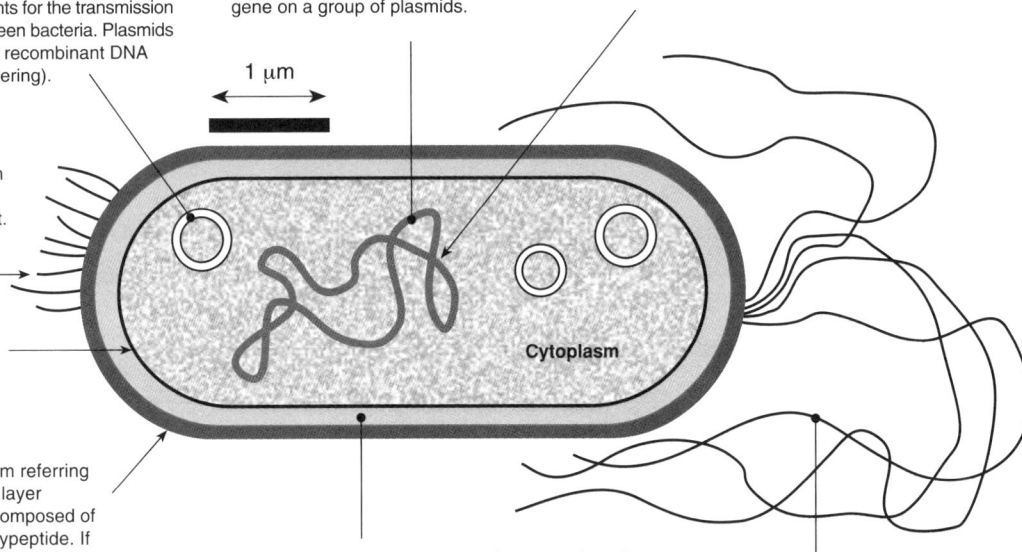

Cytoplasm

Cell wall. A complex, semi-rigid structure that gives the cell shape, prevents rupture, and serves as an anchorage point for flagella. The cell wall is composed of a macromolecule called **peptidoglycan**; repeating disaccharides attached by polypeptides to form a lattice. The wall also contains varying amounts of lipopolysaccharides and lipoproteins. The amount of peptidoglycan present in the wall forms the basis of the diagnostic **gram stain**. In many species, the cell wall contributes to their virulence (disease-causing ability).

Flagellum (pl. flagella). Some bacteria have long, filamentous appendages, called flagella, that are used for locomotion. There may be a single polar flagellum (monotrichous), one or more flagella at each end of the cell, or the flagella may be distributed over the entire cell (peritrichous).

Bacterial cell shapes

Most bacterial cells range between 0.20-2.0 μm in diameter and 2-10 μm length. Although they are a very diverse group, much of this diversity is in their metabolism. In terms of gross morphology, there are only a few basic shapes found (illustrated below). The way in which members of each group aggregate after division is often characteristic and is helpful in identifying certain species.

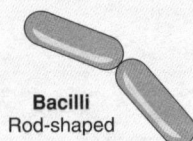

Bacilli Rod-shaped

Bacilli: Rod-shaped bacteria that divide only across their short axis. Most occur as single rods, although pairs and chains are also found. The term bacillus can refer (as here) to shape. It may also denote a genus.

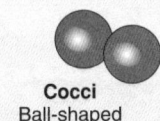

Cocci Ball-shaped

Cocci: usually round, but sometimes oval or elongated. When they divide, the cells stay attached to each other and remain in aggregates e.g. pairs (diplococci) or clusters (staphylococci), that are usually a feature of the genus.

Spirilla Spiral-shaped

Spirilla and vibrio: Bacteria with one or more twists. Spirilla bacteria have a helical (corkscrew) shape which may be rigid or flexible (as in spirochetes). Bacteria that look like curved rods (comma shaped) are called vibrios.

Bacterial conjugation

The two bacteria illustrated below are involved in 'pseudo sex'. This involves a one-way exchange of genetic information from a donor cell to a recipient cell. The plasmid, which must be of the 'conjugative' type, passes through a tube called a sex pilus to the other cell. Which is donor and which is recipient appears to be genetically determined.

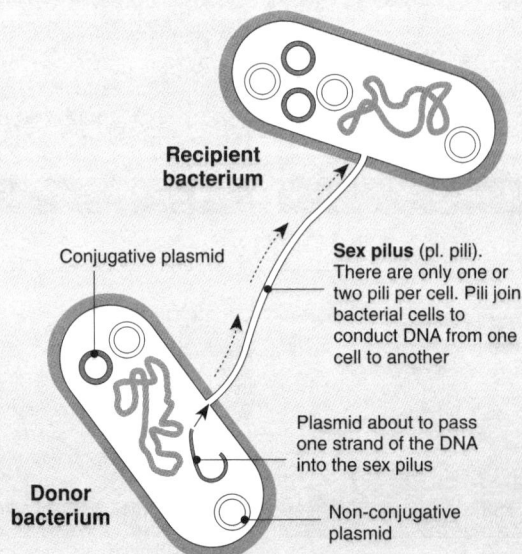

Recipient bacterium

Conjugative plasmid

Sex pilus (pl. pili). There are only one or two pili per cell. Pili join bacterial cells to conduct DNA from one cell to another

Plasmid about to pass one strand of the DNA into the sex pilus

Donor bacterium

Non-conjugative plasmid

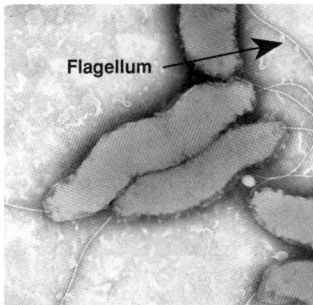

Campylobacter jejuni, a spiral bacterium responsible for foodborne intestinal disease. Note the single flagellum at each end (amphitrichous arrangement).

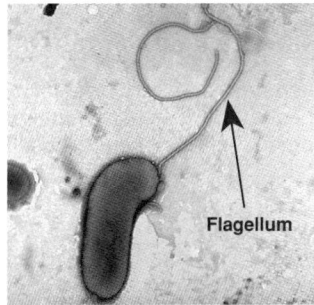

Helicobacter pylori, a comma-shaped vibrio bacterium that causes stomach ulcers in humans. This bacterium moves by means of multiple polar flagella.

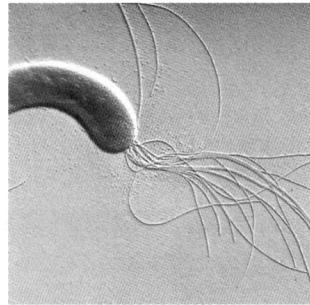

A species of *Spirillum*, a spiral shaped bacterium with a tuft of polar flagella. Most of the species in this genus are harmless aquatic organisms.

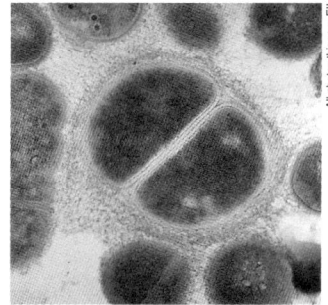

Bacterial division in gram positive cocci. Some gram positive cocci form heat-resistant endospores (dehydrated resting cells), which can survive indefinitely.

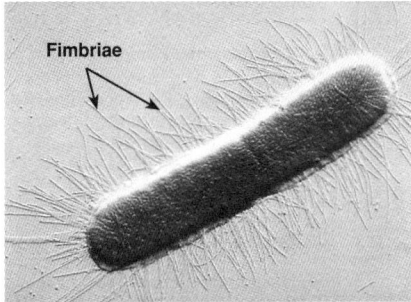

Escherichia coli, a common gut bacterium with **peritrichous** (around the entire cell) **fimbriae**. *E. coli* is a gram negative rod; it does not take up the gram stain but can be counter stained with safranin.

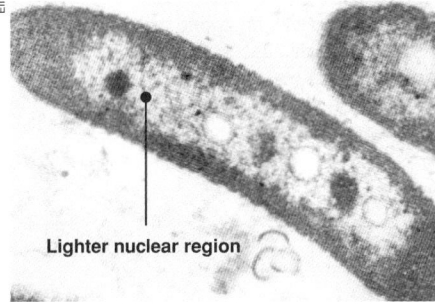

TEM showing *Enterobacter* bacteria, which belong to the family of gut bacteria commonly known as enterics. They are widely distributed in water, sewage, and soil. The family includes motile and non-motile species.

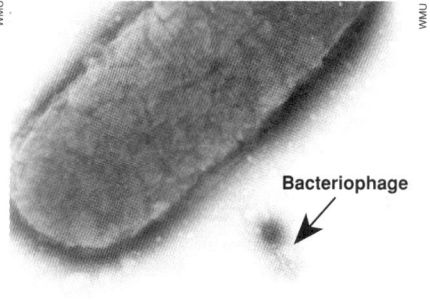

SEM showing a large rod-shaped bacterium with an approaching bacteriophage (viral particle). The bacterium has hair-like **pili** (not visible) protruding from the surface which act as phage receptors.

1. Contrast the generalized prokaryote (bacterial) cell with the eukaryotic (plant and animal) cells earlier in this topic. Describe 3 important differences between the structure of bacterial and eukaryotic cells:

   (a) _____

   (b) _____

   (c) _____

2. (a) Describe the function of flagella in bacteria: _____

   (b) Explain how fimbriae differ structurally and functionally from flagella: _____

   _____

3. Explain the basis for the gram stain: _____

   _____

4. (a) Describe the location and general composition of the glycocalyx: _____

   _____

   (b) Describe an advantageous function of capsules in bacteria: _____

   _____

5. (a) Describe the purpose of **conjugation** between compatible bacteria (recipient and donor): _____

   _____

   (b) Suggest how conjugation might facilitate rapid evolution in bacterial strains: _____

   _____

6. Briefly describe how the artificial manipulation of plasmids has been used for technological applications:

   _____

   _____

   _____

Plant Cells

RA2

Plant cells are enclosed in a cellulose cell wall. The cell wall protects the cell, maintains its shape, and prevents excessive water uptake. It does not interfere with the passage of materials into and out of the cell. The diagram below shows the structure and function of a typical plant cell and its organelles. Also see pages 83-85, where further information is provided on the organelles listed here but not described.

Starch granule: carbohydrate stored in amyloplasts (plastids for specialized storage). Plastids are unique to plants. Non-photosynthetic plastids usually store materials.

Chloroplast: specialized plastids containing the green pigment chlorophyll. They contain dense stacks of membranes (grana) within a colorless stroma. They are the sites for photosynthesis and occur mainly in leaves.

Cell wall: a semi-rigid structure outside the plasma membrane. It is composed mainly of cellulose. It supports the cell and limits its volume.

Plasma membrane: Located inside the cell wall in plants.

Large **central vacuole**: usually filled with an aqueous solution of ions. Vacuoles are prominent in plants and function in storage, waste disposal, and growth.

Mitochondrion: 1.5 μm X 2–8 μm. Mitochondria are ovoid structures bounded by a double membrane. They are the cell energy transformers, converting chemical energy into ATP.

Cytoplasm: a watery solution containing dissolved substances, enzymes, and the cell organelles and structures. The site of translation in the cell.

Endoplasmic reticulum (ER) comprises a network of tubes and flattened sacs. ER is continuous with the plasma membrane and the nuclear membrane and may be smooth or have attached ribosomes (rough ER).

Nuclear pore

Nuclear membrane is a double layered structure penetrated by holes (pores).

Nucleus containing most of the cell's DNA.

Nucleolus

Ribosomes manufacture proteins. Ribosomes are made of ribosomal RNA and protein. They may be free in the cytoplasm or associated with the surface of the endoplasmic reticulum.

Golgi apparatus

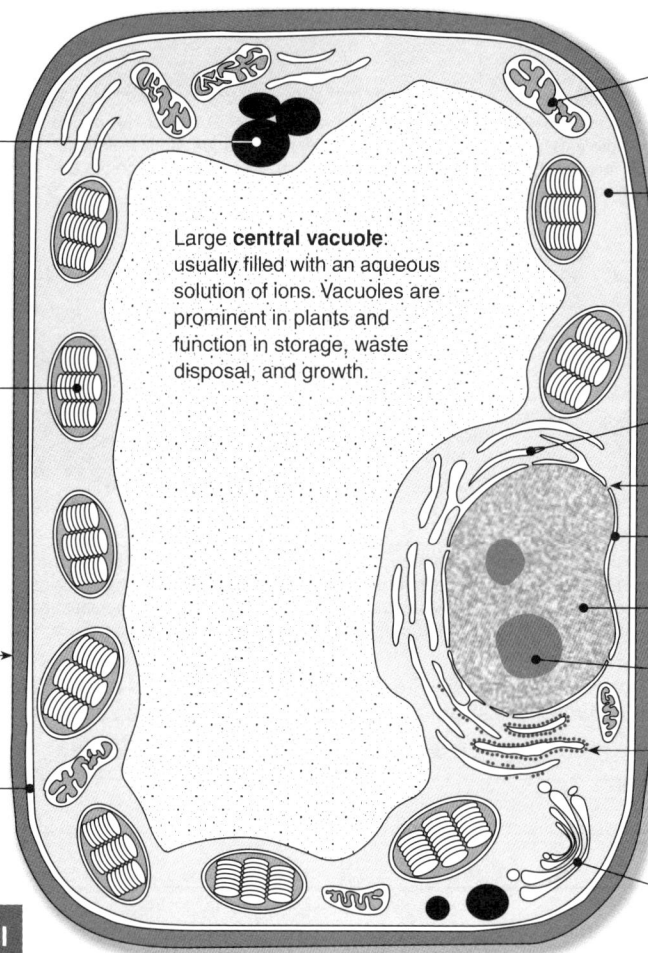

Generalized Plant Cell

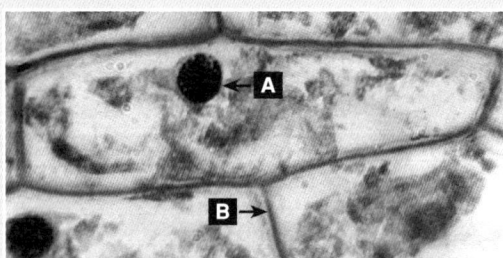

Onion epidermial cells

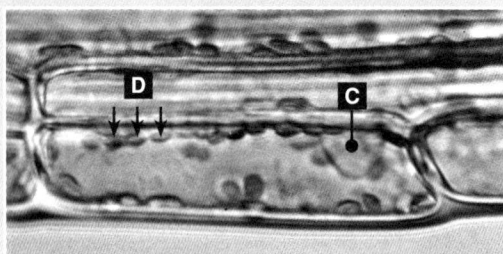

Elodea cells

Photos: RCN

1. The two photographs (left) show plant cells as seen by a light microscope. Identify the basic features labelled A-D:

   A: _____

   B: _____

   C: _____

   D: _____

2. Cytoplasmic streaming is a feature of eukaryotic cells, often clearly visible with a light microscope in plant (and algal) cells.

   (a) Explain what is meant by cytoplasmic streaming:

   _____

   _____

   (b) For the *Elodea* cell (lower, left), draw arrows to indicate cytoplasmic streaming movements.

3. Describe three structures/organelles present in generalized plant cells but absent from animal cells (also see page 83):

   (a) _____

   (b) _____

   (c) _____

Animal Cells

Animal cells, unlike plant cells, do not have a regular shape. In fact, some animal cells (such as phagocytes) are able to alter their shape for various purposes (e.g., engulfment of foreign material). The diagram below shows the structure and function of a typical animal cell and its organelles. Note the differences between this cell and the generalized plant cell. Also see pages 82 and 84-85, where further information is provided on the organelles listed here but not described.

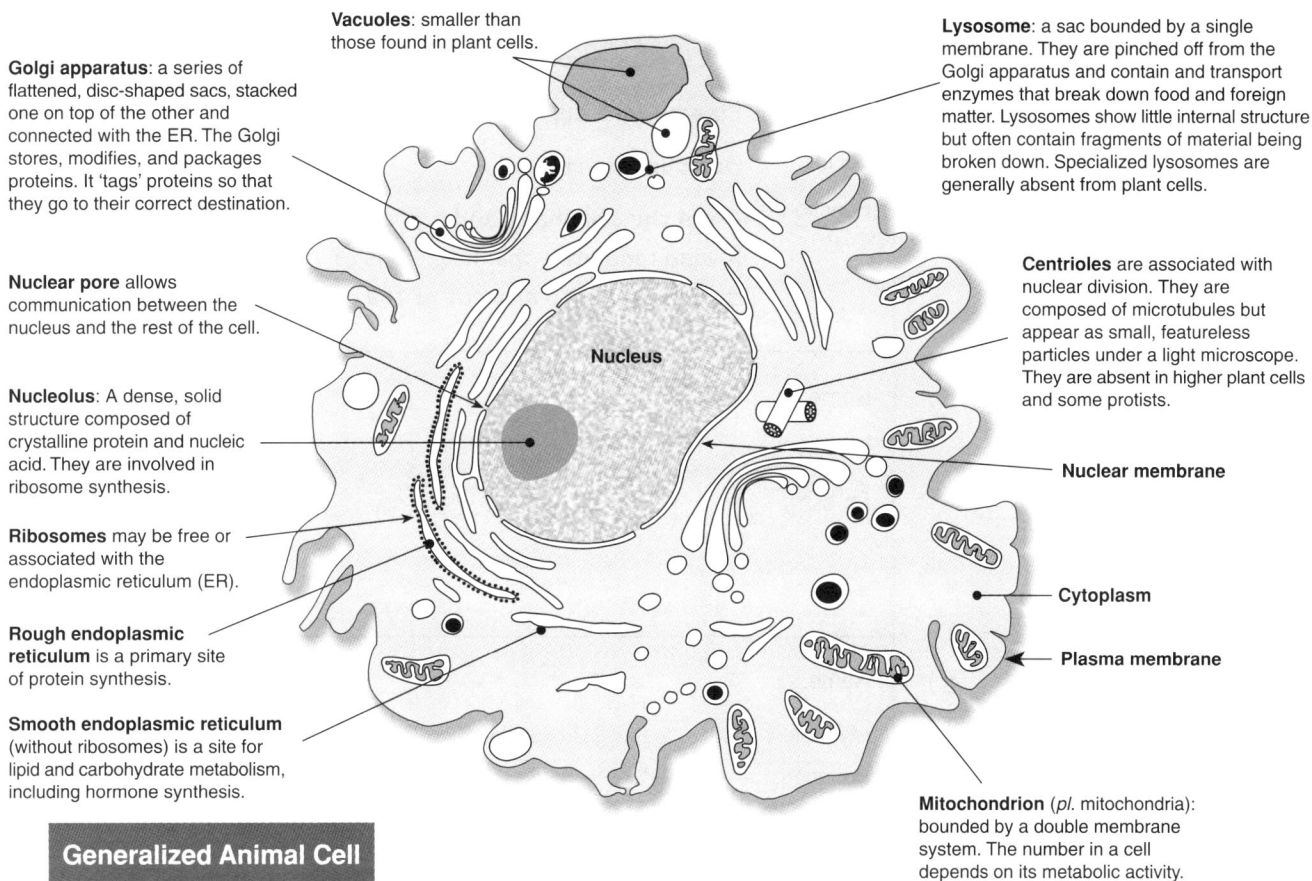

Vacuoles: smaller than those found in plant cells.

Golgi apparatus: a series of flattened, disc-shaped sacs, stacked one on top of the other and connected with the ER. The Golgi stores, modifies, and packages proteins. It 'tags' proteins so that they go to their correct destination.

Lysosome: a sac bounded by a single membrane. They are pinched off from the Golgi apparatus and contain and transport enzymes that break down food and foreign matter. Lysosomes show little internal structure but often contain fragments of material being broken down. Specialized lysosomes are generally absent from plant cells.

Nuclear pore allows communication between the nucleus and the rest of the cell.

Nucleolus: A dense, solid structure composed of crystalline protein and nucleic acid. They are involved in ribosome synthesis.

Ribosomes may be free or associated with the endoplasmic reticulum (ER).

Rough endoplasmic reticulum is a primary site of protein synthesis.

Smooth endoplasmic reticulum (without ribosomes) is a site for lipid and carbohydrate metabolism, including hormone synthesis.

Centrioles are associated with nuclear division. They are composed of microtubules but appear as small, featureless particles under a light microscope. They are absent in higher plant cells and some protists.

Nucleus

Nuclear membrane

Cytoplasm

Plasma membrane

Mitochondrion (*pl.* mitochondria): bounded by a double membrane system. The number in a cell depends on its metabolic activity.

Generalized Animal Cell

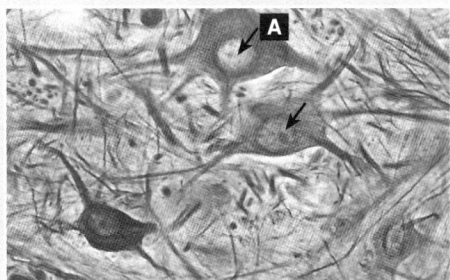

1. The two photomicrographs (left) show several types of animal cells. Identify the features indicated by the letters A-C:

   A: _____

   B: _____

   C: _____

2. White blood cells are mobile, phagocytic cells, whereas red blood cells are smaller than white blood cells and, in humans, lack a nucleus.

   (a) In the photomicrograph (below, left), circle a white blood cell and a red blood cell:

   (b) With respect to the features that you can see, explain how you made your decision.

   _____

   _____

   _____

   _____

Neurons (nerve cells) in the spinal cord

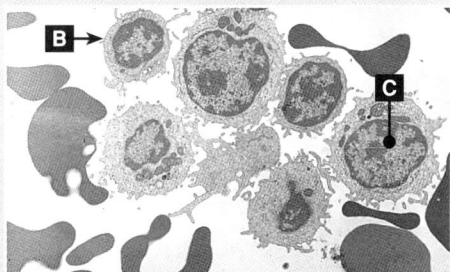

White blood cells and red blood cells (blood smear)

3. Name and describe one structure or organelle present in generalized animal cells but absent from plant cells:

_____

_____

RA 2 Cell Structures and Organelles

The table below provides a format to summarize information about structures and organelles of typical eukaryotic cells. Complete the table using the list at the top of the opposite page and by referring to a textbook and to other pages in this topic. Fill in the final three columns by writing either 'YES' or 'NO'. The first cell component has been completed for you as a guide.

Cell Component	Details	Present in		Visible under light microscope
		Plant cells	Animal cells	
(a) 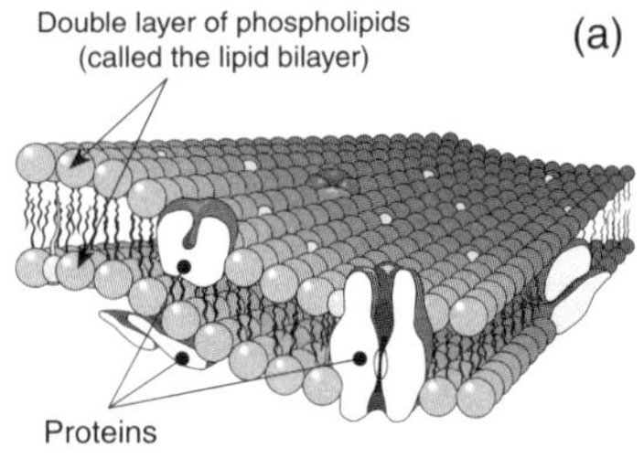 Double layer of phospholipids (called the lipid bilayer) / Proteins	Name: Plasma (cell surface) membrane Location: Surrounding the cell Function: Gives the cell shape and protection. It also regulates the movement of substances into and out of the cell.	YES	YES	YES (but not at the level of detail shown in the diagram)
(b) 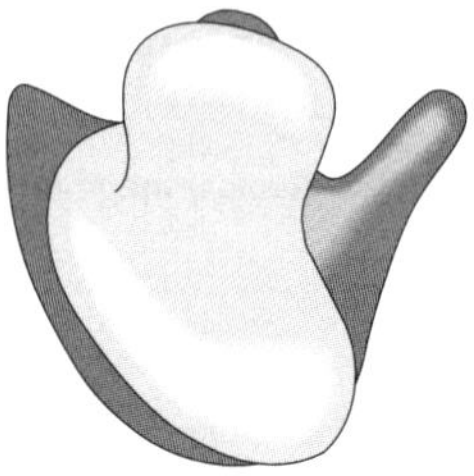	Name: Location: Function:			
(c) 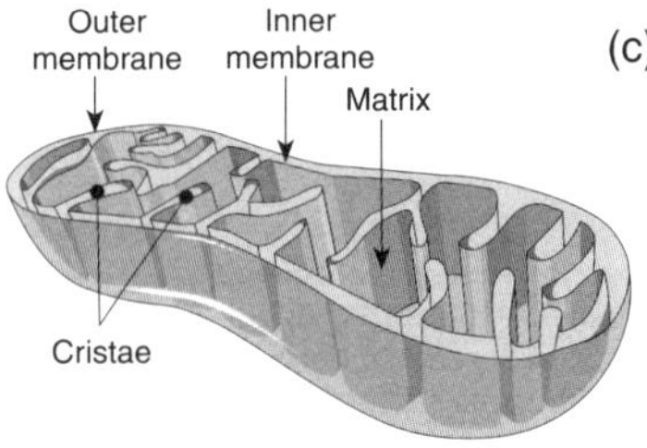 Outer membrane / Inner membrane / Matrix / Cristae	Name: Location: Function:			
(d) 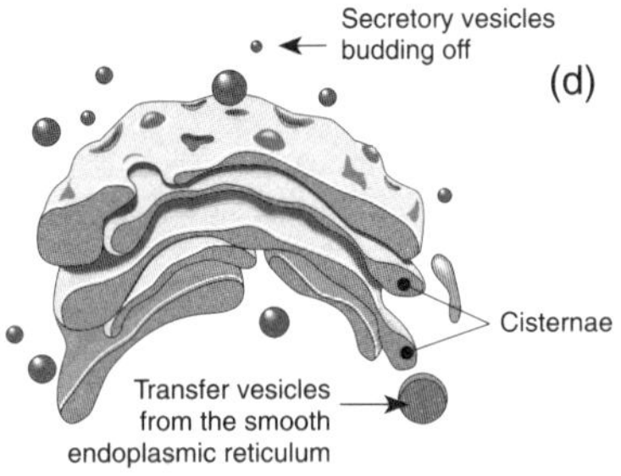 Secretory vesicles budding off / Cisternae / Transfer vesicles from the smooth endoplasmic reticulum	Name: Location: Function:			
(e) 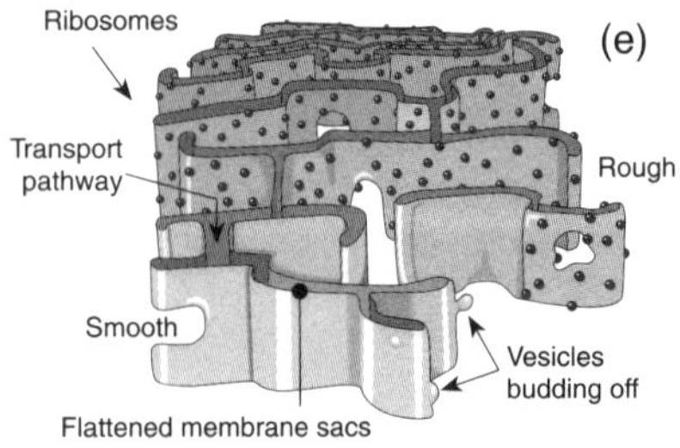 Ribosomes / Transport pathway / Rough / Smooth / Vesicles budding off / Flattened membrane sacs	Name: Location: Function:			
(f) 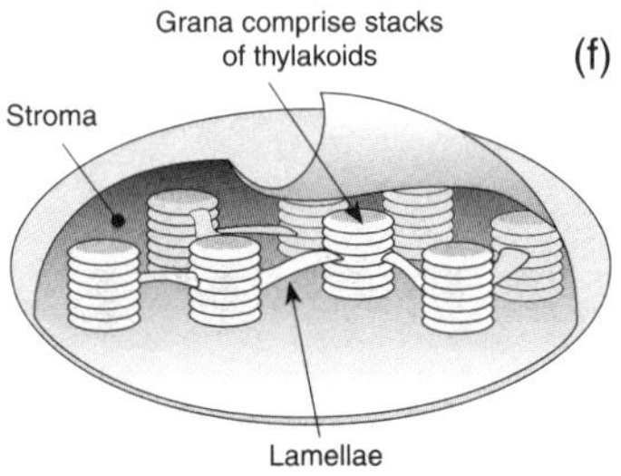 Grana comprise stacks of thylakoids / Stroma / Lamellae	Name: Location: Function:			

List of structures and organelles: *cell wall, mitochondrion, chloroplast, centrioles, ribosome, endoplasmic reticulum, and Golgi apparatus.*

Cell Component	Details	Present in		Visible under light microscope
		Plant cells	Animal cells	
(g) Microtubules 2 central, single microtubules / 9 doublets of microtubules in an outer ring Extension of plasma membrane surrounding a core of microtubules in a 9+2 pattern Basal body anchors the cilium	Name: Location: Function:			
(h)	Name: Cilia and flagella (some eukaryotic cells) Location: Function:			
(i) Cross-layering of cellulose	Name: Location: Function:			
(j) Lysosome	Name: Lysosome Location: Function:			
(k) Food Vacuole Phagocytosis	Name: Vacuole (a food vacuole is shown) Location: Function:			
(l) Nuclear membrane Nuclear pores Nucleolus Genetic material	Name: Nucleus Location: Function:			

Differential Centrifugation

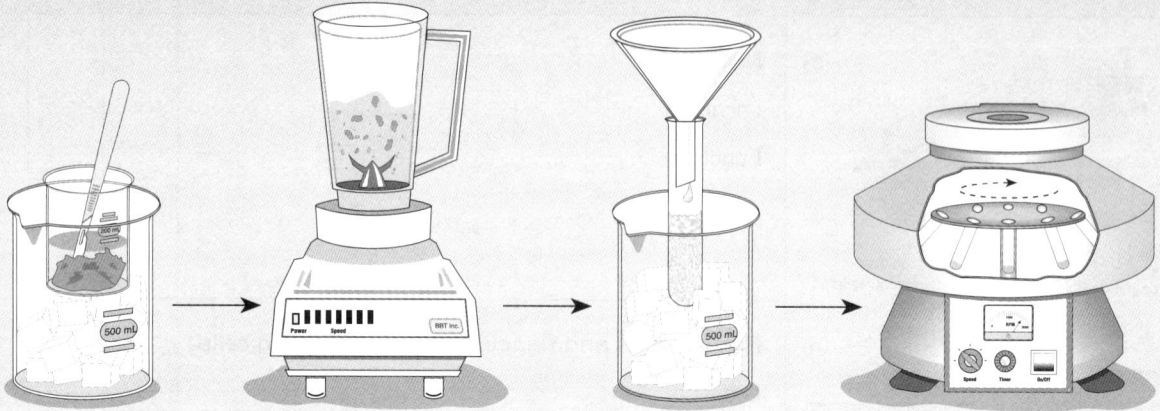

Differential centrifugation (also called cell fractionation) is a technique used to extract organelles from cells so that they can be studied. The aim is to extract undamaged intact organelles. Care must be taken to keep the sample cool so that metabolism is slowed and self digestion of the organelles is prevented. The samples must also be kept in a buffered, isotonic solution so that the organelles do not change volume and the enzymes are not denatured by changes in pH.

Differential Centrifugation

1 The sample is chilled over ice and cut into small pieces in a cold, buffered, isotonic solution.

2 The sample is homogenized by breaking down the cells' outer membranes. The cell organelles remain intact.

3 The homogenized suspension is filtered to remove cellular debris. It is kept cool throughout.

4 The filtrate is centrifuged at low speed to remove partially opened cells and small pieces of debris.

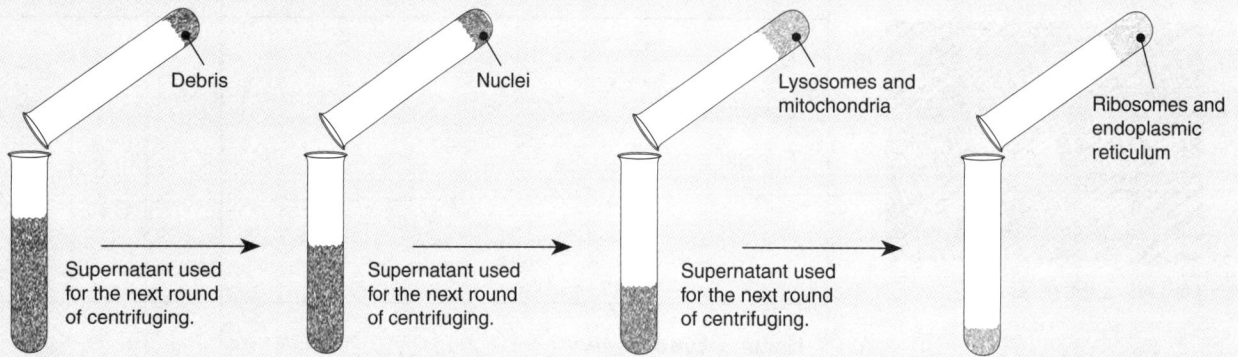

Debris

Nuclei

Lysosomes and mitochondria

Ribosomes and endoplasmic reticulum

Supernatant used for the next round of centrifuging.

Supernatant used for the next round of centrifuging.

Supernatant used for the next round of centrifuging.

5 The supernatant containing the organelles is carefully decanted off.

6 The sample is centrifuged at 500-600 g for 5-10 minutes then decanted.

7 The sample is centrifuged at 10 000-20 000 g for 15-20 minutes then decanted.

8 The sample is centrifuged at 100 000 g for 60 minutes then decanted.

NOTE: In centrifugation, the relative centrifugal force (RCF) is expressed as 'g', where g represents the gravitational field strength.

1. Explain why it is possible to separate cell organelles using centrifugation: _____

2. Define the following terms:

   (a) **Supernatant**: _____

   (b) **Homogenized**: _____

3. Explain why the sample must be kept in a solution that is:

   (a) Isotonic: _____

   (b) Cool: _____

   (c) Buffered: _____

4. **Density gradient centrifugation** is another method of cell fractionation. Sucrose is added to the sample, which is then centrifuged at high speed. The organelles will form layers according to their specific densities. Using the information above, label the centrifuge tube on the right with the organelles you would find in each layer.

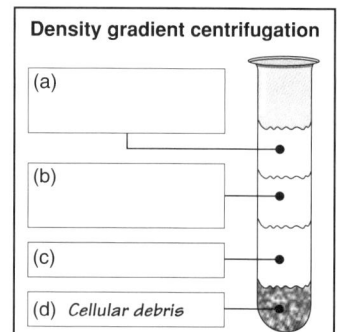

Density gradient centrifugation

(a)

(b)

(c)

(d) *Cellular debris*

Identifying Cell Structures

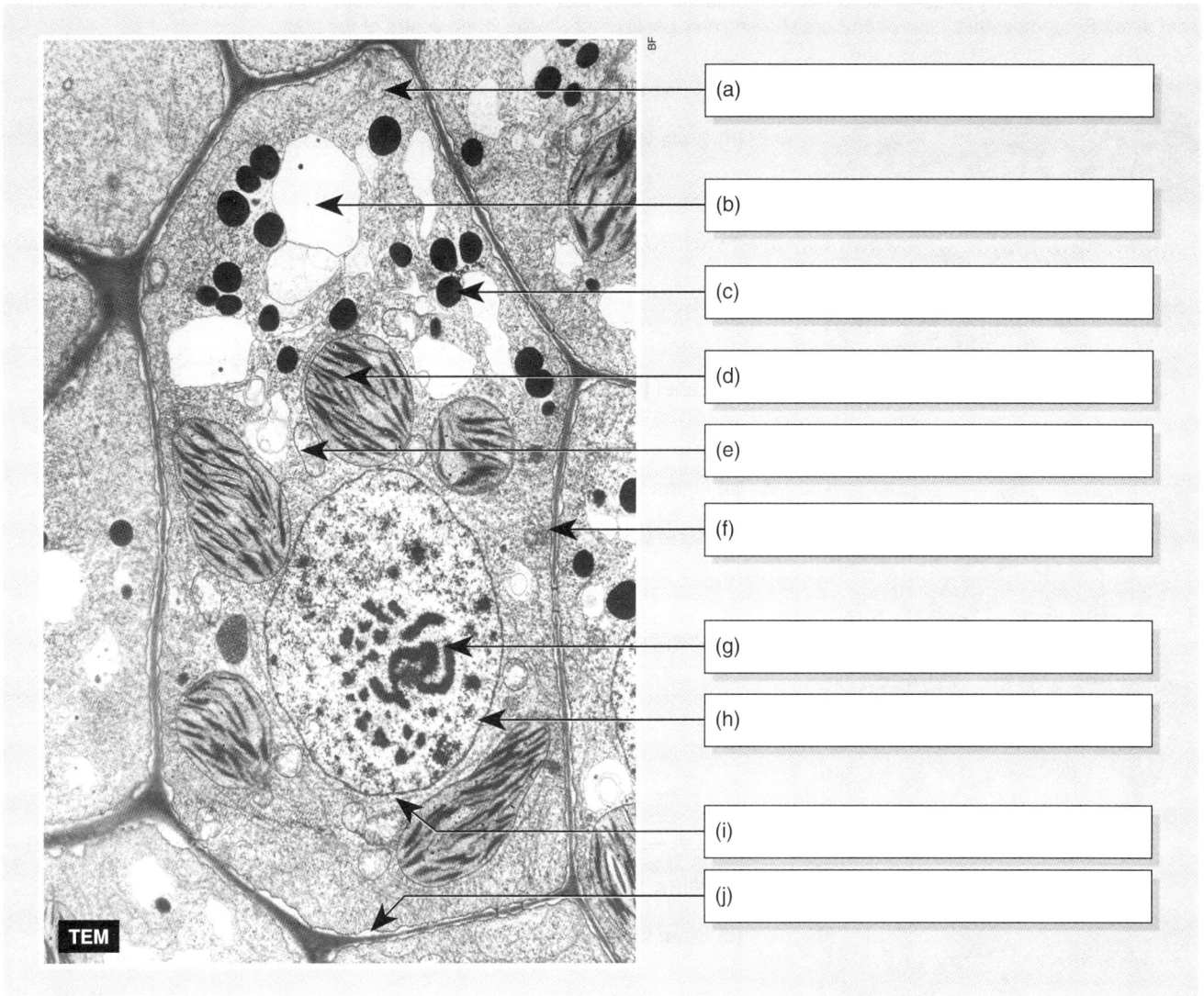

(a)

(b)

(c)

(d)

(e)

(f)

(g)

(h)

(i)

(j)

TEM

1. Study the diagrams on the previous pages to become familiar with the various structures found in plant and animal cells. Identify and label the 10 structures in the cell above using the following list of terms: *nuclear membrane, cytoplasm, endoplasmic reticulum, mitochondrion, starch granules, chromosome, vacuole, plasma membrane, cell wall, chloroplast*

2. State how many cells, or parts of cells, are visible in the photograph above: _____

3. Giving a comprehensive reason for your answer, state what **type** of cell is shown above (bacterial, plant, or animal cell):

_____

_____

_____

4. (a) Explain where cytoplasm is found in the cell: _____

_____

(b) Describe what cytoplasm is made up of: _____

_____

_____

5. Describe two important functions of **lysosomes**:

(a) _____

(b) _____

A 2   Identifying TEM Photographs

The photographs below were taken using a transmission electron microscope (TEM). They show some of the cell organelles in great detail. Remember that these photos are showing only **parts** of cells – **not whole cells**. Some of the photographs show more than one type of organelle. The questions refer to the main organelle in the centre of the photo.

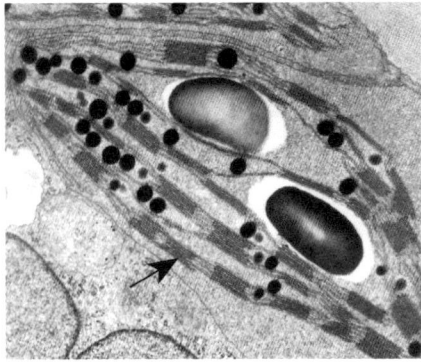

1. (a) Name this organelle (arrowed): _____

   (b) State which kind of cell(s) this organelle would be found in:

   _____

   (c) Describe the function of this organelle: _____

   _____

   _____

   (d) Label **two** structures that can be seen inside this organelle.

   _____

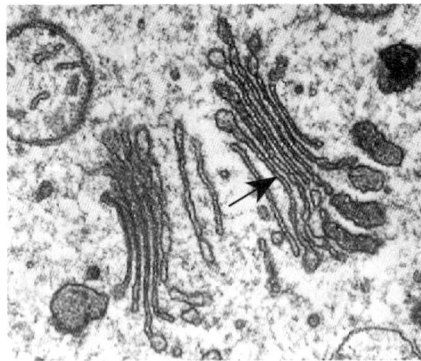

2. (a) Name this organelle (arrowed): _____

   (b) State which kind of cell(s) this organelle would be found in:

   _____

   (c) Describe the function of this organelle: _____

   _____

   _____

   _____

   _____

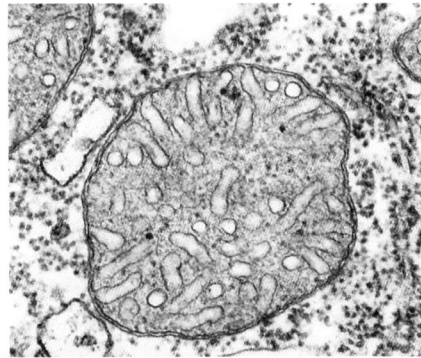

3. (a) Name the large, circular organelle: _____

   (b) State which kind of cell(s) this organelle would be found in:

   _____

   (c) Describe the function of this organelle: _____

   _____

   _____

   (d) Label **two** regions that can be seen **inside** this organelle.

   _____

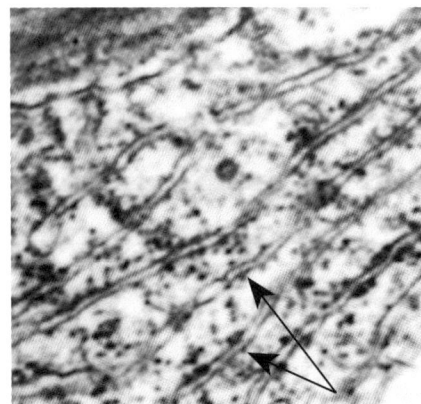

4. (a) Name and label the ribbon-like organelle in this photograph (arrowed):

   _____

   (b) State which kind of cell(s) this organelle is found in:

   _____

   (c) Describe the function of these organelles: _____

   _____

   _____

   (d) Name the dark 'blobs' attached to the organelle you have labeled:

   _____

   _____

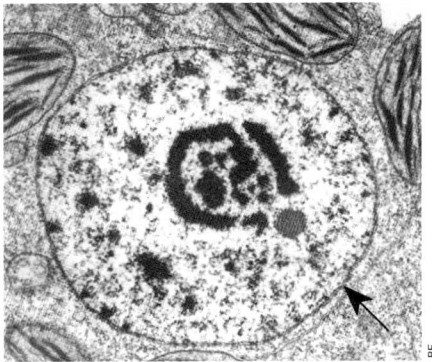

5. (a) Name this large circular structure (arrowed): _____

   (b) State which kind of cell(s) this structure would be found in:

   _____

   (c) Describe the function of this structure: _____

   _____

   _____

   (d) Label **3** features relating to this structure in the photograph.

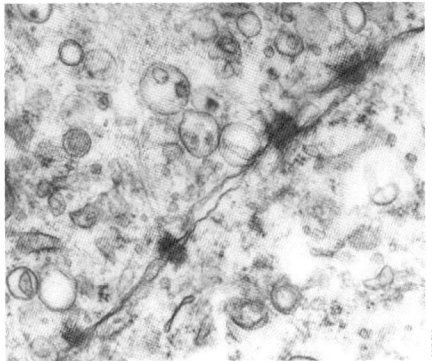

   _____

6. The four dark structures shown in this photograph are called **desmosomes**. They cause the plasma membranes of neighboring cells to stick together. Without desmosomes, animal cells would not combine together to form tissues.

   (a) Describe the functions of the plasma membrane:

   _____

   _____

   _____

   (b) Label the **plasma membrane** and the 4 **desmosomes** in the photograph.

7. In the space below, **draw** a simple, labeled diagram of a **generalized cell** to show the **relative size** and **location** of these six structures and organelles (simple outlines of the organelles will do):

RA②

Cell Division

The life cycle of **diploid sexually reproducing organisms** (such as humans) is illustrated in the diagram below. **Gametogenesis** is the process responsible for the production of male and female gametes for the purpose of sexual reproduction. The difference between meiosis in males and in females should be noted (see spermatogenesis and oogenesis in the box below).

Human embryos have cells that are rapidly dividing by **mitosis**. The term **somatic** means 'body', so the cell divisions are creating new body cells (as opposed to gametes or sex cells). The **2N** number refers to how many whole 'sets' of chromosomes are present in each body cell. For a normal human embryo, all cells will have a 2N number of 46.

Adults still continue to produce somatic cells by mitosis for cell replacement and growth. Blood cells are replaced by the body at the astonishing rate of two million per second, and a layer of skin cells is constantly lost and replaced about every 28 days.

Gamete production begins at puberty, and lasts until menopause for women, and indefinitely for men. Gametes are produced by **meiosis**; a special type of cell division, which reduces the chromosome number to half. Human males produce about 200 million sperm per day (whether they are used or not), while females usually release a single egg only once a month.

Fertilization involves the fusing of the sperm and the egg to produce a single cell called the **zygote**. This cell has all the genetic information to build a human body as well as maintain it (metabolism).

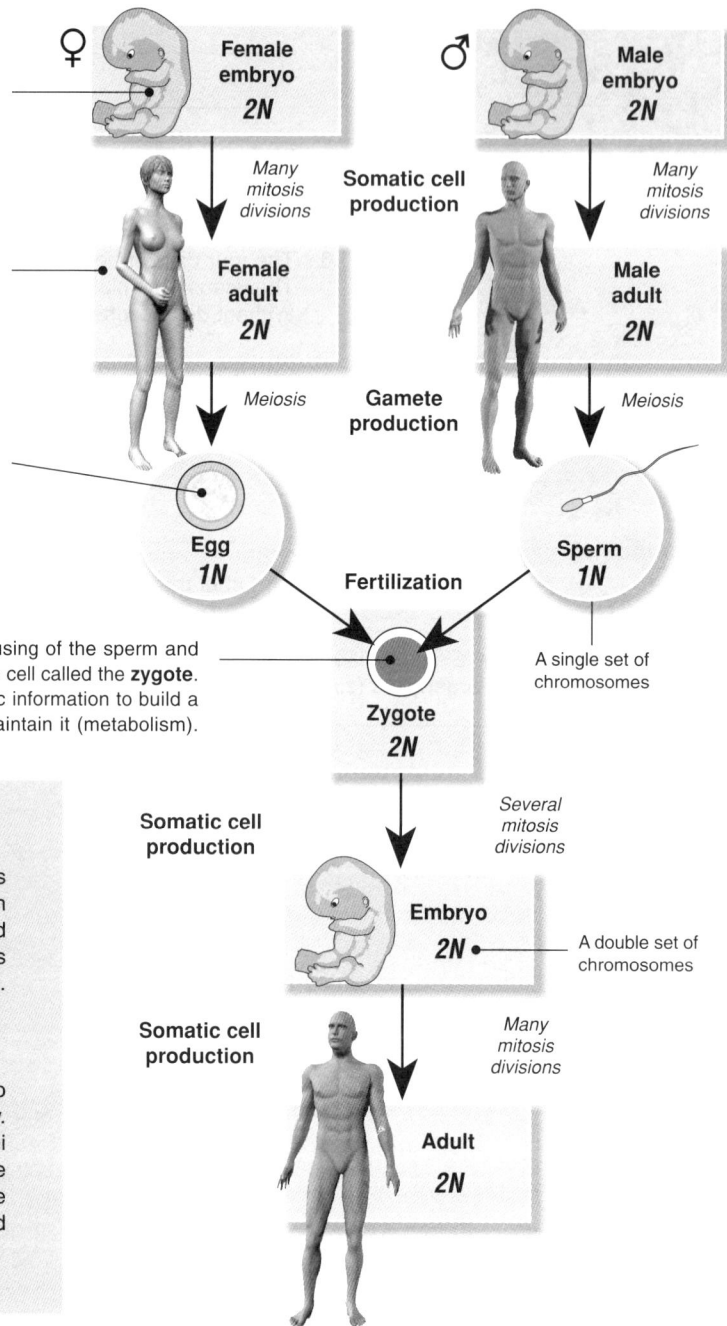

♀ Female embryo **2N** — Many mitosis divisions — **Somatic cell production** — Female adult **2N** — Meiosis — **Gamete production** — Egg **1N**

♂ Male embryo **2N** — Many mitosis divisions — Male adult **2N** — Meiosis — Sperm **1N** — A single set of chromosomes

Fertilization — Zygote **2N**

Somatic cell production — Several mitosis divisions — Embryo **2N** — A double set of chromosomes

Somatic cell production — Many mitosis divisions — Adult **2N**

Spermatogenesis

Sperm production: This type of cell division produces the male gametes. The nucleus of the **germ cell** in the male divides twice to produce four similar-sized sperm cells. Many organisms produce vast quantities of male gametes in this way (e.g. pollen and sperm).

Oogenesis

Egg production: In the female, there are also two divisions, but the cytoplasm is divided very unequally. Most of the cytoplasm and one of the four nuclei form the egg cell. The remainder, plus the other three nuclei, form much smaller polar bodies and are abortive (i.e. do not take part in fertilization and zygote formation).

1. Describe the **purpose** of the following types of cell division:

   (a) Mitosis: _____

   _____

   (b) Meiosis: _____

   _____

2. Define the term **zygote**: _____

3. Describe the basic difference between the cell divisions involved in spermatogenesis and oogenesis:

   _____

   _____

Mitosis and the Cell Cycle

A 1

Mitosis is part of the 'cell cycle' in which an existing cell (the parent cell) divides into two new ones (the daughter cells). Mitosis does not result in a change of chromosome numbers (unlike meiosis): the daughter cells are identical to the parent cell. Although mitosis is part of a continuous cell cycle, it is divided into stages (below). In plants and animals mitosis is associated with growth and repair of tissue, and it is the method by which some organisms reproduce asexually. The example below illustrates the cell cycle in a plant cell. Note that in animal cells, **cytokinesis** involves the formation of a constriction that divides the cell in two. It is usually well underway by the end of telophase and does not involve the formation of a cell plate.

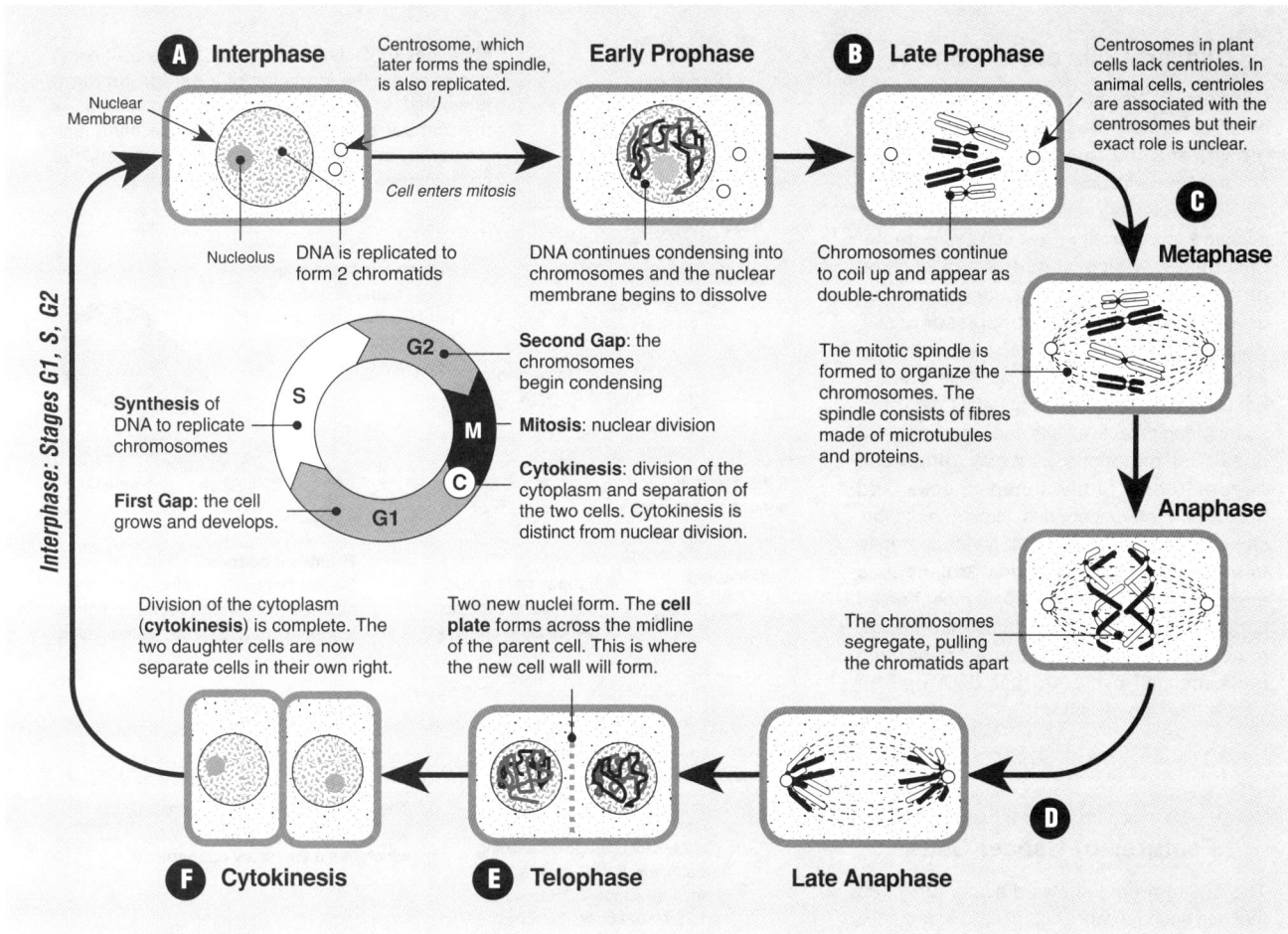

A Interphase

Centrosome, which later forms the spindle, is also replicated.

Nuclear Membrane

Nucleolus

Cell enters mitosis

DNA is replicated to form 2 chromatids

Early Prophase

DNA continues condensing into chromosomes and the nuclear membrane begins to dissolve

B Late Prophase

Chromosomes continue to coil up and appear as double-chromatids

Centrosomes in plant cells lack centrioles. In animal cells, centrioles are associated with the centrosomes but their exact role is unclear.

C

Metaphase

The mitotic spindle is formed to organize the chromosomes. The spindle consists of fibres made of microtubules and proteins.

Anaphase

The chromosomes segregate, pulling the chromatids apart

D

Interphase: Stages G1, S, G2

Synthesis of DNA to replicate chromosomes

First Gap: the cell grows and develops.

S

G2

M

C

G1

Second Gap: the chromosomes begin condensing

Mitosis: nuclear division

Cytokinesis: division of the cytoplasm and separation of the two cells. Cytokinesis is distinct from nuclear division.

Division of the cytoplasm (**cytokinesis**) is complete. The two daughter cells are now separate cells in their own right.

Two new nuclei form. The **cell plate** forms across the midline of the parent cell. This is where the new cell wall will form.

F Cytokinesis

E Telophase

Late Anaphase

1. The five photographs below were taken at various stages through the process of mitosis in a plant cell. They are not in any particular order. Study the diagram above and determine the stage that each photograph represents (eg. anaphase).

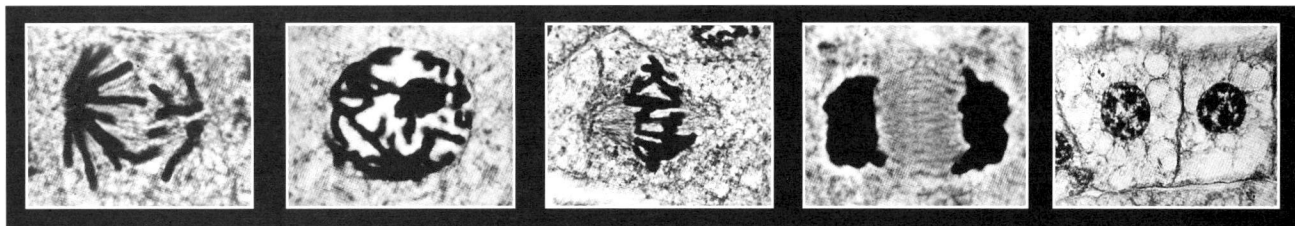

Photos: Ralph Cocklin

(a) _____   (b) _____   (c) _____   (d) _____   (e) _____

2. State two important changes that chromosomes must undergo before cell division can take place:

_____

3. Briefly summarize the stages of the cell cycle by describing what is happening at the points (A-F) in the diagram above:

A. _____

B. _____

C. _____

D. _____

E. _____

F. _____

Cancer: Cells out of Control

Normal cells do not live forever. Under certain circumstances, cells are programmed to die, particularly during development. Cells that become damaged beyond repair will normally undergo this programmed cell death (called **apoptosis** or **cell suicide**). Cancer cells evade this control and become immortal, continuing to divide regardless of any damage incurred. **Carcinogens** are agents capable of causing cancer. Roughly 90% of carcinogens are also mutagens, i.e. they damage DNA. Chronic exposure to carcinogens accelerates the rate at which dividing cells make errors. Susceptibility to cancer is also influenced by genetic make-up. Any one or a number of cancer-causing factors (including defective genes) may interact to induce cancer.

Cancer: Cells out of Control

Cancerous transformation results from changes in the genes controlling normal cell growth and division. The resulting cells become immortal and no longer carry out their functional role. Two types of gene are normally involved in controlling the cell cycle: proto-oncogenes, which start the cell division process and are essential for normal cell development, and **tumor-suppressor** genes, which switch off cell division. In their normal form, both kinds of genes work as a team, enabling the body to perform vital tasks such as repairing defective cells and replacing dead ones. But mutations in these genes can disrupt these finely tuned checks and balances. Proto-oncogenes, through mutation, can give rise to **oncogenes**; genes that lead to uncontrollable cell division. Mutations to tumor-suppressor genes initiate most human cancers. The best studied tumor-suppressor gene is **p53**, which encodes a protein that halts the cell cycle so that DNA can be repaired before division.

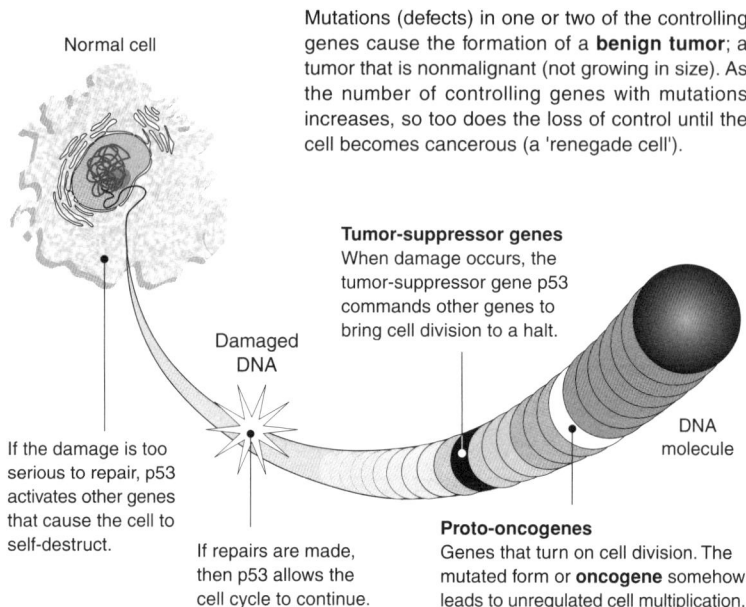

Mutations (defects) in one or two of the controlling genes cause the formation of a **benign tumor**; a tumor that is nonmalignant (not growing in size). As the number of controlling genes with mutations increases, so too does the loss of control until the cell becomes cancerous (a 'renegade cell').

Normal cell

Damaged DNA

If the damage is too serious to repair, p53 activates other genes that cause the cell to self-destruct.

If repairs are made, then p53 allows the cell cycle to continue.

Tumor-suppressor genes
When damage occurs, the tumor-suppressor gene p53 commands other genes to bring cell division to a halt.

DNA molecule

Proto-oncogenes
Genes that turn on cell division. The mutated form or **oncogene** somehow leads to unregulated cell multiplication.

Features of Cancer Cells

The diagram right shows a single **lung cell** that has become cancerous. It no longer carries out the role of a lung cell, and instead takes on a parasitic lifestyle, taking from the body what it needs in the way of nutrients and contributing nothing in return. The rate of cell division is greater than in normal cells in the same tissue because there is no *resting phase* between divisions.

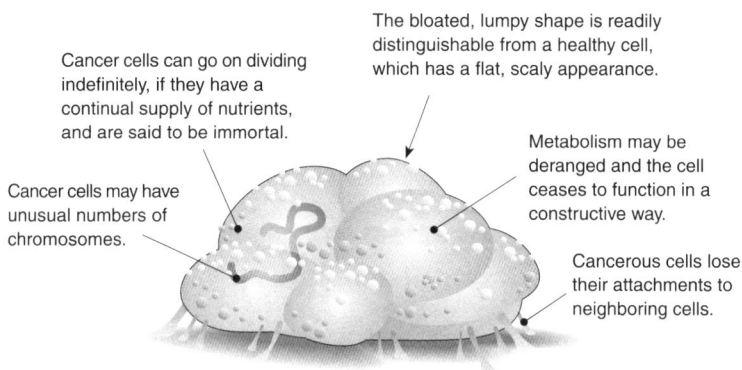

Cancer cells can go on dividing indefinitely, if they have a continual supply of nutrients, and are said to be immortal.

The bloated, lumpy shape is readily distinguishable from a healthy cell, which has a flat, scaly appearance.

Cancer cells may have unusual numbers of chromosomes.

Metabolism may be deranged and the cell ceases to function in a constructive way.

Cancerous cells lose their attachments to neighboring cells.

1. Explain how cancerous cells differ from normal cells: _____

    _____

2. Define **oncogene**: _____

3. Define **tumor-suppressor gene**: _____

4. Explain why a cell with a faulty oncogene can be likened to a car with a **stuck accelerator**: _____

    _____

    _____

5. Explain why a cell with a damaged tumor-suppressor gene can be likened to a car with **no brakes**: _____

    _____

    _____

    _____

Root Cell Development

RA②

In plants, cell division for growth (mitosis) is restricted to growing tips called **meristematic** tissue. These are located at the tips of every stem and root. This is unlike mitosis in a growing animal where cell divisions can occur all over the body. The diagram below illustrates the position and appearance of developing and growing cells in a plant root. Similar zones of development occur in the growing stem tips, which may give rise to specialized structures such as leaves and flowers.

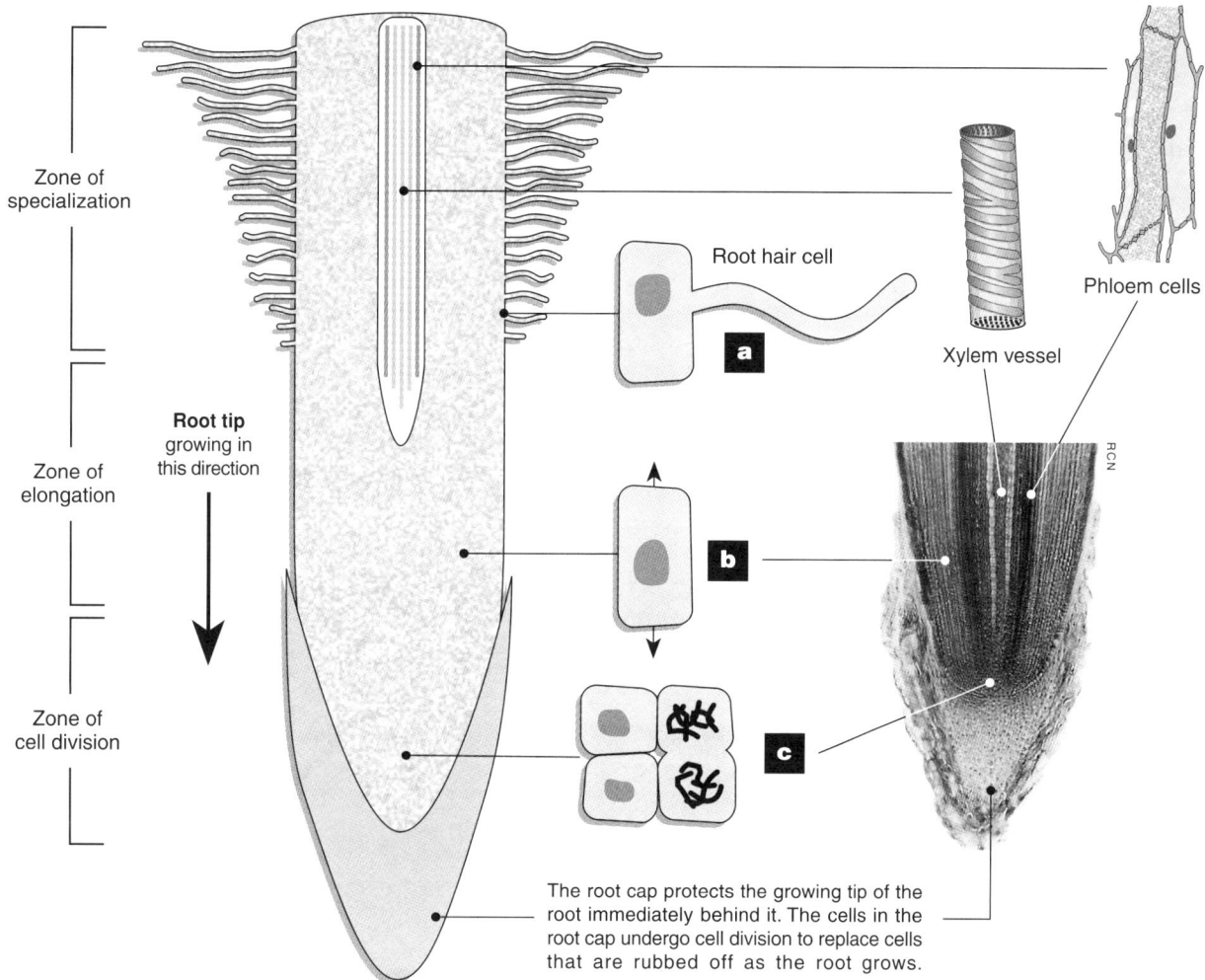

Zone of specialization

Root hair cell

a

Xylem vessel

Phloem cells

Root tip
growing in
this direction

Zone of elongation

b

Zone of cell division

c

The root cap protects the growing tip of the root immediately behind it. The cells in the root cap undergo cell division to replace cells that are rubbed off as the root grows.

1. Briefly describe what is happening to the plant cells at each of the points labeled (a) to (c) in the diagram above:

   (a) _____

   (b) _____

   (c) _____

2. The light micrograph (below) shows a section of the cells of an onion root tip, stained to show up the chromosomes.

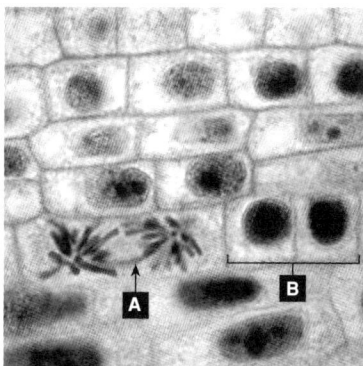

   (a) State the mitotic stage of the cell labeled A and explain your answer:

   _____

   (b) State the mitotic stage just completed in the cells labeled B and explain:

   _____

   _____

   (c) If, in this example, 250 cells were examined and 25 were found to be in the process of mitosis, state the proportion of the cell cycle occupied by mitosis:

   _____

3. Identify the cells that divide and specialize when a tree increases its girth (diameter): _____

Differentiation of Human Cells

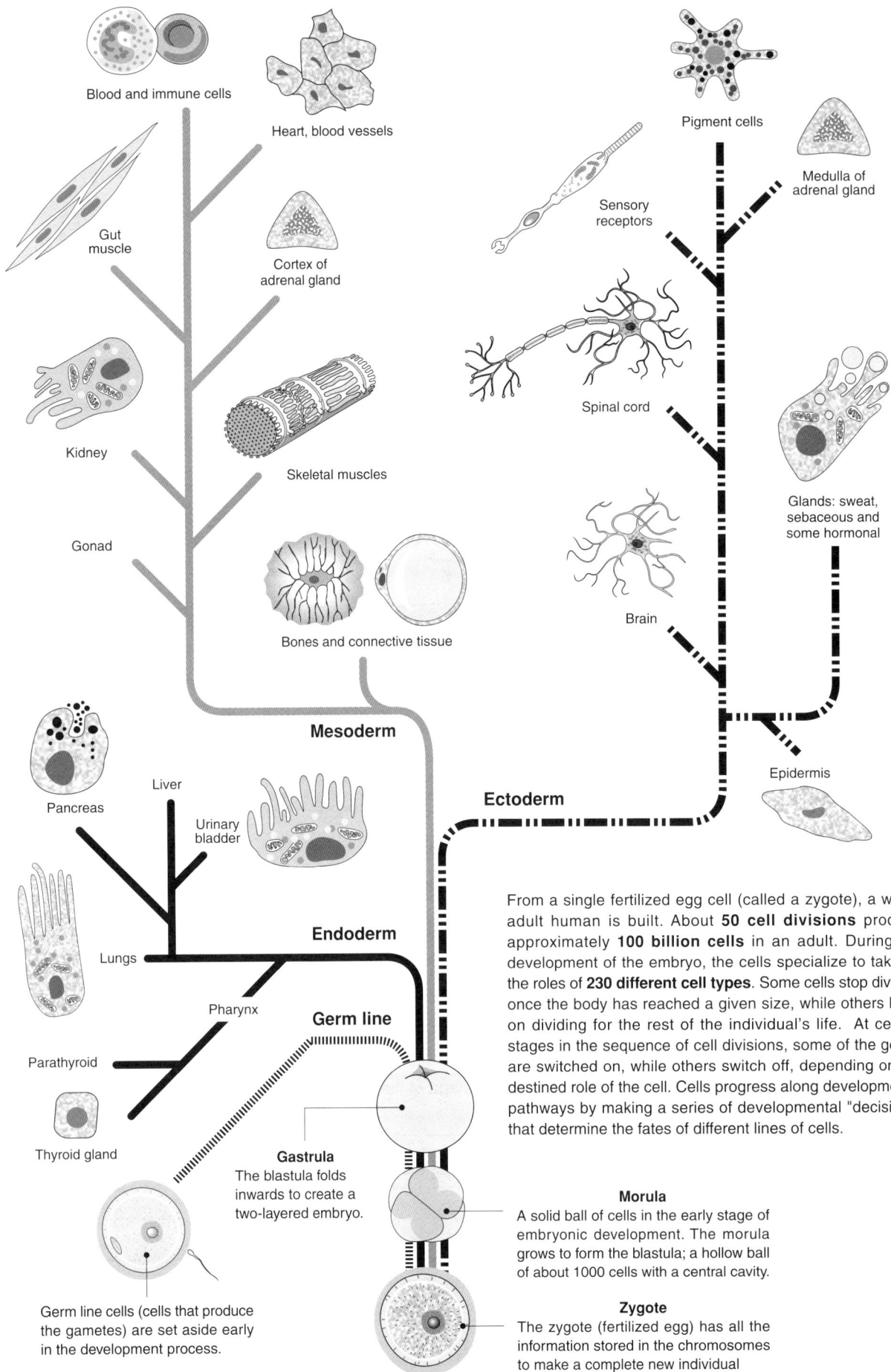

RA 2

Blood and immune cells

Heart, blood vessels

Pigment cells

Medulla of
adrenal gland

Gut
muscle

Sensory
receptors

Cortex of
adrenal gland

Kidney

Spinal cord

Skeletal muscles

Gonad

Glands: sweat,
sebaceous and
some hormonal

Bones and connective tissue

Brain

Mesoderm

Epidermis

Ectoderm

Pancreas

Liver

Urinary
bladder

From a single fertilized egg cell (called a zygote), a whole
adult human is built. About **50 cell divisions** produce
approximately **100 billion cells** in an adult. During the
development of the embryo, the cells specialize to take on
the roles of **230 different cell types**. Some cells stop dividing
once the body has reached a given size, while others keep
on dividing for the rest of the individual's life. At certain
stages in the sequence of cell divisions, some of the genes
are switched on, while others switch off, depending on the
destined role of the cell. Cells progress along developmental
pathways by making a series of developmental "decisions"
that determine the fates of different lines of cells.

Endoderm

Lungs

Pharynx

Germ line

Parathyroid

Gastrula
The blastula folds
inwards to create a
two-layered embryo.

Thyroid gland

Morula
A solid ball of cells in the early stage of
embryonic development. The morula
grows to form the blastula; a hollow ball
of about 1000 cells with a central cavity.

Germ line cells (cells that produce
the gametes) are set aside early
in the development process.

Zygote
The zygote (fertilized egg) has all the
information stored in the chromosomes
to make a complete new individual

Development is the process of progressive change through the lifetime of an organism. Part of this process involves growth (increase in size) and cell division (to generate the multicellular body). Cellular **differentiation** (the generation of specialized cells) and morphogenesis (the creation of the shape and form of the body) are also part of development. Differentiation defines the specific structure and function of a cell. As development proceeds, the possibilities available to individual cells become fewer, until each cell's **fate** is determined. The tissues and organs making up the body form from the aggregation and organization of these differentiated cells. In animals, the final body form is the result of cell migration and the programmed death of certain cells during embryonic development. The diagram opposite shows how a single fertilized egg (zygote) gives rise to the large number of specialized cell types that make up the adult human body. The morula, blastula, and gastrula stages mentioned at the bottom of the diagram show the early development of the embryo from the zygote. The gastrula gives rise to the three layers of cells (ectoderm, mesoderm, and endoderm), from which specific cell types develop.

1. State how many different **types of cell** are found in the human body: _____

2. State approximately how many **cell divisions** take place from fertilized egg (zygote) to produce an adult: _____

3. State approximately **how many cells** make up an adult human body: _____

4. Name one cell type that **continues to divide** throughout a person's lifetime: _____

   _____

5. Name one cell type that **does not continue to divide** throughout a person's lifetime: _____

   _____

6. Germ line cells diverge (become isolated) from other cells at a very early stage in embryonic development.

   (a) Explain what the germ line is: _____

   _____

   _____

   (b) Explain why it is necessary for the germ line to become separated at such an early stage of development:

   _____

   _____

   _____

7. Cloning whole new organisms is possible by taking a nucleus from a cell during the blastula stage of embryonic development and placing it into an egg cell that has had its own nucleus removed.

   (a) Explain what a clone is: _____

   _____

   _____

   (b) Explain why the cell required for cloning needs to be taken at such an early stage of embryonic development:

   _____

   _____

   _____

8. Cancer cells are particularly damaging to organisms. Explain what has happened to a cell that has become cancerous:

   _____

   _____

9. Explain the genetic events that enable so many different cell types to arise from one unspecialized cell (the zygote):

   _____

   _____

   _____

   _____

Human Cell Specialization

Animal cells are often specialized to perform particular functions. The eight specialized cell types shown below are representative of some 230 different cell types in humans. Each has specialized features that suit it to performing a specific role.

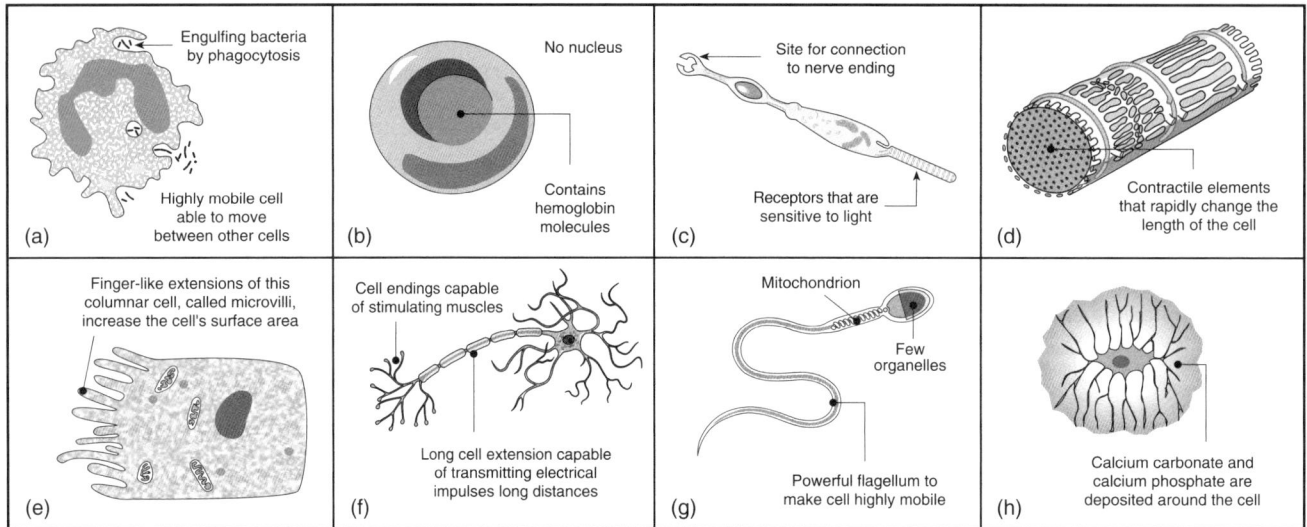

1. **Identify** each of the cells (b) to (h) pictured above, and describe their **specialized features** and **role** in the body:

    (a) Type of cell: Phagocytic white blood cell (neutrophil)

    Specialized features: Engulfs bacteria and other foreign material by phagocytosis

    Role of cell within body: Destroys pathogens and other foreign material as well as cellular debris

    (b) Type of cell: _____

    Specialized features: _____

    Role of cell within body: _____

    (c) Type of cell: _____

    Specialized features: _____

    Role of cell within body: _____

    (d) Type of cell: _____

    Specialized features: _____

    Role of cell within body: _____

    (e) Type of cell: _____

    Specialized features: _____

    Role of cell within body: _____

    (f) Type of cell: _____

    Specialized features: _____

    Role of cell within body: _____

    (g) Type of cell: _____

    Specialized features: _____

    Role of cell within body: _____

    (h) Type of cell: _____

    Specialized features: _____

    Role of cell within body: _____

RA 2   Plant Cell Specialization

Plants show a wide variety of cell types. The vegetative plant body consists of three organs: stems, leaves, and roots. Flowers, fruits, and seeds comprise additional organs that are concerned with reproduction. The eight cell types illustrated below are representatives of these plant organ systems. Each has structural or physiological features that set it apart from the other cell types. The differentiation of cells enables each specialized type to fulfill a specific role in the plant.

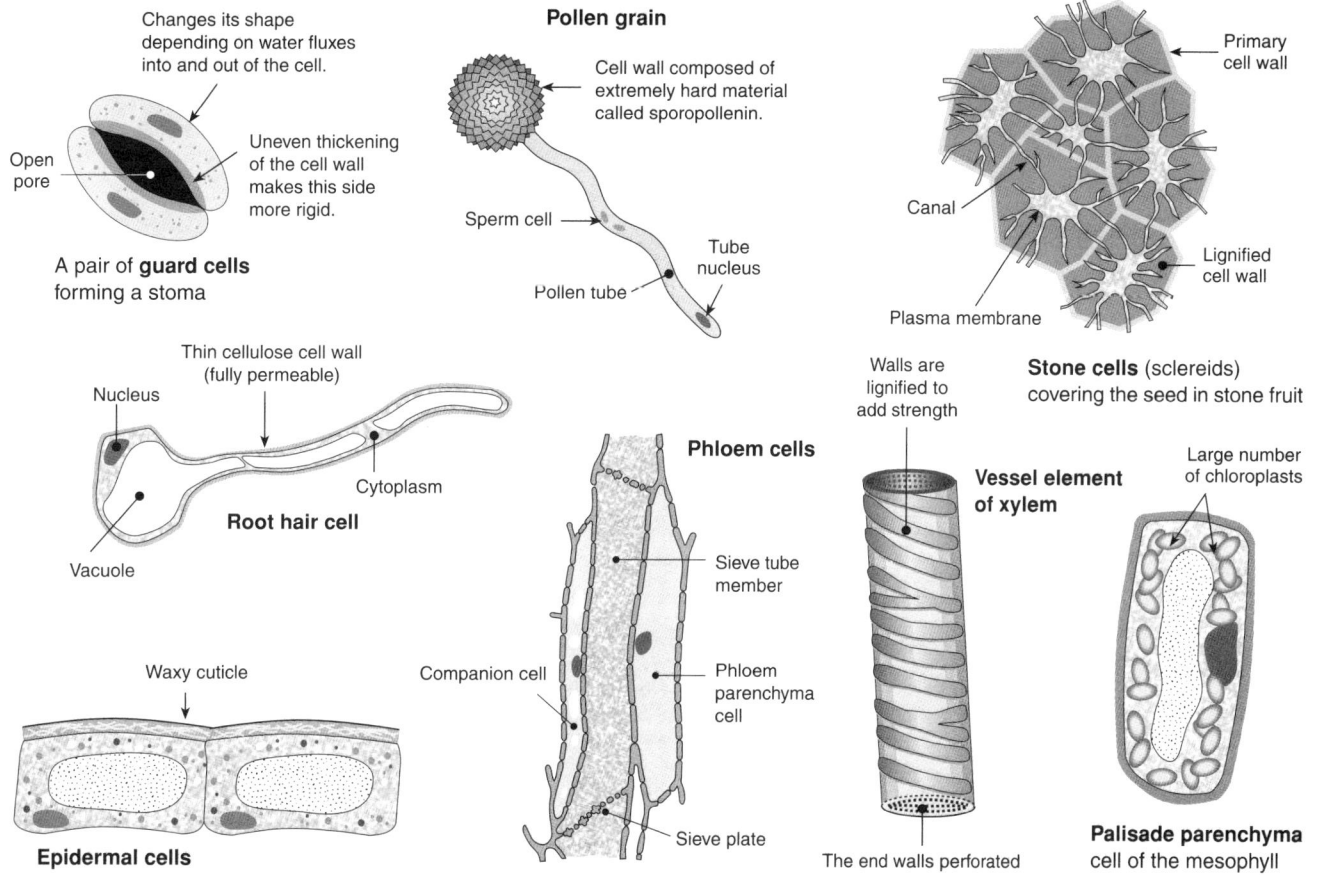

Changes its shape depending on water fluxes into and out of the cell.

Open pore

Uneven thickening of the cell wall makes this side more rigid.

A pair of **guard cells** forming a stoma

Pollen grain

Cell wall composed of extremely hard material called sporopollenin.

Sperm cell

Pollen tube

Tube nucleus

Primary cell wall

Canal

Lignified cell wall

Plasma membrane

Thin cellulose cell wall (fully permeable)

Nucleus

Cytoplasm

Root hair cell

Vacuole

Waxy cuticle

Epidermal cells

Phloem cells

Companion cell

Sieve tube member

Phloem parenchyma cell

Sieve plate

Walls are lignified to add strength

Vessel element of xylem

The end walls perforated

Stone cells (sclereids) covering the seed in stone fruit

Large number of chloroplasts

Palisade parenchyma cell of the mesophyll

1. Using the information given above, describe the **specialized features** and **role** of each of the cell types (b)-(h) below:

(a) **Guard cell**: Features: *Curved, sausage shaped cell, unevenly thickened.* _____

   Role in plant: *Turgor changes alter the cell shape to open or close the stoma.* _____

(b) **Pollen grain**: Features: _____

   Role in plant: _____

(c) **Palisade parenchyma cell**: Features: _____

   Role in plant: _____

(d) **Epidermal cell**: Features: _____

   Role in plant: _____

(e) **Vessel element**: Features: _____

   Role in plant: _____

(f) **Stone cell**: Features: _____

   Role in plant: _____

(g) **Sieve tube member**: Features: _____

   Role in plant: _____

(h) **Root hair cell**: Features: _____

   Role in plant: _____

Levels of Organization

RA 2

Organization is one of the defining features of living things. Organisms are organized according to a hierarchy of structural levels (below), each level building on the one below it. Atoms are organized into complex molecules such as proteins. These form the components of cells. Some organisms consist of single cells, but others are collections of many cells, organized into tissues and organs. Hierarchical organization allows the grouping of specialized cells together to perform a particular function.

In the spaces provided for each question below, assign each of the examples listed to one of the levels of organisation as indicated.

1. **Animals**: *adrenaline, blood, bone, brain, cardiac muscle, cartilage, collagen, DNA, heart, leucocyte, lysosome, mast cell, nervous system, neuron, phospholipid, reproductive system, ribosomes, Schwann cell, spleen, squamous epithelium.*

   (a) Organ system: _____

   _____

   (b) Organs: _____

   _____

   (c) Tissues: _____

   _____

   (d) Cells: _____

   _____

   (e) Organelles: _____

   _____

   (f) Molecular level: _____

   _____

   _____

2. **Plants**: *cellulose, chloroplasts, collenchyma, companion cells, DNA, epidermal cell, fibres, flowers, leaf, mesophyll, parenchyma, pectin, phloem, phospholipid, ribosomes, roots, sclerenchyma, tracheid.*

   (a) Organs: _____

   _____

   (b) Tissues: _____

   _____

   (c) Cells: _____

   _____

   (d) Organelles: _____

   _____

   (e) Molecular level: _____

   _____

   _____

The Organism
A complex, functioning whole that is the sum of all its component parts.

Organ System Level
In animals, organs form parts of even larger units known as organ systems. An organ system is an association of organs with a common function, e.g. digestive system, cardiovascular system, and the urinogenital system.

⇑

Organ Level
Organs are structures of definite form and structure, comprising two or more tissues.
Animal examples include: heart, lungs, brain, stomach, kidney.
Plant examples include: leaves, roots, storage organs, ovary.

⇑

Tissue Level
Tissues are composed of groups of cells of similar structure that perform a particular, related function.
Animal examples include: epithelial tissue, bone, muscle.
Plant examples include: phloem, chlorenchyma, endodermis, xylem.

⇑

Cellular Level
Cells are the basic structural and functional units of an organism. Each cell type has a different structure and function - the result of cellular differentiation during development.
Animal examples include: epithelial cells, osteoblasts, muscle fibres.
Plant examples include: sclereids, xylem vessels, sieve tubes.

⇑

Organelle Level
Many diverse molecules may associate together to form complex, highly specialized structures within cells called cellular organelles, e.g. mitochondria, Golgi apparatus, endoplasmic reticulum, chloroplasts.

⇑

Chemical and Molecular Level
Atoms and molecules form the most basic, level of organization. This level includes all the chemicals essential for maintaining life, e.g. water, ions, fats, carbohydrates, amino acids, proteins, and nucleic acids.

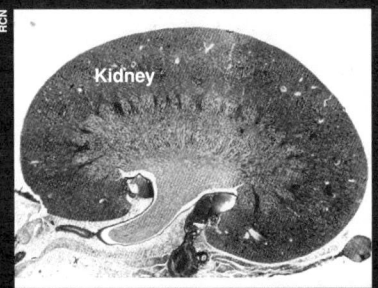

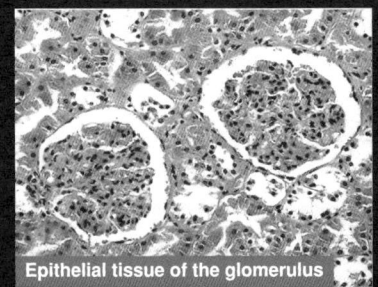

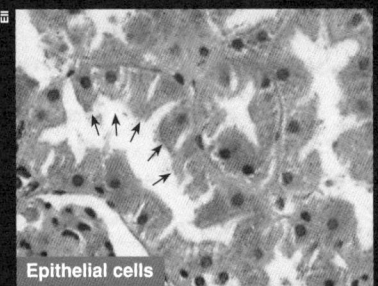

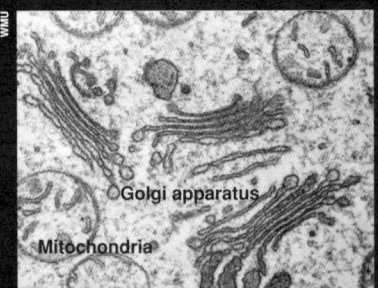

Kidney

Epithelial tissue of the glomerulus

Epithelial cells

Golgi apparatus
Mitochondria

The study of tissues is called **histology**. The cells of a tissue, and their associated intracellular substances e.g. collagen, are grouped together to perform particular functions. Tissues improve the efficiency of operation because they enable tasks to be shared amongst various specialized cells. **Animal tissues** can be divided into four broad groups: **epithelial tissues**, **connective tissues**, **muscle**, and **nervous tissues**. Some features of animal tissues are described below. Plant tissues are divided into two groups: simple and complex. Simple tissues contain only one cell type and form packing and support tissues (e.g. parenchyma). Complex tissues contain more than one cell type and form the conducting and support tissues of plants (periderm, xylem, phloem). Examples of these are illustrated in the structure and function topics in *Senior Biology 2*.

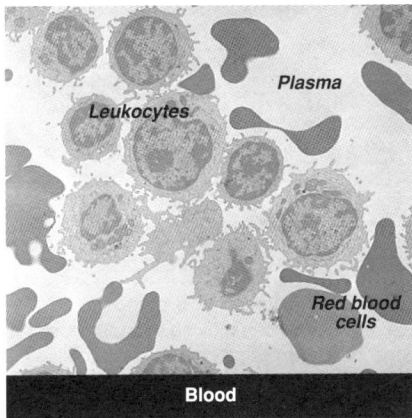

Plasma
Leukocytes
Red blood cells

Blood

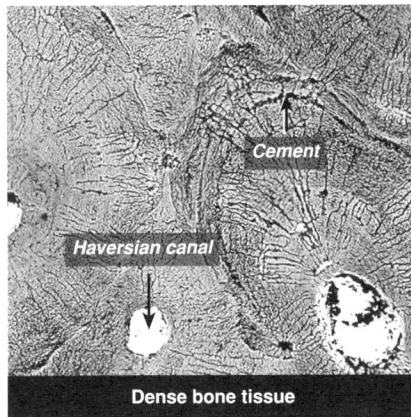

Cement
Haversian canal

Dense bone tissue

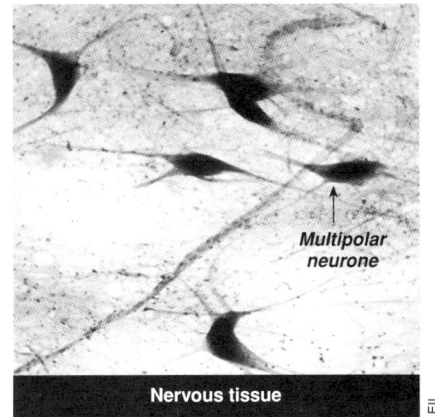

Multipolar neurone

Nervous tissue

Connective tissue is the major supporting tissue of the animal body. It comprises cells, widely dispersed in a semi-fluid matrix. Connective tissues bind other structures together and provide support, and protection against damage, infection, or heat loss. Connective tissues include dentine (teeth), adipose (fat) tissue, bone (above) and cartilage, and the tissues around the body's organs and blood vessels. Blood (above, left) is a special type of liquid tissue, comprising cells floating in a liquid matrix.

Nervous tissue contains densely packed nerve cells (neurons) which are specialized for the transmission of nerve impulses. Associated with the neurons there may also be supporting cells and connective tissue containing blood vessels.

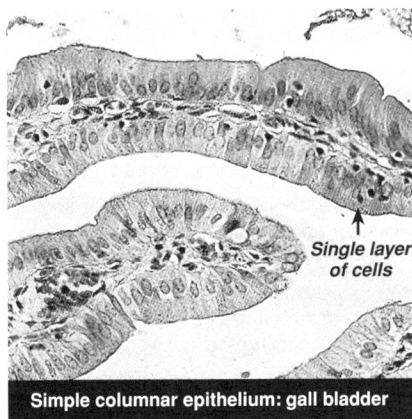

Single layer of cells

Simple columnar epithelium: gall bladder

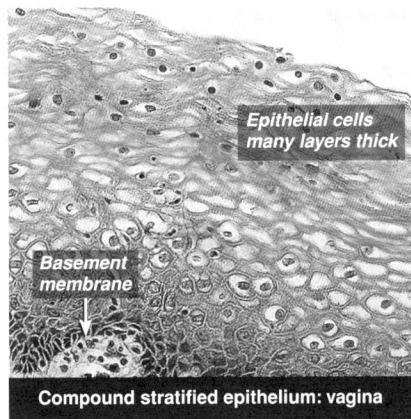

Epithelial cells many layers thick
Basement membrane

Compound stratified epithelium: vagina

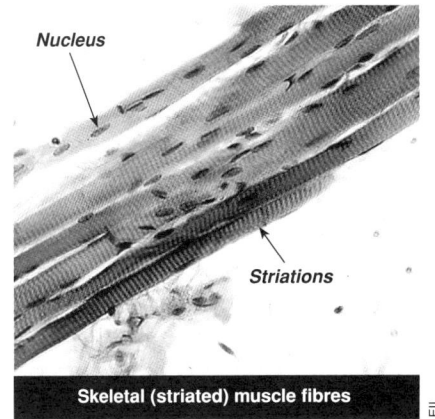

Nucleus
Striations

Skeletal (striated) muscle fibres

Epithelial tissue is organized into single (above, left) or layered (above) sheets. It lines internal and external surfaces (e.g. blood vessels, ducts, gut lining) and protects the underlying structures from wear, infection, and/or pressure. Epithelial cells rest on a basement membrane of fibres and collagen and are held together by a carbohydrate-based "glue". The cells may also be specialized for absorption, secretion, or excretion. Examples: stratified (compound) epithelium of vagina, ciliated epithelium of respiratory tract, cuboidal epithelium of kidney ducts, and the columnar epithelium of the intestine.

Muscle tissue consists of very highly specialized cells called fibres, held together by connective tissue. The three types of muscle in the body are cardiac muscle, skeletal muscle (above), and smooth muscle. Muscles bring about both voluntary and involuntary (unconscious) body movements.

3. Explain the advantage of the organization seen in living things: _____

_____

_____

4. Give an example of an organ system in an animal, stating the organs, tissues, and specialized cells that comprise it:

Organ system: _____ Organs: _____

Tissues: _____

Specialized cells: _____

5. Describe the main features of the following animal tissues:

(a) Epithelial tissues: _____

(b) Connective tissues: _____

(c) Muscle tissue: _____

(d) Nervous tissue: _____

Cell Membranes and Transport

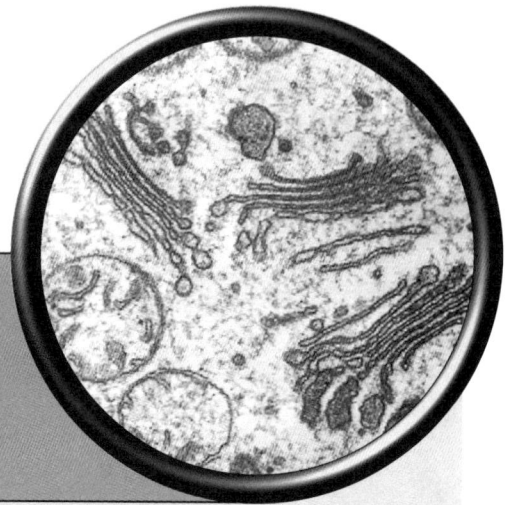

IB SL
Complete nos:
1-3, 5-7, 9-13

Extension: 4, 8, 14

IB HL
Complete nos:
1-3, 5-7, 9-13

Extension: 4, 8, 14

IB Options
Not applicable to options

AP Biology
Complete nos:
1-3, 5-7, 9-13

Extension: 4, 8, 14

Learning Objectives

☐ 1. Compile your own glossary from the **KEY WORDS** displayed in **bold type** in the learning objectives below.

Cell membranes *(pages 60, 102-105)*

☐ 2. Draw a simple labeled diagram of the structure of the **plasma membrane** (cell surface membrane), clearly identifying the arrangement of the lipids and proteins.

☐ 3. Describe and explain the current **fluid-mosaic model** of membrane structure. Define: **lipid bilayer**, **partially permeable membrane**. Explain the roles of **phospholipids**, cholesterol, glycolipids, proteins, and glycoproteins in plasma membrane structure. Explain how the **hydrophobic** and **hydrophilic** properties of phospholipids help to maintain membrane structure. Appreciate that the plasma membrane is essentially no different to the membranes of organelles.

☐ 4. Outline the evidence from **freeze-fracture studies** in support of the current model of membrane structure. Contrast this currently accepted model with the earlier Davson-Danielli model.

☐ 5. Describe the *general functions* of membranes (including the plasma membrane) in the cell, identifying their role in the structure of cellular organelles and their role in regulating the transport of materials within cells, as well as into and out of cells.

Cellular transport *(pages 101, 106-112)*

☐ 6. Summarize the types of movements that occur across membranes. Outline the role of proteins in membranes as receptors and carriers in membrane transport. Define: **passive transport**, **concentration gradient**.

☐ 7. Describe the processes of **diffusion** and **osmosis**, identifying the types of substances moving in each case. Describe **facilitated diffusion** (also called facilitated transport). Identify when and where this process might occur in a cell.

☐ 8. Identify factors determining the rate of diffusion. Explain how **Fick's law** provides a framework for determining maximum diffusion rates across cell surfaces.

☐ 9. Suggest why cell size is limited by the rate of diffusion. Discuss the significance of **surface area to volume ratio** to cell size and efficiency of function. Explain why organisms without efficient transport mechanisms remain small.

☐ 10. With respect to solutions of differing solute concentration, distinguish between: **hypotonic**, **isotonic**, **hypertonic**. Determine the net direction of water movement between solutions of different tonicity.

☐ 11. With respect to plant cells, define the terms: **turgor** and **plasmolysis**. Comment on the importance of ion concentrations in maintaining cell turgor.

☐ 12. Distinguish between passive and **active transport** mechanisms. Understand the principles involved in active transport, clearly identifying the involvement of protein molecules and energy.

☐ 13. Describe the following active transport mechanisms: **ion-exchange pumps**, **exocytosis**, **endocytosis**, **phagocytosis**, and **pinocytosis**. Give examples of when and where (in the plant or animal body) each type of transport mechanism occurs.

☐ 14. Identify the mechanisms involved in the transport of some of the most important substances: water, fatty acids, glucose, amino acids, O_2, CO_2, ions (e.g. mineral and metal ions), sucrose (in plants).

Textbooks

See the 'Textbook Reference Grid' on pages 8-9 for textbook page references relating to material in this topic.

Supplementary Texts

See pages 5-6 for additional details of this text:
■ Adds, J., *at al.*, 2000. **Molecules and Cells**, (NelsonThornes), pp. 61-66.

Software and video resources are now provided in the Teacher Resource Handbook

Periodicals

See page 6 for details of publishers of periodicals:
STUDENT'S REFERENCE
■ **Cellular Factories** New Scientist, 23 Nov. 1996 (Inside Science). *An overview of cellular processes and the role of organelles in plant and animal cells.*
■ **Border Control** New Scientist, 15 July 2000 (Inside Science). *The structure and role of the plasma membrane (includes membrane receptors).*
■ **High Tension** Biol. Sci. Rev., 13(1), Sept. 2000, pp. 14-18. *An excellent account of water and solute transport mechanisms in vascular plants.*

TEACHER'S REFERENCE
■ **Phosphate Uptake in Carrot and Yeast** The American Biology Teacher, 63(7) Sept. 2001, pp. 498-502. *A how-to-do-it activity on investigating active transport mechanisms in isolated cells.*

■ **Budding Vesicles in Living Cells** Scientific American, March 1996, pp. 50-55. *Vesicles and the role of the Golgi apparatus in cell transport.*

Internet WWW

See pages 10-11 for details of how to access **Bio Links** from our web site: **www.thebiozone.com**. From Bio Links, access sites under the topics:

GENERAL BIOLOGY ONLINE RESOURCES > Online Textbooks and Lecture Notes: • Biology online org • Kimball's biology pages • Learn.co.uk • Mr Biology's biology web site • S - cool! A level biology revision guide *and others*

CELL BIOLOGY AND BIOCHEMISTRY: • Cell and molecular biology online • Cell structure and function web links • MIT biology hypertextbook > **Cell Structure and Transport**: • CELLS alive! • The virtual cell • Transport in and out of cells

R 1

Cell Processes

All of the organelles and other structures in the cell have functions. The cell can be compared to a factory with an assembly line. Organelles in the cell provide the equivalent of the power supply, assembly line, packaging department, repair and maintenance, transport system, and the control centre. The sum total of all the processes occurring in a cell is known as **metabolism**. Some of these processes store energy in molecules (anabolism) while others release that stored energy (catabolism). Below is a summary of the major processes that take place in a cell.

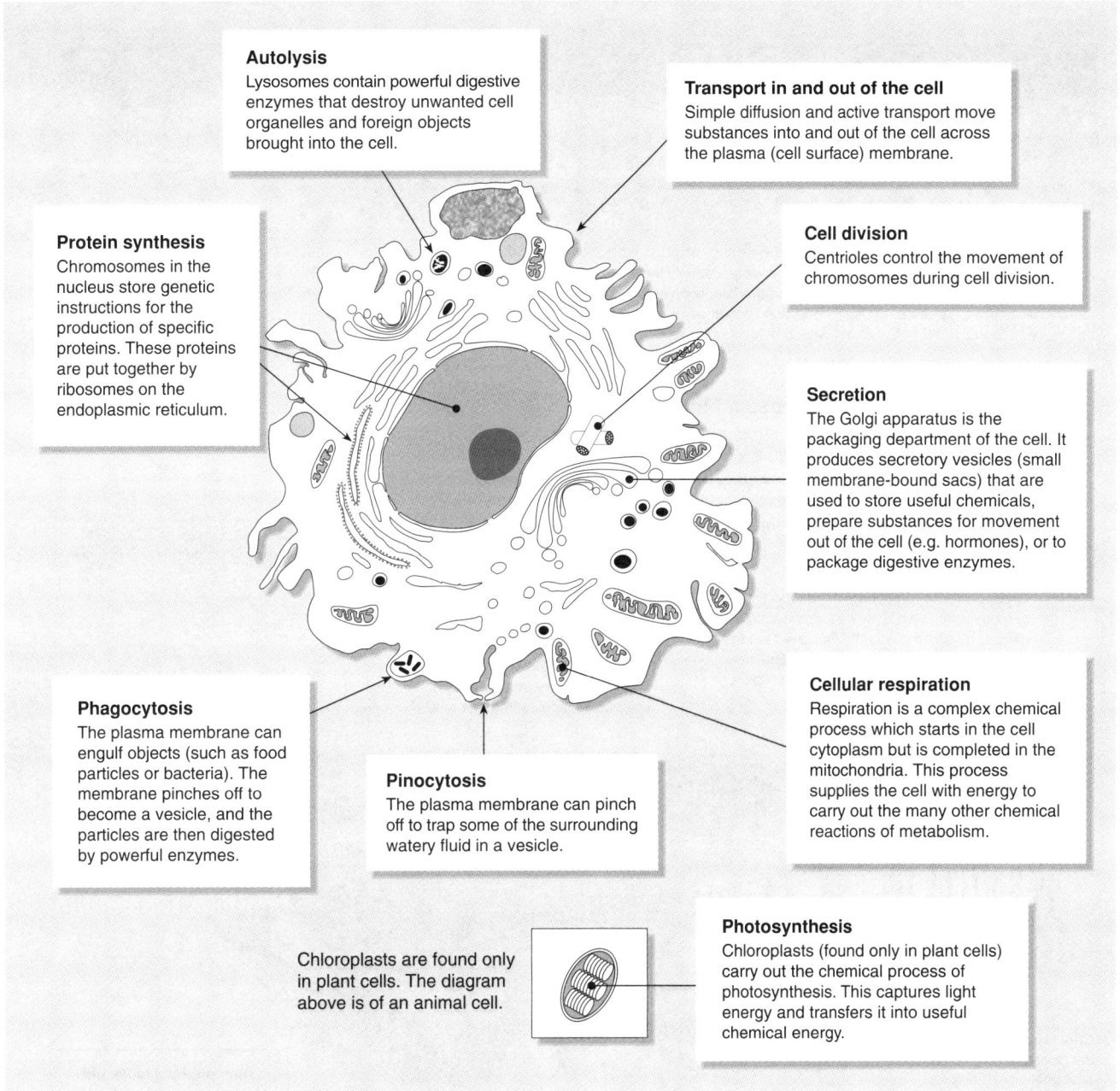

Autolysis
Lysosomes contain powerful digestive enzymes that destroy unwanted cell organelles and foreign objects brought into the cell.

Transport in and out of the cell
Simple diffusion and active transport move substances into and out of the cell across the plasma (cell surface) membrane.

Protein synthesis
Chromosomes in the nucleus store genetic instructions for the production of specific proteins. These proteins are put together by ribosomes on the endoplasmic reticulum.

Cell division
Centrioles control the movement of chromosomes during cell division.

Secretion
The Golgi apparatus is the packaging department of the cell. It produces secretory vesicles (small membrane-bound sacs) that are used to store useful chemicals, prepare substances for movement out of the cell (e.g. hormones), or to package digestive enzymes.

Phagocytosis
The plasma membrane can engulf objects (such as food particles or bacteria). The membrane pinches off to become a vesicle, and the particles are then digested by powerful enzymes.

Pinocytosis
The plasma membrane can pinch off to trap some of the surrounding watery fluid in a vesicle.

Cellular respiration
Respiration is a complex chemical process which starts in the cell cytoplasm but is completed in the mitochondria. This process supplies the cell with energy to carry out the many other chemical reactions of metabolism.

Chloroplasts are found only in plant cells. The diagram above is of an animal cell.

Photosynthesis
Chloroplasts (found only in plant cells) carry out the chemical process of photosynthesis. This captures light energy and transfers it into useful chemical energy.

1. For each of the processes listed below, state which organelles or structures are associated with that process (there may be more than one associated with a process):

(a) Secretion: _____

(f) Photosynthesis: _____

(b) Respiration: _____

(g) Cell division: _____

(c) Pinocytosis: _____

(h) Autolysis: _____

(d) Phagocytosis: _____

(i) Transport in/out of cell: _____

(e) Protein synthesis: _____

2. Explain what distinguishes anabolic and catabolic processes and give one example of each: _____

_____

_____

The Structure of Membranes

RA 2

All cells have a plasma membrane that forms the outer limit of the cell. Bacteria, fungi, and plant cells have a cell wall outside this, but it is quite distinct and outside the cell. Membranes are also found inside eukaryotic cells as part of membranous **organelles**. Present day knowledge of membrane structure has been built up as a result of many observations and experiments. The original model of membrane structure, proposed by Davson and Danielli, was the unit membrane (a lipid bilayer coated with protein). This model was later modified after the discovery that the protein molecules were embedded *within* the bilayer rather than coating the outside. The now-accepted model of membrane structure is the **fluid-mosaic model** described below.

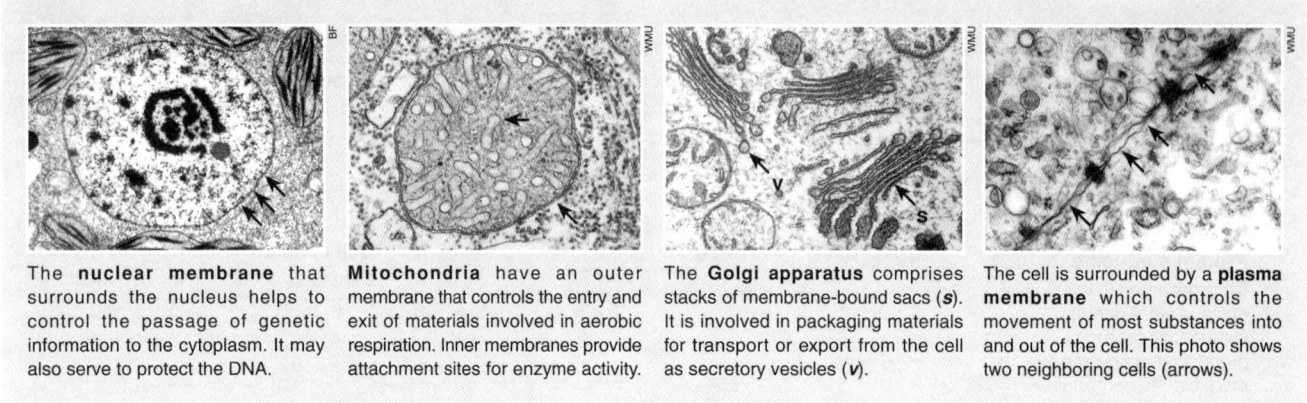

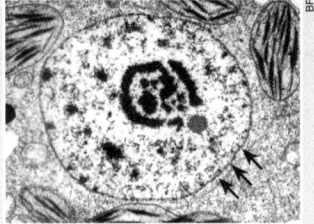

The **nuclear membrane** that surrounds the nucleus helps to control the passage of genetic information to the cytoplasm. It may also serve to protect the DNA.

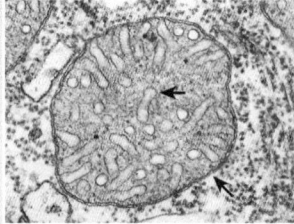

Mitochondria have an outer membrane that controls the entry and exit of materials involved in aerobic respiration. Inner membranes provide attachment sites for enzyme activity.

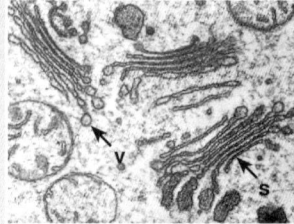

The **Golgi apparatus** comprises stacks of membrane-bound sacs (*s*). It is involved in packaging materials for transport or export from the cell as secretory vesicles (*v*).

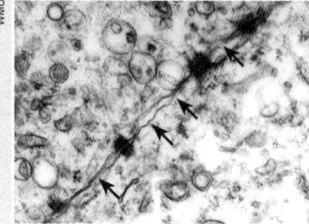

The cell is surrounded by a **plasma membrane** which controls the movement of most substances into and out of the cell. This photo shows two neighboring cells (arrows).

The Fluid Mosaic Model

The currently accepted model for the structure of membranes is called the **fluid mosaic model**. In this model there is a double layer of lipids (fats) which are arranged with their 'tails' facing inwards. The double layer of lipids is thought to be quite fluid, with proteins 'floating' in this layer. The mobile proteins are thought to have a number of functions, including a role in active transport.

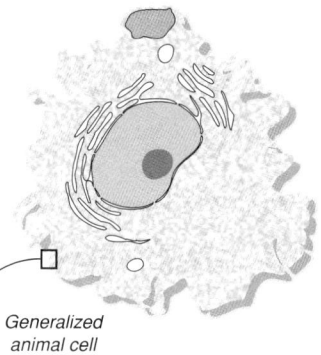

Glycoproteins (proteins with attached carbohydrate chains) play an important role in cellular recognition and the immune response, and act as receptors for hormones and neurotransmitters. Together with glycolipids, they stabilize membrane structure.

Some proteins completely penetrate the lipid layer. These proteins may control the entry and removal of specific molecules from the cell.

Generalized animal cell

Like glycoproteins, **glycolipids** act as surface receptors and stabilize the membrane.

Double layer of phospholipids (the lipid bilayer).

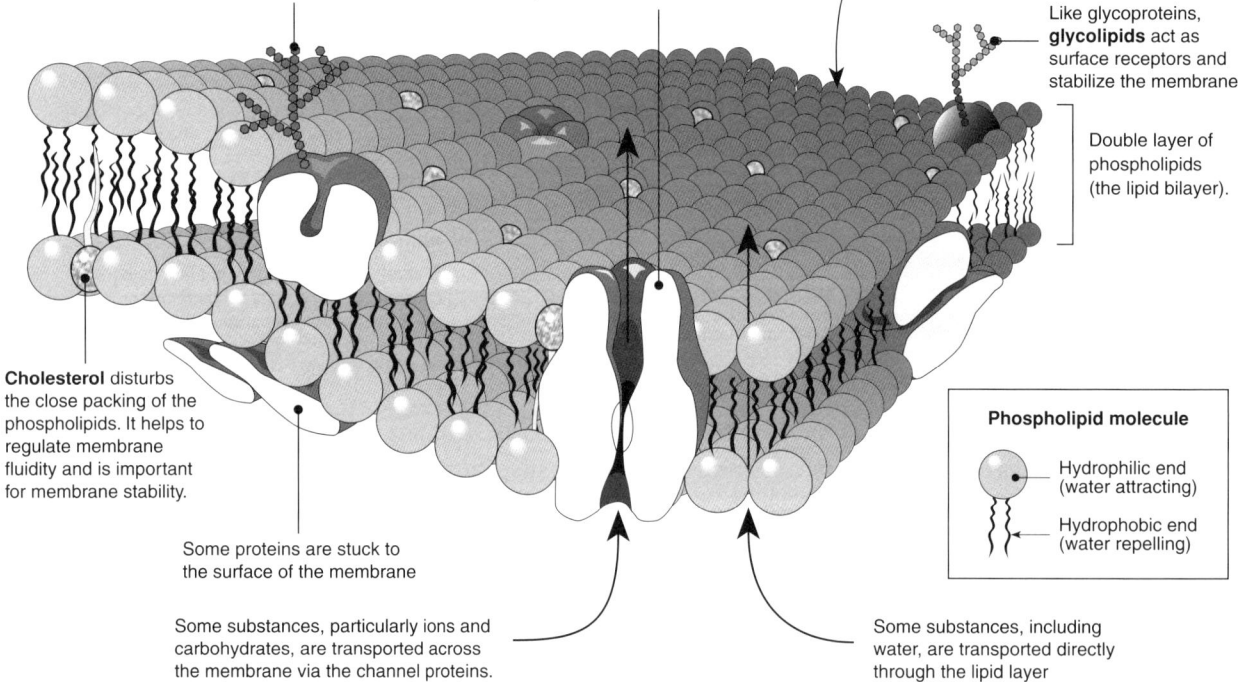

Cholesterol disturbs the close packing of the phospholipids. It helps to regulate membrane fluidity and is important for membrane stability.

Some proteins are stuck to the surface of the membrane

Some substances, particularly ions and carbohydrates, are transported across the membrane via the channel proteins.

Some substances, including water, are transported directly through the lipid layer

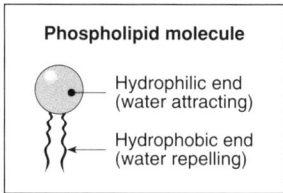

Phospholipid molecule

Hydrophilic end (water attracting)

Hydrophobic end (water repelling)

1. Briefly describe what membranes are made of: _____

_____

2. Name two general functions that membranes have in cells: _____

_____

3. (a) Name a cellular organelle that possesses a membrane: _____

    (b) Describe the membrane's purpose in this organelle: _____

4. Name three other cell organelles that are made up of membrane systems:

    (a) _____

    (b) _____

    (c) _____

5. (a) State the purpose of cholesterol in plasma membranes: _____

    _____

    (b) Suggest why marine organisms living in polar regions have a very high proportion of cholesterol in their membranes:

    _____

    _____

6. Describe how the modern fluid mosaic model of membrane structure differs from the earlier Davson-Danielli model:

    _____

    _____

7. List three substances that need to be transported **into** all kinds of animal cells, in order for them to survive:

    (a) _____

    (b) _____

    (c) _____

8. List two substances that need to be transported **out** of all kinds of animal cells, in order for them to survive:

    (a) _____

    (b) _____

9. Use the symbol for a phospholipid molecule (below) to draw a **simple labeled diagram** to show the structure of a plasma membrane (include features such as lipid bilayer and various kinds of proteins):

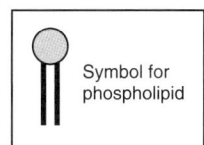

Symbol for phospholipid

The Role of Membranes in Cells

Many of the important structures and organelles in cells are composed of, or are enclosed by, membranes. These include: the endoplasmic reticulum, mitochondria, nucleus, Golgi apparatus, chloroplasts, lysosomes, vesicles and the plasma membrane itself. All membranes within eukaryotic cells share the same basic structure as the plasma membrane that encloses the entire cell. They perform a number of critical functions in the cell: serving to compartmentalize regions of different function within the cell, controlling the entry and exit of substances, and fulfilling a role in recognition and communication between cells. Some of these roles are described below. The role of membranes in the production of macromolecules (e.g. proteins) is shown opposite:

Isolation of enzymes Membrane-bound lysosomes contain enzymes for the destruction of wastes and foreign material. Peroxisomes are the site for destruction of the toxic and reactive molecule, hydrogen peroxide (formed as a result of some cellular reactions).

Role in lipid synthesis
The smooth ER is the site of lipid and steroid synthesis.

Containment of DNA
The nucleus is surrounded by a nuclear envelope of two membranes, forming a separate compartment for the cell's genetic material.

Role in protein synthesis
Some protein synthesis occurs on free ribosomes, but much occurs on membrane-bound ribosomes on the rough endoplasmic reticulum. Here the protein is synthesized directly into the space within the ER membranes.

Entry and export of substances The plasma membrane may take up fluid or solid material and form membrane-bound vesicles (or larger vacuoles) within the cell. Membrane-bound transport vesicles move substances to the inner surface of the cell where they can be exported from the cell by exocytosis.

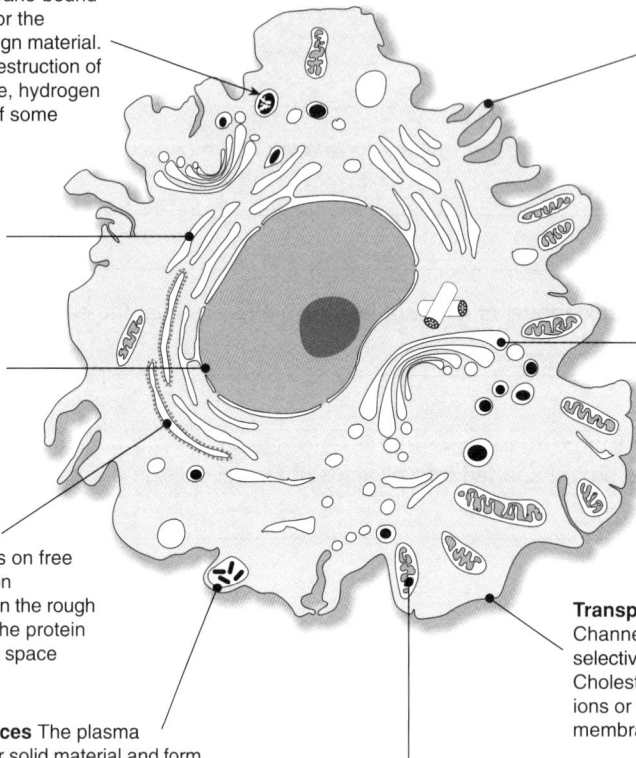

Cell communication and recognition
The proteins embedded in the membrane act as receptor molecules for hormones and neurotransmitters. Glycoproteins and glycolipids stabilize the plasma membrane and act as cell identity markers, helping cells to organize themselves into tissues, and enabling foreign cells to be recognized.

Packaging and secretion
The Golgi apparatus is a specialized membrane-bound organelle which produces lysosomes and compartmentalizes the modification, packaging, and secretion of substances such as proteins and hormones.

Transport processes
Channel and carrier proteins are involved in selective transport across the plasma membrane. Cholesterol in the membrane can help to prevent ions or polar molecules from passing through the membrane (acting as a plug).

Energy transfer The reactions of cellular respiration (and photosynthesis in plants) take place in the membrane-bound energy transfer systems occurring in mitochondria and chloroplasts respectively. See the example explained below.

Compartmentation Within Membranes

Membranes play an important role in separating regions within the cell (and within organelles) where particular reactions occur. Specific enzymes are therefore often located in particular organelles. The reaction rate is controlled by controlling the rate at which substrates enter the organelle and therefore the availability of the raw materials required for the reactions.

Example (right): *The enzymes involved in cellular respiration are arranged in different parts of the mitochondria. Reactions are localized and separated by membrane systems.*

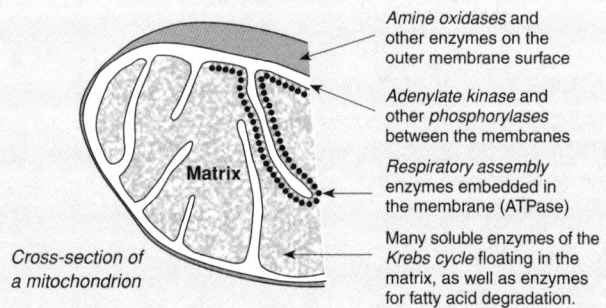

Amine oxidases and other enzymes on the outer membrane surface

Adenylate kinase and other *phosphorylases* between the membranes

Respiratory assembly enzymes embedded in the membrane (ATPase)

Many soluble enzymes of the *Krebs cycle* floating in the matrix, as well as enzymes for fatty acid degradation.

Matrix

Cross-section of a mitochondrion

1. Explain the crucial role of membrane systems and organelles in the following:

   (a) Providing compartments within the cell: _____

   _____

   _____

   (b) Increasing the total membrane surface area within the cell: _____

   _____

   _____

   _____

Cells produce a range of **macromolecules** – organic polymers made up of repeating units of smaller molecules. The synthesis, packaging and movement of these molecules inside the cell involves a number of membrane bound organelles, as indicated below. These organelles provide compartments where the enzyme systems involved can be isolated.

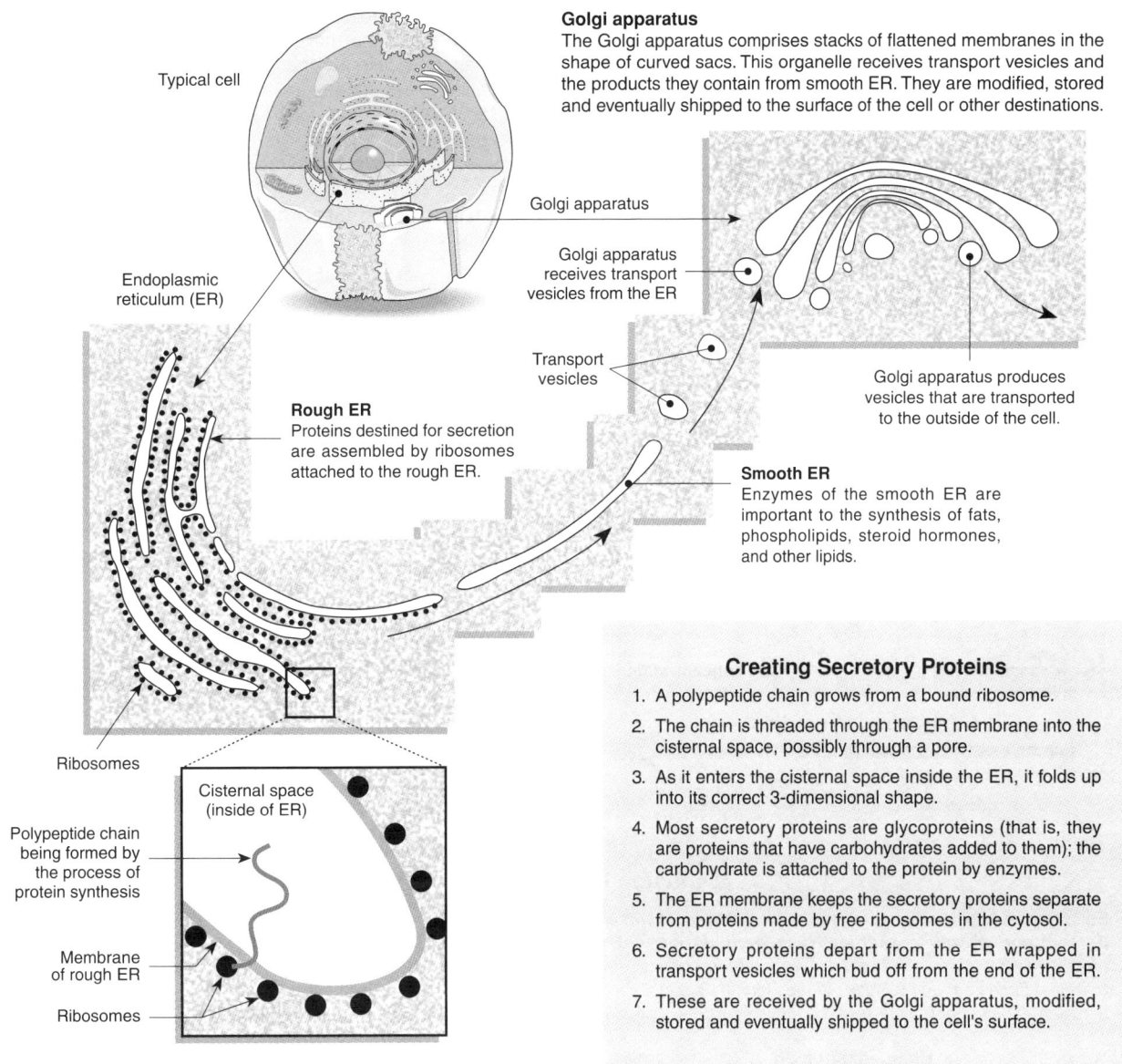

Golgi apparatus
The Golgi apparatus comprises stacks of flattened membranes in the shape of curved sacs. This organelle receives transport vesicles and the products they contain from smooth ER. They are modified, stored and eventually shipped to the surface of the cell or other destinations.

Typical cell

Golgi apparatus

Golgi apparatus receives transport vesicles from the ER

Endoplasmic reticulum (ER)

Transport vesicles

Golgi apparatus produces vesicles that are transported to the outside of the cell.

Rough ER
Proteins destined for secretion are assembled by ribosomes attached to the rough ER.

Smooth ER
Enzymes of the smooth ER are important to the synthesis of fats, phospholipids, steroid hormones, and other lipids.

Ribosomes

Cisternal space (inside of ER)

Polypeptide chain being formed by the process of protein synthesis

Membrane of rough ER

Ribosomes

Creating Secretory Proteins
1. A polypeptide chain grows from a bound ribosome.
2. The chain is threaded through the ER membrane into the cisternal space, possibly through a pore.
3. As it enters the cisternal space inside the ER, it folds up into its correct 3-dimensional shape.
4. Most secretory proteins are glycoproteins (that is, they are proteins that have carbohydrates added to them); the carbohydrate is attached to the protein by enzymes.
5. The ER membrane keeps the secretory proteins separate from proteins made by free ribosomes in the cytosol.
6. Secretory proteins depart from the ER wrapped in transport vesicles which bud off from the end of the ER.
7. These are received by the Golgi apparatus, modified, stored and eventually shipped to the cell's surface.

2. Explain the importance of the following components of plasma membranes:

(a) Glycoproteins and glycolipids: _____

(b) Channel proteins and carrier proteins: _____

3. Explain how cholesterol can play a role in membrane transport: _____

4. Non-polar (lipid-soluble) molecules diffuse more rapidly through membranes than polar (lipid-insoluble) molecules:

(a) Explain the reason for this: _____

(b) Discuss the implications of this to the transport of substances into the cell through the plasma membrane: _____

Diffusion and Osmosis

The molecules that make up substances are constantly moving in a random way. This motion causes molecules to disperse from areas of high to low concentration; a process called **diffusion**. The molecules move along a **concentration gradient**. **Osmosis** is the term describing the diffusion of water along its concentration gradient across a **partially permeable membrane**. It is the principal mechanism by which water enters and leaves cells in living organisms. Diffusion and osmosis are **passive** processes, and use no energy. Diffusion occurs freely across membranes, as long as the membrane is permeable to that molecule. Each type of molecule diffuses along its own concentration gradient; diffusion of molecules in one direction does not hinder the movement of other molecules. Diffusion is important in allowing exchanges with the environment and in the regulation of cell water content.

*NOTE: Students and teachers requiring coverage of **water potential** can download an alternative three page series of activities from*: **www.thebiozone.com/waterpotential.html**

Diffusion of Molecules Along Concentration Gradients

Diffusion is the movement of particles from regions of high to low concentration (the **concentration gradient**), with the end result being that the molecules become evenly distributed. In biological systems, diffusion often occurs across partially permeable membranes. Various factors determine the rate at which this occurs (see right).

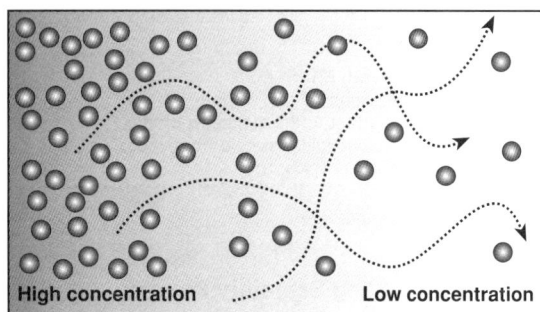

High concentration   **Low concentration**

Concentration gradient

If molecules are free to move, they move from high to low concentration until they are evenly dispersed.

Factors affecting rates of diffusion	
Concentration gradient:	Diffusion rates will be higher when there is a greater difference in concentration between two regions.
The distance involved:	Diffusion over shorter distances occurs at a greater rate than diffusion over larger distances.
The area involved:	The larger the area across which diffusion occurs, the greater the rate of diffusion.
Barriers to diffusion:	Thicker barriers slow diffusion rate. Pores in a barrier enhance diffusion.

These factors are expressed in **Fick's law**, which governs the rate of diffusion of substances within a system. It is described by:

$$\frac{\text{Surface area of membrane} \quad X \quad \text{Difference in concentration across the membrane}}{\text{Length of the diffusion path (thickness of the membrane)}}$$

Diffusion through Membranes

Each type of diffusing molecule (gas, solvent, solute) moves **along its own concentration gradient**. Two-way diffusion (below) is common in biological systems e.g. at the lung surface, carbon dioxide diffuses out and oxygen diffuses into the blood. Facilitated diffusion (below, right) increases the diffusion rate selectively and is important for larger molecules (e.g. glucose, amino acids) where a higher diffusion rate is desirable (e.g. transport of glucose into skeletal muscle fibres, transport of ADP into mitochondria). Neither type of diffusion requires energy expenditure because the molecules are not moving against their concentration gradient.

Unaided diffusion

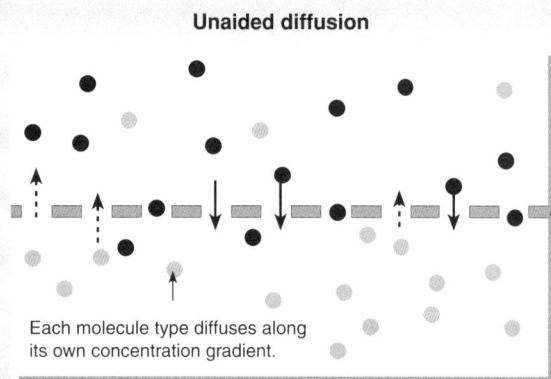

Partially permeable membrane

Each molecule type diffuses along its own concentration gradient.

Diffusion rates depend on the concentration gradient. Diffusion can occur in either direction but **net** movement is in the direction of the concentration gradient. An equilibrium is reached when concentrations are equal.

Facilitated diffusion

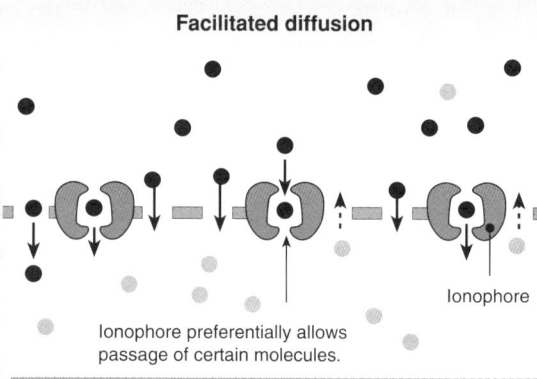

Ionophore

Ionophore preferentially allows passage of certain molecules.

Facilitated diffusion occurs when a substance is aided across a membrane by a special molecule called an **ionophore**. Ionophores allow some molecules to diffuse but not others, effectively speeding up the rate of diffusion of that molecule.

1. Define the term **diffusion**: _____

_____

2. Describe two properties of an exchange surface that would facilitate rapid diffusion rates:

(a) _____ (b) _____

Osmosis and the Concentration of Water in Cells

Osmosis is simply the diffusion of water molecules from high concentration to lower concentration, across a partially permeable membrane. *"Water always diffuses from regions of lower solute concentration to regions of higher solute concentration"* (i.e. from higher concentration of water molecules to lower concentration of water molecules). When the external solute concentration is the same as that of the cell there is no net movement of water. Two systems (cell and environment) with the same solute concentration are termed **isotonic**. The diagram below illustrates two situations: when the external solute concentration is lower than the cell (**hypotonic**) and when it is higher than the cell (**hypertonic**).

Plasmolysis in a plant cell

Hypertonic salt solution

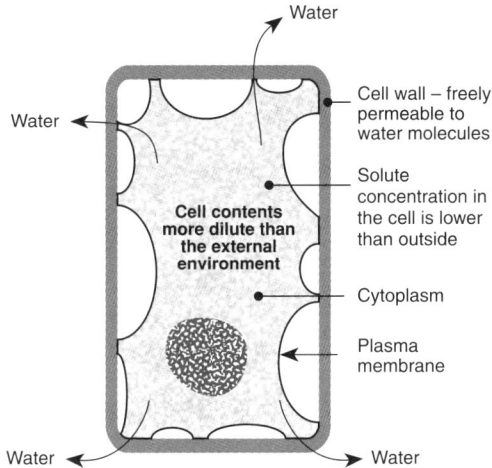

In a **hypertonic** solution, the external solute concentration is higher than the solute concentration of the cell. Water leaves the cell and, because the cell wall is rigid, the plasma membrane shrinks away from the cell wall. This process is termed **plasmolysis** and the cell becomes **flaccid** (turgor pressure =0). Full plasmolysis is irreversible – the cell cannot recover by taking up water.

Turgor in a plant cell

Pure water (hypotonic)

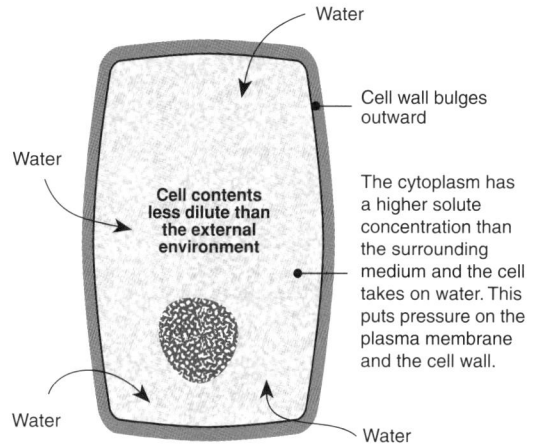

In a **hypotonic** solution, the external solute concentration is lower than that of the cell cytoplasm. Water enters the cell causing it to swell. A wall (turgor) pressure is generated when enough water has been taken up to cause the cell contents to press against the cell wall. Turgor pressure rises until it offsets further net influx of water. The rigid wall prevents rupture. Cells in this state are called **turgid**.

3. Identify one way in which organisms maintain concentration gradients across membranes:

4. State how facilitated diffusion is achieved:

5. Name two biological processes where diffusion plays an important role:

   (a) _____ (b) _____

6. Explain the role of cell wall pressure in generating cell turgor in plants:

7. Explain how animal cells differ from plant cells with respect to the effects of net water movements:

8. Describe what would happen to an animal cell (e.g. a red blood cell) if it was placed into:

   (a) Pure water:

   (b) A hypertonic solution:

9. Fluid replacements are usually provided for heavily perspiring athletes after endurance events:

   (a) Identify the preferable tonicity of these replacement drinks (isotonic/hypertonic/hypotonic):

   (b) Give a reason for your answer:

DA① # Surface Area and Volume

When an object (e.g. a cell) is small it has a large surface area in comparison to its volume. In this case diffusion will be an effective way to transport materials (e.g. gases) into the cell. As an object becomes larger, its surface area compared to its volume is smaller. Diffusion is no longer an effective way to transport materials to the inside. For this reason, there is a physical limit for the size of a cell, with the effectiveness of diffusion being the controlling factor.

Diffusion in Organisms of Different Sizes

Respiratory gases and some other substances are exchanged with the surroundings by diffusion or active transport across the plasma membrane.

The **plasma membrane**, which surrounds every cell, functions as a selective barrier that regulates the cell's chemical composition. For each square micrometer of membrane, only so much of a particular substance can cross per second.

The surface area of an elephant is increased, for radiating body heat, by large flat ears.

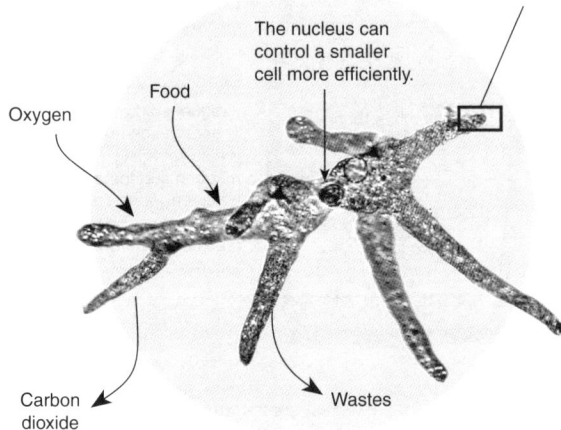

The nucleus can control a smaller cell more efficiently.

Food

Oxygen

A specialized gas exchange surface (lungs) and circulatory (blood) system are required to speed up the movement of substances through the body.

Carbon dioxide

Wastes

Respiratory gases cannot reach body tissues by diffusion alone.

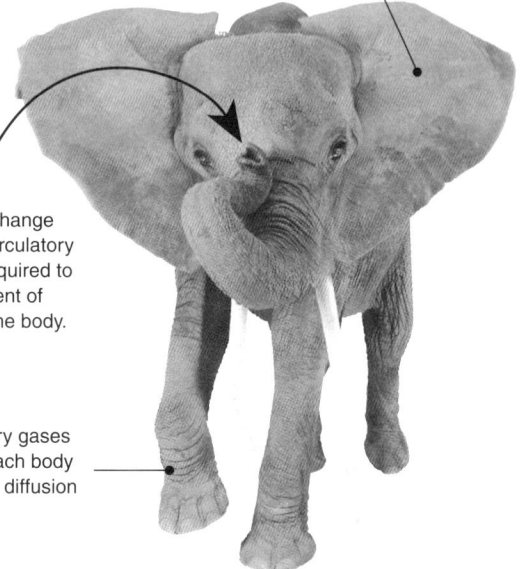

Amoeba: The small size of the single-celled amoeba provides a large surface area compared to the cell's volume. This is adequate for many materials to be moved into and out of the cell by diffusion or active transport.

Multicellular organisms: To overcome the problems of small cell size, plants and animals became multicellular. They provide a small surface area compared to their volume but have evolved various adaptive features to improve their effective surface area.

Smaller is Better for Diffusion

One large cube

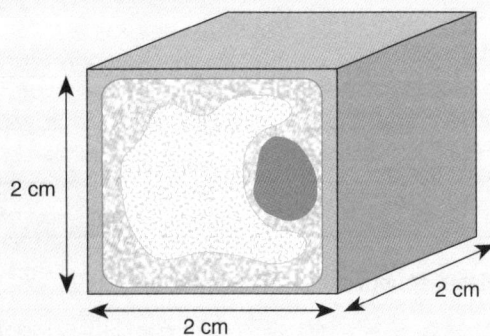

2 cm

2 cm

2 cm

Volume: = 8 cm^3
Surface area: = 24 cm^2

Eight small cubes

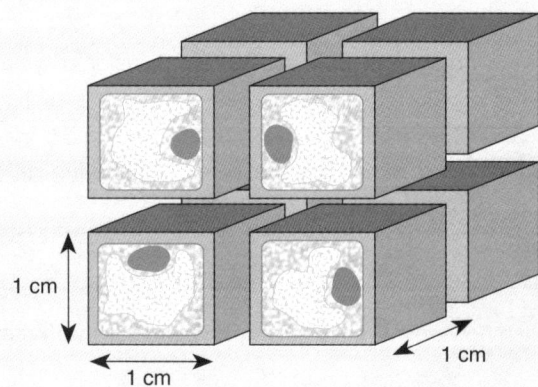

1 cm

1 cm

1 cm

Volume: = 8 cm^3 for 8 cubes
Surface area: = 6 cm^2 for 1 cube
= 48 cm^2 for 8 cubes

The eight small cells and the single large cell have the same total volume, but their surface areas are different. The small cells together have twice the total surface area of the large cell, because there are more exposed (inner) surfaces. Real organisms have complex shapes, but the same principles apply.

The surface-area volume relationship has important implications for processes involving transport into and out of cells across membranes. For activities such as gas exchange, the surface area available for diffusion is a major factor limiting the rate at which oxygen can be supplied to tissues.

The diagram below shows four imaginary cells of different sizes (cells do not actually grow to this size, their large size is for the sake of the exercise). They range from a small 2 cm cube to a larger 5 cm cube. This exercise investigates the effect of cell size on the efficiency of diffusion.

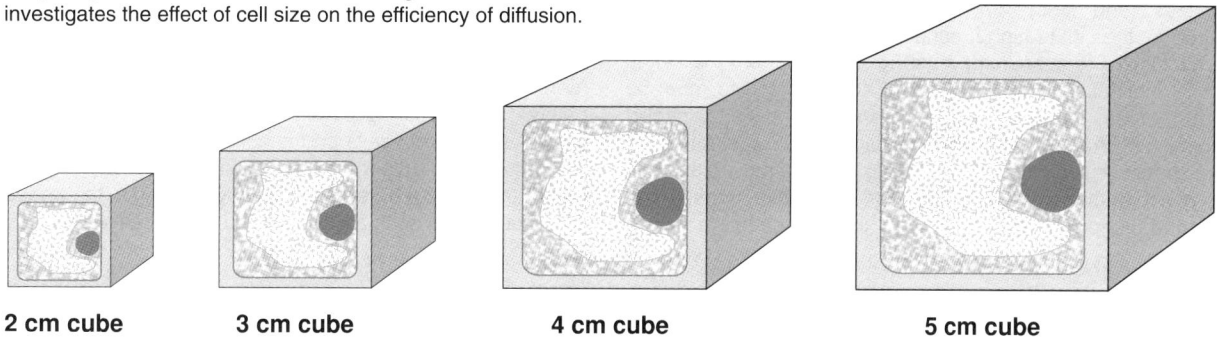

2 cm cube   **3 cm cube**   **4 cm cube**   **5 cm cube**

1. Calculate the volume, surface area and the ratio of surface area to volume for each of the four cubes above (the first has been done for you). When completing the table below, show your calculations.

Cube size	Surface area	Volume	Surface area / volume ratio
2 cm cube	$2 \times 2 \times 6 = 24\,cm^2$ (2 cm x 2 cm x 6 sides)	$2 \times 2 \times 2 = 8\,cm^3$ (height x width x depth)	$24\ to\ 8 = 3{:}1$
3 cm cube			
4 cm cube			
5 cm cube			

2. Create a graph, plotting the surface area against the volume of each cube, on the grid on the right. Draw a line connecting the points and label axes and units.

3. State which increases the fastest with increasing size - the **volume** or **surface area**.

_____

4. Explain what happens to the ratio of surface area to volume with increasing size.

_____

_____

_____

_____

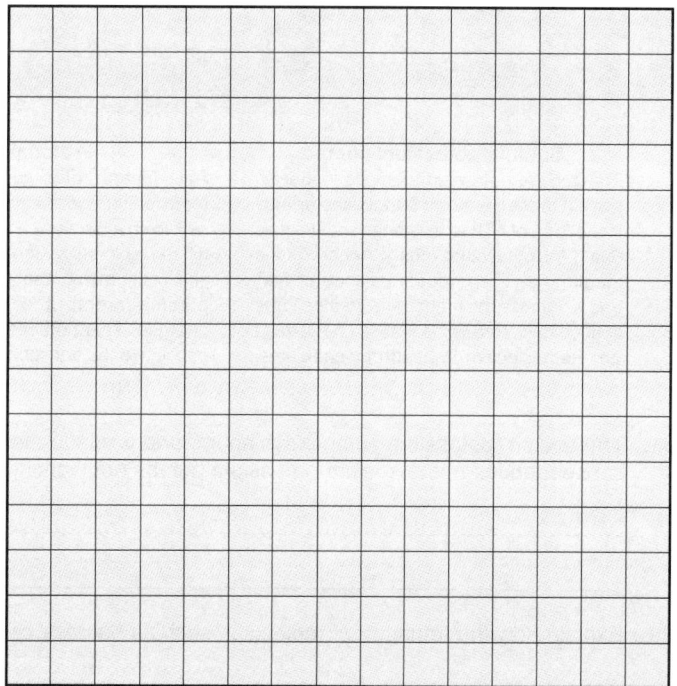

5. Diffusion of substances into and out of a cell occurs across the cell surface. Describe how increasing the size of a cell will affect the ability of diffusion to transport materials into and out of a cell:

_____

_____

_____

_____

Ion Pumps

A 2

Diffusion alone cannot supply the cell's entire requirements for molecules (and ions). Some molecules (e.g. glucose) are required by the cell in higher concentrations than occur outside the cell. Others (e.g. sodium) must be removed from the cell in order to maintain cell fluid balance. These molecules must be moved across the plasma membrane by active transport mechanisms. **Active transport** requires the expenditure of energy because the molecules (or ions) must be moved **against** their concentration gradient. The work of active transport is performed by specific carrier proteins in the membrane. These transport proteins harness the energy of ATP to pump molecules from a low to a high concentration. When ATP transfers a phosphate group to the carrier protein, the protein changes its shape in such a way as to move the bound molecule across the membrane. Three types of membrane pump are illustrated below. The sodium-potassium pump (below, left) is almost universal in animal cells and is common in plant cells also. The concentration gradient created by ion pumps such as this and the proton pump (center) is frequently coupled to the transport of other molecules such as glucose and sucrose (below, right).

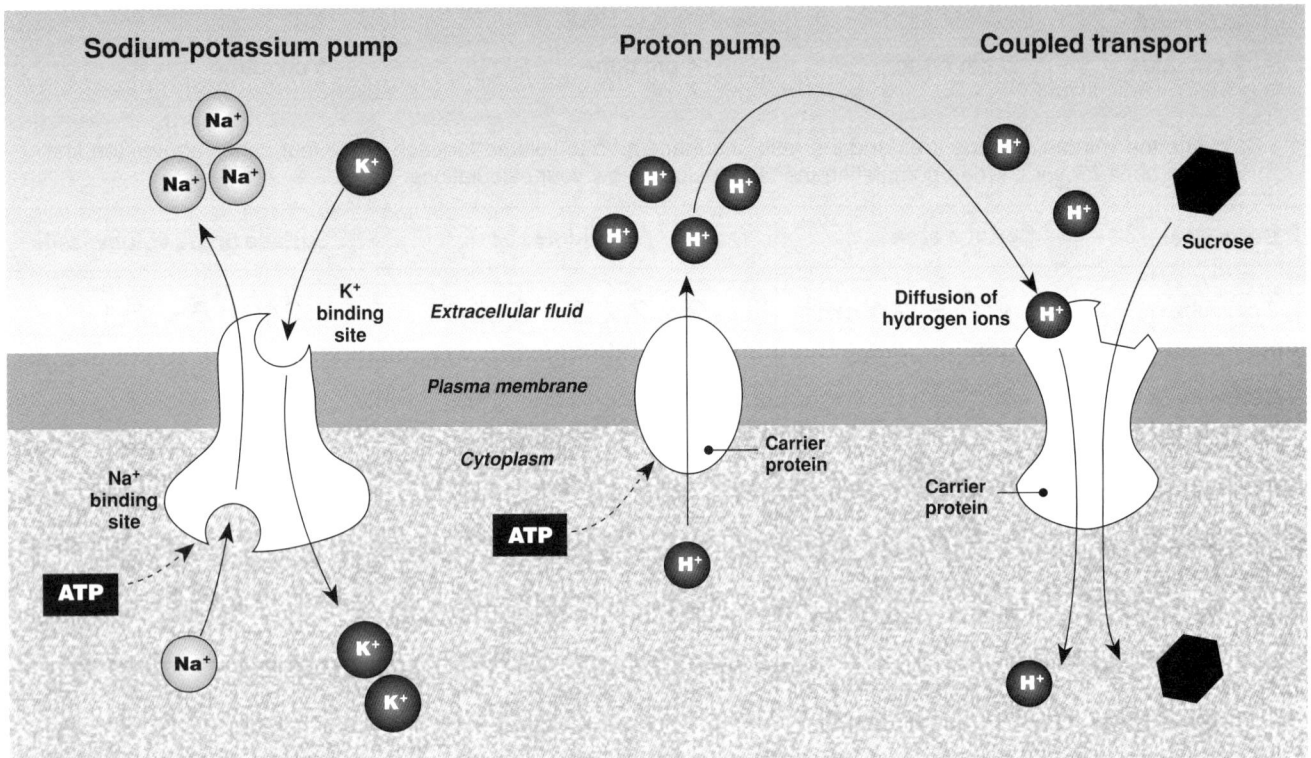

Sodium-potassium pump
The sodium-potassium pump is a specific protein in the membrane that uses energy in the form of ATP to exchange sodium ions (Na^+) for potassium ions (K^+) across the membrane. The unequal balance of Na^+ and K^+ across the membrane creates large concentration gradients that can be used to drive other active transport mechanisms.

Proton pumps
ATP driven proton pumps use energy to remove hydrogen ions (H^+) from inside the cell to the outside. This creates a large difference in the proton concentration either side of the membrane, with the inside of the plasma membrane being negatively charged. This potential difference can be coupled to the transport of other molecules.

Coupled transport (cotransport)
Plant cells use the gradient in hydrogen ions created by proton pumps to drive the active transport of nutrients into the cell. The specific transport protein couples the return of H^+ to the transport of sucrose into the phloem cells. The sucrose rides with the H^+ as it diffuses down the concentration gradient maintained by the proton pump.

1. The sodium-potassium pump plays an important role in the water balance of cells. In terms of osmosis, explain the consequences of the sodium-potassium pumps not working:

   _____

   _____

2. Explain how the transport of molecules such as sucrose can be coupled to the activity of an ion exchange pump:

   _____

   _____

3. Explain why the ATP is required for membrane pump systems to operate: _____

   _____

   _____

4. Name a type of cell that relies on coupled transport to perform its function: _____

Exocytosis and Endocytosis

Most cells carry out **cytosis**: a form of **active transport** involving the in- or outfolding of the plasma membrane. The ability of cells to do this is a function of the flexibility of the plasma membrane. Cytosis results in the bulk transport into or out of the cell and is achieved through the localized activity of microfilaments and microtubules in the cell cytoskeleton. Engulfment of material is

termed **endocytosis.** Endocytosis typically occurs in protozoans and certain white blood cells of the mammalian defense system (e.g neutrophils, macrophages). **Exocytosis** is the reverse of endocytosis and involves the release of material from vesicles or vacuoles that have fused with the plasma membrane. Exocytosis is typical of cells that export material (secretory cells).

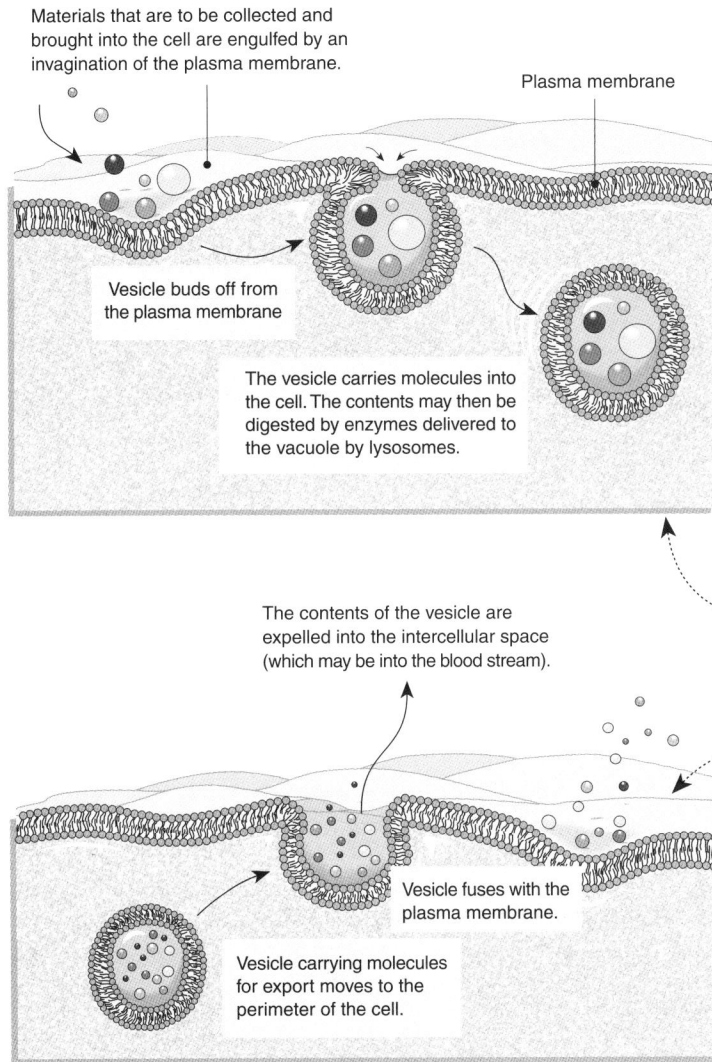

Materials that are to be collected and brought into the cell are engulfed by an invagination of the plasma membrane.

Plasma membrane

Vesicle buds off from the plasma membrane

The vesicle carries molecules into the cell. The contents may then be digested by enzymes delivered to the vacuole by lysosomes.

The contents of the vesicle are expelled into the intercellular space (which may be into the blood stream).

Vesicle fuses with the plasma membrane.

Vesicle carrying molecules for export moves to the perimeter of the cell.

Endocytosis

Endocytosis (left) occurs by invagination (infolding) of the plasma membrane, which then forms vesicles or vacuoles that become detached and enter the cytoplasm. There are two main types of endocytosis:

Phagocytosis: "cell-eating"
Examples: Feeding method of *Amoeba*, phagocytosis of foreign material and cell debris by neutrophils and macrophages. Phagocytosis involves the engulfment of **solid material** and results in the formation of vacuoles (e.g. food vacuoles).

Pinocytosis: "cell-drinking"
Examples: Uptake in many protozoa, some cells of the liver, and some plant cells. Pinocytosis involves the uptake of **liquids** or fine suspensions and results in the formation of pinocytic vesicles.

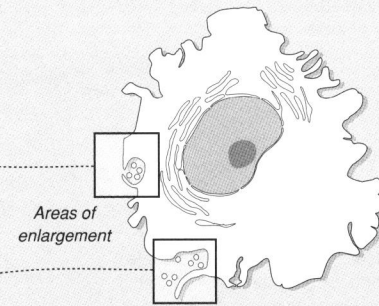

Areas of enlargement

Exocytosis

Exocytosis (left) is the reverse process to endocytosis. In multicellular organisms, various types of cells are specialised to manufacture and export products (e.g. proteins) from the cell to elsewhere in the body or outside it. Exocytosis occurs by fusion of the vesicle membrane and the plasma membrane, followed by release of the vesicle contents to the outside of the cell.

1. Distinguish between **phagocytosis** and **pinocytosis**: _____

2. Describe an example of phagocytosis and identify the cell type involved: _____

3. Describe an example of exocytosis and identify the cell type involved: _____

4. Explain why cytosis is affected by changes in oxygen level, whereas diffusion is not: _____

5. Identify the processes by which the following substances enter a living macrophage:

(a) Oxygen: _____ (c) Water: _____

(b) Cellular debris: _____ (d) Glucose: _____

RA❶ Active and Passive Transport

Cells need to transport substances: the raw materials necessary for metabolism must be accumulated from the extracellular environment, and wastes and molecules for use elsewhere must be exported from the cell. Some substances (e.g. gases and water) move into and out of the cell by **passive transport** processes, without the expenditure of energy. Other molecules (e.g. sucrose) are moved against their concentration gradients using **active transport**. Active transport processes involve the expenditure of energy in the form of ATP (and in aerobic organisms, therefore the use of oxygen also). The diagram below provides a summary of the various passive and active transport processes described earlier in this chapter.

Passive Transport

Diffusion
Molecules of liquids, dissolved solids, and gases are able to move into or out of a cell without any expenditure of energy. These molecules move because they follow a **concentration gradient**.

Molecules

Facilitated diffusion
Diffusion involving a carrier system but without any energy expenditure.

Water

Osmosis
Water can also follow a concentration gradient, across a **partially permeable membrane**, by diffusion. This is called **osmosis**. Osmosis causes cells in fresh water to puff up as water seeps in. This water must be continually expelled.

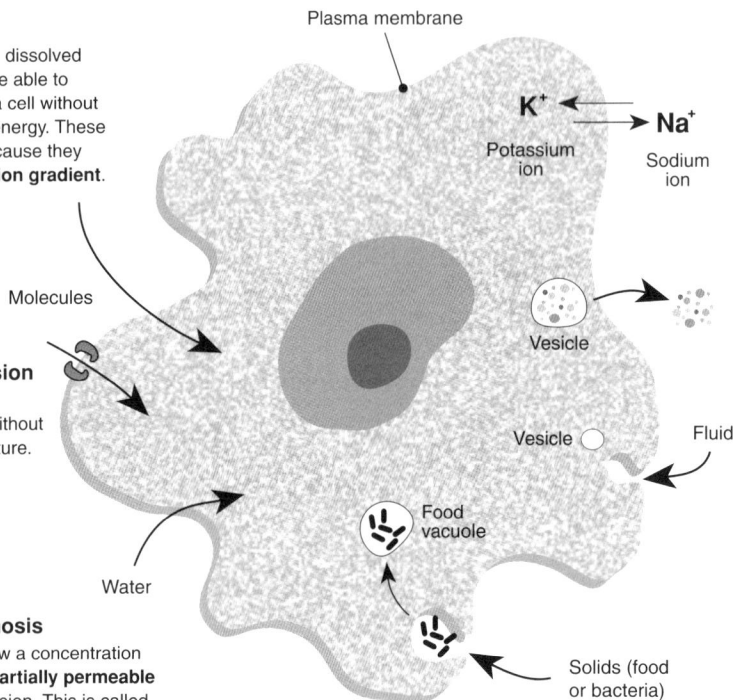

Plasma membrane

K^+ ⟵⟶ Na^+
Potassium ion   Sodium ion

Vesicle

Vesicle ○   Fluid

Food vacuole

Solids (food or bacteria)

Active Transport

Ion pumps
Some cells need to control the amount of a certain ion inside the cell. Proteins in the plasma membrane can actively accumulate specific ions on one side of the membrane.

Exocytosis
Vesicles budded off from the Golgi apparatus or endoplasmic reticulum can fuse with the plasma membrane, expelling their contents. Common in secretory cells e.g. in glands.

Pinocytosis
Ingestion of a fluid or a suspension into the cell. The plasma membrane encloses some of the fluid and pinches off to form a vesicle.

Phagocytosis
Ingestion of solids from outside the cell. The plasma membrane encloses a particle and buds off to form a vacuole. Lysosomes will fuse with it to enable digestion of the contents.

1. In general terms, describe the energy requirements of **passive** and **active** transport: _____

_____

_____

2. Name **two** gases that move into or out of our bodies by **diffusion**: _____

_____

3. Name a gland which has cells where **exocytosis** takes place for the purpose of secretion:

_____

4. **Phagocytosis** is a process where solid particles are enveloped by the cell membrane and drawn inside the cell.

   (a) Name a protozoan that would use this technique for feeding: _____

   (b) Describe how it uses the technique: _____

   _____

   _____

   (c) Name a type of cell found in human blood that uses this technique for capturing and destroying bacteria:

   _____

Cellular Energetics

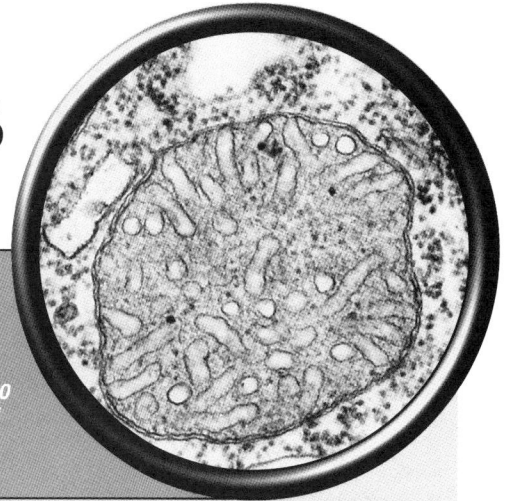

IB SL
Complete nos:
1-3, 6-10, 12-13, 17-18, 22-23, 25, 29
Extension:
4, 21

IB HL
Complete nos:
1-4, 6-12, 14-18, 22-30
Extension:
19-21

IB Options
Complete nos:
Option C: 14-16, 24, 26-28, 30

AP Biology
Complete nos:
1-12, 13 or 14, 15-30
31 as extension if required

Learning Objectives

☐ 1. Compile your own glossary from the **KEY WORDS** displayed in **bold type** in the learning objectives below.

The role of ATP (pages 115-116)

☐ 2. Explain the need for energy in living things and the universal role of ATP in **metabolism**, as illustrated by specific examples e.g. **glycolysis**, **active transport**, **anabolic reactions**, movement, and thermoregulation.

☐ 3. Describe the structure of **ATP** as a phosphorylated nucleotide. Describe its synthesis from ADP and inorganic hosphate (P_i) and explain how it stores and releases its energy.

☐ 4. Recall the role of enzymes in the control of **metabolic pathways** as illustrated by specific examples (e.g. in photosynthesis and cellular respiration).

☐ 5. Recall what is meant by the terms **endergonic** and **exergonic**. Provide examples of endergonic and exergonic reactions in biological systems.

☐ 6. Outline the principles involved in **photosynthesis** and **cellular respiration**, explaining in which way the two processes can be considered opposites.

☐ 7. Appreciate that both photosynthesis and cellular respiration involve the molecule **ATP** and hydrogen carriers, and identify these for each process.

Cellular respiration (pages 115-120)

Introduction to respiration

☐ 8. Draw and label the structure of a **mitochondrion**, including the **matrix**, the outer and inner membrane and the **cristae**. Explain the relationship between the structure of the mitochondrion and its function.

☐ 9. Identify the main steps in cellular respiration: **glycolysis**, **Krebs cycle** (*tricarboxylic acid cycle*) **electron transport system** (*electron transport chain, ETS, or respiratory chain*). On a diagram of a mitochondrion, indicate where each stage occurs. Recognise glycolysis as first stage in cellular respiration and the major anaerobic pathway in cells.

☐ 10. Identify **glucose** as the main respiratory substrate. Appreciate that other substrates can, through conversion, act as substrates for cellular respiration.

☐ 11. Describe the central role of **acetyl CoA** in carbohydrate and fat metabolism.

☐ 12. Outline **glycolysis** as the phosphorylation of glucose and the subsequent splitting of a 6C sugar into two triose phosphate molecules (2 X **pyruvate**). State the net yield of ATP and $NADH_2$ from glycolysis and appreciate that the subsequent metabolism of pyruvate depends on the availability of oxygen.

Aerobic respiration

☐ 13. Describe the complete oxidation of glucose to CO_2, with reference to:
- The conversion of pyruvate to **acetyl-coenzyme A**.
- The stepwise oxidation of intermediates.
- Generation of **ATP** in the electron transport chain.
- The role of oxygen as the terminal electron acceptor and the formation of water.
- The net yield of ATP from aerobic respiration compared to the yield from glycolysis.

☐ 14. Describe the complete oxidation of glucose to CO_2, with reference to:
- The conversion of pyruvate to **acetyl-coenzyme A**.
- The entry of acetyl CoA into the Krebs cycle by combination with **oxaloacetate**.
- The **Krebs cycle** (as a series of oxidation reactions involving release of CO_2, the production of $NADH_2$ or $FADH_2$, and the regeneration of oxaloacetate).
- The *role* of the coenzymes NAD and FAD.
- In simple terms, the synthesis of **ATP** by **oxidative phosphorylation** in the electron transport chain.
- The role of oxygen as the terminal electron acceptor and the formation of water.
- The net yield of ATP from aerobic respiration compared to the yield from glycolysis.

☐ 15. Explain oxidative phosphorylation in terms of **chemiosmosis** (the coupling of electron transport and the movement of hydrogen ions to the synthesis of ATP). Identify the role of the **electron carriers** and **ATP synthetase** (ATPase) in this process.

☐ 16. Understand the terms **decarboxylation** and **dehydrogenation** as they relate to the Krebs cycle.

Fermentation

☐ 17. Understand the situations in which the pyruvate formed in glycolysis may not undergo complete oxidation. Describe the following examples of **fermentation**, identifying the H^+ acceptor to each case:
(a) Formation of **lactic acid** in muscle.
(b) Formation of **ethanol** in yeast.

NOTE: Although fermentation is often used synonymously with anaerobic respiration, they are not the same. Respiration always involves hydrogen ions passing down a chain of carriers to a terminal acceptor, and this does not occur in fermentation. In anaerobic respiration, the terminal H^+ acceptor is a molecule other than oxygen, e.g. Fe^{2+} or nitrate.

☐ 18. Compare and explain the differences in the yields of ATP from aerobic respiration and from fermentation.

Respiratory quotients

☐ 19. Describe the relative energy values of carbohydrate, lipid, and protein as respiratory substrates. Explain the term **respiratory quotient** (RQ). Explain what RQ reveals about the substrate being respired.

☐ 20. Use a simple respirometer to measure RQ.

Photosynthesis *(pages 121-125)*

The structure of the dicot leaf

☐ 21. Recognise the leaf as the main photosynthetic organ in plants. Appreciate structural features of the dicot leaf related to its functional role. *See Senior Biology 2: Plant Science for coverage of this material.*

Chloroplasts

☐ 22. Describe the structure of **chloroplasts**, identifying the **stroma**, **grana**, lamellae (**thylakoids**), and location of the chlorophylls and other pigments. Relate the chloroplast structure you have described to function.

☐ 23. Describe the role of **chlorophyll a** and **b**, and **accessory pigments** (e.g. carotenoids) in light capture. Outline the differences in absorption of red, green, and blue light by chlorophyll.

☐ 24. In more detail than in #23 above, describe the absorption of light by **chlorophyll a** and **b**, and **accessory pigments**. In particular, explain what is meant by the terms **absorption spectrum** and **action spectrum** with respect to the light absorbing pigments.

Photosynthesis in C3 plants

Describe, using diagrams, the reactions of photosynthesis in a C3 plant with reference to:

☐ 25. The *light dependent phase (LDP)* with reference to:
  • Where in the chloroplast the LDP occurs.
  • The generation of ATP and NADPH2 for use in the light independent phase.

☐ 26. In more detail than in #25 above describe the light dependent phase (LDP) with reference to:
  • The location and role of the photosystems.
  • The **photoactivation** of chlorophyll.

  • The splitting of water (**photolysis**) to produce protons and electrons.
  • The production of O_2 as a result of photolysis.
  • The transfer of energy to ATP (photophosphorylation) and the formation of $NADPH_2$ (reduced NADP).

☐ 27. In greater detail than in #26 above, explain photophosphorylation in terms of **chemiosmosis** (the coupling of electron transport and the movement of hydrogen ions to the synthesis of ATP). Relate the accumulation of H^+ inside the thylakoid to the generation of ATP by **ATP synthetase** (ATPase).

☐ 28. Distinguish between cyclic and non-cyclic (photo)phosphorylation:
  • **Cyclic photophosphorylation**: electrons leaving photosystem I return to photosystem I with the generation of ATP but no $NADPH_2$.
  • **Non-cyclic photophosphorylation**: electrons leaving photosystem I are replaced by the photolysis of water by photosystem II with the generation of ATP and $NADPH_2$. This normal flow of electrons is linear from photosystem II to photosystem I.

☐ 29. The *light independent phase (LIP)* with reference to:
  • Where in the chloroplast the LIP occurs.
  • The **Calvin cycle** and the fixation of carbon dioxide using ATP and $NADPH_2$ generated in the light dependent phase.

☐ 30. In more detail than in #29 above describe the light independent phase (LIP) with reference to the **Calvin cycle** including the following:
  • The fixation of carbon dioxide into a 5C compound, **ribulose bisphosphate** (RuBP).
  • The reduction of **glycerate-3-phosphate** (PGA) to **carbohydrate** and the role of **ATP** and **NADPH$_2$** (formed in the light dependent phase) in this.
  • The regeneration of the ribulose bisphosphate.

☐ 31. Appreciate how scientific ideas and theories relating to the biochemistry of photosynthesis have developed. Relate the development of these ideas to our current understanding of the biochemistry of photosynthesis.

Textbooks

See the 'Textbook Reference Grid' on pages 8-9 for textbook page references relating to material in this topic.

Supplementary Texts

See pages 5-6 for additional details of this text:

■ Adds, J. *et al.*, 2001. **Respiration and Coordination** (NelsonThornes), pp. 1-8 (respiration).

Periodicals

See page 6 for details of publishers of periodicals:

STUDENT'S REFERENCE

Chlorophyll and photosynthesis

■ **Growing Plants in the Perfect Environment** Biol. Sci. Rev., 15(2) November 2002, pp. 12-16. *To manipulate the growth of plants in controlled environments, one must understand how plants grow and what influences photosynthetic rate.*

■ **Chlorophyll** Biol. Sci. Rev., 8(3) January 1996, pp. 28-30. *The chlorophyll molecule: how it absorbs light and its role in photosynthesis.*

■ **Why Don't Plants Wear Sunhats?** Biol. Sci. Rev., 9(3) Jan. 1997, pp. 32-35. *Plants need light, but too much is damaging - how do they cope?*

ATP and cellular respiration

■ **Fat Burns in the Flame of Carbohydrate** Biol. Sci. Rev., 15(3) February 2003, pp. 37-41. *A thorough account of both carbohydrate metabolism and how fatty acid oxidation feeds into the Krebs cycle. Starvation and ketosis are described and several points for discussion are included.*

■ **Glucose Catabolism** Biol. Sci. Rev., 10(3) January 1998, pp. 22-24. *The biological role of glucose in cells: oxidative phosphorylation and the role of mitochondria.*

TEACHER'S REFERENCE

■ **Learn about Cellular Respiration** The American Biology Teacher, 60(9) Nov. 1998, pp. 681-683. *Ideas on how to explore the concepts relating to cellular respiration.*

■ **The Bigger Picture** New Scientist, June 2000, pp. 54-61. *Understanding the complexity of biochemical pathways and the effects of altering genetic constitution.*

■ **Measuring the Metabolism of Small Organisms** Scientific American, December 1995, pp. 84-85. *Methods of measuring and monitoring respiration and metabolic rate in small organisms.*

■ **The Photosynthetic Dark Reactions do not Operate in the Dark** The American Biology Teacher, 62(3) March 2000, pp. 166-170. *This account explores the misconception that the 'dark'*

reactions occur in the dark: some of the the the enzymes are indirectly dependent on the light.

■ **Green Miracle** New Scientist, 14 August 1999, pp. 26-30. *The mechanism by which plants split water to make oxygen remains a mystery.*

Internet

See pages 10-11 for details of how to access **Bio Links** from our web site: **www.thebiozone.com**. From Bio Links, access sites under the topics:

GENERAL BIOLOGY ONLINE RESOURCES > **Online Textbooks and Lecture Notes**: • S-Cool! A level biology revision guide • Learn.co.uk • Mark Rothery's biology web site ... *and others*

CELL BIOLOGY AND BIOCHEMISTRY: • Cell and molecular biology online • MIT biology hypertextbook ... *and others* > **Biochemistry and Metabolic Pathways**: • Calvin cycle (C3 cycle) • Cellular energy references • Cellular respiration • Cycle (Krebs cycle, Citric Acid Cycle) • Electron transport chain • Energy, enzymes, and catalysis problem set • Glycolysis • Learning about photosynthesis • Chapter 7: Metabolism and biochemistry ... *and others*

Software and video resources are now provided in the Teacher Resource Handbook

Energy in Cells

RA❷

A summary of the flow of energy within a plant cell is illustrated below. Animal cells have a similar flow except the glucose is supplied by ingestion rather than by photosynthesis. The energy not immediately stored in chemical bonds is lost as heat. Note the role of ATP; it is made in cellular respiration and provides the energy for metabolic reactions, including photosynthesis.

Energy Transformations in a Photosynthetic Plant Cell

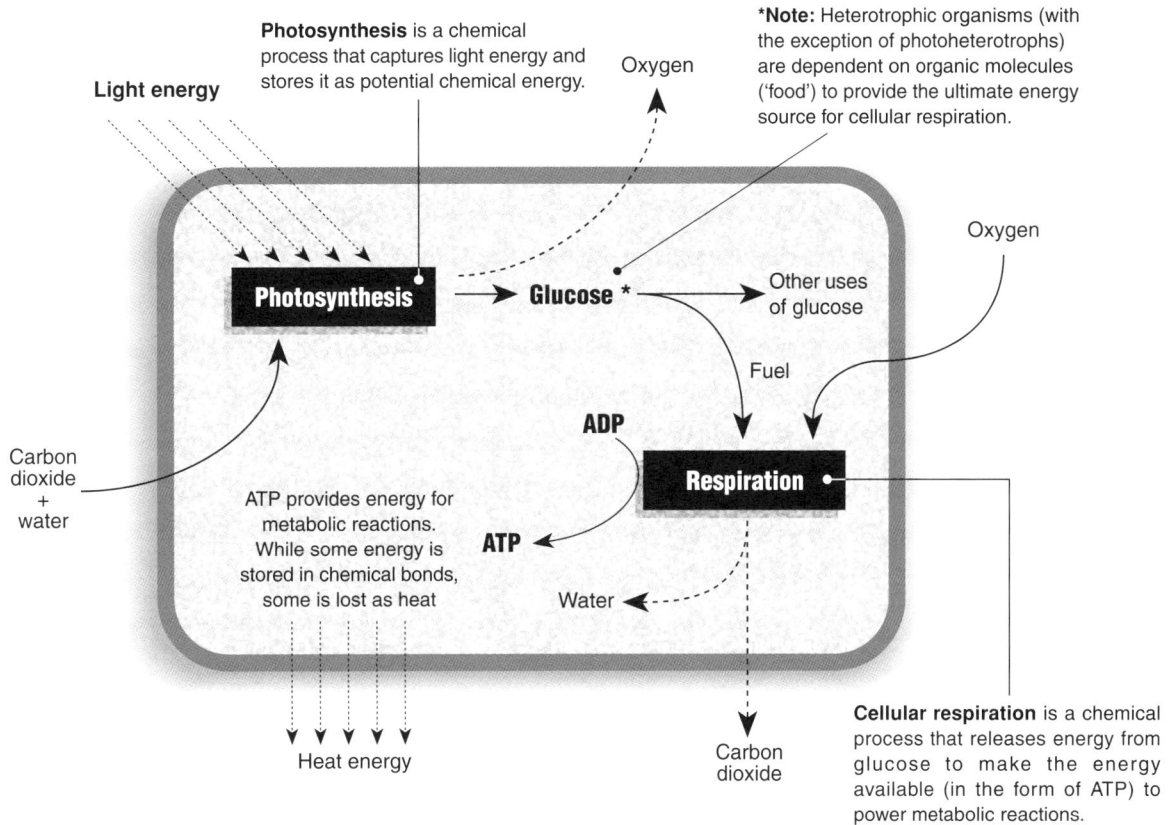

Photosynthesis is a chemical process that captures light energy and stores it as potential chemical energy.

Light energy

*Note: Heterotrophic organisms (with the exception of photoheterotrophs) are dependent on organic molecules ('food') to provide the ultimate energy source for cellular respiration.

Oxygen

Oxygen

Photosynthesis → **Glucose *** → Other uses of glucose

Fuel

Carbon dioxide + water

ADP

ATP provides energy for metabolic reactions. While some energy is stored in chemical bonds, some is lost as heat

ATP ←

Respiration

Water ←

Heat energy

Carbon dioxide

Cellular respiration is a chemical process that releases energy from glucose to make the energy available (in the form of ATP) to power metabolic reactions.

1. Define the following terms that classify how organisms derive their source of energy for metabolism:

   (a) Heterotrophs: _____

   _____

   (b) Photosynthetic autotrophs: _____

   _____

   (c) Chemosynthetic autotrophs: _____

   _____

2. In 1977, scientists working near the Galapagos Islands in the equatorial eastern Pacific found warm water spewing from cracks in the mid-oceanic ridges 2600 meters below the surface. Clustered around these hydrothermal vents were strange and beautiful creatures new to science. The entire community depends on sulfur-oxidizing bacteria that use hydrogen sulfide dissolved in the venting water as an energy source to manufacture carbohydrates. This process is similar to photosynthesis, but does not rely on sunlight to provide the energy for generating ATP and fixing carbon:

   (a) Explain why a community based on photosynthetic organisms is not found at this site: _____

   _____

   (b) Name the ultimate energy source for the bacteria: _____

   (c) This same chemical that provides the bacteria with energy is also toxic to the process of cellular respiration; a problem that the animals living in the habitat have resolved by evolving various adaptations. Explain what would happen if these animals did not possess adaptations to reduce the toxic effect on cellular respiration:

   _____

   (d) Name the energy source classification for these sulfur-oxidizing bacteria: _____

The Role of ATP in Cells

RA 2

The molecule ATP (adenosine triphosphate) is the universal energy carrier for the cell. ATP can release its energy quickly; only one chemical reaction (hydrolysis of the terminal phosphate) is required. This reaction is catalyzed by the enzyme ATPase. Once ATP has released its energy, it becomes ADP (adenosine diphosphate), a low energy molecule that can be recharged by adding a phosphate. This requires energy, which is supplied by the controlled breakdown of respiratory substrates in cellular respiration. The most common respiratory substrate is glucose, but other molecules (e.g., fats or proteins) may also be used.

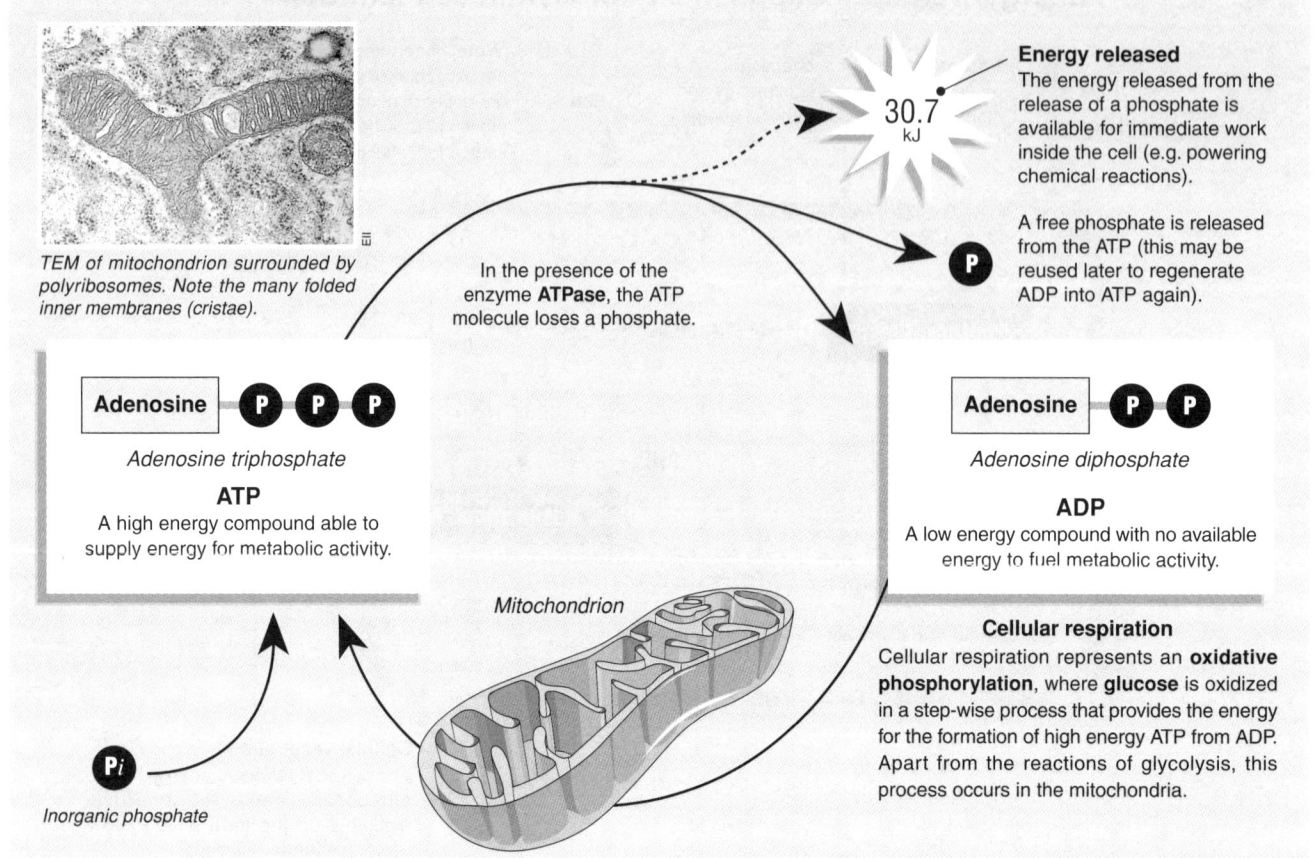

TEM of mitochondrion surrounded by polyribosomes. Note the many folded inner membranes (cristae).

Energy released
The energy released from the release of a phosphate is available for immediate work inside the cell (e.g. powering chemical reactions).

30.7 kJ

A free phosphate is released from the ATP (this may be reused later to regenerate ADP into ATP again).

In the presence of the enzyme **ATPase**, the ATP molecule loses a phosphate.

Adenosine P P P
Adenosine triphosphate
ATP
A high energy compound able to supply energy for metabolic activity.

Adenosine P P
Adenosine diphosphate
ADP
A low energy compound with no available energy to fuel metabolic activity.

Mitochondrion

Cellular respiration
Cellular respiration represents an **oxidative phosphorylation**, where **glucose** is oxidized in a step-wise process that provides the energy for the formation of high energy ATP from ADP. Apart from the reactions of glycolysis, this process occurs in the mitochondria.

P*i*
Inorganic phosphate

1. Describe how ATP acts as a supplier of energy to power metabolic reactions: _____

   _____

2. Name the **immediate** source of energy used to reform ATP from ADP molecules: _____

3. Name the process of re-energizing ADP into ATP molecules: _____

4. Name the **ultimate** source of energy for plants: _____

5. Name the **ultimate** source of energy for animals: _____

6. Explain in what way the ADP/ATP system can be likened to a rechargeable battery: _____

   _____

7. In the following table, use brief statements to contrast photosynthesis and respiration in terms of the following:

Feature	Photosynthesis	Cellular respiration
Starting materials		
Waste products		
Role of hydrogen carriers: NAD, NADP		
Role of ATP		
Overall biological role		

Measuring Respiration

In small animals or germinating seeds, the rate of cellular respiration can be measured using a simple respirometer: a sealed unit where the carbon dioxide produced by the respiring tissues is absorbed by soda lime and the volume of oxygen consumed is detected by fluid displacement in a manometer. Germinating seeds are also often used to calculate the **respiratory quotient** (RQ): the ratio of the amount of carbon dioxide produced during cellular respiration to the amount of oxygen consumed. RQ provides a useful indication of the respiratory substrate being used.

Respiratory Substrates and RQ

The respiratory quotient (RQ) can be expressed simply as:

$$RQ = \frac{CO_2 \text{ produced}}{O_2 \text{ consumed}}$$

When pure carbohydrate is oxidized in cellular respiration, the RQ is 1.0; more oxygen is required to oxidize fatty acids (RQ = 0.7). The RQ for protein is about 0.9. Organisms usually respire a mix of substrates, giving RQ values of between 0.8 and 0.9 (see table 1, below).

Using RQ to determine respiratory substrate

Fig. 1: RQ in relation to germination stage in wheat

Modified after Clegg and MacKean 1994

Fig. 1, above, shows how experimental RQ values have been used to determine the respiratory substrate utilized by germinating wheat seeds (*Triticum sativum*) over the period of their germination.

Table 1: RQ values for the respiration of various substrates

RQ	Substrate
> 1.0	Carbohydrate with some anaerobic respiration
1.0	Carbohydrates e.g. glucose
0.9	Protein
0.7	Fat
0.5	Fat with associated carbohydrate synthesis
0.3	Carbohydrate with associated organic acid synthesis

Table 2: Rates of O_2 consumption and CO_2 production in crickets

Time after last fed (h)	Temperature (°C)	Rate of O_2 consumption ($mlg^{-1}h^{-1}$)	Rate of CO_2 production ($mlg^{-1}h^{-1}$)
1	20	2.82	2.82
48	20	2.82	1.97
1	30	5.12	5.12
48	30	5.12	3.57

Table 2 shows the rates of oxygen consumption and carbon dioxide production of crickets kept under different experimental conditions.

1. Table 2 above shows the results of an experiment to measure the rates of oxygen consumption and carbon dioxide production of crickets 1 hour and 48 hours after feeding at different temperatures:

   (a) Calculate the RQ of a cricket kept at 20°C, 48 hours after feeding (show working): _____

   (b) Compare this RQ to the RQ value obtained for the cricket 1 hour after being fed (20°C). Explain the difference:

   _____

   _____

2. The RQs of two species of seeds were calculated at two day intervals after germination. Results are tabulated to the right:

   (a) Plot the change in RQ of the two species during early germination:

   (b) Explain the values in terms of the possible substrates being respired:

   _____

   _____

   _____

   _____

   _____

   _____

   _____

Days after germination	RQ	
	Seedling A	Seedling B
2	0.65	0.70
4	0.35	0.91
6	0.48	0.98
8	0.68	1.00
10	0.70	1.00

Cellular Respiration

Cellular respiration is the process by which organisms break down energy rich molecules (e.g. glucose) to release the energy in a useable form (ATP). All living cells respire in order to exist, although the substrates they use may vary. **Aerobic respiration** requires oxygen. Forms of cellular respiration that do not require

oxygen are said to be **anaerobic**. Some plants and animals can generate ATP anaerobically for short periods of time. Other organisms use only anaerobic respiration and live in oxygen-free environments. For these organisms, there is some other final electron acceptor other than oxygen (e.g. nitrate or Fe^{2+}).

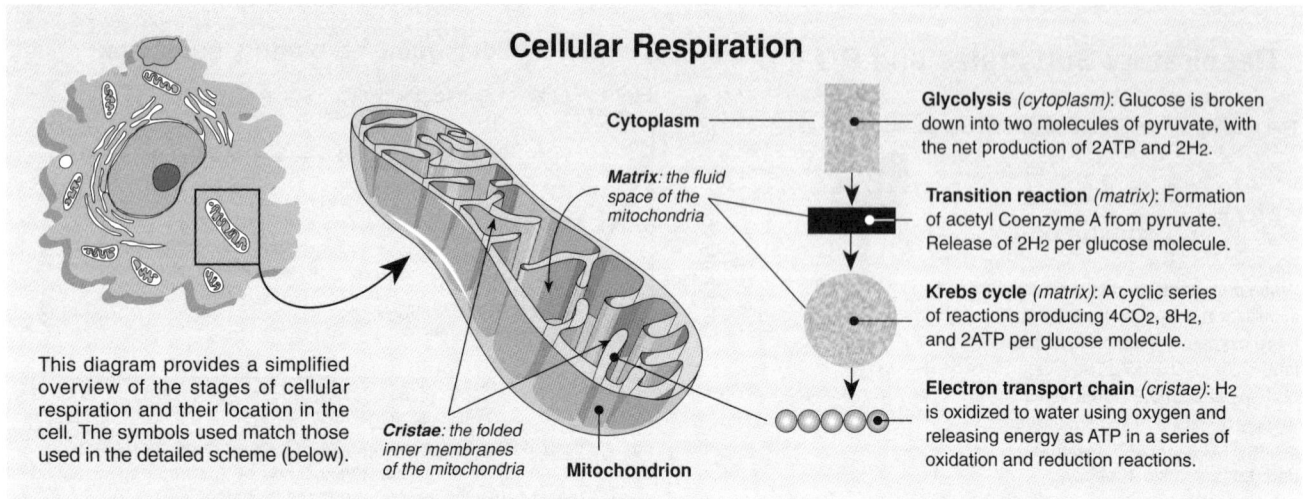

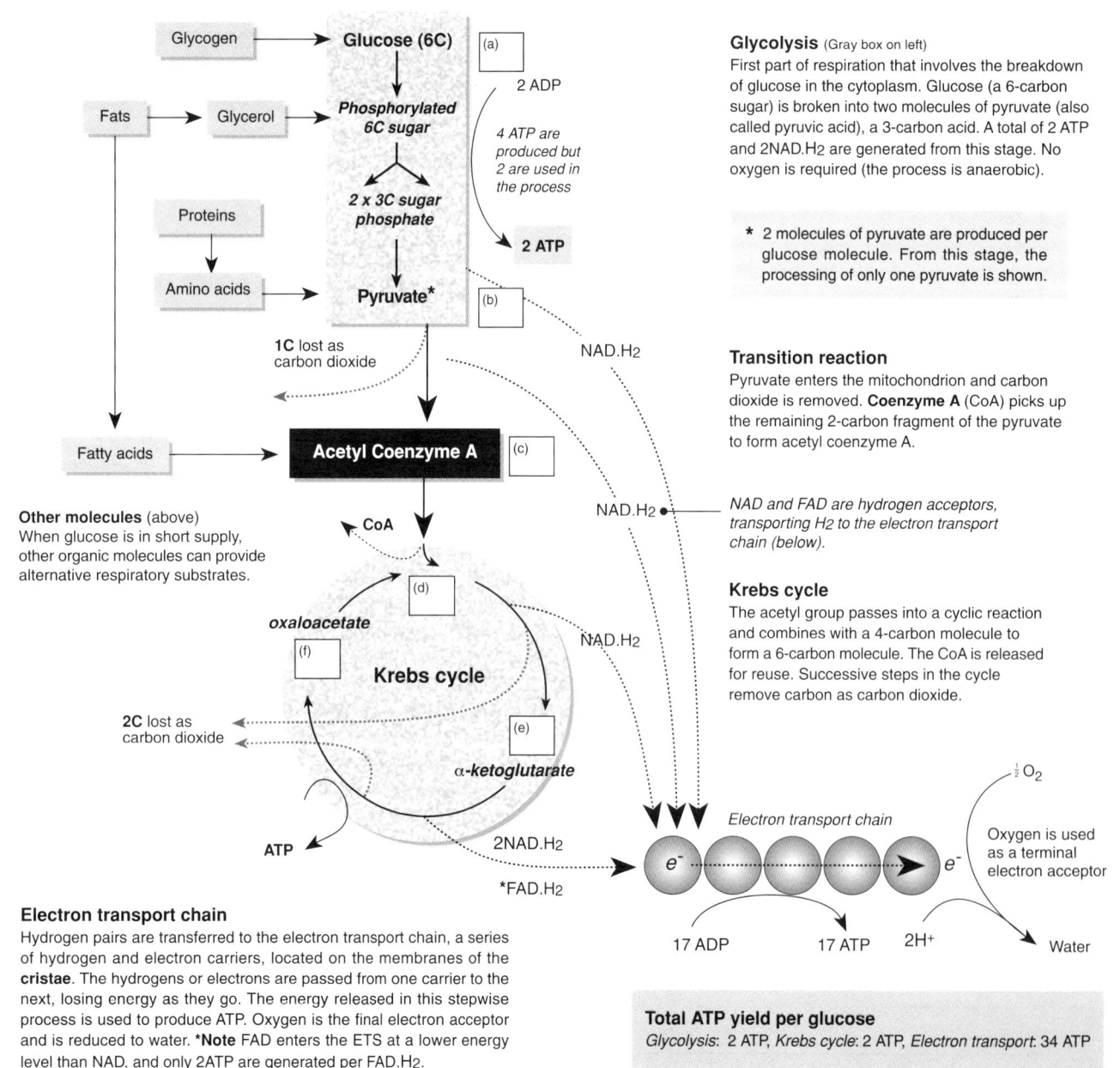

Cellular Respiration

Cytoplasm

Glycolysis *(cytoplasm)*: Glucose is broken down into two molecules of pyruvate, with the net production of 2ATP and $2H_2$.

Transition reaction *(matrix)*: Formation of acetyl Coenzyme A from pyruvate. Release of $2H_2$ per glucose molecule.

Krebs cycle *(matrix)*: A cyclic series of reactions producing $4CO_2$, $8H_2$, and 2ATP per glucose molecule.

Electron transport chain *(cristae)*: H_2 is oxidized to water using oxygen and releasing energy as ATP in a series of oxidation and reduction reactions.

Matrix: the fluid space of the mitochondria

This diagram provides a simplified overview of the stages of cellular respiration and their location in the cell. The symbols used match those used in the detailed scheme (below).

Cristae: the folded inner membranes of the mitochondria

Mitochondrion

Glycogen → **Glucose (6C)** (a)

Fats → Glycerol

Proteins

Amino acids →

Phosphorylated 6C sugar

2 x 3C sugar phosphate

Pyruvate* (b)

2 ADP

4 ATP are produced but 2 are used in the process

2 ATP

1C lost as carbon dioxide

NAD.H_2

Fatty acids → **Acetyl Coenzyme A** (c)

Other molecules (above)
When glucose is in short supply, other organic molecules can provide alternative respiratory substrates.

CoA

(d)

oxaloacetate

(f)

Krebs cycle

2C lost as carbon dioxide

(e)

α-*ketoglutarate*

ATP

2NAD.H_2

*FAD.H_2

NAD.H_2

NAD.H_2

Glycolysis (Gray box on left)
First part of respiration that involves the breakdown of glucose in the cytoplasm. Glucose (a 6-carbon sugar) is broken into two molecules of pyruvate (also called pyruvic acid), a 3-carbon acid. A total of 2 ATP and 2NAD.H_2 are generated from this stage. No oxygen is required (the process is anaerobic).

* 2 molecules of pyruvate are produced per glucose molecule. From this stage, the processing of only one pyruvate is shown.

Transition reaction
Pyruvate enters the mitochondrion and carbon dioxide is removed. **Coenzyme A** (CoA) picks up the remaining 2-carbon fragment of the pyruvate to form acetyl coenzyme A.

NAD and FAD are hydrogen acceptors, transporting H_2 to the electron transport chain (below).

Krebs cycle
The acetyl group passes into a cyclic reaction and combines with a 4-carbon molecule to form a 6-carbon molecule. The CoA is released for reuse. Successive steps in the cycle remove carbon as carbon dioxide.

Electron transport chain

e^- ····· → e^-

$\frac{1}{2}O_2$

Oxygen is used as a terminal electron acceptor

17 ADP   17 ATP $2H^+$ Water

Electron transport chain
Hydrogen pairs are transferred to the electron transport chain, a series of hydrogen and electron carriers, located on the membranes of the **cristae**. The hydrogens or electrons are passed from one carrier to the next, losing energy as they go. The energy released in this stepwise process is used to produce ATP. Oxygen is the final electron acceptor and is reduced to water. *Note FAD enters the ETS at a lower energy level than NAD, and only 2ATP are generated per FAD.H_2.

Total ATP yield per glucose
Glycolysis: 2 ATP, *Krebs cycle*: 2 ATP, *Electron transport*: 34 ATP

Chemiosmosis

Chemiosmosis is the process whereby the synthesis of ATP is coupled to electron transport and the movement of protons (H+ ions). **Electron transport carriers** are arranged over the inner membrane of the mitochondrion and oxidize NADH + H+ and FADH$_2$. Energy from this process forces protons to move, against their concentration gradient, from the mitochondrial matrix into the space between the two membranes. Eventually the protons flow back into the matrix via ATP synthetase molecules in the membrane. As the protons flow down their concentration gradient, energy is released and ATP is synthesized. Chemiosmotic theory also explains the generation of ATP in the light dependent phase of photosynthesis.

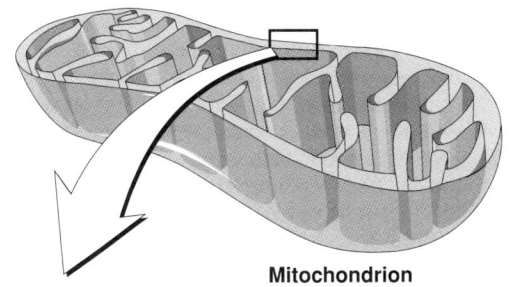

Mitochondrion

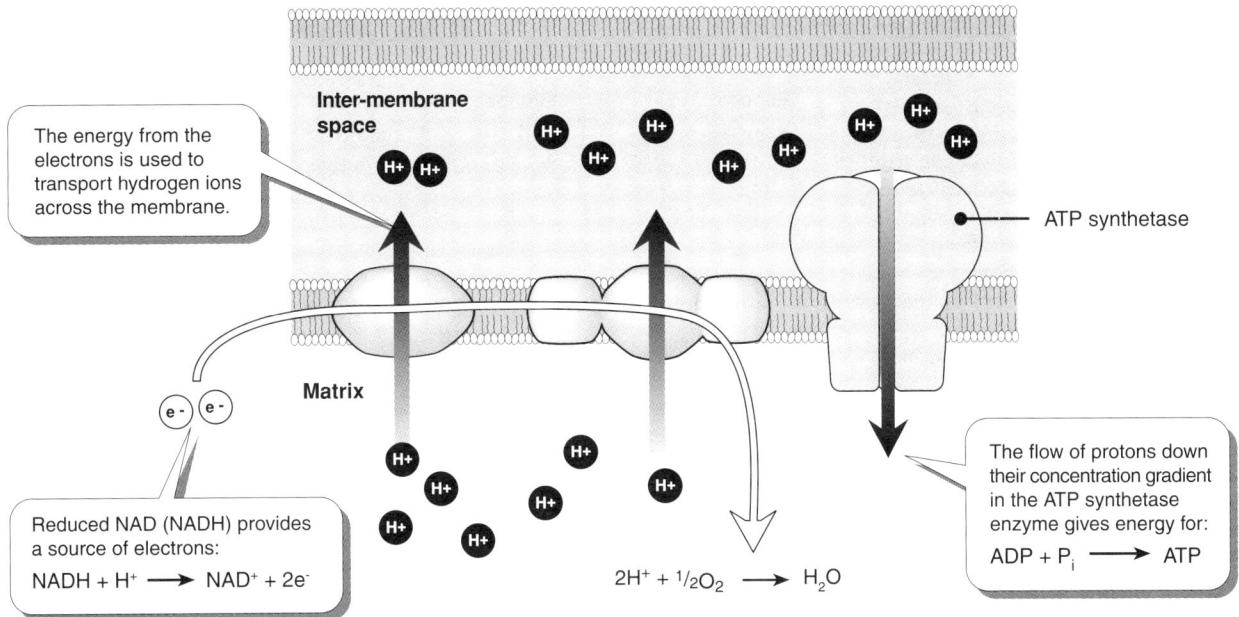

The energy from the electrons is used to transport hydrogen ions across the membrane.

Inter-membrane space

ATP synthetase

Matrix

Reduced NAD (NADH) provides a source of electrons:

$$NADH + H^+ \longrightarrow NAD^+ + 2e^-$$

$$2H^+ + \tfrac{1}{2}O_2 \longrightarrow H_2O$$

The flow of protons down their concentration gradient in the ATP synthetase enzyme gives energy for:

$$ADP + P_i \longrightarrow ATP$$

1. Describe precisely in which part of the cell the following take place:

    (a) Glycolysis: _____

    (b) Krebs cycle reactions: _____

    (c) Transition reaction: _____

    (d) Electron transport chain: _____

2. On the diagram of cellular respiration (previous page), state the number of carbon atoms in each of the molecules (a) – (f):

3. Determine how many ATP molecules **per molecule of glucose** are generated during the following stages of respiration:

    (a) Glycolysis: _____ (b) Krebs cycle: _____ (c) Electron transport chain: _____ (d) Total: _____

4. State what happens to the carbon atoms lost during respiration: _____

5. Describe the role of the following in aerobic cellular respiration:

    (a) Hydrogen atoms: _____

    _____

    (b) Oxygen: _____

    _____

6. (a) Name the process by which ATP is synthesized in respiration: _____

    (b) Briefly summarize this process: _____

    _____

    _____

    _____

RA 2   Anaerobic Pathways

All organisms can metabolize glucose anaerobically (without oxygen) using glycolysis in the cytoplasm, but the energy yield from this process is low and few organisms can obtain sufficient energy for their needs this way. In the absence of oxygen, glycolysis soon stops unless there is an alternative acceptor for the electrons produced from the glycolytic pathway. In yeasts and the root cells of higher plants this acceptor is ethanal, and the pathway is called alcoholic fermentation. In the skeletal muscle of mammals, the acceptor is pyruvate itself and the end product is lactic acid. In both cases, the duration of the fermentation is limited by the toxic effects of the organic compound produced. Although fermentation is often used synonymously with anaerobic respiration, they are not the same. Respiration always involves hydrogen ions passing down a chain of carriers to a terminal acceptor, and this does not occur in fermentation. In anaerobic respiration, the terminal H^+ acceptor is a molecule other than oxygen, e.g. Fe^{2+} or nitrate.

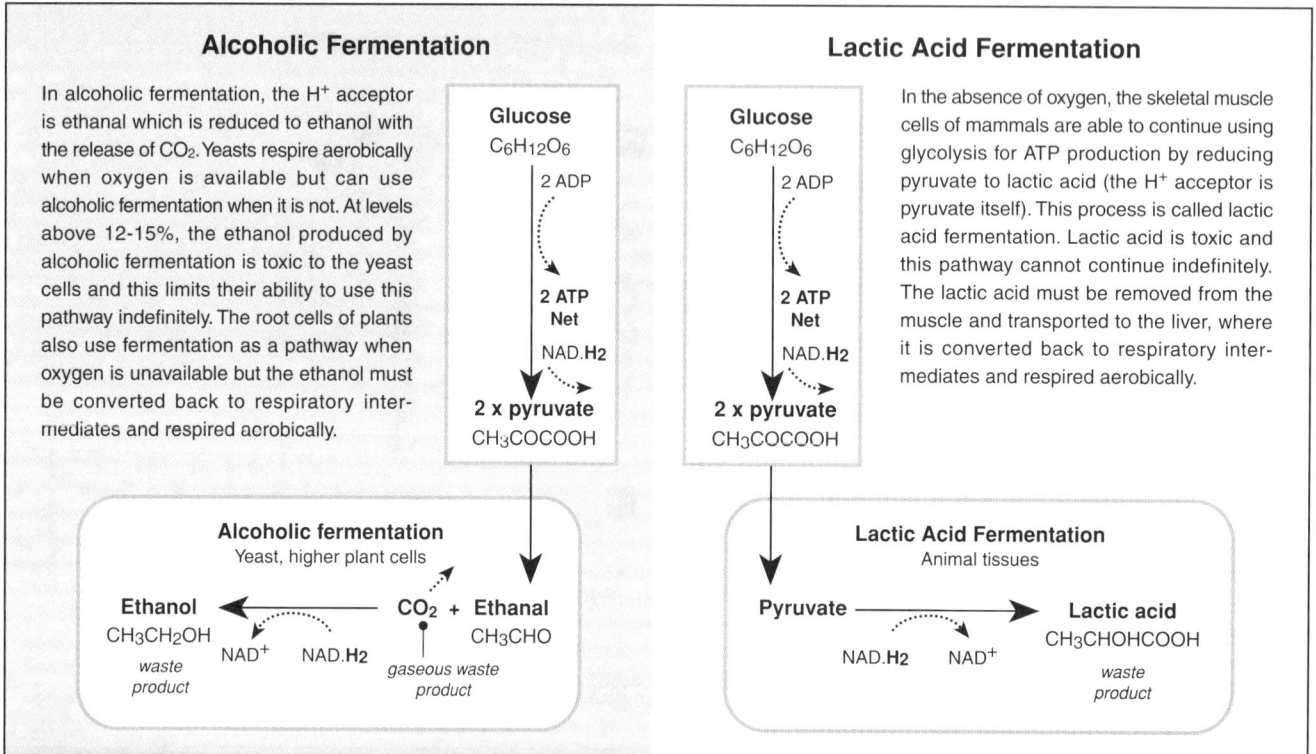

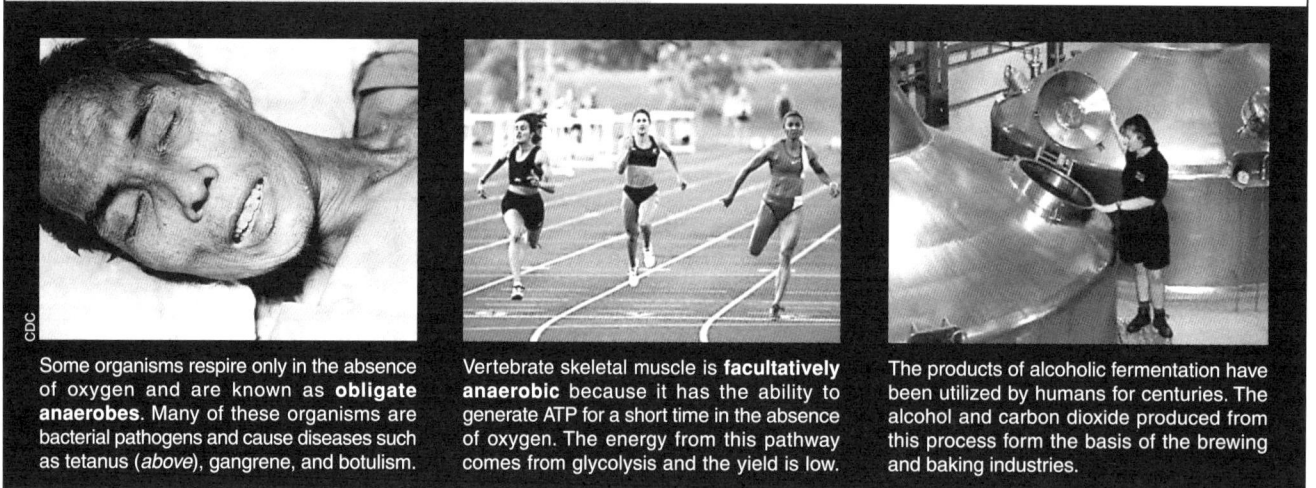

Alcoholic Fermentation

In alcoholic fermentation, the H^+ acceptor is ethanal which is reduced to ethanol with the release of CO_2. Yeasts respire aerobically when oxygen is available but can use alcoholic fermentation when it is not. At levels above 12-15%, the ethanol produced by alcoholic fermentation is toxic to the yeast cells and this limits their ability to use this pathway indefinitely. The root cells of plants also use fermentation as a pathway when oxygen is unavailable but the ethanol must be converted back to respiratory intermediates and respired aerobically.

Glucose
$C_6H_{12}O_6$

2 ADP

2 ATP Net

NAD.**H2**

2 x pyruvate
$CH_3COCOOH$

Alcoholic fermentation
Yeast, higher plant cells

Ethanol
CH_3CH_2OH
waste product

NAD^+ NAD.**H2**

CO_2 + Ethanal
CH_3CHO
gaseous waste product

Lactic Acid Fermentation

In the absence of oxygen, the skeletal muscle cells of mammals are able to continue using glycolysis for ATP production by reducing pyruvate to lactic acid (the H^+ acceptor is pyruvate itself). This process is called lactic acid fermentation. Lactic acid is toxic and this pathway cannot continue indefinitely. The lactic acid must be removed from the muscle and transported to the liver, where it is converted back to respiratory intermediates and respired aerobically.

Glucose
$C_6H_{12}O_6$

2 ADP

2 ATP Net

NAD.**H2**

2 x pyruvate
$CH_3COCOOH$

Lactic Acid Fermentation
Animal tissues

Pyruvate

NAD.**H2** NAD^+

Lactic acid
$CH_3CHOHCOOH$
waste product

Some organisms respire only in the absence of oxygen and are known as **obligate anaerobes**. Many of these organisms are bacterial pathogens and cause diseases such as tetanus (*above*), gangrene, and botulism.

Vertebrate skeletal muscle is **facultatively anaerobic** because it has the ability to generate ATP for a short time in the absence of oxygen. The energy from this pathway comes from glycolysis and the yield is low.

The products of alcoholic fermentation have been utilized by humans for centuries. The alcohol and carbon dioxide produced from this process form the basis of the brewing and baking industries.

1. Describe the key difference between aerobic respiration and fermentation: _____

_____

2. (a) Refer to page 118 and determine the efficiency of fermentation compared to aerobic respiration: _____ %

   (b) In simple terms, explain why the efficiency of anaerobic pathways is so low: _____

_____

3. Explain why fermentation cannot go on indefinitely: _____

_____

_____

Pigments and Light Absorption

As light meets matter, it may be reflected, transmitted, or absorbed. Substances that absorb visible light are called **pigments**, and different pigments absorb light of different wavelengths. The ability of a pigment to absorb particular wavelengths of light can be measured with a spectrophotometer. The light absorption vs the wavelength is called the **absorption spectrum** of that pigment. The absorption spectrum of different photosynthetic pigments provides clues to their role in photosynthesis, since light can only perform work if it is absorbed. An **action spectrum** profiles the effectiveness of different wavelength light in fuelling photosynthesis. It is obtained by plotting wavelength against some measure of photosynthetic rate (e.g. CO_2 production). Some features of photosynthetic pigments and their light absorbing properties are outlined below.

The Electromagnetic Spectrum

Light is a form of energy known as electromagnetic radiation. The segment of the electromagnetic spectrum most important to life is the narrow band between about 380 and 750 nanometres (nm). This radiation is known as visible light because it is detected as colors by the human eye (although some other animals, such as insects, can see in the ultraviolet range). It is the visible light that drives photosynthesis.

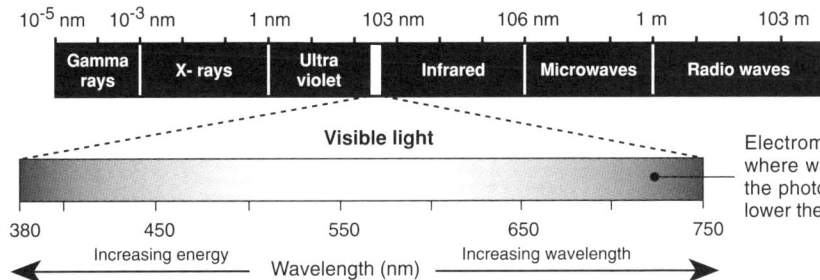

10^{-5} nm	10^{-3} nm	1 nm	103 nm	106 nm	1 m	103 m

| Gamma rays | X- rays | Ultra violet | | Infrared | Microwaves | Radio waves |

Visible light

380   450   550   650   750

Increasing energy ← Wavelength (nm) → Increasing wavelength

Electromagnetic radiation (EMR) travels in waves, where wavelength provides a guide to the energy of the photons; the greater the wavelength of EMR, the lower the energy of the photons in that radiation.

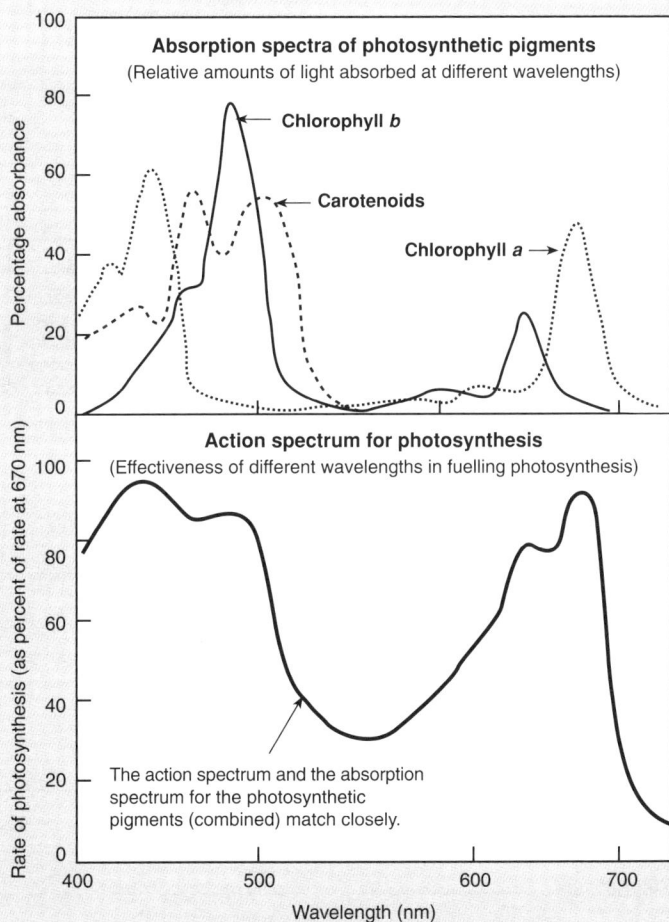

Absorption spectra of photosynthetic pigments
(Relative amounts of light absorbed at different wavelengths)

Percentage absorbance

Chlorophyll *b*

Carotenoids

Chlorophyll *a* →

Action spectrum for photosynthesis
(Effectiveness of different wavelengths in fuelling photosynthesis)

Rate of photosynthesis (as percent of rate at 670 nm)

The action spectrum and the absorption spectrum for the photosynthetic pigments (combined) match closely.

400   500   600   700

Wavelength (nm)

The Photosynthetic Pigments of Plants

The photosynthetic pigments of plants fall into two categories: **chlorophylls** (which absorb red and blue-violet light) and **carotenoids** (which absorb strongly in the blue-violet and appear orange, yellow, or red). The pigments are located on the chloroplast membranes (the thylakoids) and are associated with membrane transport systems.

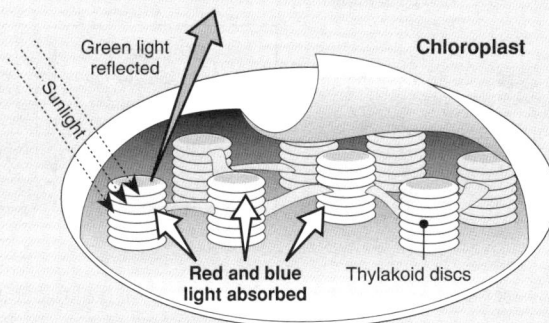

Green light reflected

Sunlight

Chloroplast

Red and blue light absorbed

Thylakoid discs

The pigments of chloroplasts in higher plants (above) absorb blue and red light, and the leaves therefore appear green (which is reflected). Each photosynthetic pigment has its own characteristic **absorption spectrum** (left, top graph). Although only chlorophyll *a* can participate directly in the light reactions of photosynthesis, the **accessory pigments** (chlorophyll *b* and carotenoids) can absorb wavelengths of light that chlorophyll *a* cannot. The accessory pigments pass the energy (photons) to chlorophyll *a*, thus broadening the spectrum that can effectively drive photosynthesis.

Left: Graphs comparing absorption spectra of photosynthetic pigments compared with the action spectrum for photosynthesis.

1. Explain what is meant by the absorption spectrum of a pigment: _____

_____

2. Explain why the action spectrum for photosynthesis does not exactly match the absorption spectrum of chlorophyll *a*:

_____

_____

Photosynthesis

Photosynthesis is of fundamental importance to living things because it transforms sunlight energy into chemical energy stored in molecules. This becomes part of the energy available in food chains. The molecules that trap the energy in their chemical bonds are also used as building blocks to create other molecules. Finally, photosynthesis releases free oxygen gas – essential for the survival of advanced life forms. Below is a diagram summarizing the process of photosynthesis.

Summary of Photosynthesis in a C₃ Plant

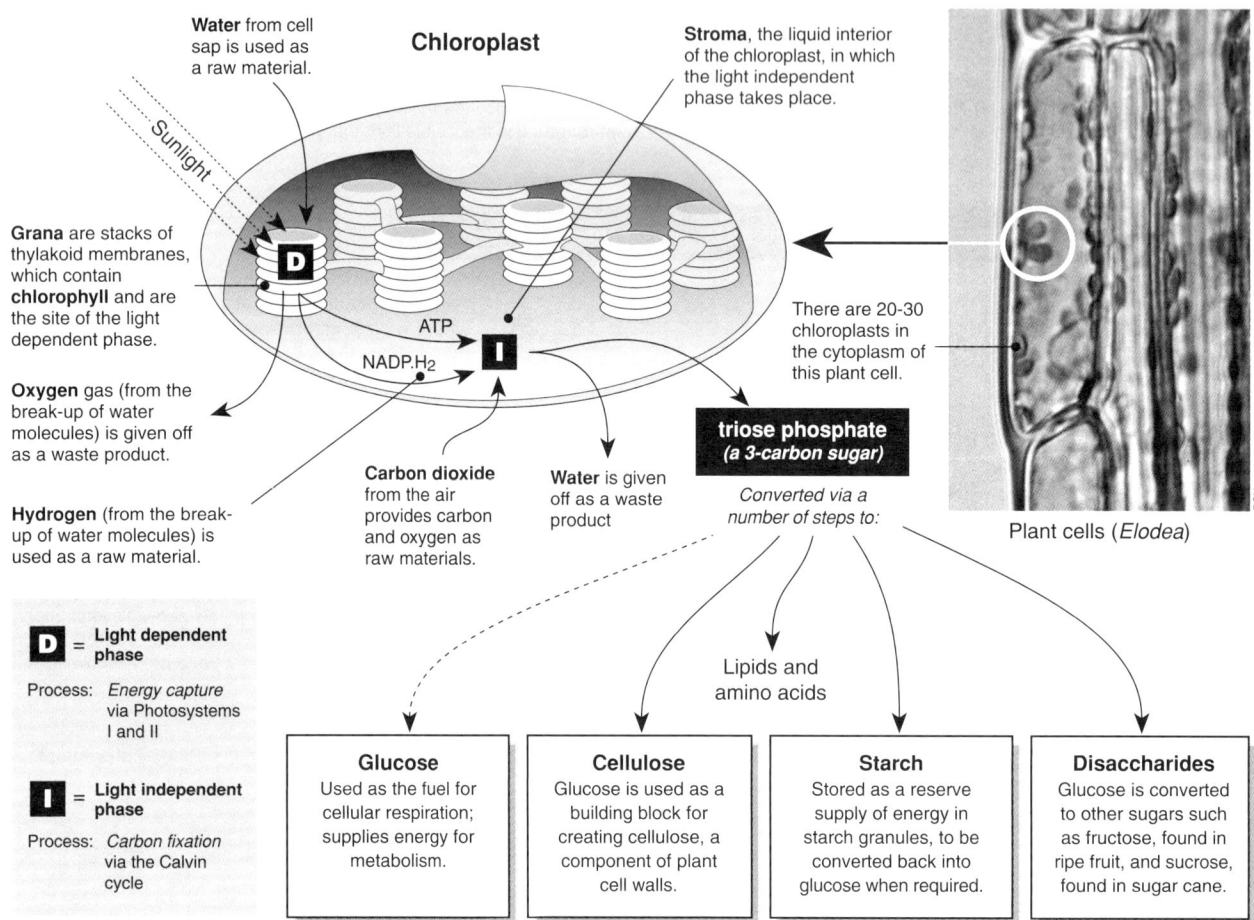

Water from cell sap is used as a raw material.

Chloroplast

Stroma, the liquid interior of the chloroplast, in which the light independent phase takes place.

Sunlight

Grana are stacks of thylakoid membranes, which contain **chlorophyll** and are the site of the light dependent phase.

D

ATP

NADP.H₂

I

Oxygen gas (from the break-up of water molecules) is given off as a waste product.

Hydrogen (from the break-up of water molecules) is used as a raw material.

Carbon dioxide from the air provides carbon and oxygen as raw materials.

Water is given off as a waste product

There are 20-30 chloroplasts in the cytoplasm of this plant cell.

triose phosphate
(a 3-carbon sugar)

Converted via a number of steps to:

Plant cells (*Elodea*)

D = **Light dependent phase**

Process: *Energy capture via Photosystems I and II*

I = **Light independent phase**

Process: *Carbon fixation via the Calvin cycle*

Lipids and amino acids

Glucose
Used as the fuel for cellular respiration; supplies energy for metabolism.

Cellulose
Glucose is used as a building block for creating cellulose, a component of plant cell walls.

Starch
Stored as a reserve supply of energy in starch granules, to be converted back into glucose when required.

Disaccharides
Glucose is converted to other sugars such as fructose, found in ripe fruit, and sucrose, found in sugar cane.

1. Describe the three things of fundamental biological importance provided by photosynthesis:

    (a) _____

    (b) _____

    (c) _____

2. Write the overall chemical equation for photosynthesis using:

    (a) Words: _____

    (b) Chemical symbols: _____

3. Describe the role of the carrier molecule **NADP** in photosynthesis: _____

    _____

    _____

4. Explain the role of chlorophyll molecules in the process of photosynthesis: _____

    _____

    _____

    _____

Light Dependent Phase
(Energy capture)

Electron transport chain: each electron is passed from one electron carrier to another, losing energy as it goes. This energy is used to pump hydrogen ions across the thylakoid membrane.

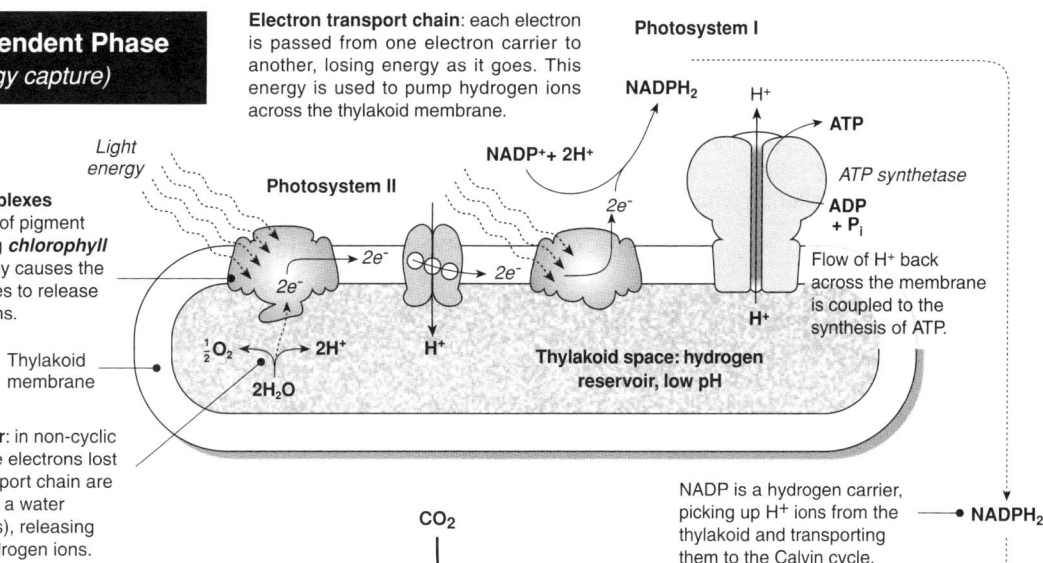

Photosystem I

NADPH$_2$

H$^+$

ATP

ATP synthetase

ADP + P$_i$

Light energy

Photosystem complexes comprise hundreds of pigment molecules, including *chlorophyll a* and *b*. Light energy causes the chlorophyll molecules to release high energy electrons.

Photosystem II

NADP$^+$+ 2H$^+$

2e$^-$

2e$^-$

2e$^-$

2e$^-$

Flow of H$^+$ back across the membrane is coupled to the synthesis of ATP.

Thylakoid membrane

$\frac{1}{2}$O$_2$

2H$^+$

H$^+$

2H$_2$O

H$^+$

Thylakoid space: hydrogen reservoir, low pH

Photolysis of water: in non-cyclic phosphorylation, the electrons lost to the electron transport chain are replaced by splitting a water molecule (photolysis), releasing oxygen gas and hydrogen ions.

NADP is a hydrogen carrier, picking up H$^+$ ions from the thylakoid and transporting them to the Calvin cycle.

NADPH$_2$

CO$_2$

Light Independent Phase
(Carbon fixation)

The light independent reaction, called the **Calvin cycle**, has also been labelled the 'dark phase' of photosynthesis. This is not a good label as it is not necessary that the phase occur in darkness; it simply does not require light to proceed. In the Calvin cycle, hydrogen (H$^+$) is added to CO$_2$ and a 5C intermediate to make carbohydrate. The H$^+$ and ATP are supplied by the light dependent phase above.

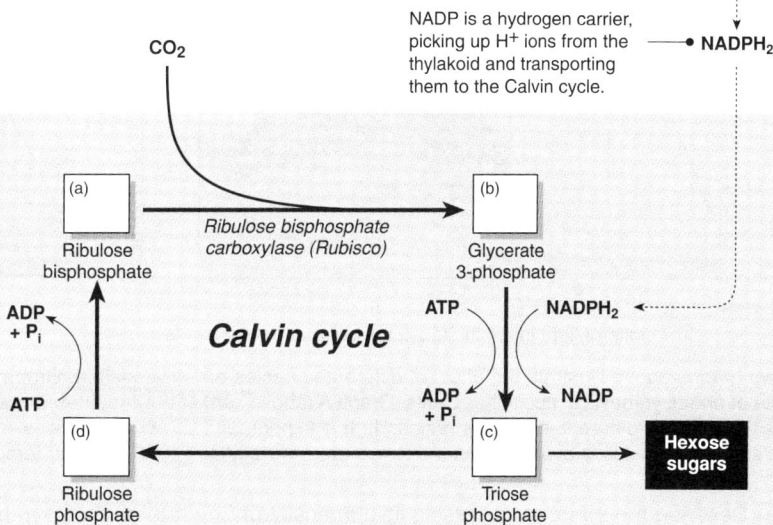

(a) Ribulose bisphosphate

Ribulose bisphosphate carboxylase (Rubisco)

(b) Glycerate 3-phosphate

ATP

NADPH$_2$

Calvin cycle

ADP + P$_i$

ATP

ADP + P$_i$

NADP

(d) Ribulose phosphate

(c) Triose phosphate

Hexose sugars

5. On the diagram above, write the number of carbon atoms each molecule has at each stage of the Calvin cycle (a) to (d).

6. During the process of photosynthesis, energy gets converted to different states. Name the three energy states in order of occurrence, starting with the initial input of energy:

_____

7. Explain what is meant by the following phases in photosynthesis:

    (a) **Light dependent phase (D)**: _____

    _____

    (b) **Light independent phase (I)**: _____

    _____

8. The final product of photosynthesis is triose phosphate. Describe precisely where the carbon, hydrogen and oxygen molecules originate from to make this molecule:

_____

_____

9. Describe how ATP is produced as a result of light striking chlorophyll molecules during the light dependent phase:

_____

_____

_____

_____

_____

Photosynthetic Rate

DA ②

The rate at which plants can make food (the photosynthetic rate) is dependent on environmental factors, particularly the amount of **light** available, the level of **carbon dioxide** (CO_2) and the **temperature**. The effect of these factors can be tested experimentally by altering one of the factors while holding others constant (a controlled experiment). In reality, a plant is subjected to variations in all three factors at the same time. The interaction of the different factors can also be examined in the same way, as long as only one factor at a time is altered. The results can be expressed in a graph.

Factors Affecting Photosynthetic Rate

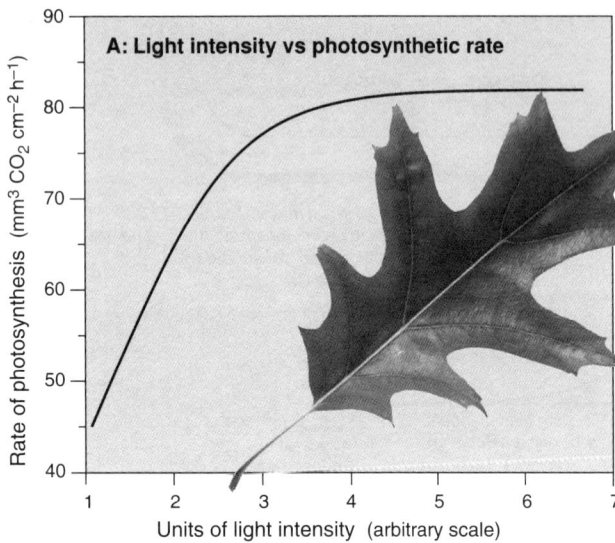

A: Light intensity vs photosynthetic rate

Rate of photosynthesis (mm^3 CO_2 cm^{-2} h^{-1})

Units of light intensity (arbitrary scale)

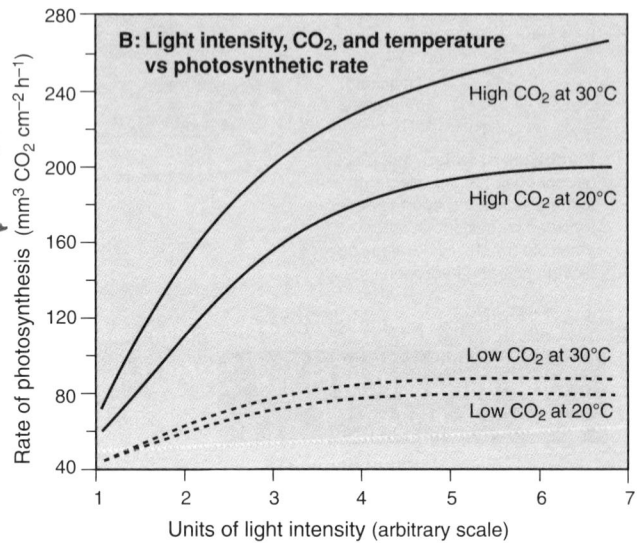

B: Light intensity, CO_2, and temperature vs photosynthetic rate

High CO_2 at 30°C
High CO_2 at 20°C
Low CO_2 at 30°C
Low CO_2 at 20°C

Rate of photosynthesis (mm^3 CO_2 cm^{-2} h^{-1})

Units of light intensity (arbitrary scale)

The two graphs above illustrate the effect of different variables on the rate of photosynthesis in cucumber plants. Graph A (above, left) shows the effect of different intensities of light. In this experiment, the level of carbon dioxide available and the temperature were kept constant. Graph B (above, right) shows the effect of different light intensities at two temperatures and two carbon dioxide (CO_2) concentrations. In each of these experiments either the carbon dioxide level or the temperature was raised at each light intensity in turn.

1. (a) Describe the effect of increasing light intensity on the rate of photosynthesis (temperature and CO_2 constant):

_____

_____

   (b) Give a possible explanation for the shape of the curve: _____

_____

2. (a) Describe the effect of increasing the temperature on the rate of photosynthesis: _____

_____

   (b) Suggest a reason for this response: _____

_____

3. Explain why the rate of photosynthesis declines when the CO_2 level is reduced: _____

_____

_____

4. (a) In the graph above right, explain how the effects of CO_2 level were separated from the effects of temperature:

_____

_____

   (b) State which of the two factors, CO_2 level or temperature, has the greatest effect on photosynthetic rate:

_____

   (c) Explain how you can tell this from the graph: _____

_____

Events in Biochemistry

RA 2

Our current knowledge of photosynthesis is the result of the investigations of trained and lay scientists over more than 300 years. Many new developments in theory relied on and utilised the ideas and techniques developed by previous workers. Some key events in this development of ideas are outlined below (name first, with details below). Dates refer to the date of the work or to its publication.

The historical development of ideas relating to photosynthesis

(a)

1662: Publication of a famous experiment showing that a tree's increase in mass did not come from the soil.

(b) **Stephen Hales**

1727: Demonstrated experimentally that plants take in part of the air for their nutrition. Showed that water loss is through the leaves and caused an upward flow of sap.

(c)

1774: Discovered oxygen when attempting to make gases by heating mercury oxide. He found the gas (O_2) to be colourless, breathable, and able to restore a flame.

(d) **Jan Ingen-Housz**

1779: Discovered two cycles in the light and dark in green plants and concluded that light is needed for the production of oxygen by leaves.

(e) **Jean Senebier**

1779/1788: First to demonstrate the basic principle of photosynthesis and to establish precise experimental method.

(f) **Nicholas de Saussure**

1804: Performed a series of experiments on carbonic acid in plant tissues. His *Chemical Researches on Vegetation* established the science of plant biochemistry and showed that plants require carbon dioxide from the air and nitrogen from the soil.

(g)

1842/1845: Extended his *Principles of Conservation of Energy* (1842) to show that living things are powered by processes that use energy from the sun (1845). He identified plants as the converters of the sun's energy into food.

(h) **Julius von Sachs**

1861-1865: Discovered chlorophyll in small "bodies" (chloroplasts), identified chlorophyll as the key compound in carbon dioxide fixation, and showed that the first 'visible' product of carbon dioxide uptake in green plants is starch.

(i) **Thomas W. Engelmann**

1882: Famous for an elegant experiment that revealed the action spectrum for photosynthesis.

Engelmann's experiment: A filament of the alga *Spirogyra* was illuminated with light that had been passed through a prism. The aggregation pattern of aerobic bacteria was used to determine which parts of the filament were releasing the most O_2. The action spectrum revealed by the experiment paralleled the absorption spectrum for chlorophyll. Engelmann concluded that photosynthesis depends on the light absorbed by chlorophyll.

(j) **Frederick Frost Blackman**

1895: Demonstrated conclusively by experiment that gas exchange between plants and the air occurs through stomata. Also proposed the principle of limiting factors in 1905 and applied it to photosynthesis.

(k)

1906: Developed paper chromatography as a method of separating dyes (later used extensively for organic molecules).

(l) **Cornelius van Niel**

1930s: Investigated photosynthesis in bacteria that make carbohydrate from CO_2 but do not release O_2. He reasoned that all photosynthetic organisms required a hydrogen source, but the source varied, and hypothesised that (therefore) the O_2 given off by plants was derived from water and not CO_2.

(m) **Robert Emerson and William Arnold**

1932: Measured oxygen yield when *Chlorella* cells were exposed to light flashes of a few μs. They observed that a saturating light flash produced one O_2 molecule per 2,500 chlorophyll molecules. The experiment led to the concept of the *photosynthetic unit*.

(n) **Hans Gaffron**

Mid 1930s: Advanced the ideas of Emerson and Arnold by proposing that light is absorbed by hundreds of chlorophyll molecules, which transfer their energy to a site where the chemical reactions occur (the reaction centre).

(o)

1939: Discovered that isolated chloroplasts evolve oxygen when they are illuminated in the presence of a suitable electron acceptor such as ferricyanide. The experiments confirmed that the O_2 evolved in photosynthesis came from water (not CO_2).

(p)

1940s: Discovered, isolated, and used the radioactive isotope of carbon (^{14}C). Studying photosynthesis, he also confirmed that the O_2 evolved in photosynthesis did not come from CO_2.

(q) **Albert Claude**

1942: Developed cell fractionation techniques and applied electron microscopy to the study of biology, leading to important advances in understanding the ultrastructure of cells.

(r)

1946: Used radioisotope labelling and chromatography to investigate carbon fixation. He allowed *Chlorella* to absorb radioactive CO_2 for a few seconds and detected the early products of the reaction. His investigations led to the discovery of the light independent reactions that fix CO_2.

1. Use the word list provided here to match each missing scientist in the timeline above with the experiments in photosynthesis for which they are most noted (surnames are in bold). Write the name in the blank spaces provided:
   Word list: Mikhail **Tsvett**, Joseph **Priestly**, Melvin **Calvin**, Johann van **Helmont**, Robert **Hill**, Martin **Kamen**, Julius von **Mayer**.

   The following questions should be answered on a separate sheet and attached to this page after completion:

2. Choosing **either** chromatography **or** isotope labelling, write a short (150 word) summary of the basis of the technique and its significance to the advancement of our understanding of photosynthesis.

3. Investigate in detail the experimental work of one of the people whose findings are summarized above.

Molecular Genetics

IB SL
Complete nos:
1, 3-4, 7, 9(a), 11, 13(a)-(d),14-15, 20-22 Extension: 2, 12

IB HL
Complete nos:
1-26, 28-29, 31-32, 34
Extension: 27, 30, 33

IB Options
Complete nos:
Option D: 30

AP Biology
Complete nos:
1-34
Some numbers as extension as appropriate

Learning Objectives

☐ 1. Compile your own glossary from the **KEY WORDS** displayed in **bold type** in the learning objectives below.

The genetic blueprint

Nucleic acid structure *(pages 128-130, 132-135, also see 150)*

☐ 2. Name some examples of **nucleic acids** and describe their role in biological systems.

☐ 3. Describe the components of a (mono)**nucleotide**: a *5C sugar* (ribose or deoxyribose), a *nitrogenous base* (**purine** or **pyrimidine**), and a *phosphate*. Identify the bases that form nucleotides.

☐ 4. Understand the role of **condensation** reactions in joining the components of nucleotides and in the formation of di- and **polynucleotides** (nucleic acids).

☐ 5. Outline the structure of **nucleosomes**, including reference to the role of **histone proteins** in packaging of the DNA in the nucleus.

☐ 6. Understand that DNA contains **repetitive sequences** and that only a small proportion constitutes **genes**. Appreciate the role of repetitive sequences in DNA technologies such as DNA profiling.

☐ 7. Describe the Watson-Crick **double-helix** model of DNA structure and the **base pairing rule**. Explain the importance of **complementary base pairing** to the conservation of the base sequence in DNA. Contrast the structure and function of **DNA** and **RNA**.

☐ 8. In more detail than #7 above, describe the structure of DNA including the **antiparallel strands**, the 3'–5' linkages, and the role of the **hydrogen bonding** between **purines** and **pyrimidines**.

DNA replication *(pages 136-137)*

☐ 9. Describe the **semi-conservative** replication of DNA, and interpret experimental evidence for this process. Explain the role of the following in DNA replication:

   (a) **DNA polymerase, helicase, DNA ligase**.

   (b) **DNA polymerase III, RNA primase, DNA polymerase I, Okazaki fragments**, and **deoxynucleoside triphosphates**.

☐ 10. Understand that DNA replication proceeds only in the 5' → 3' direction and explain the significance of this. Explain the term: **replication fork**, and explain its significance in eukaryotic chromosomes.

☐ 11. Demonstrate an understanding of the base-pairing rule for creating a **complementary strand** from a **template strand**.

☐ 12. Appreciate the role of polymerase chain reaction (PCR) as an artificially induced form of DNA replication, used as a tool in molecular biology (see the topic *Aspects of Biotechnology* for coverage of this technique).

The genetic code *(page 131)*

☐ 13. Explain the main features of the **genetic code**, including reference to the following:

   (a) The 4-letter alphabet and the 3-letter **triplet code** (**codon**) of base sequences.

   (b) The **non-overlapping**, linear nature of the code.

   (c) The **universal nature** of the code.

   (d) The **degeneracy** of the code.

   (e) The way in which the code is always read from a start point to a finish point in a 3' → 5' direction.

   (f) Specific punctuation codons and their significance.

Gene expression *(pages 138-143)*

☐ 14. Outline the basis by which information is transferred from DNA to protein. Distinguish clearly between **allele** and **gene**. Explain what is meant by **gene expression** and define its two distinct stages: **transcription** and **translation**. *Note that gene expression is sometimes used to refer just to transcription.*

☐ 15. Recall the structure and role of messenger RNA (**mRNA**). In simple terms, describe the process of **transcription**, identifying the role of **RNA polymerase**.

☐ 16. In more detail than in #15 above, describe the process of transcription. Demonstrate an understanding of the direction of transcription (5' → 3' direction).

☐ 17. Distinguish between the **coding (sense) strand**, **template (antisense) strand**. Relate the base sequence on each of these strands to the sequence on the mRNA molecule.

☐ 18. Distinguish between **introns** and **exons**. Explain the significance of introns with the respect to the production of a functional mRNA molecule.

☐ 19. Understand how **reverse transcriptase** catalyzes the production of DNA from RNA. Explain how this enzyme is used by retroviruses. Appreciate the use of reverse transcriptase in molecular biology.

☐ 20. Recall the structure of **proteins** as **polypeptides** with a complex (post-translational) structure.

☐ 21. Explain how the 4-letter alphabet of bases provides the code for the 20 amino acids needed to assemble proteins. Explain the relationship between one **gene** and one polypeptide.

☐ 22. In simple terms, describe the process of **translation**. Describe the role of transfer RNA (**tRNA**) molecules in translation, with reference to the significance of the **anticodons**. Understand and explain the general role of ribosomes in translation.

☐ 23. With respect to the process of **translation**, describe how the structure of transfer RNA (**tRNA**) molecules allows recognition by a tRNA-activating enzyme. Explain the role of this enzyme in binding specific amino acids to their tRNAs and identify the role of ATP in this process.

□ 24. Outline the structure of ribosomes with reference to: small and large subunits, RNA and protein, tRNA binding sites, and mRNA binding sites. Relate the functional role of ribosomes to their specific structure.

□ 25. Describe translation as a process involving **initiation**, **elongation**, and **termination**, occurring in a 5' → 3' direction. In more detail than in #22 above, explain the process of translation including more detailed reference to **ribosomes**, **polysomes** (polyribosomes), **start codons**, and **stop codons**.

□ 26. Distinguish between protein synthesis on free ribosomes and on those bound to the endoplasmic reticulum. Explain why proteins are synthesized in these different locations in the cell.

□ 27. Contrast **gene expression** in prokaryotic and eukaryotic cells, identifying differences in mRNA processing after transcription, movement of the mRNA to the site of translation, and the speed at which translation can take place.

Control of metabolic pathways

Metabolic Pathways (pages 144-145)

□ 28. Recognize **enzymes** as proteins whose synthesis is controlled by DNA. Appreciate the role of enzymes in the control of **metabolic pathways** and in determining the phenotype of an organism.

□ 29. Explain clearly how enzymes control metabolic pathways as illustrated by specific examples e.g. **oxidoreductases**, **anabolism** and **catabolism**. With respect to this control, explain how the amount or activity of an enzyme regulating a metabolic pathway can itself be controlled. Define the terms: **end-product** and **end-product inhibition**.

□ 30. Identify major **metabolic disorders** that are inherited in humans. Explain, using an example, how the malfunction of enzymes are responsible in many cases.

Exemplar case study: metabolism of phenylalanine. Describe the metabolic breakdown of the essential amino acid phenylalanine by liver enzymes. Describe how malfunctioning of specific enzymes can interrupt this metabolic pathway, causing a variety of metabolic defects e.g. phenylketonuria (**PKU**).

Regulation of gene action (pages 146-147)

□ 31. Understand the term **operon** as being a unit of genes in prokaryotes that function in a coordinated way under the control of an operator gene. Comment on the extent to which the operon model is universally applicable.

□ 32. Explain how simple metabolic pathways are regulated in bacteria, as illustrated by the **lac operon** in E. coli. Outline the principles involved in **gene induction** in the lac operon, identifying how lactose activates transcription and how metabolism of the substrate is achieved. Explain the adaptive value of gene induction.

□ 33. Appreciate that the end-product of a metabolic pathway can activate a repressor and switch genes off (**gene repression**). Appreciate the adaptive value of gene repression for the control of a metabolic end-product.

□ 34. Describe the regulation of gene action (transcriptional control only) in **eukaryotes**. Identify the roles of the **promoter** region, **RNA polymerase**, and the **terminator** (not to be confused with terminator codons in translation). Appreciate that the energy for the incorporation of the nucleotides into the mRNA strand in mRNA synthesis is provided by the hydrolysis of nucleoside triphosphates (ATP, GTP, CTP, and UTP). *NOTE: In DNA replication, the nucleoside triphosphates are dATP, dGTP, dCTP, and dTTP. For simplicity, often the nucleotide only is shown).*

See the 'Textbook Reference Grid' on pages 8-9 for textbook page references relating to material in this topic.

Supplementary Texts

See pages 5-6 for additional details of these texts:

■ Adds, J., *et al.*, 2000. **Molecules and Cells**, (NelsonThornes), pp. 19-32.

■ Clegg, C.J., 1999. **Genetics & Evolution**, (John Murray), pp. 40-42, 44-47.

■ Jones, N., *et al.*, 2001. **Essentials of Genetics**, (John Murray), pp. 123-155 as required.

See page 6 for details of publishers of periodicals:

STUDENT'S REFERENCE

Gene structure and expression

■ **Gene Structure and Expression** Biol. Sci. Rev., 12 (5) May 2000, pp. 22-25. *An account of gene function, including a comparison of gene regulation in pro- and eukaryotes.*

■ **What is a Gene?** Biol. Sci. Rev., 15(2) Nov. 2002, pp. 9-11. *A good synopsis of genes and their role in heredity, mutations, and transcriptional control of gene expression.*

■ **Transfer RNA** Biol. Sci. Rev., 15(3) Feb. 2003, pp. 26-29. *A good account of the structure and role of tRNA in protein synthesis.*

■ **DNA in a Spin** Biol. Sci. Rev., 11(3) Jan. 1999, pp. 15-17. *A short account of the methods used to establish the mechanism for DNA replication.*

■ **Control Centre** New Scientist, 17 July 1999, (Inside Science). *The organization of DNA in eukaryotic cells, the nucleus, how genes code for proteins, and the role of ribosomes and RNA.*

Metabolic pathways and their control

■ **Tyrosine** Biol. Sci. Rev., 12 (4) March 2000, pp. 29-30. *The central metabolic role of the amino acid tyrosine (includes errors in tyrosine metabolism).*

■ **Genes that Control Genes** New Scientist, 3 Nov. 1990 (Inside Science). *The control of gene expression in prokaryotes by gene induction and repression. The operon model is explained.*

TEACHER'S REFERENCE

■ **DNA 50** SSR, 84(308), March 2003, pp. 17-80. *A special issue celebrating 50 years since the discovery of DNA. There are various articles examining the practical and theoretical aspects of teaching molecular genetics and inheritance.*

■ **DNA: 50 Years of the Double Helix** New Scientist, 15 March 2003, pp. 35-51. *A special issue on DNA: structure and function, repair, the new-found role of histones, and the functional significance of chromosome position in the nucleus.*

■ **Modeling the Classic Meselson and Stahl Experiment** The American Biology Teacher, 63(5), May 2001, pp. 358-361. *An account of how to model the experiments of Meselson and Stahl to demonstrate semi-conservative replication of DNA.*

■ **A Working Model of Protein Synthesis using Lego™ Building Blocks** The American Biology Teacher, 64(9), Nov. 2002, pp. 673-678. *Using a hands-on project to demonstrate the various stages of protein synthesis.*

■ **Deciphering the Code of Life** Scientific American, December 1999, pp. 50-55. *An exploration of what will be gained from the study of the genomes of humans and other organisms.*

■ **Stuff or Nonsense** New Scientist, 1 April 2000, pp. 38-41. *The functional and evolutionary role of introns (junk DNA) in the genomes of organisms.*

■ **Molecular Machines that Control Genes** Scientific American, Feb. 1995, pp. 38-45. *How gene action is regulated by protein complexes that assemble on DNA.*

■ **A Discovery Lab for Studying Gene Regulation** The American Biology Teacher, 59(8), Oct. 1997, pp. 522-526. *Investigating gene regulation in prokaryotes: a how-to-do-it account.*

See pages 10-11 for details of how to access **Bio Links** from our web site: **www.thebiozone.com**. From Bio Links, access sites under the topics:

GENERAL BIOLOGY ONLINE RESOURCES > Online Textbooks and Lecture Notes: • S-Cool! A level biology revision guide • Learn.co.uk • Mark Rothery's biology web site ... *and others*

CELL BIOLOGY AND BIOCHEMISTRY: • Cell and molecular biology online • MIT biology hypertextbook ... *and others*

GENETICS: • DNA basics • MIT biology hypertextbook • Gene almanac • Virtual library on genetics • Prokaryotic genetics and gene expression chapter ... *and others* > **Molecular Genetics (DNA)**: • Beginners guide to molecular biology • Basic genetics • DNA and molecular genetics • DNA from the beginning • DNA workshop • E!Mouse • Primer on molecular genetics • Protein synthesis • Model of Lac operon (animation) • Induction of the Lac operon • Molecular genetics of prokaryotes

> **Software and video resources are now provided in the Teacher Resource Handbook**

Nucleic Acids

A 1

Nucleic acids are a special group of chemicals in cells concerned with the transmission of inherited information. They have the capacity to store the information that controls cellular activity. The central nucleic acid is called **deoxyribonucleic acid** (DNA). DNA is a major component of chromosomes and is found primarily in the nucleus, although a small amount is found in mitochondria and chloroplasts. Other **ribonucleic acids** (RNA) are involved in the 'reading' of the DNA information. All nucleic acids are made up of simple repeating units called **nucleotides**, linked together to form chains or strands, often of great length (see the activity *DNA Molecules*). The strands vary in the sequence of the bases found on each nucleotide. It is this sequence which provides the 'genetic code' for the cell. In addition to nucleic acids, certain nucleotides and their derivatives are also important as suppliers of energy (**ATP**) or as hydrogen ion and electron carriers in respiration and photosynthesis (NAD, NADP, and FAD).

Chemical Structure of a Nucleotide

Phosphate   Sugar   Base

Symbolic Form of a Nucleotide

Phosphate: Links neighboring sugars together.

Base: One of four types possible (see box on right). This part of the nucleotide comprises the coded genetic message.

Sugar: One of two types possible: ribose in RNA and deoxyribose in DNA.

Nucleotides are the building blocks of DNA. Their precise sequence in a DNA molecule provides the genetic instructions for the organism to which it governs. Accidental changes in nucleotide sequences are a cause of mutations, usually harming the organism, but occasionally providing benefits.

Bases

Purines:
Adenine   Guanine

Pyrimidines:
Cytosine   Thymine   Uracil
                  (DNA only)   *(RNA only)*

The two-ringed bases above are **purines** and make up the longer bases. The single-ringed bases are **pyrimidines**. Although only one of four kinds of base can be used in a nucleotide, **uracil** is found only in RNA, replacing **thymine**. DNA contains: A, T, G, and C, while RNA contains A, U, G, and C.

Sugars

OH   H

Ribose   Deoxyribose

Deoxyribose sugar is found only in DNA. It differs from **ribose** sugar, found in RNA, by the lack of a single oxygen atom (arrowed).

RNA Molecule

In RNA, uracil replaces thymine in the code.

Ribose sugar

DNA Molecule

Deoxyribose sugar

Hydrogen bonds hold the two strands together. Only certain bases can pair.

Symbolic representation

DNA Molecule

Space filling model

Ribonucleic acid (RNA) comprises a *single strand* of nucleotides linked together.

Deoxyribonucleic acid (DNA) comprises a *double strand* of nucleotides linked together. It is shown unwound in the symbolic representation (left). The DNA molecule takes on a twisted, double helix shape as shown in the space filling model on the right.

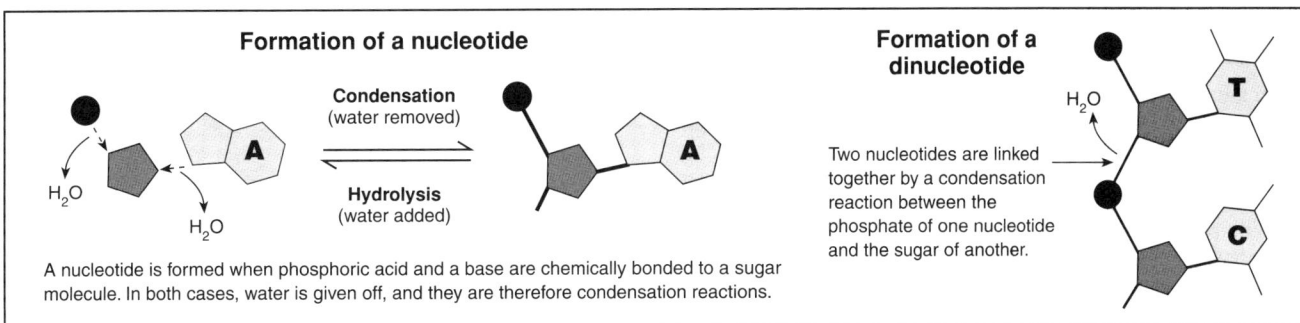

Formation of a nucleotide

Condensation
(water removed)

Hydrolysis
(water added)

A nucleotide is formed when phosphoric acid and a base are chemically bonded to a sugar molecule. In both cases, water is given off, and they are therefore condensation reactions.

Formation of a dinucleotide

Two nucleotides are linked together by a condensation reaction between the phosphate of one nucleotide and the sugar of another.

Double-stranded DNA molecule

The **double-helix** structure of DNA is like a ladder twisted into a corkscrew shape around its longitudinal axis. It is 'unwound' here to show the relationships between the bases.

- The way the correct pairs of bases are attracted to each other to form hydrogen bonds is determined by the number of bonds they can form and the shape (length) of the base.

- The **template strand** is the side of the DNA molecule that stores the information that is transcribed into mRNA.

- The other side (sometimes called the **coding strand**) has the same nucleotide sequence as the mRNA except that T in DNA substitutes for U in mRNA. The coding strand is also called the sense strand.

1. The diagram above depicts a double-stranded DNA molecule. Label the following parts on the diagram:
   (a) **Sugar** (deoxyribose)
   (b) **Phosphate**
   (c) **Hydrogen bonds** (points of attraction between bases)
   (d) **Purine** bases
   (e) **Pyrimidine** bases

2. State the 'base-pairing rule' which describes which bases can pair up opposite each other to form a double-stranded DNA molecule:

3. State the functional role of the following nucleic acids:
   (a) Nucleotides:
   (b) ATP:
   (c) NAD/NADP:
   (d) Coenzyme A:

4. Complete the following table that summarizes the differences between DNA and RNA molecules:

	DNA	RNA
Sugar present		
Bases present		
Number of strands		
Relative length		

DNA Molecules

Even the smallest DNA molecules are extremely long. The DNA from the small *Polyoma* virus, for example, has a length of 1.7μm (about 3 times longer than the longest proteins). The DNA comprising a bacterial chromosome is 1000 times longer than the cell into which it has to fit. The amount of DNA present in the nucleus of the cells of eukaryotic organisms varies widely from one species to another. The quantity of DNA in vertebrate sex cells ranges from 40 000 **kb** to 80 000 000 **kb**, with humans in the middle of the range. There is good reason to believe that most proteins (or polypeptide chains) are coded for by only one gene in each set of chromosomes. Proteins that are found in relatively large concentrations within the cell usually have multiple copies of their gene. About 50-75% of the DNA consists of base sequences that are long enough to code for proteins (around 1000 bases). Current estimates suggest that as little as 10% of the human **genome** (the total DNA complement of a cell) encodes proteins or structural RNA and is therefore made up of **genes**. Of the remaining 90% of the DNA, some is used for the structural aspects of *gene expression*, *DNA replication*, *chromosome division*, and *organizing chromatin* within the chromosome. Some regions of the DNA appear to have no function, although this view may change with further research.

Sizes of DNA Molecules			
Group	**Organism**	**Base pairs** (in 1000s, or kb)	**Length**
Viruses	Polyoma or SV40	5.1	1.7 μm
	Lambda phage	48.6	17 μm
	T2 phage	166	56 μm
	Vaccinia	190	65 μm
Bacteria	Mycoplasma	760	260 μm
	E. coli (from human gut)	4 600	1.56 mm
Eukaryotes	Yeast	13 500	4.6 mm
	Drosophila (fruit fly)	165 000	5.6 cm
	Human	2 900 000	99 cm

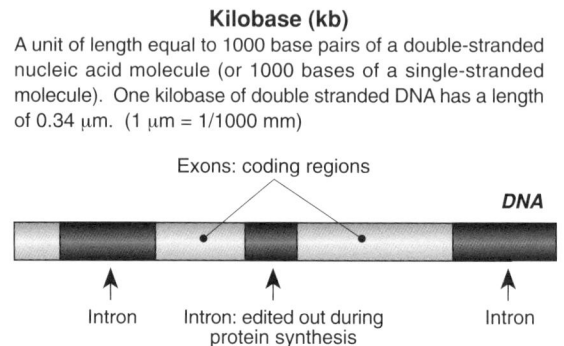

Kilobase (kb)
A unit of length equal to 1000 base pairs of a double-stranded nucleic acid molecule (or 1000 bases of a single-stranded molecule). One kilobase of double stranded DNA has a length of 0.34 μm. (1 μm = 1/1000 mm)

Exons: coding regions

DNA

Intron   Intron: edited out during   Intron
                protein synthesis

Most genes in eukaryotic DNA are not continuous and may be interrupted by 'intrusions' of other pieces of DNA. Coding regions (**exons**) are interrupted by non-coding regions called **introns**. Introns range in frequency from 1 to over 30 in a single gene and also in size (100 to more than 10 000 bases). They are edited out of the genetic instructions during protein synthesis.

Giant lampbrush chromosomes
Lampbrush chromosomes are large chromosomes found in amphibian eggs, with lateral loops of DNA that produce a brushlike appearance under the microscope. The two scanning electron micrographs (below and right) show minute strands of DNA giving a fuzzy appearance in the high power view.

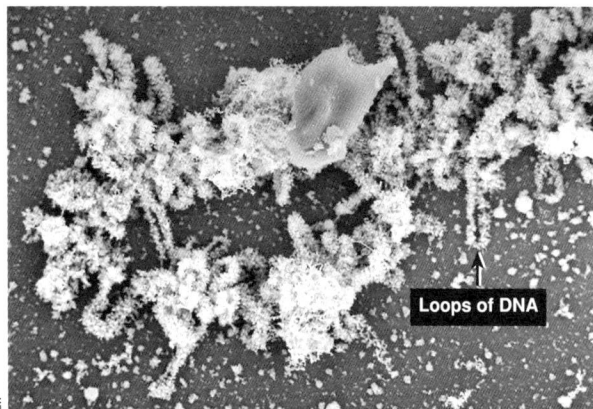

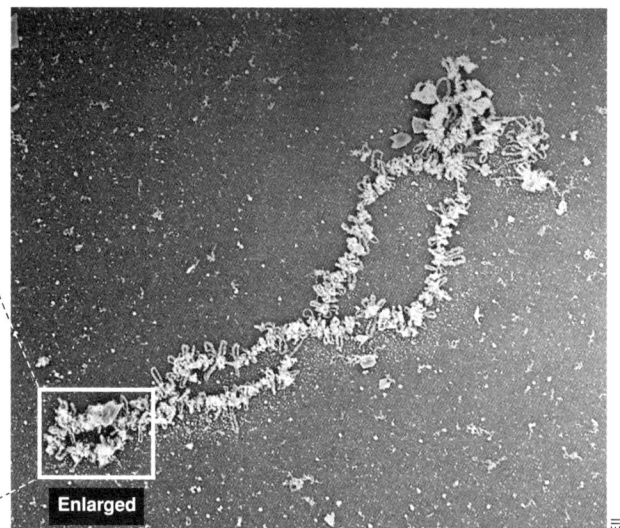

Loops of DNA

Enlarged

1. Consult the table above and make the following comparisons. Determine how much more DNA is present in:

    (a) The bacterium *E. coli* compared to the Lambda phage virus: _____

    (b) Human cells compared to the bacteria *E. coli:* _____

2. State what proportion of DNA in a eukaryotic cell is used to code for proteins or structural RNA: _____

3. List three functions for some of the remaining (noncoding) DNA:

    (a) _____

    (b) _____

    (c) _____

4. State the length of all the DNA (genome) from a single human cell: _____

The Genetic Code

A 2

The genetic information that codes for the assembly of amino acids is stored as three-letter codes, called **codons**. Each codon represents one of 20 amino acids used in the construction of polypeptide chains. The **mRNA amino acid table** (bottom of page) can be used to identify the amino acid encoded by each of the mRNA codons. Note that the code is **degenerate** in that for

each amino acid, there may be more than one codon. Most of this degeneracy involves the third nucleotide of a codon. The genetic code is **universal**; all living organisms on Earth, from viruses and bacteria, to plants and humans, share the same genetic code book (with a few minor exceptions representing mutations that have occurred over the long history of evolution).

Amino acid		Codons that code for this amino acid	No.	Amino acid		Codons that code for this amino acid	No.
Ala	Alanine	GCU, GCC, GCA, GCG	4	**Leu**	Leucine		
Arg	Arginine			**Lys**	Lysine		
Asn	Asparagine			**Met**	Methionine		
Asp	Aspartic acid			**Phe**	Phenylalanine		
Cys	Cysteine			**Pro**	Proline		
Gln	Glutamine			**Ser**	Serine		
Glu	Glutamic acid			**Thr**	Threonine		
Gly	Glycine			**Try**	Tryptophan		
His	Histidine			**Tyr**	Tyrosine		
Iso	Isoleucine			**Val**	Valine		

1. Use the **mRNA amino acid table** (below) to list in the table above all the **codons** that code for each of the amino acids and the number of different codons that can code for each amino acid (the first amino acid has been done for you).

2. (a) State how many amino acids could be coded for if a codon consisted of just TWO bases: _____

   (b) Explain why this number of bases is inadequate to code for the 20 amino acids required to make proteins:

   _____

   _____

3. There are multiple codons for a single amino acid. Comment on the significance of this with respect to point mutations:

   _____

   _____

mRNA-Amino Acid Table

How to read the table: The table on the right is used to 'decode' the genetic code as a sequence of amino acids in a polypeptide chain, from a given mRNA sequence. To work out which amino acid is coded for by a codon (triplet of bases) look for the first letter of the codon in the row label on the left hand side. Then look for the column that intersects the same row from above that matches the second base. Finally, locate the third base in the codon by looking along the row from the right hand end that matches your codon.

Example: Determine **CAG**

C on the left row, A on the top column, G on the right row
CAG is Gln (**glutamine**)

Read second letter here
Read first letter here
Read third letter here

		Second Letter				
		U	**C**	**A**	**G**	
First Letter	**U**	UUU Phe UUC Phe UUA Leu UUG Leu	UCU Ser UCC Ser UCA Ser UCG Ser	UAU Tyr UAC Tyr UAA STOP UAG STOP	UGU Cys UGC Cys UGA STOP UGG Try	U C A G
	C	CUU Leu CUC Leu CUA Leu CUG Leu	CCU Pro CCC Pro CCA Pro CCG Pro	CAU His CAC His CAA Gln CAG Gln	CGU Arg CGC Arg CGA Arg CGG Arg	U C A G
	A	AUU Iso AUC Iso AUA Iso AUG Met	ACU Thr ACC Thr ACA Thr ACG Thr	AAU Asn AAC Asn AAA Lys AAG Lys	AGU Ser AGC Ser AGA Arg AGG Arg	U C A G
	G	GUU Val GUC Val GUA Val GUG Val	GCU Ala GCC Ala GCA Ala GCG Ala	GAU Asp GAC Asp GAA Glu GAG Glu	GGU Gly GGC Gly GGA Gly GGG Gly	U C A G

Third Letter

Creating a DNA Model

PA ②

Although DNA molecules can be enormous in terms of their molecular size, they are made up of simple repeating units called **nucleotides**. A number of factors control the way in which these nucleotide building blocks are linked together. These factors cause the nucleotides to join together in a predictable way. This is referred to as the **base pairing rule** and can be used to construct a complementary DNA strand from a template strand, as illustrated in the exercise below:

DNA Base Pairing Rule			
Adenine	is always attracted to	**Thymine**	A ←→ T
Thymine	is always attracted to	**Adenine**	T ←→ A
Cytosine	is always attracted to	**Guanine**	C ←→ G
Guanine	is always attracted to	**Cytosine**	G ←→ C

1. Cut out the facing page and separate each of the 24 nucleotides by cutting along the columns and rows (see arrows indicating 2 such cutting points). Although drawn as geometric shapes, these symbols represent chemical structures.

2. Place one of each of the four kinds of nucleotide on their correct spaces below:

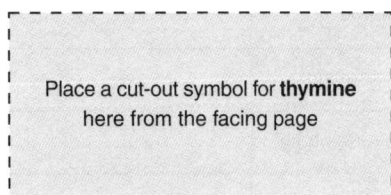

Thymine

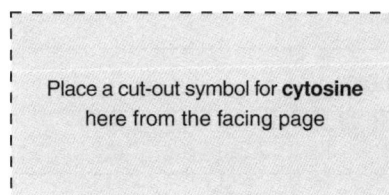

Cytosine

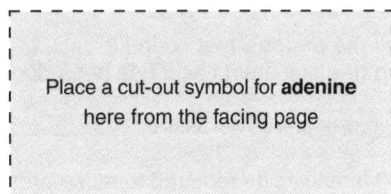

Adenine

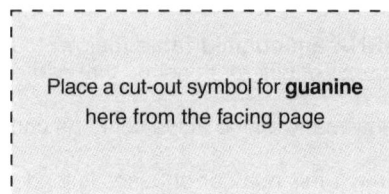

Guanine

3. Identify and **label** each of the following features on the *adenine* nucleotide immediately above:
   phosphate, sugar, base, hydrogen bonds

4. Create one strand of the DNA molecule by placing the 9 correct 'cut out' nucleotides in the labeled spaces on the now facing page (DNA Molecule). Make sure these are the right way up (with the **P** on the left) and are aligned with the left hand edge of each box. Begin with thymine and end with guanine.

5. Create the complementary strand of DNA by using the base pairing rule above. Note that the nucleotides have to be arranged upside down.

6. Under normal circumstances, it is not possible for *adenine* to pair up with *guanine* or *cytosine*, nor for any other mismatches to occur. Describe the **two factors** that prevent a mismatch from occurring:

   Factor 1: _____

   _____

   Factor 2: _____

   _____

7. Once you have checked that the arrangement is correct, you may glue, paste or tape these nucleotides in place.

> **NOTE:** There may be some value in keeping these pieces loose in order to practise the base pairing rule. For this purpose, *removable tape* would be best.

Nucleotides

Tear out this page along the perforation and separate each of the 24 nucleotides
by cutting along the columns and rows (see arrows indicating the cutting points).

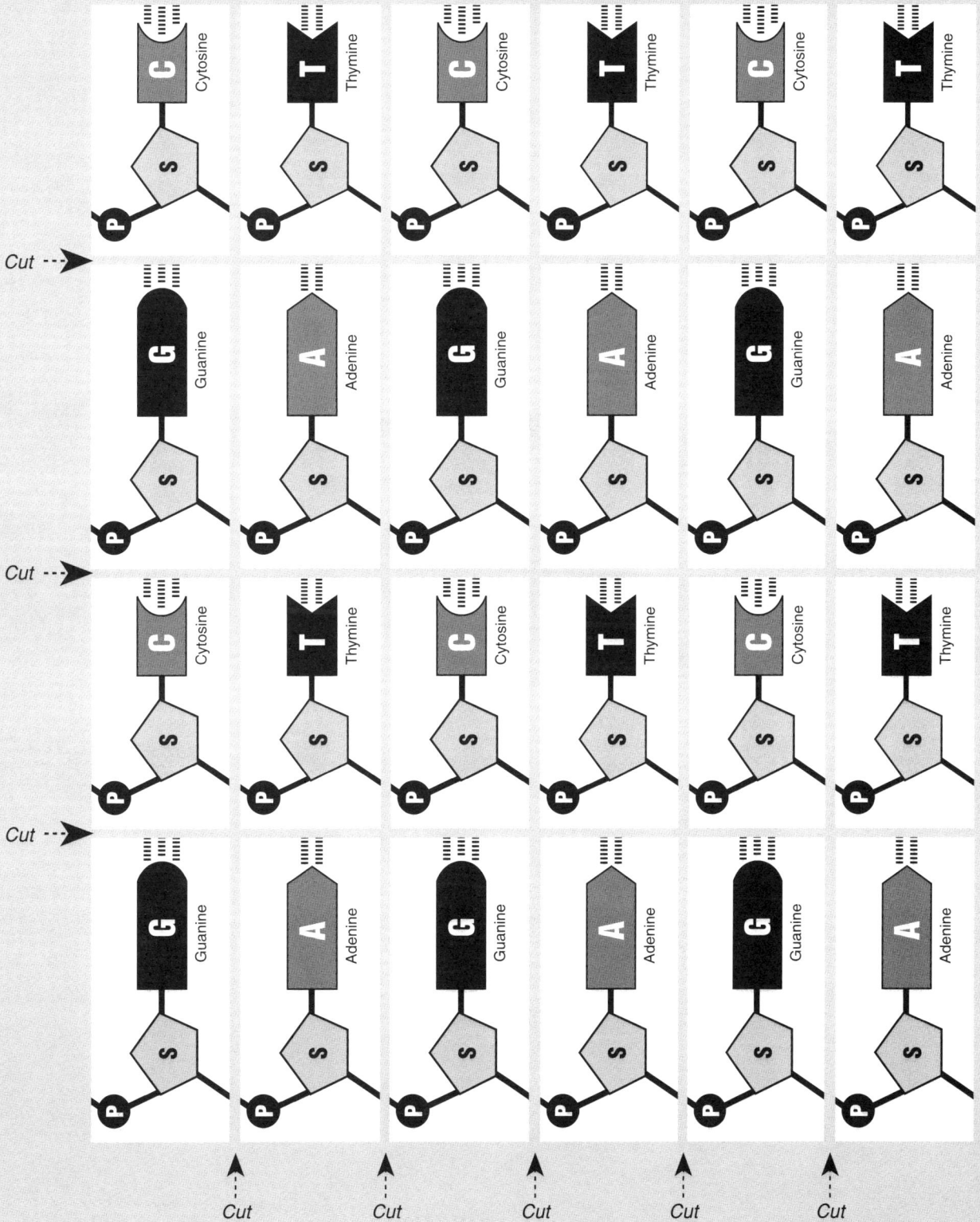

Cut ⟶

Cut ⟶

Cut ⟶

Cut   Cut   Cut   Cut   Cut

This page is deliberately left blank

DNA Molecule

Put the named nucleotides on the left hand side to create the template strand

Put the matching **complementary** nucleotides opposite the template strand

Thymine

Cytosine

Adenine

Adenine

Guanine

Thymine

Thymine

Cytosine

Guanine

DNA Replication

The replication of DNA is a necessary preliminary step for cell division (both mitosis and meiosis). This process creates the **two chromatids** that are found in chromosomes that are preparing to divide. By this process, the whole chromosome is essentially duplicated, but is still held together by a common centromere. Enzymes are responsible for all of the key events. The diagram below shows the essential steps in the process. The diagram on the facing page shows how enzymes are involved at each stage.

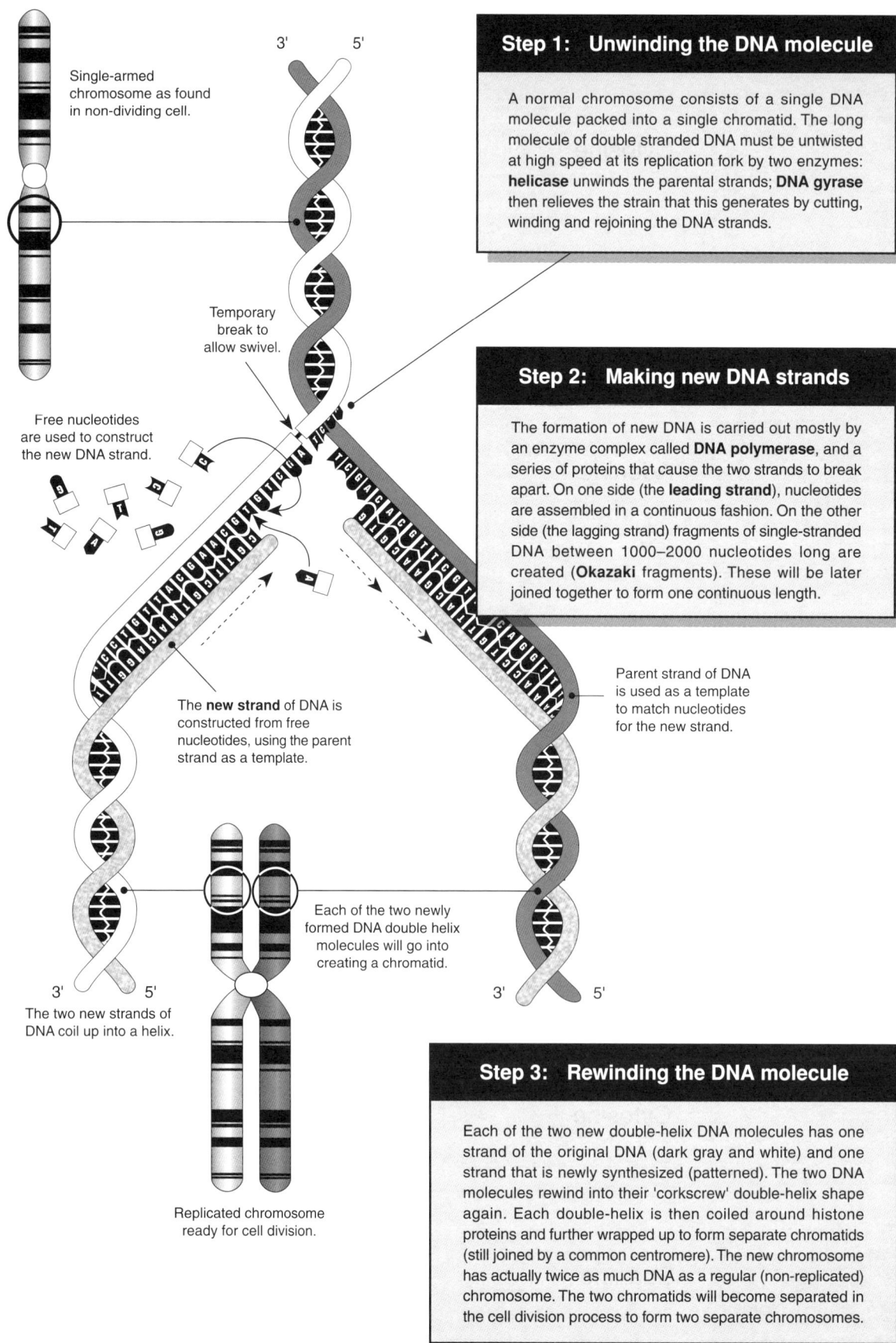

Single-armed chromosome as found in non-dividing cell.

3'   5'

Temporary break to allow swivel.

Free nucleotides are used to construct the new DNA strand.

Step 1:   Unwinding the DNA molecule

A normal chromosome consists of a single DNA molecule packed into a single chromatid. The long molecule of double stranded DNA must be untwisted at high speed at its replication fork by two enzymes: **helicase** unwinds the parental strands; **DNA gyrase** then relieves the strain that this generates by cutting, winding and rejoining the DNA strands.

Step 2:   Making new DNA strands

The formation of new DNA is carried out mostly by an enzyme complex called **DNA polymerase**, and a series of proteins that cause the two strands to break apart. On one side (the **leading strand**), nucleotides are assembled in a continuous fashion. On the other side (the lagging strand) fragments of single-stranded DNA between 1000–2000 nucleotides long are created (**Okazaki** fragments). These will be later joined together to form one continuous length.

The **new strand** of DNA is constructed from free nucleotides, using the parent strand as a template.

Parent strand of DNA is used as a template to match nucleotides for the new strand.

Each of the two newly formed DNA double helix molecules will go into creating a chromatid.

3'   5'

3'   5'

The two new strands of DNA coil up into a helix.

Replicated chromosome ready for cell division.

Step 3:   Rewinding the DNA molecule

Each of the two new double-helix DNA molecules has one strand of the original DNA (dark gray and white) and one strand that is newly synthesized (patterned). The two DNA molecules rewind into their 'corkscrew' double-helix shape again. Each double-helix is then coiled around histone proteins and further wrapped up to form separate chromatids (still joined by a common centromere). The new chromosome has actually twice as much DNA as a regular (non-replicated) chromosome. The two chromatids will become separated in the cell division process to form two separate chromosomes.

Enzyme Control of DNA Replication

This process of DNA replication occurs at an astounding rate. As many as 4000 nucleotides per second are replicated. This explains how under ideal conditions, bacterial cells with as many as 4 million nucleotides, can complete a cell cycle in about 20 minutes. See the section on **polymerase chain reaction** for a useful application of this process.

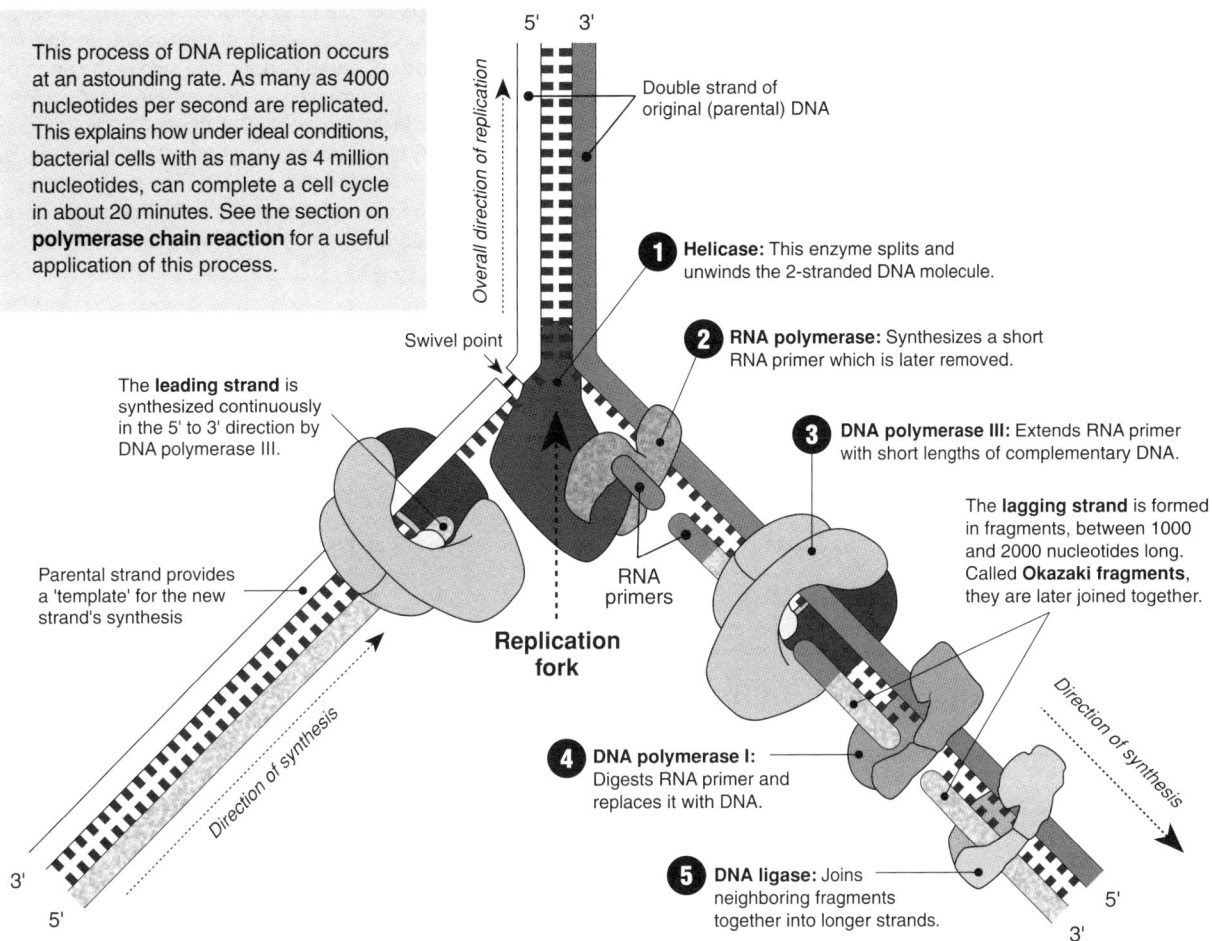

5'   3'

Overall direction of replication

Double strand of original (parental) DNA

Swivel point

1 **Helicase:** This enzyme splits and unwinds the 2-stranded DNA molecule.

2 **RNA polymerase:** Synthesizes a short RNA primer which is later removed.

The **leading strand** is synthesized continuously in the 5' to 3' direction by DNA polymerase III.

3 **DNA polymerase III:** Extends RNA primer with short lengths of complementary DNA.

The **lagging strand** is formed in fragments, between 1000 and 2000 nucleotides long. Called **Okazaki fragments**, they are later joined together.

Parental strand provides a 'template' for the new strand's synthesis

RNA primers

Replication fork

Direction of synthesis

Direction of synthesis

4 **DNA polymerase I:** Digests RNA primer and replaces it with DNA.

3'

5'

5 **DNA ligase:** Joins neighboring fragments together into longer strands.

5'

3'

The sequence of enzyme controlled events in DNA replication is shown above. Although shown as separate, many of the enzymes are found clustered together as enzyme complexes. These enzymes are also able to 'proof-read' the new DNA strand as it is made and correct mistakes. The polymerase enzyme can only work in one direction, so that one new strand is constructed as a continuous length (the leading strand) while the other new strand is made in short segments to be later joined together (the lagging strand). **NOTE** that the nucleotides are present as deoxynucleoside triphosphates. When hydrolyzed, these provide the energy for incorporating the nucleotide into the strand.

1. Briefly summarize the steps involved in DNA replication (on the facing page):

    (a) Step 1: _____

    _____

    (b) Step 2: _____

    _____

    (c) Step 3: _____

    _____

2. Explain the role of the following enzymes in DNA replication:

    (a) Helicase: _____

    (b) DNA polymerase I: _____

    (c) DNA polymerase III: _____

    (d) Ligase: _____

3. Briefly explain the purpose of DNA replication: _____

    _____

4. Determine the time it would take for a bacteria to replicate its DNA (see note in diagram above): _____

Genes Code For Proteins

A2

The genetic code is responsible for the construction of proteins, which may be structural components of cells or metabolism controlling enzymes. The various levels of genetic instructions are illustrated below, together with their 'protein equivalents'. **Nucleotides** are the simplest basic unit of genetic information, that are read in groups of three (called **triplets**). One triplet provides information to bring in a single amino acid during protein construction. Series of triplets in a long string allow the synthesis of **polypeptide chains** and are called **genes**. Some triplets have a special controlling function in the making of a polypeptide chain. The equivalent of the triplet on the mRNA molecule is the **codon**. Three codons can signify the end point of polypeptide chain construction in the mRNA: UAG, UAA and UGA (also called STOP codons). The triplet ATG is found at the beginning of every gene (codon AUG on mRNA) and marks the starting position for reading the gene. Several polypeptide chains may be needed to form a functional protein. The genes required to do this are collectively called a **transcription unit**.

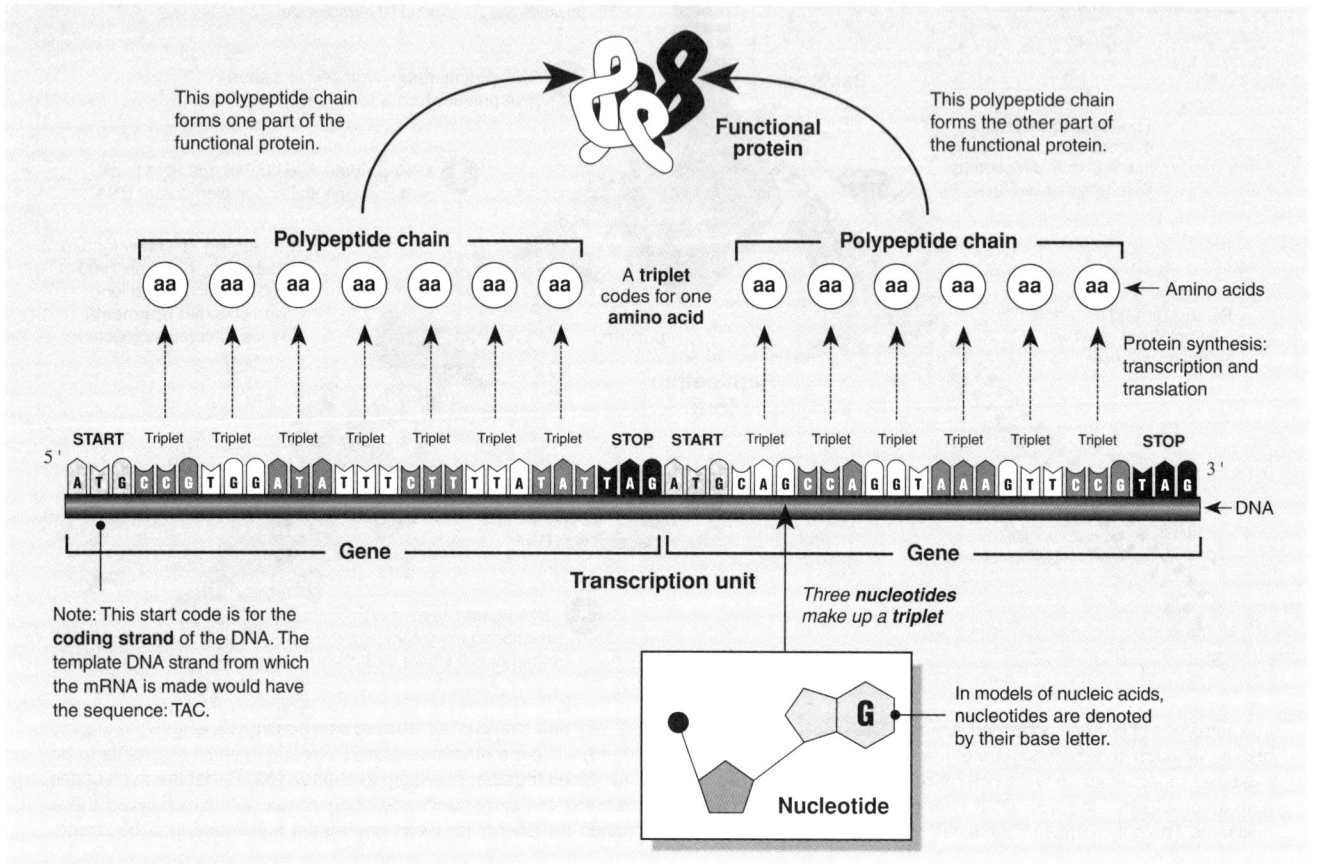

This polypeptide chain forms one part of the functional protein.

Functional protein

This polypeptide chain forms the other part of the functional protein.

Polypeptide chain

aa aa aa aa aa aa aa

A **triplet** codes for one **amino acid**

Polypeptide chain

aa aa aa aa aa aa ← Amino acids

Protein synthesis: transcription and translation

START Triplet Triplet Triplet Triplet Triplet Triplet Triplet **STOP** **START** Triplet Triplet Triplet Triplet Triplet Triplet **STOP**

5' ATGCCGTGGATATTTCTTTTATATTAGATGCAGCCAGGTAAAGTTCCGTAG 3' ←DNA

Gene — Transcription unit — Gene

Note: This start code is for the **coding strand** of the DNA. The template DNA strand from which the mRNA is made would have the sequence: TAC.

*Three **nucleotides** make up a **triplet***

G

In models of nucleic acids, nucleotides are denoted by their base letter.

Nucleotide

1. The following exercise is designed to establish an understanding of the terms used in describing protein structure and the genetic information that determines them. Your task is to consult the diagram above and match the structure in the level of protein organization with its equivalent genetic information:

    (a) Nucleotide   codes for: _____

    (b) Triplet   codes for: _____

    (c) Gene   codes for: _____

    (d) Transcription unit   codes for: _____

2. Name the basic building blocks for each of the following levels of genetic information:

    (a) **Nucleotide** is made up of: _____

    _____

    (b) **Triplet** is made up of: _____

    _____

    (c) **Gene** is made up of: _____

    _____

    (d) **Transcription unit** is made up of: _____

    _____

Gene Expression

RA 2

The process of **protein synthesis** is fundamental to the understanding of how a cell can control its activities. Genetic instructions, in the form of DNA, are used as a blueprint for designing and manufacturing proteins. Some of these proteins are the enzymes that control the complex biochemical reactions in the cell, while others take on a variety of other roles. The process of transferring the information encoded in a gene to its functional gene product is called **gene expression**. It is divided up into two distinct stages: **transcription** and **translation**. These are summarized below and detailed in the following pages. For the sake of simplicity, the involvement of introns in gene expression has been omitted from the following pages.

Chromosomal DNA

DNA contains the master copy of all the genetic information to produce proteins for the cell. Most eukaryotic genes contain segments of coding sequences (exons) interrupted by non-coding sequences (introns).

Primary RNA Transcript

Both exons and introns are transcribed to produce a long primary RNA transcript.

Messenger RNA

The introns are then removed by splicing to form a mature mRNA. Messenger RNA is an edited copy of the DNA molecule (now excluding the introns) that codes for the making of a single protein.

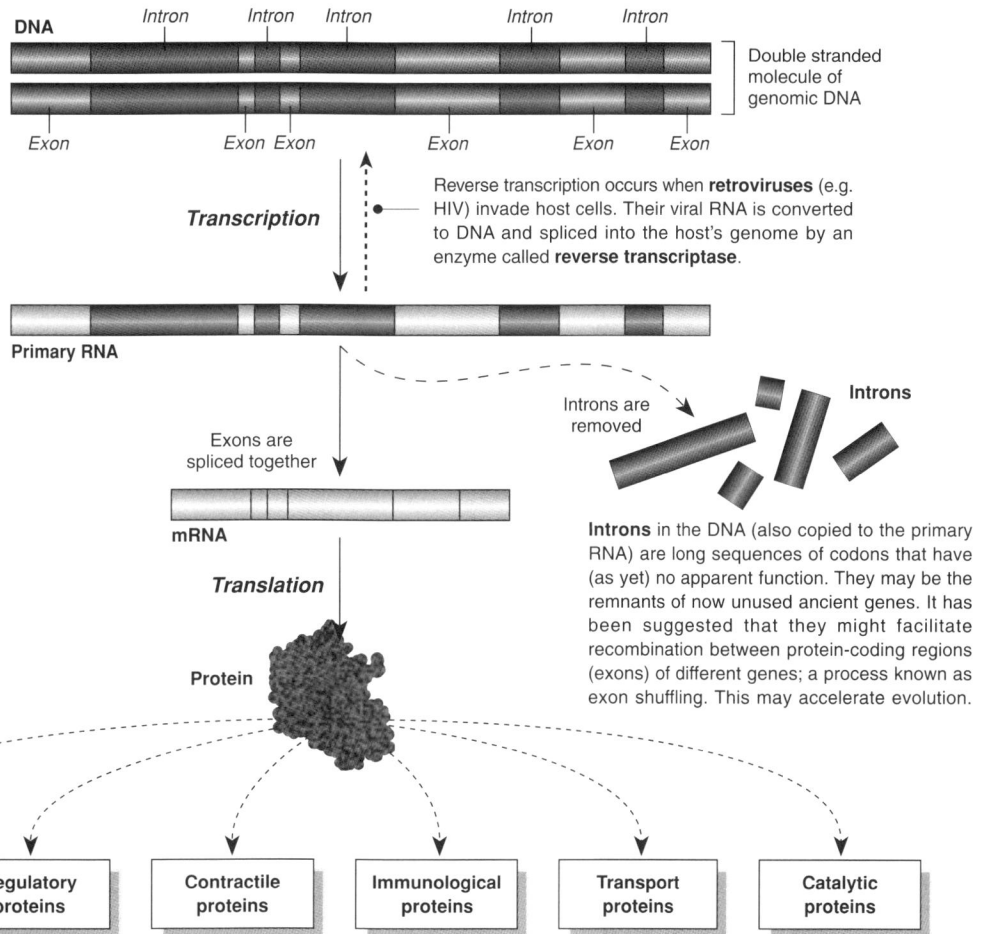

DNA *Intron   Intron   Intron   Intron   Intron*

Double stranded molecule of genomic DNA

Exon   Exon Exon   Exon   Exon   Exon

Transcription

Reverse transcription occurs when **retroviruses** (e.g. HIV) invade host cells. Their viral RNA is converted to DNA and spliced into the host's genome by an enzyme called **reverse transcriptase**.

Primary RNA

Exons are spliced together

Introns are removed

Introns

mRNA

Translation

Introns in the DNA (also copied to the primary RNA) are long sequences of codons that have (as yet) no apparent function. They may be the remnants of now unused ancient genes. It has been suggested that they might facilitate recombination between protein-coding regions (exons) of different genes; a process known as exon shuffling. This may accelerate evolution.

Protein

| Structural proteins | Regulatory proteins | Contractile proteins | Immunological proteins | Transport proteins | Catalytic proteins |

1. The hypothesis known as the **central dogma** of biology states that: "*genetic information can only flow in the direction of DNA to proteins and not in the opposite direction*". Accounting for the ideas in the diagram above, form a discussion group with 2-3 of your classmates and discuss the merits of this statement. Summarize your group's response below:

_____

_____

_____

_____

_____

2. Explain the significance of introns and exons found in DNA and primary RNA:

(a) Intron: _____

_____

_____

(b) Exon: _____

_____

_____

Transcription

Transcription is the process by which the code contained in the DNA molecule is transcribed (rewritten) into a **mRNA** molecule. Transcription is under the control of the cell's metabolic processes which must activate a gene before this process can begin. The enzyme that directly controls the process is RNA polymerase, which makes a strand of mRNA using the single antisense (template) strand of DNA as a template. The enzyme transcribes only a gene length of DNA at a time and therefore recognizes start and stop signals (codes) at the beginning and end of the gene. Only RNA polymerase is involved in mRNA synthesis; it causes the unwinding of the DNA as well. It is common to find several RNA polymerase enzyme molecules on the same gene at any one time, allowing a high rate of mRNA synthesis to occur.

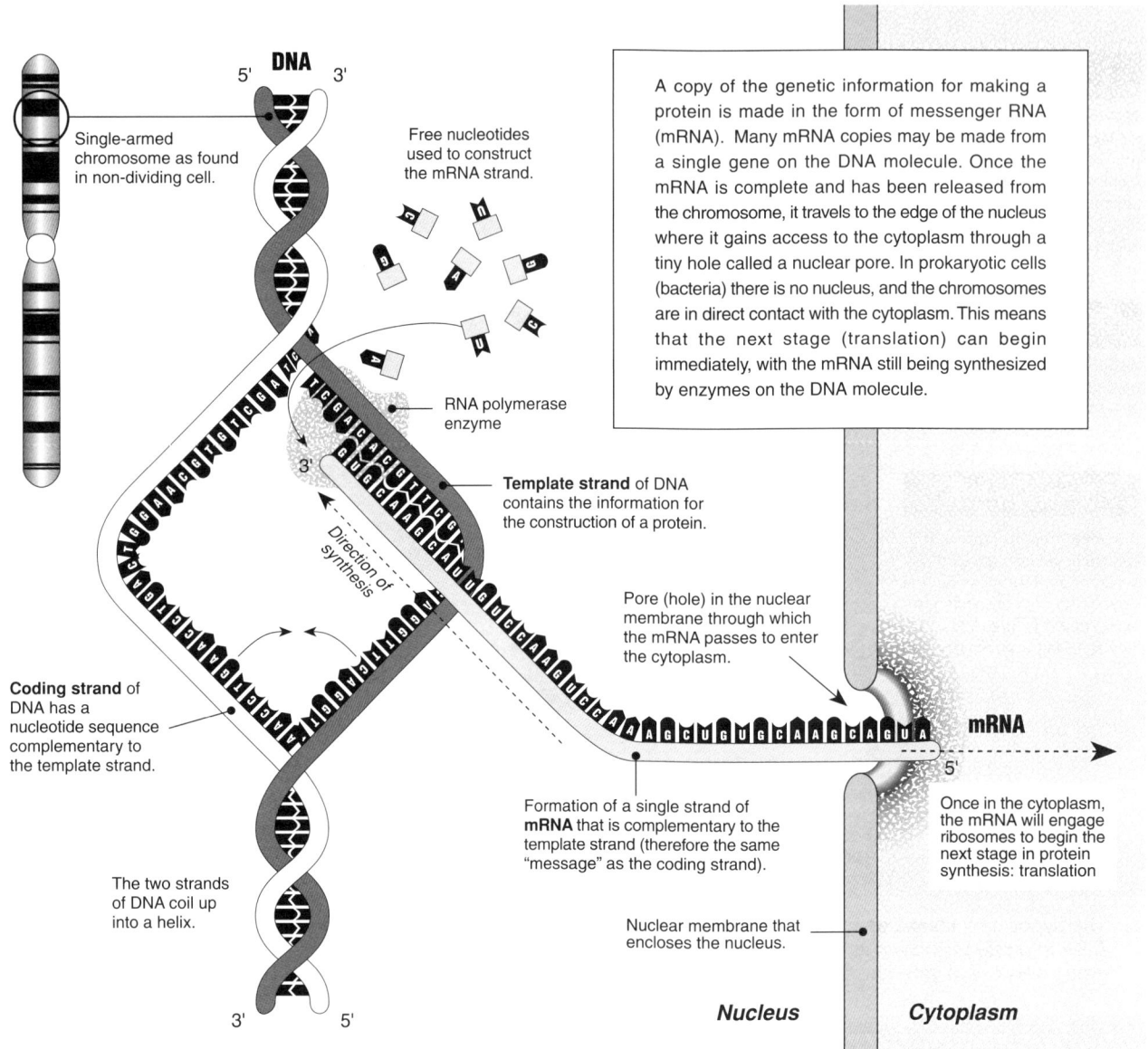

DNA

Single-armed chromosome as found in non-dividing cell.

Free nucleotides used to construct the mRNA strand.

RNA polymerase enzyme

Direction of Synthesis

Template strand of DNA contains the information for the construction of a protein.

Coding strand of DNA has a nucleotide sequence complementary to the template strand.

A copy of the genetic information for making a protein is made in the form of messenger RNA (mRNA). Many mRNA copies may be made from a single gene on the DNA molecule. Once the mRNA is complete and has been released from the chromosome, it travels to the edge of the nucleus where it gains access to the cytoplasm through a tiny hole called a nuclear pore. In prokaryotic cells (bacteria) there is no nucleus, and the chromosomes are in direct contact with the cytoplasm. This means that the next stage (translation) can begin immediately, with the mRNA still being synthesized by enzymes on the DNA molecule.

Pore (hole) in the nuclear membrane through which the mRNA passes to enter the cytoplasm.

Formation of a single strand of **mRNA** that is complementary to the template strand (therefore the same "message" as the coding strand).

mRNA

Once in the cytoplasm, the mRNA will engage ribosomes to begin the next stage in protein synthesis: translation

The two strands of DNA coil up into a helix.

Nuclear membrane that encloses the nucleus.

Nucleus   *Cytoplasm*

1. Explain the role of messenger RNA (mRNA) in protein synthesis: _____

    _____

    _____

2. The genetic code contains punctuation codons to mark the starting and finishing points of the code for synthesis of polypeptide chains and proteins. Consult the mRNA–amino acid table earlier in this manual and state the codes for:

    (a) Start codon: _____ (b) Stop (termination) codons: _____

3. For the following triplets on the DNA, determine the **codon** sequence for the mRNA that would be synthesized:

    (a) Triplets on the DNA: T A C   T A G   C C G   C G A   T T T

        Codons on the mRNA: _____

    (b) Triplets on the DNA: T A C   A A G   C C T   A T A   A A A

        Codons on the mRNA: _____

Translation

The diagram below shows the translation phase of protein synthesis. The scene shows how a single mRNA molecule can be 'serviced' by many ribosomes at the same time. The ribosome on the right is in a more advanced stage of constructing a polypeptide chain because it has 'translated' more of the mRNA than the ribosome to the left. The anti-codon at the base of each tRNA must make a perfect complementary match with the codon on the mRNA before the amino acid is released. Once released, the amino acid is added to the growing polypeptide chain by enzymes.

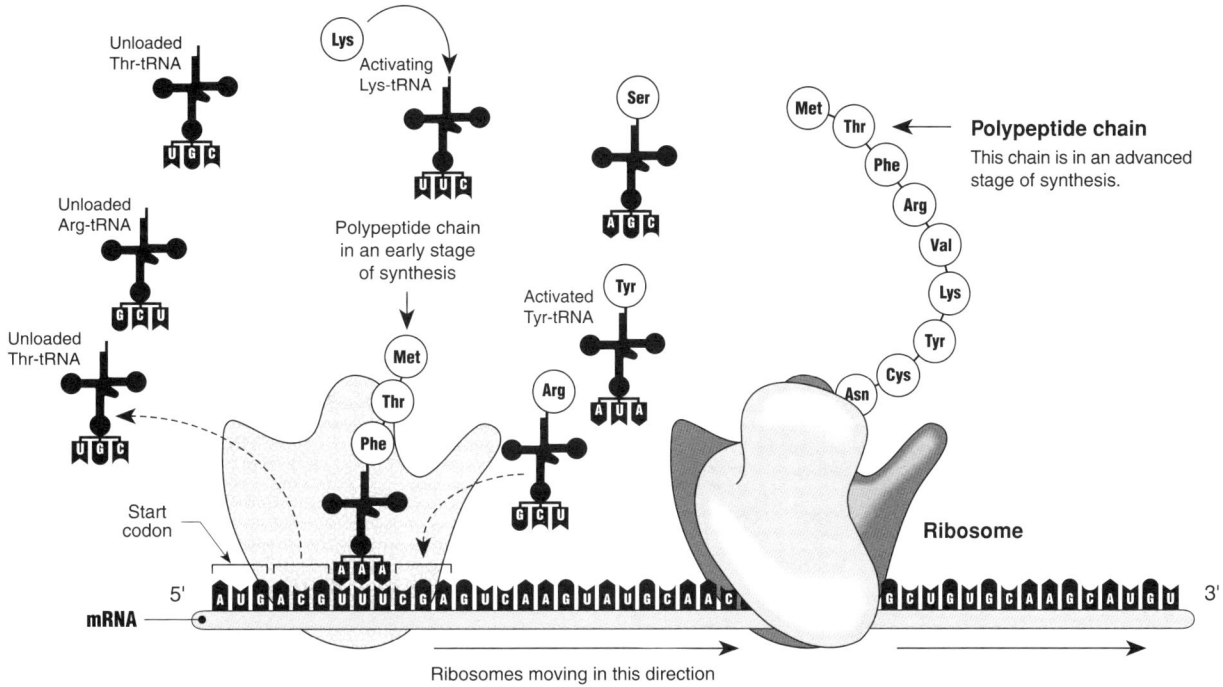

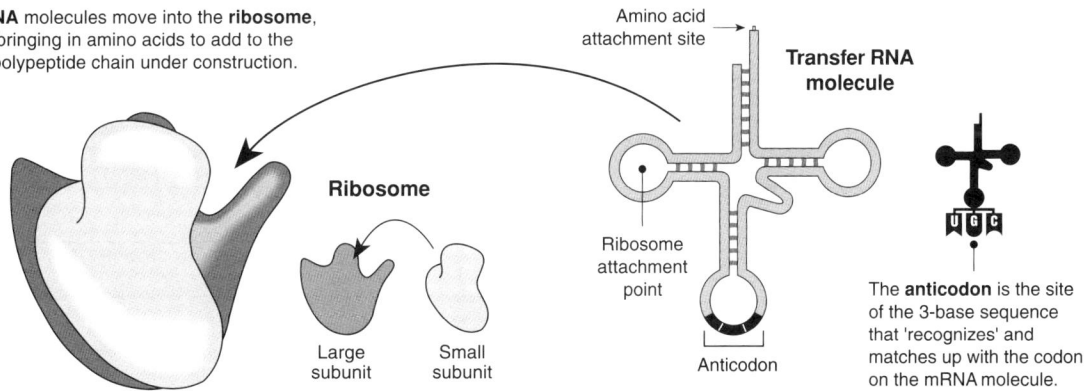

Ribosomes are made up of a complex of ribosomal RNA (rRNA) and proteins. They exist as two separate sub-units until they are attracted to a binding site on the mRNA molecule, when they join together. Ribosomes have binding sites that attract tRNA molecules loaded with amino acids. The transfer RNA (tRNA) molecules are about 80 nucleotides in length and are made under the direction of genes in the chromosomes. There is a different tRNA molecule for each of the different possible anticodons (there may be up to six different tRNAs carrying the same amino acid).

1. For the following codons on the mRNA, determine the **anti-codons** for each tRNA that would deliver the amino acids:

   Codons on the mRNA: U A C   U A G   C C G   C G A   U U U

   Anti-codons on the tRNAs: _____

2. There are many different types of tRNA molecules, each with a different anti-codon (HINT: see the mRNA table).

   (a) State how many different tRNA types there are, each with a unique anticodon: _____

   (b) Give a reason for your answer in (a) above: _____

Protein Synthesis Summary

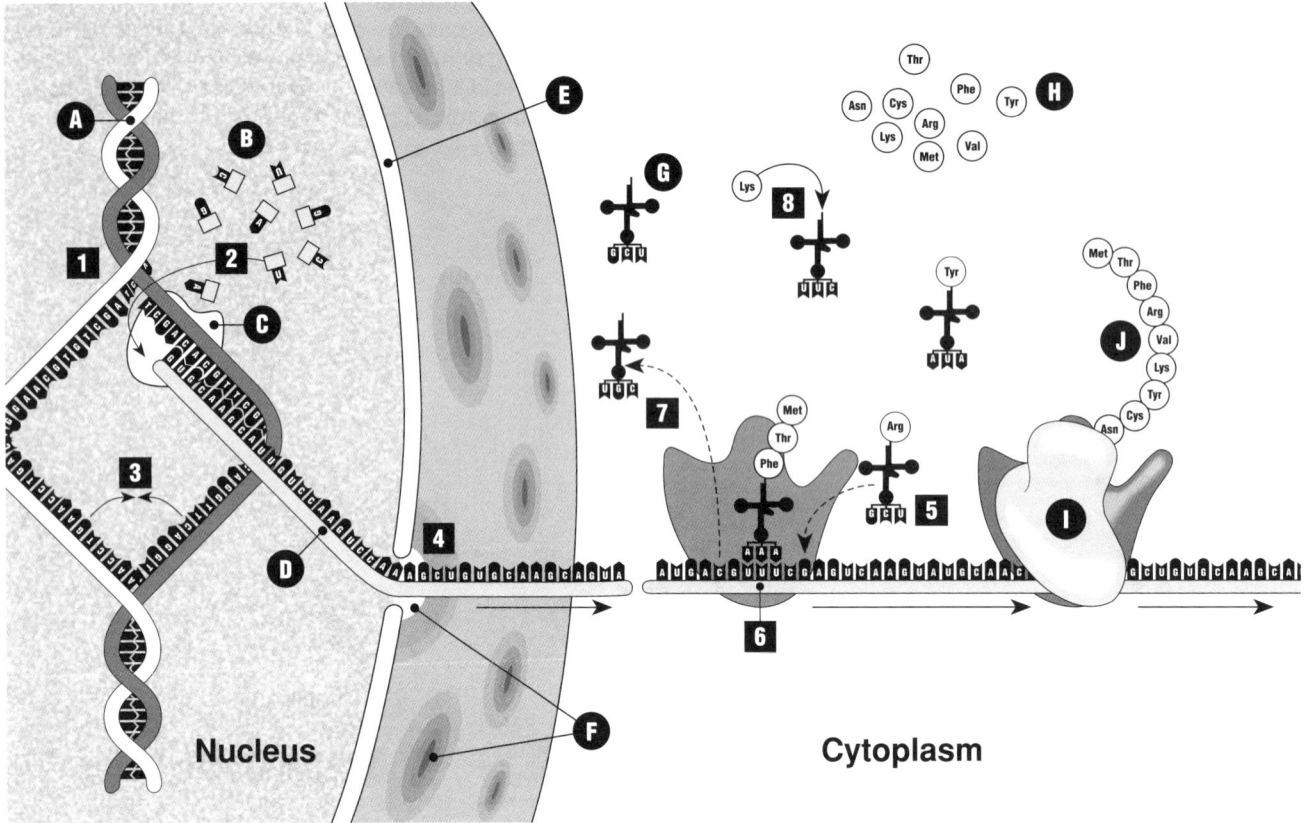

Nucleus

Cytoplasm

The diagram above shows an overview of the process of protein synthesis. It is a combination of the diagrams from the previous two pages. Each of the major steps in the process are numbered, while structures are labeled with letters.

1. Write a brief description of each numbered process in the diagram above:

   (a) Process 1: _____

   (b) Process 2: _____

   (c) Process 3: _____

   (d) Process 4: _____

   (e) Process 5: _____

   (f) Process 6: _____

   (g) Process 7: _____

   (h) Process 8: _____

2. Identify each of the structures marked with a letter and write their names below in the spaces provided:

   (a) Structure A: _____   (f) Structure F: _____

   (b) Structure B: _____   (g) Structure G: _____

   (c) Structure C: _____   (h) Structure H: _____

   (d) Structure D: _____   (i) Structure I: _____

   (e) Structure E: _____   (j) Structure J: _____

3. Explain the purpose of protein synthesis (gene expression): _____

   _____

   _____

Analyzing a DNA Sample

A②

The nucleotide (base sequence) of a section of DNA can be determined using DNA sequencing techniques. The base sequence determines the amino acid sequence of the resultant protein therefore the DNA tells us what type of protein that gene encodes. This exercise reviews the areas of DNA replication,

transcription, and translation using an analysis of a gel electrophoresis column. **Attempt it after you have completed the rest of this topic.** Remember that the gel pattern represents the sequence in the synthesized strand.

1. Determine the amino acid sequence of a protein from the nucleotide sequence of its DNA, with the following steps:
   (a) Determine the sequence of **synthesized DNA** in the gel
   (b) Convert it to the complementary sequence of the **sample DNA**
   (c) Complete the **mRNA** sequence
   (d) Determine the **amino acid** sequence by using the 'mRNA-amino acid table' in this manual.

   NOTE: The nucleotides in the gel are read from bottom to top and the sequence is written in the spaces provided from left to right (the first four have been done for you).

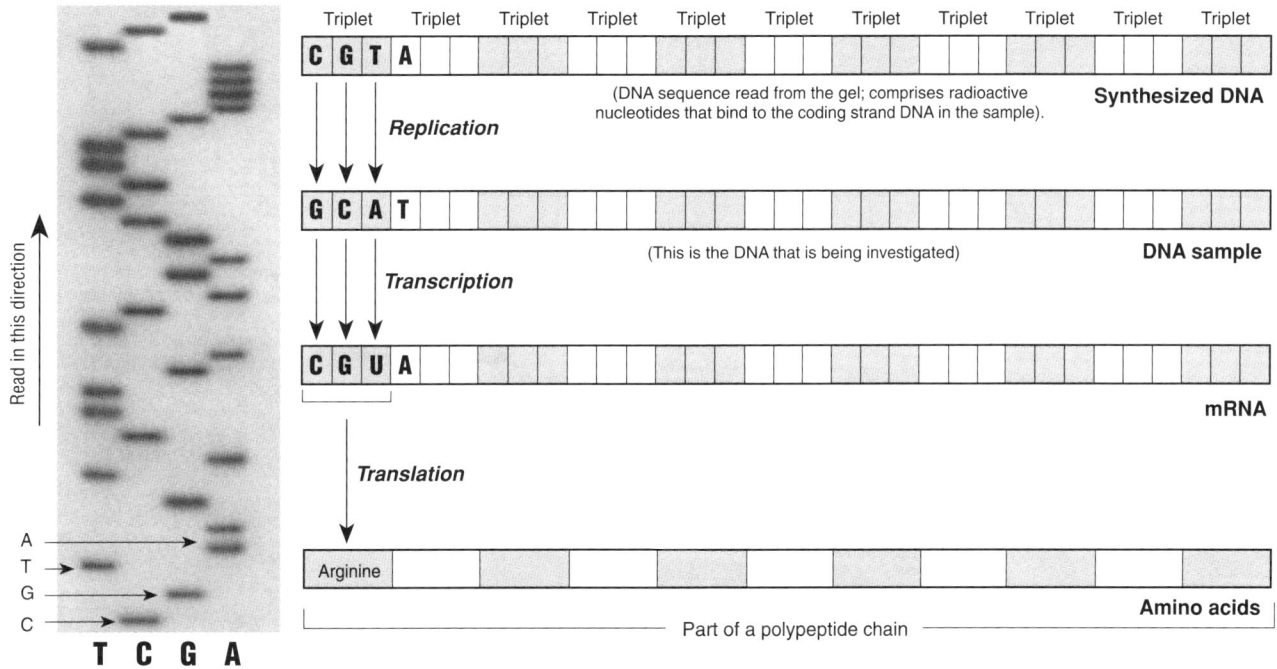

2. For each single strand DNA sequence below, write the base sequence for the **complementary DNA** strand:

   (a) DNA: T A C   T A G   C C G   C G A   T T T   A C A   A T T

       DNA: _____

   (b) DNA: T A C   G C C   T T A   A A G   G G C   C G A   A T C

       DNA: _____

   (c) Name the cell process that this exercise represents: _____

3. For each single strand DNA sequence below, write the base sequence for the **mRNA** strand and the **amino acid** that it codes for (refer to the mRNA-amino acid table to determine the amino acid sequence):

   (a) DNA: T A C   T A G   C C G   C G A   T T T   A C A   A T T

       mRNA: _____

       Amino
       acids: _____

   (b) DNA: T A C   G C C   T T A   A A G   G G C   C G A   A T C

       mRNA: _____

       Amino
       acids: _____

   (c) Name the cell process that this exercise represents: _____

Metabolic Pathways

RA③

Metabolism is all the chemical activities of life. The myriad enzyme-controlled **metabolic pathways** that are described as metabolism form a tremendously complex network that is necessary in order to 'maintain' the organism. Errors in the step-wise regulation of enzyme-controlled pathways can result in metabolic disorders that in some cases can be easily identified. An example of a well studied metabolic pathway, the metabolism of phenylalanine, is described below.

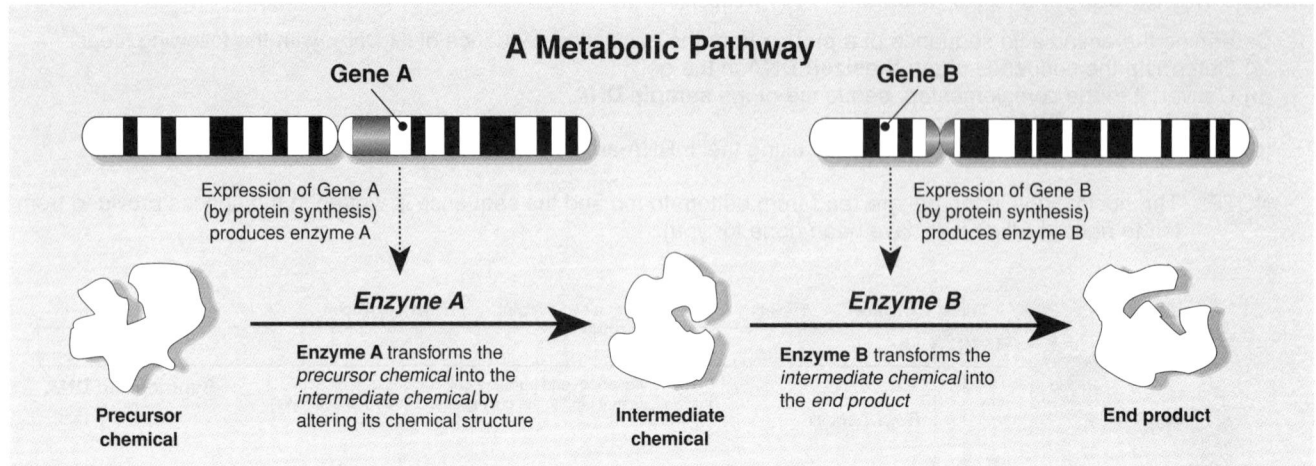

A Metabolic Pathway

Gene A

Expression of Gene A
(by protein synthesis)
produces enzyme A

Enzyme A

Enzyme A transforms the *precursor chemical* into the *intermediate chemical* by altering its chemical structure

Precursor chemical

Intermediate chemical

Gene B

Expression of Gene B
(by protein synthesis)
produces enzyme B

Enzyme B

Enzyme B transforms the *intermediate chemical* into the *end product*

End product

Case Study: The Metabolism of Phenylalanine

Protein

Proteins are broken down to release free amino acids, one of which is phenylalanine.

• Phenylalanine

Phenylalanine hydroxylase

Faulty enzyme causes buildup of:

Phenylketonuria

Symptoms: Mental retardation, mousy body odor, light skin color, excessive muscular tension and activity, eczema.

This in turn causes:

Phenylpyruvic acid

a series of enzymes

Thyroxine

Tyrosine

Tyrosinase

Melanin

Faulty enzymes cause:

Cretinism

Trans-aminase

Faulty enzyme causes:

Albinism

Symptoms: Complete lack of the pigment melanin in body tissues, including skin, hair, and eyes.

Symptoms: Dwarfism, mental retardation, low levels of thyroid hormones, retarded sexual development, yellow skin color.

Hydroxyphenylpyruvic acid

Hydroxyphenylpyruvic acid oxidase

Faulty enzyme causes:

Tyrosinosis

Symptoms: Death from liver failure, or (if surviving) chronic liver and kidney disease.

Homogentisic acid

Carbon dioxide & water

Homogentisic acid oxidase

Faulty enzyme causes:

Alkaptonuria

Symptoms: Dark urine, pigmentation of cartilage and other connective tissues. In later years, arthritis.

Maleylacetoacetic acid

A well-studied metabolic pathway is the metabolic breakdown of the essential amino acid **phenylalanine**. The first step is carried out by an enzyme produced in the liver, called phenylalanine hydroxylase. This enzyme converts phenylalanine to the amino acid **tyrosine**. Tyrosine, in turn, through a series of intermediate steps, is converted into **melanin**, the skin pigment, and other substances. If phenylalanine hydroxylase is absent, phenylalanine is in part converted into phenylpyruvic acid, which accumulates, together with phenylalanine, in the blood stream. Phenylpyruvic acid and phenylalanine are toxic to the central nervous system and produce some of the symptoms of the genetic disease **phenylketonuria**. Other genetic metabolic defects in the tyrosine pathway are also known. As indicated above, absence of enzymes operating between tyrosine and melanin, is a cause of **albinism**. **Tyrosinosis** is a rare defect that causes hydroxyphenylpyruvic acid to accumulate in the urine. **Alkaptonuria** makes urine turn black on exposure to air, causes pigmentation to appear in the cartilage, and produces symptoms of arthritis. A different block in another pathway from tyrosine produces thyroid deficiency leading to goiterous **cretinism** (due to lack of thyroxine).

1. Explain what is meant by a **metabolic pathway**: _____

    _____

    _____

2. Describe the role that enzymes play in metabolic pathways: _____

    _____

    _____

    _____

    _____

3. List three **final products** of the metabolism of phenylalanine: _____

    _____

4. Name the enzyme failures (faulty enzymes) responsible for the following conditions:

    (a) Albinism: _____

    (b) Phenylketonuria: _____

    (c) Cretinism: _____

    (d) Tyrosinosis _____

    (e) Alkaptonuria: _____

5. Explain why people with **phenylketonuria** have light skin coloring: _____

    _____

6. Explain the role of the hormone thyroxine in causing the symptoms of **cretinism**: _____

    _____

    _____

    _____

    _____

7. The five conditions illustrated in the diagram are due to too much or too little of a chemical in the body. For each
    condition listed below, state which chemical (absent or in excess), causes the problem:

    (a) Albinism: _____

    (b) Phenylketonuria: _____

    (c) Cretinism: _____

    (d) Tyrosinosis _____

    (e) Alkaptonuria: _____

8. If you suspected that a person suffered from phenylketonuria, suggest how could you test for the condition:

    _____

    _____

9. The diagram at the top of the previous page represents the normal condition for a simple metabolic pathway. A starting
    chemical, called the **precursor**, is progressively changed into a final chemical called the **end product**.

    Consider the effect on this pathway if **gene A** underwent a mutation and the resulting **enzyme A** did not function:

    (a) Name the chemicals that would be present in **excess**: _____

    (b) Name the chemicals that would be **absent**: _____

Control of Metabolic Pathways

The **operon** mechanism was proposed by **Jacob and Monod** to account for the regulation of gene activity in response to the needs of the cell. Their work was carried out with the bacterium *Escherichia coli* and the model is not applicable to eukaryotic cells where the genes are not found as operons (see opposite for the eukaryote model). An operon consists of a group of closely linked genes that act together and code for the enzymes that control a particular **metabolic pathway**. These may be for the metabolism of an energy source (e.g. lactose) or the synthesis of a molecule such as an amino acid. The structural genes contain the information for the production of the enzymes themselves and they are transcribed as a single **transcription unit**. These structural genes are controlled by a **promoter**, which initiates the formation of the mRNA, and a region of the DNA in front of the

structural genes called the **operator**. A gene outside the operon, called the **regulator gene**, produces a **repressor** molecule that can bind to the operator and block the transcription of the structural genes. It is the repressor that switches the structural genes on or off and controls the metabolic pathway. Two mechanisms operate in the operon model: gene induction and gene repression. **Gene induction** occurs when genes are switched on by an inducer binding to the repressor molecule and deactivating it. In the *Lac* **operon model** based on *E.coli*, lactose acts as the **inducer**, binding to the repressor and permitting transcription of the structural genes for the utilization of lactose. **Gene repression** occurs when genes that are normally switched on (e.g. genes for synthesis of an amino acid) are switched off by activation of the repressor.

Control of Gene Expression Through Induction: the *Lac* Operon

Structure of the operon

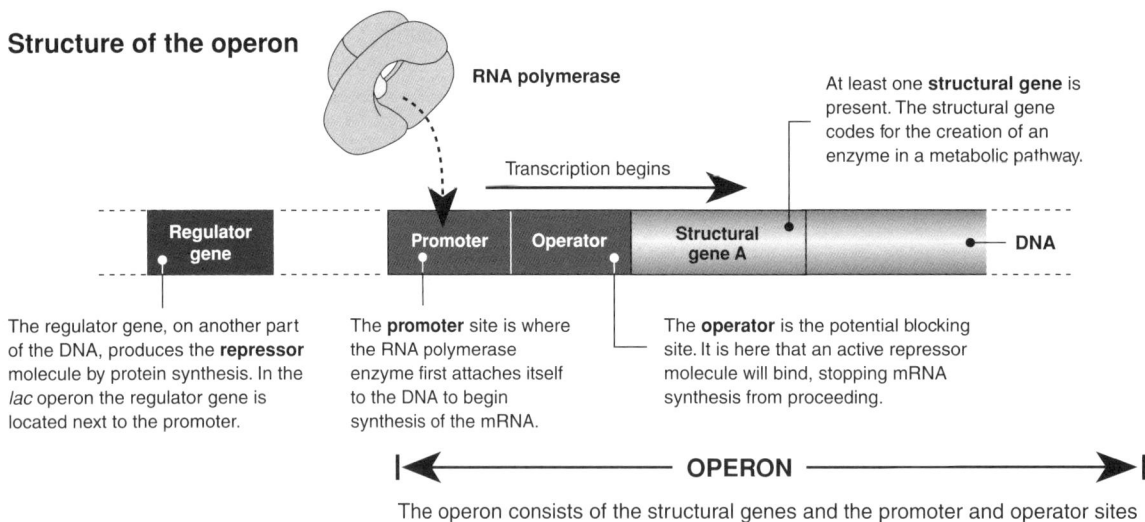

RNA polymerase

Transcription begins

At least one **structural gene** is present. The structural gene codes for the creation of an enzyme in a metabolic pathway.

Regulator gene | Promoter | Operator | Structural gene A | DNA

The regulator gene, on another part of the DNA, produces the **repressor** molecule by protein synthesis. In the *lac* operon the regulator gene is located next to the promoter.

The **promoter** site is where the RNA polymerase enzyme first attaches itself to the DNA to begin synthesis of the mRNA.

The **operator** is the potential blocking site. It is here that an active repressor molecule will bind, stopping mRNA synthesis from proceeding.

$\blacktriangleleft$——————— **OPERON** ———————$\blacktriangleright$

The operon consists of the structural genes and the promoter and operator sites

Structural genes switched off

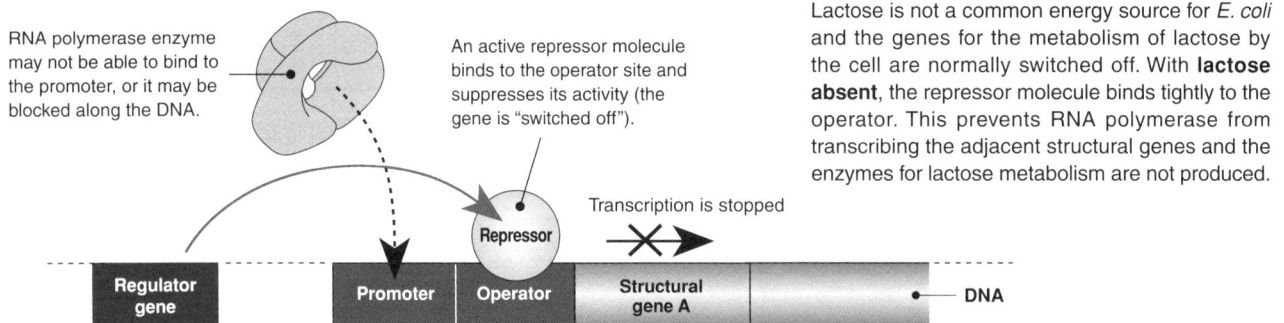

RNA polymerase enzyme may not be able to bind to the promoter, or it may be blocked along the DNA.

An active repressor molecule binds to the operator site and suppresses its activity (the gene is "switched off").

Lactose is not a common energy source for *E. coli* and the genes for the metabolism of lactose by the cell are normally switched off. With **lactose absent**, the repressor molecule binds tightly to the operator. This prevents RNA polymerase from transcribing the adjacent structural genes and the enzymes for lactose metabolism are not produced.

Repressor

Transcription is stopped

Regulator gene | Promoter | Operator | Structural gene A | DNA

Gene induction

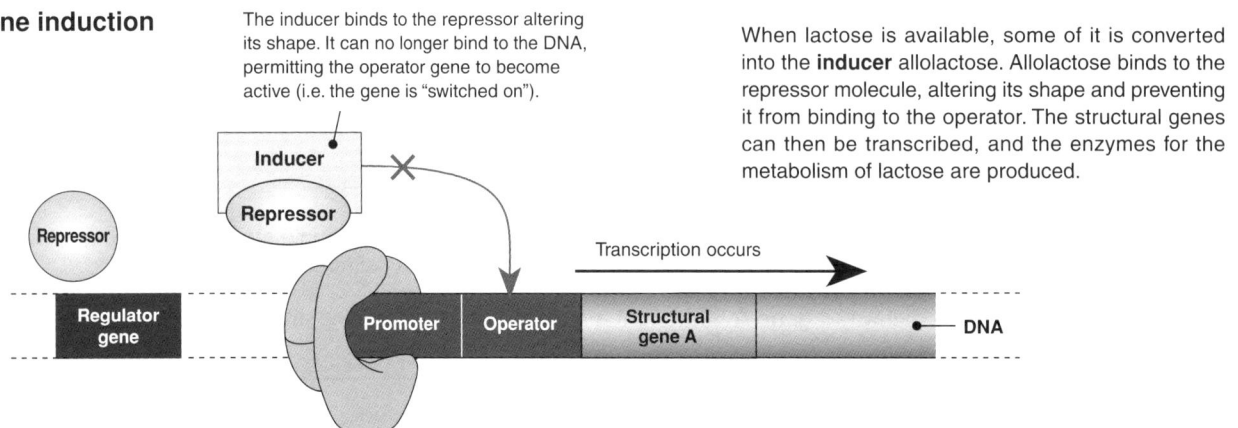

The inducer binds to the repressor altering its shape. It can no longer bind to the DNA, permitting the operator gene to become active (i.e. the gene is "switched on").

When lactose is available, some of it is converted into the **inducer** allolactose. Allolactose binds to the repressor molecule, altering its shape and preventing it from binding to the operator. The structural genes can then be transcribed, and the enzymes for the metabolism of lactose are produced.

Inducer

Repressor

Repressor

Transcription occurs

Regulator gene | Promoter | Operator | Structural gene A | DNA

Control of Gene Expression in Eukaryotes

Although all the cells in your body contain identical copies of your genetic instructions, these cells appear very different. Morphological differences between cell types reflect profound differences in gene expression. For example, nerve cells express proteins responsible for propagating electrical signals, whereas muscle cells express the proteins that make up the contractile elements. This variety of cell structure and function reflects the precise control over the time, location and extent of expression of a huge variety of genes.

The role of transcription factors: RNA polymerase requires additional proteins called transcription factors in order to recognize and bind to the promoter region at the upstream end of the gene. According to one hypothesis, transcription is activated when a hairpin loop in the DNA brings the transcription factors attached to the enhancer in contact with the transcription factors bound to RNA polymerase at the promoter. Transcription is deactivated when a terminator sequence is encountered. Terminators are nucleotide sequences that function to stop transcription. *Do not confuse these with terminator codons, which are the stop signals for translation.*

A range of transcription factors and enhancer sequences throughout the genome may selectively activate the expression of specific genes at appropriate stages in cell development.

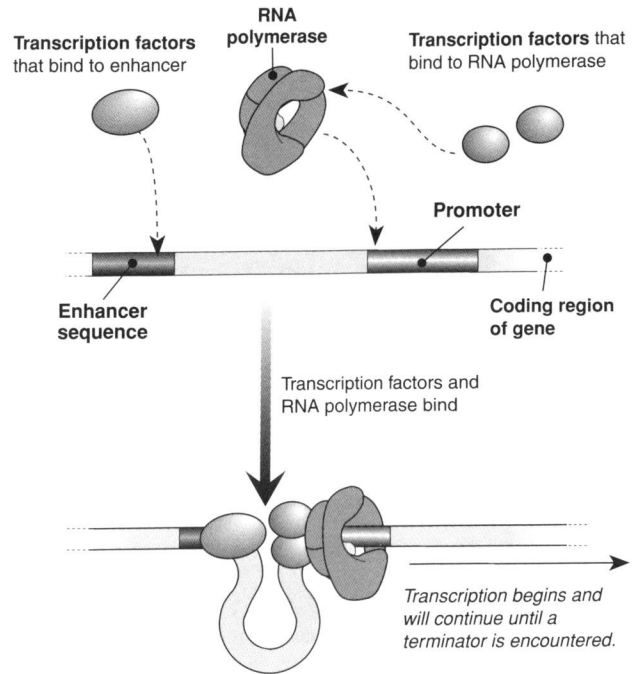

1. Explain the functional role of each of the following in relation to gene regulation in a prokaryote e.g. *E. coli*:

(a) Operon:

(b) Regulator gene:

(c) Operator:

(d) Promoter:

(e) Structural genes:

2. (a) Explain the advantage in having an inducible enzyme system that is regulated by the presence of a substrate:

(b) Suggest when it would **not** be adaptive to have an inducible system for metabolism of a substrate:

3. With reference to eukaryotes, briefly explain why the control of gene expression is necessary:

Genes and Chromosomes

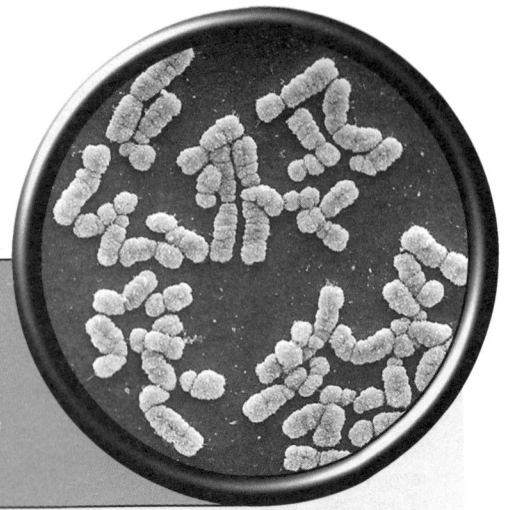

IB SL	IB HL	IB Options	AP Biology
Complete nos: 1-2, 4, 6-11(a)-(c), 12, 16, 21-22(a), 23, 27-28, 30, 33	Complete nos: 1-2, 4, 6-16, 21-22(a), 23, 27-28, 30, 33 Extension: 3, 5, 17-20, 31	Complete nos: Option D: 16-31 Extension: as appropriate	Complete nos: 1-33 Some numbers as extension as appropriate

Learning Objectives

☐ 1. Compile your own glossary from the **KEY WORDS** displayed in **bold type** in the learning objectives below.

Chromosome structure (pages 150-157, 184)

☐ 2. Describe the structure and morphology of eukaryote **chromosomes**, identifying the role of **histone proteins** in packaging the DNA in the nucleus.

☐ 3. With respect to structure and organization, distinguish between prokaryote and eukaryote chromosomes.

☐ 4. Explain what is meant by a **karyotype**. Explain the basis of karyotyping and describe one application of this process. Define: **autosomes**, **sex chromosomes**.

☐ 5. Explain, in general terms, how a karyotype is prepared.

☐ 6. Define, and recall the difference between, **gene** and **allele**. Clearly define the following terms: **genome**, **homologous chromosomes** (=homologues), **chromatid**, **centromere**.

Sources of variation (pages 160-163)

☐ 7. Appreciate that both genes and environment contribute to **phenotypic variation**. With reference to specific examples, identify sources of genetic and environmental variation.

Meiosis, linkage, and recombination

Meiosis (pages 160, 164-165)

☐ 8. Appreciate the general significance of meiosis in generating genetic variation. Identify how meiosis creates new allele combinations in the gametes.

☐ 9. Describe how chromosome numbers can vary between somatic cells (**diploid** 2N) and gametes (**haploid** 1N).

☐ 10. Recognize that meiosis, like mitosis, involves DNA replication during interphase in the parent cell, but that this is followed by *two* cycles of nuclear division.

☐ 11. Using simple diagrams, summarize the principal events associated with meiosis, to include:
(a) Pairing of **homologous chromosomes** (synapsis) and the formation of **bivalents**.
(b) **Chiasma** formation and exchange between **chromatids** in the first, (**reduction**) **division**.
(c) Separation of chromatids in the second division and the production of **haploid cells**.
(d) The associated behavior of the **nuclear envelope**, plasma membrane, and **centrioles**.
(e) Identification of the names of the main stages.

☐ 12. Describe the behavior of homologous chromosomes (and their associated alleles) during meiosis and fertilization, with reference to:
• The **independent assortment** of maternal and paternal chromosomes. Chance governs which pole

each chromosome of a bivalent moves to, ensuring random combinations of non-homologous chromosomes in the haploid nuclei.
• The **recombination** of segments of maternal and paternal homologous chromosomes in **crossing over**.
• The **random fusion** of gametes during fertilization.

Explain how these events in meiosis and fertilization give rise to genetic variety in the gametes.

Linkage and recombination (pages 160, 165-168)

☐ 13. With respect to inheritance, explain what is meant by the terms: **linkage** and **linkage group**. Explain the *consequences* of linkage to the inheritance of alleles.

☐ 14. Recall that **recombination** refers to the exchange of alleles between homologous chromosomes as a result of **crossing over**. Explain the *consequences* of recombination to the inheritance of alleles.

☐ 15. In general terms, explain the effect of linkage and recombination on the phenotypic ratios from dihybrid crosses (see the topic *Inheritance*).

Mutations as a source of variation (pages 169-172)

☐ 16. Explain what is meant by the general term **mutation** and understand the significance of mutations as the ultimate source of all new alleles.

☐ 17. Define: **spontaneous mutation**. Recognize that each species has its own frequency of naturally occurring mutations (called the **background mutation rate**).

☐ 18. Define the terms: **mutagen**, **induced mutation**. Identify the environmental factors that can cause mutations. Describe the effects of chemical mutagens and radiation on DNA and the rate of mutation.

☐ 19. Mutations may occur in different types of cell. The location of a mutation can have a different significance in terms of producing heritable change. Clearly define: **germ line**, **somatic mutation**, **gametic mutation**.

☐ 20. Recognize that mutations may have different survival value in different environments. Explain, with examples, how mutations may be **harmful**, **beneficial**, or **neutral** (silent) in their effect on the organism. Recognize the evolutionary importance of **neutral mutations**.

Types of mutations

Gene mutations (pages 173-176)

☐ 21. Explain what is meant by a **single gene mutation** and provide examples. Distinguish between single gene mutations involving change in a single nucleotide (commonly called **point mutations**), and those involving changes to a triplet (e.g. triplet deletion, triplet repeat). Understand why single gene mutations offer the greatest evolutionary potential.

☐ 22. Understand the cause and effect of single gene mutations as illustrated by **base**:
(a) **Substitution** (b) **Deletion**

☐ 23. Describe the effect of a base substitution mutation on the resulting amino acid sequence and the phenotype, as illustrated by the **sickle cell mutation** in humans.

☐ 24. Recognize other disorders that arise as a result of single gene mutations: β-**thalassemia**, **cystic fibrosis**, and **Huntington disease**. Describe the genetic basis of one or more of these diseases.

Chromosome mutations (page 177)

☐ 25. Explain what is meant by a **chromosome** (block) **mutation**, and contrast chromosome mutations and single gene mutations.

☐ 26. Using symbolic diagrams in which genes are identified, describe the nature and genetic consequences of chromosome mutations, with reference to:
(a) **Translocation**: movement of a group of genes between different chromosomes.
(b) **Inversion**: rotation and rejoining of a segment of a chromosome.
(c) **Duplication**: one chromosome loses a segment, and the segment is added to its homologue.
(d) **Deletion**: loss of part of a chromosome.

Aneuploidy (pages 178-181)

☐ 27. Recognize **aneuploidy** as a condition in which the chromosome number of an individual is not an exact multiple of the typical haploid set for the species. Explain how aneuploidy may arise as a result of **non-disjunction** during meiosis. Define the term **polysomy**

and recognize polysomies as types of aneuploidy. Appreciate that certain aneuploidies occur with a predictable frequency.

☐ 28. With respect to chromosomal disorders, explain what is meant by a **syndrome**. Explain why chromosomal abnormalities are typically characterized by a suite of abnormal phenotypic characteristics.

☐ 29. Describe examples of aneuploidy in human sex chromosomes, e.g., Turner or Klinefelter syndrome.

☐ 30. Describe examples of **polysomy** in human autosomes, e.g., the common form of Down syndrome (trisomy 21).

☐ 31. Explain what is meant by the **maternal age effect**. Describe an example of a chromosomal disorder that shows a maternal age effect.

Genetic Screening (pages 158-159, 224-227, 240)

☐ 32. Discuss the role of **genetic counseling** in managing the occurrence of inherited genetic disorders in families. Describe the circumstances under which couples might seek genetic counseling.

☐ 33. Appreciate the implications of **genome projects**, and the **Human Genome Project** in particular, for the detection and diagnosis of genetic disorders. Recognize that our deeper knowledge of the basis of genetic disorders will assist in **genetic screening** and counseling in the future (see *Gene Technology*).

Textbooks

See the 'Textbook Reference Grid' on pages 8-9 for textbook page references relating to material in this topic.

Supplementary Texts

See pages 5-6 for additional details of these texts:

■ Adds, J., *et al.*, 2001. **Genetics, Evolution and Biodiversity**, (NelsonThornes), pp. 80-81, 88-100.

■ Clegg, C.J., 1999. **Genetics & Evolution**, (John Murray), pp. 19-22, 34-39, 41, 43.

■ Jones, N., *et al.*, 2001. **Essentials of Genetics**, (JM), pp. 17-25, 61-73, 131-34, 157-71, 257.

Internet

See pages 10-11 for details of how to access **Bio Links** from our web site: **www.thebiozone.com**. From Bio Links, access sites under the topics:
GENERAL BIOLOGY ONLINE RESOURCES > Online Textbooks and Lecture Notes

CELL BIOLOGY AND BIOCHEMISTRY: • Cell & molecular biology online • MIT biology hypertextbook • Molecular biology web book

GENETICS: • DNA basics • MIT biology hypertextbook • Gene almanac • Virtual library on genetics ... *and others* > **Molecular Genetics (DNA):** • Beginners guide to molecular biology • Basic genetics • DNA and molecular genetics • DNA from the beginning • DNA workshop • E!Mouse • Primer on molecular genetics • Protein synthesis ... *and others* > **Mutations and Genetic Disorders:** • Blazing a genetic trail • Mutant fruit flies • Mutations • Facts about cystic fibrosis • Cystic fibrosis • Mutations causing cystic fibrosis • Joint center for sickle cell and thalassemic disorders • Sickle cell disease • Sickle cell information center ... *and others*

Periodicals

See page 6 for details of publishers of periodicals:

STUDENT'S REFERENCE

Sources of genetic variation

■ **Mechanisms of Meiosis** Biol. Sci. Rev., 15(4), April 2003, pp. 20-24. *A clear and thorough account of the events and mechanisms of meiosis.*

■ **Radiation and Risk** New Scientist, 18 March 2000 (Inside Science). *In large doses radiation can kill you in hours. In low doses, it can lead to slow death by cancer. How do we quantify the effects?*

■ **Secrets of The Gene** National Geographic, October 1999, pp. 42-75. *A comprehensive article covering the nature of genes and mutations, including inherited defects, screening & treatment.*

■ **The Biological Aspects of Down's Syndrome** Biol. Sci. Rev., 10(5) May 1998, pp. 11-15. *Chromosome trisomy: how it arises and its phenotypic effects. Includes methods of diagnosis.*

■ **Antibiotic Resistance** Biol. Sci. Rev., 12(2) November 1999, pp. 28-30. *The genetic basis of antibiotic resistance in bacteria.*

Genetic screening and counseling

■ **Genetic Screening - Controlling the Future** Biol. Sci. Rev., 12 (4) March 2000, pp. 36-38. *The techniques, applications, and ethical questions posed by genetic screening.*

TEACHER'S REFERENCE

Genes and genetic variation

■ **DNA 50** SSR, 84(308), March 2003, pp. 17-80. *A special issue with various articles examining the practical and theoretical aspects of teaching molecular genetics and inheritance.*

■ **Investigating Polyploidy** The American Biology Teacher, 64(5), May 2002, pp. 364-368. *Polyploidy and its occurrence in plants, and the effects of chromosome number on cell size.*

■ **Doing the Meiosis Shuffle** The American Biology Teacher, 61(1), January 1999, pp. 60-61. *Describes a short experiment with cards that can be used to clarify ideas in meiosis and cell division.*

■ **DNA: 50 Years of the Double Helix** New Scientist, 15 March 2003, pp. 35-51. *A special issue on DNA: structure and function, repair, the new-found role of histones, and the functional significance of chromosome position in the nucleus.*

■ **Mystery of the Crooked Cell** The American Biology Teacher, 61(2), Feb. 1999, pp. 137-148. *Sickle cell disease and gene mutations; an experiment to establish the link between hemoglobin and symptoms of sickle cell disease.*

■ **Modeling Mitosis and Meiosis** The American Biology Teacher, 62(3), March 2000, pp. 204-206. *An activity where students solve problems to develop a better understanding of nuclear division.*

■ **Making the Chromosome-Gene-Protein Connection** The American Biology Teacher, 58(6), Sept. 1996, pp. 364-366. *Sickle cell disease as a model for understanding the relationships between chromosome, gene, and protein (excellent).*

■ **Weapons of Mass Disruption** Sci. American, Nov. 2002, pp. 58-635. *The effects of radiation on the human body and an account of the new threat posed by the "weapons of mass destruction".*

■ **Cystic Fibrosis** Scientific American, December 1995, pp. 36-43. *The basis of the cystic fibrosis mutation: the nature of the mutation and how it brings about the symptoms of the disease.*

■ **The Challenge of Antibiotic Resistance** Sci. American, March 1998, pp. 32-39. *An excellent article covering the basis of antibiotic resistance in bacteria. Such resistance confers an advantage.*

Genetic screening and counseling

■ **The Price of Prevention** Scientific American, April 1995, pp. 98-103. *Diagnostic techniques and the use of screening as a preventative measure.*

■ **Vital Data** Scientific American, March 1996, pp. 76-81. *Ethics of genetic screening and the use of screening in the Human Genome Project.*

■ **I See a Long Life and a Healthy One** New Scientist, 23 Nov. 2002, pp. 42-45. *An examination of the ethical issues surrounding genetic testing.*

Software and video resources are now provided in the Teacher Resource Handbook

Eukaryote Chromosome Structure

A2

The chromosomes of eukaryote cells (such as those from plants and animals) are complex in their structure compared to those of prokaryotes. The illustration below shows a chromosome during the early stage of meiosis. Here it exists as a chromosome consisting of two chromatids. A non-dividing cell would have chromosomes with the 'equivalent' of a single chromatid only. The chromosome consists of a protein coated strand which coils in three ways during the time when the cell prepares to divide.

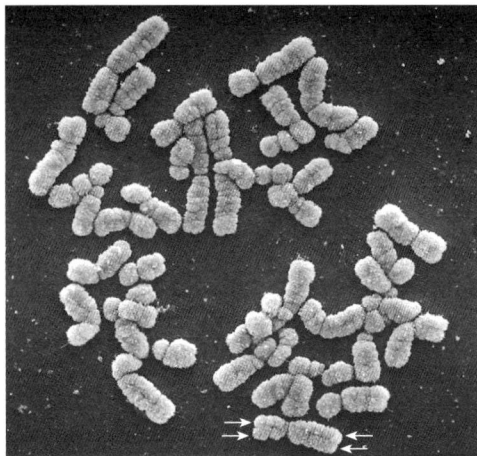

A cluster of human chromosomes during metaphase of cell division as seen with a scanning electron microscope. Individual chromatids are difficult to discern on these double chromatid chromosomes (a visible one is arrowed).

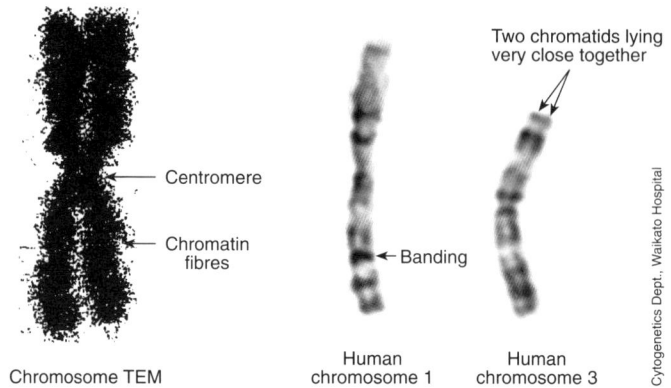

Chromosome TEM

Centromere

Chromatin fibres

Two chromatids lying very close together

Banding

Human chromosome 1

Human chromosome 3

Cytogenetics Dept., Waikato Hospital

Human chromosomes: To the left is a TEM of a human chromosome from a dividing white blood cell. Note the compact arrangement of the chromatin and the two chromatids (see how a chromosome is tightly packaged in the diagram below). The two photographs on the right have been taken through a light microscope and show the banding patterns on chromosomes 1 and 3.

Metaphase Chromosome

This chromosome has two chromatids (one shown dark and one light) indicating that it is taking part in cell division. Each chromatid contains an identical copy of the DNA molecule.

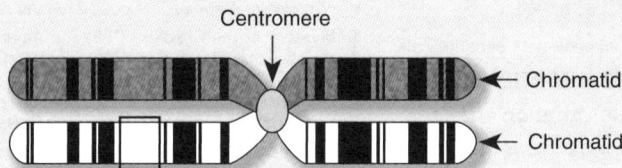

Centromere

Chromatid

Chromatid

Enlarged view of segment of chromosome above

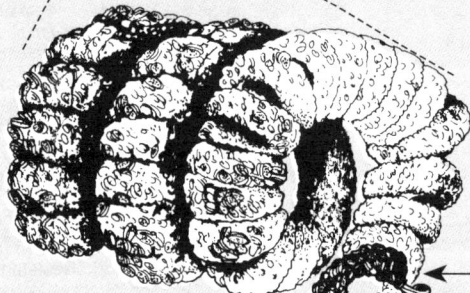

Chromosome in a Non-Dividing Cell

In non-dividing cells, chromosomes exist as single-armed structures (each is the equivalent of one of the chromatids in a metaphase chromosome prepared for cell division). It would not be visible as a coiled structure like the one below, but would be 'unwound' to make the genes accessible (see the TEM of the nucleus below).

Nuclear membrane

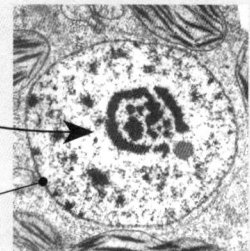

TEM photo of nucleus

Coiling of chromosome

Chromosomes are made up of **chromatin** (a complex of DNA and protein). The DNA is coiled at several levels so that long DNA molecules can fit inside the nucleus. This condensation is achieved by the wrapping of DNA around protein cores and the folding and further wrapping of the chromatin fibre.

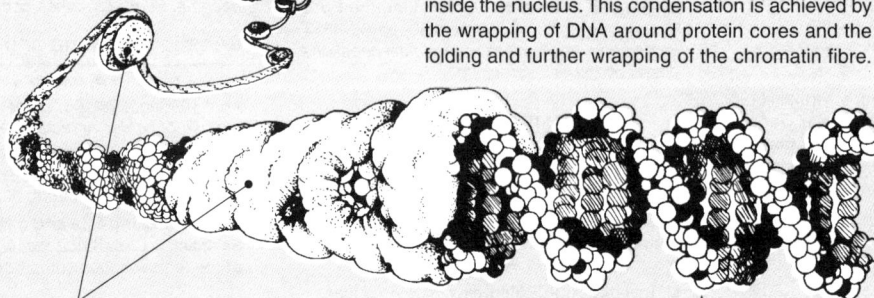

Histone proteins

The DNA is wrapped around ball-shaped histone protein core. Some are attached to the strand of DNA. These proteins may regulate DNA functioning in some way.

DNA molecule

The DNA molecule is a double-helix arrangement of atoms containing genes that comprise many millions of base pairs forming the genetic code.

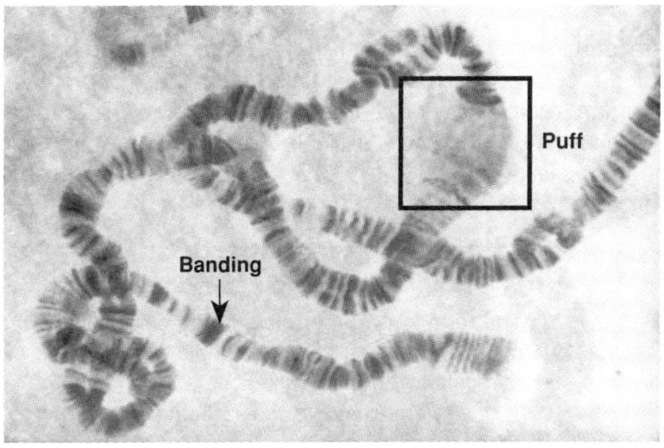

Banded chromosome: This light microscope photo is a view of the polytene chromosomes in a salivary gland cell of a sandfly. It shows a banding pattern that is thought to correspond to groups of genes. Regions of chromosome **puffing** are thought to occur where the genes are being transcribed into mRNA (see SEM on right).

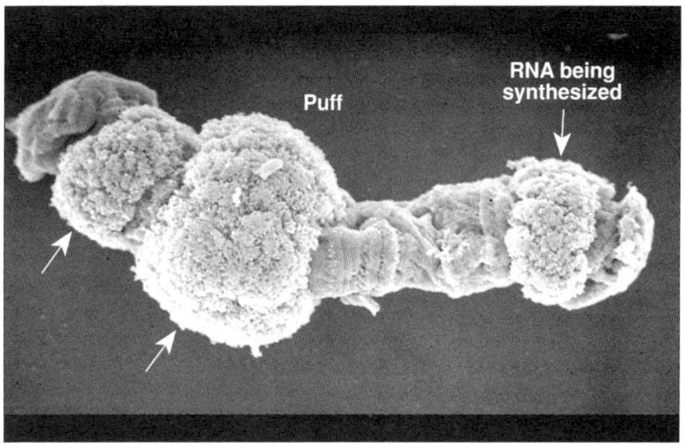

A **polytene chromosome** viewed with a scanning electron microscope (SEM). The arrows indicate localized regions of the chromosome that are uncoiling to expose their genes (puffing) to allow transcription of those regions. Polytene chromosomes are a special type of chromosome consisting of a large bundle of chromatids bound tightly together.

1. Explain the significance of the following terms used to describe the structure of chromosomes:

(a) DNA: _____

_____

(b) Chromatin: _____

_____

(c) Histone: _____

_____

(d) Centromere: _____

_____

(e) Chromatid: _____

_____

2. Each human cell has about a 1 meter length of DNA in its nucleus. Explain how it is possible to fit all of this DNA into the nucleus of a cell and organize it in such a way that it does not get ripped apart during cell division:

_____

_____

_____

_____

_____

_____

_____

_____

_____

_____

_____

_____

_____

Karyotypes

The diagram below shows the **karyotype** of a normal human. Karyotypes are prepared from the nuclei of cultured white blood cells that are 'frozen' at the metaphase stage of mitosis (see the photo circled opposite). A photograph of the chromosomes is then cut up and the chromosomes are rearranged on a grid so that the homologous pairs are placed together. Homologous pairs are identified by their general shape, length, and the pattern of banding produced by a special staining technique. Karyotypes for a human male and female are shown below. The **male karyotype** has 44 autosomes, a single X chromosome, and a Y chromosome (written as 44 + XY), whereas the **female karyotype** shows two X chromosomes (written as 44 + XX).

Typical Layout of a Human Karyotype

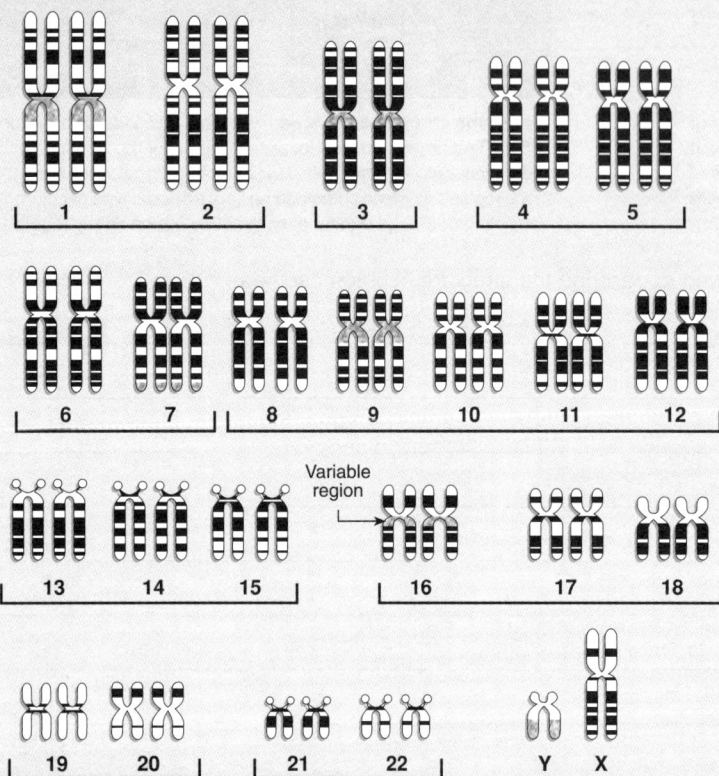

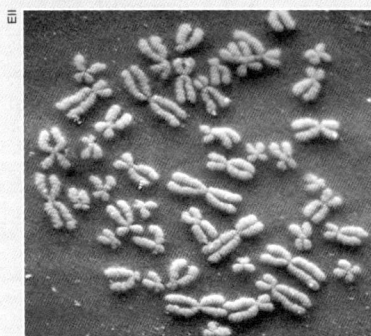

Karyotypes for different species

The term **karyotype** refers to the chromosome complement of a cell or a whole organism. In particular, it shows the number, size, and shape of the chromosomes as seen during metaphase of mitosis. The diagram on the left depicts the human karyotype. Chromosome numbers vary considerably among organisms and may differ markedly between closely related species:

Organism	Chromosome number (2N)
Vertebrates	
human	46
chimpanzee	48
gorilla	48
horse	64
cattle	60
dog	78
cat	38
rabbit	44
rat	42
turkey	82
goldfish	94
Invertebrates	
fruit fly, *Drosophila*	8
housefly	12
honey bee	32 or 16
Hydra	32
Plants	
cabbage	18
broad bean	12
potato	48
orange	18, 27 or 36
barley	14
garden pea	14
Ponderosa pine	24

NOTE: The number of chromosomes is not a measure of the quantity of genetic information.

A scanning electron micrograph (SEM) of human chromosomes clearly showing their double chromatids

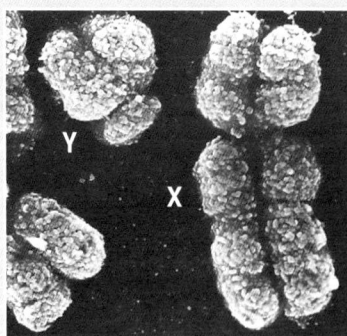

This SEM shows the human X and Y chromosomes. Although these two are the sex chromosomes, they are not homologous.

1. Explain what a karyotype is:

2. Briefly define the following terms:

(a) Autosome:

(b) Sex chromosome:

Preparing a Karyotype

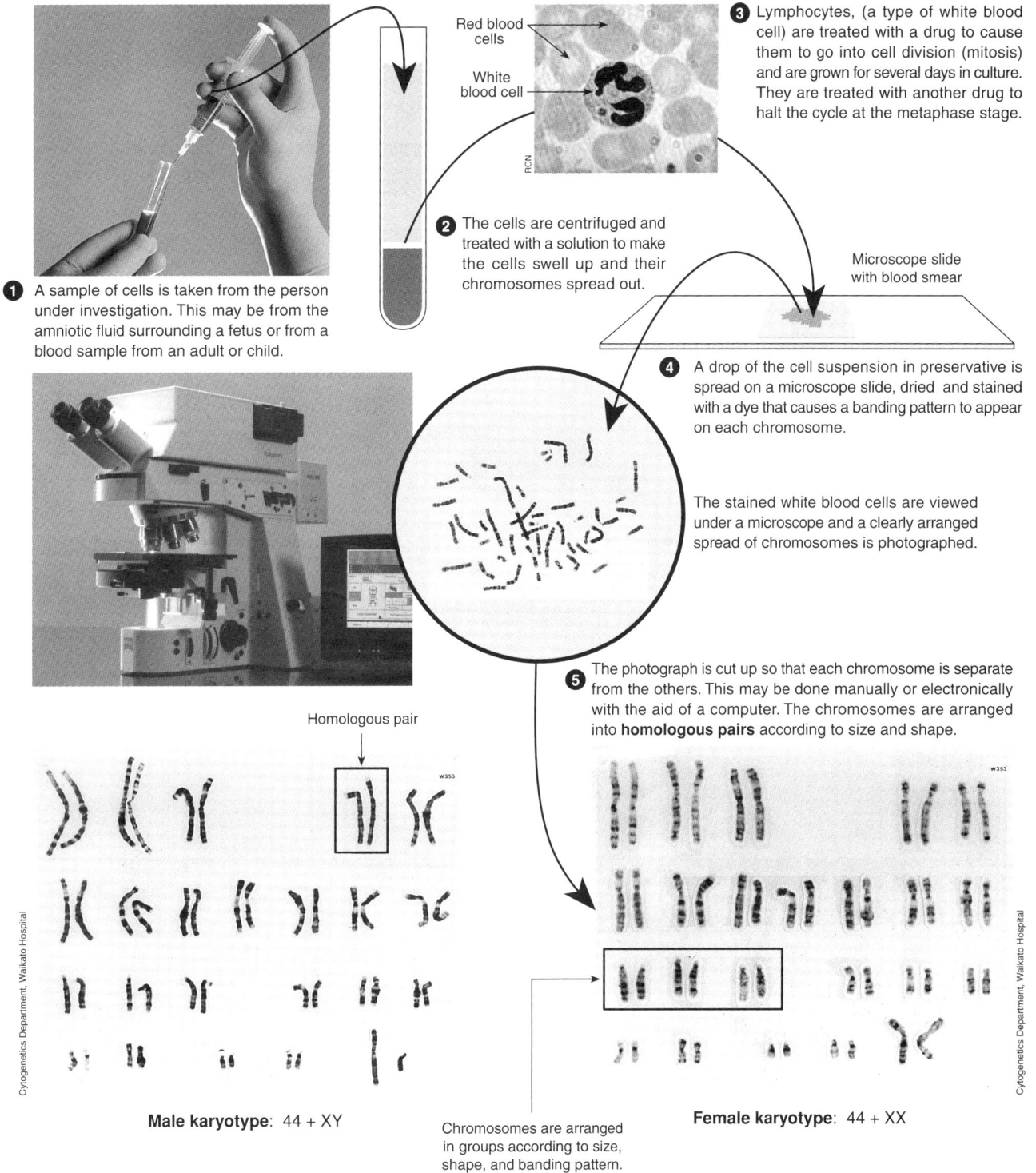

1 A sample of cells is taken from the person under investigation. This may be from the amniotic fluid surrounding a fetus or from a blood sample from an adult or child.

2 The cells are centrifuged and treated with a solution to make the cells swell up and their chromosomes spread out.

Red blood cells

White blood cell

3 Lymphocytes, (a type of white blood cell) are treated with a drug to cause them to go into cell division (mitosis) and are grown for several days in culture. They are treated with another drug to halt the cycle at the metaphase stage.

Microscope slide with blood smear

4 A drop of the cell suspension in preservative is spread on a microscope slide, dried and stained with a dye that causes a banding pattern to appear on each chromosome.

The stained white blood cells are viewed under a microscope and a clearly arranged spread of chromosomes is photographed.

5 The photograph is cut up so that each chromosome is separate from the others. This may be done manually or electronically with the aid of a computer. The chromosomes are arranged into **homologous pairs** according to size and shape.

Homologous pair

Male karyotype: 44 + XY

Chromosomes are arranged in groups according to size, shape, and banding pattern.

Female karyotype: 44 + XX

Cytogenetics Department, Waikato Hospital

3. On the male and female karyotype photographs *above* **number** each homologous pair of chromosomes using the diagram on the facing page as a guide.

4. **Circle** the sex chromosomes (**X** and **Y**) in the female karyotype and male karyotype.

5. Write down the number of *autosomes* and the arrangement of *sex chromosomes* for each sex:

    (a) **Female**:   No. of autosomes: _____   Sex chromosomes: _____

    (b) **Male**:   No. of autosomes: _____   Sex chromosomes: _____

6. State how many chromosomes are found in a:

    (a) Normal human (somatic) body cell: _____   (b) Normal human sperm or egg cell: _____

PA 2   Human Karyotype Exercise

Determine the sex and chromosome condition of the individual whose chromosomes are displayed on the facing page. The karyotypes presented on the previous pages, and the hints on how to recognize chromosome pairs, can be used to help you complete this activity.

1. Cut out the chromosomes on the facing page and arrange them on this record sheet in their homologous pairs.

2. (a) Determine the sex of this individual: **Male** or **Female**   (circle one)

   (b) State whether the individual's *chromosome arrangement* is: **Normal** or **Abnormal**   (circle one)

   (c) If the arrangement is *abnormal*, state in what way: _____

1	2	3	4	5

6	7	8	9	10	11	12

13	14	15	16	17	18

19	20	21	22	Sex chromosomes

Cut out the chromosomes below and arrange them on the Record Sheet provided on the facing page

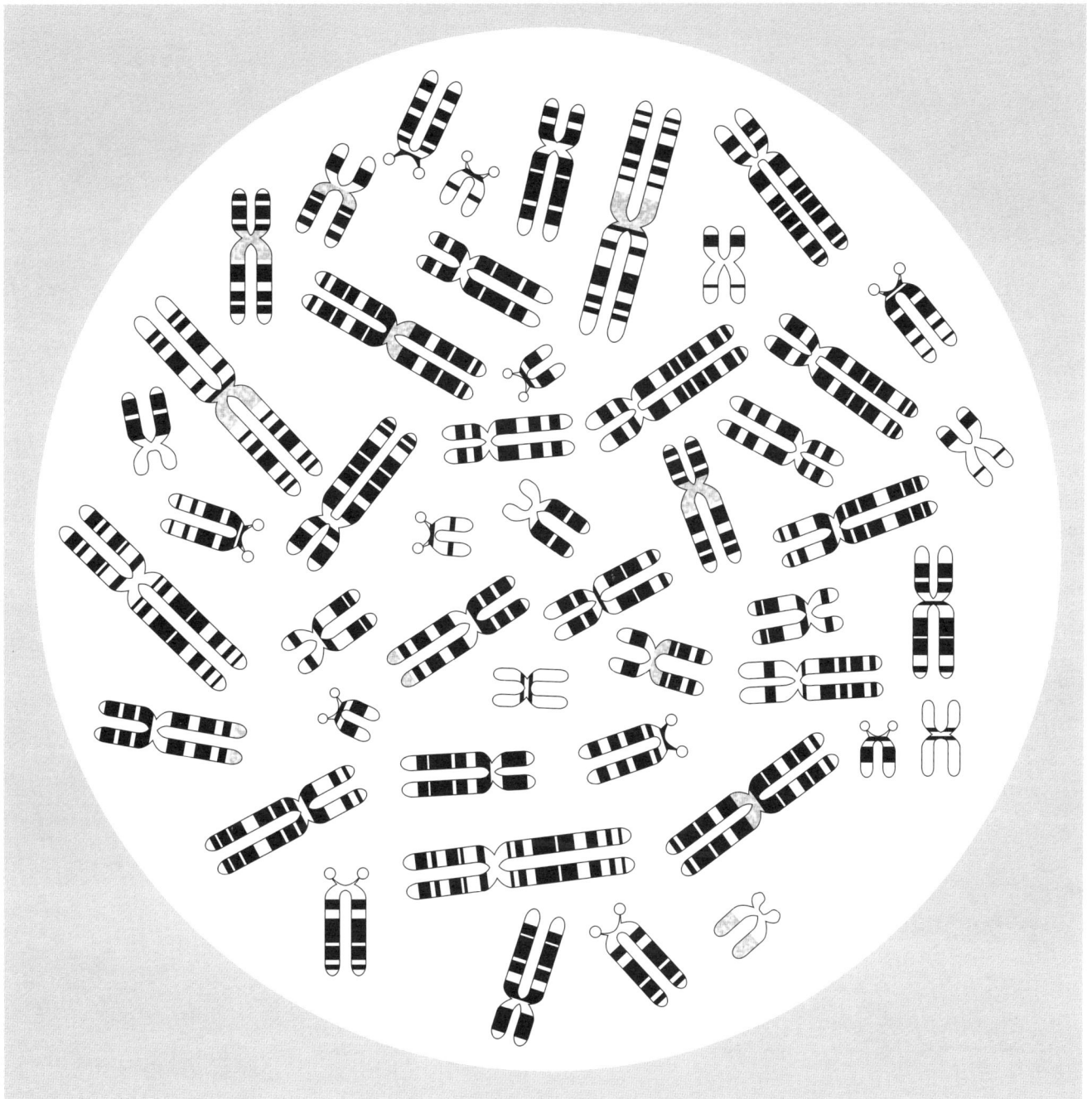

Distinguishing Characteristics of Chromosomes

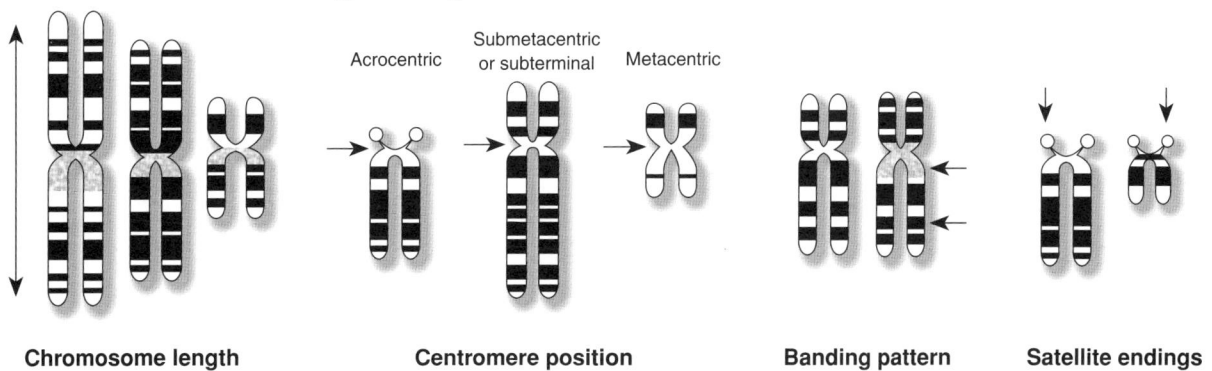

| Chromosome length | Centromere position | Banding pattern | Satellite endings |

Acrocentric

Submetacentric or subterminal

Metacentric

Each chromosome has distinctive features that enable it to be identified and distinguished from others. The banding pattern does not represent individual genes, but regions of the chromosome that would contain up to many hundreds of genes. They are 'stained' in a special technique that gives them their banded appearance.

This page is left blank deliberately

Genomes

Genome research has become an important field of genetics. A **genome** is the entire haploid complement of genetic material of a cell or organism. Each species has a unique genome, although there is a small amount of genetic variation between individuals within a species. For example, in humans the average genetic difference is one in every 500-1000 bases. Every cell in an individual has a complete copy of the genome. The base sequence shown below is the total DNA sequence for the

genome of a virus. There are nine genes in the sequence, coding for nine different proteins. At least 2000 times this amount of DNA would be found in a single bacterial cell. Half a million times this quantity of DNA would be found in the genome of a single human cell. In the viral genome below, the first gene has been highlighted gray, while the start and stop codes are in black rectangles. As is common in viral and bacterial genomes, some of the genes overlap. This increases the efficiency of DNA usage.

Genome for the φX174 bacterial virus

Start ↓

The gray area represents the nucleotide sequence for a single gene

```
CCGTCAGGATTGACACCCTCCCAATTGTATGTTTTCATGCCTCCAAATCTTGGAGGCTTTT ATG GGTTCGTTCTTATTACCCTTCTGAATGTCACGCTG
ACGAATACCTTCGGTTCGTAACCCCTAACTCTTTCTCATCTTTACGGTGTTCGGAGTTATCGTCCAAATTCTGGGAGCTATGGGAGTTTCAGTTTTATTA
GATGGATAACCGCATCAAGCTCTTGGAAGAGATTCTGTCTTTTCGTATGCAGGCCCTTGAGTTCGATAATGGTGATATGTATGTTGACGGCCATAAGGCT
ACAATAATTATAGTTCAACCCCCTCGTGTAACATCGTAACACGGTTAAGTAGGTAATTGAAGAGTCATTGTCTATGTTTGAGTAGTGCTTGGAGTCTTGG
CTATAGACCACCGCCCCGAAGGGGACGAAAAATGGTTTTTACAGAACGAGAAGACGGTTACGCAGTTTTGCCGCAAGCTGGCTGGTGAACGCCCTCTTAA
TTTCGGACATGCGCTATAGAATCAGGTCCGGACCTCGTTAGACATTGTGAGTAGGAATTATGGAAAGAAAAACCCCATTAATATGAGTAGCGCTTATAGG
GCTATTCAGCGTTTGATGAATGCAATGCGACAGGCTCATGCTGATGGTTGGTTTATCGTTTTTGACAGTCTCACGTTGGCTGACGACCGATTAGAGGCGT
GTGAGGCGCACAGTTAGTAATCGGAACGCTCGGAGCCGTGGTTCTTGGTATGCTGGTTATAGTGCTTTTATCAGTGCGTTTCGTAACCCTAATAGTATTT
GTATCAGTATTTTTGTGTGGCTGAGTATCGTAGAGCTAATGGCCGTCTTCATTTCCATGCGGTGCACTTTATGGGGACACTTCGTAGAGGTAGCGTTGAG
CGCACATGGGTTGAGGCTACCCGTATGAGATTGGTATTCCGGTGCATAAAAGGTTCGATAAATTGAGCCGCGGTAACGCATAGGCTGCTGGTTTTAATCG
AGGACGCTTTTTCACGTTGTCGTTGGTTGTGGCCTGTTGATGCTAAAGGTGAGCGCTTAAAGGTACCAGTTATATGGCTGTTGGTTTCTATGTGGCTAA
GAAGGCTTCATGGGTGTCGAACCAAAAATCAGTCAACAAGGTAAGAAATGGAACAACTCGAAATGGTCGTTCCAGGTATAGAGTGAAAAAGAATTGCATA
AAGGTGTTCAGAATCAGAATGAGCCGCAAGTTCGGGATGAAAATGGCTCACAATGACGAAATCTCTCCACGGAGTGGTTAATCGAAGTTAGCAAGGTGGGTT
ACGCGGCGGTTTTGCAGCCGATGTCATTGAAAAGGGTCGGAGTTAGAGTACAGAGAAAAAGGCAAGACGAAGTTATAGACCAACTTGCCGCAGCGCAGCA
AGCTGTGACGAGAAATCTGGTCAAATTTATGCGCGCTTGGATAAAAATGATTGGCGTATCCAACCTGGAGAGTTTTATCGGTTCCATGAGGCAGAAGTTA
AAGGGGGTCGTCAGGTGAAGGTAAATTAAGCATTTGTTCGTCATCATTAAGGACGAAATAGTTCTATTAAAAAGGTGAGTAGTCTTTATAGGCTTTCACA
AAT TGA GAAAATTCGACCTATCCTTGCGCAGCTCGAGAAGCTCTTAGTTTGCGACGTTTCGCCATCAACTAACGATTGTGTCAAAAAGTGACGCGTTGGAT
AATTTTAGAGTTGTTGTTTAGAGATGGTACTTGTTTTTACAGTGACTATAGATTTGGTCAGGAAGTGCTTGCAGGGTTCGTATAATTCGGTGAAGAGGAG
AAGAGCGTGGATTACTATCTGAGTCCGATGCTGTTCAAGGAGTAATAGGTAAGAAATCATGAGTCAAGTTAGTGAACAATCCGTACGTTTCCAGACCGCT
GCAGTCATCGTTAGGTTTGAAACAATGAGGAGTCTTTTAGCTTTAGTAGAAGCCAATTTAGGTTTTGCCGTCTTCGGACTTACTCGAATTATCTCCGGTT
GCTCTCGTGCTCGTCGCTGCGTTGAGGCTTGCGTTTATGGTACGC...
GCCTGCGAGGTGCGGTAATTATTCACAAAAGGGGATTTAAGTCGCGGA...
GTTAAAGCCGGTGAATTGTTCGGGGTTTACCTTGCGTGTAGGCGGA...
TCGCCGGAAATGGGAACGGAAATCATCGAGGGTTGCCGACGGCTGC...
CGTGTTTGGTATGTAGGTGGTCAACAATTTTAATTGCAGGGGCTT...
TAGAGCTTCGTCAGCGGTCGCTATTGGCCTCATCAACTTTAGCAT...
GGACGCCGTTGGCGCTGTCCGTCTTTGTGGATTGCGTCGTGGCGT...
GTTCTTTTCGCCGTAGGAGTTATATTGGTCATCACAATTGTCAGC...
GCACGATTAAGCCTGATACCAATAAAATCCCTAAGCATTTGTTTC...
GAGTCCTCGTTCGCGTGGTCAGGTTTACAAAAAGTGTAGGGTGGT...
ACTGAGCTTTCTGGCCAAATGAGGAGTTCTACCAGATCTATTGAC...
GTCTCTAATGTCGCGTACTGTTCATTTCGTGCGAACAGTCGCAGT...
GGCATCTGGGTATGATGTTGATGGAACTGAGCAAACGTCGTTAGG...
TTCAGTTTCGTGGAAATCGCAATTCCATGACTTAGAGAAATCAGC...
ATACCGATATTGGTGGCGACCCTGTTTTGTATGGCAACTTGGCGC...
TCTTCGGCCAAGGAGTTACTTAGCCTTCGGAAGTTCTTCCACTAT...
GGTGATTTGCAAGAACGCGTACTTATTCGCAACCATGATTATGAC...
GGCCGTTTTTAATTTTAAAAATGGCGAAGCGAATATTGGAGTGTGAGTTAGAAAATAGTGGTT[?]AGTAGTAACTTAGCGGTCACCAGCCGTGTAACGCTA
TGAGGGGTTGACCAAGCGAAGCGGGGTAGGTTTTGTGCTTAGGAGTTTAATCATGTTTCAGA[?]TTTTATTTGTCGCCACAATTGAAAGTTTTTTTCTGAT
ATTGGGAGTTTGATAGTTTTATATTGGAACTGGTACATCGAAATCCACAGACATTTTGTC[?]ACGGCTTCTTCGAGGTGATTGTCTTCAGTCTTGGTGGAA
ATGCTGGTAATGGTGGTTTTCTTCATTGCATTCAGATGGATACATCTGTCAAGGCCG[?]AATCAGGTTGTTTCAGTTGGTGCTGATATTGCTTTTGATGG
TACGGCTGGTAGGTTTCCTATTTGTAGTATCCGTCAGCCCTCCCATCAGCCTT[?]G[?]TTCTTCTGAGTTTCGGTTGGTTTGTCGGTTTTTTAAATCCCAGC
GATGGTGGTTATTATACGGTCAAGGACTGTGACTATTGACGTCCTTCCC[?]ACGCCCCGCAATAACGTGACGTTGGTTTCATGGTTTGGTCTAAGT
TCGTGGTTTGTATTTAGTGGAGTGAATTCACCGACCTCTGTTTTATTAGAGAAATTATTGGACTAAGTCGCTTTGGTTAGGGGCCGTAAATCATCGCCATT
ATTGGTGGCGGTATTGCTTGTGCTCTTGGTGGTGGCGCCATGTCTAAATTGTTTGGAGCCGGTCAAAAAGCGGCCTCCGGTGGCATTCAAGGTGATGTGG
TTTGATCCCGCCGGACTAGTCCCAATCCTTGTAATGTCGGAAGTTACCGTCTAAATTATGGTCGTAGTGGGTACGGATGTCATAAGAATAGCCATCGTT
TGTTTCTGGTGGTATGGGTAAAGGTCGTAAAGGAGTTCTTGAAGGTACGTTGGAGGGTGGGAGTTCTGCCGTTTGTGATAAGTTGGTTGATTTGGTTGGA
GTACTCGTGGTCGTGGGAGGGTTCGTAATTCGAGTCCCTTAGGTCGTCGTTCTATTAGTGCTCATAGGAAAGGAAATAGTCGGCGTCTGAACGGTGGTTC
GTTCGTCTGCTGGTATCGTTGACGGCGGATTTGAGAATCAAAAAGAGCTTAGTAAAATGGAACTGGACAATCAGAAAGAGATTGCCGAGATGCAAAATGA
GAAGACAACTATTCGTTCGTAGAGTAAAAGACGTATATGGACCAGAAAGCATAAGACCGCACTTGAGCGGGTGAGTTACGGTCGTTAGAGAAAAAGTCAG
GAGTCTAGTGCTCGGCTTGCGTCTATTATGGAAAAGACCAATCTTTCCAAGCAACAGCAGGTTTCCGAGATTATGGGCGAAATGCTTACTCAAGCTCAAA
ATGGGGAGTAAGAGGCAAAGGACTACTTGATTCAGTTGGAGTCCTGATTGGAACGGTCAGTAAAGAAAGTAAACCAGTAACCATTTTATGACTGGTCGGC
TGGCTGTTGTCATATTGGCGCTAGTGCAAAGGATATTTCTAATGTCGTCACTGATGCTGCTTCTGGTGTGGTTGATATTTTTCATCGTATTGATAAAGCT
AATAAAGGATGTGTTTAATCTCGGTTATGGTAGTGGAAATGGGAGAAAGGTCTTTAACAAGGTTCATAGCCGTTG
```

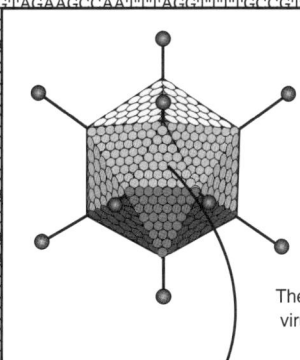

φX174 bacterial virus

This virus consists of a protein coat made up of a 20-sided polyhedron. Spikes made of protein at each of the 12 corners are used to attach itself to a bacterial cell.

The entire DNA sequence for the virus is made up of just 9 genes

1. Define the term **genome**: _____

    _____

2. Determine the number of bases, kilobases, and megabases in this genome (100 bases in each row, except the last):

    1 kb = 1 kilobase = 1000 bases   **1 Mb** = 1 megabase = 1 000 000 bases

    (a) Bases: _____ (b) Kilobases: _____ (c) Megabases: _____

3. State whether the genome of the virus above is **small, average** or **large** in size compared to those viruses listed in the table on the earlier page *DNA Molecules* (in the topic Molecular Genetics):

    _____

4. Determine how many bases are present in the gene shown above (in the gray area): _____

RDA② Genome Projects

There are many genome projects underway around the world, including the Human Genome Project. The aim of most genome projects is to determine the DNA sequence of the organism's entire genome. Over one hundred bacterial and viral genomes, as well as a number of larger genomes (including fruit fly, mouse, nematode worm, African clawed frog, pufferfish, zebra fish, rice, and rat) have already been sequenced. Genomes that are, for a variety of reasons, high priority for DNA sequencing include the cow, dog, honeybee, sea urchin, kangaroo, pig, cat, baboon, silkworm, and chicken. Genome sequencing is very costly, so candidates are carefully chosen. Important factors in this choice include the value of the knowledge to practical applications, the degree of technical difficulty involved, and the size of the genome (currently very large genomes are avoided). Genome sizes and the number of genes per genome vary, and are not necessarily correlated with the size and structural complexity of the organism itself. Once completed, genome sequences are analyzed by computer to identify genes.

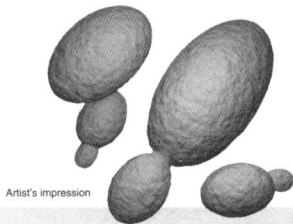

Artist's impression

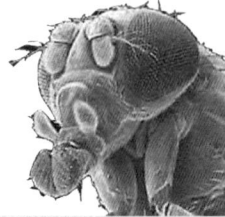

Yeast (*Saccharomyces cerevisiae*)

Status: Completed in 1996
Number of genes: 6000
Genome size: 13 Mb

The first eukaryotic genome to be completely sequenced. Yeast is used as a model organism to study human cancer.

Bacteria (*Escherichia coli*)

Status: Completed in 1997
Number of genes: 4403
Genome size: 4.6 Mb

E. coli has been used as a laboratory organism for over 70 years. Various strains of *E. coli* are responsible for several human diseases.

Fruit fly (*Drosophila melanogaster*)

Status: Completed in 2000
Number of genes: 14 000
Genome size: 150 Mb

Drosophila has been used extensively for genetic studies for many years. About 50% of all fly proteins show similarities to mammalian proteins.

Mouse (*Mus musculus*)

Status: Completed in 2002
Number of genes: 30 000
Genome size: 2500 Mb

New drugs destined for human use are often tested on mice because more than 90% of their proteins show similarities to human proteins.

Chimpanzee (*Pan troglodytes*)

Status: In progress
Genome size: 3000 Mb

The chimp and human genomes differ by less than 5%. Identification of differences could provide clues to the genetics of malaria and cancer, as chimps are less prone than humans to these conditions.

Banana (*Musa acuminata*)

Status: In progress
Genome size: 500-600 Mb

The first tropical crop to be sequenced. Bananas have high economic importance. Knowledge of the genome will assist in producing disease resistant varieties of banana.

Maize (*Zea mays*)

Status: In progress
Genome size: 2500 Mb

Maize is a major world crop and an important model organism for studying monocotyledons (including other cereals). The genome contains many repeats, so it will not be fully sequenced.

Chicken (*Gallus domesticus*)

Status: High priority (needs funds)
Genome size: 1200 Mb

Various human viruses were first found in chickens making this species important for the study of human disease and cross-species transfers. It will be the first bird genome to be sequenced.

1. Calculate the number of genes per Mb of DNA for the organisms above:

    (a) Yeast: _____ (b) *E. coli*: _____ (c) Fruit fly: _____ (d) Mouse: _____

2. Suggest why the number of genes per Mb of DNA varies between organisms (hint: consider relative sizes of introns):

    _____

    _____

3. Suggest why researchers want to sequence the genomes of plants such as wheat, rice, and maize:

    _____

    _____

4. Using a web engine search (or other research tool), find the following:

    (a) **First multicellular animal genome** to be sequenced: _____ Date: _____

    (b) **First plant genome** to be sequenced: _____ Date: _____

Genetic Counseling

A 3

Genetic counseling provides an analysis of the risk of producing offspring with known gene defects. It involves presenting available options to family members so that the potential risks can be avoided or reduced. **Screening tests** (analyses of a patient's DNA) are often used for the identification of specific defective genes. The use of these tests is still an area of great debate.

Autosomal Recessive Conditions		Autosomal Dominant Conditions	
The list of inherited disorders below are all caused by recessive alleles on autosomes (non-sex chromosomes). Because they are recessive, they will bring about the condition only in homozygous recessive genotypes.		*The inherited disorders below are all caused by dominant alleles on autosomes. Because they are dominant, they will bring about the condition in heterozygous genotypes, as well as homozygous dominant individuals. Any dominant allele present in the person will cause the disease.*	
Trait	**Description**	**Trait**	**Description**
Color blindness (total)	Perception only in gray due to missing cones in the retina.	Centralopathic epilepsy	Seizures primarily between ages 4 and 16, thereafter less frequently and usually disappearing by age 40.
Cystic fibrosis	Malfunction of the pancreas and other glands; thick mucus in various body passages, leading to pneumonia and emphysema. Death usually occurs in childhood. It is the most frequent lethal genetic disorder in childhood (about 1 case in 3,700 live births).	Diabetes insipidus	Inadequate output of antidiuretic hormone, leading to production of large amount of urine, accompanied by extreme thirst. (Also produced by an x-linked gene).
Galactosemia	Decreased levels of galactose-1-phosphate uridyl transferase, produce enlargement of the liver, cataracts, and mental retardation.	Dwarfism	Inhibited growth caused by a number of different genes, and accompanied by a variety of other symptoms.
Hydrocephalus	Excessive accumulation of fluid in the skull, with many genetic and non-genetic causes.	Glaucoma	Blindness caused by increased fluid pressure in the eye, with degeneration of the nerve cells. (Also caused by recessive genes).
Deafness	About half of severe childhood deafness is caused by this allele.	Hemoglobin types	At least five different genes code for this protein, with over 200 different known variations.
Maple syrup urine disease	Mental and physical retardation produced by a block in amino acid metabolism. Isoleucine in the urine produces the characteristic odor.	Huntington's disease	Involuntary movements of the face and limbs, later general mental deterioration. Beginning of symptoms is highly variable, usually between 30 to 40 years of age.
Niemann-Pick disease	Accumulation of lipids in nerve cells causing mental retardation. Other symptoms include enlarged liver and retarded growth. Death usually occurs by three years of age.	Muscular dystrophy	Abnormal muscle function with deterioration. (Also caused by autosomal recessive and by x-linked genes).
Pernicious anemia	Digestive system defect prevents normal absorption of vitamin B12, leading to a number of symptoms including greatly decreased numbers of red blood cells.	Intestinal polyposis	Formation of many small bulges in the colon, usually leading to cancer.
Tay-Sachs disease	Progressive developmental paralysis, mental deterioration, and blindness, resulting in death, usually by three years of age. A lipid storage disease similar to Niemann-Picks.	Psoriasis	Eruption of reddish bumps covered by silvery scales, primarily on the elbow, knees, scalp and trunk.
Xeroderm pigmentosum	Inability of skin cells to repair DNA damage done by sunlight: it produces heavy freckling, becoming cancerous in childhood.	Retinitis pigmentosa	Inflammation of the retina with increased pigmentation, leading to blindness.

Consult the table above describing autosomal dominant and recessive conditions. Form a discussion group with one or two other classmates and answer the following questions, summarizing your conclusions in the spaces provided.

1. A man with **psoriasis** who marries a normal woman consults you about the probability that his children will have the disorder. Explain what you would tell him:

_____

_____

2. A normal couple have had three children, one normal and two with **Tay-Sachs** disease. As their genetic counselor, describe what you would tell them about the probability of their next child being normal:

_____

_____

3. Debate whether DNA tests should be used for identifying defective genes for which there is no effective treatment:

_____

_____

Sources of Genetic Variation

RA 2

The genetic variability between individuals is what makes us all different from each other. Brothers and sisters may look similar to each other but there are always significant differences between them (unless they happen to be identical twins). The differences between close relatives is due mostly to a **shuffling** of the existing genetic material into new combinations. In addition to this is the new variation that originates from the **mutation** of existing genes. While most mutations are harmful, there are a significant number that are thought to be 'silent' and do not appear to have any effect on the individual. On rare occasions, a mutation may even prove to be beneficial. Mutations create new **alleles** and form an important part of the evolutionary process.

Mutations
Gene mutations; chromosome mutations

Mutations are the source of all **new** genetic information. Existing genes are modified by base substitutions and deletions, causing the formation of new alleles.

Mutation: Substitute **T** instead of **C**

Original DNA
A A A A T G C T T C T C

Mutant DNA
A A A A T G T T T C T C

Single Gene Mutations

Mutations may cause alterations in the genetic instructions coded in the DNA of chromosomes. Most mutations are harmful, some are neutral (no effective change), while a very few may provide some improvement on the earlier version of the gene. Mutations may be accumulated (inherited) over many generations.

Chromosome Mutations

Pieces of chromosome may be rearranged during meiosis. Pieces may be turned upside-down, duplicated, moved from one chromosome to another or lost altogether. Most instances are harmful, but occasionally they may be beneficial.

Sexual Reproduction
Independent assortment; crossing over and recombination; mate selection

Sexual reproduction provides a rearrangement and shuffling of the genetic material into new combinations.

Independent Assortment

Genes are carried on chromosomes – 23 pairs in the case of humans. Each chromosome pair is sorted independently of the other pairs during meiosis. This random shuffling produces a huge variety of gametes from a single individual (parent).

Recombination

Pieces of chromosome are often exchanged with a chromosome's homologue (its paired chromosome with equivalent genes). This increases shuffling of allele combinations.

Mate Selection

Variation is further enhanced by the choice of mate to produce offspring. Different combinations of genes will come together in the offspring, depending on which two parents mate together.

Genotype

Determines the **genetic potential** of an individual

Dominant, recessive, codominant and multiple allele systems, as well as interactions between genes, combine in their effects.

Phenotype

The phenotype expressed in an individual is the result of all the factors listed on this page. The genetic instructions for creating the individual may be modified along the way, or at least modified by environmental influences.

Environmental Factors

Environmental factors may influence the expression of the genotype. These factors may include physical factors such as temperature, light intensity, presence of groundwater, diet or nutrients, wind exposure, and pH. The presence of other organisms may also affect the expression of the genotype.

1. Describe three ways in which sexual reproduction can provide genetic variation in individuals:

   (a) _____

   _____

   (b) _____

   _____

   (c) _____

   _____

2. Explain how the environment of a particular genotype can affect its expression (the phenotype):

   _____

   _____

   _____

3. Name three common ways by which humans can choose to alter their phenotype:

   (a) _____

   (b) _____

   (c) _____

4. Explain why siblings (brothers and sisters) have a family similarity but are not identical (unless they happen to be identical twins):

   _____

   _____

   _____

   _____

   _____

5. Describe the evolutionary significance of mutations: _____

   _____

   _____

6. (a) Explain what is meant by a neutral (silent) mutation: _____

   _____

   _____

   (b) Explain how neutral mutations can be important in the evolution of populations: _____

   _____

   _____

   _____

   _____

   _____

   _____

   _____

Gene-Environment Interactions

RA2

External environmental factors can modify the phenotype encoded by genes. This can occur both in the development of the embryo and later in life. Even identical twins, which are essentially clones, have minor differences in their appearance due to factors such as diet. Environmental factors that affect the phenotype pf plants and animals include nutrient availability or diet, temperature, and the presence of other organisms (especially of one particular gender or other).

The Effect of Temperature

The sex of some animals is determined by the temperature at which they were incubated during their embryonic development. Examples include turtles, crocodiles, and the American alligator. In some species, high incubation temperatures produce males and low temperatures produce females. In other species, the opposite is true. The advantages of temperature regulated sex determination may arise through prevention of inbreeding (since all siblings will tend to be of the same sex).

The Effect of Other Organisms

The presence of other individuals of the same species may control the determination of sex in other individuals of the group. Some fish species, including some in the wrasse family (e.g. *Coris sandageri,* above), show such a change in phenotype. The fish live in groups consisting of a single male with attendant females and juveniles. In the presence of a male, all juvenile fish of this species grow into females. When the male dies, the dominant female will undergo physiological changes to become a male for the group. The male has distinctive vertical bands behind the gills. The female is pale in color and has very faint markings.

Severe stunting (krummholz)

Growth to genetic potential

Cline

The Effect of Altitude

Increasing altitude can stunt the phenotype of plants with the same genotype. In some conifers, e.g. Engelmann spruce (*Picea engelmannii*), plants at low altitude grow to their full genetic potential, but become progressively more stunted as elevation increases, forming krummholz (gnarled bushy growth forms) at the highest, most severe sites. This situation, where there is a continuous, or nearly continuous, gradation in a phenotypic character within a species, associated with a change in an environmental variable, is called a **cline**.

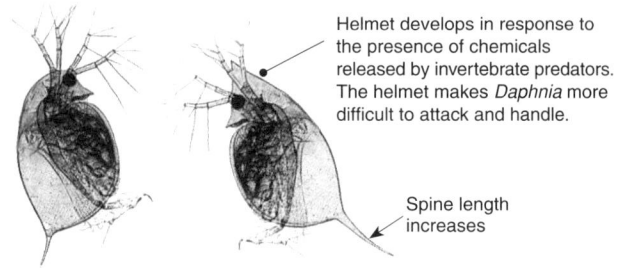

Helmet develops in response to the presence of chemicals released by invertebrate predators. The helmet makes *Daphnia* more difficult to attack and handle.

Spine length increases

Non-helmeted form   **Helmeted form with long tail spine**

Some organisms respond to the presence of other, potentially harmful, organisms by changing their morphology or body shape. Invertebrates such as *Daphnia* will grow a large helmet when a predatory midge larva (*Chaoborus*) is present. Such responses are usually mediated through the action of chemicals produced by the predator (or competitor), and are common in plants as well as animals.

1. One controversial theory concerning the extinction of the dinosaurs suggests a global change in temperature is involved. Briefly state how this might be explained in terms of the sex determination effect described above:

_____

_____

2. List some of the physical factors associated with altitude that would affect the plant phenotype: _____

_____

3. The hydrangea is a plant that exhibits a change in the color of its flowers, depending on the state of the soil. Name the physical factor that causes hydrangea flowers to be blue or pink:

_____

4. There has been much amusement over the size of record-breaking vegetables produced for competitions, such as enormous pumpkins. List the factors that you would control if you wanted the phenotype of a vegetable plant such as a pumpkin to grow to its maximum genetic potential:

_____

5. Color pointing in some breeds of cats such as the siamese, involves the activity of a temperature sensitive enzyme that produces the pigment melanin. Explain why the darker patches of fur are found only on the face, paws and tail:

_____

_____

At conception (the formation of the zygote), an organism possesses a genetic potential to grow into an adult form with certain characteristics. The exact form it takes is determined largely by the genes in its chromosomes, but it is also strongly influenced by a vast range of environmental factors acting upon it. These factors may subject an organism to stresses and may limit its growth to something less than it is capable of (e.g. plants that are grown at high altitude or in very exposed locations will often have stunted growth). Changes in the phenotype due solely to environmental factors are not inherited. Traumatic events such as the loss of a limb on a tree, or the removal of the tail in a young mammal (e.g. lambs, pups), does not affect the phenotype of the next generation (trees do not grow with limbs missing, and not one lamb has been born without a tail).

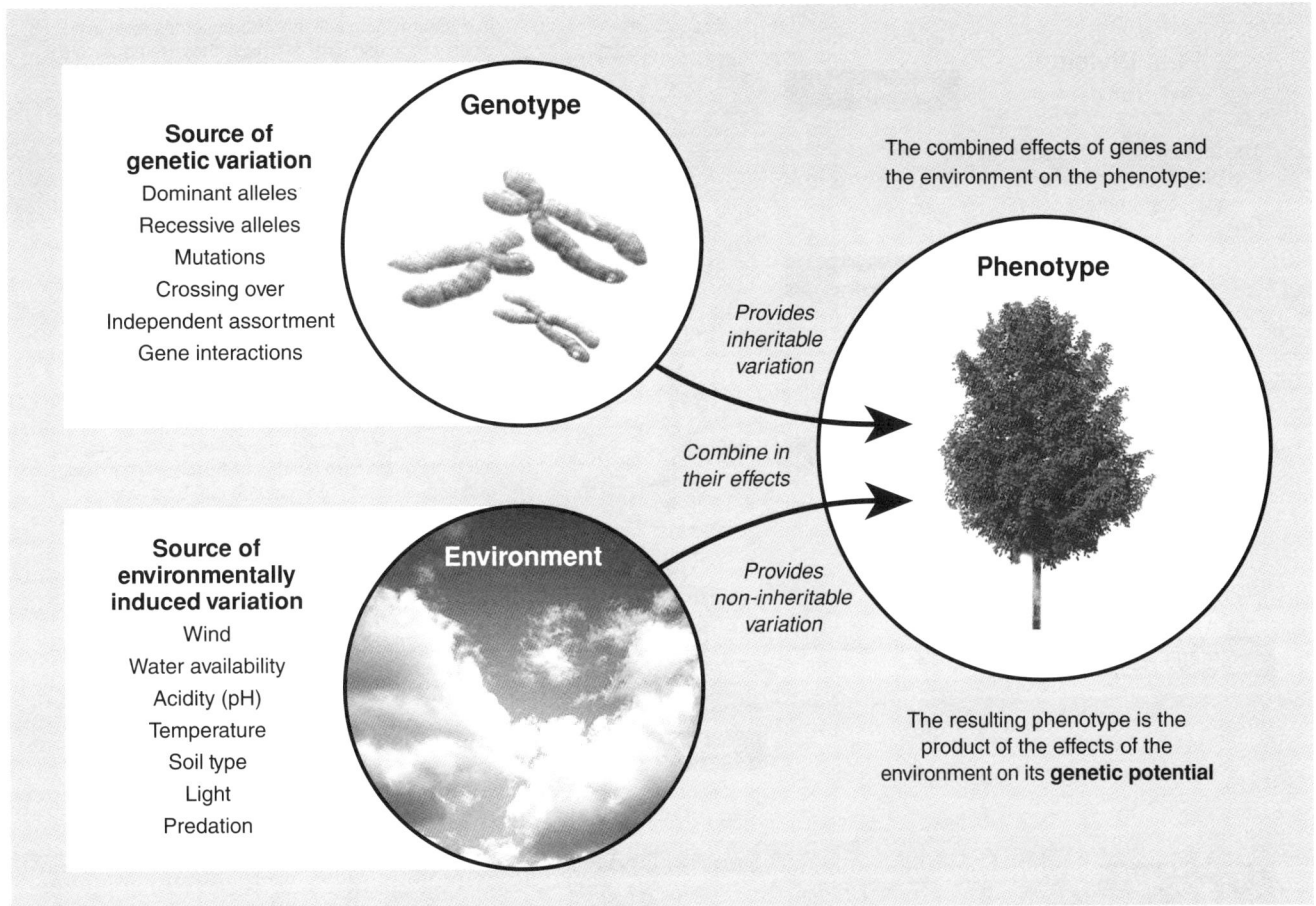

Genotype

Source of genetic variation

Dominant alleles
Recessive alleles
Mutations
Crossing over
Independent assortment
Gene interactions

Provides inheritable variation

The combined effects of genes and the environment on the phenotype:

Phenotype

Combine in their effects

Source of environmentally induced variation

Wind
Water availability
Acidity (pH)
Temperature
Soil type
Light
Predation

Environment

Provides non-inheritable variation

The resulting phenotype is the product of the effects of the environment on its **genetic potential**

6. On a windswept portion of a coast, two different species of plant (species A and species B) were found growing together. Both had a low growing (prostrate) phenotype. One of each plant type was transferred to a greenhouse where "ideal" conditions were provided to allow maximum growth. In this controlled environment, species B continued to grow in its original prostrate form, but species A changed its growing pattern and became erect in form.

Describe what you can conclude about the **cause** of the prostrate phenotype of each of the coastal grown plant species:

(a) Plant species A: _____

_____

_____

(b) Plant species B: _____

_____

_____

7. Provide a definition for the following terms:

(a) Genotype: _____

_____

(b) Phenotype: _____

_____

_____

A 1

Meiosis

The process of **meiosis** is a special type of cell division concerned with producing sex cells (gametes) for the purpose of sexual reproduction. This cell division occurs in the sex organs of plants and animals. If genetic mistakes (**single gene** and **block mutations**) occur here, they will be passed on to the offspring (they will be inherited).

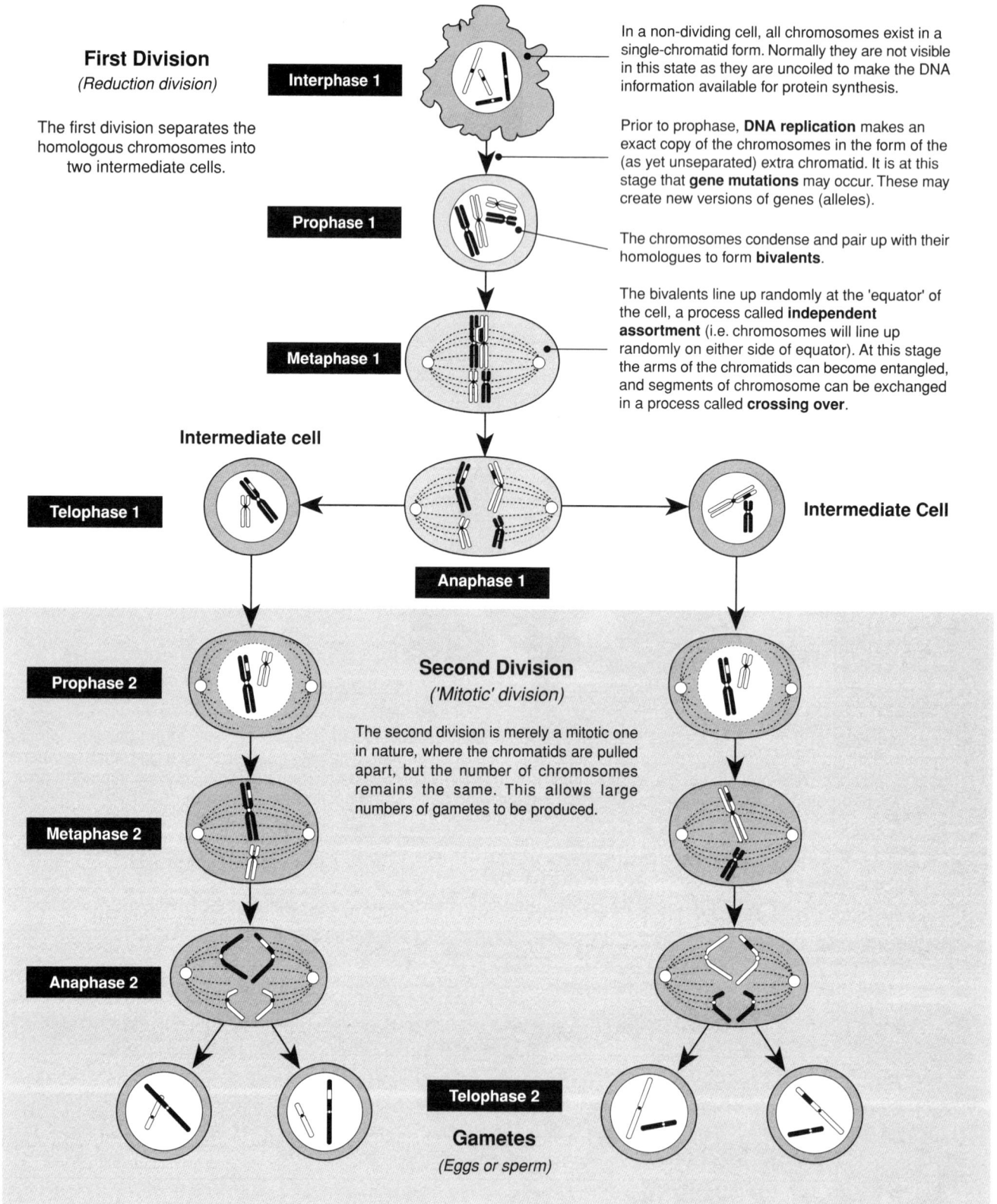

First Division
(Reduction division)

The first division separates the homologous chromosomes into two intermediate cells.

Interphase 1

In a non-dividing cell, all chromosomes exist in a single-chromatid form. Normally they are not visible in this state as they are uncoiled to make the DNA information available for protein synthesis.

Prophase 1

Prior to prophase, **DNA replication** makes an exact copy of the chromosomes in the form of the (as yet unseparated) extra chromatid. It is at this stage that **gene mutations** may occur. These may create new versions of genes (alleles).

The chromosomes condense and pair up with their homologues to form **bivalents**.

Metaphase 1

The bivalents line up randomly at the 'equator' of the cell, a process called **independent assortment** (i.e. chromosomes will line up randomly on either side of equator). At this stage the arms of the chromatids can become entangled, and segments of chromosome can be exchanged in a process called **crossing over**.

Intermediate cell

Telophase 1

Anaphase 1

Intermediate Cell

Prophase 2

Second Division
('Mitotic' division)

The second division is merely a mitotic one in nature, where the chromatids are pulled apart, but the number of chromosomes remains the same. This allows large numbers of gametes to be produced.

Metaphase 2

Anaphase 2

Telophase 2

Gametes
(Eggs or sperm)

1. This imaginary organism has a chromosome number of 4, or 2 pairs. Write the number of chromosomes and the **N** numbers next to each stage on the diagram. For this organism: **1N** = 2 chromosomes and **2N** = 4 chromosomes.

2. Briefly describe what is happening to chromosome numbers for the:

(a) First division: _____

(b) Second division: _____

Crossing Over

Crossing over refers to the mutual exchange of pieces of chromosome and involves the swapping of whole groups of genes between the **homologous** chromosomes. This process can occur only during the first division of **meiosis**. Errors in crossing over can result in **block mutations** (see activity *Chromosome Mutations*), which can be very damaging to development. Crossing over can upset expected frequencies of offspring in dihybrid crosses. The frequency of crossing over (COV) for different genes (as followed by inherited, observable traits) can be used to determine the relative positions of genes on a chromosome and provide a genetic map. There has been a recent suggestion that crossing over may be necessary to ensure accurate cell division.

Pairing of Homologous Chromosomes

Every somatic cell has a pair of each type of chromosome in its nucleus. These chromosome pairs, one derived from each parent, are called **homologous** pairs. At the first division of **meiosis**, homologous pairs line up at the equator (middle part) of the cell to form **bivalents**. This event, called **synapsis**, allows the chromatids of the homologous chromosomes to come in very close contact.

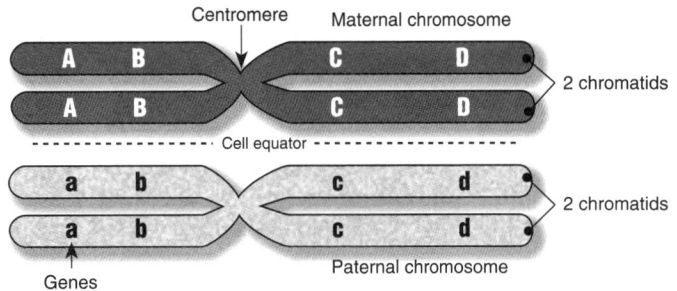

Chiasma Formation

Chiasma (the intertwining of chromatids from neighbouring chromosomes) forms at one or several points along the chromatids. Before the homologous chromosomes are pulled in opposite directions during the first meiotic division, some of the chromatin from homologous chromosomes becomes tangled (perhaps at several points along the same chromatid). In the diagram, the chiasma are in the process of forming and the exchange of pieces of chromosome have not yet taken place.

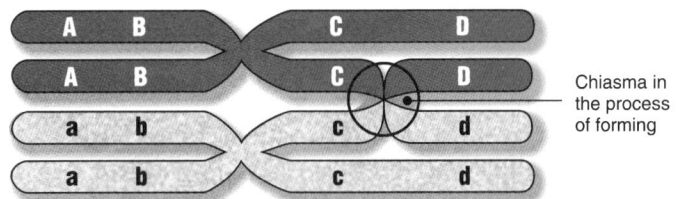

Separation

Every point where the chromatids have crossed over is called a **chiasma**. New combinations of genes result from this process, resulting in what is called **recombination**. Both of the chromosomes pictured have new genetic material (mixed types) that will be passed into the gametes about to be formed. This process of recombination is an important source of variation for the gene pool of a population.

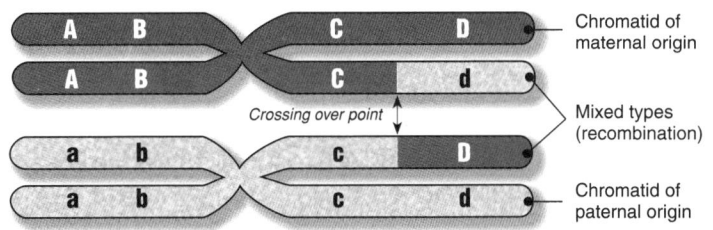

Gamete Formation

Once the final division of meiosis is complete, the two chromatids comprising each chromosome become separated. Because chromatid segments were exchanged, **four** chromatids that are quite different (genetically) are produced. If no crossing over had occurred, there would have been only two types (two copies of each). Each of these chromatids will end up in a different gamete (sperm or egg).

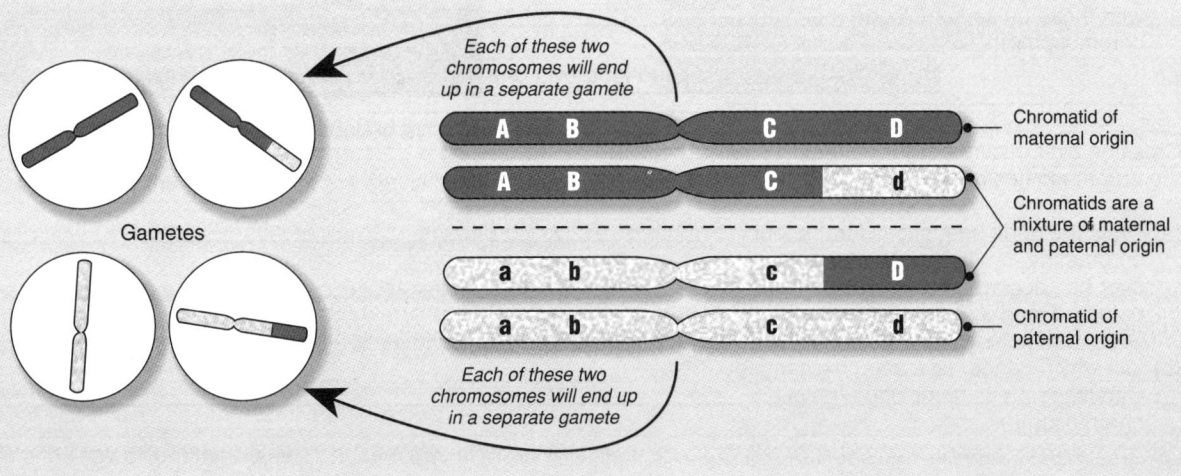

1. Briefly explain how the process of crossing over is going to alter the genotype of gametes: _____

_____

2. Describe the importance of crossing over in the process of evolution: _____

_____

A 3

Crossing Over Problems

The diagram below shows a pair of homologous chromosomes about to undergo chiasma formation during the first division of meiosis. There are known crossover points along the length of the chromatids (same on all four chromatids shown in the diagram). In the prepared spaces below, draw the gene sequences after crossing over has occurred on three unrelated and separate occasions (it would be useful to use different colored pens to represent the genes from the two different chromosomes). See the diagrams on the previous page as a guide.

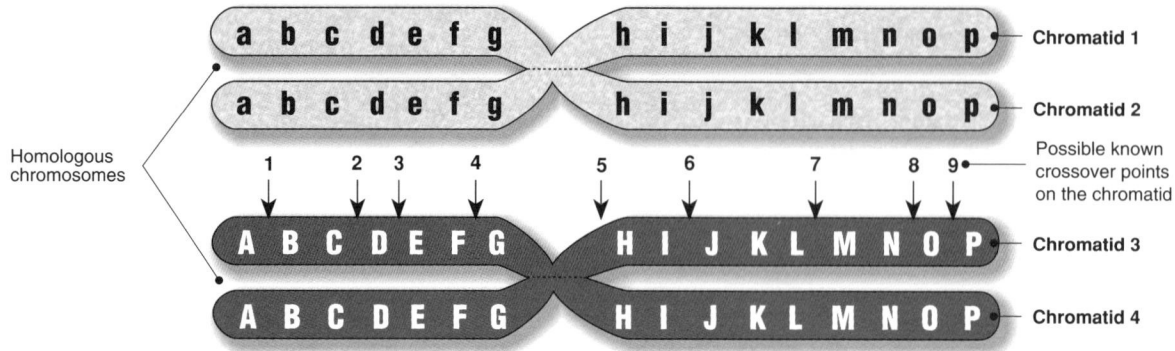

| a b c d e f g | h i j k l m n o p | Chromatid 1 |
| a b c d e f g | h i j k l m n o p | Chromatid 2 |

Homologous chromosomes

Possible known crossover points on the chromatid

1   2 3   4   5   6   7   8 9

| A B C D E F G | H I J K L M N O P | Chromatid 3 |
| A B C D E F G | H I J K L M N O P | Chromatid 4 |

1. Crossing over occurs at a **single** point between the chromosomes above.

   (a) Draw the gene sequences for the four chromatids (on the right), after crossing over has occurred at crossover point: **2**

   (b) List which genes have been exchanged with those on its homologue (neighbor chromosome):

   _____

2. Crossing over occurs at **two** points between the chromosomes above.

   (a) Draw the gene sequences for the four chromatids (on the right), after crossing over has occurred between crossover points: **6** and **7**

   (b) List which genes have been exchanged with those on its homologue (neighbor chromosome):

   _____

3. Crossing over occurs at **four** points between the chromosomes above.

   (a) Draw the gene sequences for the four chromatids (on the right), after crossing over has occurred between crossover point:s **1** and **3, 5**, and **7**

   (b) List which genes have been exchanged with those on its homologue (neighbor chromosome):

   _____

4. Explain the genetic significance of **crossing over**: _____

_____

_____

_____

Linkage

A 3

Linkage refers to genes that are located on the same chromosome. Linked genes tend to be inherited together and fewer genetic combinations of their alleles are possible. Linkage reduces the variety of offspring that can be produced (contrast this with recombination). In genetic crosses, linkage is indicated when a greater proportion of the progeny resulting from a cross are of the parental type (than would be expected if the alleles were assorting independently). If the genes in question had been on separate chromosomes, there would have been more genetic variation in the gametes and therefore in the offspring. Note that

in the example below, wild type alleles are dominant and are denoted by an upper case symbol of the mutant phenotype (Cu or Eb). This symbology used for *Drosophila* departs from the convention of using the dominant gene to provide the symbol. This is necessary because there are many mutant alternative phenotypes to the wild type (e.g curled and vestigial wings). A lower case symbol of the wild type (e.g. ss for straight wing), would not indicate the mutant phenotype involved. Alternatively, the wild type is sometimes denoted with a raised plus sign, e.g. cu^+cu^+ and all symbols are in lower case.

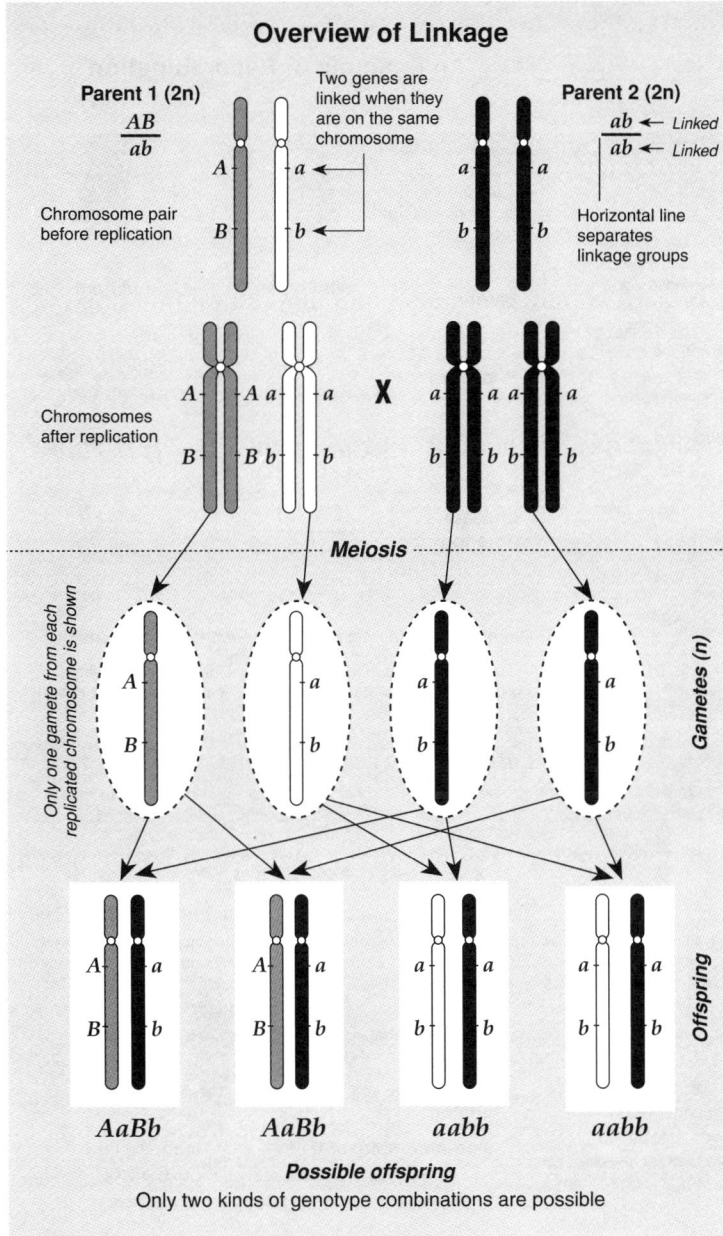

Overview of Linkage

Parent 1 (2n)
$$\frac{AB}{ab}$$

Two genes are linked when they are on the same chromosome

Chromosome pair before replication

Parent 2 (2n)
$$\frac{ab}{ab} \leftarrow \text{Linked}$$
$$\leftarrow \text{Linked}$$

Horizontal line separates linkage groups

Chromosomes after replication

X

Only one gamete from each replicated chromosome is shown

-------- **Meiosis** --------

Gametes (n)

Offspring

AaBb   *AaBb*   *aabb*   *aabb*

Possible offspring
Only two kinds of genotype combinations are possible

An Example of Linked Genes in *Drosophila*

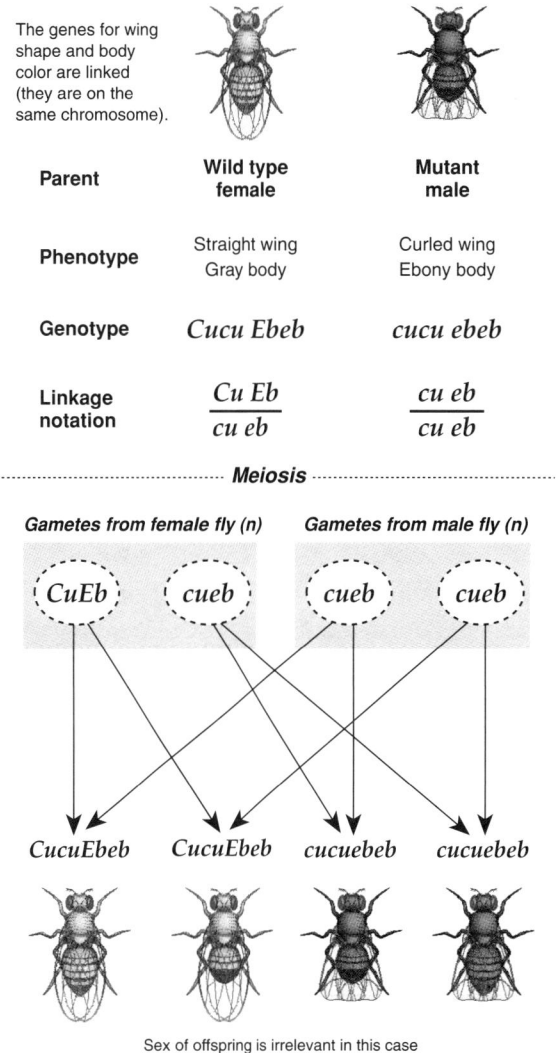

The genes for wing shape and body color are linked (they are on the same chromosome).

Parent	Wild type female	Mutant male
Phenotype	Straight wing Gray body	Curled wing Ebony body
Genotype	*Cucu Ebeb*	*cucu ebeb*
Linkage notation	$\dfrac{Cu\ Eb}{cu\ eb}$	$\dfrac{cu\ eb}{cu\ eb}$

-------- **Meiosis** --------

Gametes from female fly (n)   **Gametes from male fly (n)**

(*CuEb*)   (*cueb*)   (*cueb*)   (*cueb*)

CucuEbeb   *CucuEbeb*   *cucuebeb*   *cucuebeb*

Sex of offspring is irrelevant in this case

Contact **Newbyte Educational Software** for details of their superb *Drosophila Genetics* software package which includes coverage of linkage and recombination. *Drosophila* images © Newbyte Educational Software.

1. Define what is meant by **linkage**: _____

_____

2. (a) List the possible genotypes in the offspring (above, left) if genes A and B had been on **separate chromosomes**:

_____

(b) If the female *Drosophila* had been homozygous for the dominant wild type alleles (CuCu EbEb), state:

The genotype(s) of the F1: _____ The phenotype(s) of the F1: _____

3. Explain how linkage decreases the amount of genetic variation in the offspring: _____

_____

Recombination

Genetic recombination refers to the exchange of alleles between homologous chromosomes as a result of **crossing over**. The alleles of parental linkage groups separate and new associations of alleles are formed in the gametes. Offspring formed from these gametes show new combinations of characteristics and are known as **recombinants**; they are offspring with genotypes unlike either parent. The proportion of recombinants in the offspring can be used to calculate the frequency of recombination (crossover value). These values are fairly constant for any given pair of alleles and can be used to produce gene maps indicating the relative positions of genes on a chromosome. In contrast to linkage, recombination increases genetic variation. Recombination between the alleles of parental linkage groups is indicated by the appearance of recombinants in the offspring, although not in the numbers that would be expected had the alleles been on separate chromosomes (independent assortment). The example below uses the same genotypes as the previous activity (Linkage), but in this case crossing over occurs between the alleles in a linkage group in one parent. The symbology is the same for both activities.

Overview of Recombination

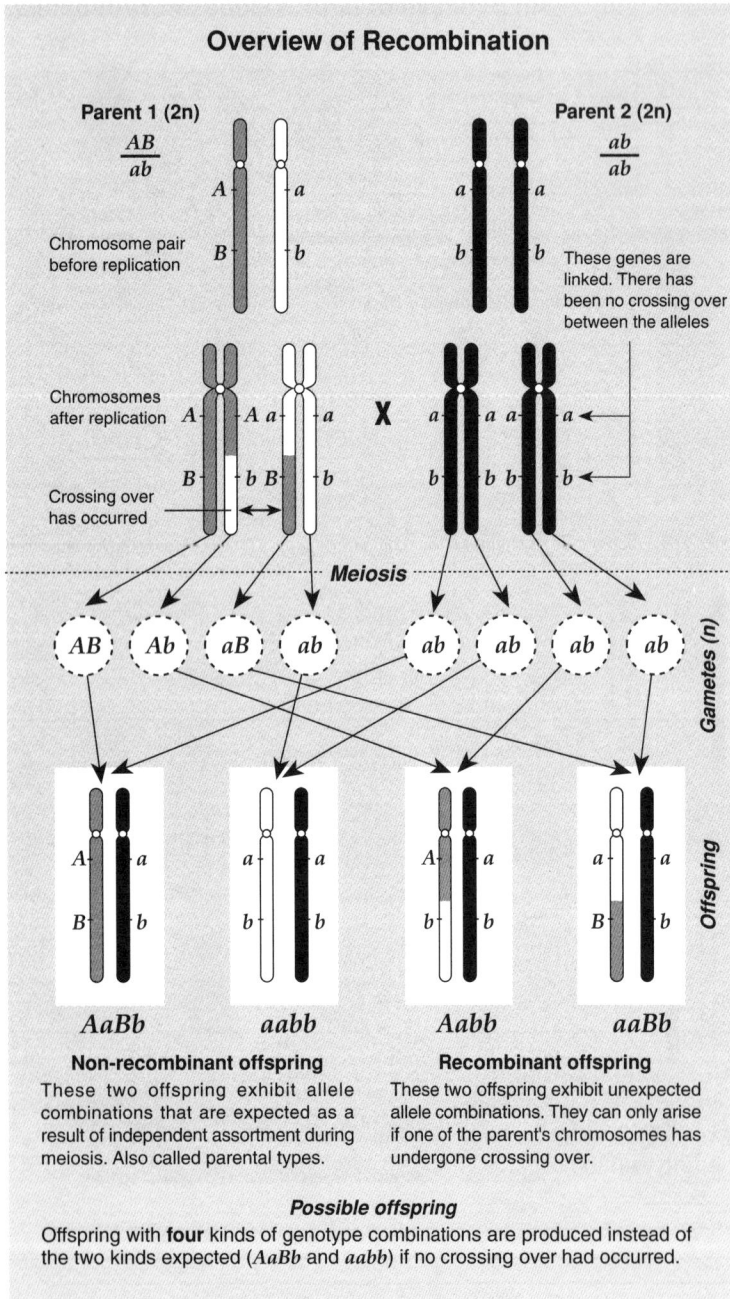

Parent 1 (2n) $\dfrac{AB}{ab}$

Parent 2 (2n) $\dfrac{ab}{ab}$

Chromosome pair before replication

These genes are linked. There has been no crossing over between the alleles

Chromosomes after replication

Crossing over has occurred

········ *Meiosis* ········

Gametes (n)

AB   Ab   aB   ab   ab   ab   ab   ab

Offspring

AaBb   *aabb*   *Aabb*   *aaBb*

Non-recombinant offspring

These two offspring exhibit allele combinations that are expected as a result of independent assortment during meiosis. Also called parental types.

Recombinant offspring

These two offspring exhibit unexpected allele combinations. They can only arise if one of the parent's chromosomes has undergone crossing over.

Possible offspring

Offspring with **four** kinds of genotype combinations are produced instead of the two kinds expected (*AaBb* and *aabb*) if no crossing over had occurred.

An Example of Recombination

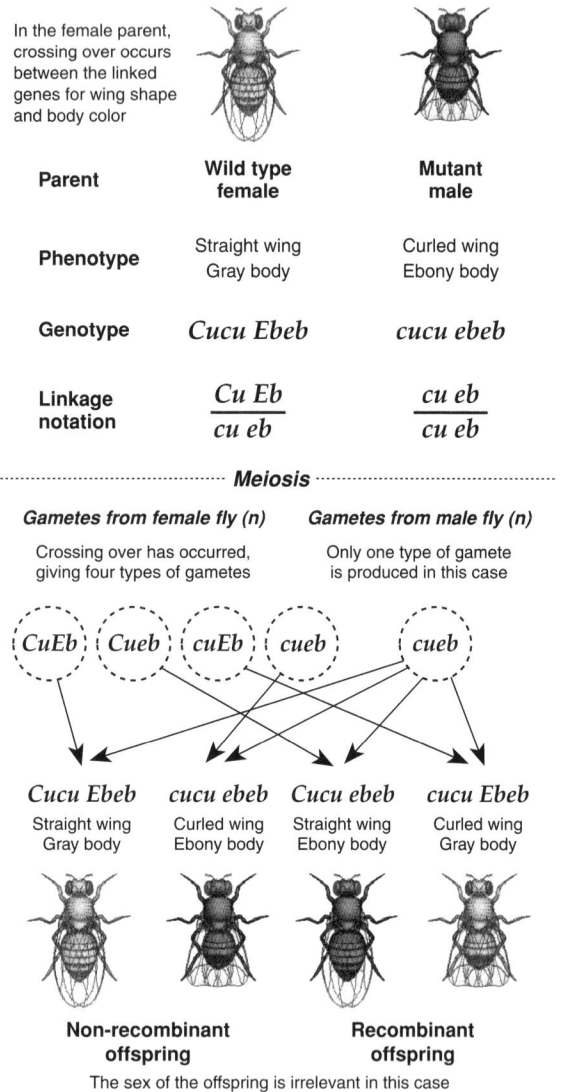

In the female parent, crossing over occurs between the linked genes for wing shape and body color

	Wild type female	Mutant male
Parent		
Phenotype	Straight wing Gray body	Curled wing Ebony body
Genotype	*Cucu Ebeb*	*cucu ebeb*
Linkage notation	$\dfrac{Cu\ Eb}{cu\ eb}$	$\dfrac{cu\ eb}{cu\ eb}$

········ *Meiosis* ········

Gametes from female fly (n)

Crossing over has occurred, giving four types of gametes

CuEb   *Cueb*   *cuEb*   *cueb*

Gametes from male fly (n)

Only one type of gamete is produced in this case

cueb

Cucu Ebeb   *cucu ebeb*   *Cucu ebeb*   *cucu Ebeb*

Straight wing Gray body

Curled wing Ebony body

Straight wing Ebony body

Curled wing Gray body

Non-recombinant offspring   **Recombinant offspring**

The sex of the offspring is irrelevant in this case

Contact **Newbyte Educational Software** for details of their superb *Drosophila Genetics* software package which includes coverage of linkage and recombination. *Drosophila* images © Newbyte Educational Software.

1. Define what is meant by **recombination**: _____

_____

2. State how recombination increases the amount of genetic variation in offspring: _____

_____

3. Explain why it is not possible to have a recombination frequency of greater than 50% (half recombinant progeny):

_____

Mutagens

Mutagens are chemicals or radiation that increase the likelihood of a mutation occurring. The rate of mutation induced by a mutagen is directly proportional to the dose received. Mutagens have a cumulative effect on an individual (i.e small doses over a long period may be just as harmful as a single, larger dose). The four main classes of mutagens are outlined below.

Mutagen and Effect	Those Most at Risk
Ionizing radiation Nuclear radiation from nuclear fallout, ultraviolet radiation from the sun and tanning lamps, X-rays and gamma rays from medical diagnosis and treatment. Ionizing radiation is associated with the development of cancers e.g. thyroid cancers and leukemia (nuclear fallout), and skin cancer (high UV exposure).	• Nuclear radiation: Those working with radioisotopes, or living near nuclear plants, waste dumps, or testing sites. • UV radiation: Fair skinned people in tropical and sub-tropical regions. Those using tanning beds excessively. • X-rays, gamma rays: Early workers in radiology. Today, better protection and safer equipment has considerably lowered the risks to technicians and patients.
Viruses and microorganisms Some viruses integrate into the human chromosome, upsetting genes and triggering cancers. Examples include hepatitis B virus (liver cancer), HIV (Kaposi's sarcoma), and Epstein-Barr virus (Burkitt's lymphoma, Hodgkin's disease). Aflatoxins produced by the fungus *Aspergillus flavus* are potent inducers of liver cancer.	• Hepatitis B: Intravenous drug users. • HIV: Intravenous drug users, those with unsafe sexual activity (i.e. unprotected sex with new partners). • The development of Burkitt's lymphoma in response to infection with Epstein-Barr virus is triggered only after infection with malaria. Children in low-lying tropical regions are most at risk.
Alcohol and dietary components Diets high in fat, especially those containing burned and/or fatty, highly preserved meat, slow the passage of food through the gut giving time for mutagenic irritants to form in the bowel. High alcohol intake increases the risk of some cancers and also increases susceptibility to tobacco-smoking related cancers.	• Those with a diet high in total fats (particularly saturated fat) are at higher risk of developing bowel or rectal cancers. The risks may be increased by obesity. • The risks associated with specific dietary factors may be compounded by familial (inherited) susceptibility. • The risks associated with specific dietary factors may be compounded by other lifestyle choices e.g. smoking.
Environmental poisons and irritants Many chemicals are mutagenic. Synthetic and natural examples include: organic solvents like benzene, asbestos, formaldehyde, tobacco tar, vinyl chlorides, coal tars, some dyes, and nitrites.	• Those working in the chemicals industries, including the glue, paint, rubber, resin, and leather industries. • Smokers • Those in coal and other mining industries • Petrol pump attendants exposed to petroleum volatiles and vehicle exhaust emissions.

Tobacco smoking: Tobacco tar is one of the most damaging constituents of tobacco smoke. Tobacco tars contain at least 17 known carcinogens (cancer inducing mutagens) that cause chronic irritation of the respiratory system and are a major cause of cancer in smokers. In the last 5 years, there has been acknowledgement by the tobacco-producing companies that tobacco smoke is not only addictive but also carcinogenic.

Nuclear reactor failures: The most famous nuclear accident is that of Chornobyl, in the Ukraine, which suffered a catastrophic explosion and fire in 1986 during routine tests. Two explosions ejected some 8 tonnes of plutonium and other highly radioactive materials from the reactor. This led to widespread contamination of food sources, an increase in radiation-linked diseases, and ongoing environmental problems throughout northern parts of western Europe.

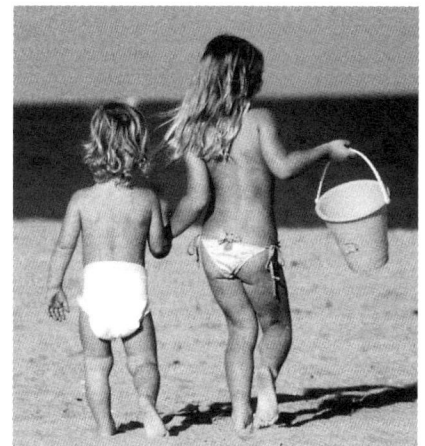

Ultraviolet rays from the sun: The ultraviolet rays (UV-A and UV-B) from the sun are particularly damaging to the skin and the retina of the eyes. The development of the ozone depleted region over Antarctica each year has increased the mutagenic effect from this source. One of the main diseases caused by this radiation is a form of skin cancer called melanoma. This is often an aggressive cancer that may be fatal if left untreated.

1. Define the following terms :

    (a) **Mutagen**: _____

    (b) **Carcinogen**: _____

2. Explain briefly how a high fat diet may lead to an increased risk of a mutation occurring: _____

_____

The Effect of Mutations

Mutations add, delete, or rearrange genetic material. Not all mutations are inherited. Mutations can happen spontaneously due to DNA replication errors, or they can be induced by mutagens. Only those mutations taking place in cells that produce gametes will be inherited. If they occur in a body cell after the organism has begun to develop beyond the zygote stage, then they may give rise to **chimaeras** (mixture of gene types in a single organism). In some cases, mutations trigger the onset of **cancer**, through the disruption of the normal controls regulating cell division. It is not correct to assume that all mutations are harmful. There are many documented cases where mutations conferring a survival advantage have arisen in a population. Such **beneficial mutations** are most common among viruses and bacteria, but occur in multicellular organisms also (e.g. the development of pesticide resistance in insects). Sometimes, a mutation may be neutral and have no immediate effect. If there is no selective pressure against it, a mutation may be carried in the population and be of benefit (or harm) at some future time.

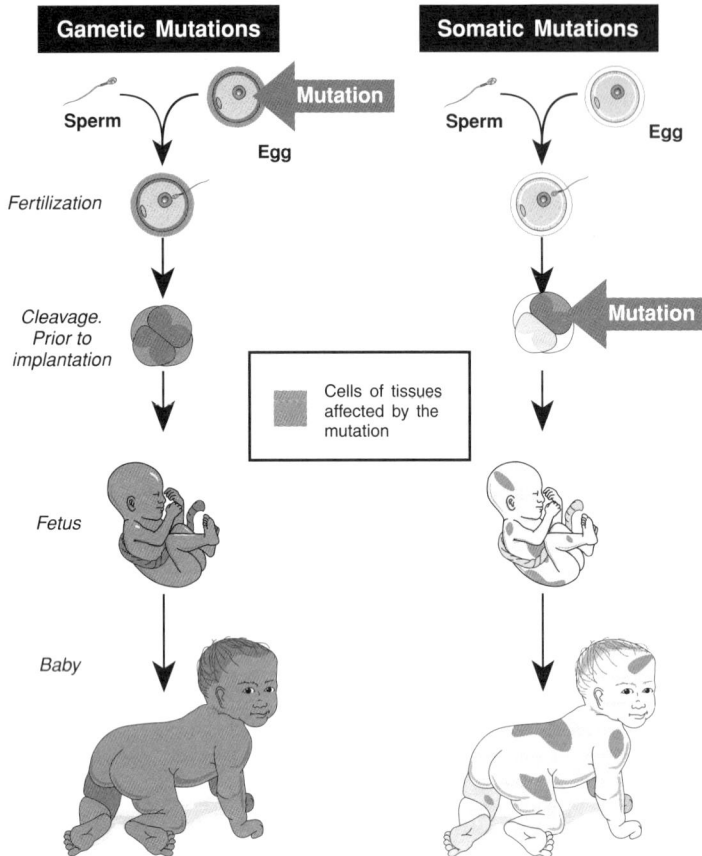

Gametic Mutations

Sperm   Mutation   Egg

Fertilization

Cleavage. Prior to implantation

Cells of tissues affected by the mutation

Fetus

Baby

Gametic mutations are *inherited* and occur in the testes of males and the ovaries of females.

Somatic Mutations

Sperm   Egg

Mutation

Somatic mutations occur in body cells. They are *not inherited* but may affect the person during their lifetime.

The Effect of Mutagens on DNA

UV Light   Thymine dimer

DNA of tumor suppressor gene

G C T T G C A G T A
C G A A C G T C A T

An example of how mutagens cause damage to the genes controlling the normal cell cycle is shown above. After exposure to UV light (a potent mutagen), adjacent thymine bases in DNA become cross-linked to form a 'thymine dimer'. This disrupts the normal base pairing and throws the controlling gene's instructions into chaos.

Normal phenotype (red color)

Mutant phenotype (gold color)

The photo above shows an example of a somatic mutation in a red delicious apple. A mutation occurred in the part of the flower that eventually developed into the fleshy part of the apple. The seeds would not be mutant.

1. Define the term **mutation**: _____

2. Explain how **somatic mutations** differ from **gametic mutations** and comment on the significance of the difference:

3. Outline why the mutation seen in the red delicious apple (above right) will not be inherited: _____

4. Explain why organisms such as *Drosophila* (fruit fly) and microorganisms are often used in the study of mutations:

Harmful Mutations

There are many well-documented examples of mutations that cause harmful effects. Examples are the mutations giving rise to **cystic fibrosis** (CF) and **sickle cell disease**. The sickle cell mutation involves a change to only one base in the DNA sequence, whereas the CF mutation involves the loss of a single triplet (three nucleotides). The malformed proteins that result from these mutations cannot carry out their normal biological functions. The example, right, shows an albino python. **Albinism** is caused by a mutation in the gene that produces an enzyme in the metabolic pathway to produce melanin. It occurs in a large number of animals. Albinos are not common in the wild because they tend to be more vulnerable to predation.

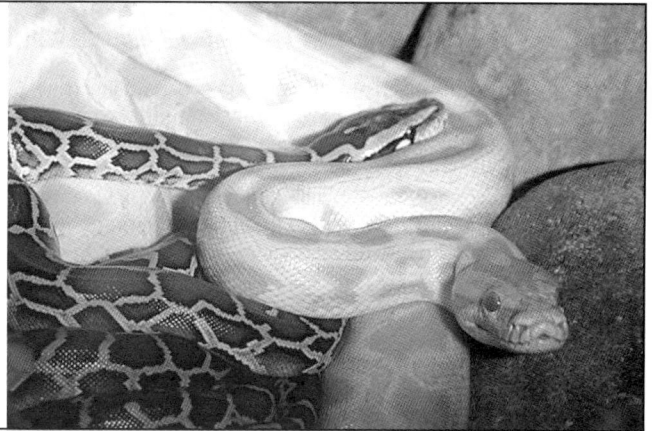

Beneficial Mutations

Tolerance to high cholesterol levels in humans: In the small village of **Limone**, northern Italy, about 40 villagers have extraordinarily high levels of blood cholesterol, with no apparent harmful effects on their coronary arteries.

The village has a population of 980 inhabitants and was, until recently, largely isolated from the rest of the world. The villagers possess a mutation that alters the protein produced by just **one amino acid**. This improved protein is ten times more effective at mopping up excess cholesterol. No matter how much excess cholesterol is taken in by eating, it can always be disposed of. All carriers of the mutation are related and descended from one couple who arrived in Limone in 1636. Generally, the people of Limone live longer and show a high resistance to heart disease.

High blood cholesterol and dietary fat are implicated in the formation of plaques in the coronary arteries and in the development of cardiovascular disease.

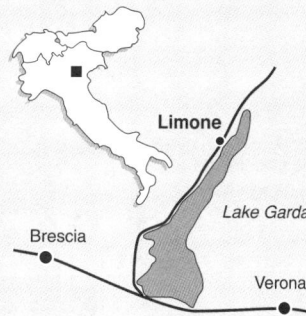

Neutral Mutations

Some mutations are neither harmful nor beneficial to the organism in which they occur. However, they may be very important in an evolutionary sense. A mutation may have no 'adaptive value' when it occurs but this may not be the case in the future. Neutral or **silent** mutations are virtually impossible to detect because they have no observable effect. The example below shows how a change to the DNA sequence can be silenced if no change to the amino acid sequence occurs.

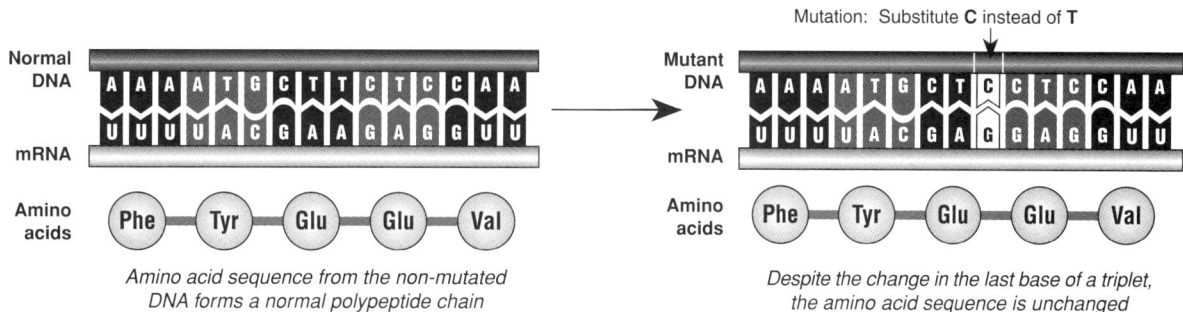

Mutation: Substitute **C** instead of **T**

Amino acid sequence from the non-mutated DNA forms a normal polypeptide chain

Despite the change in the last base of a triplet, the amino acid sequence is unchanged

5. (a) Explain the difference between neutral (silent), beneficial, and harmful mutations: _____

(b) State which of these mutations is the most common and suggest a reason why this would be the case:

6. Explain how the mutation that 40 of the villagers of Limone possess is beneficial under current environmental conditions:

RA 2 Antibiotic Resistance

Antibiotics are drugs that fight bacterial infections. After being discovered in the 1940s, they rapidly transformed medical care and dramatically reduced illness and death from bacterial disease. However, many bacteria have developed **drug resistance**. Genes for resistance may arise through mutation and, in an environment of widespread antibiotic use, confer a **selective advantage** to the bacteria possessing them. The increasing number of **multi-drug**

resistant strains is particularly worrying; resistant infections inhibit the treatment of patients and increase mortality. Antibiotic resistance also adds considerably to the costs of treating disease and, as resistance spreads, new drugs have an increasingly limited life span during which they are effective. Resistant bacteria include *Klebsiella*, *Enterococcus*, *E. coli*, *Staphylococcus aureus*, *Enterobacter*, *Pseudomonas*, and *Mycobacterium tuberculosis*.

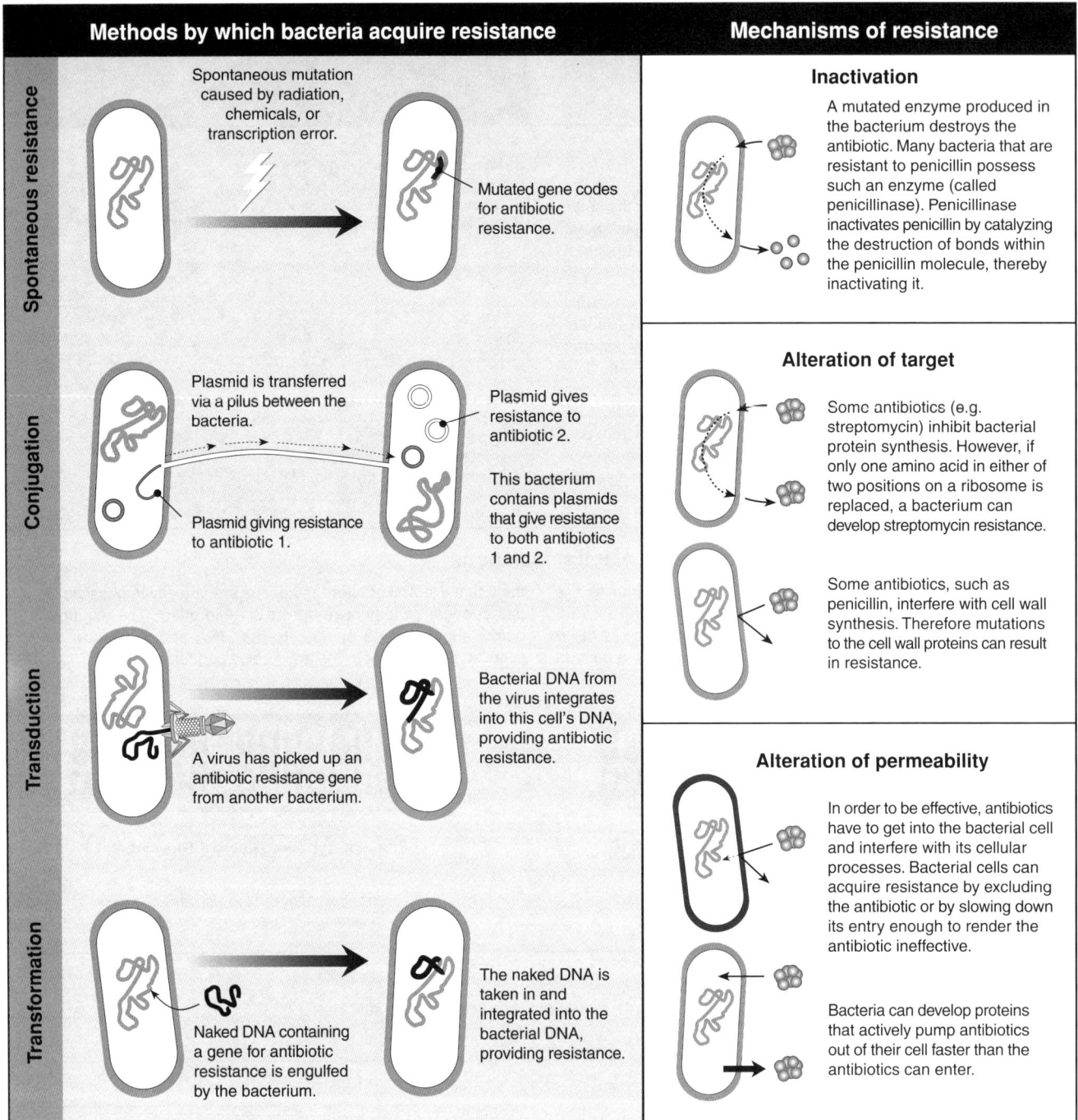

Methods by which bacteria acquire resistance

Mechanisms of resistance

Spontaneous resistance

Spontaneous mutation caused by radiation, chemicals, or transcription error.

Mutated gene codes for antibiotic resistance.

Conjugation

Plasmid is transferred via a pilus between the bacteria.

Plasmid giving resistance to antibiotic 1.

Plasmid gives resistance to antibiotic 2.

This bacterium contains plasmids that give resistance to both antibiotics 1 and 2.

Transduction

A virus has picked up an antibiotic resistance gene from another bacterium.

Bacterial DNA from the virus integrates into this cell's DNA, providing antibiotic resistance.

Transformation

Naked DNA containing a gene for antibiotic resistance is engulfed by the bacterium.

The naked DNA is taken in and integrated into the bacterial DNA, providing resistance.

Inactivation

A mutated enzyme produced in the bacterium destroys the antibiotic. Many bacteria that are resistant to penicillin possess such an enzyme (called penicillinase). Penicillinase inactivates penicillin by catalyzing the destruction of bonds within the penicillin molecule, thereby inactivating it.

Alteration of target

Some antibiotics (e.g. streptomycin) inhibit bacterial protein synthesis. However, if only one amino acid in either of two positions on a ribosome is replaced, a bacterium can develop streptomycin resistance.

Some antibiotics, such as penicillin, interfere with cell wall synthesis. Therefore mutations to the cell wall proteins can result in resistance.

Alteration of permeability

In order to be effective, antibiotics have to get into the bacterial cell and interfere with its cellular processes. Bacterial cells can acquire resistance by excluding the antibiotic or by slowing down its entry enough to render the antibiotic ineffective.

Bacteria can develop proteins that actively pump antibiotics out of their cell faster than the antibiotics can enter.

1. Briefly state four cellular mechanisms by which bacteria become resistant to antibiotics:

(a) _____ (c) _____

(b) _____ (d) _____

2. Describe how the misuse of antibiotics by patients can lead to the development of antibiotic resistant bacteria:

_____

_____

_____

Gene Mutations

RA 3

Gene mutations are small, localized changes in the structure of a DNA strand. These mutations may involve change in a single nucleotide (sometimes called point mutations), or they may involve changes to a triplet (e.g. deletion or triplet repeat). If one amino acid in a protein is wrong, the biological function of the entire protein can be disrupted. Not all mutations may result in altered proteins. Because of the degeneracy of the genetic code,

a substitution of the 3rd base in a codon may code for the same amino acid. The diagrams below show how various point mutations can occur. These alterations in the DNA are at the **nucleotide** level where individual **codons** are affected. Alteration of the precise nucleotide sequence of a coded gene in turn alters the mRNA transcribed from the mutated DNA and may affect the polypeptide chain that it is designed to create.

During DNA replication mistakes occur in the copying process. If non-corrected, these can result in an altered sequence of DNA bases and the formation of an alternative allele of a gene. These **gene mutations** can be of three types: substitution

mutations; deletion mutations, and insertion mutations. The latter two of these often cause a major change in the amino acid sequence of the protein structure. A normal (non-mutated) sequence is shown at the top for comparison.

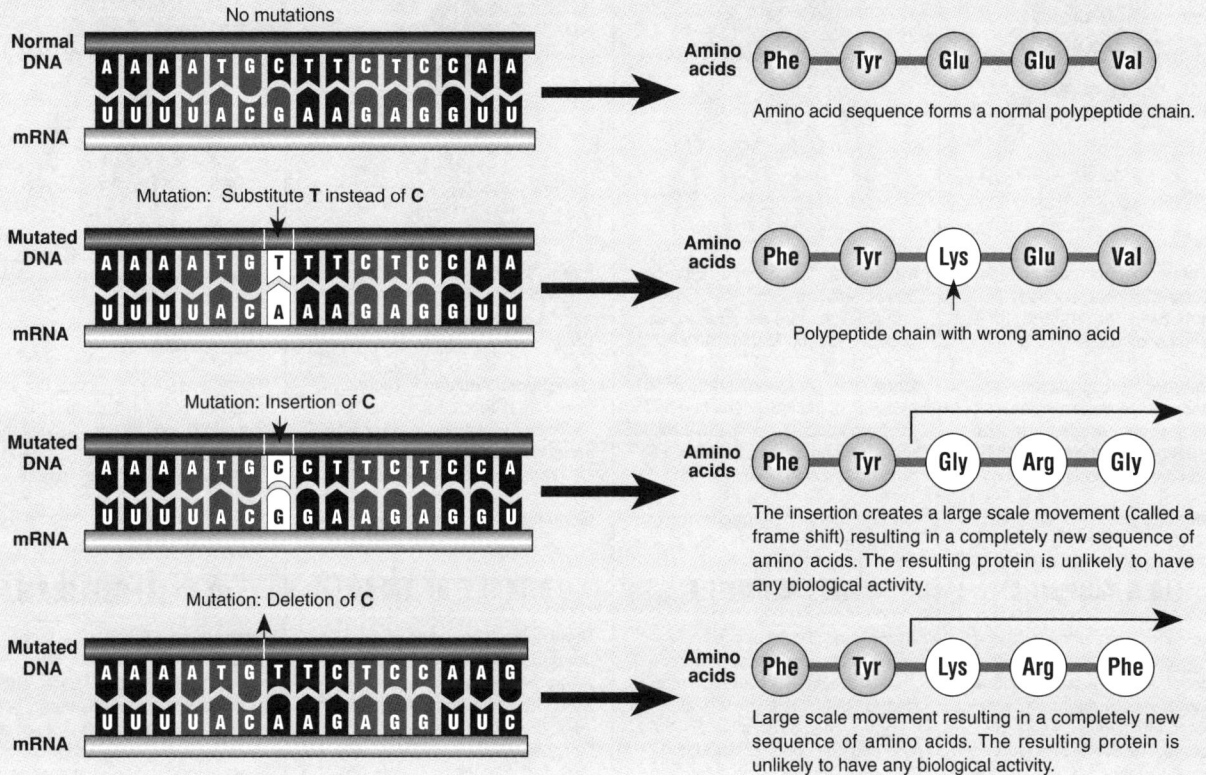

No mutations

Normal DNA

A A A A T G C T T C T C C A A
U U U U A C G A A G A G G U U

mRNA

Amino acids Phe — Tyr — Glu — Glu — Val

Amino acid sequence forms a normal polypeptide chain.

Mutation: Substitute T instead of C

Mutated DNA

A A A A T G T T T C T C C A A
U U U U A C A A A G A G G U U

mRNA

Amino acids Phe — Tyr — Lys — Glu — Val

Polypeptide chain with wrong amino acid

Mutation: Insertion of C

Mutated DNA

A A A A T G C C T T C T C C A
U U U U A C G G A A G A G G U

mRNA

Amino acids Phe — Tyr — Gly — Arg — Gly

The insertion creates a large scale movement (called a frame shift) resulting in a completely new sequence of amino acids. The resulting protein is unlikely to have any biological activity.

Mutation: Deletion of C

Mutated DNA

A A A A T G T T C T C C A A G
U U U U A C A A G A G G U U C

mRNA

Amino acids Phe — Tyr — Lys — Arg — Phe

Large scale movement resulting in a completely new sequence of amino acids. The resulting protein is unlikely to have any biological activity.

1. Describe how the following gene mutations upset the normal amino acid sequence:

   (a) Substitution: _____

   _____

   (b) Deletion: _____

   _____

   (c) Insertion: _____

   _____

2. Not all gene mutations have the same effect on the organism; some are more disruptive than others.

   (a) State which types of gene mutations are the most damaging to an organism: _____

   (b) Explain why they are the most disruptive: _____

   _____

3. Explain what is meant by **biological activity** of a protein: _____

   _____

4. Name a disease where a gene mutation has a large detrimental effect: _____

Examples of Gene Mutations

Humans have more than 6000 physiological diseases attributed to mutations in single genes and over one hundred syndromes known to be caused by chromosomal abnormality. The number of genetic disorders identified increases every year. Rapid progress of the Human Genome Project is enabling the identification of the genetic basis of these disorders. This will facilitate the development of new drug therapies and gene therapies. Four genetic disorders are summarized below.

Sickle Cell Disease	β-Thalassemia	Cystic Fibrosis	Huntington Disease
Synonym: Sickle cell anemia	**Synonyms**: Cooley anemia, Mediterranean anemia	**Synonyms**: Mucoviscidosis, CF	**Synonyms**: Huntington's chorea, HD (abbreviated)
Incidence: Occurs most commonly in people of African ancestry. West Africans: 1% (10-45% carriers) West Indians: 0.5%	**Incidence**: Most common type of thalassemia affecting 1% of some populations. More common in Asia, Middle East and Mediterranean.	**Incidence**: Varies with populations: United States: 1 in 1000 (0.1%) Asians in England: 1 in 10 000 Caucasians: 1 in 20-28 are carriers	**Incidence**: An uncommon genetic disease present in 1 in 20 000.
Gene type: Autosomal recessive mutation which results in the substitution of a single nucleotide in the HBB gene that codes for the beta chain of hemoglobin.	**Gene type**: Autosomal recessive mutation of the HBB gene coding for the hemoglobin beta chain. It may arise through a gene deletion or a nucleotide deletion or insertion.	**Gene type**: Autosomal recessive. Over 500 different recessive mutations (deletions, missense, nonsense, terminator codon) of the CFTR gene have been identified.	**Gene type**: An autosomal dominant mutation of the HD gene (IT15) caused by an increase in the length (36-125) of a CAG repeat region (normal range is 11-30 repeats).
Gene location: Chromosome 11 HBB p q	**Gene location**: Chromosome 11 HBB p q	**Gene location**: Chromosome 7 CFTR p q	**Gene location**: Chromosome 4 IT15 p q
Symptoms: Include the following: pain, ranging from mild to severe, in the chest, joints, back, or abdomen; swollen hands and feet; jaundice; repeated infections, particularly pneumonia or meningitis; kidney failure; gallstones (at an early age); strokes (at an early age), anemia.	**Symptoms**: The result of hemoglobin with few or no beta chains, causes a severe anemia during the first few years of life. People with this condition are tired and pale because not enough oxygen reaches the cells.	**Symptoms**: Disruption of glands: the *pancreas*; *intestinal glands*; *biliary tree* (biliary cirrhosis); *bronchial glands* (chronic lung infections); and *sweat glands* (high salt content of which becomes depleted in a hot environment); *infertility* occurs in males/females.	**Symptoms**: Mutant gene forms defective protein: **Huntingtin**. Progressive, selective *nerve cell death* associated with chorea (jerky, involuntary movements), *psychiatric disorders,* and *dementia* (memory loss, disorientation, impaired ability to reason, and personality changes).
Treatment and outlook: Patients are given folic acid. Acute episodes may require oxygen therapy, intravenous infusions of fluid, and antibiotic drugs. Experimental therapies include bone marrow transplants and gene therapy.	**Treatment and outlook**: Patients require frequent blood transfusions which causes iron build-up in their heart, liver, and other organs. Bone marrow transplants and gene therapy hold promise and are probable future treatments.	**Treatment and outlook**: Conventional: chest physiotherapy, a modified diet, and the use of TOBI antibiotic to control lung infections. Outlook: Gene transfer therapy inserting normal CFTR gene using adenovirus vectors and liposomes.	**Treatment and outlook**: Surgical treatment may be possible. Research is underway to discover drugs that interfere with *Huntingtin* protein. Genetic counselling coupled with genetic screening of embryos may be developed into the future.

1. Suggest why there is a considerable difference in the incidence rates for some genetic disorders based on the racial types or geographic origin of peoples' ancestors:

_____

_____

2. For each of the genetic disorder below, indicate the following:

   (a) Sickle cell disease: Gene name: __HBB__   Chromosome: __11__   Mutation type: _Substitution___

   (b) β-thalassemia: Gene name: _____   Chromosome: _____   Mutation type: _____

   (c) Cystic fibrosis: Gene name: _____   Chromosome: _____   Mutation type: _____

   (d) Huntington disease: Gene name: _____   Chromosome: _____   Mutation type: _____

3. Explain the cause of the symptoms for people suffering from β-thalassemia: _____

Cystic Fibrosis Mutation

A 3

Cystic fibrosis is an inherited disorder caused by a faulty gene which in turn codes for a faulty **CFTR protein**. This is the most common lethal genetic mutation of caucasians with

5% of the population thought to be carriers (heterozygous). The DNA sequence below is part of the transcribing sequence for the **normal** cystic fibrosis gene.

Normal CFTR protein *(1480 amino acids)*
Correctly controls chloride ion balance in the cell

Abnormal CFTR protein *(1479 amino acids)*
Does not control chloride ion balance in the cell

The CFTR gene on chromosome 7

The CFTR gene is located on chromosome 7. Cystic fibrosis results from a deletion mutation where 3 nucleotides are lost. This in turn causes the loss of a single **amino acid** (the 508th in a total chain of 1480) from an important protein called CFTR. This protein normally regulates the chloride channels in cell membranes, but the mutant form fails to achieve this adequately. The portion of the DNA containing the mutation site is shown below:

The CFTR protein consists of 1480 amino acids

CFTR protein

The mutant form of the CFTR (Cystic Fibrosis Transmembrane Conductance Regulator) protein does not work properly and excessive amounts of chloride ions remain in the cell. This in turn leads to water from the tissue fluid outside the cell entering the cell. This accounts for the symptoms of this genetic disease, where mucus-secreting glands, particularly in the lungs and pancreas, become fibrous and produce abnormally thick mucus.

Base 1630

CFTR gene

DNA C C G T G G T A A T T T C T T T T T A T A G T A G A A A C C A C C A

This triplet codes for the 500th amino acid

The 508th triplet is lost (not present) in the mutant form

1. Identify how many of the following are exhibited in the DNA sequence above:

    (a) Bases: _____   (b) Triplets: _____   (c) Amino acids coded for: _____

2. Write the mRNA sequence for the transcribing DNA strand above:

    _____

3. Determine the amino acid sequence coded by the mRNA (in question 2 above) for the fragment of the normal protein we are studying here. Use the mRNA-amino acid table in this manual (consult the index):

    _____

4. The mutation that causes cystic fibrosis has nucleotide bases missing at positions 1654-1656.

    (a) Rewrite the transcribing DNA sequence from the above diagram, but without the 508th triplet shown (white):

    _____

    (b) State what kind of mutation this is: _____

5. Write the mRNA sequence for the mutant DNA strand above:

    _____

6. Determine the amino acid sequence coded by the mRNA (in question 5 above) for the fragment of the mutant protein we are studying here. Use the mRNA-amino acid table in this manual (consult the index):

    _____

7. Name the amino acid that has been removed from the protein by this mutation: _____

Sickle Cell Mutation

RA ❸

Sickle cell disease (formerly called sickle cell anemia) is an inherited disorder caused by a gene mutation which codes for a faulty beta (ß) chain haemoglobin (Hb) protein. This in turn causes the red blood cells to deform causing a whole range of medical problems. The DNA sequence below is the beginning of the transcribing sequence for the **normal** β-chain Hb molecule.

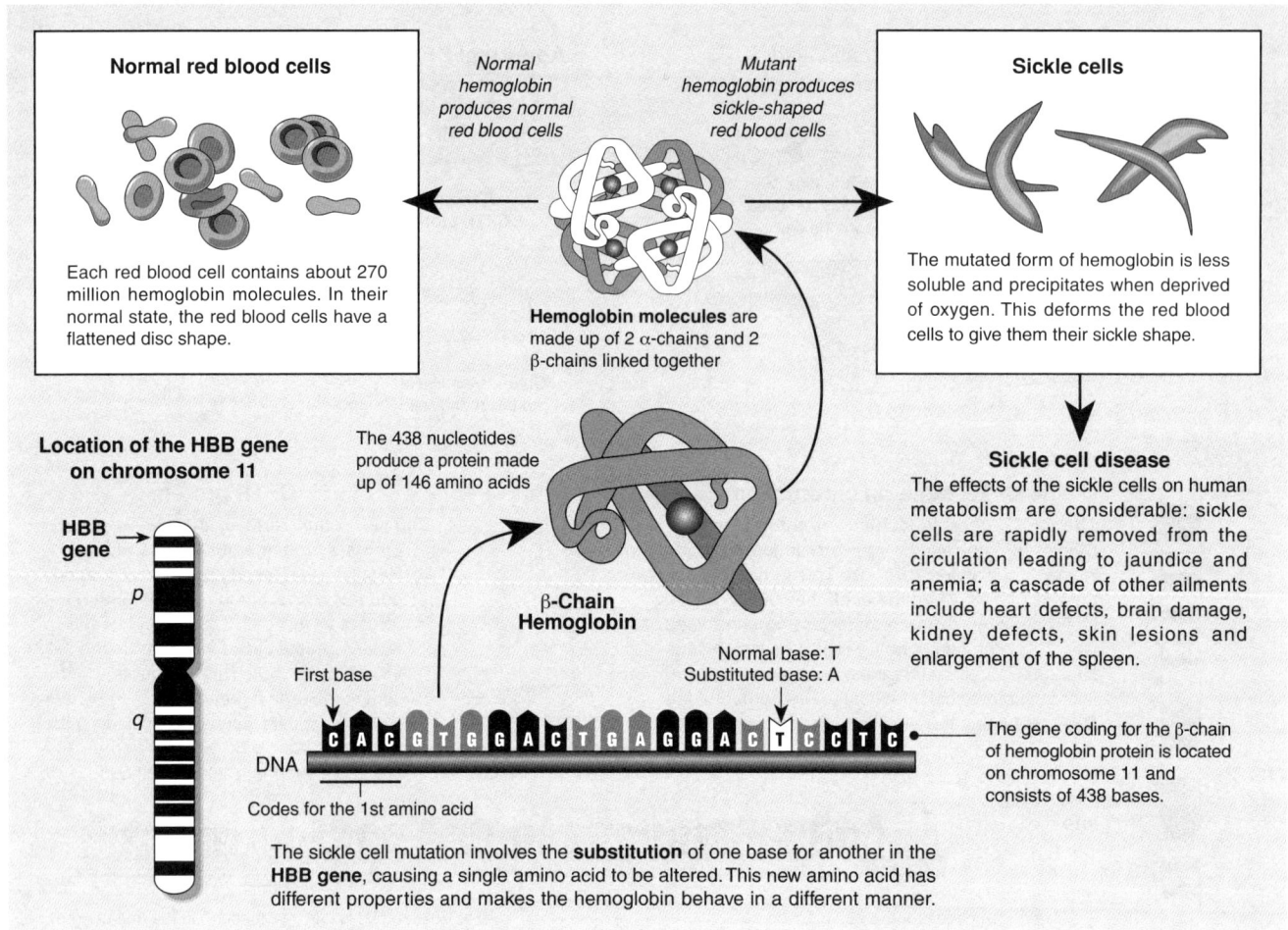

Normal red blood cells

Each red blood cell contains about 270 million hemoglobin molecules. In their normal state, the red blood cells have a flattened disc shape.

Normal hemoglobin produces normal red blood cells

Mutant hemoglobin produces sickle-shaped red blood cells

Sickle cells

The mutated form of hemoglobin is less soluble and precipitates when deprived of oxygen. This deforms the red blood cells to give them their sickle shape.

Hemoglobin molecules are made up of 2 α-chains and 2 β-chains linked together

Location of the HBB gene on chromosome 11

HBB gene →

p

q

The 438 nucleotides produce a protein made up of 146 amino acids

β-Chain Hemoglobin

First base

Normal base: T
Substituted base: A

DNA — C A C G T G G A C T G A G G A C T C C T C

Codes for the 1st amino acid

Sickle cell disease
The effects of the sickle cells on human metabolism are considerable: sickle cells are rapidly removed from the circulation leading to jaundice and anemia; a cascade of other ailments include heart defects, brain damage, kidney defects, skin lesions and enlargement of the spleen.

The gene coding for the β-chain of hemoglobin protein is located on chromosome 11 and consists of 438 bases.

The sickle cell mutation involves the **substitution** of one base for another in the **HBB gene**, causing a single amino acid to be altered. This new amino acid has different properties and makes the hemoglobin behave in a different manner.

1. Identify how many of the following are exhibited or coded for in the DNA sequence above:

   (a) Bases: _____   (b) Triplets: _____   (c) Amino acids coded for: _____

2. Write the mRNA sequence for the transcribing DNA strand above.

   _____

3. Determine the amino acids coded by the mRNA (in question 2 above) for the fragment of the **normal** protein we are studying here. Use the mRNA-amino acid table in this manual (consult the index):

   Amino acids: _____

4. Rewrite the transcribing DNA sequence above with the 17th nucleotide (base) changed from a **T** to **A.** This is the mutation that causes sickle cell disease.

   Mutant DNA: _____   Type of mutation: _____

5. Write the mRNA sequence for the **mutant** DNA strand above.

   _____

6. Determine the amino acids coded by the mRNA (in question 5 above) for the fragment of the **mutant** protein we are studying here. Use the mRNA-amino acid table in this manual (consult the index):

   _____

7. Briefly explain what causes sickle cell disease: _____

   _____

   _____

Chromosome Mutations

The diagrams below show the different types of chromosome mutation that can occur only during **meiosis**. These mutations (sometimes also called block mutations) involve the rearrangement of whole blocks of genes, rather than individual bases within a gene. Each type of mutation results in an alteration in the number and/or sequence of whole sets of genes (represented by letters) on the chromosome. In humans, **translocations** occur with varying frequency (several rare types of Down syndrome occur in this way). Individuals with a **balanced translocation** have the correct amount of genetic material and appear phenotypically normal but have an increased chance of producing faulty gametes. Translocation may sometimes involve the fusion of whole chromosomes, thereby reducing the chromosome number of an organism. This is thought to be an important mechanism by which **instant speciation** can occur.

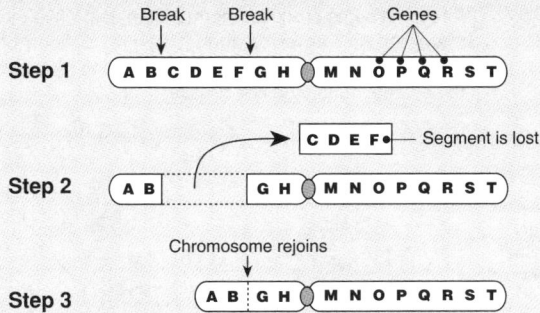

Deletion

A break may occur at two points on the chromosome and the middle piece of the chromosome falls out. The two ends then rejoin to form a chromosome deficient in some genes. Alternatively, the end of a chromosome may break off and is lost.

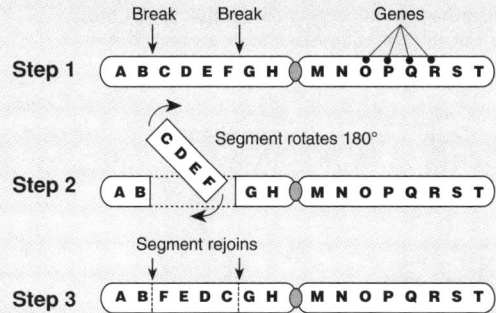

Inversion

The middle piece of the chromosome falls out and rotates through 180° and then rejoins. There is no loss of genetic material. The genes will be in a reverse order for this segment of the chromosome.

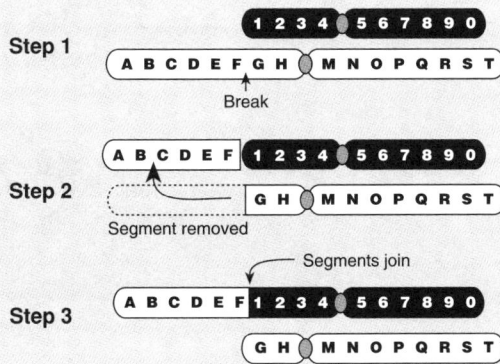

Translocation

Translocation involves the movement of a group of genes between different chromosomes. The large chromosome (white) and the small chromosome (black) are not homologous. A piece of one chromosome breaks off and joins onto another chromosome. This will cause major problems when the chromosomes are passed to gametes. Some will receive extra genes, while some will be deficient.

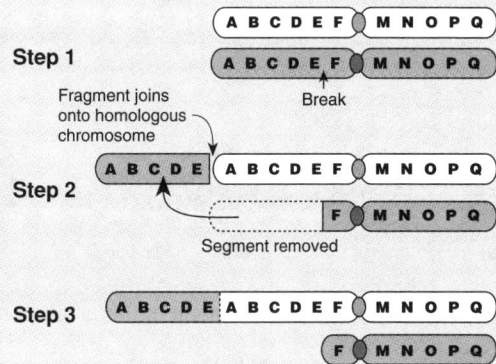

Duplication

A segment is lost from one chromosome and is added to its homologue. In this diagram, the darker chromosome on the bottom is the 'donor' of the duplicated piece of chromosome. The chromosome with the segment removed is deficient in genes. Some gametes will receive double the genes while others will have no genes for the affected segment.

1. For each of the chromosome (block) mutations illustrated above, write the original gene sequence and the new gene sequence after the mutation has occurred (the first one has been done for you):

	Original sequence(s)	Mutated sequence(s)
(a) Deletion:	A B C D E F G H M N O P Q R S T	A B G H M N O P Q R S T
(b) Inversion:		
(c) Translocation:		
(d) Duplication:		

2. State which of the above types of block mutation is likely to be the least damaging to the organism, giving a reason:

_____

RA② Aneuploidy in Humans

Euploidy is the condition of having an exact multiple of the haploid number of chromosomes. Normal euploid humans have 46 chromosomes (2N). **Aneuploidy** is the condition where the chromosome number is not an exact multiple of the normal haploid set for the species (the number may be more, e.g., 2N+2, or less, e.g., 2N–1). **Polysomy** is aneuploidy involving

reduplication of some of the chromosomes beyond the normal diploid number (e.g. 2N+1). Aneuploidy usually results from the **non-disjunction** (failure to separate) of homologous chromosomes during meiosis. The two most common forms are monosomy (e.g. Turner syndrome) and trisomy (e.g. Down and Klinefelter syndrome) as outlined on the next few pages.

Faulty Egg Production

The male has produced normal gametes, but the female has not. The two X-sex chromosomes failed to separate during the first division of meiosis.

Faulty Sperm Production

The female has produced normal gametes, while the male has had an error during the first division of meiosis. The two sex chromosomes (**X** and **Y**) failed to separate during the first division.

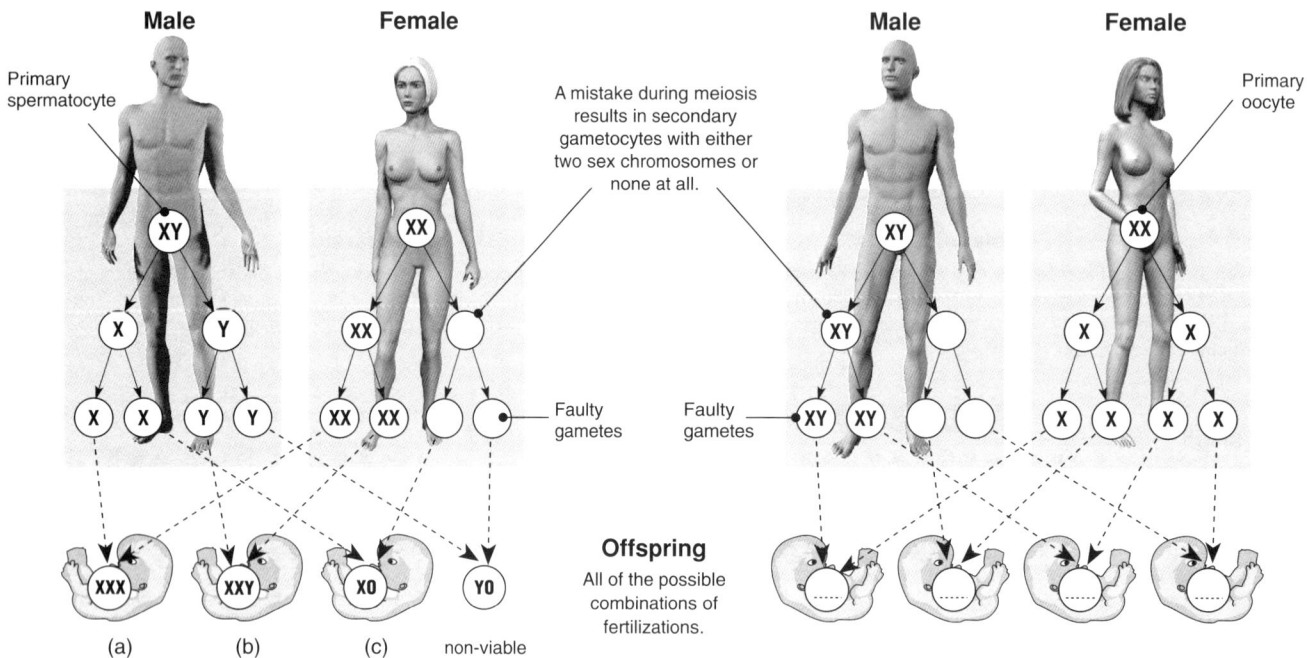

A mistake during meiosis results in secondary gametocytes with either two sex chromosomes or none at all.

Offspring
All of the possible combinations of fertilizations.

1. Identify the sex chromosomes in each of the unlabeled embryos (above, right):

2. Using the table opposite, identify the syndrome for each of the offspring labeled (a) to (c) above:

   (a) _____ (b) _____ (c) _____

3. Explain why the YO configuration (above) is non-viable (i.e., there is no embryonic development): _____

4. (a) For karyotype A, below, circle the sex chromosomes and state:

   Chromosome configuration: _____ Sex of individual (M/F): ___ Syndrome: _____

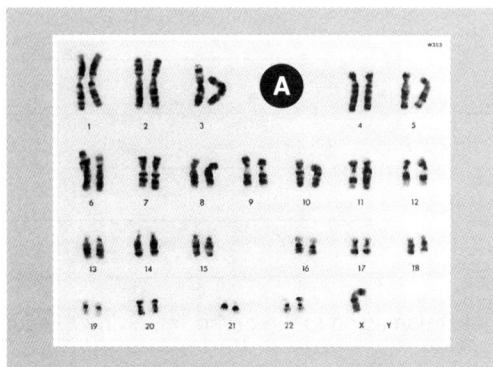

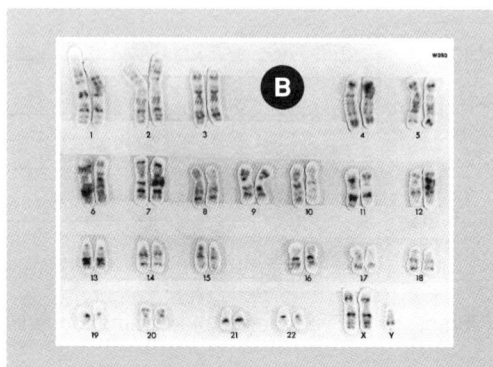

   (b) For karyotype B, below, circle the sex chromosomes and state:

   Chromosome configuration: _____ Sex of individual (M/F): ___ Syndrome: _____

Examples of Aneuploidy in Human Sex Chromosomes

Sex chromosomes and chromosome condition	Apparent sex	Phenotype
XO, monosomic	Female	Turner syndrome
XX, disomic	Female	**Normal female**
XXX, trisomic	Female	Most appear physically and mentally normal; greater tendency to criminality
XXXX, tetrasomic	Female	Rather like Down syndrome, low fertility and intelligence
XY, disomic	Male	**Normal male**
XYY, trisomic	Male	Jacob syndrome, apparently normal male, tall, aggressive
XXY, trisomic	Male	Klinefelter syndrome (infertile). Incidence rate 1 in 1000 live male births, with a maternal age effect.
XXXY, tetrasomic	Male	Extreme Klinefelter, mentally retarded

Above: Features of selected aneuploidies in humans. Note that this list represents only a small sample of the possible sex chromosome aneuploidies in humans.

Right: Symbolic representation of Barr body occurrence in various human karyotypes. The chromosome number is given first, and the inactive X chromosomes are framed by a black box. Note that in aneuploid syndromes, such as those described here, all but one of the X chromosomes are inactivated, regardless of the number present.

Barr Bodies

In the nucleus of any non-dividing somatic cell, one of the X chromosomes condenses to form a visible piece of chromatin, called a **Barr body**. This chromosome is inactivated, so that only one X chromosome in a cell ever has its genes expressed. The inactivation is random, and the inactive X may be either the maternal homologue (from the mother) or the paternal homologue (from the father).

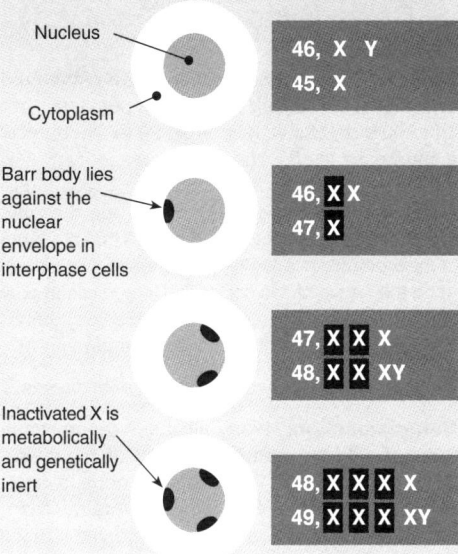

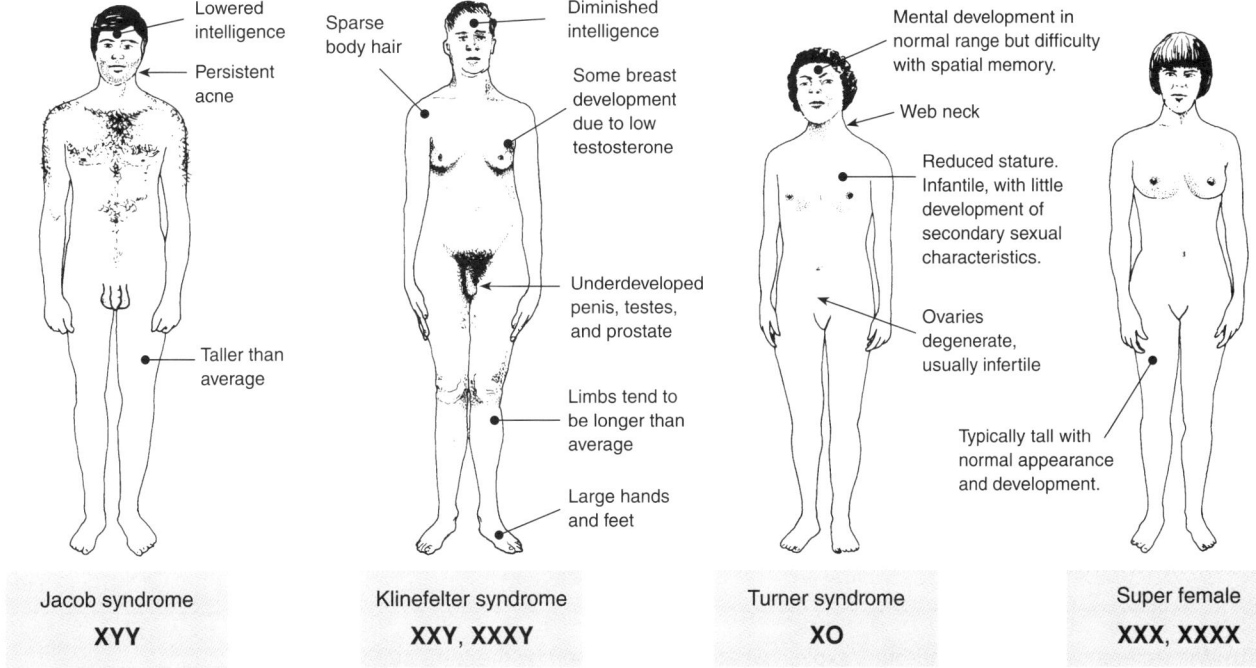

Jacob syndrome **XYY**

Klinefelter syndrome **XXY, XXXY**

Turner syndrome **XO**

Super female **XXX, XXXX**

5. State how many Barr bodies are present in each somatic cell for each of the following syndromes:

(a) Jacob syndrome: _____ (b) Klinefelter syndrome: _____ (c) Turner syndrome: _____

6. Describe two phenotypic traits that have resulted from underdeveloped **testes** in individuals with Klinefelter syndrome:

7. State how many chromosomes for each set of homologues are present for the following forms of aneuploidy:

(a) Nullisomy: _____ (c) Trisomy: _____

(b) Monosomy: _____ (d) Polysomy: _____

Down Syndrome

A 2

Trisomy is a form of **polysomy** where the nucleus of the cells have one chromosome pair represented by three chromosomes (2N+1). The extra chromosome disturbs the overall chromosomal balance causing abnormalities or death. In humans, about 50% of all spontaneous abortions result from chromosomal abnormalities, and trisomies are responsible for about half of these (25% of all

spontaneous abortions). About 6% of live births involve children with chromosomal abnormalities. Autosomal trisomies make up only 0.1% of all pregnancies. Of the three autosomal trisomies surviving to birth, trisomy 21 (**Down** syndrome) is the most common. The other two, **Edward** and **Patau**, show severe physical and mental abnormalities. Trisomies in other autosomes are rare.

Down Syndrome (Trisomy 21)

Down syndrome is the most common of the human aneuploidies. The incidence rate in humans is about 1 in 800 births for women aged 30 to 31 years, with a maternal age effect (the rate increases rapidly with maternal age). The most common form of this condition arises when meiosis fails to separate the pair of chromosome number 21s in the eggs that are forming in the woman's ovaries (it is apparently rare for males to be the cause of this condition). In addition to growth failure and mental retardation, there are a number of well known phenotypic traits (see diagram right).

Down syndrome may arise from several causes:

Non-disjunction: Nearly all cases (approximately 92%) result from **non-disjunction** of chromosome 21 during **meiosis**. When this happens, a gamete (usually the oocyte) ends up with 24 rather than 23 chromosomes, and fertilization produces a trisomic offspring (see the karyotype photo, above right).

Translocation: Fewer than 5% of Down syndrome cases arise from a **translocation** mutation where one parent is a translocation carrier (chromosome 21 is fused to another chromosome, usually number 14).

Mitotic errors: A very small proportion of cases (fewer than 3%) arise from the failure of the pair of chromosomes 21 to separate during **mitosis** at an early embryonic stage. The resulting individual is a **mosaic** in which two cell lines exist, one of which is trisomic. If the mitotic abnormality occurs very early in development, a large number of cells are affected and the full Down syndrome is expressed. If only a few cells are affected, there are only mild expressions of the syndrome.

A child showing features of the Down syndrome phenotype.

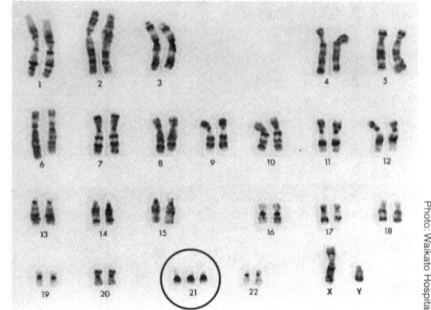

Photo: Waikato Hospital

The karyotype of a trisomic 21 individual that produces the phenotype known as Down syndrome.

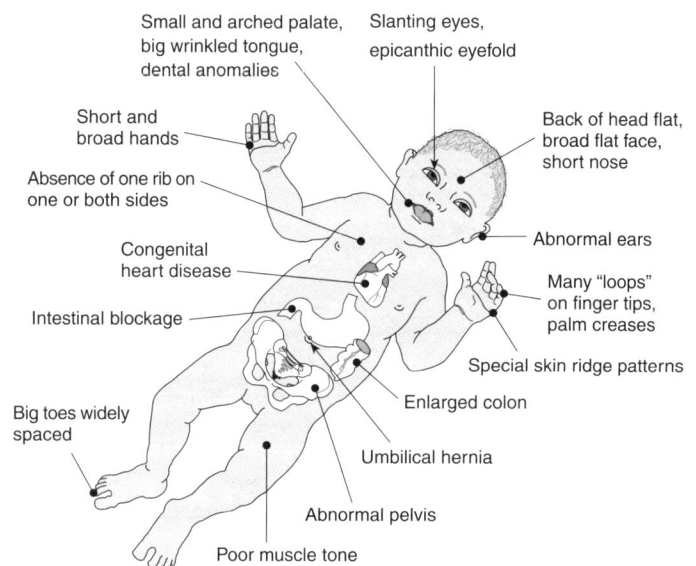

Small and arched palate, big wrinkled tongue, dental anomalies

Slanting eyes, epicanthic eyefold

Short and broad hands

Absence of one rib on one or both sides

Congenital heart disease

Intestinal blockage

Big toes widely spaced

Back of head flat, broad flat face, short nose

Abnormal ears

Many "loops" on finger tips, palm creases

Special skin ridge patterns

Enlarged colon

Umbilical hernia

Abnormal pelvis

Poor muscle tone

1. Define the term trisomy: _____

   _____

2. (a) Suggest a possible reason why the presence of an extra chromosome causes such a profound effect on the development of a person's phenotype:

   _____

   (b) With reference to Down syndrome, explain what you understand by the term **syndrome**: _____

   _____

3. (a) Describe the main cause of Down syndrome: _____

   _____

   (b) Describe the features of the Down phenotype: _____

   _____

4. Describe one other cause of Down syndrome: _____

   _____

5. State how many chromosomes would be present in the somatic cells of an individual with Down syndrome: _____

The Fate of Conceptions

RA 2

A significant number of conceptions do not end in live births. Even those that do may still have problems. A large proportion of miscarriages, which are spontaneous natural abortions, are caused by **chromosome disorders**: trisomy, polyploidy, and missing pieces of chromosomes. Some chromosome abnormalities are less severe than others and those affected survive into childhood or beyond. There is a strong correlation between the age of the mother and the incidence in chromosome abnormalities, called the **maternal age effect**. Prospective mothers older than 35-40 years of age are therefore encouraged to have a prenatal test (e.g. **amniocentesis** or **CVS**) to establish whether the fetus has a normal chromosome complement.

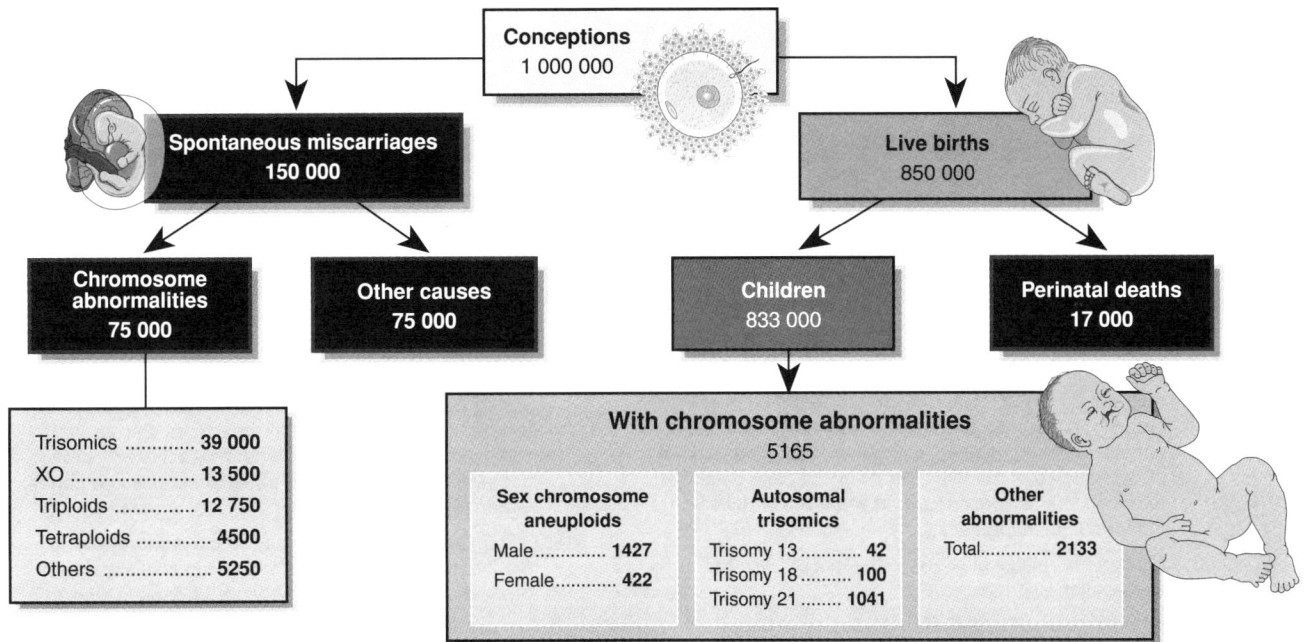

```
                         Conceptions
                          1 000 000

   Spontaneous miscarriages                    Live births
          150 000                               850 000

Chromosome        Other causes          Children          Perinatal deaths
abnormalities       75 000              833 000               17 000
   75 000
```

Trisomics **39 000**
XO **13 500**
Triploids **12 750**
Tetraploids **4500**
Others **5250**

With chromosome abnormalities
5165

Sex chromosome aneuploids	Autosomal trisomics	Other abnormalities
Male.............. **1427**	Trisomy 13 .... **42**	Total.............. **2133**
Female............ **422**	Trisomy 18 .... **100**	
	Trisomy 21 .... **1041**	

(Source: A.J.F. Griffiths et al, 1993, Freeman)

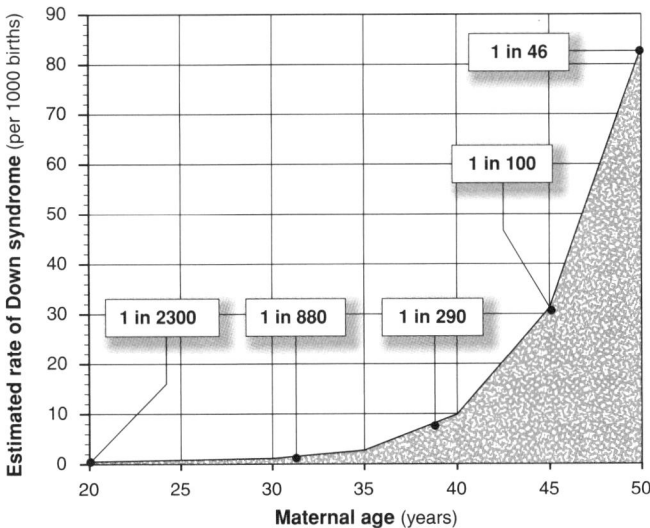

Graph axes: Estimated rate of Down syndrome (per 1000 births) vs Maternal age (years)

Labels on graph: 1 in 46, 1 in 100, 1 in 2300, 1 in 880, 1 in 290

Incidence of Down syndrome related to maternal age

Maternal age (years)	Incidence per 1000 live births
< 30	< 1
30 - 34	1 - 2
35 - 39	2 - 5
40 - 44	5 - 10
> 44	10 - 20

(data for European women)

The table (above) and the graph (left) show different representations of the maternal age effect on the incidence of **Down syndrome**. The older the prospective mother is, the more likely it is that she will have an affected child.

1. Explain what 'maternal age effect' means in relation to the incidence rate of Down syndrome and other trisomic syndromes (see the graph and table above, and the activity *Down Syndrome*):

_____

_____

2. Explain what **amniocentesis** is and why it is used: _____

_____

_____

3. In recent times, most Down syndrome babies are born to younger mothers. State a reason for this:

_____

_____

Inheritance

IB SL	IB HL	IB Options	AP Biology
Complete nos: 1-13, 18-20(a), 27	**Complete nos:** 1-20(a), 23-25, 27-28	**Not applicable to options**	**Complete nos:** 1-28 Some numbers as extension as appropriate
Extension: 20(b), 28	*Extension:* 20(b), 21, 26		

Learning Objectives

☐ 1. Compile your own glossary from the **KEY WORDS** displayed in **bold type** in the learning objectives below.

The study of inheritance *(pages 184-187)*

☐ 2. Summarize the outcomes of Gregor **Mendel**'s historical breeding experiments with peas. Outline Mendel's principles of inheritance, stating their importance to the understanding of heredity: the *theory of particulate inheritance*, the *law of segregation*, and the *law of independent assortment*.

☐ 3. Explain the relationship between Mendel's law of segregation and meiosis.

☐ 4. Appreciate that Mendelian principles were important in providing a mechanism through which natural selection could act upon the genetic variation in populations.

☐ 5. Define the terms: **allele** and **locus**. Distinguish between **dominant**, **recessive**, and **codominant** alleles. Appreciate how *new* alleles are formed.

☐ 6. Define the term **trait** with respect to the study of genetics.

☐ 7. Describe how genes, and their dominant and recessive alleles, are represented symbolically by letters of the alphabet. Explain clearly what is meant by the terms: **heterozygous** and **homozygous**.

☐ 8. Distinguish between **genotype** and **phenotype** and use these terms appropriately when discussing the outcomes of genetic crosses.

☐ 9. Demonstrate an ability to use a **Punnett square** in the solution of different inheritance problems. Define the terms: **monohybrid**, and **dihybrid cross**.

☐ 10. Define and demonstrate an understanding of the terms commonly used in inheritance studies: **cross**, **carrier**, **selfing**, **pure-breeding**, **test-cross**, **back-cross**, **offspring** (progeny), **F₁ generation**, **F₂ generation**.

Inheritance patterns *(pages 188-95, 197-201, 207-209)*

For each of the cases below, use a Punnett square through to the F_2 generation and determine the probability (expressed as a number between 0 and 1) of the occurrence of a particular genetic outcome (genotype and phenotype ratios).

☐ 11. Describe **monohybrid inheritance** involving a single trait or gene locus. Solve problems involving the inheritance of phenotypic traits that follow a simple **dominant-recessive** pattern.

☐ 12. Solve problems involving the inheritance of phenotypic traits that follow a pattern of **codominance**.

☐ 13. Recognize that **multiple alleles** (alternative alleles) may exist for a single gene, e.g. ABO blood groups. Solve problems involving the inheritance of phenotypic traits involving multiple alleles.

☐ 14. Describe **dihybrid inheritance** involving two **unlinked genes** for two independent traits, where the genes described are carried on different chromosomes (**unlinked, autosomal genes**). Solve problems involving dihybrid inheritance of unlinked genes.

☐ 15. Describe **dihybrid inheritance** involving two **linked genes** for two traits, where the genes described are carried on the same chromosome (**linked, autosomal genes**). Explain how, from the results of a cross, you would decide whether or not genes are linked. Solve problems involving dihybrid inheritance of linked genes, demonstrating proper notation in your working.

☐ 16. Demonstrate an ability to use the **chi-square test** to test the significance of differences observed between the observed and expected results of genetic crosses.

☐ 17. Explain why experimental results may be expected only to approximate Mendelian ratios.

Sex determination in humans *(page 196)*

☐ 18. Understand the basis of **sex determination** in humans. Recognize humans as being of the **XX / XY** type. Distinguish **sex chromosomes** from **autosomes**.

Sex linkage *(pages 189, 202-203)*

☐ 19. Define the term: **sex linked**. Describe examples and solve problems involving different patterns of sex linked inheritance involving sex linked genes (e.g. inheritance of red-green color-blindness, hemophilia, and the sex linked form of rickets).

☐ 20. Contrast the pattern of inheritance of:
   (a) **Sex-linked recessive traits** (e.g. hemophilia).
   (b) **Sex linked dominant traits** (e.g. rickets).

Gene interactions *(pages 201, 204-206)*

☐ 21. Explain what is meant by **pleiotropy** and describe an example of a gene with pleiotropic effects e.g. **sickle cell gene mutation**. Describe how the phenotype is affected by the presence of the sickle cell mutation.

☐ 22. Explain what is meant by **epistasis**, **epistatic gene**, and **hypostatic gene**. Solve problems involving the inheritance of phenotypic traits involving epistasis.

   Example of epistasis: coat color in mice. Several genes determine coat color in mice. Mice that are homozygous recessive for the albino gene are white regardless of their genotype for coat color.

☐ 23. Describe the distribution pattern of phenotypic variation produced by **polygenic inheritance**. Understand why **polygenes** are also called multiple genes. Provide examples of traits that follow this type of **quantitative inheritance** pattern.

☐ 24. Demonstrate genetic crosses for the inheritance of a

polygenic trait (e.g. skin color) using a Punnett square through to the F2 generation and determine the probability (expressed as a number between 0 and 1) of the occurrence of a particular genetic outcome (i.e. genotype and phenotype ratios).

☐ 25. Distinguish between **continuous** and **discontinuous variation** in phenotypes and explain the genetic basis for each pattern.

☐ 26. Collect data related to a continuous phenotypic variable in your class. Plot the data, and calculate the mean and standard deviation for the sample. Describe the distribution obtained.

Pedigree analysis *(pages 210-211, also see 159)*

☐ 27. Describe the symbols and notation used in **pedigree analysis** charts. Use pedigree analysis charts to illustrate the inheritance of genetically determined traits in a 'family tree'. Use the charts to determine the probability of certain offspring having particular traits.

☐ 28. Appreciate the importance of **genetic counseling**. Describe the circumstances under which couples seek genetic counseling. Explain how this field has been expanded in the light of new technologies.

Textbooks

See the 'Textbook Reference Grid' on pages 8-9 for textbook page references relating to material in this topic.

Supplementary Texts

See pages 5-6 for additional details of these texts:

■ Adds, J., *et al.*, 2001. **Genetics, Evolution and Biodiversity**, (NelsonThornes), pp. 72-80, 83-86.

■ Clegg, CJ., 1999. **Genetics and Evolution**, (John Murray), pp. 4-39 (in part).

■ Jones, N., *et al.*, 2001. **Essentials of Genetics**, pp. 29-56, 61-74 (review), 77-110.

Internet

See pages 10-11 for details of how to access **Bio Links** from our web site: **www.thebiozone.com**. From Bio Links, access sites under the topics:

GENERAL BIOLOGY ONLINE RESOURCES > see under **Online Textbooks and Lecture Notes**. **GENETICS**: • DNA basics • Genetest • Genetic science learning center • MIT biology hypertextbook • Virtual library on genetics > **Molecular Genetics:** • Basic genetics > **Inheritance:** • BioLogica • Coat color and pattern genetics of the domestic cat • Cat color genetics • Drag and drop genetics • Funny types of gene interactions • Gene interactions • MendelWeb homework sets • Online Mendelian inheritance in man • Patterns of inheritance • The role of genes ... *and others* **Mutations & Genetic Disorders:** • Fragile X syndrome • PKU fact sheet • Sickle cell disease • What are metabolic disorders? ... *and others*

Periodicals

See page 6 for details of publishers of periodicals:

STUDENT'S REFERENCE

■ **What is a Gene?** Biol. Sci. Rev., 15(2) Nov. 2002, pp. 9-11. *A good introduction to genes and their role in heredity. This article provides a useful overview and an historical perspective.*

■ **What is Variation?** Biol. Sci. Rev., 13(1) Sept. 2000, pp. 30-31. *The nature of continuous and discontinuous variation in particular characters. The distribution pattern of traits that show continuous variation as a result of polygeny is discussed.*

■ **It Takes Two** New Scientist, 5 October 2002, pp. 34-37. *The relative influence of genes and environment. Studies of twins may help to clarify the nature versus nurture debate.*

Gender determination

■ **Boy Meets Girl / The Gender Police** New Scientist, 12 May 2001, pp. 28-35, 38-41. *Two part special report examining the nature of gender.*

■ **Determinedly Male** Biol. Sci. Rev., 7(3) Jan. 1995, pp. 28-31. *The basis of gender determination and sexual differentiation in animals.*

Inheritance Patterns

■ **Pay Attention Rover** New Scientist, 10 May 1997, pp. 30-33. *Genes account for about 25% of the differences between dogs in their ability to learn.*

■ **Secrets of The Gene** National Geographic, 196(4) Oct. 1999, pp. 42-75. *Thorough coverage of the nature of genes and the inheritance of particular genetic traits through certain populations.*

■ **Upwardly Mobile** New Scientist, 7 Nov. 1998, p. 6. *Recent studies indicate that 70% of the variation in adult height is due to one gene.*

■ **Blood Group Antigens** Biol. Sci. Rev., 9(5) May 1997, pp. 10-13. *Blood group antigens illustrate human genetic diversity at the molecular level.*

TEACHER'S REFERENCE

Gender determination

■ **Why the Y is so Weird** Scientific American, Feb. 2001, pp. 42-47. *A comparison of the features of the X and Y chromosomes: why they look so different and how they behave during division.*

■ **Decoding the Ys and Wherefores of Males** New Scientist, 21 June 2003, p. 15. *The publication of the genetic sequence of the Y chromosome has unveiled surprising information; the Y chromosome contains about 78 genes, and has mechanisms by which it can repair itself, generation to generation.*

■ **The Double Life of Women** New Scientist, 10 May 2003, pp. 42-45. *Two X chromosomes make you a girl, but why are women not overloaded by having two. A good account of the role of X inactivation in embryonic development.*

Inheritance patterns

■ **Fair Enough** New Scientist, 12 October 2002, pp. 34-37. *The inheritance of skin color in humans. This article examines why humans have such varied skin pigmentation and looks at the argument for there being a selective benefit to being dark or pale in different environments.*

■ **Relating Enzyme Function to Concepts of Dominance and Recessiveness** The American Biology Teacher, 63(6), August 2001, pp. 432-436. *Integrating concepts related to genes and inheritance in an experiment imitating the action of functional and non-functional enzymes.*

■ **Wrinkled Peas and White-Eyed Fruit Flies** The American Biology Teacher, 59(2), Feb. 1997, pp. 92-95. *The basis of genetic variation and its inheritance: Mendelian inheritance of mutant alleles; one arising in peas and one in Drosophila.*

■ **A Simulation of X-Linked Inheritance** The American Biology Teacher, 59(4), April 1997, pp. 224-228. *A simulation of X-linked inheritance in humans using examples of commonly occurring sex linked disorders in humans.*

■ **Inheritance of Kernel Color in Corn** The American Biology Teacher, 62(3), March 2000, pp. 181-188. *A class practical using corn can enhance understanding of basic Mendelian inheritance.*

■ **Mending Mendelism** The American Biology Teacher, 62(9), Nov. 2000, pp. 633-639. *An examination of the concepts proposed by Mendel, including his laws of segregation and independent assortment, and the concept of dominance.*

■ **Managing the Fruit Fly Experiment** The American Biology Teacher, 59(5), May 1997, pp. 292-294. *The use of Drosophila in the study of Mendelian genetics in the classroom.*

■ **An Interdisciplinary Approach to Teaching Dihybrid and Multifactorial Crosses** The American Biology Teacher, 63(9), Nov. 2001, pp. 655-659. *An integration of mathematics and biology in the teaching of Mendelian inheritance.*

■ **Hidden Inheritance** New Scientist, 28 Nov. 1998, pp. 27-30. *Epigenetic inheritance - the study of imprinted genes may help to explain why inheritance patterns are not always as predicted.*

■ **Where Did You Get Your Brains?** New Scientist, 3 May 1997, pp. 34-39. *What features do we inherit from our mothers and which from our fathers? The study of imprinted genes can make maternal/paternal inheritance clearer.*

■ **Why Genes Have a Gender** New Scientist, 22 May 1993, pp. 34-38. *Without knowing it, parents stamp their authority on the DNA of their children.*

■ **Mitochondrial DNA in Aging and Disease** Scientific American, August 1997, pp. 22-29. *The use of mitochondrial DNA inheritance patterns to study human evolution and dispersal.*

■ **Spot Marks the X** Scientific American, April 1993, pp. 12-13. *The broad black and yellow patches in the calico cat's fur are the outward manifestations of a more subtle genetic quirk.*

Gene interactions

■ **Using the Biochemical Pathway Model to Teach the Concepts of Gene Interaction and Epistasis** The American Biology Teacher, 61(3), March 1999, pp. 207-211. *Teaching dihybrid inheritance involving gene interaction based on various biochemical pathways.*

■ **The Molecular Architects of Body Design** Scientific American, February 1994, pp. 36-42. *Patterns of expression, homeobox genes and the genetic regulation of development (requires good subject comprehension and a high reading level).*

Pedigree analysis and genealogy

■ **Back to Your Roots** New Scientist, 16 March 2002, 32-36. *Commercial genetic profiling is being used to determine family lineages and establish accurate genealogies.*

Software and video resources are now provided in the Teacher Resource Handbook

Alleles

A 1

Sexually reproducing organisms in nearly all cases have paired sets of chromosomes, one set coming from each parent. The equivalent chromosomes that form a pair are termed **homologues**. They contain equivalent sets of genes on them. But there is the potential for different versions of a gene to exist in a population and these are termed **alleles**.

Homologous Chromosomes

In sexually reproducing organisms, most cells have a homologous pair of chromosomes (one coming from each parent). The diagram below shows the position of 3 different genes on the same chromosome that control three different traits (A, B and C).

These two different versions of *gene A* create a condition known as **heterozygous**. Only the dominant allele (A) will be expressed.

When both chromosomes have identical copies of the dominant allele for *gene B* the organism is said to be **homozygous dominant** for that gene

When both chromosomes have identical copies of the recessive allele for *gene C* the organism is said to be **homozygous recessive** for that gene

Maternal chromosome that originated from the egg of this person's mother

The diagram above shows the complete chromosome complement for a hypothetical organism. It has a total of 10 chromosomes, comprising five, nearly identical, pairs (each pair is numbered). One chromosome of each pair was supplied by each parent (mother and father). These pairs are called **homologues** or **homologous pairs**. Each homologue carries an identical assortment of genes, but the version (allele) of the gene from each parent may differ.

Genes occupying the same **locus** or position on a chromosome code for the same trait

Paternal chromosome that originated from the sperm of this person's father

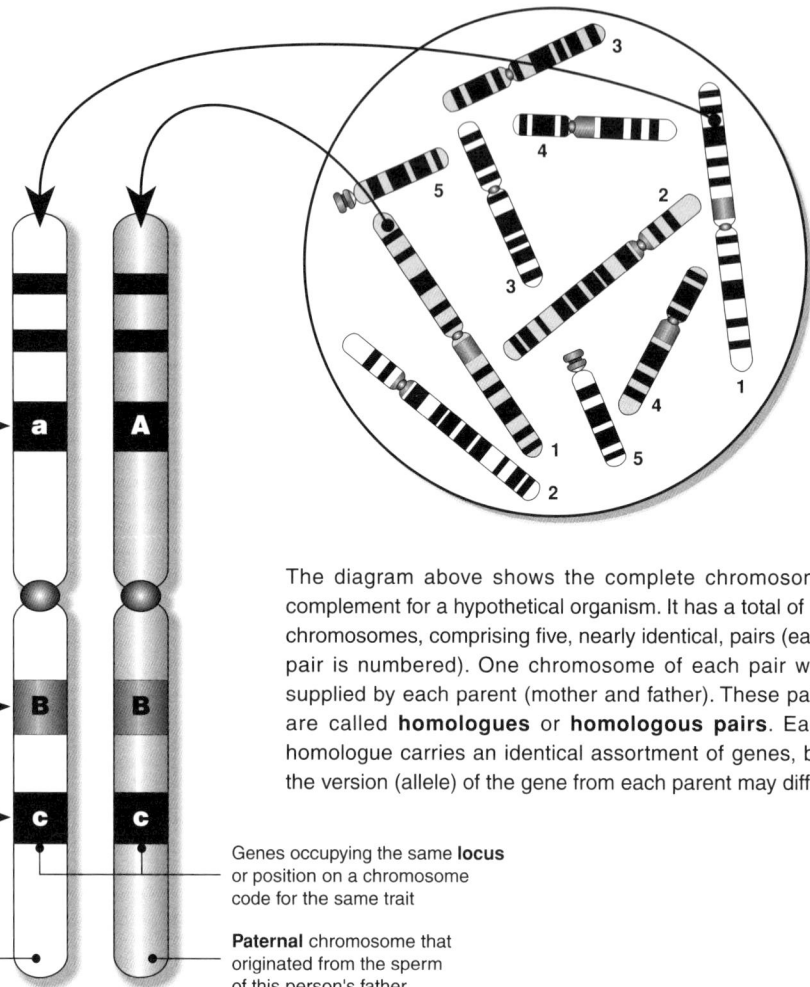

1. Explain what an allele is: _____

   _____

   _____

2. Define the following terms used to describe the allele combinations in the genotype for a given gene:

   (a) Heterozygous: _____

   (b) Homozygous dominant: _____

   (c) Homozygous recessive: _____

3. For a gene given the symbol 'A', name the alleles present in an organism that is identified as:

   (a) Heterozygous: _____

   (b) Homozygous dominant: _____

   (c) Homozygous recessive: _____

4. Explain what a homologous pair of chromosomes is: _____

   _____

   _____

(DA 2) Mendel's Pea Plant Experiments

Gregor Mendel (1822-84), pictured on the right, was an Austrian monk who is regarded as the 'father of genetics'. He carried out some pioneering work using pea plants to study the inheritance patterns of a number of **traits** (characteristics). Mendel observed that characters could be masked in one generation of peas but could reappear in later generations. He showed that inheritance involved the passing on to offspring of discrete units of inheritance – what we now call genes. Mendel examined 7 phenotypic traits and found that they were inherited in predictable ratios, depending on the phenotype of the parents. Below are some of his results from crossing heterozygous plants (eg. tall plants that were the offspring of tall and dwarf parent plants: Tt x Tt). The numbers in the results column represent how many offspring had those phenotypic features.

1. Study the **results** for each of the seven experiments below. Determine which of the two phenotypes is the dominant one, and which is the recessive. Place your answers in the spaces in the **dominance** column in the table below.

2. Calculate the ratio of dominant phenotypes to recessive phenotypes (to 2 decimal places). The first one (for seed coat color) has been done for you (705 ÷ 224 = 3.15). Place your answers in the spaces provided in the table below:

Trait	Possible Phenotypes		Results		Dominance	Ratio
Seed coat color	*Gray*	*White*	Gray White **TOTAL**	705 224 **929**	Dominant: *Gray* Recessive: *White*	**3.15 : 1**
Seed shape	*Wrinkled*	*Round*	Wrinkled Round **TOTAL**	1850 5474 **7324**	Dominant: Recessive:	
Seed color	*Green*	*Yellow*	Green Yellow **TOTAL**	2001 6022 **8023**	Dominant: Recessive:	
Pod color	*Green*	*Yellow*	Green Yellow **TOTAL**	428 152 **580**	Dominant: Recessive:	
Flower position	*Axial*	*Terminal*	Axial Terminal **TOTAL**	651 207 **858**	Dominant: Recessive:	
Pod shape	*Constricted*	*Inflated*	Constricted Inflated **TOTAL**	299 882 **1181**	Dominant: Recessive:	
Stem length	*Tall*	*Dwarf*	Tall Dwarf **TOTAL**	787 277 **1064**	Dominant: Recessive:	

3. Mendel's experiments identified that two heterozygous parents should produce offspring in the ratio of 3 times as many dominant offspring to those showing the recessive phenotype.
   (a) State which two or three of Mendel's experiments provided ratios closest to the theoretical 3:1 ratio:

   _____

   (b) Suggest a possible reason why these results deviated less from the theoretical ratio than the others:

   _____

   _____

Mendel's Laws of Inheritance

From his work on the inheritance of phenotypic traits in peas, Mendel formulated a number of ideas about the inheritance of characters. These were later given formal recognition as Mendel's laws of inheritance. These are outlined below.

The Theory of Particulate Inheritance
Mendel recognized that characters are determined by discrete units that are inherited intact down through the generations. This model explained many observations that could not be explained by the idea of blending inheritance that was universally accepted prior to this. The diagram on the right illustrates this principle, showing that the trait for flower color appears to take on the appearance of only one parent plant in the first generation, but reappears in later generations.

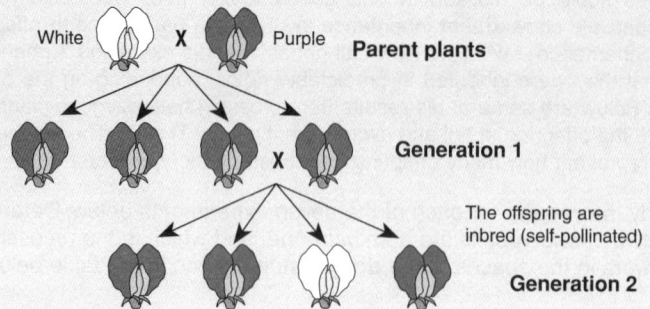

White ⚘ X ⚘ Purple **Parent plants**

Generation 1

The offspring are inbred (self-pollinated)

Generation 2

Law of Segregation
The diagram on the right illustrates how, during meiosis, the two members of any pair of alleles segregate unchanged by passing into different gametes. These gametes are eggs and sperm in animals, and pollen grains and ova in plants. The allele in the gamete will be passed on to the offspring.

> NOTE: This diagram has been simplified, omitting the stage where the second chromatid is produced for each chromosome.

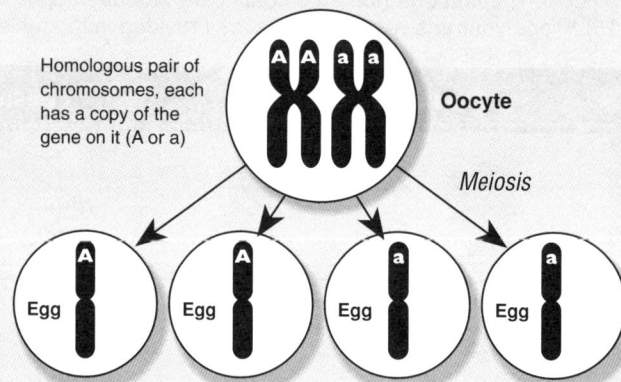

Homologous pair of chromosomes, each has a copy of the gene on it (A or a)

Oocyte

Meiosis

Egg   Egg   Egg   Egg

Law of Independent Assortment
The diagram on the right illustrates how genes are carried on chromosomes. There are two genes shown (A and B) that code for different traits. Each of these genes is represented twice, one copy (allele) on each of two homologous chromosomes. The genes A and B are located on different chromosomes and, because of this, they will be inherited independently of each other, i.e., the gametes may contain any combination of the parental alleles.

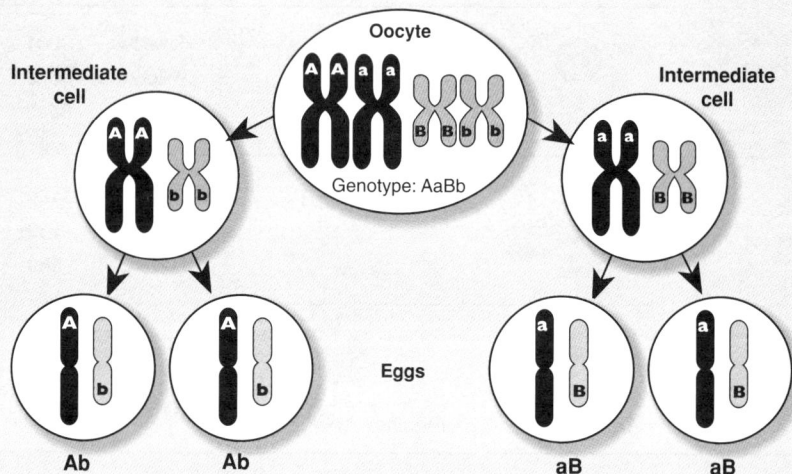

Intermediate cell

Oocyte

Genotype: AaBb

Intermediate cell

Eggs

Ab   Ab   aB   aB

1. Briefly state what **property of genetic inheritance** allows parent pea plants that differ in flower color to give rise to flowers of a single color in the first generation, with both parental flower colors reappearing in the following generation:

   _____

2. The oocyte is the egg producing cell in the ovary of an animal. In the diagram illustrating the **law of segregation** above:

   (a) State the genotype for the oocyte (adult organism): _____

   (b) State the genotype of each of the **four** gametes: _____

   (c) State how many different kinds of gamete can be produced by this oocyte: _____

3. The diagram illustrating the **law of independent assortment** (above) shows only one possible result of the random sorting of the chromosomes to produce: Ab and aB in the gametes.
   (a) List another possible combination of genes (on the chromosomes) ending up in gametes from the same oocyte:

   _____

   (b) State how many different gene combinations are possible for the oocyte: _____

Basic Genetic Crosses

For revision purposes, examine the diagrams below on monohybrid crosses and complete the exercise for dihybrid (two gene) inheritance. A test cross is also provided to show how the genotype of a dominant phenotype can be determined. A test cross will yield one of two different results, depending on the genotype of the dominant individual.

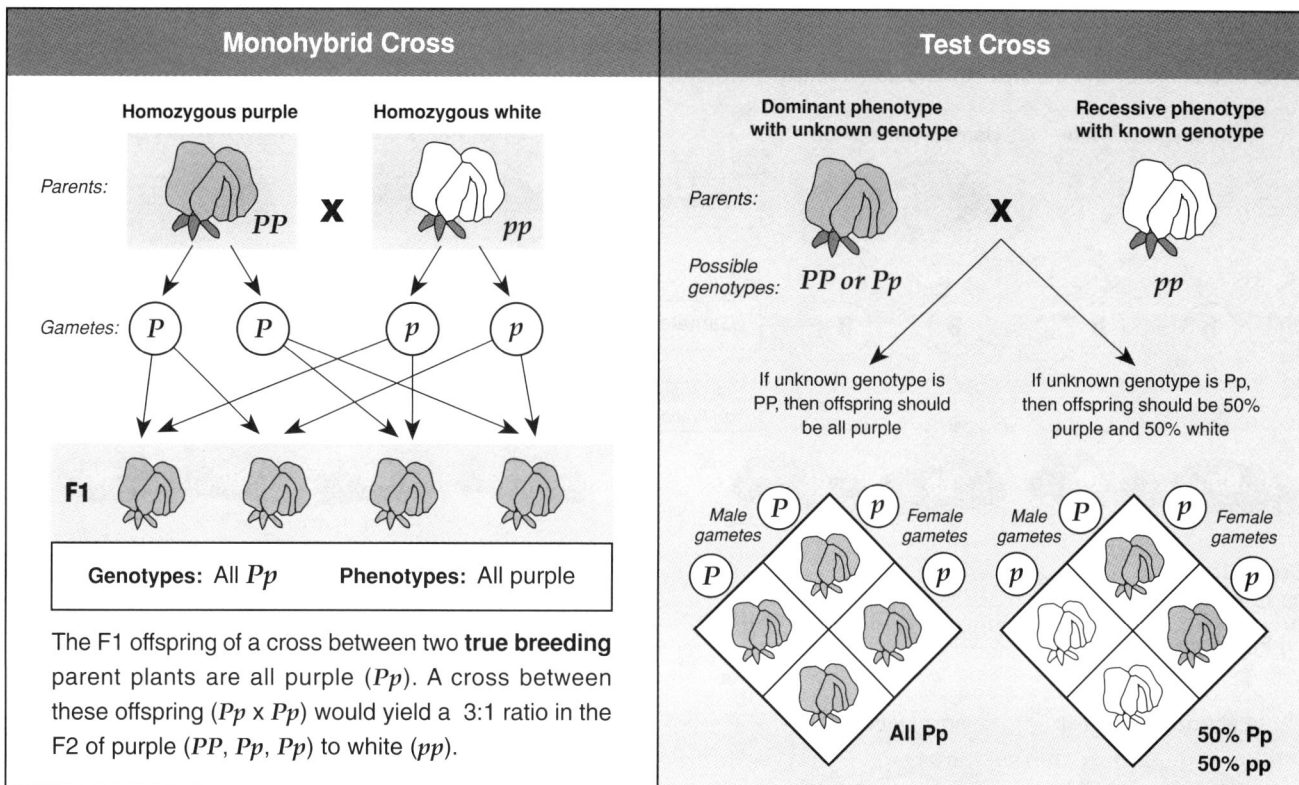

Monohybrid Cross

Homozygous purple **Homozygous white**

Parents: PP **X** pp

Gametes: P P p p

F1

Genotypes: All Pp **Phenotypes:** All purple

The F1 offspring of a cross between two **true breeding** parent plants are all purple (Pp). A cross between these offspring (Pp x Pp) would yield a 3:1 ratio in the F2 of purple (PP, Pp, Pp) to white (pp).

Test Cross

Dominant phenotype with unknown genotype **Recessive phenotype with known genotype**

Parents:

Possible genotypes: PP or Pp **X** pp

If unknown genotype is PP, then offspring should be all purple

If unknown genotype is Pp, then offspring should be 50% purple and 50% white

Male gametes P p Female gametes
P p

All Pp

Male gametes P p Female gametes
p p

50% Pp
50% pp

Dihybrid Cross

In pea seeds, yellow color (Y) is dominant to green (y) and round shape (R) is dominant to wrinkled (r). Each **true breeding** parental plant has matching alleles for each of these characters ($YYRR$ or $yyrr$). F1 offspring will all have the same genotype and phenotype (yellow-round: $YyRr$).

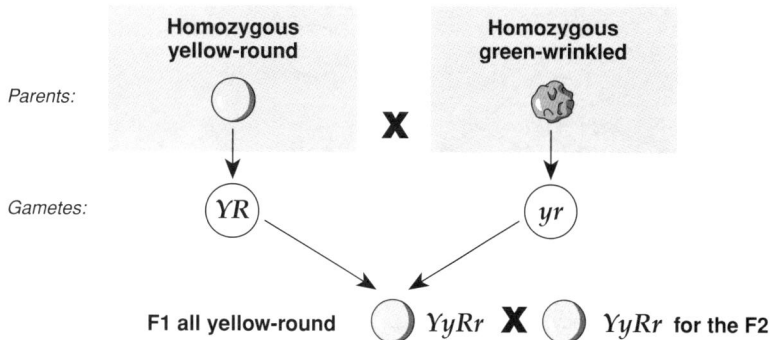

Homozygous yellow-round   **Homozygous green-wrinkled**

Parents:

Gametes: YR yr

F1 all yellow-round $YyRr$ **X** $YyRr$ for the F2

1. Fill in the Punnett square (below right) to show the genotypes of the F2 generation.

2. In the boxes below, use fractions to indicate the numbers of each phenotype produced from this cross.

Yellow-round

Green-round

Yellow-wrinkled

Green-wrinkled

3. Express these numbers as a ratio:

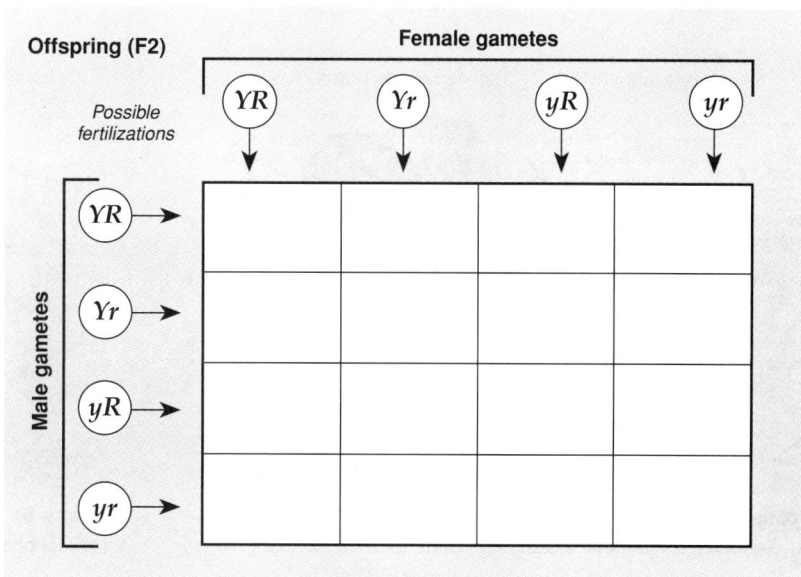

Offspring (F2)

Female gametes

Possible fertilizations YR Yr yR yr

Male gametes YR Yr yR yr

A 1

Monohybrid Cross

The study of **single-gene inheritance** is achieved by performing **monohybrid crosses**. The six basic types of matings possible among the three genotypes can be observed by studying a pair of alleles that govern coat color in the guinea pig. A dominant allele: given the symbol **B** produces **black** hair, and its recessive allele: **b**, produces white. Each of the parents can produce two types of gamete by the process of **meiosis** (in reality there are four, but you get identical pairs). Determine the **genotype** and **phenotype frequencies** for the crosses below (enter the frequencies in the spaces provided). For crosses 3 to 6, you must also determine gametes produced by each parent (write these in the circles), and offspring (F1) genotypes and phenotypes (write in the genotype inside the offspring and state if black or white).

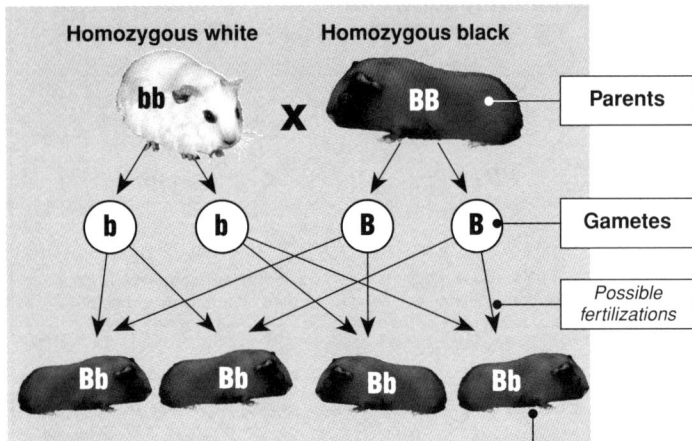

Cross 1:
(a) Genotype frequency: _100% Bb_

(b) Phenotype frequency: _100% black_

Offspring (F₁)

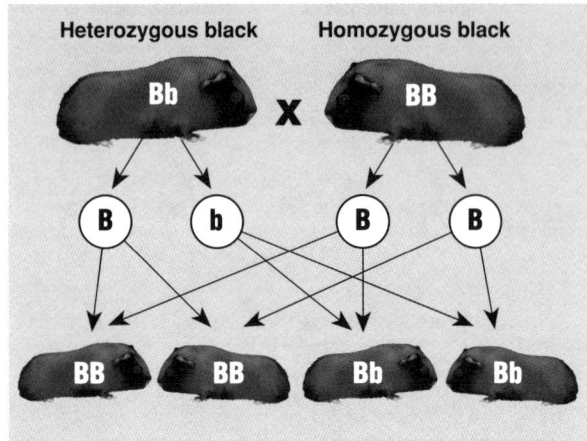

Cross 2:
(a) Genotype frequency: _____

(b) Phenotype frequency: _____

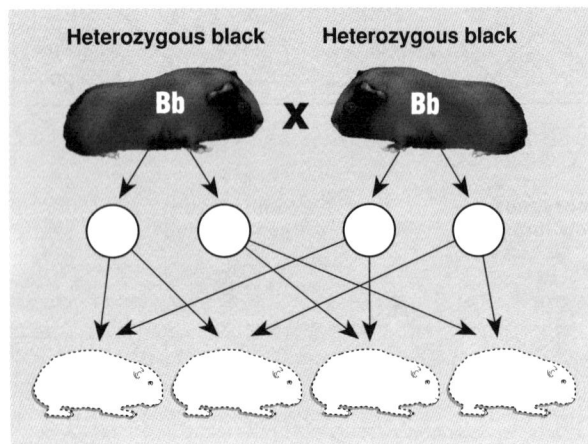

Cross 3:
(a) Genotype frequency: _____

(b) Phenotype frequency: _____

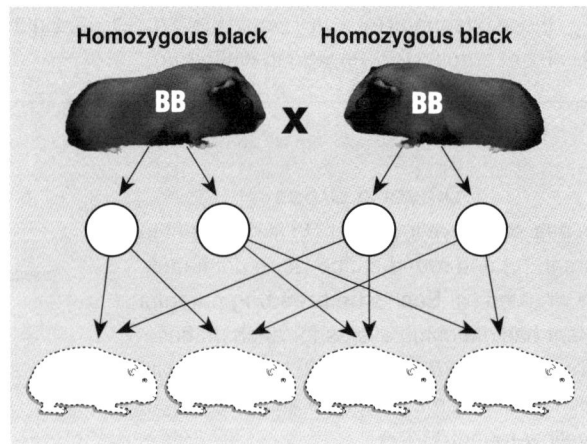

Cross 4:
(a) Genotype frequency: _____

(b) Phenotype frequency: _____

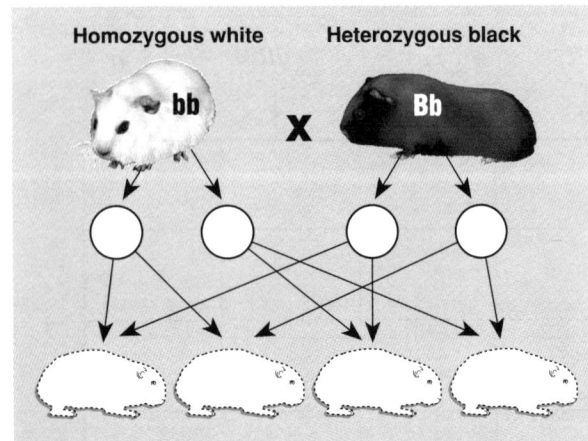

Cross 5:
(a) Genotype frequency: _____

(b) Phenotype frequency: _____

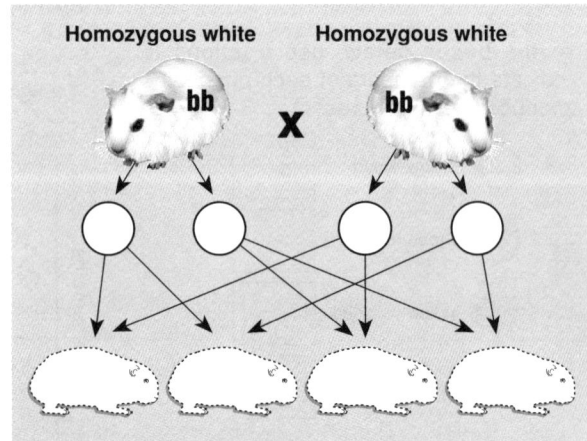

Cross 6:
(a) Genotype frequency: _____

(b) Phenotype frequency: _____

Inheritance Patterns

Complete the following monohybrid crosses for different types of inheritance patterns in humans: autosomal recessive, autosomal dominant, sex linked recessive, and sex linked dominant inheritance.

1. Inheritance of autosomal recessive traits

Example: *Albinism*

Albinism (lack of pigment in hair, eyes and skin) is inherited as an autosomal recessive allele (not sex-linked).

Using the codes: **PP**   (normal)
                          Pp   (carrier)
                          pp   (albino)

(a) Enter the parent phenotypes and complete the Punnett square for a cross between two carrier genotypes.

(b) Give the ratios for the phenotypes from this cross.

Phenotype ratios: _____

_____

Female parent phenotype: ☐

Male parent phenotype: ☐

P p *eggs*

P
sperm
p

2. Inheritance of autosomal dominant traits

Example: *Woolly hair*

Woolly hair is inherited as an autosomal dominant allele. Each affected individual will have at least one affected parent.

Using the codes: **WW**   (woolly hair)
                          wW   (woolly hair, heterozygous)
                          ww   (normal hair)

(a) Enter the parent phenotypes and complete the Punnett square for a cross between two heterozygous individuals.

(b) Give the ratios for the phenotypes from this cross.

Phenotype ratios: _____

_____

Female parent phenotype: ☐

Male parent phenotype: ☐

w W *eggs*

w
sperm
W

3. Inheritance of sex linked recessive traits

Example: *Hemophilia*

Inheritance of hemophilia is sex linked. Males with the recessive (hemophilia) allele, are affected. Females can be carriers.

Using the codes: $X_o X_o$ (normal female)
                          $X_o X_h$ (carrier female)
                          $X_h X_h$ (hemophiliac female)
                          $X_o Y$ (normal male)
                          $X_h Y$ (hemophiliac male)

(a) Enter the parent phenotypes and complete the Punnett square for a cross between a normal male and a carrier female.

(b) Give the ratios for the phenotypes from this cross.

Phenotype ratios: _____

_____

Female parent phenotype: ☐

Male parent phenotype: ☐

X_o X_h *eggs*

X_o
sperm
Y

4. Inheritance of sex linked dominant traits

Example: *Sex linked form of rickets*

A rare form of rickets is inherited on the X chromosome.

Using the codes: $X_o X_o$ (normal female); $X_o Y$ (normal male)
                          $X_R X_o$ (affected heterozygote female)
                          $X_R X_R$ (affected female)
                          $X_R Y$ (affected male)

(a) Enter the parent phenotypes and complete the Punnett square for a cross between an affected male and heterozygous female.

(b) Give the ratios for the phenotypes from this cross.

Phenotype ratios: _____

_____

Female parent phenotype: ☐

Male parent phenotype: ☐

X_R X_o *eggs*

X_R
sperm
Y

Dominance of Alleles

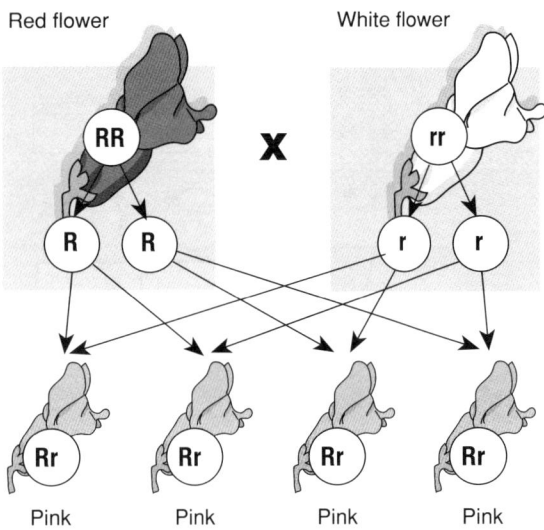

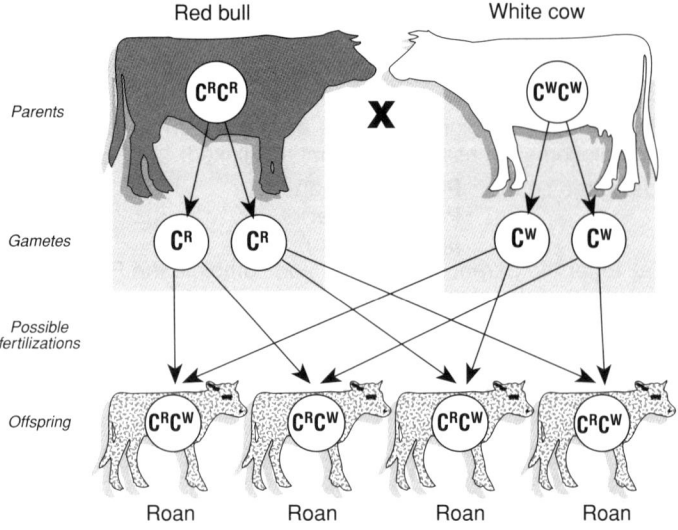

A 2

Red flower   White flower   Red bull   White cow

RR   X   rr   C^{R}C^R X   C^{W}C^W Parents

R   R   r   r   C^R C^R C^W C^W Gametes

Possible
fertilizations

Rr   Rr   Rr   Rr   C^{R}C^W C^{R}C^W C^{R}C^W C^{R}C^W Offspring

Pink   Pink   Pink   Pink   Roan   Roan   Roan   Roan

Incomplete Dominance

Incomplete dominance refers to the situation where the action of one allele does not completely mask the action of the other and neither allele has dominant control over the trait. The heterozygous offspring is **intermediate** In phenotype between the contrasting homozygous parental phenotypes. In crosses involving incomplete dominance the phenotype and genotype ratios are identical. Examples include snapdragons (*Antirrhinum*), where red and white-flowered parent plants are crossed to produce pink-flowered offspring. In this type of inheritance the phenotype of the offspring results from the partial influence of both alleles.

Codominance

Codominance refers to inheritance patterns when both alleles in a heterozygous organism contribute to the phenotype. Both alleles are **independently** and **equally** **expressed**. One example includes the human blood group AB which is the result of two alleles: A and B, both being equally expressed. Other examples include certain coat colors in horses and cattle. Reddish coat color is not completely dominant to white. Animals that have both alleles have coats that are **roan**-colored (coats with a mix of red and white hairs). The red hairs and white hairs are expressed equally and independently (not blended to produce pink).

1. In incomplete and codominance, two parents of differing phenotype produce offspring different from either parent. Explain the mechanism by which this occurs in:

   (a) Incomplete dominance: _____

   _____

   (b) Codominance: _____

   _____

2. For each situation below, explain how the heterozygous individuals differ in their phenotype from homozygous ones:

   (a) Incomplete dominance: _____

   (b) Codominance: _____

3. Describe the classical phenotypic ratio for a codominant gene resulting from the cross of two heterozygous parents (in the case of the cattle described above, this would be a cross between two roan cattle). Use the Punnett square (provided right) to help you:

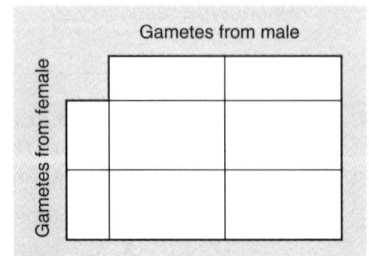

   _____

   _____

   _____

   Gametes from male

   Gametes from female

4. A plant breeder wanted to produce flowers for sale that were only pink or white (i.e., no red). Determine the phenotypes of the two parents necessary to produce these desired offspring. Use the Punnett square (provided right) to help you:

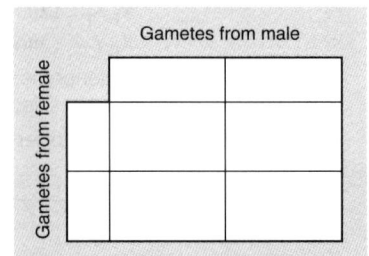

   _____

   _____

   Gametes from male

   Gametes from female

In the shorthorn cattle breed coat color is inherited. White shorthorn parents always produce calves with white coats. Red parents always produce red calves. But when a red parent mates with a white one the calves have a coat color that is different from either parent, called roan (a mixture of red hairs and white hairs). Look at the example on the previous page for guidance and determine the offspring for the following two crosses. In the cross on the left, you are given the phenotype of the parents. From this information, their genotypes can be determined, and therefore the gametes and genotypes and phenotypes of the calves. In the cross on the right, only one parent's phenotype is known. Work out the genotype of the cow and calves first, then trace back to the unknown bull via the gametes, to determine its genotype.

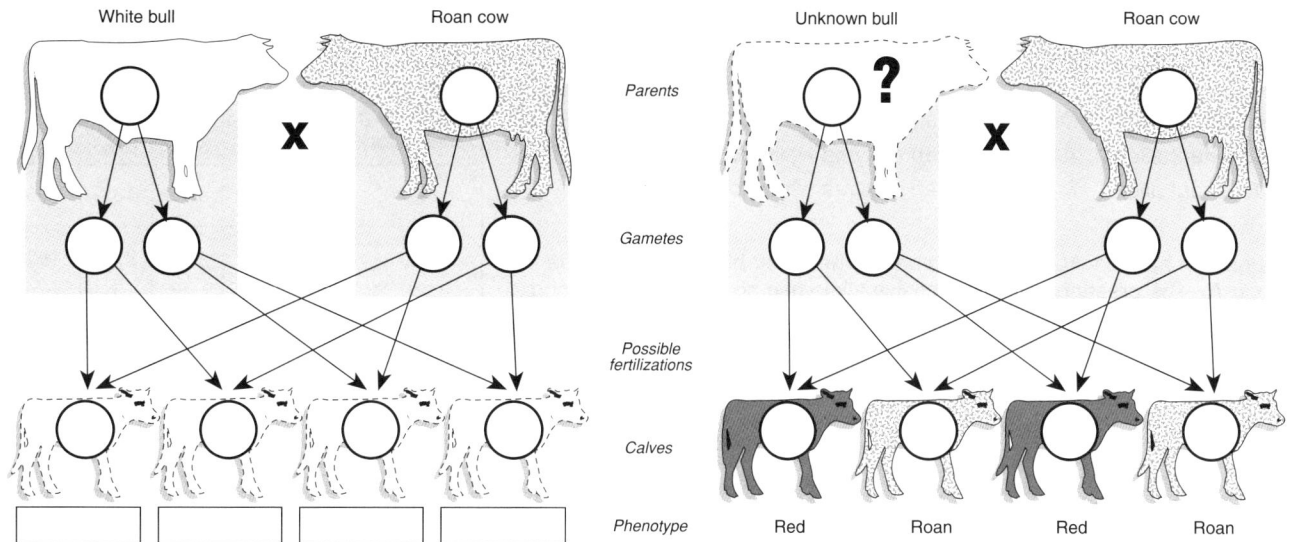

White bull Roan cow Unknown bull Roan cow

X X ?

Parents

Gametes

Possible fertilizations

Calves

Phenotype Red Roan Red Roan

5. A white bull is mated with a roan cow (above, left).
   (a) Fill in the spaces on the diagram (above, left) to show the genotype and phenotype for parents and calves.

   (b) State the phenotype ratio for this cross: _____

   (c) Suggest how the farmer who owns these cattle could control the breeding so that the herd ultimately consisted of red colored cattle only:

   _____
   _____
   _____

6. A unknown bull is mated with a roan cow (above, right). A farmer has only roan shorthorn cows on his farm. He suspects that one of the bulls from his next door neighbors may have jumped the fence to mate with his cows earlier in the year. All the calves born were either red or roan. One neighbor has a red bull, the other has a roan bull.
   (a) Fill in the spaces on the diagram (above, right) to show the genotype and phenotype for parents and calves.

   (b) State which of the neighbor's bulls must have mated with the cows: **red** or **white**   (*delete one*)

7. A plant breeder crossed two plants of the plant variety known as Japanese four o'clock. This plant is known to have its flower color controlled by a gene which possesses incomplete dominant alleles. Pollen from a pink flowered plant was placed on the stigma of a red flowered plant.

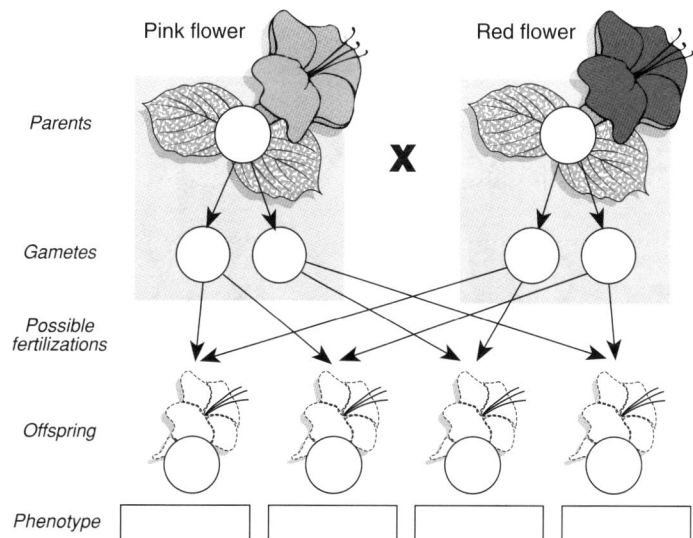

   Pink flower Red flower

   Parents X

   (a) Fill in the spaces on the diagram on the right to show the genotype and phenotype for parents and offspring.

   Gametes

   (b) State the phenotype ratio:

   Possible fertilizations

   Offspring

   _____
   _____
   _____
   _____

   Phenotype

Multiple Alleles in Blood Groups

The four common blood groups of the human 'ABO blood group system' are determined by three alleles: *A*, *B*, and *O* (also represented in some textbooks as: I^A, I^B, and i^O or just *i*). This is an example of a **multiple allele** system for a gene. The ABO antigens consist of sugars attached to the surface of red blood cells. The alleles code for enzymes (proteins) that join together these sugars. The allele *O* produces a non-functioning enzyme

that is unable to make any changes to the basic antigen (sugar) molecule. The other two alleles *(A, B)* are **codominant** and are expressed equally. They each produce a different functional enzyme that adds a different, specific sugar to the basic sugar molecule. The blood group A and B antigens are able to react with antibodies present in the blood from other people and must be matched for transfusion.

Recessive allele:	**O** produces a non-functioning protein
Dominant allele:	**A** produces an enzyme which forms **A antigen**
Dominant allele:	**B** produces an enzyme which forms **B antigen**

Blood group (phenotype)	Possible genotypes	Frequency*		
		White	Black	Native American
O	*OO*	45%	49%	79%
A	*AA AO*	40%	27%	16%
B		11%	20%	4%
AB		4%	4%	1%

* Frequency is based on North American population
Source: www.kcom.edu/faculty/chamberlain/Website/MSTUART/Lect13.htm

If a person has the *AO* allele combination then their blood group will be group **A**. The presence of the recessive allele has no effect on the blood group in the presence of a dominant allele. Another possible allele combination that can create the same blood group is *AA*.

1. Use the information above to complete the table for the possible genotypes for blood group B and group AB.

2. Below are six crosses possible between couples of various blood group types. The first example has been completed for you. Complete the genotype and phenotype for the other five crosses below:

Blood group: **AB** **Cross 1** Blood group: **AB**

Parental genotypes: AB X AB

Gametes: A   B   A   B

Possible fertilizations

Children's genotypes: AA   AB   AB   BB

Blood groups: A   AB   AB   B

Blood group: **O** **Cross 2** Blood group: **O**

Parental genotypes: OO X OO

Blood group: **AB** **Cross 3** Blood group: **A**

Parental genotypes: AB X AO

Blood group: **A** **Cross 4** Blood group: **B**

Parental genotypes: AA X BO

Blood group: A   **Cross 5**   Blood group: O

Blood group: B   **Cross 6**   Blood group: O

Parental genotypes   (AO) X (OO)   (BO) X (OO)

Gametes

Possible fertilizations

Children's genotypes

Blood groups

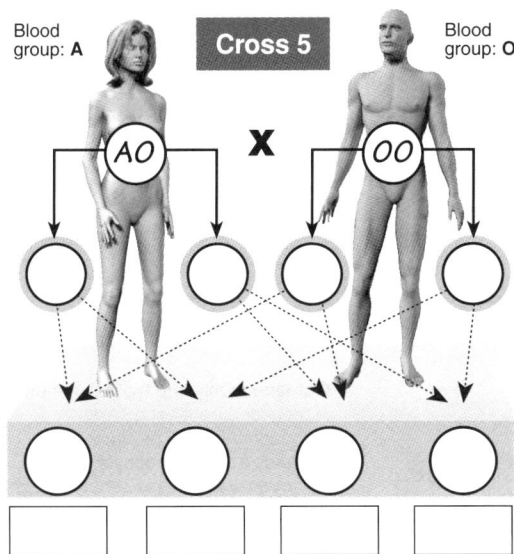

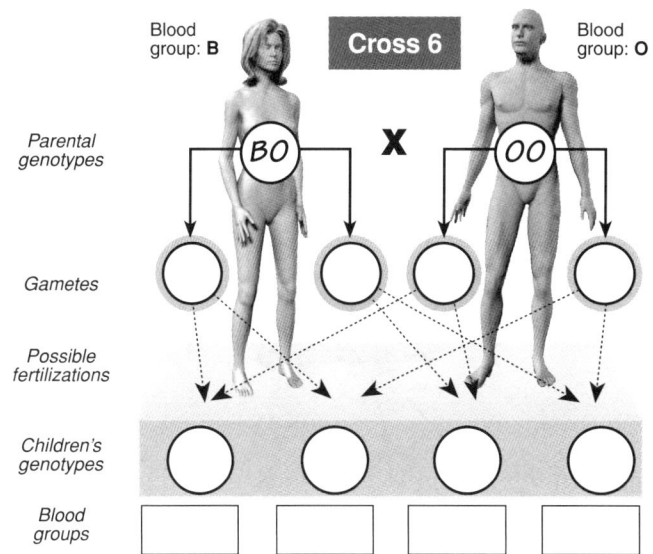

3. A wife is heterozygous for blood group **A** and the husband has blood group **O**.

(a) Give the genotypes of each parent (fill in spaces on the diagram on the right).

Determine the probability of:

(b) One child having blood group **O**:

_____

(c) One child having blood group **A**:

_____

(d) One child having blood group **AB**:

_____

Blood group A   X   **Blood group O**

Parental genotypes

Gametes

Possible fertilizations

Children's genotypes

Blood groups

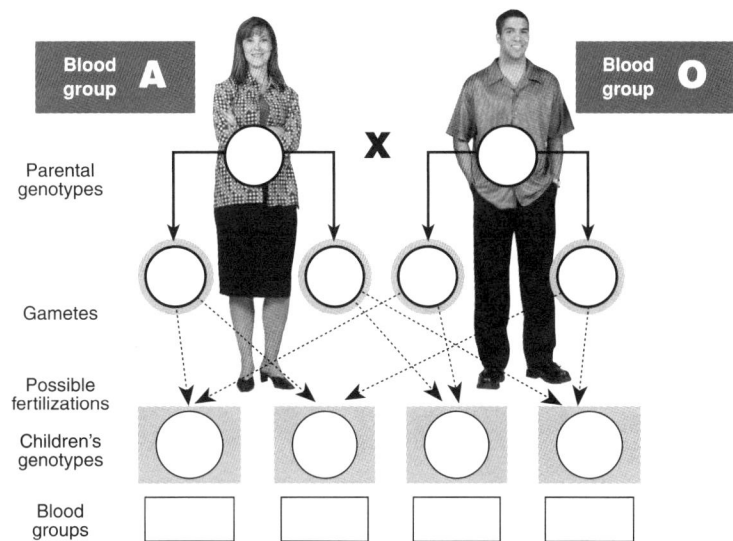

4. In a court case involving a paternity dispute (i.e. who is the father of a child) a man claims that a male child (blood group **B**) born to a woman is his son and wants custody. The woman claims that he is not the father.

(a) If the man has a blood group **O** and the woman has a blood group **A**, could the child be his son? Use the diagram on the right to illustrate the genotypes of the three people involved.

(b) State with reasons whether the man can be correct in his claim:

_____

_____

_____

Blood group A   X   **Blood group O**

Parental genotypes

Gametes

Child's genotype

Blood group   **B**

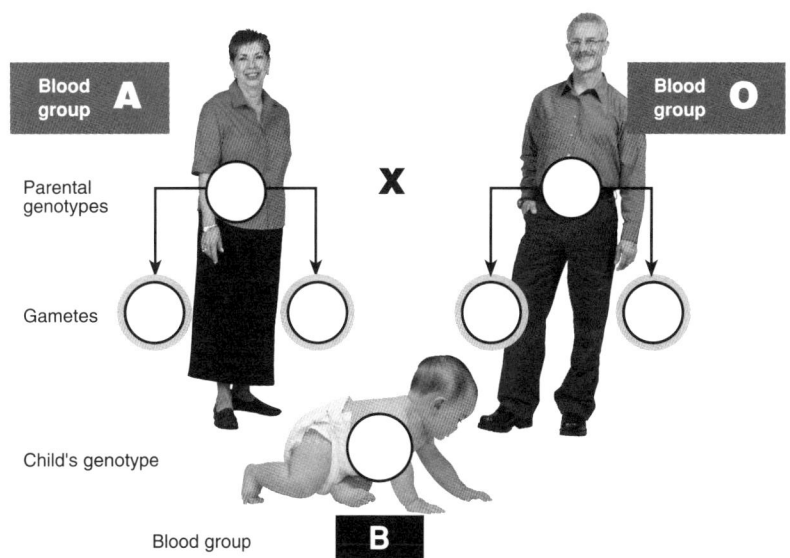

5. Give the blood groups which are possible for children of the following parents (remember that in some cases you don't know if the parent is homozygous or heterozygous).

(a) Mother is group **AB** and father is group **O**: _____

(b) Father is group **B** and mother is group **A**: _____

Dihybrid Cross

A cross (or mating) between two organisms where the inheritance patterns of **two genes** are studied is called a **dihybrid cross** (compared with the study of one gene in a monohybrid cross). There are a greater number of gamete types produced when two genes are considered - four types.

Remember that the genes described are being carried by separate chromosomes and are sorted independently of each other during meiosis (that is why you get four kinds of gamete). The two genes below control two unrelated characteristics **hair color** and **coat length**. Black and short are dominant.

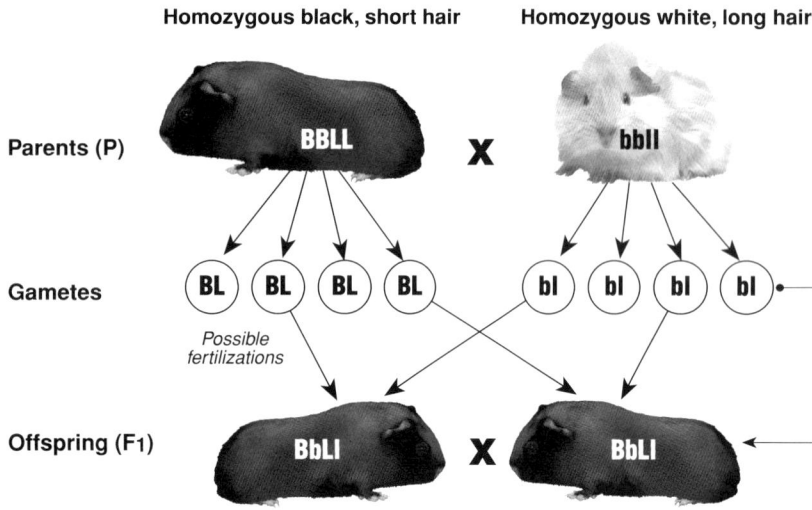

Homozygous black, short hair   **Homozygous white, long hair**

Parents (P)   BBLL   X   bbll

Parents: The notation **P**, is only used for a cross between **true breeding** (homozygous) parents.

Gametes   BL BL BL BL   bl bl bl bl

Possible fertilizations

Gametes: Only one type of gamete is produced from each parent (although they will produce four gametes from each oocyte or spermatocyte). This is because each parent is homozygous for both traits.

Offspring (F1)   BbLl   X   BbLl

F1 offspring: There is only one **kind** of gamete from each parent, therefore only one kind of offspring produced in the first generation. The notation **F1** is only used to denote the heterozygous offspring of a cross between two true breeding parents.

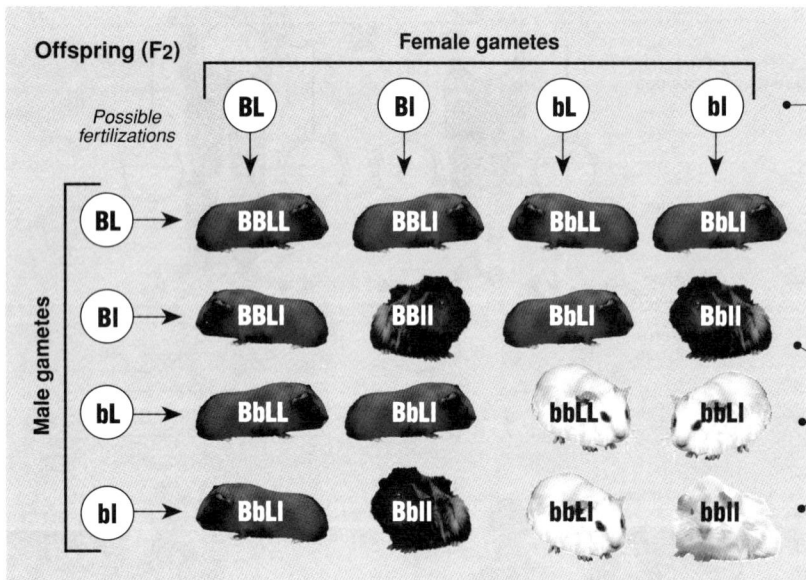

Offspring (F2)

Female gametes

Possible fertilizations

	BL	Bl	bL	bl
BL	BBLL	BBLl	BbLL	BbLl
Bl	BBLl	BBll	BbLl	Bbll
bL	BbLL	BbLl	bbLL	bbLl
bl	BbLl	Bbll	bbLl	bbll

Male gametes

F2 offspring: The F1 were mated with each other (**selfed**). Each individual from the F1 is able to produce four different kinds of gamete. Using a grid called a **Punnett square** (left), it is possible to determine the expected genotype and phenotype ratios in the F2 offspring. The notation **F2** is only used to denote the offspring produced by crossing F1 heterozygotes.

Each of the 16 animals shown here represents the possible zygotes formed by different combinations of gametes coming together at fertilization.

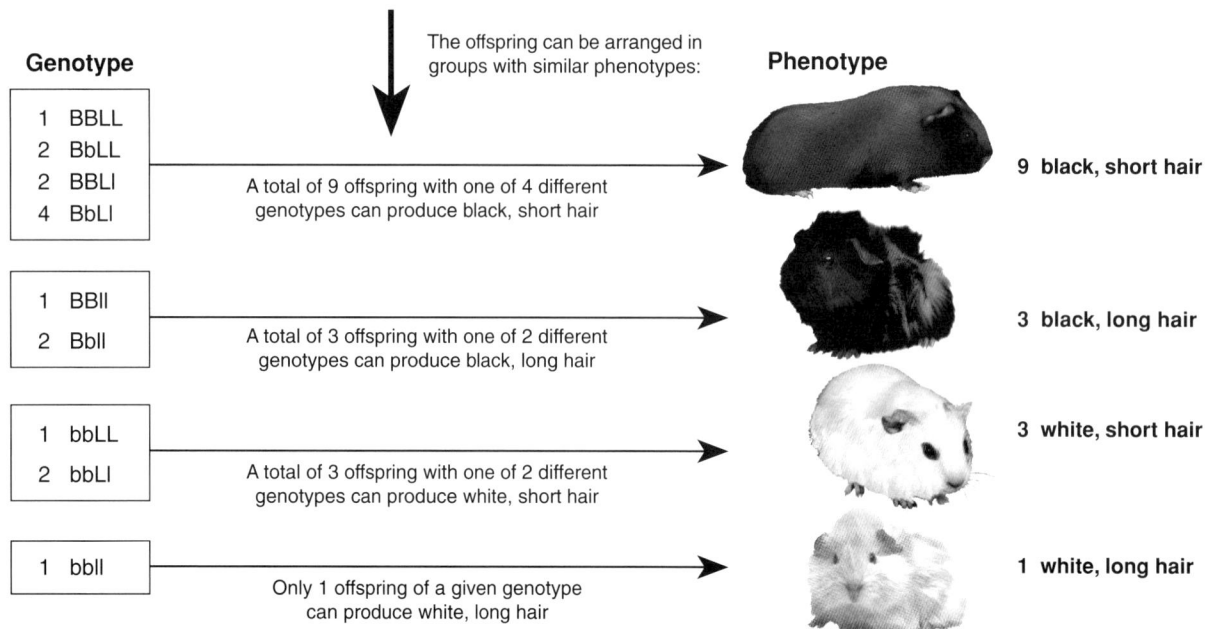

The offspring can be arranged in groups with similar phenotypes:

Genotype   **Phenotype**

1	BBLL
2	BbLL
2	BBLl
4	BbLl

A total of 9 offspring with one of 4 different genotypes can produce black, short hair

→ **9 black, short hair**

1	BBll
2	Bbll

A total of 3 offspring with one of 2 different genotypes can produce black, long hair

→ **3 black, long hair**

1	bbLL
2	bbLl

A total of 3 offspring with one of 2 different genotypes can produce white, short hair

→ **3 white, short hair**

1	bbll

Only 1 offspring of a given genotype can produce white, long hair

→ **1 white, long hair**

Cross Nº· 1

The dihybrid cross on the right has been partly worked out for you. You must determine:

1. The genotype and phenotype for each animal (write your answers in its dotted outline).

2. Genotype **ratio** of the offspring:

_____
_____
_____
_____

3. Phenotype **ratio** of the offspring:

_____
_____
_____
_____

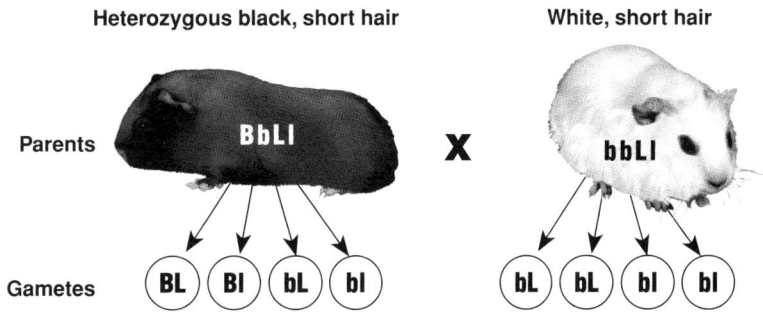
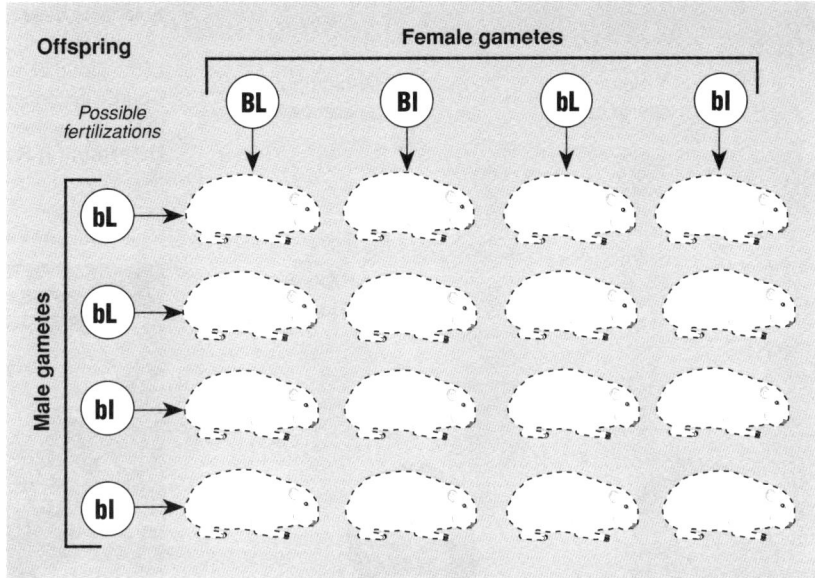

Cross Nº· 2

For the dihybrid cross on the right, determine:

1. Gametes produced by each parent (write these in the circles).

2. The genotype and phenotype for each animal (write your answers in its dotted outline).

3. Genotype **ratio** of the offspring:

_____
_____
_____
_____

4. Phenotype **ratio** of the offspring:

_____
_____
_____
_____

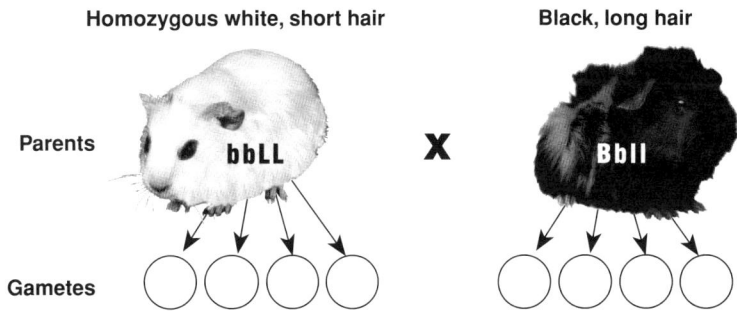
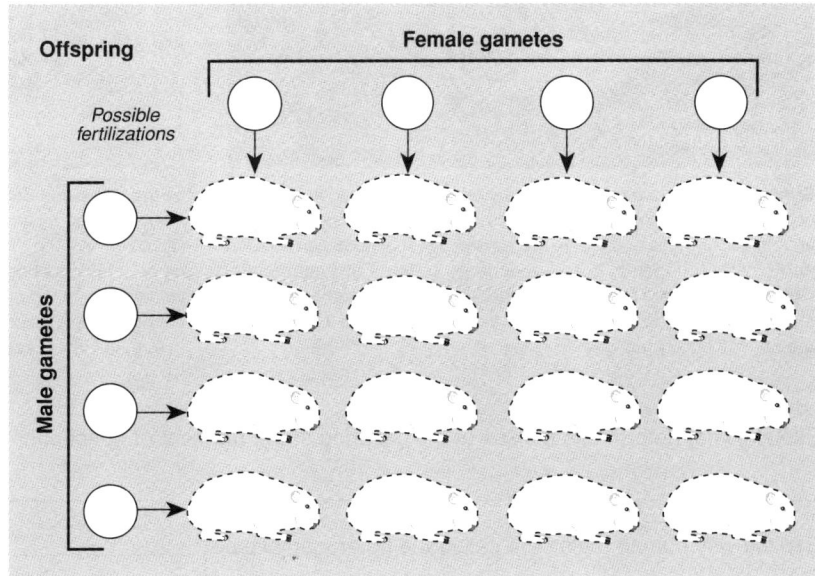

Sex Determination

The determination of the sex (gender) of an organism is controlled in most cases by the sex chromosomes provided by each parent. These have evolved to regulate the ratios of males and females produced and preserve the genetic differences between the sexes. In humans, males are referred to as the **heterogametic sex** because each somatic cell has one X chromosome and one Y chromosome. The determination of sex is based on the presence or absence of the Y chromosome. Without the Y chromosome, an individual will develop into a **homogametic** female (each somatic cell with two X chromosomes). In mammals, the male is always the hetero-gametic sex, but this is not necessarily the case in other taxa. In birds and butterflies, the female is the heterogametic sex, and in some insects the male is simply X whereas the female is XX.

Sex Determination in Humans

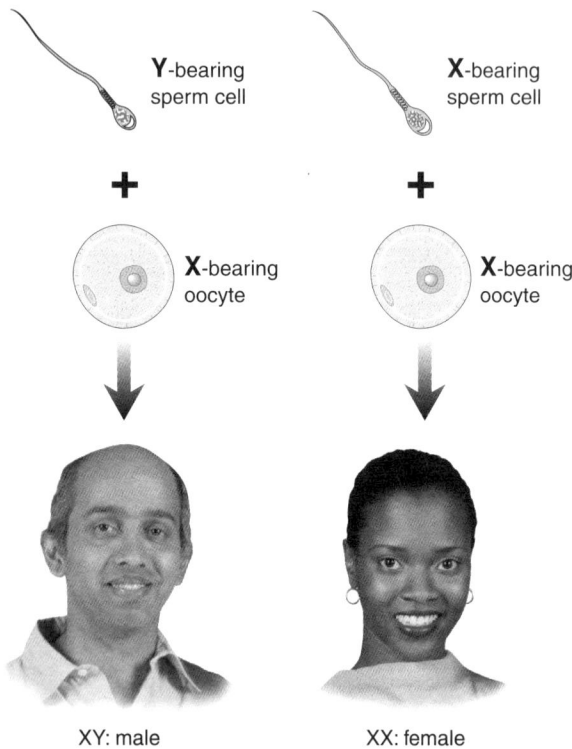

Y-bearing sperm cell

X-bearing sperm cell

+

+

X-bearing oocyte

X-bearing oocyte

XY: male

XX: female

The Sex Determining Region of the Y Chromosome

Scientists have known since 1959 that the Y chromosome is associated with being male. However, it was not until 1990 that a group of researchers, working for the Medical Research Council in London, discovered the gene on the Y chromosome that determines maleness. It was named **SRY**, for **Sex Determining Region of the Y**. The SRY gene produces a type of protein called a **transcription factor**. This transcription factor switches on the genes that direct the development of male structures in the embryo.

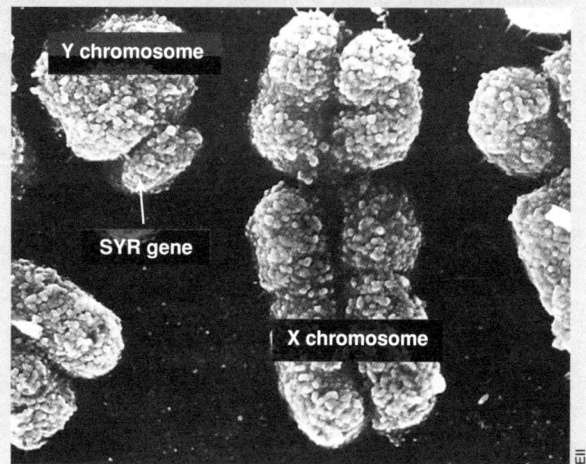

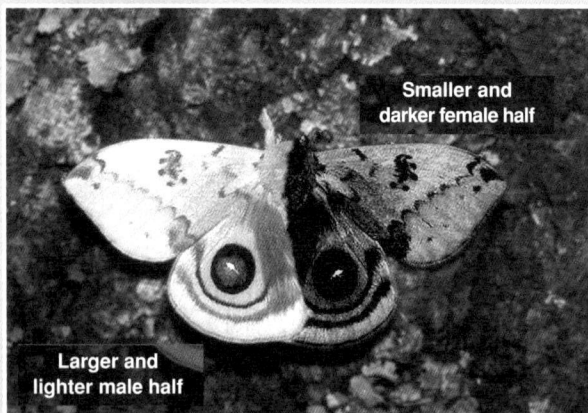

Y chromosome

SYR gene

X chromosome

Gynandromorphism occurs when an animal is a genetic mosaic and possesses both male and female characteristics (i.e. some of its cells are genetically male and others are female). This phenomenon is found particularly in insects, but also appears in birds and mammals. Gynandromorphism occurs due to the loss of an X chromosome in a stem cell of a female (XX), so that all the tissues derived from that cell are phenotypically male.

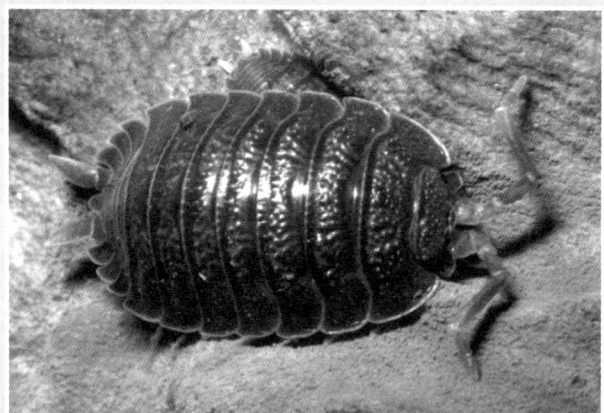

Smaller and darker female half

Larger and lighter male half

In the pill woodlouse, *Armadillium vulgare*, sex determination is characterized by female heterogamety (ZW) and male homogamety (ZZ). However, in several wild populations this system is overridden by an infectious bacterium. This bacterium causes genetically male woodlice to change into females. The bacteria are transmitted through the egg cytoplasm of the woodlouse. Therefore the conversion of males to females increases the propagation of the bacterium.

1. Explain what determines the sex of the offspring at the moment of conception in humans: _____

_____

2. Explain why human males are called the heterogametic sex: _____

_____

Breeding Pet Varieties

The following problems examine the outcome of matings in domestic breeds. They involve following the breeding through to the F₂ generation. The alleles involved are associated with hair color or length in a number of named mammals.

1. The Himalayan color-pointed, long-haired cat is a breed developed by crossing a pedigree (true-breeding), uniform-colored, long-haired Persian with a pedigree color-pointed (darker face, ears, paws, and tail) short-haired Siamese.
The genes controlling hair coloring and length are on separate chromosomes: uniform color **U**, color pointed **u**, short hair **S**, long hair **s**.

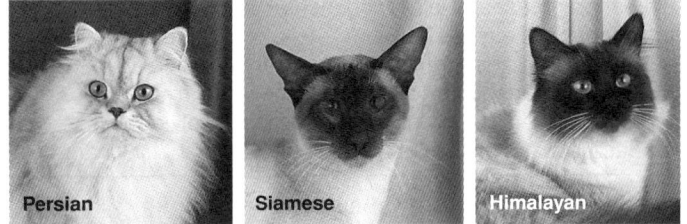

Persian   Siamese   Himalayan

   (a) Using the symbols above, indicate the genotype of each breed below its photograph (above, right). _____ _____ _____

   (b) State the genotype and phenotype of the **F₁**: _____

   (c) Use the Punnett square to show the outcome of a cross between F₁ offspring (the F₂):

   (d) State the ratio of the F₂ that would be Himalayan: _____

   (e) State whether the Himalayan (mated together) would be true breeding: _____

   (f) State the ratio of the F₂ that would be color-pointed, short-haired cats: _____

   (g) Explain how two F₂ cats of the same phenotype could have different genotypes:

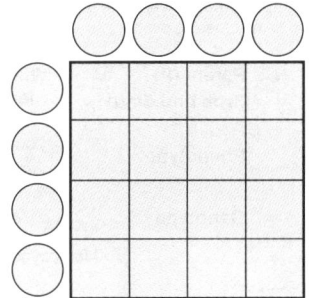

   _____

   (h) Explain how would you discover which of the F₂ color-pointed, short-haired cats were true breeding for these characters:

   _____

For the problems below, use a separate sheet to determine the outcomes of the crosses using Punnett squares. Staple the sheet into your manual to provide a permanent record of your workings:

2. In rabbits, spotted coat **S** is dominant to solid color **s,** while for coat color: black **B** is dominant to brown **b**. A brown spotted rabbit is mated with a solid black one and all the offspring are black spotted (the genes are not linked).

   (a) State the genotypes: Male parent: _____ Female parent: _____ Offspring: _____

   (b) Using ratios, state the phenotypes of the F₂ generation if two of these F₁ black spotted rabbits were mated:

   _____

   (c) State the name given to this type of cross: _____

3. In guinea pigs, rough coat **R** is dominant over smooth coat **r** and black coat **B** is dominant over white **b**. The genes for coat texture and color are independent genes (not linked). If a homozygous rough, black animal is crossed with a homozygous smooth white one, state the appearance (phenotype) of the:

   (a) **F₁** generation: _____ (b) **F₂** generation: _____

   (c) Offspring of a back-cross of the **F1** to the rough, black parent (include ratios of each phenotype if applicable):

   _____

   (d) Offspring of a test-cross of the **F1** to the smooth, white parent (include ratios of each phenotype if applicable):

   _____

4. In Manx cats, the allele for taillessness (**M**) is incompletely dominant over the recessive allele for normal tail (**m**). Tailless Manx cats are heterozygous (**Mm**) and carry a recessive allele for normal tail. Normal tailed cats are **mm**. A cross between two Manx (tailless) cats, produces two Manx to every one normal tailed cat (not three to one as would be expected).

   (a) State the genotypes arising from this type of cross: _____

   (b) Explain why the ratio of Manx to normal cats is not as expected: _____

Dihybrid Cross with Linkage

In a normal case of Mendelian dihybrid inheritance with independent assortment of alleles, a cross between two heterozygotes produces the expected 9:3:3:1 ratio in the offspring. In cases of dihybrid inheritance involving linkage, the offspring of a cross between two heterozygotes produces a 3:1 ratio of the parental types with no recombinants. However, because total linkage is uncommon, this 3:1 ratio is rarely achieved. Most dihybrid crosses involving linkage produce equal numbers of parental types and a significantly smaller number of recombinants. The examples below show the inheritance of body color (gray or black) and wing shape (long or vestigial) in *Drosophila*. The genes for these two characters are linked and do not assort independently. The example on the left shows the expected phenotype ratios from a mating between heterozygotes without crossing over. The example on the right shows the results of a test cross involving recombination of alleles. A test cross reveals the frequency of recombination for the gene involved.

Dihybrid Inheritance Involving Linkage
Genetic explanation for the 3:1 ratio in F_2 as a result of linkage

The genes for wing shape and body color are linked (they are on the same chromosome and there is no crossing over).

	Wild type female	Mutant male
Parent (P) (true breeding)		
Phenotype	Long wing Gray body	Vestigial wing Black body
Genotype	*VgVg BkBk*	*vgvg bkbk*
	Homozygous dominant	Homozygous recessive
Linkage notation	$\dfrac{Vg\ Bk}{Vg\ Bk}$	$\dfrac{vg\ bk}{vg\ bk}$

- - - - - Meiosis - - - - -

Gametes (n)

(*VgBk*)   Only one type of gamete is produced from each parent   (*vgbk*)

F_1   Sex of offspring is irrelevant in this case   *Vgvg Bkbk*

Long wing, grey body

The F_1 (heterozygous, wild type) progeny are allowed to interbreed

F_1 selfed | *Vgvg Bkbk*   X   *Vgvg Bkbk* |

- - - - - Meiosis - - - - -

Gametes (n)

(*VgBk*)   (*vgbk*)   X   (*VgBk*)   (*vgbk*)

F_2

VgVgBkBk   *VgvgBkbk*   *vgVgbkBk*   *vgvgbkbk*

Sex of offspring is irrelevant in this case | 3 Long wing Gray body | 1 Vestigial wing Black body

Expected ratio of phenotypes with linkage and no crossing over: 3: 1 ratio of the two parental phenotypes

---

Dihybrid Test Cross Involving Linkage
Explaining the appearance of recombinant alleles

The genes for wing shape and body color are linked but crossing over occurs between linked alleles in one parent

	Wild type female	Mutant male
Parent (P) (true breeding)		
Phenotype	Long wing Gray body	Vestigial wing Black body
Genotype	*VgVg BkBk*	*vgvg bkbk*
	Homozygous dominant	Homozygous recessive
Linkage notation	$\dfrac{Vg\ Bk}{Vg\ Bk}$	$\dfrac{vg\ bk}{vg\ bk}$

- - - - - Meiosis - - - - -

Gametes (n)

(*VgBk*)   Only one type of gamete is produced from each parent   (*vgbk*)

F_1   Sex of offspring is irrelevant in this case   *Vgvg Bkbk*

Long wing, grey body

A test cross was performed between the F_1 females and the black, vestigial winged male parent

Test cross | *Vgvg Bkbk*   X   *vgvg bkbk* |

- - - - - Meiosis - - - - -

Crossing over produces four types of female gametes

Gametes (n) ♀	*VgBk*	*Vgbk*	*vgBk*	*vgbk*
♂ *vgbk*	*VgvgBkbk*	*Vgvgbkbk*	*vgvgBkbk*	*vgvgbkbk*

	Long wing Gray body	Long wing Black body	Vestigial wing Gray body	Vestigial wing Black body
From 300 offspring, numbers of each phenotype were:	**123**	**21**	**27**	**129**

Sex of offspring is irrelevant in this case

Possible offspring with crossing over: the majority of the offspring are the parental type, with smaller proportions of recombinants

---

1. Calculate the crossover (value) for the offspring of the test cross, above:_____

DA 2 Using Chi-Square in Genetics

The following problems examine the use of the chi-square(χ^2) test in genetics. A worked example illustrating the use of the chi-square test for a genetic cross is provided on page 43, in the topic "Skills in Biology".

1. In a tomato plant experiment, two heterozygous individuals were crossed (the details of the cross are not relevant here). The predicted Mendelian ratios for the offspring of this cross were **9:3:3:1** for each of the **four following phenotypes**: purple stem-jagged leaf edge, purple stem-smooth leaf edge, green stem-jagged leaf edge, green stem-smooth leaf edge.

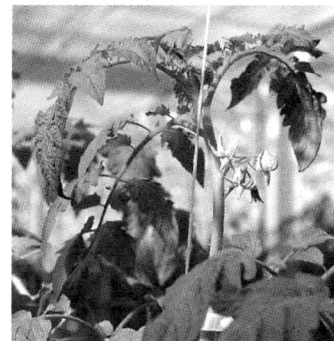

   The observed results of the cross were not exactly as predicted. The numbers of offspring with each phenotype are provided below:

Observed results of the tomato plant cross			
Purple stem-jagged leaf edge	12	Green stem-jagged leaf edge	8
Purple stem-smooth leaf edge	9	Green stem-smooth leaf edge	0

   (a) State your null hypothesis for this investigation (H0): _____

   _____

   (b) State the alternative hypothesis (HA): _____

   _____

2. Use the chi-squared (χ^2) test to determine if the differences observed between the phenotypes are significant. The table of critical values of χ^2 at different *P* values is provided in the topic "Skills in Biology", earlier in this manual.

   (a) Enter the observed values (number of individuals) and complete the table to calculate the χ^2 value:

Category	O	E	O – E	(O – E)^2	$\frac{(O - E)^2}{E}$
Purple stem, jagged leaf					
Purple stem, smooth leaf					
Green stem, jagged leaf					
Green stem, smooth leaf					
Σ					Σ

   (b) Calculate χ^2 value using the equation:

   $$\chi^2 = \sum \frac{(O - E)^2}{E} \qquad \chi^2 = \underline{\qquad}$$

   (c) Calculate the degrees of freedom: _____

   (d) Using the χ^2 table, state the *P* value corresponding to your calculated χ^2 value:

   _____

   (e) State your decision: reject H0 / accept H0

   (circle one)

3. Students carried out a pea plant experiment, where two heterozygous individuals were crossed. The predicted Mendelian ratios for the offspring were **9:3:3:1** for each of the **four following phenotypes**: round-yellow seed, round-green seed, wrinkled-yellow seed, wrinkled-green seed.

   The observed results were as follows:

Round-yellow seed	441	Wrinkled-yellow seed	143
Round-green seed	159	Wrinkled-green seed	57

   Use a separate piece of paper to complete the following:

   (a) State the null and alternative hypotheses (H0 and HA).

   (b) Calculate the χ^2 value.

   (c) Calculate the degrees of freedom and state the *P* value corresponding to your calculated χ^2 value.

   (d) State whether you accept or reject your null hypothesis: reject H0 / accept H0   (circle one)

4. Comment on the whether the χ^2 values obtained above are similar. Suggest a reason for any difference:

   _____

   _____

PDA❷ Types of Human Variation

An estimated 80 000 or so genes determine all human characteristics (traits). Some human traits are determined by a single gene (see examples below). Single gene traits show **discontinuous variation** in a population: individuals show only one of a limited number of phenotypes (usually 2 or 3). Other traits, such as skin color, are polygenic (controlled by more than one gene). Polygenic traits show **continuous variation** in a population, with a spread of phenotypes across a normal distribution range. Height is usually regarded as a polygenic trait, although recent findings indicate that 70% of the variation in adult height may be due to a single gene. It is possible to classify a small part of your own genotype for the six traits below:

Trait: Eye color

Dominant	Recessive

Phenotype:	Brown, green, hazel or gray	**Phenotype:**	Blue
Allele:	**B**	**Allele:**	**b**

The determination of eye color is complex, involving perhaps many genes. Any eye color other than pure blue is determined by a dominant allele that codes for the production of the pigment melanin. Hazel, green, gray, and brown eyes are dominant over blue.

Trait: Handedness

Dominant	Recessive

Phenotype:	Right-handed	**Phenotype:**	Left-handed
Allele:	**R**	**Allele:**	**r**

The trait of left or right handedness is genetically determined. Right-handed people have the dominant allele. People that consider themselves ambidextrous can assume they have the dominant allele for this trait.

Trait: Tongue roll

Dominant	Recessive

Phenotype:	Can roll tongue	**Phenotype:**	Cannot roll tongue
Allele:	**R**	**Allele:**	**r**

The ability to roll the tongue into a U-shape (viewed from the front) is controlled by a dominant allele. There are rare instances where a person can roll it in the opposite direction (to form an n-shape).

Trait: Middle digit hair

Dominant	Recessive

Phenotype:	Hair on middle segment	**Phenotype:**	No hair on mid segment
Allele:	**M**	**Allele:**	**m**

Some people have a dominant allele that causes hair to grow on the middle segment of their fingers. It may not be present on all fingers, and in some cases may be very fine and hard to see.

Trait: Ear lobe shape

Dominant	Recessive

Phenotype:	Lobes free	**Phenotype:**	Lobes attached
Allele:	**F**	**Allele:**	**f**

In people with only the recessive allele (homozygous recessive), ear lobes are attached to the side of the face. The presence of a dominant allele causes the ear lobe to hang freely.

Trait: Thumb hyperextension

Dominant	Recessive

Phenotype:	'Hitchhiker's thumb'	**Phenotype:**	Normal thumb
Allele:	**H**	**Allele:**	**h**

There is a gene that controls the trait known as 'hitchhiker's thumb" which is technically termed distal hyperextensibility. People with the dominant phenotype are able to curve their thumb backwards without assistance, so that it forms an arc shape.

1. Define the following types of variation and give two examples of each:

   (a) Discontinuous variation: _____

   _____

   Examples: _____

   (b) Continuous variation: _____

   _____

   Examples: _____

2. Carry out a survey of a minimum of 20 people to determine the frequency of the following traits:

Trait	Dominant	Recessive	Total sample size	Ratio
(a) Handedness				
(b) Eye color				
(c) Mid-digital hair				
(d) Ear lobes				
(e) Hitchiker's thumb				
(f) Tongue roll				

3. Carry out another survey of no less than 20 people and either ask them or actually measure an example of a continuous variable (i.e. height, shoe size, or hand span). Record your results and plot the frequency on the graph below:

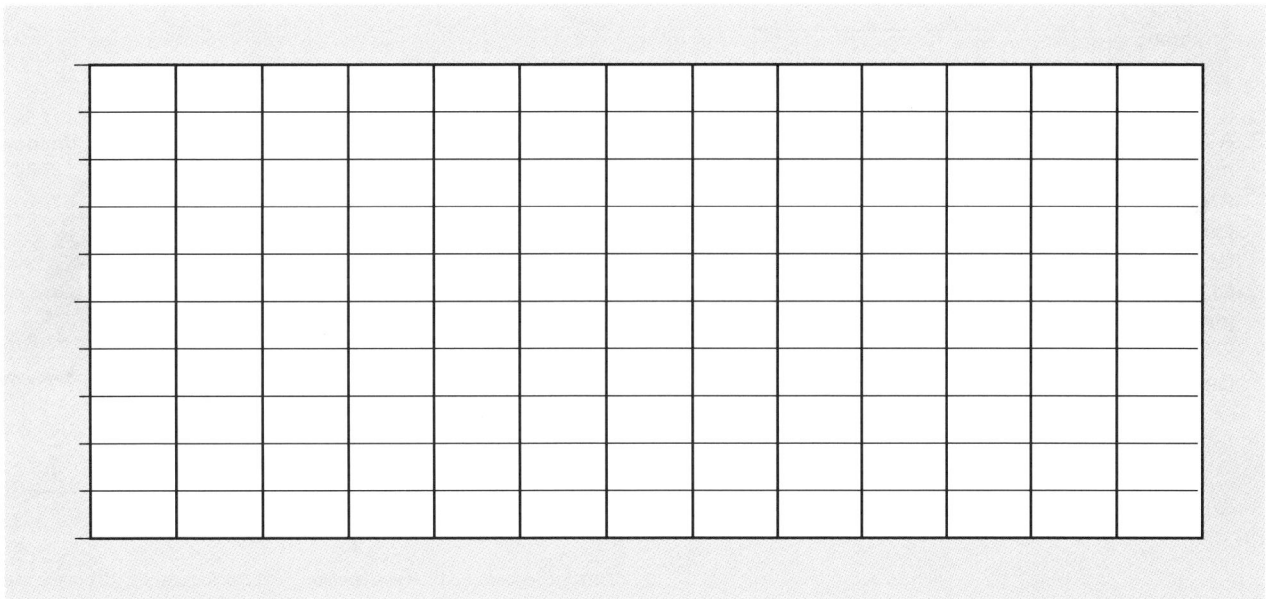

4. (a) Describe the pattern of distribution shown by the graph: _____

   (b) Explain the genetic basis of this distribution: _____

   _____

   (c) From the data obtained in (3) above and using a textbook for guidance, calculate:

   The mean: _____

   _____

   The standard deviation: _____

   _____

   (d) Suggest why a sample of at least 20 people is preferable for this exercise: _____

   _____

RA ③   Sex-Linked Genes

Codominant alleles in cats: One of the genes controlling coat color in cats is sex-linked. The two alleles, black and orange, are found only on the X-chromosome. Note that tortoiseshell phenotype is only possible in female cats because two X-chromosomes have to be present to carry the black and orange alleles.

Allele types

X_B = Black pigment
X_O = Orange pigment

Genotypes **Phenotypes**

X_BX_B, X_BY	= Black coated female, male
X_OX_O, X_OY	= Orange coated female, male
X_BX_O	= Tortoiseshell coat (intermingled black and orange in fur) in female cats only

1. An owner of a cat is thinking of mating her black female cat with an orange male cat. Before she does this, she would like to know what possible coat colors could result from such a cross. Use the symbols above to fill in the diagram on the right. Summarize the possible genotypes and phenotypes of the kittens in the tables below.

	Genotypes	Phenotypes
Male kittens		

	Genotypes	Phenotypes
Female kittens		

Parent cats

Black female X **Orange male**

Gametes

Possible fertilizations (kittens)

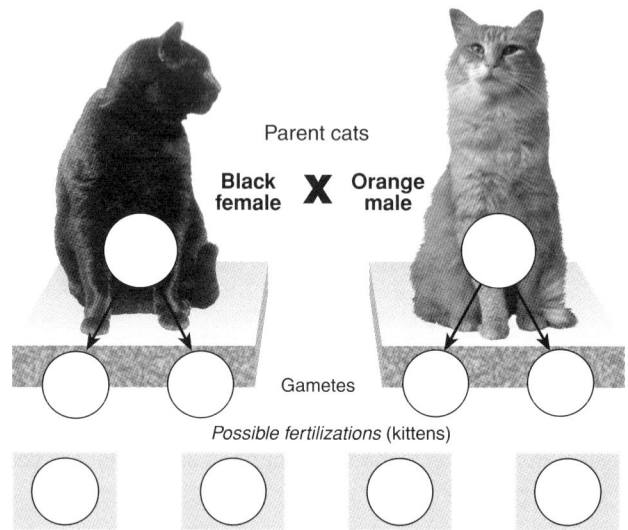

2. A female tortoiseshell cat mated with an unknown male cat in the neighborhood and has given birth to a litter of six kittens. The owner of this female cat wants to know what the appearance and the genotype of the father was of these kittens. Use the symbols above to fill in the diagram on the right. Also show the possible fertilizations by placing appropriate arrows.

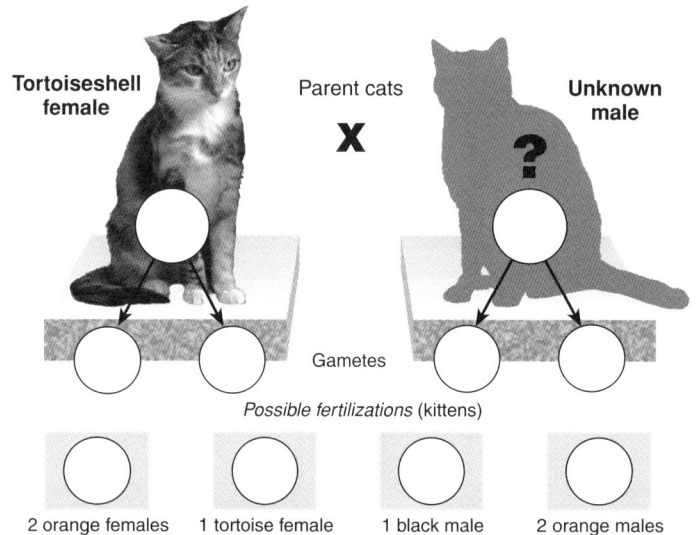

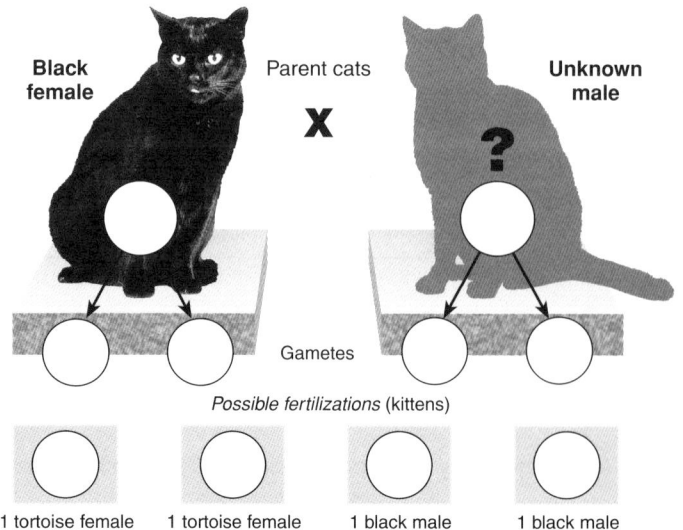

Describe the father cat's:

(a) Genotype: _____

(b) Phenotype: _____

Tortoiseshell female   **Parent cats**   **Unknown male**

X   ?

Gametes

Possible fertilizations (kittens)

2 orange females   1 tortoise female   1 black male   2 orange males

3. The owner of another cat, a black female, also wants to know which cat fathered her two tortoiseshell female and two black male kittens. Use the symbols above to fill in the diagram on the right. Show the possible fertilizations by placing appropriate arrows.

Describe the father cat's:

(a) Genotype: _____

(b) Phenotype: _____

(c) Was it the same male cat that fathered both this litter and the one above?
YES / NO *(delete one)*

Black female   **Parent cats**   **Unknown male**

X   ?

Gametes

Possible fertilizations (kittens)

1 tortoise female   1 tortoise female   1 black male   1 black male

Dominant allele in humans

A rare form of rickets in humans is determined by a **dominant** allele of a gene on the **X chromosome** (it is not found on the Y chromosome). This condition is not successfully treated with vitamin D therapy. The allele types, genotypes, and phenotypes are as follows:

Allele Types	Genotypes	Phenotypes
X_R = affected by rickets	$X_R X_R$, $X_R X$ =	Affected female
X = normal	$X_R Y$ =	Affected male
	XX, XY =	Normal female, male

As a genetic counselor you are presented with a married couple where one of them has a family history of this disease. The husband is affected by this disease and the wife is normal. The couple, who are thinking of starting a family, would like to know what their chances are of having a child born with this condition. They would also like to know what the probabilities are of having an affected boy or affected girl. Use the symbols above to complete the diagram right and determine the probabilities stated below (expressed as a proportion or percentage).

4. Determine the probability of having:

   (a) Affected children: _____

   (b) An affected girl: _____

   (c) An affected boy: _____

Normal wife   X   Affected husband

Parents

Gametes

Possible fertilizations

Children

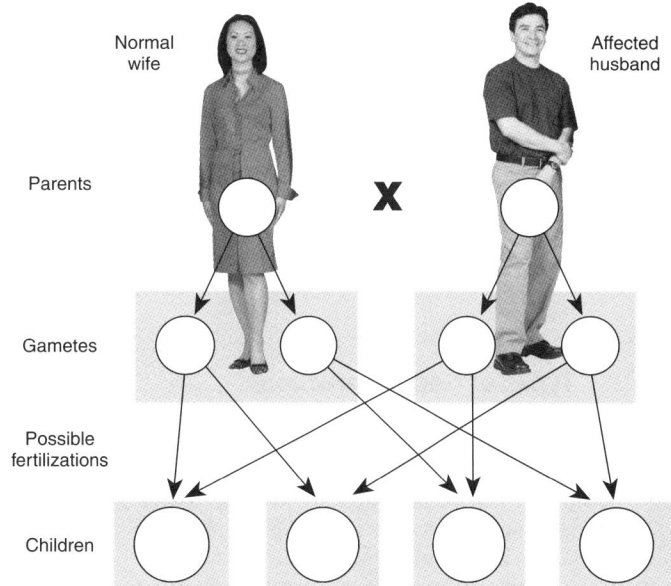

Another couple with a family history of the same disease also come in to see you to obtain genetic counseling. In this case the husband is normal and the wife is affected. The wife's father was not affected by this disease. Determine what their chances are of having a child born with this condition. They would also like to know what the probabilities are of having an affected boy or affected girl. Use the symbols above to complete the diagram right and determine the probabilities stated below (expressed as a proportion or percentage).

5. Determine the probability of having:

   (a) Affected children: _____

   (b) An affected girl: _____

   (c) An affected boy: _____

Affected wife
(normal whose father was normal)   X   Normal husband

Parents

Gametes

Possible fertilizations

Children

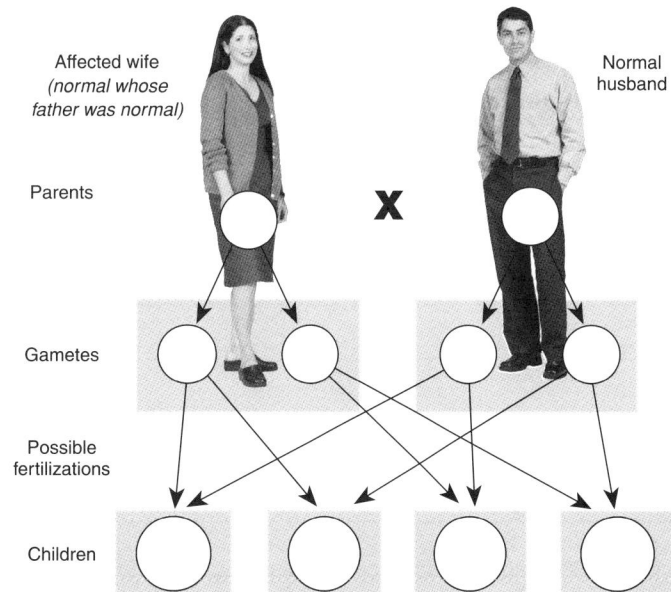

6. Explain the term **sex-linked genes**, identifying their significance to inheritance: _____

_____

_____

7. Name two examples of a sex-linked gene found in humans (not including the example above): _____

_____

Interactions Between Genes

RA 2

Genes   Product   Character

Protein synthesis

Pleiotropy
Several characters are affected by the single gene

Polygeny
Several genes control the expression of the same character

No interaction
Some genes only control the expression of a single character with no other input from other genes

Sickle Cell Disease as an Example of Pleiotropy

A person homozygous recessive (**Hb^{S}Hb^S**) for the sickle cell allele produces mutant hemoglobin. This affects a number of organs.

Brain damage leading to seizures, stroke, or loss of consciousness.

Skin lesions

Heart and blood vessel damage

Spleen enlarges in childhood but atrophies later, leading to susceptibility to infection.

Kidney damage leading to blood in the urine.

Types of Gene Interaction

Some genes may not just control a single characteristic or trait in the phenotype of an organism. It is thought that most genes probably have an effect on one or more phenotypic traits, a phenomenon known as **pleiotropy**. In some cases a single characteristic may be controlled by more than one gene; a situation known as **polygeny**. A further possible type of gene interaction, called **epistasis**, involves two non-allelic genes (at different loci), where the action of one gene masks or otherwise alters the expression of other genes. An example is albinism, which appears in rodents that are homozygous recessive for color even if they have the alleles for agouti or black fur (the gene for color is epistatic and the hypostatic gene determines the nature of the color).

Pleiotropy

A single gene may produce a product that can influence a number of traits or characteristics in the phenotype of an organism. Such a gene is said to be **pleiotropic**. The gene Hb codes for production of hemoglobin, an important oxygen-carrying molecule in the blood. A point mutation to this gene produces sickle cell disease. The phenotype has poor oxygen-carrying capability and deformed red blood cells leading to hemolytic anemia. A range of other organ abnormalities (above) also occur as a result of the mutant hemoglobin. In the diagram above, **Hb^S** stands for the single gene that codes for the mutated hemoglobin molecule. A person with sickle cell disease is homozygous recessive: **Hb^{S}Hb^S**. This condition is eventually fatal. The normal genotype is HbHb.

1. Distinguish between **polygeny** and **pleiotropy**: _____

_____

_____

_____

2. Define the term **epistasis**: _____

_____

3. (a) Outline the cause of sickle cell disease: _____

_____

(b) State the genotype of an affected individual: _____

(c) Describe the phenotype of an individual who is homozygous recessive for the sickle cell mutation: _____

_____

(d) Suggest why the sickle cell gene is regarded as pleiotropic: _____

_____

A 3

Epistasis

In its narrowest definition, **epistatic genes** are those that mask the effect of other genes. Typically there are **three possible phenotypes** for a dihybrid cross involving this type of gene interaction. One well studied example of epistasis occurs between the genes controlling coat color in rodents and other mammals. Skin and hair color is the result of melanin, a pigment which may be either black/brown (eumelanin) or reddish/yellow (phaeomelanin). Melanin itself is made up through several biochemical steps from the amino acid tyrosine. The control of

coat color and patterning in mammals is complex and involves at least five major interacting genes. One of these genes (gene C), controls the production of the pigment melanin, while another gene (gene B), is responsible for whether the color is black or brown. The interaction between these genes in determining coat color in mice is illustrated below. Epistasis literally means "standing upon". In albinism, the homozygous recessive condition, cc, "stands upon" the other coat color genes, blocking their expression.

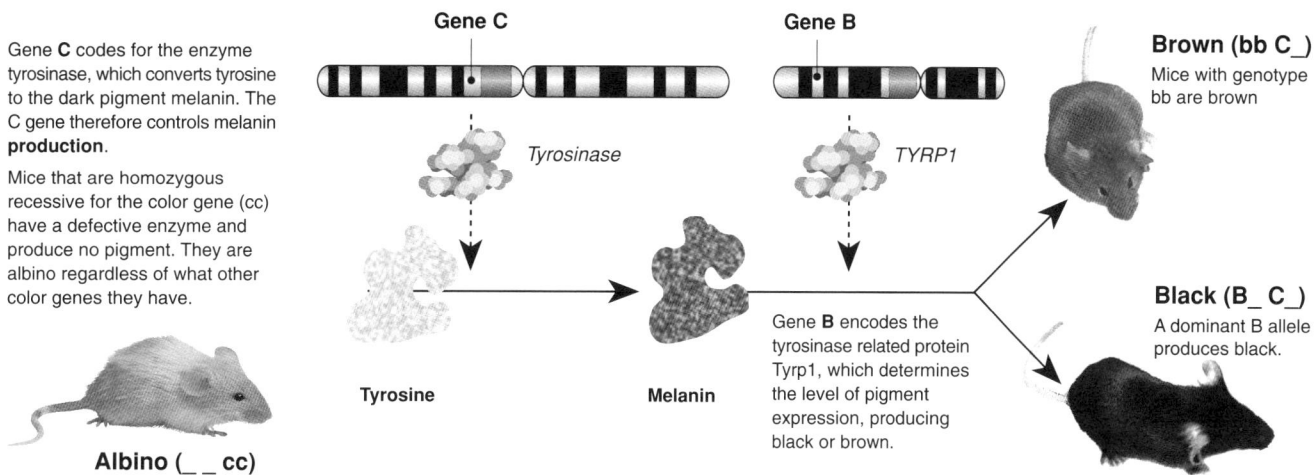

Gene **C** codes for the enzyme tyrosinase, which converts tyrosine to the dark pigment melanin. The C gene therefore controls melanin **production**.

Mice that are homozygous recessive for the color gene (cc) have a defective enzyme and produce no pigment. They are albino regardless of what other color genes they have.

Albino (_ _ cc)

Gene C

Tyrosinase

Tyrosine

Gene B

TYRP1

Melanin

Gene **B** encodes the tyrosinase related protein Tyrp1, which determines the level of pigment expression, producing black or brown.

Brown (bb C_)
Mice with genotype bb are brown

Black (B_ C_)
A dominant B allele produces black.

1. State how many phenotypes are possible for a dihybrid cross involving epistasis:

    _____

2. State which alleles must be present/absent for the following phenotypes:

    Black: _____

    Brown: _____

    Albino: _____

3. Complete the Punnett square (on the right) by entering the **genotype** and **phenotype** for each possible offspring. Determine the **ratio** of the phenotypes in this type of cross (BbCc x BbCc):

    _____

    _____

    _____

For the following crosses between parent rats (all homozygous for the genes involved), determine the **phenotypes** and possible **genotypes** of the offspring:

4. A mating of albino with black:

    _____

    _____

5. A mating of brown with black:

    _____

    _____

Parent generation
(true breeding)

X

Brown (bbCC)   **Albino** (BBcc)

Inbred (mated with siblings)

Black (BbCc)

Sperm

	BC	Bc	bC	bc
BC				
Bc				
bC				
bc				

Eggs

Polygenes

A single phenotype may be influenced, or determined, by more than one gene. Such phenotypes exhibit continuous variation in a population. Examples are skin color and height, although the latter has now been found to be influenced primarily by one gene.

A light-skinned person   A dark-skinned person

In the diagram (right), the five possible phenotypes for skin color are represented by nine genotypes. The production of the skin pigment melanin is controlled by two genes. The amount of pigment produced is directly proportional to the number of dominant alleles for either gene. No dominant allele results in an **albino** (aabb). Full pigmentation (black) requires four dominant alleles (AABB).

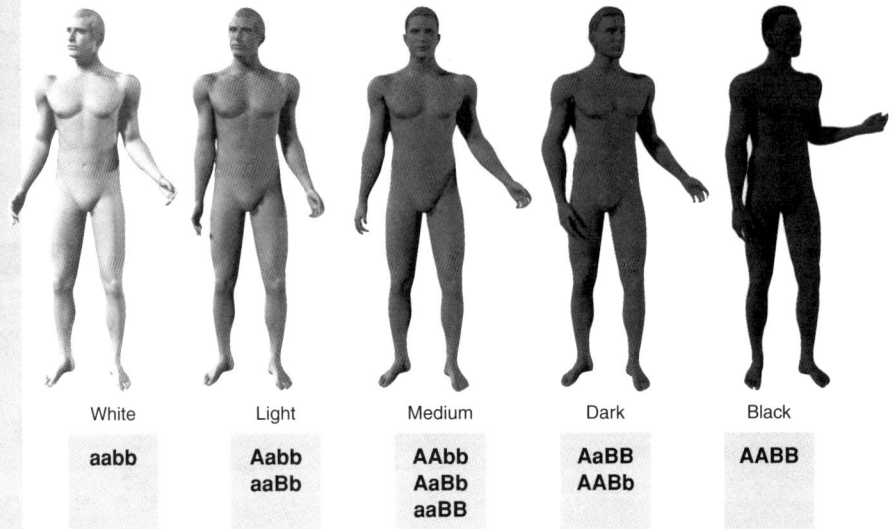

White	Light	Medium	Dark	Black
aabb	**Aabb** **aaBb**	**AAbb** **AaBb** **aaBB**	**AaBB** **AABb**	**AABB**

1. State **how many** phenotypes are possible for this type of gene interaction:

_____

2. State which alleles must be present/absent for the following phenotypes:

   Black: _____

   Medium: _____

   White: _____

3. Complete the Punnett square (on the right) by entering the **genotype** and **phenotype** for each possible offspring. Determine the **ratio** of the phenotypes in this type of cross, between heterozygous parents (AaBb x AaBb):

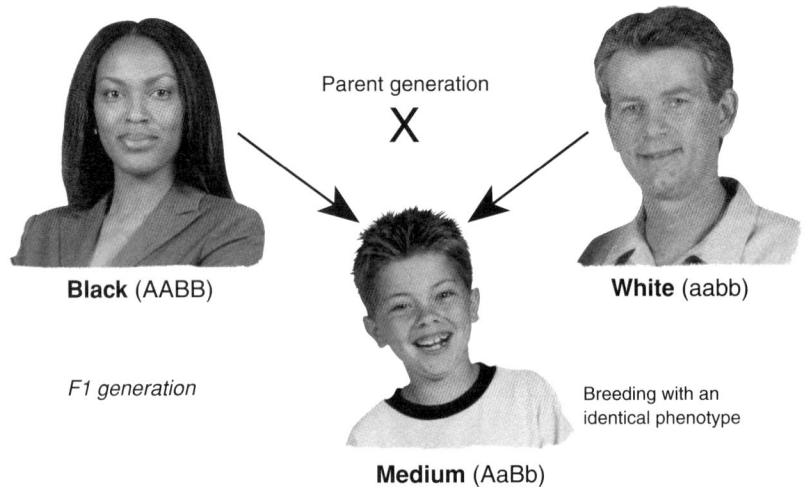

_____
_____
_____

For the following two crosses between humans, determine the phenotypes of the offspring:

4. A mating of white with black:

_____

5. A mating between two individuals of medium skin color:

_____

6. In a polygenic inheritance illustrated above, two genes (A and B) are able to produce 5 phenotypes. Determine how many possible phenotypes could be produced if **three** genes were involved (i.e. genes A, B and C produce genotypes aabbcc, Aabbcc, etc.):

Parent generation
X

Black (AABB)   **White** (aabb)

F1 generation

Breeding with an identical phenotype

Medium (AaBb)

F2 generation | Sperm: AB, Ab, aB, ab

Eggs: AB, Ab, aB, ab

_____
_____
_____

Inheritance in Domestic Cats

Cats have been domesticated for thousands of years. During this time, certain traits or characteristics have been considered fashionable or desirable in a cat by people in different parts of the world. In the domestic cat, the 'wild type' is the short-haired tabby. All the other coat colors found in cats are modifications of this ancestral tabby pattern. Inheritance of coat characteristics and a few other features in cats is interesting because they exhibit the most common genetic phenomena. Some selected traits for domestic cats are identified below, together with a list of the kinds of genetic phenomena easily demonstrated in cats.

Inheritance Patterns in Domestic Cats

Dominance The polydactylism gene with the dominant allele (Pd) produces a paw with extra digits.

Recessiveness The dilution gene with the recessive allele (d) produces a diluted black to produce gray, or orange to cream.

Epistasis The dominant agouti gene (A) must be present for the tabby gene (T) to be expressed.

Multiple alleles The albino series (C) produces a range of phenotypes from full pigment intensity to true albino.

Incomplete dominance The spotting gene (S) has three phenotypes ranging from extensive spotting to no spotting at all.

Lethal genes The Manx gene (M) that produces a stubby or no tail is lethal when in the homozygous dominant condition (MM causes death in the womb).

Pleiotropism The white gene (W) also affects eye color and can cause congenital deafness (one gene with three effects).

Sex linkage The orange gene is X-linked and can convert black pigment to orange. Since female cats have two X chromosomes they have three possible phenotypes (black, orange and tortoiseshell) whereas males can normally only exhibit two phenotypes (black and orange).

Environmental effects The dark color pointing in Siamese and Burmese cats where the gene (cs) is only active in the cooler extremities such as the paws, tail and face.

(NOTE: Some of these genetic phenomena are covered elsewhere)

Eyes
May have a range of coloring for the irises: blue, yellow, pink.

Ears
May be normal pointed ears, or the ears may be folded.

Coat color
A wide range of coat colors are available, controlled by a variety of genes. Basic colors include black, white, orange and agouti. Color patterns can range from solid, patched, spotted or tabby.

Coat length
Hair is usually either long or short. There is a breed with extremely short hair - so much so that it looks hairless (sphynx).

Coat texture
Smooth hair is the common phenotype, but there is an allele that causes curly hair.

Tail
Most cats have a long tail. An allele for short, stubby tails is almost completely restricted to the bobcat and Manx breeds.

Paws
Most cats have 5 digits on the front paw and 4 on the rear. The occurrence of polydactyly with as many as 6 or 7 digits affects as many as one out of five cats (in some parts of the world it is even higher than this).

Genes controlling inherited traits in domestic cats			
Wild forms	**Mutant forms**	**Wild forms**	**Mutant forms**
Allele *Phenotype*	*Allele* *Phenotype*	*Allele* *Phenotype*	*Allele* *Phenotype*
A Agouti	**a** Black (non-agouti)	**m** Normal tail	**M** Manx tail, shorter than normal (stubby)
B Black pigment	**b** Brown pigment	**o** Normal colors (no red, usually black)	**O** Orange (sex-linked)
C Unicolored	**cch** Silver **cs** Siamese (pointing: dark at extremities) **ca** Albino with blue eyes **c** Albino with pink eyes	**pd** Normal number of toes	**Pd** Polydactylism; has extra toes
		R Normal, smooth hair	**R** Rex hair, curly
D Dense pigment	**d** Dilute pigment	**s** Normal coat color without white spots	**S** Color interspersed with white patches or spots (piebald white spotting)
fd Normal, pointed ears	**Fd** Folded ears		
Hr Normal, full coat	**h** Hairlessness	**T** Tabby pattern (mackerel striped)	**Ta** Abyssinian tabby **tb** Blotched tabby, classic pattern of patches or stripes
i Fur colored all over	**I** Inhibitor: part of the hair is not colored (silver)		
L Short hair	**l** Long hair, longer than normal	**w** Normal coat color, not all white	**W** All white coat color (dominant white) **Wh** Wirehair

Variation in Coat Color in Domestic Cats

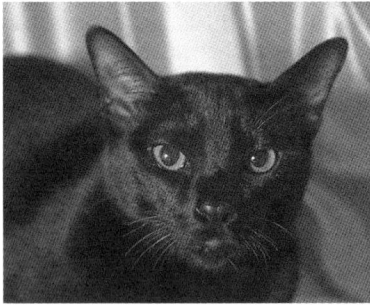

Non-agouti
A completely jet black cat has no markings on it whatsoever. It would have the genotype: **aaB–D–** since no dominant agouti allele must be present, and the black pigment is not diluted

Agouti hair
Enlarged view of agouti hair. Note that the number of darkly pigmented stripes can vary on the same animal.

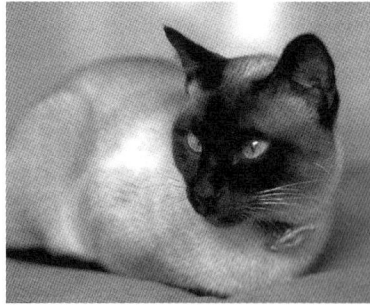

Stripes of dark pigment

Lighter color

Wild type
Mackerel (striped) tabby (**A–B–T–**) with evenly spaced, well-defined, vertical stripes. The background color is **agouti** with the stripes being areas of completely black hairs.

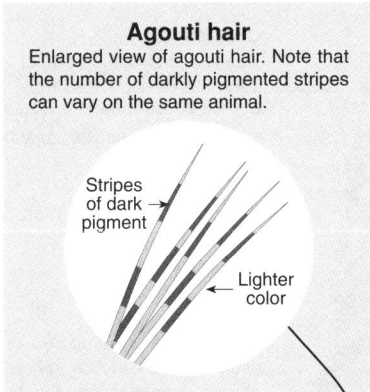

Siamese
The color pointing of Siamese cats is caused by warm temperature deactivation of a gene that produces melanin pigment. Cooler parts of the body are not affected and appear dark.

Sex-linked orange
The orange (**XO, XO**) cat has an orange coat with little or no patterns such as tabby showing.

Orange

Black   White

Calico
Similar to a tortoiseshell, but with substantial amounts of white fur present as well. Black, orange and white fur.

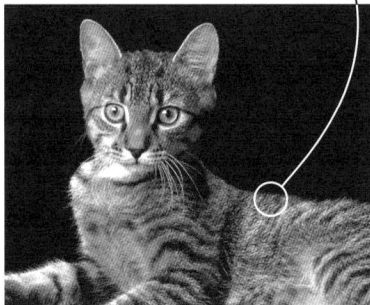

Tortoiseshell
Because this is a sex-linked trait, it is normally found only in female cats (**XO, Xo**). The coat is a mixture of orange and black fur irregularly blended together.

Blotched tabby
Lacks stripes but has broad, irregular bands arranged in whorls (**tb**)

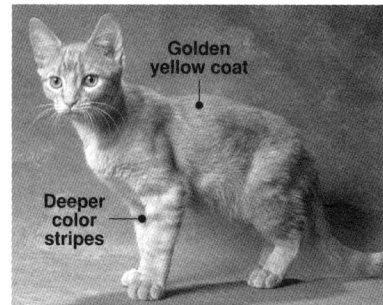

Golden yellow coat

Deeper color stripes

Marmalade
The orange color (**XO, XO**) is expressed, along with the alleles for the tabby pattern. The orange allele shows epistatic dominance and overrides the expression of the normal agouti color so that the tabby pattern appears dark orange.

Other Inherited Features in Domestic Cats

No tail

Manx tail (Mm)
The Manx breed of cat has little or no tail. This dominant allele is lethal if it occurs in the homozygous condition.

6 digits on the paw

Polydactylism (Pd–)
This is a dominant mutation. The number of digits on the front paw should be 5, with 4 digits on the rear paw.

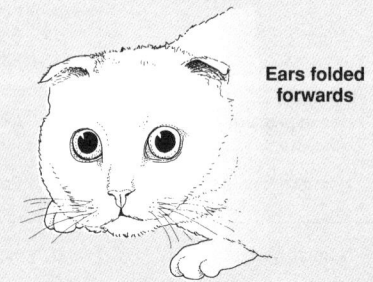

Ears folded forwards

Ear fold (Fd–)
Most cats have normal pointed ears. A dominant mutation exists where the ear is permanently folded forwards.

What Genotype Has That Cat?

Consult the table of genes listed on the previous pages and enter the allele symbols associated with each of the phenotypes in the column headed 'Alleles'. For this exercise, study the appearance of real cats around your home or look at color photographs of different cats. For each cat, complete the checklist of traits listed below by simply placing a tick in the appropriate spaces. These traits are listed in the same order as the genes for **wild forms** and **mutant forms** on the page opposite. On a piece of paper, write each of the cat's genotypes. Use a dash (-) for the second allele for characteristics that could be either heterozygous or homozygous dominant (see the sample at the bottom of the page).

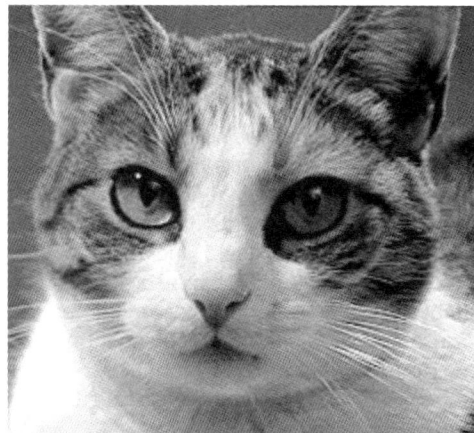

NOTES:
1. *Agouti* fur coloring is used to describe black **hairs** with a light band of pigment close to its tip.
2. Patches of silver fur (called chinchilla) produces the silver tabby phenotype in agouti cats. Can also produce "smoke" phenotype in Persian long-haired cats, causing reduced intensity of the black.
3. Describes the dark extremities (face, tail and paws) with lighter body (e.g. Siamese).
4. The recessive allele makes black cats blue-gray in color and yellow cats cream.
5. Spottiness involving less than half the surface area is likely to be heterozygous.

Phenotype Record Sheet for Domestic Cats

Gene	Phenotype	Allele	Sample	Cat 1	Cat 2	Cat 3	Cat 4
Agouti color	Agouti[1]						
	Non-agouti		✔				
Pigment color	Black		✔				
	Brown						
Color present	Uncolored		✔				
	Silver patches[2]						
	Pointed[3]						
	Albino with blue eyes						
	Albino with pink eyes						
Pigment density	Dense pigment						
	Dilute pigment[4]		✔				
Ear shape	Pointed ears		✔				
	Folded ears						
Hairiness	Normal, full coat		✔				
	Hairlessness						
Hair length	Short hair		✔				
	Long hair						
Tail length	Normal tail (long)		✔				
	Stubby tail or no tail at all						
Orange color	Normal colors (non-orange)		✔				
	Orange						
Number of digits	Normal number of toes		✔				
	Polydactylism (extra toes)						
Hair curliness	Normal, smooth hair		✔				
	Curly hair (rex)						
Spottiness	No white spots						
	White spots (less than half)[5]		✔				
	White spots (more than half)						
Stripes	Mackerel striped (tabby)						
	Blotched stripes						
White coat	Not all white		✔				
	All white coat color						

Sample cat (see ticks in chart above)

To give you an idea of how to read the chart you have created, here is an example genotype of the author's cat with the following features: *A smoky gray uniform-colored cat, with short smooth hair, normal tail and ears, with 5 digits on the front paws and 4 on the rear paws, small patches of white on the feet and chest.* (Note that the stripe genotype is completely unknown since there is no agouti allele present).

GENOTYPE: aa B– C– dd fdfd Hr– ii L– mm oo pdpd R– Ss ww

Pedigree Analysis

A ③

Sample Pedigree Chart

Pedigree charts are a way of graphically illustrating inheritance patterns over a number of generations. They are used to study the inheritance of genetic disorders. The key (below the chart) should be consulted to make sense of the various symbols. Particular individuals are identified by their generation number and their order number in that generation. For example, **II-6** is the sixth person in the second row. The arrow indicates the **propositus**; the person through whom the pedigree was discovered (ie. who reported the condition).

If the chart on the right were illustrating a human family tree, it would represent three generations: grandparents (I-1 and I-2) with three sons and one daughter. Two of the sons (II-3 and II-4) are identical twins, but did not marry or have any children. The other son (II-1) married and had a daughter and another child (sex unknown). The daughter (II-5) married and had two sons and two daughters (plus a child that died in infancy).

For the particular trait being studied, the grandfather was expressing the phenotype (showing the trait) and the grandmother was a carrier. One of their sons and one of their daughters also show the trait, together with one of their granddaughters.

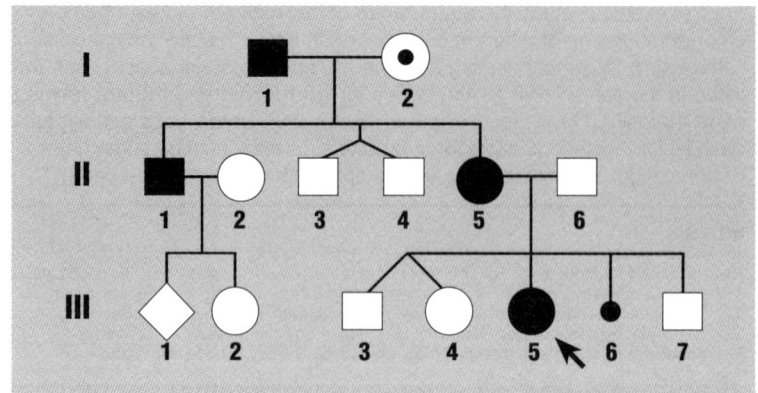

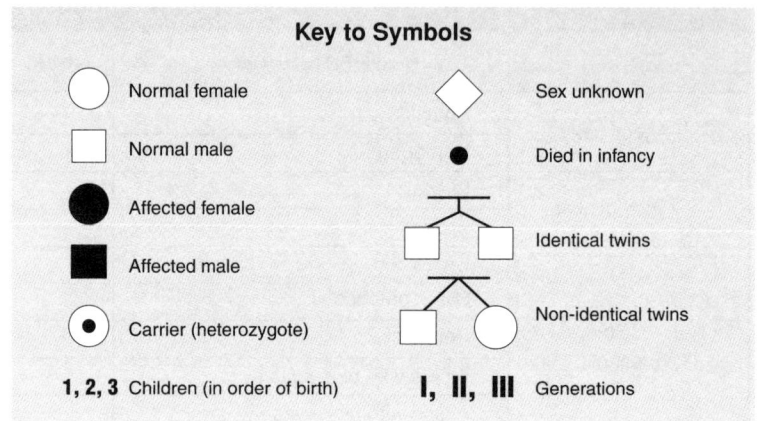

Key to Symbols

○	Normal female	◇	Sex unknown
□	Normal male	●	Died in infancy
●	Affected female		Identical twins
■	Affected male		
⊙	Carrier (heterozygote)		Non-identical twins
1, 2, 3 Children (in order of birth)		**I, II, III** Generations	

1. Pedigree chart of your family

Using the symbols in the key above and the example illustrated as a guide, construct a pedigree chart of your own family (or one that you know of) starting with the grandparents of your mother and/or father on the first line. Your parents will appear on the second line (II) and you will appear on the third line (III). There may be a fourth generation line (IV) if one of your brothers or sisters has had a child. Use a ruler to draw up the chart carefully.

2. The pedigree chart below illustrates the inheritance of a trait (darker symbols) in two families joined in marriage.

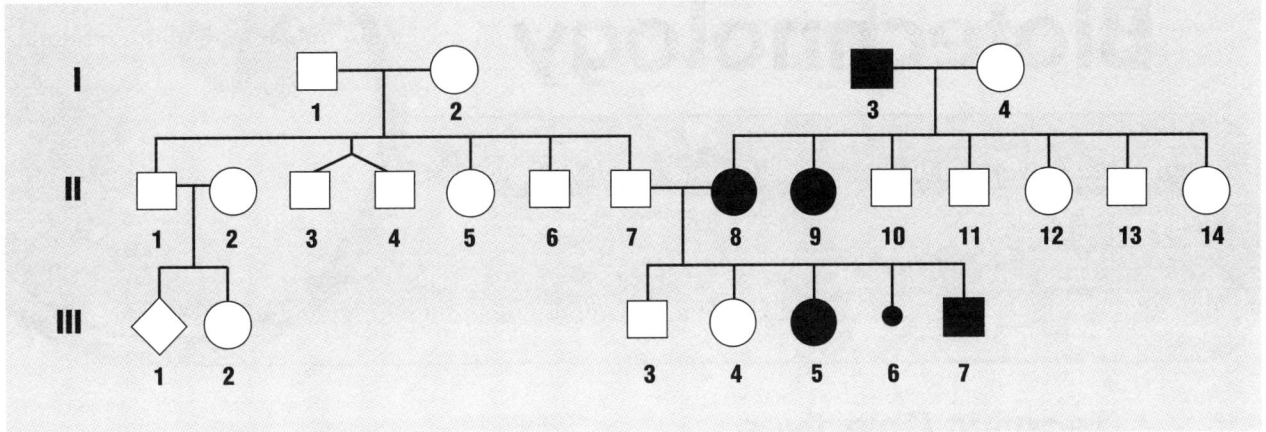

(a) State whether the trait is **dominant** or **recessive**, providing a reason for your choice: _____

_____

_____

(b) State whether the trait is **sex-linked** or not, providing a reason for your choice: _____

_____

_____

3. The recessive sex-linked gene (h) prolongs the blood-clotting time, resulting in the genetically inherited disease called hemophilia. From the information in the pedigree chart (right), answer the following questions:

Hemophilia in humans

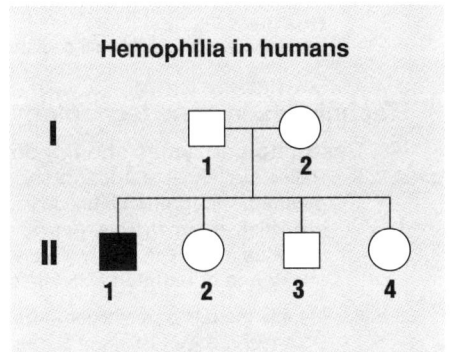

(a) If **II2** marries a normal man, what is the probability of her first child being a hemophiliac?

_____

(b) Suppose her first child is actually a hemophiliac. What is the chance that her second child will be a boy with hemophilia?

_____

(c) If **II4** has children with a hemophiliac man, what is the probability that her first child will be phenotypically normal?

_____

(d) If the mother of **I2** was phenotypically normal, what phenotype was her father? _____

4. The phenotypic expression of a dominant gene in Ayrshire cattle is a notch in the tips of the ears. In the pedigree chart on the right, notched animals are represented by the solid symbols.

Ear notches in Ayrshire cattle

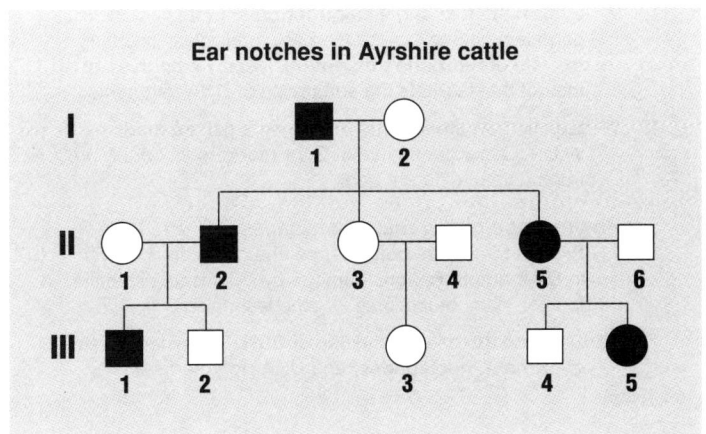

Determine the probability of notched offspring being produced from the following matings:

(a) III1 x III3 _____

(b) III3 x II2 _____

(c) III3 x III4 _____

(d) III1 x III5 _____

(e) III2 x III5 _____

Aspects of Biotechnology

IB SL

Complete nos:
1-9, 11, 13-15, 18-20, 23-24, 26, 30-32 (a)-(c), 33-34, 36 Extension: 35

IB HL

Complete nos:
1-9, 11, 13-15, 18-20, 23-24, 26, 30-32 (a)-(c), 33-34, 36 Extension: 35

IB Options

Complete nos:
Option F (HL): 27, 29, 32 Extension: 28

AP Biology

Complete nos:
1-15, 16 or 17, 18-25, 26 or 27, 28-36 Some as extension as appropriate

Learning Objectives

☐ 1. Compile your own glossary from the **KEY WORDS** displayed in **bold type** in the learning objectives below.

Introduction to gene technology *(page 230)*

☐ 2. Define: **gene technology**. Appreciate that not all **biotechnology** involves gene technology (although it often does). Distinguish between **recombinant DNA technology** (**genetic engineering**) and other forms of **genetic manipulation**.

☐ 3. Recognize that four basic techniques (*restriction digestion, DNA ligation, gel electrophoresis, and PCR*) are used in a number of different processes (e.g. *gene cloning, transformation, DNA profiling*). Appreciate that these processes have wide application.

☐ 4. Appreciate the various *applications* of gene technology in modern medicine, agriculture, and industry. Recognize the pivotal role of microorganisms in the development and application of this technology.

Techniques in gene technology

Restriction enzymes and ligation *(pages 214-216)*

☐ 5. Define the terms: **restriction enzyme** (**endonuclease**), **plasmid**, **recognition site**. Outline the basis by which restriction enzymes work. Appreciate that restriction enzymes are of different types and may produce either **sticky end** or **blunt end** DNA fragments.

☐ 6. Identify the role of restriction enzymes in recombinant DNA technology. List some commonly used restriction enzymes and give their recognition sites.

☐ 7. Explain what is meant by **DNA ligation** and **annealing**. Explain the purpose of DNA ligation and describe how it is achieved, identifying the role of **DNA ligase**.

☐ 8. Understand how **recombinant DNA** is produced by the ligation of DNA from different sources.

Gel electrophoresis of DNA *(page 217)*

☐ 9. Explain the role of **gel electrophoresis** (of DNA) in gene technology. Outline the basic principles, including the role of **restriction digestion**. Identify properties of the gel that facilitate the separation of DNA fragments.

☐ 10. Explain how the DNA fragments on a gel are made visible. Describe the role of **DNA markers** in identifying fragments of different size.

Polymerase chain reaction *(pages 218-219)*

☐ 11. Explain the role of **polymerase chain reaction** (PCR) in **DNA amplification**. Identify why PCR is an essential tool for many procedures in gene technology.

☐ 12. Describe the basic technique of PCR, including the role of **primers**, **nucleotides**, and **DNA polymerase**.

Processes

DNA sequencing *(pages 220-223, 240-241)*

☐ 13. Define the term **DNA sequencing**. Understand that determining the sequence of nucleotides in DNA involves the use of **PCR**, **radioactive labeling**, and **gel electrophoresis**.

☐ 14. Recognize the **Human Genome Project** as an international cooperative venture to sequence the entire human genome. Appreciate the role of rapid automated sequencing in the feasibility of the HGP. Explain what is meant by a **genome library**. Describe two possible advantageous outcomes of the HGP.

DNA profiling *(pages 224-227)*

☐ 15. Explain what is meant **DNA profiling** (also called genetic/DNA fingerprinting). Distinguish clearly between DNA profiling and sequencing.

☐ 16. Describe the process of DNA profiling using **Southern blotting**. Take care to explain the role of the following:
   - *Gel electrophoresis* to separate DNA fragments.
   - *The Blot* to transfer the DNA fragments to a filter.
   - *Radioactively labeled probes* to localize and visualize the sought-after fragments.

☐ 17. Describe the process of DNA profiling using PCR. Explain the role of the following in this process:
   - *Microsatellites* in providing identifiable variation.
   - *PCR* in amplifying the microsatellites.
   - *Gel electrophoresis* in visualizing the PCR products so that they can be compared.

☐ 18. Describe two applications of DNA profiling, e.g. in paternity suits and criminal investigations.

Genetic screening *(pages 159, 224-225, 240-241)*

☐ 19. Explain what is meant by **genetic screening** and understand the basic principles involved. Discuss three advantages and/or disadvantages of genetic screening.

Gene cloning *(pages 228-229)*

☐ 20. Define the term: **gene cloning** and briefly describe the application of this process. Recognize the stages involved in gene cloning (see #21-22).

☐ 21. Outline the steps in *preparation of a gene for cloning*.
   - **Isolation** of the desired gene from cells.
   - Use of **reverse transcriptase** to create the gene for insertion into the plasmid vector.
   - Insertion of the gene into an appropriate vector (e.g. plasmid) to create a **molecular clone**.

☐ 22. Outline how the prepared molecular clone (containing the desired gene) is introduced into the host cells (e.g. bacterial cells). Understand that these bacteria are then grown in culture to produce multiple copies of the gene.

Transgenic organisms *(pages 230-234)*

☐ 23. Define: **transformation** and **transgenic organism**. With respect to the nature of the genetic code, explain why DNA can be transferred between species.

☐ 24. Outline the basic techniques for gene transfer involving plasmid vectors, including the role of restriction enzymes and DNA ligation. Define **host cell** and identify the types of host cells commonly involved.

☐ 25. Appreciate the role of **marker genes** (genetic markers) in identifying transformed cells. These may be genes for antibiotic resistance or ability to grow on specific media.

Meeting human needs

Using transgenics *(page 230-231, 234, 238-239)*

☐ 26. **State** two examples of current uses of genetically modified crops or animals.

☐ 27. **Describe** three examples of the use of transgenic techniques in agriculture, including at least one plant and one animal example. Examples could include: *salt tolerance in a named crop plant, production of frost resistance in fruit, transfer of Bt toxin to tomatoes, viral resistance in tomatoes, herbicide resistance in crop plants, production of α-1-antitrypsin in milk.*

☐ 28. Appreciate the role of genetically modified microbes in the mass production of valuable human proteins (e.g. *human insulin, factor VIII*), antibiotics, and enzymes. Explain how this application of gene technology can meet human needs safely, efficiently, and at low cost.

☐ 29. Discuss gene manipulation involving sense/antisense technology, with reference to the **Flvr Savr tomatoes**.

Gene therapy *(pages 235-237)*

☐ 30. Explain what is meant by **gene therapy** and outline the procedures involved, including the role of gene cloning and **vectors**. Citing examples, explain why successful gene therapy is feasible but difficult.

☐ 31. Describe an example of current or proposed gene therapies (e.g. for **SCID** and **cystic fibrosis**). For your chosen example, outline the vectors that could be used to introduce healthy genes into patients and describe probable mechanisms for *delivering* those vectors.

Ethics of gene technology *(pages 242-243)*

☐ 32. Discuss (in a balanced way) the relevant ethical, social, and/or economic issues associated with the use of GMOs. You may wish to consider all or some of:
  • **Transposons** and the risks of jumping genes.
  • The advantages and disadvantages of using transgenic organisms in agriculture and industry.
  • The social/moral implications of gene technology, e.g. for *non-therapeutic genetic manipulation, gene therapy, genetic screening,* and *animal welfare.*
  • The economic issues associated with the use of gene technology. Consider: the impact of **patents** for GMOs and consequent control over a product (e.g. seeds), insurance for GMO accidents or problems, and the cost of staying GM-free.

Cloning *(pages 244-247)*

☐ 33. Explain clearly what is meant by a **clone**. Appreciate the current and potential uses of cloning technology.

☐ 34. Outline a technique for cloning using differentiated cells i.e. using the **nuclear transfer technique**. Explain the principles involved and identify the purpose of each step in the process. Describe the benefits and disadvantages involved with this technique.

☐ 35. Appreciate that cloning has traditionally been achieved through **embryo splitting**. Explain the principles involved and contrast embryo splitting with nuclear transfer, identifying the advantages of the latter.

☐ 36. Discuss, in a balanced way, the ethics of human cloning.

Textbooks

See the 'Textbook Reference Grid' on pages 8-9 for textbook page references relating to material in this topic.

Supplementary Texts

See pages 5-6 for additional details of these texts:
■ Adds, J. *et al.*, 1999. **Tools, Techniques and Assessment in Biology** (NelsonThornes), pp. 56-71.
■ Adds, J., *et al.*, 2001. **Genetics, Evolution and Biodiversity**, (NelsonThornes), pp. 109-120.
■ Clegg, C.J., 1999. **Genetics and Evolution** (John Murray), pp. 48-59.
■ Jones, N., *et al.*, 2001. **Essentials of Genetics** (John Murray), pp. 235-260.

Periodicals

See page 6 for details of publishers of periodicals:

STUDENT'S REFERENCE

Gene technology and cloning

■ **Recombinant Protein Production in Milk** Biol. Sci. Rev., 15(2) Nov. 2002, pp. 39-41. *A useful synopsis of the development and uses of transgenic livestock, including historical milestones.*
■ **Genetic Manipulation of Plants** Biol. Sci. Rev., 15(1) Sept. 2002, pp. 10-13. *The aims, methods, and applications of plant genetic engineering.*
■ **Tailor-Made Proteins** Biol. Sci. Rev., 13(4) March 2001, pp. 2-6. *Recombinant proteins and their uses in industry and medicine.*

■ **Beyond the Genome** New Scientist, 4 Nov. 2000, pp. 28-55. *A series of articles examining the applications of genomics and its offshoots.*
■ **Genes Can Come True** New Scientist, 30 Nov. 2002, pp. 30-33. *An overview of the current state of gene therapy, and a note about future directions.*
■ **Bioinformatics** Biol. Sci. Rev., 15(4), April 2003, pp. 2-6. *An account of how bioinformatics will provide new approaches to research in biology and medicine (also see "Bioinformatics", 15(3), p. 13).*
■ **Genes, the Genome, and Disease** New Scientist, 17 Feb. 2001, (Inside Science). *The human genome: genome maps, the role of introns in gene regulation, and the future of genomics.*
■ **Sequence Me!** New Scientist, 21 Dec. 2002, pp. 44-47. *Which organisms have had their genomes sequenced and why? Which are next?*

Ethical issues

■ **Live and Let Live** New Scientist, 31 Oct. 1998, pp. 46-49. *Scientific and ethical arguments for and against genetically engineered crops.*
■ **Food / How Altered?** National Geographic, May 2002, pp. 32-50. *The issue of "biotech foods". How altered are they and how safe are they?*

TEACHER'S REFERENCE

■ **Ready for Your Close-Up?** New Scientist, 20 July 2002, pp. 34-37. *A person's appearance can now be deduced from their DNA profile.*
■ **Making Gene Therapy Work** Scientific American Jun. 1997, pp. 79-103. *A thorough report on the technology involved in gene therapies.*
■ **The Business of the Human Genome** Sci. American, July 2000, pp. 38-57. *The HGP: where will the research progress from here?*
■ **A DNA Fingerprinting Simulation Laboratory** The American Bio. Teacher, 63(8), Oct. 2001, pp. 596-605. *How-to-do-it; using a DNA fingerprinting simulation to solve a mock forensic investigation.*

■ **A Paternity Testing Simulation Laboratory** The American Bio. Teacher, 64(3), March 2002, pp. 212-218. *Simulation involving PCR amplification, DNA profiling, and blood group analysis.*
■ **GM Food Safety Special Report** Scientific American, April 2001. *Special issue examining aspects of the GM food debate (excellent).*
■ **Genetically Modified Foods and Teaching Critical Thinking** The American Biology Teacher, 65(3), March 2003, pp. 180-184. *Using two case studies, corn and potato, to examine GM ethics.*
■ **Human Gene Therapy** The American Biology Teacher, 64(4), April 2002, pp. 264-270. *The latest advances and setbacks in gene therapy.*

Internet

See pages 10-11 for details of how to access **Bio Links** from our web site: **www.thebiozone.com**. From Bio Links, access sites under the topics:
BIOTECHNOLOGY > General Biotechnology Sites: • ABelgoBiotech • Molecular genetics ...& *others* > **Biotechnology Techniques:** • Molecular techniques • DNA ... & *many others* > **Biotechnology Processes:** • Animal and plant transformation • Transgenic organisms ... & *many others* > **Applications in Biotechnology:** access sites under > *Cloning and tissue culture* > *HGP* > *Food biotechnology* > *Medical biotechnology* > *Industrial biotechnology* > **Issues & Ethics in Biotechnology:** • Bioethics for beginners ... & *others*
also see sites under > **DNA Software Download**

Software and video resources are now provided in the Teacher Resource Handbook

Restriction Enzymes

One of the essential tools of genetic engineering is a group of special **restriction enzymes** (also known as restriction endonucleases). These have the ability to cut DNA molecules at very precise sequences of 4 to 8 base pairs called **recognition sites**. These enzymes are the "molecular scalpels" that allow genetic engineers to cut up DNA in a controlled way. Although first isolated in 1970, these enzymes were discovered earlier in many bacteria (see panel opposite). The purified forms of these bacterial restriction enzymes are used today as tools to cut DNA

(see table on the facing page for examples). Enzymes are named according to the bacterial species from which they were first isolated. By using a 'tool kit' of over 400 restriction enzymes recognizing about 100 recognition sites, genetic engineers can isolate, sequence, and manipulate individual genes derived from any type of organism. The sites at which the fragments of DNA are cut may result in overhanging "sticky ends" or non-overhanging "blunt ends". Pieces may later be joined together using an enzyme called *DNA ligase* in a process called **ligation**.

Sticky End Restriction Enzymes

1 A **restriction enzyme** cuts the double-stranded DNA molecule at its specific **recognition site** (see the table opposite for a representative list of restriction enzymes and their recognition sites).

2 The cuts produce a DNA fragment with two **sticky ends** (ends with exposed nucleotide bases at each end). The piece it is removed from is also left with sticky ends.

Restriction enzymes may cut DNA leaving an overhang or sticky end, without its complementary sequence opposite. DNA cut in such a way is able to be joined to other exposed end fragments of DNA with matching sticky ends. Such joins are specific to their recognition sites.

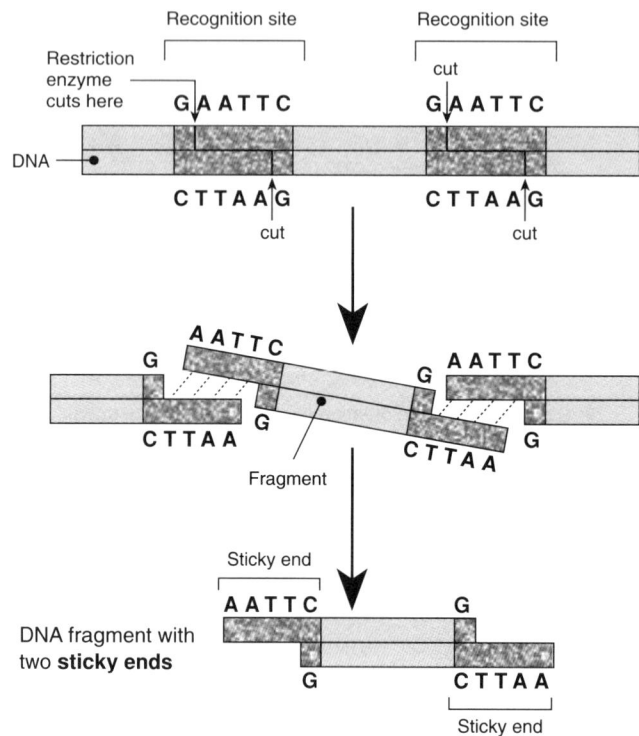

DNA fragment with two **sticky ends**

Blunt End Restriction Enzymes

1 A **restriction enzyme** cuts the double-stranded DNA molecule at its specific **recognition site** (see the table opposite for a representative list of restriction enzymes and their recognition sites).

2 The cuts produce a DNA fragment with two **blunt ends** (ends with no exposed nucleotide bases at each end). The piece it is removed from is also left with blunt ends.

It is possible to use restriction enzymes that cut leaving no overhang. DNA cut in such a way is able to be joined to any other blunt end fragment, but tends to be nonspecific because there are no sticky ends as recognition sites.

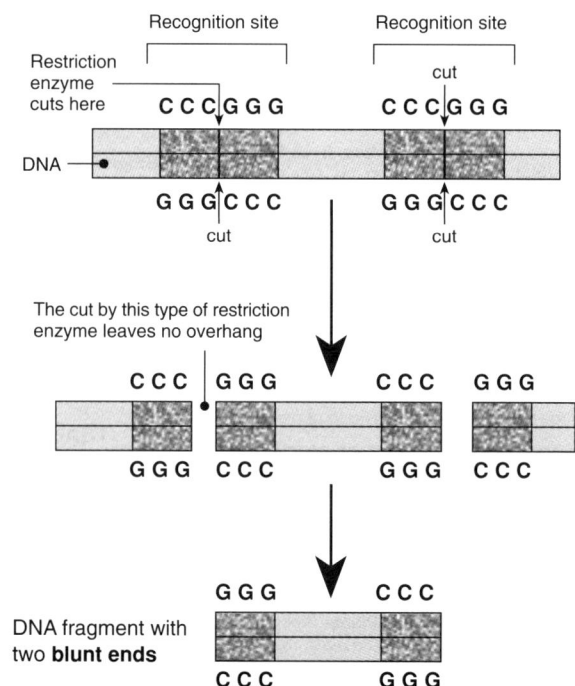

DNA fragment with two **blunt ends**

Origin of Restriction Enzymes

Restriction enzymes have been isolated from many bacteria. It was observed that certain *bacteriophages* (viruses that infect bacteria) could not infect bacteria other than their usual hosts. The reason was found to be that other potential hosts could destroy almost all of the phage DNA using *restriction enzymes* present naturally in their cells; a defense mechanism against the entry of foreign DNA. Restriction enzymes are named according to the species they were first isolated from, followed by a number to distinguish different enzymes isolated from the same organism.

Recognition sites for selected restriction enzymes

Enzyme	Source	Recognition Sites
*Eco*RI	*Escherichia coli* RY13	G A A T T C
*Bam*HI	*Bacillus amyloliquefaciens* H	G G A T C C
*Hae*III	*Haemophilus aegyptius*	G G C C
*Hind*III	*Haemophilus influenzae* Rd	A A G C T T
*Hpa*I	*Haemophilus parainfluenzae*	G T T A A C
*Hpa*II	*Haemophilus parainfluenzae*	C C G G
*Mbo*I	*Moraxella bovis*	G A T C
*Not*I	*Norcardia otitidis-caviarum*	G C G G C C G C
*Taq*I	*Thermus aquaticus*	T C G A

1. Explain the following terms:

(a) Restriction enzyme: _____

_____

(b) Recognition site: _____

_____

(c) Sticky end: _____

_____

(d) Blunt end: _____

_____

2. The action of a specific sticky end restriction enzyme is illustrated on the opposite page (top). Use the table above to:

(a) Name the **restriction enzyme** used: _____

(b) **Name** the **organism** from which it was first isolated: _____

(c) State the **base sequence** for this restriction enzyme's recognition site: _____

3. A genetic engineer wants to use the restriction enzyme *Bam*HI to cut the DNA sequence below:

(a) Consult the table above and state the recognition site for this enzyme: _____

(b) Place a circle around every **recognition site** on the DNA sequence below that could be cut by the enzyme *Bam*HI:

```
          10              20              30              40              50              60
|AATGGGTACG|CACAGTGGAT|CCACGTAGTA|TGCGATGCGT|AGTGTTTATG|GAGAGAAGAA|
          70              80              90             100             110             120
|AACGCGTCGC|CTTTTATCGA|TGCTGTACGG|ATGCGGAAGT|GGCGATGAGG|ATCCATGCAA|
         130             140             150             160             170             180
|TCGCGGCCGA|TCGXGTAATA|TATCGTGGCT|GCGTTTATTA|TCGTGACTAG|TAGCAGTATG|
         190             200             210             220             230             240
|CGATGTGACT|GATGCTATGC|TGACTATGCT|ATGTTTTTAT|GCTGGATCCA|GCGTAAGCAT|
         250             260             270             280             290             300
|TTCGCTGCGT|GGATCCCATA|TCCTTATATG|CATATATTCT|TATACGGATC|GCGCACGTTT|
```

(c) State how many fragments of DNA were created by this action: _____

4. State approximately how many different kinds of restriction enzymes are in use today: _____

5. When restriction enzymes were first isolated in 1970 there were not many applications to which they could be put to use. They are now an important tool in genetic engineering. Briefly list the human needs and demands that have driven the development and use of restriction enzymes in genetic engineering:

_____

_____

Ligation

DNA fragments produced using restriction enzymes may be reassembled by a process called **ligation**. Pieces are joined together using an enzyme called *DNA ligase*. DNA of different origins produced in this way is called **recombinant DNA** (because it is DNA that has been *recombined* from different sources). The combined techniques of using restriction enzymes and ligation are the basic tools of genetic engineering (also known as recombinant DNA technology).

Creating a Recombinant DNA Plasmid

1 If two pieces of DNA are cut by the same restriction enzyme, they will produce fragments with matching **sticky ends** (ends with exposed nucleotide bases at each end).

2 When two such matching sticky ends come together, they can join by base-pairing. This process is called **annealing**. This can allow DNA fragments from a different source, perhaps a **plasmid**, to be joined to the DNA fragment.

3 The joined fragments will usually form either a linear molecule or a circular one, as shown here for a **plasmid**. However, other combinations of fragments can occur.

4 The fragments of DNA are joined together by the enzyme **DNA ligase**, producing a molecule of **recombinant DNA**.

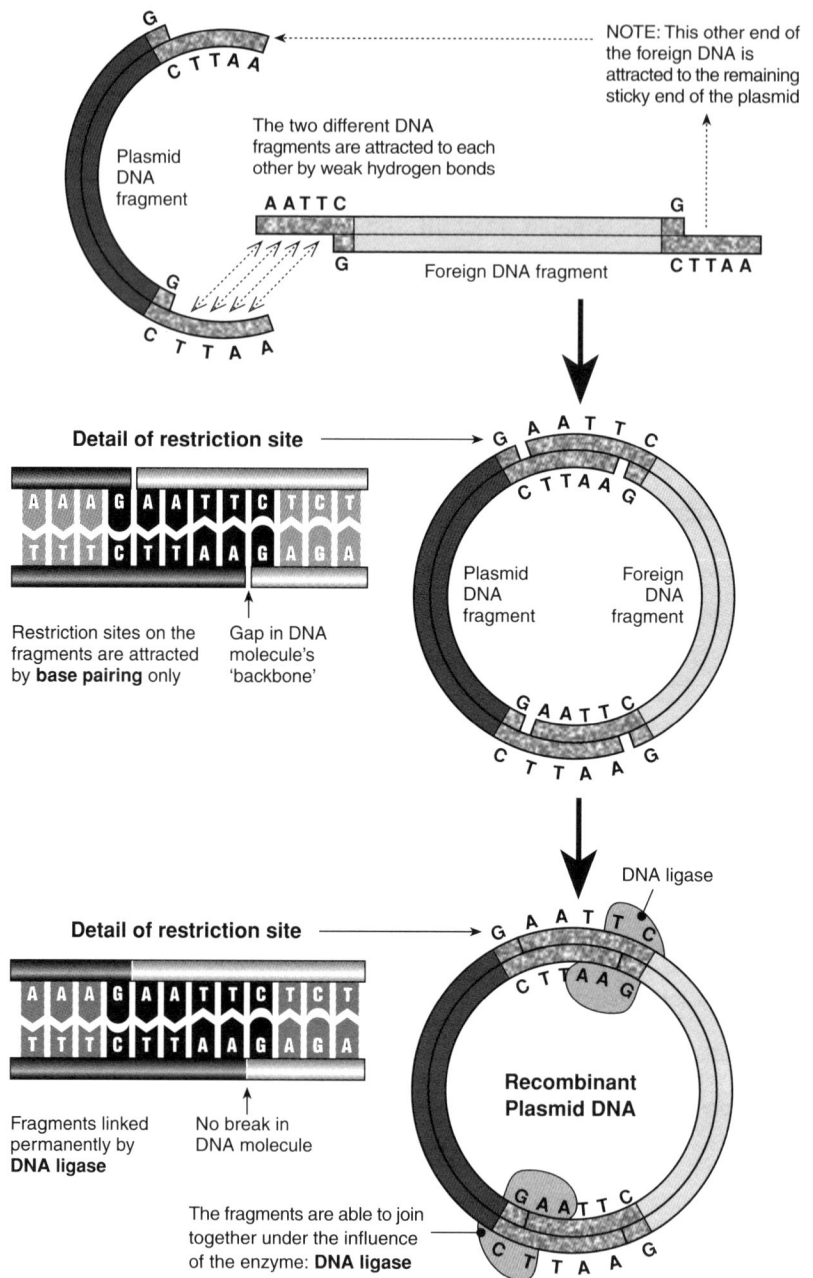

NOTE: This other end of the foreign DNA is attracted to the remaining sticky end of the plasmid

The two different DNA fragments are attracted to each other by weak hydrogen bonds

Plasmid DNA fragment

A A T T C   G

Foreign DNA fragment   C T T A A

G   G

C T T A A

Detail of restriction site

Restriction sites on the fragments are attracted by **base pairing** only

Gap in DNA molecule's 'backbone'

G A A T T C
C T T A A G

Plasmid DNA fragment   Foreign DNA fragment

G A A T T C
C T T A A G

DNA ligase

Detail of restriction site

Fragments linked permanently by **DNA ligase**

No break in DNA molecule

G A A T T C
C T T A A G

Recombinant Plasmid DNA

The fragments are able to join together under the influence of the enzyme: **DNA ligase**

G A A T T C
C T T A A G

1. Explain in your own words the two main steps in the process of joining two DNA fragments together:

   (a) Annealing: _____

   _____

   (b) DNA ligase: _____

   _____

2. Refer to the activity "DNA Replication", in the topic *Molecular Genetics,* and state the **usual role** of DNA ligase in a cell:

   _____

3. Explain why **ligation** can be considered the *reverse* of the **restriction enzyme** process: _____

   _____

Gel Electrophoresis

A 3

Gel electrophoresis is a method that separates large molecules (including nucleic acids or proteins) on the basis of size, electric charge, and other physical properties. Such molecules possess a slight electric charge (see DNA below). To prepare DNA for gel electrophoresis the DNA is often cut up into smaller pieces. This is done by mixing DNA with restriction enzymes in controlled conditions for about an hour. Called **restriction digestion**, it produces a range of DNA fragments of different lengths. During electrophoresis, molecules are forced to move through the pores of a **gel** (a jelly-like material), when the electrical current is

applied. Active electrodes at each end of the gel provide the driving force. The electrical current from one electrode repels the molecules while the other electrode simultaneously attracts the molecules. The frictional force of the gel material resists the flow of the molecules, separating them by size. Their rate of migration through the gel depends on the strength of the electric field, size and shape of the molecules, and on the ionic strength and temperature of the buffer in which the molecules are moving. After staining, the separated molecules in each lane can be seen as a series of bands spread from one end of the gel to the other.

Analyzing DNA using Gel Electrophoresis

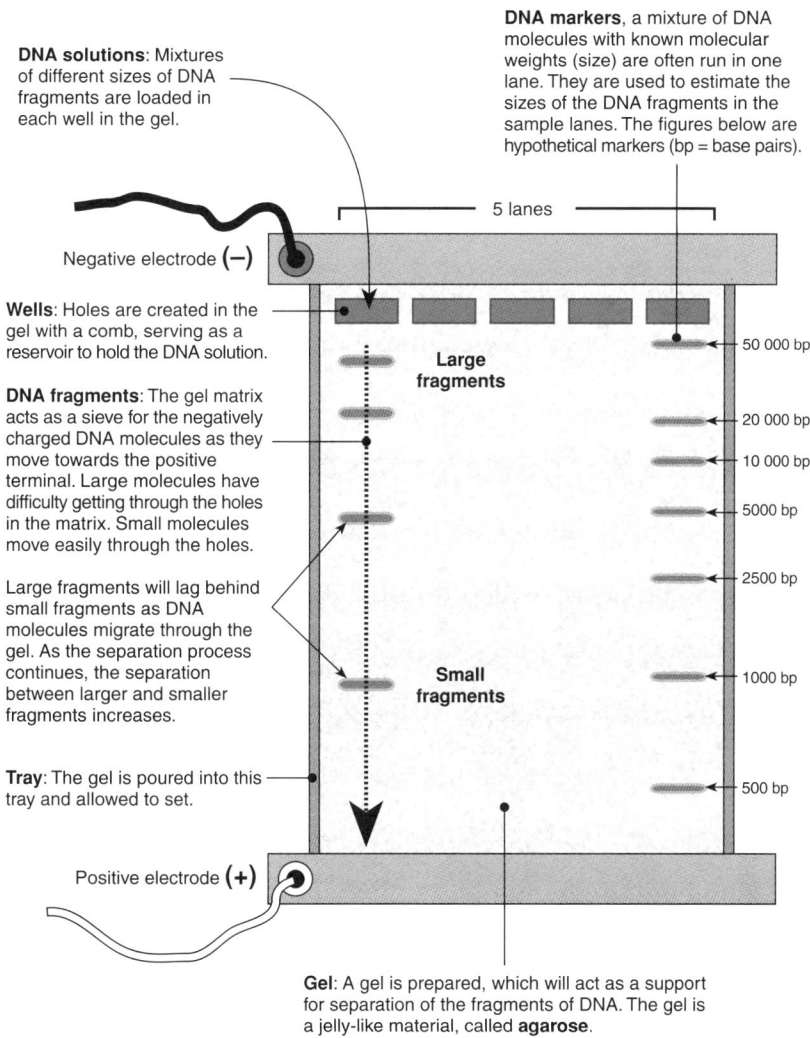

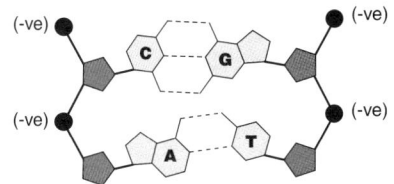

DNA solutions: Mixtures of different sizes of DNA fragments are loaded in each well in the gel.

DNA markers, a mixture of DNA molecules with known molecular weights (size) are often run in one lane. They are used to estimate the sizes of the DNA fragments in the sample lanes. The figures below are hypothetical markers (bp = base pairs).

(-ve)   C   G   (-ve)

(-ve)   A   T   (-ve)

DNA is negatively charged because the phosphates (black) that form part of the backbone of a DNA molecule have a negative charge.

Negative electrode (−)

5 lanes

Wells: Holes are created in the gel with a comb, serving as a reservoir to hold the DNA solution.

DNA fragments: The gel matrix acts as a sieve for the negatively charged DNA molecules as they move towards the positive terminal. Large molecules have difficulty getting through the holes in the matrix. Small molecules move easily through the holes.

Large fragments will lag behind small fragments as DNA molecules migrate through the gel. As the separation process continues, the separation between larger and smaller fragments increases.

Tray: The gel is poured into this tray and allowed to set.

Positive electrode (+)

Large fragments

Small fragments

50 000 bp
20 000 bp
10 000 bp
5000 bp
2500 bp
1000 bp
500 bp

Steps in gel electrophoresis of DNA

1. A tray is prepared to hold the gel matrix.

2. A gel comb is used to create holes in the gel. The gel comb is placed in the tray.

3. Agarose gel powder is mixed with a buffer solution (the liquid used to carry the DNA in a stable form). The solution is heated until dissolved and poured into the tray and allowed to cool.

4. The gel tray is placed in an electrophoresis chamber and the chamber is filled with buffer, covering the gel. This allows the electric current from electrodes at either end of the gel to flow through the gel.

5. DNA samples are mixed with a "loading dye" to make the DNA sample visible. The dye also contains glycerol or sucrose to make the DNA sample heavy so that it will sink to the bottom of the well.

6. A safety cover is placed over the gel, electrodes are attached to a power supply and turned on.

7. When the dye marker has moved through the gel, the current is turned off and the gel is removed from the tray.

8. DNA molecules are made visible by staining the gel with ethidium bromide which binds to DNA and will fluoresce in UV light.

Gel: A gel is prepared, which will act as a support for separation of the fragments of DNA. The gel is a jelly-like material, called **agarose**.

1. Explain the purpose of gel electrophoresis: _____

_____

_____

2. Describe the two forces that control the speed at which fragments pass through the gel: _____

_____

_____

3. Explain why the smallest fragments travel through the gel the fastest: _____

_____

_____

Polymerase Chain Reaction

Many procedures in DNA technology (such as DNA sequencing and DNA profiling) require substantial amounts of DNA to work with. Some samples, such as those from a crime scene or fragments of DNA from a long extinct organism, may be difficult to get in any quantity. The diagram below describes the laboratory process called **polymerase chain reaction** (**PCR**). Using this technique, vast quantities of DNA identical to trace samples can be created. This process is often termed **DNA amplification**. Although only two cycles of replication are shown below, following cycles replicate DNA at an exponential rate. PCR can be used to make literally billions of copies in only a few hours. **Linear PCR** differs from regular PCR in that the same original DNA templates are used repeatedly. It is used to make many radio-labeled DNA fragments for DNA sequencing.

A Single Cycle of the Polymerase Chain Reaction

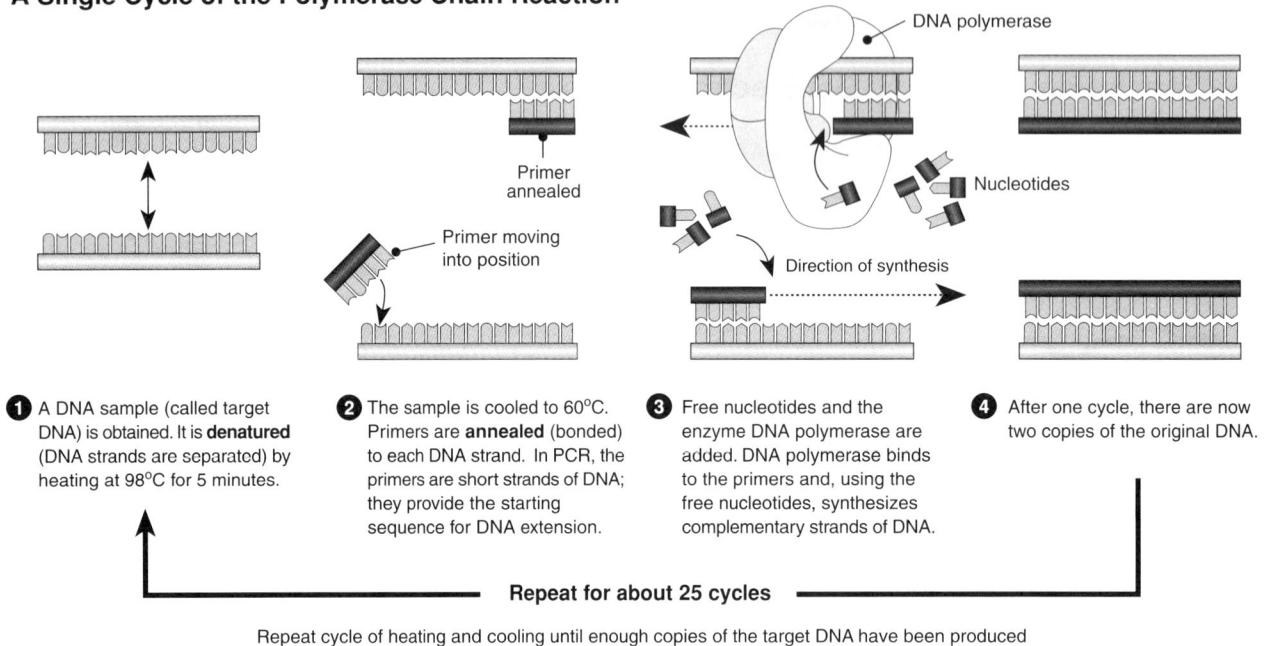

Primer annealed

Primer moving into position

DNA polymerase

Nucleotides

Direction of synthesis

1 A DNA sample (called target DNA) is obtained. It is **denatured** (DNA strands are separated) by heating at 98°C for 5 minutes.

2 The sample is cooled to 60°C. Primers are **annealed** (bonded) to each DNA strand. In PCR, the primers are short strands of DNA; they provide the starting sequence for DNA extension.

3 Free nucleotides and the enzyme DNA polymerase are added. DNA polymerase binds to the primers and, using the free nucleotides, synthesizes complementary strands of DNA.

4 After one cycle, there are now two copies of the original DNA.

Repeat for about 25 cycles

Repeat cycle of heating and cooling until enough copies of the target DNA have been produced

Loading tray
Prepared samples in tiny PCR tubes are placed in the loading tray and the lid is closed.

Temperature control
Inside the machine are heating and refrigeration mechanisms to rapidly change the temperature

Dispensing pipette
Pipettes with disposable tips are used to dispense DNA samples into the PCR tubes.

Thermal Cycler

Amplification of DNA can be carried out with simple-to-use machines called **thermal cyclers**. Once a DNA sample has been prepared, in just a few hours the amount of DNA can be increased billions of times. Thermal cyclers are in common use in the biology departments of universities, as well as other kinds of research and analytical laboratories. The one pictured on the left is typical of this modern piece of equipment.

DNA quantitation

The amount of DNA in a sample can be determined by placing a known volume in this quantitation machine. For many genetic engineering processes, a minimum amount of DNA is required.

Controls

The control panel allows a number of different PCR programs to be stored in the machine's memory. Carrying out a PCR run usually just involves starting one of the stored programs.

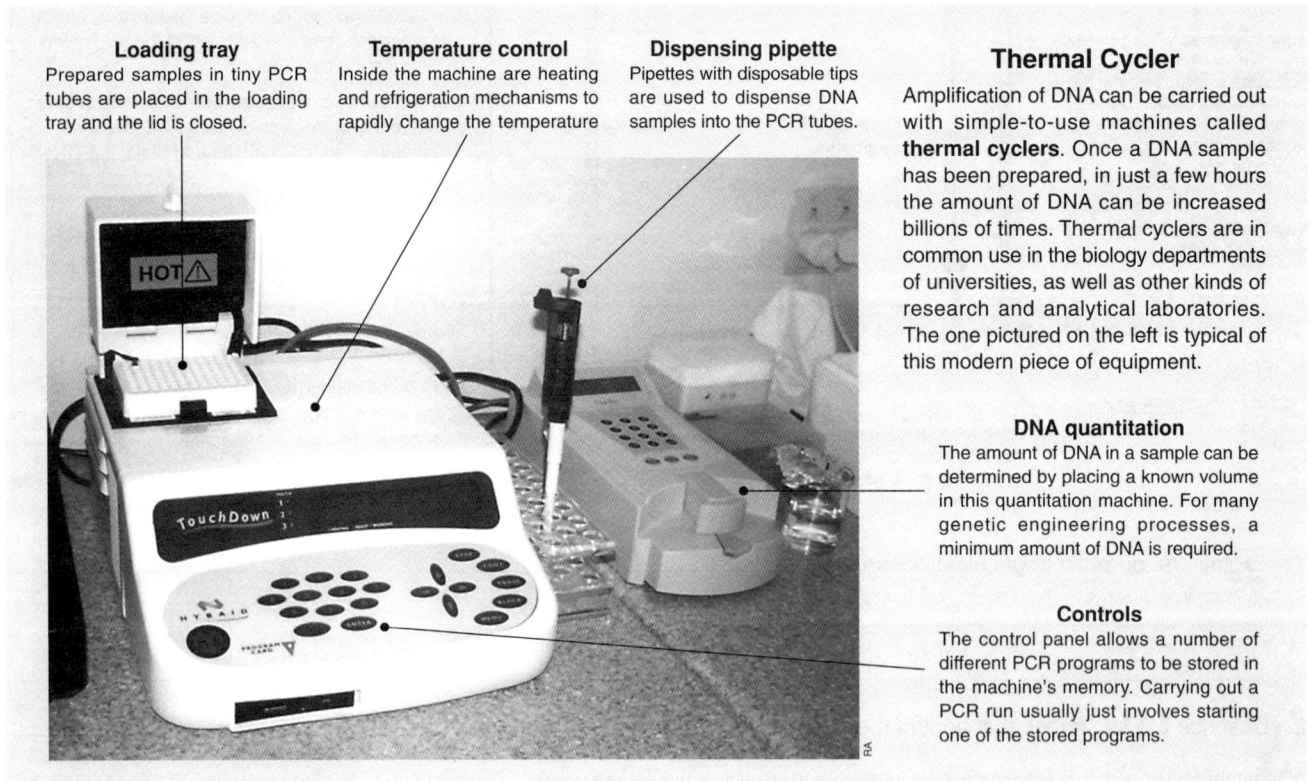

1. Explain the purpose of PCR:

_____

_____

_____

2. Briefly describe how the **polymerase chain reaction** (PCR) works: _____

_____

_____

_____

_____

_____

_____

_____

3. List three situations where only minute DNA samples may be available for sampling and PCR could be used:

   (a) _____

   _____

   (b) _____

   _____

   (c) _____

   _____

4. After only two cycles of replication, four copies of the double-stranded DNA exist. Calculate how much a DNA sample will have increased after:

   (a) 10 cycles: _____   (b) 25 cycles: _____

5. The risk of contamination in the preparation for PCR is considerable.

   (a) Explain what the effect would be of having a single molecule of unwanted DNA in the sample prior to PCR:

   _____

   _____

   _____

   (b) Describe two possible sources of DNA contamination in preparing a PCR sample:

   _____

   _____

   (c) State two precautions that could be taken to reduce the risk of DNA contamination:

   Precaution 1: _____

   _____

   Precaution 2: _____

   _____

6. Describe two other genetic engineering/genetic manipulation procedures that require PCR amplification of products:

   (a) _____

   _____

   _____

   (b) _____

   _____

   _____

Manual DNA Sequencing

RA❸

DNA sequencing techniques are used to determine the nucleotide (base) sequence of DNA. Two manual methods are in current use: the **Maxim-Gilbert** procedure and the most common method, the **Sanger** procedure (illustrated below). Both methods use a procedure called **electrophoresis**. The Sanger method is based on the premature termination of DNA synthesis resulting from the inclusion of specially modified nucleotides. DNA synthesis is initiated from a **primer** which is **radio-labeled** (contains a radioactive isotope that will appear on a photographic film called an **autoradiograph**). Four separate reactions are run, each containing a modified nucleotide mixed with its normal counterpart, as well as the three other normal nucleotides. When a modified nucleotide is added to the growing complementary DNA, synthesis stops. Each reaction yields a series of different sized fragments extending from the radioactive primer. The fragments from the four reactions are separated by electrophoresis and analyzed by autoradiography to determine the DNA sequence.

The Sanger Method for DNA Sequencing

Four sequencing reactions

Using the same DNA sample to be sequenced (example used: **A C T G G T C T A G**), a separate sequencing reaction is carried out for each of the 4 bases: T, C, G, and A. In addition to the DNA sample, each reaction has normal (unaltered) copies of nucleotides: **T**, **C**, **G**, and **A**, plus a small quantity of one of the modified nucleotides:

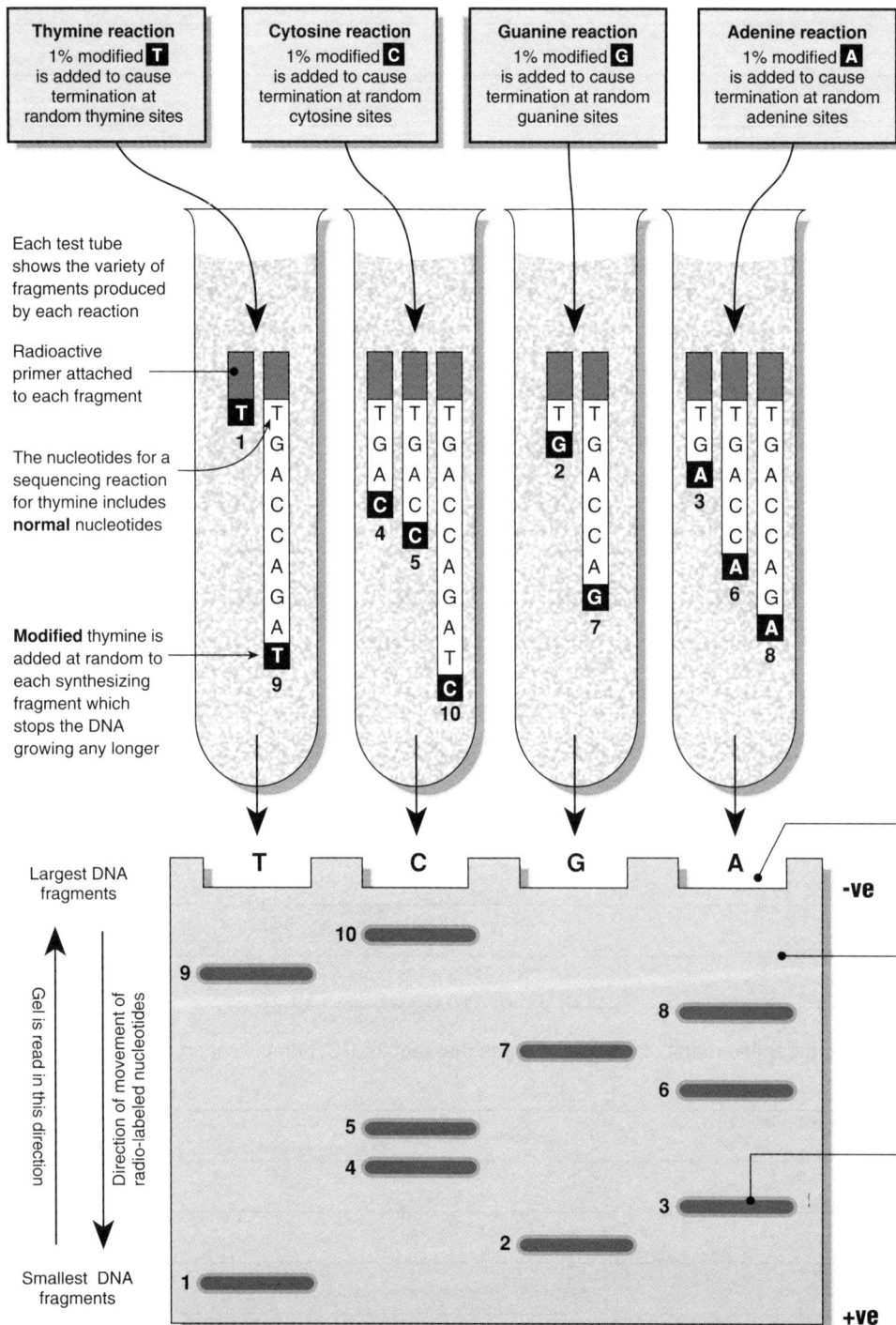

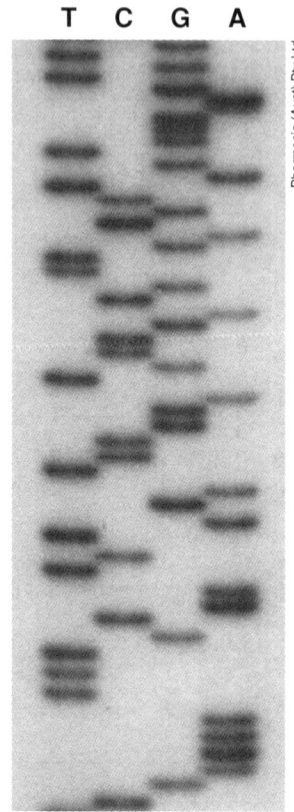

Thymine reaction
1% modified **T** is added to cause termination at random thymine sites

Cytosine reaction
1% modified **C** is added to cause termination at random cytosine sites

Guanine reaction
1% modified **G** is added to cause termination at random guanine sites

Adenine reaction
1% modified **A** is added to cause termination at random adenine sites

Each test tube shows the variety of fragments produced by each reaction

Radioactive primer attached to each fragment

The nucleotides for a sequencing reaction for thymine includes **normal** nucleotides

Modified thymine is added at random to each synthesizing fragment which stops the DNA growing any longer

T C G A

A typical **autoradiograph** showing a DNA sequence. The unexposed film is laid in contact with the gel after it has run. Radioactivity from the clustered DNA fragments create the dark shadows (blobs). Each blob contains millions of fragments.

DNA samples The four reactions containing DNA fragments are placed in separate wells at the top of the gel.

Electrophoresis gel A jelly-like material that allows DNA fragments to move through it when an electric charge is applied. It is usually made of a material called *acrylamide*.

Radio-labeled DNA fragments Attracted to the positive terminal, millions of DNA fragments of similar size and sequence move as a dark shadow down the gel. Larger pieces move more slowly and therefore do not travel as far.

Positive terminal Attracts the fragments of DNA that are negatively charged.

Largest DNA fragments

Gel is read in this direction

Direction of movement of radio-labeled nucleotides

Smallest DNA fragments

-ve

+ve

How Fragments Are Formed

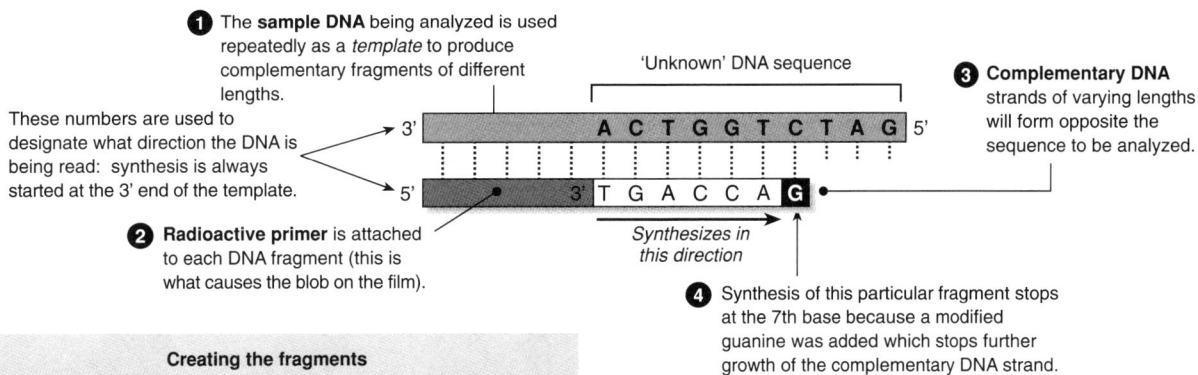

1 The **sample DNA** being analyzed is used repeatedly as a *template* to produce complementary fragments of different lengths.

'Unknown' DNA sequence

3 **Complementary DNA** strands of varying lengths will form opposite the sequence to be analyzed.

These numbers are used to designate what direction the DNA is being read: synthesis is always started at the 3' end of the template.

3'   A C T G G T C T A G   5'

5'   3' T G A C C A G

Synthesizes in this direction

2 **Radioactive primer** is attached to each DNA fragment (this is what causes the blob on the film).

4 Synthesis of this particular fragment stops at the 7th base because a modified guanine was added which stops further growth of the complementary DNA strand.

Creating the fragments

How long each fragment will be depends on what position one of the *chemically altered nucleotides* is incorporated into the sequence:

T Thymine
C Cytosine
G Guanine
A Adenine

Chemically altered so that they prevent further synthesis of the complementary DNA

What must be realized is that the DNA sample being analyzed consists of many millions of individual molecules, each being used as a template to make fragments. Each template molecule itself will produce thousands of complementary DNA fragments of varying lengths. In the sample DNA above, the guanine reaction can produce two fragments of different lengths.

1. Briefly describe how PCR, DNA sequencing, DNA profiling, or DNA screening may assist the following areas of study:

(a) Forensic science: _____

_____

_____

(b) Legal disputes: _____

_____

_____

(c) Medical applications: _____

_____

_____

(d) Investigations into evolutionary relationships and taxonomy: _____

_____

_____

(e) Archaeology and anthropology: _____

_____

_____

(f) Conservation of endangered species: _____

_____

_____

(g) Management of livestock breeding programs: _____

_____

_____

2. Explain why the Human Genome Project provided a large stimulus for the automation of DNA sequencing technology:

_____

_____

Automated DNA Sequencing

The process of DNA sequencing can be automated using **gel electrophoresis** machines that can sequence up to 600 bases at a time. Automation improves the speed at which samples can be sequenced and has made large scale sequencing projects (such as the **Human Genome Project**) possible. Instead of using radio-labeled DNA fragments, automated sequencing uses nucleotides labeled with **fluorescent dyes**; a different color is used for each of the four types of bases. Another advantage is that the entire base sequence for a sample can be determined from a single lane on the gel (not four lanes as with the manual method). Computer software automatically interprets the data from the gel and produces a base sequence.

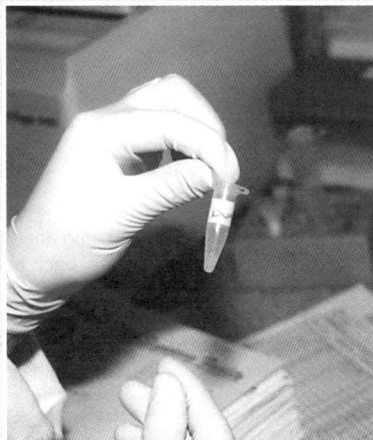

All photos are RA (unless indicated otherwise)

1. DNA sample arrives

Purified DNA samples may contain linear DNA or plasmids. The sample should contain about 1×10^{11} DNA molecules. The sample is checked to ensure that there is enough DNA present in the sample to work with.

2. Primer and reaction mix added

A **DNA primer** is added to the sample which provides a starting sequence for synthesis. Also added is the **sequencing reaction mix** containing the *polymerase enzyme* and free nucleotides, some which are labeled with dye.

3. Create dye-labeled fragments

A PCR machine creates fragments of DNA complementary to the original template DNA. Each fragment is tagged with a fluorescent dye-labeled nucleotide. Running for 25 cycles, it creates 25×10^{11} single-stranded DNA molecules.

4. Centrifuge to create DNA pellet

The sample is chemically precipitated and centrifuged to settle the DNA fragments as a solid pellet at the bottom of the tube. Unused nucleotides, still in the liquid, are discarded.

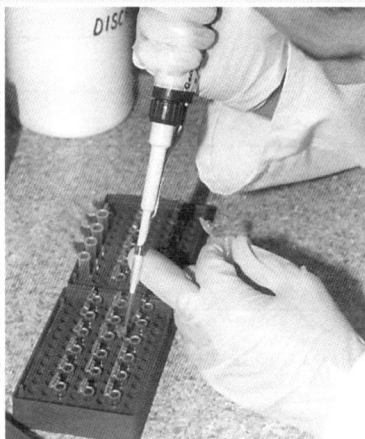

5. DNA pellet washed, buffer added

The pellet is washed with ethanol, dried, and a gel loading buffer is added. All that remains now is single stranded DNA with one dye-labeled nucleotide at the end of each molecule.

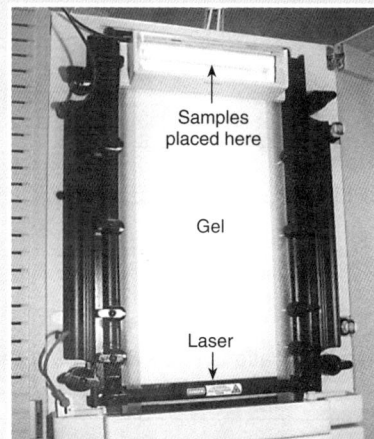

6. Acrylamide gel is loaded

The DNA sequencer is prepared by placing the gel (sandwiched between two sheets of glass) into position. A 36 channel 'comb' for receiving the samples is placed at the top of the gel.

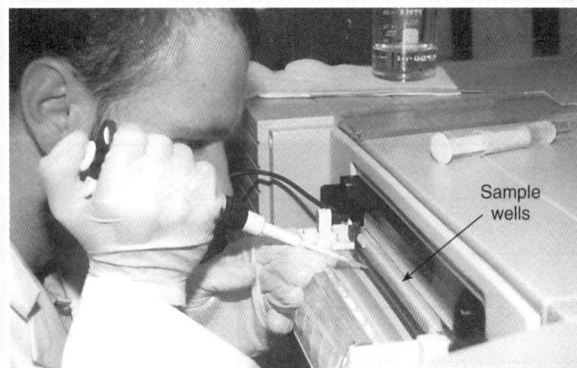

Samples placed here

Gel

Laser

7. Loading DNA samples onto gel

Sample wells

Different samples can be placed in each of the 36 wells (funnel shaped receptacles) above the gel. A control DNA sample of known sequence is applied to the first lane of the sequencer. If there are problems with the control sequence then results for all other lanes are considered invalid.

8. Running the DNA sequencer

Powerful computer software controls the activity of the DNA sequencer. The gel is left to run for up to 10 hours. During this time an argon laser is constantly scanning across the bottom of the gel to detect the passing of dye-labeled nucleotides attached to DNA fragments.

How a DNA Sequencer Operates

The gel is loaded following preparation of the samples and the gel (see steps 1-7 opposite and box, right).

Comb with 36 lanes into which different samples can be placed.

DNA fragments with dye-labeled nucleotides move down the gel over a period of 10 hours.

The smallest fragments move fastest down the gel and reach the argon laser first. Larger fragments arrive later.

DNA fragments separate into bands (see box below)

Argon laser excites fluorescent dye labels on nucleotides.

Lenses collect the emitted light and focus it into a spectrograph. An attached digital camera detects the light. See 'data collection' (below, right).

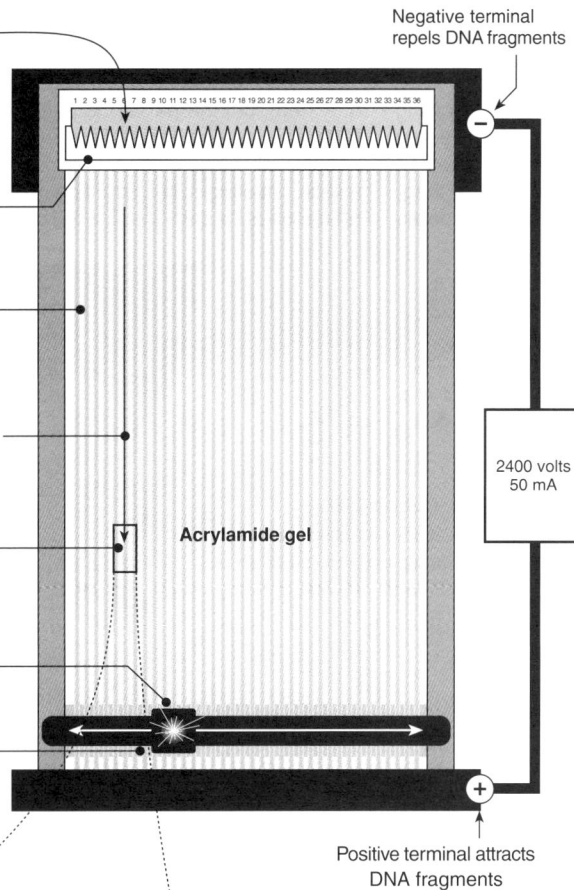

Negative terminal repels DNA fragments

Acrylamide gel

2400 volts
50 mA

Positive terminal attracts DNA fragments

Creating the dye labeled fragments
for gel electrophoresis is outlined in step 3, opposite. Key ingredients are:

(a) Original DNA template (the sample)

A C C G T A T G A T T C

(b) Many normal unlabelled nucleotides:

A   T   G   C

(c) Terminal nucleotides labeled with fluorescent dye (a different color for each of the 4 bases). The structure of the nucleotides is altered so they act as terminators to stop further synthesis of the strand:

A⬤ T⬤ G◯ C⬤

Two examples of synthesized DNA fragments are shown below. One is relatively short, the other is longer:

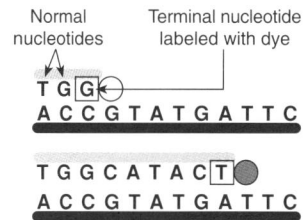

Normal nucleotides   Terminal nucleotide labeled with dye

T G **G**◯
A C C G T A T G A T T C

T G G C A T A C **T**⬤
A C C G T A T G A T T C

Data collection: The data from the digital camera are collected by computer software. The first of 23 samples is highlighted below in lane 1 with base sequences appearing on the far left.

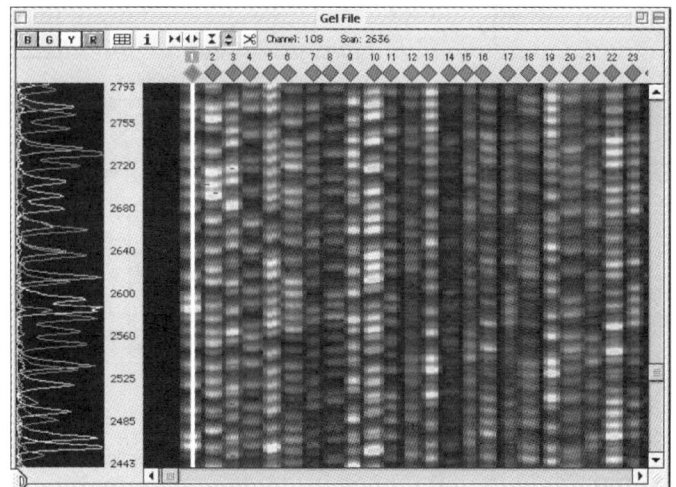

DNA fragments of different sizes are drawn down through the gel, separating into distinct bands of color as they are illuminated by the laser:

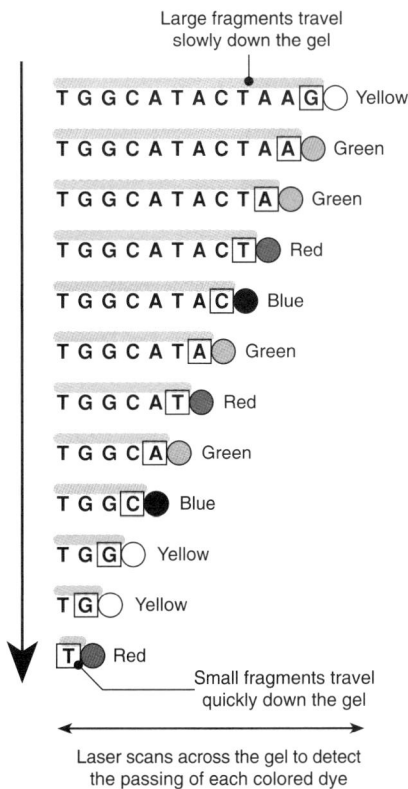

Large fragments travel slowly down the gel

T G G C A T A C T A A **G**◯ Yellow
T G G C A T A C T A **A**◯ Green
T G G C A T A C T **A**◯ Green
T G G C A T A C **T**⬤ Red
T G G C A T A **C**⬤ Blue
T G G C A T **A**◯ Green
T G G C A **T**⬤ Red
T G G C **A**◯ Green
T G G **C**⬤ Blue
T G **G**◯ Yellow
T **G**◯ Yellow
T⬤ Red

Small fragments travel quickly down the gel

Laser scans across the gel to detect the passing of each colored dye

Data analysis: The data can be saved as a computer file which can then be analyzed by other computer software. Such software can provide a printout of the base sequence as well as carry out comparisons with other DNA sequences (such as when looking for mutations).

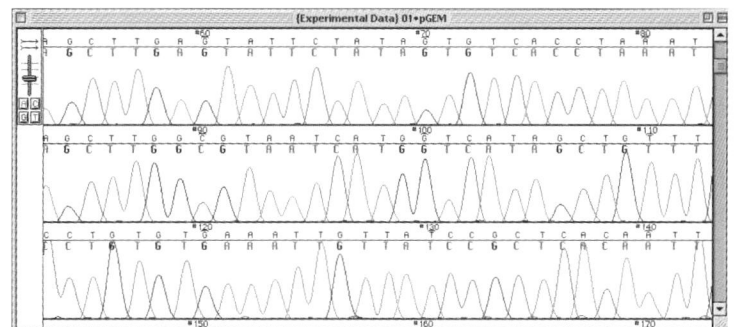

DNA Profiling using Probes

DNA profiling is a technique used to identify the natural variation, caused by repeating sequences of non-coding DNA, that is found in every person's DNA. There are several profiling techniques in common application, each targeting repeat sequences of different length. The Southern blotting method (below) uses repeating units (a few tens of nucleotides long) called **minisatellites** or **variable number tandem repeats**

(VNTRs). Equivalent sequences in different people have the same core sequence of 10-15 bases (to which a DNA **probe** is attached), but thereafter the patterns vary considerably in length from one person to another. In humans, the chance that two people will have identical DNA profiles is less than one in a million, making DNA profiling useful for investigating genetic relatedness or crime, or for **genetic screening**.

Southern Blotting Method

① Extract DNA from sample

Gene of interest

A sample of tissue from a living or dead organism is treated with chemicals and enzymes to extract the DNA, which is separated and purified.

② Cut up DNA

Using **restriction enzymes**, the DNA is cut up into thousands of fragments of all different sizes.

③ Separate fragments

The fragments are separated by length, using **gel electrophoresis**. DNA, which is negatively charged, moves toward the positive terminal. The shorter fragments travel faster and further than longer ones.

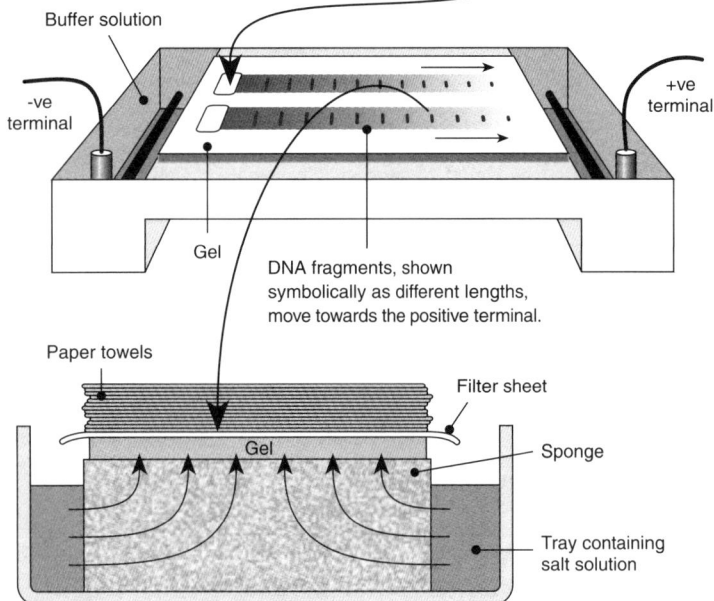

Buffer solution

-ve terminal

+ve terminal

Gel

DNA fragments, shown symbolically as different lengths, move towards the positive terminal.

Paper towels

Filter sheet

Gel

Sponge

Tray containing salt solution

④ Transfer DNA fragments to filter sheet

DNA molecules are split into single strands using alkaline chemicals. The DNA is transferred onto a nitrocellulose filter sheet by pressing it against the gel. The salt solution passes through the gel, carrying the DNA fragments onto the surface of the filter sheet. This is the blot.

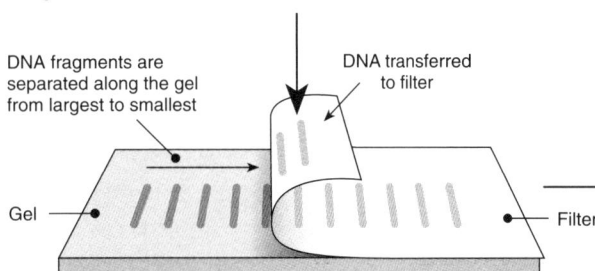

DNA fragments are separated along the gel from largest to smallest

DNA transferred to filter

Gel

Filter

⑤ Remove filter sheet

The gel with filter sheet still attached is removed and separated. The DNA fragments that have now moved to the filter sheet are in exactly the same position as on the gel.

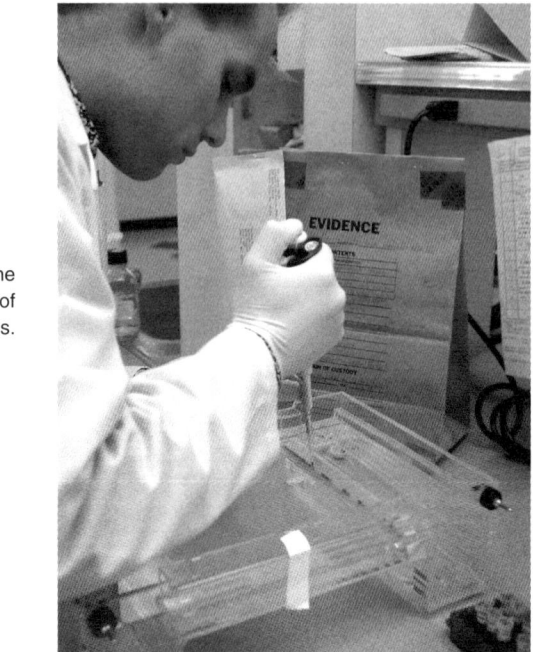

A technician carrying out a DNA profiling test of samples taken from the scene of a crime. Such tests are admissible in a court of law as forensic evidence.

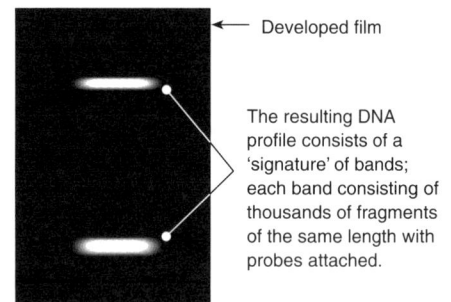

Developed film

The resulting DNA profile consists of a 'signature' of bands; each band consisting of thousands of fragments of the same length with probes attached.

⑦ Create autoradiograph

When using radioactive probes, the filter sheet is exposed to X-ray film. The radioactive probes attached to the sorted fragments show up as dark bands on the film. The spacing of these bands is the **DNA profile**, which is used as evidence.

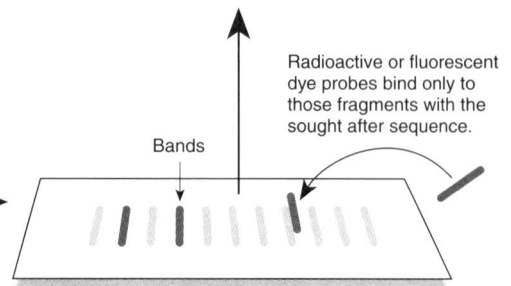

Radioactive or fluorescent dye probes bind only to those fragments with the sought after sequence.

Bands

⑥ Attach radioactively labeled probes

The filter sheet is immersed in a bath with **radioactive probes** (synthetic complementary DNA). Many thousands of these segments bind to the sample DNA fragments where they are localized as bands.

How DNA probes may be used

Artificially constructed DNA probes work by binding to a specific sequence on DNA that is of interest to the investigator. Gene probes may be used to search for:

- The presence of a specific allele of a gene (e.g. cystic fibrosis gene).

- The approximate location of a gene on a chromosome (i.e. which chromosome and what position on its *p* or *q* arm it binds to).

- The 'genetic fingerprint' of a person to tell them apart from others (e.g. paternity testing, forensic identification of suspects).

How a DNA probe works

A **DNA probe** is a small fragment of nucleic acid (either cloned or artificially synthesized), that is labelled with an *enzyme*, a *radioactive* tag, or a *fluorescent dye* tag.

Fluorescent dye tag: Shows up as fluorescent bands when gel is exposed to ultraviolet light source.

or

Radioactive tag: Shows up as a dark band when the gel is exposed to photographic film.

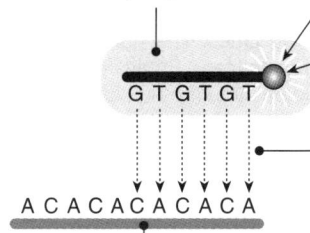

G T G T G T

Under appropriate conditions, the probe will bind to a complementary DNA sequence by base pairing, identifying the presence and location of the **target DNA** sequence for further analysis.

A C A C A C A C A C A

Target DNA strand (such as a tandem repeat) with a complementary sequence that is being searched for by the probe.

1. The DNA profile on the right is a hypothetical example of a forensic result where the victim was raped and murdered. There were 3 suspects in the case. A semen sample was taken from the body of the victim and this was used as the evidence (see arrow on the X-ray film). Two probes were used in this investigation. The three suspects were required to give blood samples and a sample was also taken from the victim.

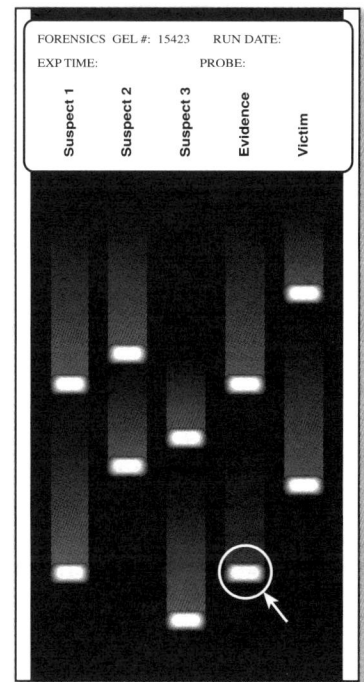

(a) Which of the three suspects was probably the killer: _____

(b) Explain with what degree of certainty do you give this verdict (give a reason for your answer):

_____

_____

(c) Explain why a sample from the **victim** was also taken and analyzed:

_____

_____

(d) Explain what the term **forensic** means: _____

_____

FORENSICS GEL #: 15423   RUN DATE:
EXP TIME: PROBE:

Suspect 1 | Suspect 2 | Suspect 3 | Evidence | Victim

2. Explain why DNA profiling is a more useful forensic diagnostic tool than simply using **blood types**:

_____

_____

3. In some well-known criminal trials in recent years (e.g. the trial of 'O.J. Simpson' for the murder of his wife, USA, 1995) the prosecution cases relied heavily on DNA evidence. Despite providing a DNA profile of the accused that clearly implicated them in the crime, the evidence was successfully challenged by defense counsel on technical grounds (concerning what is called the '**chain of evidence**'). Explain why such DNA evidence has failed to gain a prosecution:

_____

_____

_____

4. Forensic applications of DNA profiling are well known. Briefly describe two other applications of DNA profiling:

(a) _____

_____

(b) _____

_____

DNA Profiling using PCR

In chromosomes, some of the DNA contains simple, repetitive sequences. These *noncoding* nucleotide sequences repeat themselves over and over again and are found scattered throughout the genome. Some repeating sequences are short (2-6 base pairs) called **microsatellites** or **short tandem repeats** (STRs) and can repeat up to 100 times. The human genome has numerous different microsatellites. Equivalent sequences in different people vary considerably in the numbers of the repeating unit. This phenomenon has been used to develop **DNA profiling**, which identifies the natural variations found in every person's DNA. Identifying such differences in the DNA of individuals is a useful tool for forensic investigations. In 1998, the FBI's Combined Offender DNA Index System (CODIS) was established, providing a national database of DNA samples from convicted criminals, suspects, and crime scenes. In the USA, there are many laboratories approved for forensic DNA testing. Increasingly, these are targeting the 13 core STR loci recommended by the FBI; enough to guarantee that the odds of someone else sharing the same result are extremely unlikely (less than one in a million). The CODIS may be used to solve previously unsolved crimes and to assist in current and future investigations. DNA profiling can also be used to establish genetic relatedness (e.g., in disputes over paternity or pedigree), or when searching for a specific gene (e.g., screening for disease).

Microsatellites (Short Tandem Repeats)

Microsatellites consist of a variable number of tandem repeats of a 2 to 6 base pair sequence. In the example below it is a two base sequence (CA) that is repeated.

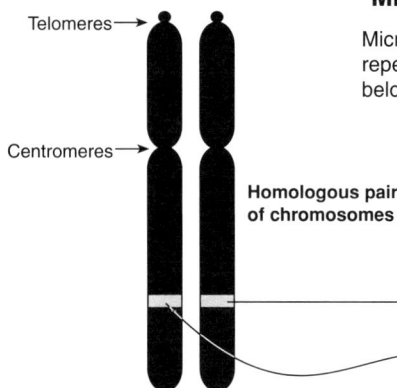

The human genome contains about 100 000 separate blocks of tandem repeats of the dinucleotide: **CA**. One such block at a known location on a chromosome is shown below:

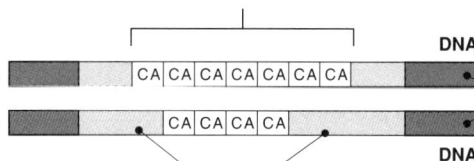

The tandem repeat may exist in two versions (alleles) in an individual; one on each homologous chromosome. Each of the strands shown left is a double stranded DNA, but only the CA repeat is illustrated.

Microsatellites are found throughout the genome: within genes (introns) and between genes, and particularly near **centromeres** and **telomeres**.

Flanking regions to which PCR primers can be attached

How short tandem repeats are used in DNA profiling

This diagram shows how three people can have quite different microsatellite arrangements at the same point (locus) in their DNA. Each will produce a different DNA profile using gel electrophoresis:

1 **Extract DNA from sample**

A sample collected from the tissue of a living or dead organism is treated with chemicals and enzymes to extract the DNA, which is separated and purified.

2 **Amplify microsatellite using PCR**

Specific primers (arrowed) that attach to the flanking regions (light gray) either side of the microsatellite are used to make large quantities of the microsatellite and flanking regions sequence only (no other part of the DNA is amplified/replicated).

3 **Visualize fragments on a gel**

The fragments are separated by length, using **gel electrophoresis**. DNA, which is negatively charged, moves toward the positive terminal. The smaller fragments travel faster than larger ones.

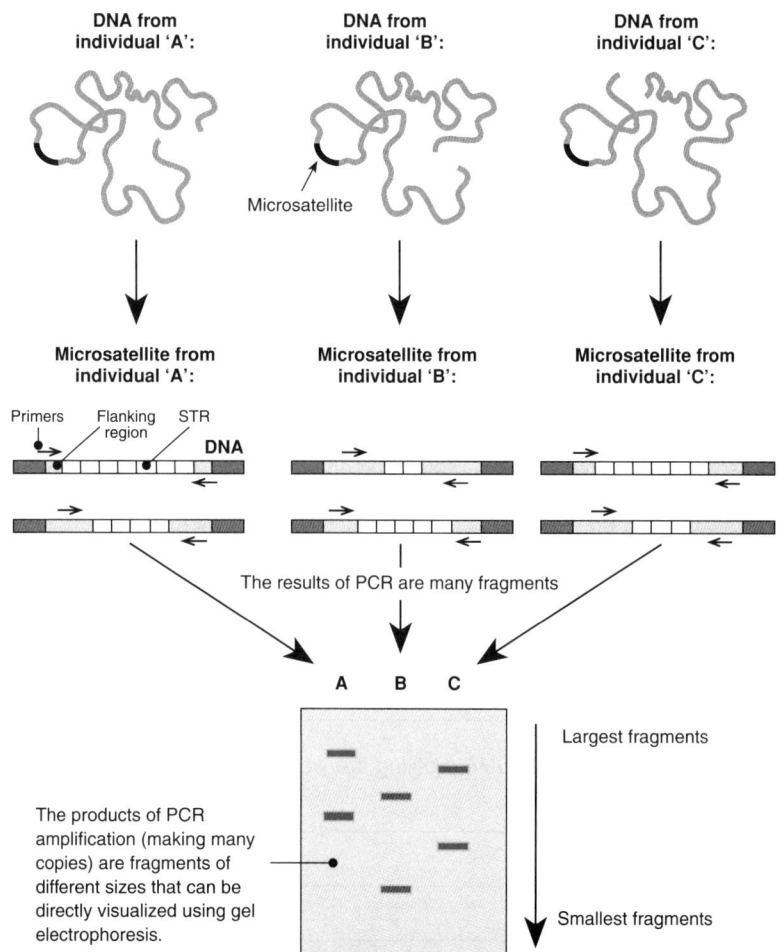

DNA from individual 'A':

DNA from individual 'B':

DNA from individual 'C':

Microsatellite

Microsatellite from individual 'A':

Microsatellite from individual 'B':

Microsatellite from individual 'C':

Primers   Flanking region   STR

The results of PCR are many fragments

The products of PCR amplification (making many copies) are fragments of different sizes that can be directly visualized using gel electrophoresis.

Largest fragments

Smallest fragments

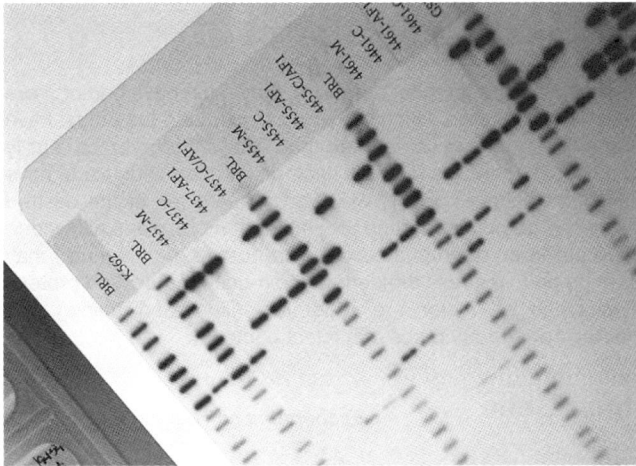

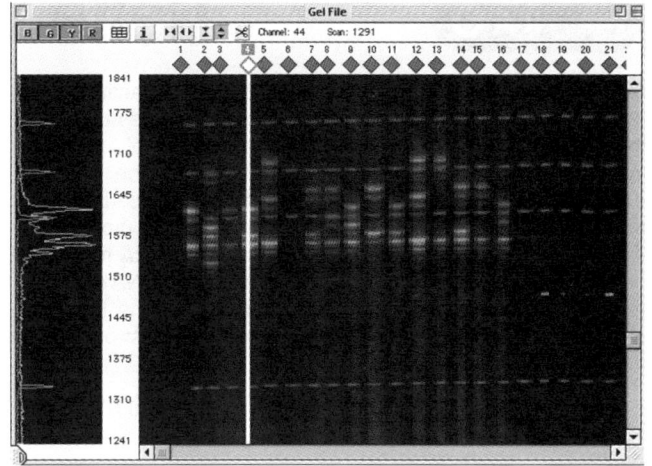

The photo above shows a film output from a DNA profiling procedure. Those lanes with many regular bands are used for calibration; they contain DNA fragment sizes of known length. These calibration lanes can be used to determine the length of fragments in the unknown samples.

DNA profiling can be automated in the same way as DNA sequencing. Computer software is able to display the results of many samples that are run at the same time. In the photo above, the sample in lane 4 has been selected. It displays fragments of different length on the left of the screen.

1. Define the following terms:

   (a) DNA profiling: _____

   _____

   (b) Short tandem repeats (STRs): _____

   _____

   (c) Microsatellites: _____

2. Explain the **role** of each of the following techniques in the process of DNA profiling:

   (a) Gel electrophoresis: _____

   _____

   _____

   (b) PCR: _____

   _____

   _____

3. Briefly summarize the three main steps in DNA profiling using PCR:

   (a) _____

   _____

   _____

   _____

   (b) _____

   _____

   _____

   _____

   (c) _____

   _____

   _____

4. Explain why as many as 10 STR sites are used to gain a DNA profile for forensic evidence:

   _____

   _____

![RA 3]

Gene Cloning

Gene cloning is a process of making large quantities of a desired piece of DNA once it has been isolated. The purpose of this process is often to yield large quantities of either an individual gene or its protein product when the gene is expressed. Methods have been developed to insert a DNA fragment of interest (e.g. a human gene for a desired protein) into the DNA of a vector, resulting in a **recombinant DNA molecule** or **molecular clone**. A **vector** is a self-replicating DNA molecule (e.g. plasmid or viral DNA) used to transmit a gene from one organism into another. To be useful, all vectors must be able to

replicate inside their host organism, they must have one or more sites at which a restriction enzyme can cut, and they must have some kind of genetic marker that allows them to be easily identified. Organisms such as bacteria, viruses and yeasts have DNA that behaves in this way. Large quantities of the desired gene can be obtained if the recombinant molecule is allowed to replicate in an appropriate host. The host (e.g. bacterium) may then go on to express the gene and produce the desired protein. Two types of vector are **plasmids** (illustrated below) and **bacteriophages** (viruses that infect bacteria).

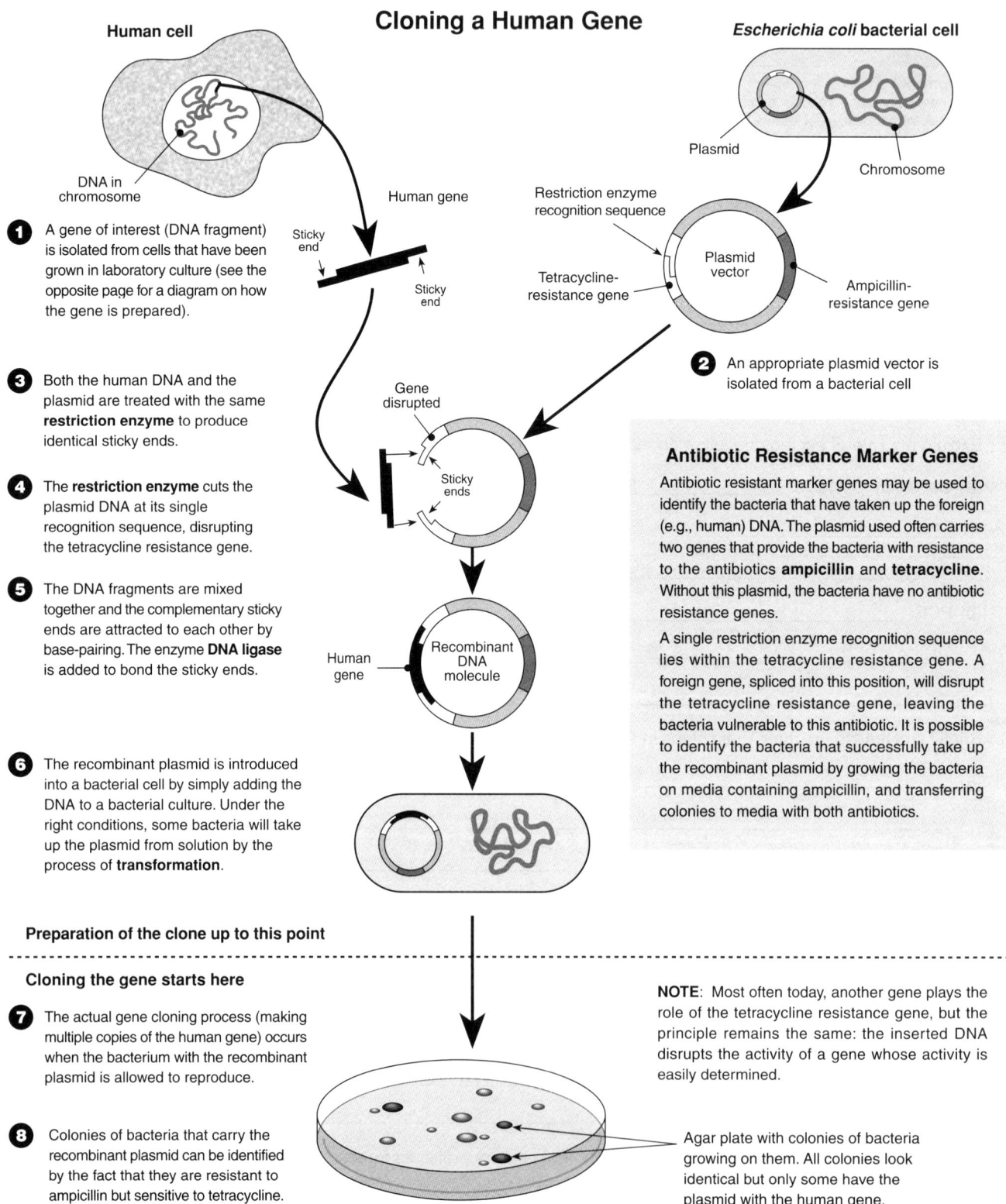

Cloning a Human Gene

Human cell

DNA in chromosome

Human gene

Escherichia coli bacterial cell

Plasmid

Chromosome

Sticky end

Sticky end

Restriction enzyme recognition sequence

Tetracycline-resistance gene

Plasmid vector

Ampicillin-resistance gene

1 A gene of interest (DNA fragment) is isolated from cells that have been grown in laboratory culture (see the opposite page for a diagram on how the gene is prepared).

2 An appropriate plasmid vector is isolated from a bacterial cell

3 Both the human DNA and the plasmid are treated with the same **restriction enzyme** to produce identical sticky ends.

Gene disrupted

Sticky ends

4 The **restriction enzyme** cuts the plasmid DNA at its single recognition sequence, disrupting the tetracycline resistance gene.

5 The DNA fragments are mixed together and the complementary sticky ends are attracted to each other by base-pairing. The enzyme **DNA ligase** is added to bond the sticky ends.

Human gene

Recombinant DNA molecule

Antibiotic Resistance Marker Genes

Antibiotic resistant marker genes may be used to identify the bacteria that have taken up the foreign (e.g., human) DNA. The plasmid used often carries two genes that provide the bacteria with resistance to the antibiotics **ampicillin** and **tetracycline**. Without this plasmid, the bacteria have no antibiotic resistance genes.

A single restriction enzyme recognition sequence lies within the tetracycline resistance gene. A foreign gene, spliced into this position, will disrupt the tetracycline resistance gene, leaving the bacteria vulnerable to this antibiotic. It is possible to identify the bacteria that successfully take up the recombinant plasmid by growing the bacteria on media containing ampicillin, and transferring colonies to media with both antibiotics.

6 The recombinant plasmid is introduced into a bacterial cell by simply adding the DNA to a bacterial culture. Under the right conditions, some bacteria will take up the plasmid from solution by the process of **transformation**.

Preparation of the clone up to this point

- -

Cloning the gene starts here

7 The actual gene cloning process (making multiple copies of the human gene) occurs when the bacterium with the recombinant plasmid is allowed to reproduce.

NOTE: Most often today, another gene plays the role of the tetracycline resistance gene, but the principle remains the same: the inserted DNA disrupts the activity of a gene whose activity is easily determined.

8 Colonies of bacteria that carry the recombinant plasmid can be identified by the fact that they are resistant to ampicillin but sensitive to tetracycline.

Agar plate with colonies of bacteria growing on them. All colonies look identical but only some have the plasmid with the human gene.

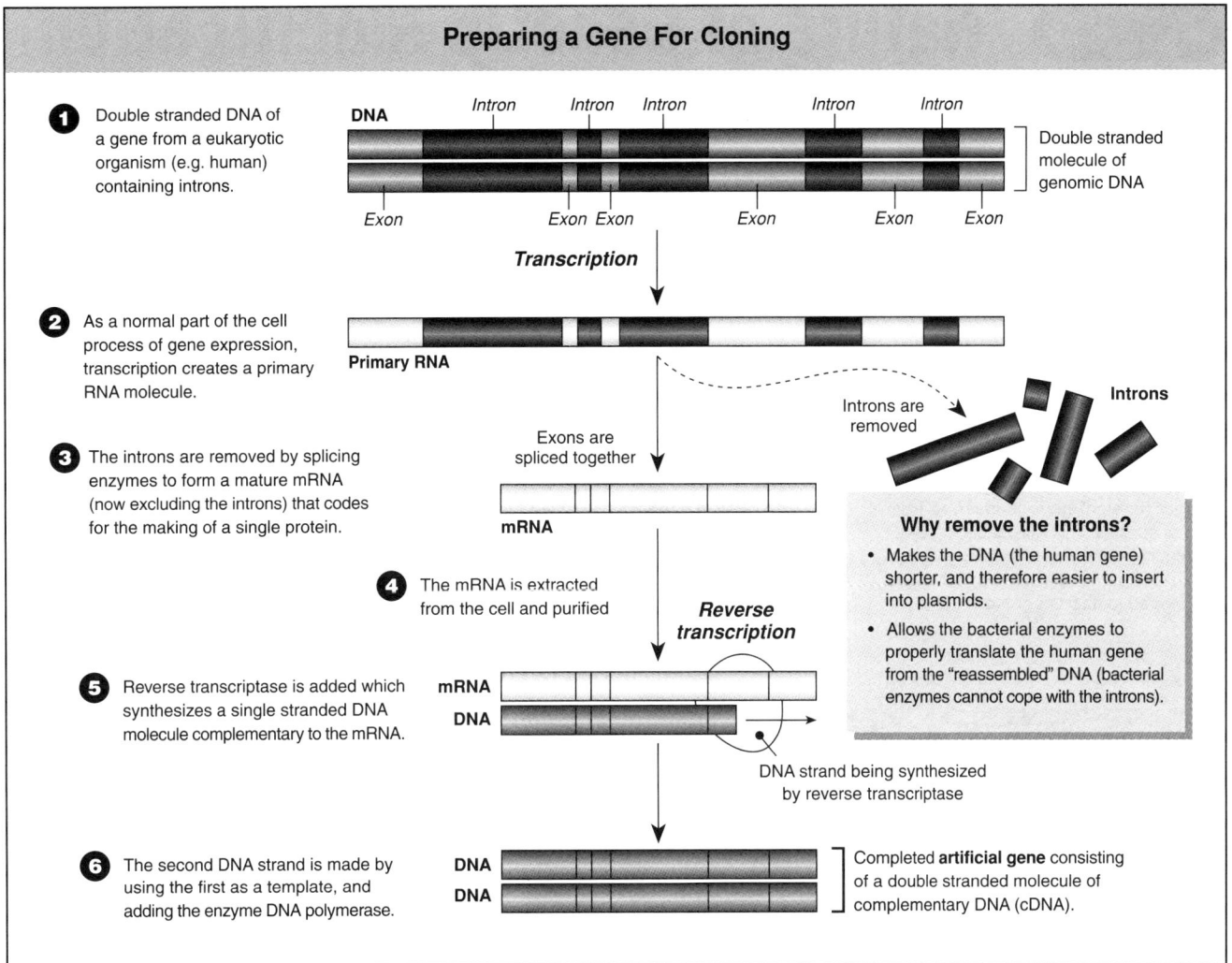

Preparing a Gene For Cloning

1 Double stranded DNA of a gene from a eukaryotic organism (e.g. human) containing introns.

DNA — Intron Intron Intron Intron Intron

Double stranded molecule of genomic DNA

Exon — Exon Exon Exon Exon Exon

Transcription

2 As a normal part of the cell process of gene expression, transcription creates a primary RNA molecule.

Primary RNA

Introns are removed

Introns

3 The introns are removed by splicing enzymes to form a mature mRNA (now excluding the introns) that codes for the making of a single protein.

Exons are spliced together

mRNA

Why remove the introns?
- Makes the DNA (the human gene) shorter, and therefore easier to insert into plasmids.
- Allows the bacterial enzymes to properly translate the human gene from the "reassembled" DNA (bacterial enzymes cannot cope with the introns).

4 The mRNA is extracted from the cell and purified

Reverse transcription

5 Reverse transcriptase is added which synthesizes a single stranded DNA molecule complementary to the mRNA.

mRNA

DNA

DNA strand being synthesized by reverse transcriptase

6 The second DNA strand is made by using the first as a template, and adding the enzyme DNA polymerase.

DNA

DNA

Completed **artificial gene** consisting of a double stranded molecule of complementary DNA (cDNA).

1. Explain what is meant by **cloning genes**: _____

_____

_____

2. Describe a possible **application** of gene cloning (i.e. a reason for wanting to clone a gene): _____

_____

_____

3. Explain the role that **restriction enzymes** play in the preparation of a clone: _____

_____

_____

4. Explain what **recombinant DNA** is: _____

_____

5. When cloning a gene using **plasmid vectors**, the bacterial colonies containing recombinant plasmids are mixed up with colonies that have none. All the colonies look identical, but some have received plasmids with the human gene, some without, while others receive no plasmid at all. Explain how the colonies with the recombinant plasmids are identified:

_____

_____

_____

_____

Nature of Genetic Modification

The genetic modification of organisms is a vast industry, and the applications of the technology are exciting and far reaching. It brings new hope for medical cures, promises to increase yields in agriculture, and has the potential to help solve the world's pollution and resource crises. Organisms with artificially altered DNA are referred to as **genetically modified organisms** or

GMOs. They may be modified in one of three ways (outlined below). Some of the current and proposed applications of gene technology raise complex ethical and safety issues, where the benefits of their use must be carefully weighed against the risks to human health, as well as the health and well-being of other organisms and the environment as a whole.

Producing Genetically Modified Organisms (GMOs)

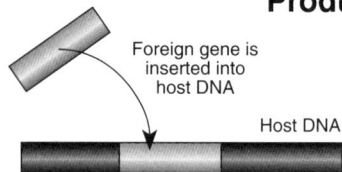

Foreign gene is inserted into host DNA

Host DNA

Existing gene is altered

Host DNA

Gene is deleted or deactivated

Host DNA

Add a foreign gene

A novel (foreign) gene is inserted from another species. This will enable the GMO to express the trait coded by the new gene. Organisms genetically altered in this way are referred to as **transgenic**.

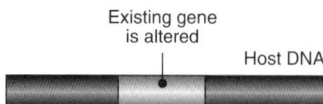

Alter an existing gene

An existing gene may be altered to make it express at a higher level (e.g. growth hormone) or in a different way (in tissue that would not normally express it). This method is also used for gene therapy.

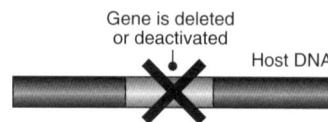

Delete or 'turn off' a gene

An existing gene may be deleted or deactivated to prevent the expression of a trait (e.g. the deactivation of the ripening gene in tomatoes).

Applications of GMOs

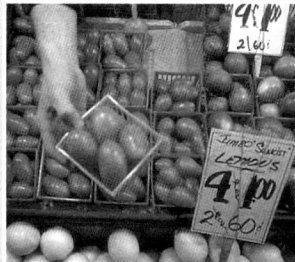

Extending shelf life
Some fresh produce (e.g. tomatoes) have been engineered to have an extended keeping quality. In the case of tomatoes, the gene for ripening has been switched off, delaying the natural process of softening in the fruit.

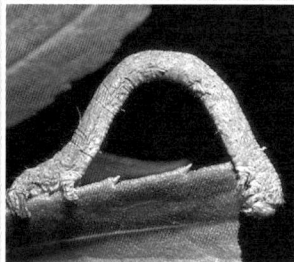

Pest or herbicide resistance
Plants can be engineered to produce their own insecticide and become pest resistant. Genetically engineered herbicide resistance is also common. In this case, chemical weed killers can be used freely without crop damage.

Crop improvement
Gene technology is now an integral part of the development of new crop varieties. Crops can be engineered to produce higher protein levels or to grow in inhospitable conditions (e.g. salty or arid conditions).

Environmental clean-up
Some bacteria have been engineered to thrive on waste products, such as liquefied newspaper pulp or oil. As well as degrading pollutants and wastes, the bacteria may be harvested as a commercial protein source.

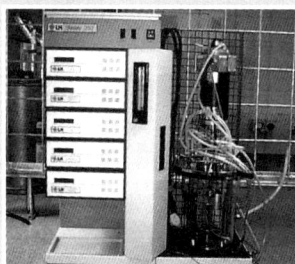

Biofactories
Transgenic bacteria are widely used to produce desirable products: often hormones or proteins. Large quantities of a product can be produced using bioreactors (above). Examples: insulin production by recombinant yeast, production of bovine growth hormone.

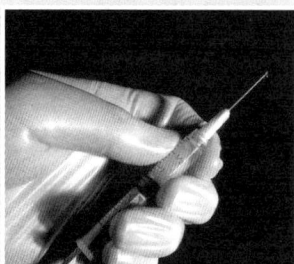

Vaccine development
The potential exists for multipurpose vaccines to be made using gene technology. Genes coding for vaccine components (e.g. viral protein coat) are inserted into an unrelated live vaccine (e.g. polio vaccine), and deliver proteins to stimulate an immune response.

Livestock improvement using transgenic animals
Transgenic sheep have been used to enhance wool production in flocks (above, left). The keratin protein of wool is largely made of a single amino acid, cysteine. Injecting developing sheep with the genes for the enzymes that generate cysteine produces woollier transgenic sheep. In some cases, transgenic animals have been used as biofactories. Transgenic sheep carrying the human gene for a protein, α-1-antitrypsin produce the protein in their milk. The antitrypsin is extracted from the milk and used to treat hereditary emphysema.

1. Briefly distinguish the three ways in which an organism may be genetically modified (to produce a GMO):

   (a) _____

   (b) _____

   (c) _____

2. On a separate sheet, write a short account of describing one of the applications of GMOs described above.

Genetically Modified Plants

RA②

Plants with **novel traits** (i.e. traits that are new to the species) may be produced by traditional methods, such as accelerated mutagenesis or plant breeding (creating hybrids from two species). Recombinant DNA techniques have allowed a much more controlled and directed approach to introducing new genetic material into plants. The table below illustrates how extensive the adoption of this genetic engineering tool has become. It has enabled important agricultural crops to be endowed with new traits that improve their pest resistance, reduce the need for agrichemicals, and improve their market appeal (e.g. new colors). Genetic engineering may also be used to improve the world's ability to feed a rapidly growing population.

Transformation using a Ti Plasmid in *Agrobacterium*

The **Ti plasmid** from the soil bacteria, *Agrobacterium tumefaciens,* causes tumors (galls) in plants. It can be successfully transferred to plant cells where a segment of its DNA can be integrated into the plant's chromosome.

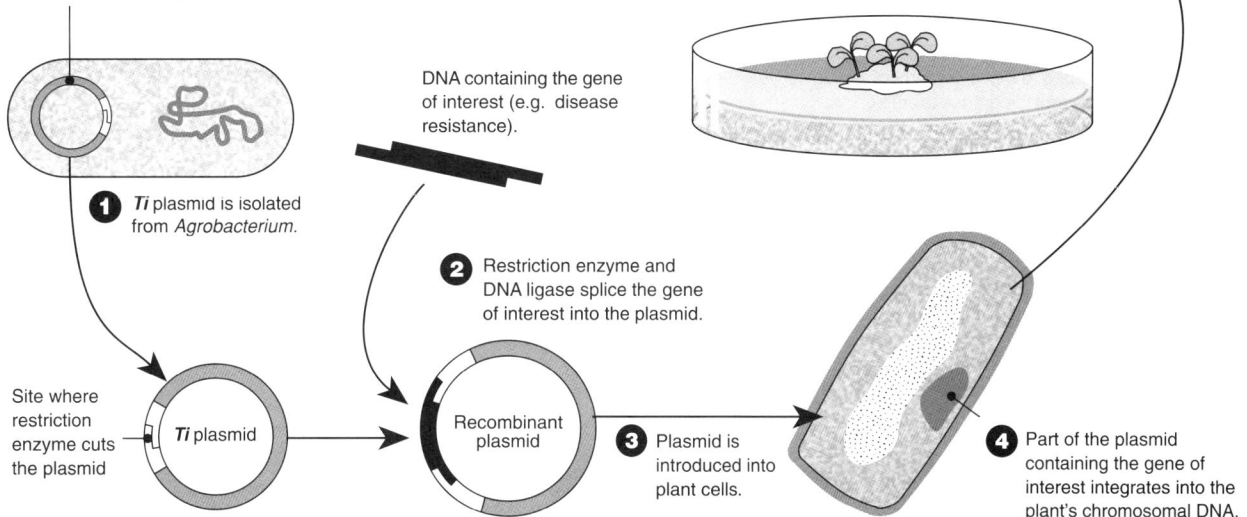

5 Transformed plant cells are grown by tissue culture and are later planted out to grow normally.

DNA containing the gene of interest (e.g. disease resistance).

1 *Ti* plasmid is isolated from *Agrobacterium.*

2 Restriction enzyme and DNA ligase splice the gene of interest into the plasmid.

Site where restriction enzyme cuts the plasmid

Ti plasmid

Recombinant plasmid

3 Plasmid is introduced into plant cells.

4 Part of the plasmid containing the gene of interest integrates into the plant's chromosomal DNA.

Examples of Genetically Modified Plants*			
Crop	**Phenotypic trait altered**	**Crop**	**Phenotypic trait altered**
Argentine canola	Herbicide tolerance, modified seed fatty acid content (high oleic acid/low linolenic acid expression), pollination control system (male sterility, fertility restoration).	**Potato**	Resistance to: Colorado potato beetle, leafroll *luteovirus*, potato virus Y.
		Rice	Herbicide resistance, adding provitamin A.
Carnation	Increased shelf-life (delayed senescence), herbicide tolerance, modified flower color.	**Soybean**	Herbicide resistance, modified fatty acid content (high oleic acid/low linolenic acid expression), herbicide tolerance.
Chicory	Male sterility, herbicide tolerance.		
Cotton	Herbicide tolerance, resistance to lepidopteran insect pests (including cotton worm, pink bollworm, tobacco budworm).	**Squash**	Resistance to infection: cucumber mosaic virus, watermelon mosaic virus, zucchini yellow mosaic virus.
Flax (linseed)	Herbicide tolerance.	**Sugar beet**	Herbicide tolerance.
Maize	Herbicide tolerance, male sterility, resistance to European corn borer.	**Tobacco**	Herbicide tolerance.
		Tomato	Increased shelf-life through delayed ripening and delayed softening. Resistance to lepidopteran pests.
Melon	Delayed ripening.		
Papaya	Resistance to infection by papaya ringspot virus.	**Wheat**	Herbicide tolerance.

* NOTE: This list includes not only plants produced using recombinant DNA techniques (i.e. genetically engineered or transgenic plants), but also plants with novel traits that may have been produced using more traditional methods, such as accelerated mutagenesis or plant breeding.

1. Describe the property of *Agrobacterium tumefaciens* that makes it an ideal vector for introducing new genes into plants:

_____

_____

2. Explain why the following traits are considered desirable in food crops:

   (a) Modified seed fatty acid content: _____

   (b) Herbicide tolerance: _____

Transgenic Organisms

An organism developing from a cell into which foreign DNA has been inserted is called a **transgenic organism**. Transgenic techniques have been applied to plants, animals, and bacteria. Such techniques allow direct modification of a genome and enable traits to be introduced that are not even naturally present in a species. The applications of this technology are various, e.g. improvement of crop yields, production of herbicide resistant plants, enhancement of desirable features in livestock, production of human proteins, and the treatment of genetic defects through **gene therapy**. Cloning technology can be used to propagate transgenic organisms so that introduced genes quickly become part of the germ line (and are inherited). Some methods commonly involved in the production of transgenic organisms are described below:

Liposomes

Liposomes, small spherical vesicles made of a single membrane, can be made commercially to precise specifications. When they are coated with appropriate surface molecules, they are attracted to specific cell types in the body. DNA carried by the liposome can enter the cell by *endocytosis* or *fusion*. They can be used to deliver genes to these cells to correct defective or missing genes, providing gene therapy.

Liposome membrane — Surface molecule — Gene carried inside liposome — Liposome fusing with plasma membrane — DNA — Animal cell — Nucleus

Plasmid Vectors

Plasmids are naturally occurring accessory chromosomes found in bacteria. Plasmids are usually transferred between closely related microbes by cell-to-cell contact (conjugation). Simple chemical treatments can make mammalian cells, yeast cells and some bacterial cells that do not naturally transfer DNA, able to take up external DNA. *Agrobacterium tumefaciens* (a bacterium) can insert part of its plasmid directly into plant cells.

Plasmid with foreign gene — Bacterium — Plant infected by bacterium with foreign gene

Viral Vectors

Viruses, such as those shown on the right, are well suited for gene therapy. They can accommodate up to 7500 bases of inserted DNA in their protein capsule. When viruses infect and reproduce inside the target cells, they are also spreading the recombinant DNA. They have already been used in several clinical trials of gene therapy for different diseases. A problem with this method involves the host immune reaction to the virus.

Retrovirus with normal human gene — Normal gene introduced into human cell by virus — Cell transplanted into body to correct genetic disease

Pronuclear Injection

DNA can be introduced directly into an animal cell by microinjection. Multiple copies of the desired transgene are injected via a glass micropipette into a recently fertilized egg cell, which is then transferred to a surrogate mother. Transgenic mice and livestock are produced in this way, but the process is inefficient: only 2-3% of eggs give rise to transgenic animals and only a proportion of these animals express the added gene adequately.

Micropipette injects gene — Egg cell — Blunt holding pipette — Egg nucleus

Ballistic DNA Injection

This remarkable way of introducing foreign DNA into living tissue literally shoots it directly into the organism using a "gene gun" (e.g., Helios gene gun made by Bio-Rad). Microscopic particles of gold or tungsten are coated with DNA. They are propelled by a burst of helium into the skin and organs of animals (e.g., rabbit, mouse, pig, fish, etc.) and tissues of intact plants. Some of the cells express the introduced DNA as if it were their own.

HELIOS GENE GUN — Gold pellets coated with DNA — Nucleus — Compressed helium gun — Target plant or animal cell

Protoplast Fusion

This process requires the cell walls of plants to be removed by enzymatic digestion. The resulting protoplasts (cells that have lost their cell walls) are then treated with polyethylene glycol which increases their frequency of fusion. In the new hybrid cell, the DNA derived from the two "parent" cells may undergo natural recombination (they may merge).

Enzymes digest cell walls — Polyethylene glycol stimulates fusion — Plasma membrane — DNA from two different cells

Microinjection of DNA to Create Transgenic Mice

2b Micropipette injects rat growth hormone gene into a fertilized egg.

This was a trial experiment of the technology involved and produced the world's first transgenic animal.

3b **Transformed egg** is cultured to an embryo, then implanted in a surrogate mother.

1 Two eggs are removed from a single female mouse and are fertilized artificially in a test tube.

Weight: 44 g

Weight: 29 g

4 The mice above are siblings, but the mouse on the right was transformed by the introduction of a rat growth hormone gene.

2a One fertilized egg is left unaltered.

3a **Normal egg** is cultured to an embryo, then implanted in a surrogate mother.

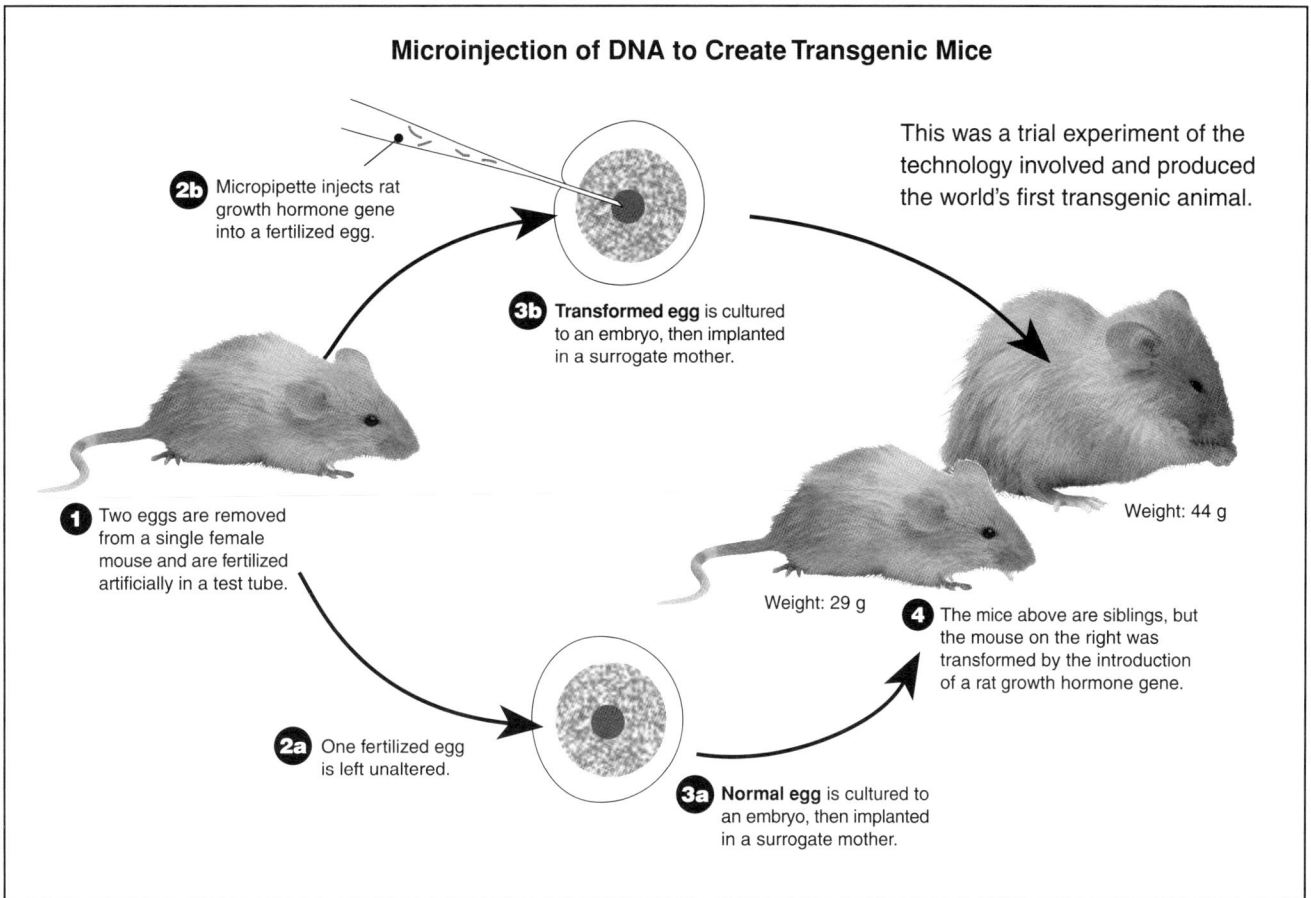

1. In the context of recombinant DNA technology, define the terms:

   (a) Transformation: _____

   (b) Foreign DNA: _____

2. Outline the basic principles (not the techniques) involved in the production of a transgenic organism:

   _____

   _____

3. Describe an example of improvement in a **commercial crop** brought about by the application of transgenic techniques:

   _____

   _____

4. Identify three human needs that have *encouraged* the development of transgenic techniques:

   (a) _____

   (b) _____

   (c) _____

5. Outline two advantages and one disadvantage of using viruses as vectors for gene delivery:

   Advantages: _____

   _____

   _____

   Disadvantage: _____

6. Explain the purpose behind the transgenic mice experiment (above): _____

   _____

Using Recombinant Bacteria

RA 2

In 1990 Pfizer, Inc. produced one of the first two products of recombinant DNA technology to enter the human food supply – the "CHY-MAX" brand of chymosin. This was a protein purified from bacteria that had been given a copy of the chymosin gene from cattle. Traditionally extracted from "chyme" or stomach secretions of suckling calves, chymosin (also called rennin) is an enzyme that digests milk proteins. Chymosin is the active ingredient in rennet, used by cheesemakers to clot milk into curds. CHY-MAX extracted from bacteria grown in a vat is identical in chemical composition to the chymosin extracted from cattle. Pfizer's product quickly won over half the market for rennet because cheesemakers found it to be a cost-effective source of high-quality chymosin in consistent supply. A recombinant form of the fungus, *Mucor*, is also used to manufacture chymosin.

Chymosin Production using Recombinant Bacteria

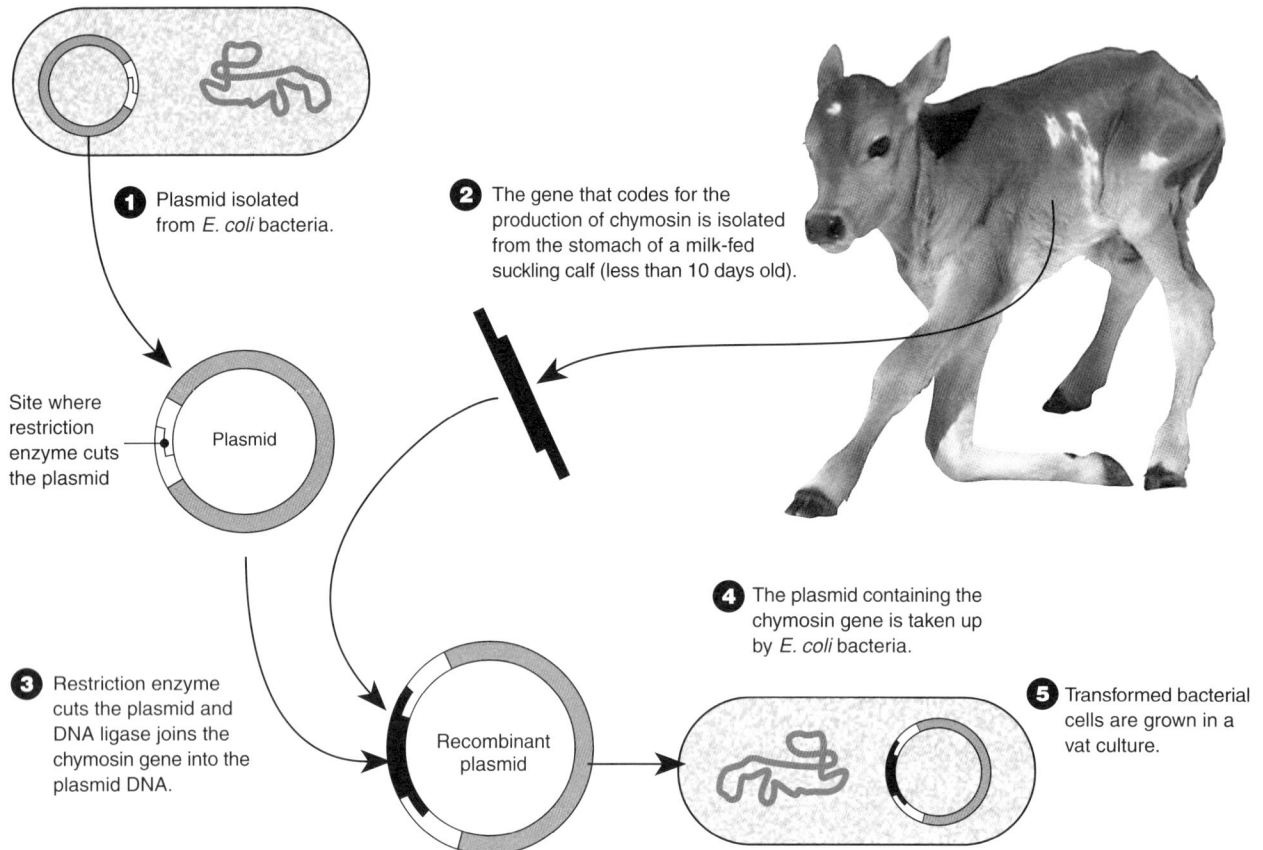

1 Plasmid isolated from *E. coli* bacteria.

2 The gene that codes for the production of chymosin is isolated from the stomach of a milk-fed suckling calf (less than 10 days old).

Site where restriction enzyme cuts the plasmid

Plasmid

3 Restriction enzyme cuts the plasmid and DNA ligase joins the chymosin gene into the plasmid DNA.

Recombinant plasmid

4 The plasmid containing the chymosin gene is taken up by *E. coli* bacteria.

5 Transformed bacterial cells are grown in a vat culture.

1. Describe the main use of chymosin: _____

   _____

2. State the traditional source of chymosin: _____

   _____

3. Describe how the following are involved in the preparation of a plasmid for chymosin production:

   (a) Restriction enzymes: _____

   _____

   (b) DNA ligase: _____

   _____

4. Outline three advantages of using chymosin produced by genetically modified bacteria over chymosin from traditional sources:

   (a) _____

   (b) _____

   (c) _____

Gene Therapy

RA 2

Gene therapy (the delivery of selected genes into a patient's cells) is a relatively recent technology that promises to revolutionize medicine this century. As the genetic basis of more diseases becomes known, their treatment or cure with gene therapy becomes feasible. This applies even to diseases that have so far resisted all conventional treatments. Traditional drugs act by altering the phenotype of the target cell, and are called **phenotypic drugs**. Gene therapies alter the genetic makeup of the cell, and are referred to as **genotypic drugs**. Initially, gene therapy was envisioned for the treatment of genetic disorders, but it could be used to treat a wide range of diseases, including cancer, arthritis, peripheral vascular disease, and neuro-degenerative disorders. Gene therapy employs **recombinant DNA technology** to insert a gene into a patient's body. Sometimes (as in the treatment of HIV) a novel gene is inserted

to interfere with the progress of a disease. In recent times, the number of patients being treated with gene therapy has rapidly increased, but no one has yet been cured. To date, only severe combined immune deficiency syndrome (**SCID**) has shown improvement after gene therapy. Infants treated for this inherited, normally lethal, condition have become healthy young adults. Gene therapy is technically difficult. Once a gene has been identified and cloned, it must be transferred to the patient and expressed. Much current research is centered on improving the efficiency of gene transfer and expression. Currently, inserted genes reach only a tiny proportion (about 1%) of target cells. Those that reach their destination may work inefficiently and produce too little protein, too slowly, to be of benefit. There may also be side effects; many patients react immunologically to the viral vectors used in gene transfer.

Target Tissues for Therapeutic Genes

Nervous system
Trials for the treatment of *Canavan disease* and *cancer*.

Respiratory tract
Disorders of the respiratory tract are a major target, including: *cystic fibrosis* and *lung cancer*.

Other solid organs
Genetic disorders of solid organs: lungs, heart, liver, bowel, and bone tissue. Gene therapy for only two disorders of the liver have been approved: *familial hypercholesterolemia* (inherited high blood cholesterol) and *partial ornithine transcarbamylase deficiency* (a faulty enzyme in the urea cycle).

Vascular system
Gene therapy trials for the treatment and prevention of *atherosclerosis*: one treatment stimulates the growth of new blood vessels in blocked arteries, while another prevents blockages in vessels already treated.

Blood stem cells and T cells
Used for the correction of genetic disorders of the immune system, such as *chronic granulomatous disease* (caused by a defective enzyme in white blood cells), as well as the treatment of *hemophilia*, *HIV infection* and *cancer*.

Muscle
Target for the correction of genetic disorders affecting skeletal muscle, such as *muscular dystrophy*. Naked DNA technology has introduced pathogen-specific genes into muscle as vaccines against infectious disease.

Potential Routes of Administration

Infusion directly into **brain** tissue (intracerebral).

Administered via an aerosol as a **nasal spray** or via a **nebulizer** into the airways. Airway delivery of the CF gene (in adenoviral vectors or liposomes) is being investigated for the treatment of cystic fibrosis.

Sprays administered via the airways are usually targeting the **lungs** (intrapulmonary), as is the case for cystic fibrosis.

Direct injection into the site of a **tumor** (intratumor).

Direct injection into an **organ** (intraorgan).

Infusion into the **peritoneal cavities** surrounding organs (intraperitoneal).

Direct injection into the **veins** (intravenous).

Direct injection under the **skin** (subcutaneous).

Direct injection into **muscle** tissue (intramuscular)

Source: Culver K.W., **Measuring success in clinical gene therapy research** [poster]. *Mol Med Today* 1996 Jun; 2: 225-67

1. State the general purpose of gene therapy and explain why its is so promising in the treatment of disease:

2. Identify three general categories of disease currently targeted for gene therapy:

Gene Delivery Systems

A 2

Gene therapy requires the transfer of a gene to a patient. This is often achieved using an infectious agent (**vector**) such as a virus; a technique called **transfection**. A gene delivered to a patient often operates by providing a correctly working version of a faulty gene or by adding a new (novel) gene to perform a corrective role. In other cases, expression of a gene may be blocked in order to control cellular (or viral) activity. One of the first clinical trials of gene therapy was for cystic fibrosis patients. Cystic fibrosis was an obvious candidate for gene therapy because the disease is controlled by a single, known gene mutation. Gene therapy involving **somatic cells** may be therapeutic, but the genetic changes produced are not inherited. The transfection of **stem cells** (immortal, undifferentiated cells), rather than mature somatic cells, achieves a longer persistence of therapy in patients. The introduction of new or altered genes into **germline** (reproductive) **cells** will enable genetic changes to be inherited. This will provide the opportunity to cure diseases.

Using Gene Therapy to Treat Cystic Fibrosis (CF)

In cystic fibrosis, a gene mutation causes the body to produce an abnormally thick, sticky mucus that accumulates in the lungs and intestines. The identification and isolation of the CF gene in 1989 meant that scientists could look for ways in which to correct the genetic defect rather than just treating the symptoms using traditional therapies.

In trials, normal genes were isolated and inserted into patients using vectors such as **adenoviruses** and **liposomes**.

In order to prevent the progressive and ultimately lethal lung damage, the main target of CF gene therapy is the lung. The viral vector was piped directly into the lung, whereas the liposomes were inhaled in a spray formulation. The results of these trials were disappointing; on average, there was only a 25% correction, the effects were short lived, and the benefits were quickly reversed. Alarmingly, the adenovirus used in one of the trials led to the death of one patient.

Source: Cystic Fibrosis Trust, UK.

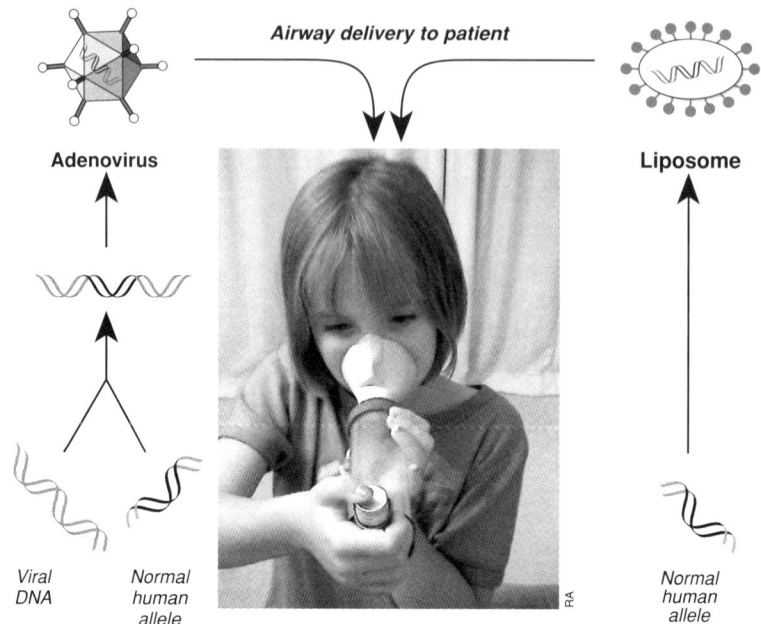

Airway delivery to patient

Adenovirus

Liposome

Viral DNA   *Normal human allele*   *Normal human allele*

An **adenovirus** that normally causes colds is genetically modified to make it safe and to carry the normal (unmutated) CFTR ('cystic fibrosis') gene.

Liposomes are tiny fat globules. Normal CF genes are enclosed in liposomes, which fuse with plasma membranes and deliver the genes into the cells.

Gene Delivery Systems Used In Human Patients

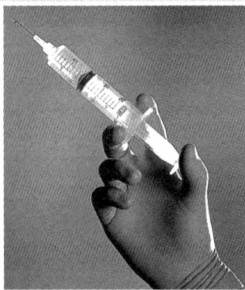

Hypodermic needle injection

- Injection of the vectors directly into the bloodstream or other organs of the patient. Vectors injected into the blood travel throughout the body and may be taken up by the target cells.

- Injections of plasmid DNA into thymus, skin, cardiac muscle and skeletal muscle have already proved successful in non-human trials (mice and primates).

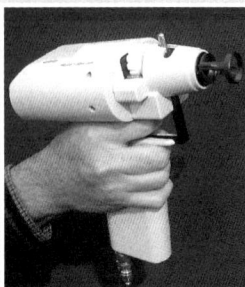

Aerosol

- Aerosols and nebulizers offer an effective spread and efficient delivery of the vector to the site of certain target cells (especially in the respiratory tract).

- Only effective on epithelial cells that can be reached by the aerosol.

Ballistic DNA injection

- Plasmid DNA encoding the gene of interest is coated onto microbeads, and these are 'fired' at the target cells using gas pressure or a high voltage discharge.

- Used to transfer genes to a wide variety of cell lines *(ex vivo)* or directly into surgically exposed tissue *(in vivo)*.

- May be used in DNA-based immunization to prevent infectious diseases or cancer.

- Allows delivery of precise DNA dosages. However, genes delivered by this method are expressed transiently and there is considerable cell damage at the center of the discharge site.

Ballistic DNA injection is also called microprojectile gene transfer, the gene-gun, or particle bombardment method.

Gene delivery to extracted cells and cell culture

- Target cells are isolated from tissue. Non-specific gene delivery is applied to the total cell population or as a microinjection of DNA into the nucleus of a single cell.

- Cells that have taken up the normal allele are cultured outside the body *(ex-vivo)* and re-injected into the patient.

- The expression of the normal allele relieves symptoms of the disease.

An incubator for culturing cell lines (ex-vivo).

©1999 University of Kansas Office of University Relations

Vectors That Can Be Used For Gene Therapy

	Retrovirus	Adenovirus	Liposome	"Naked" DNA
Insert size:	8000 bases	8000 bases	>20 000 bases	>20 000 bases
Integration:	Yes	No	No	No
In vivo delivery:	Poor	High	Variable	Poor
Advantages	• Integrate genes into the chromosomes of the human host cell. • Offers chance for long-term stability.	• Modified for gene therapy, they infect human cells and express the normal gene. • Most do not cause disease. • Have a large capacity to carry foreign genes.	• Liposomes seek out target cells using sugars in their membranes that are recognized by cell receptors. • Have no viral genes that may cause disease.	• Have no viral genes that may cause disease. • Expected to be useful for vaccination.
Disadvantages	• Many infect only cells that are dividing. • Genes integrate randomly into chromosomes, so might disrupt useful genes in the host cell.	• Viruses may have poor survival due to attack by the host's immune system. • Genes may function only sporadically because they are not integrated into host cell's chromosome.	• Less efficient than viruses at transferring genes into cells, but recent work on using sugars to aid targeting have improved success rate.	• Unstable in most tissues of the body. • Inefficient at gene transfer.

There are at least 150 approved clinical gene therapy protocols worldwide, 125 of which are approved in the United States. The majority of these (63%) employ retroviral vectors to deliver the selected gene to the target cells. Other widely used vectors include adenoviral vectors (16%), and liposomes (13%). The remaining 8% employ a variety of vector systems, the majority of which include injection of naked plasmid DNA. In the table above, the following terms are defined as follows: **"Naked" DNA**: genes applied by ballistic injection or by regular hypodermic injection of plasmid DNA. **Insert size**: size of gene that can be inserted into the vector. **Integration**: whether or not the gene is integrated into the host DNA (chromosomes). **In vivo delivery**: can/cannot transfer a gene directly into a patient.

1. (a) Describe the features of viruses that make them well suited as **vectors** for gene therapy:

_____

_____

(b) Describe a problem with using viral vectors for gene therapy and suggest why liposomes might offer an advantage:

_____

_____

2. A great deal of current research is being devoted to discovering a gene therapy solution to treat **cystic fibrosis** (CF):

(a) Describe the symptoms of CF: _____

_____

(b) Explain why this genetic disease has been so eagerly targeted: _____

_____

(c) Identify two vectors for introducing healthy CFTR genes into CF patients and outline how these might be delivered:

_____

_____

(d) Outline some of the problems so far encountered with gene therapy for CF: _____

_____

Production of Human Proteins

Transgenic microorganisms are now widely used as **biofactories** for the production of human proteins. These proteins are often used to treat metabolic protein-deficiency disorders. **Type I diabetes mellitus** is a metabolic disease caused by a lack of insulin and is treatable only with insulin injection. Before the advent of genetic engineering, insulin was extracted from the pancreatic tissue of pigs or cattle. This method was expensive and problematic in that the insulin caused various side effects and was often contaminated. Since the 1980s, human insulin has

been mass produced using genetically modified (GM) bacteria (*Escherichia coli*) and yeast (*Saccharomyces cerevisiae*). Similar methods are used for the genetic manipulation of both microorganisms, although the size of the bacterial plasmid requires that the human gene be inserted as two, separately expressed, nucleotide sequences (see below). The use of insulin from GM sources has greatly improved the management of Type I diabetes, and the range of formulations now available has allowed diabetics to live much more normal lives than previously.

Synthesis of human insulin using recombinant DNA technology

Type I diabetes is treated with regular injections of insulin according to daily needs (right). Since the 1980s, human insulin has been mass produced using genetically modified (GM) microorganisms and marketed under various trade names. Various methodologies are employed to produce the insulin, but all involve inserting a human gene into a plasmid (bacterial or yeast), followed by secretion of a protein product from which the active insulin can be derived.

❶ Identify and synthesize the human gene

Insulin is a small, simple protein. It comprises a total of 51 amino acids in two polypeptide chains (A and B). The two chains are linked by disulfide bonds. The nucleotide sequence of the gene for human insulin has been determined from the amino acid sequence. The first step in insulin production is to chemically synthesize the DNA chains that carry the specific nucleotide sequences for the A and B chains of insulin (the A and B 'genes').

❷ Insert the synthetic DNA into plasmids

Using a tool kit of restriction enzymes and DNA ligase, the synthetic A and B nucleotide sequences are separately inserted into the gene for the bacterial enzyme, β-galactosidase, which is carried on the bacterial plasmid. In *E. coli*, β-galactosidase controls the transcription of genes. To make the bacteria produce insulin, the insulin gene needs to be tied to the gene for this enzyme.

❸ Insert plasmid into the bacterial cell

The recombinant plasmids are then introduced to *E. coli* cells in culture conditions that favor the bacterial uptake of plasmid DNA. In practical terms, the synthesis of human insulin requires millions of copies of bacteria whose plasmid has been combined with the insulin gene. The insulin gene is expressed as it replicates with the β-galactosidase in the cell undergoing mitosis.

❹ Make the functional protein

The protein formed consists partly of β-galactosidase, joined either to the A or B chain of insulin. The A and B chains are then extracted from the β-galactosidase fragment and purified. The two chains are then mixed and reconnected in a reaction that forms the disulfide cross bridges and the functional human protein, insulin. The final purified product is made suitable for injection and provided in a number of different formulations.

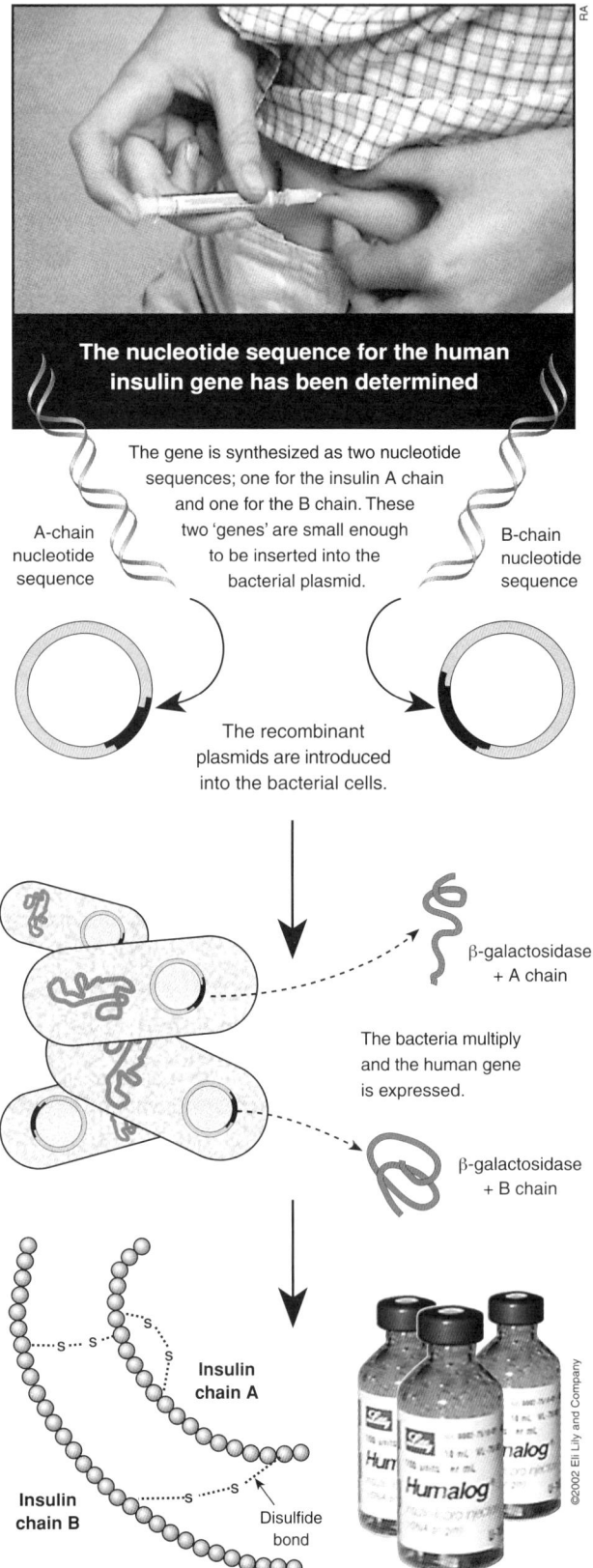

The nucleotide sequence for the human insulin gene has been determined

The gene is synthesized as two nucleotide sequences; one for the insulin A chain and one for the B chain. These two 'genes' are small enough to be inserted into the bacterial plasmid.

A-chain nucleotide sequence

B-chain nucleotide sequence

The recombinant plasmids are introduced into the bacterial cells.

β-galactosidase + A chain

The bacteria multiply and the human gene is expressed.

β-galactosidase + B chain

Insulin chain A

Insulin chain B

Disulfide bond

Human Proteins Produced using Genetic Engineering and their Applications

Human protein and biological role	Traditional production method	Current production
Erythropoetin A hormone, produced by kidneys, which stimulates red blood cell production. Used to treat anemia in patients with kidney failure.	Not applicable. Previous methods to treat anemia in patients with kidney failure was through repeated blood transfusions.	Cloned gene grown in hamster ovary cells
Human Growth Hormone Pituitary hormone promoting normal growth in height (deficiency results in dwarfism). Injection used to treat pituitary dwarfism.	Extracted from the pituitary glands of corpses. Many patients developed Creutzfeldt-Jacob disease (CJD) as a result. CJD is a degenerative brain disease, transmitted via infected tissues or their extracts.	Genetically engineered bacteria
Insulin Regulates the uptake of glucose by cells. Used (via injection) in the treatment of Type I (insulin-dependent) diabetes mellitus.	Physical extraction from the pancreatic tissue of pigs or cattle. Problems included high cost, sample contamination, and severe side effects.	Genetically engineered bacteria or yeast
Interferon Anti-viral substance produced by virus-infected cells. Used in the treatment of hepatitis b and c, some cancers, and multiple sclerosis.	Not applicable. Relatively recent discovery of the role of these proteins in human physiology.	Genetically engineered bacteria
Factor VIII One of the blood clotting factors normally present in blood. Used in the treatment of hemophilia caused by lack of factor VIII.	Blood donation. Risks of receiving blood contaminated with infective viruses (HIV, hepatitis), despite better screening procedures.	Genetically engineered bacteria

1. Explain the three major problems associated with the traditional method of obtaining insulin to treat diabetes:

   (a) _____

   (b) _____

   (c) _____

2. State why the insulin gene is synthesized as two separate A and B chain nucleotide sequences: _____

3. State why the synthetic nucleotide sequences ('genes') are inserted into the β-galactosidase gene: _____

4. Yeast (*Saccharomyces cerevisiae*) is also used in the production of human insulin. It is a eukaryote with a larger plasmid than *E. coli*. Its secretory pathways are more similar to those of humans and β-galactosidase is not involved in gene expression. **Predict** how these differences might change the procedure for insulin production with respect to:

   (a) Insertion of the gene into the plasmid: _____

   (b) Secretion and purification of the protein product: _____

5. Briefly describe the benefits to patients of using GMOs to produce human proteins: _____

6. When delivered to a patient, artificially produced human proteins only alleviate disease symptoms; they cannot cure the disease. Give a brief statement describing how this situation might change in the future: _____

The Human Genome Project

The **Human Genome Project** (HGP) is a publicly funded venture involving many different organizations throughout the world. In 1998, Celera Genomics in the USA began a competing project, as a commercial venture, in a race to be the first to determine the human genome sequence. In 2000, both organizations reached the first draft stage, and the entire genome is due to be available as a high quality (golden standard) sequence during 2003. In addition to determining the order of bases in the human genome, genes are being identified, sequenced, and mapped (their specific chromosomal location identified). With this new knowledge on gene sequences, it has become easier to identify protein products of many genes, and

gain a better understanding of many genetic disorders. Long term benefits of the HGP are both medical and non-medical (see opposite). Many biotechnology companies have taken out patents on gene sequences. This practice is controversial because it restricts usage of the sequence information to the patent holders only. Other genome sequencing projects have arisen as a result of the initiative to sequence the human one. A controversial project to map the differences between different racial and ethnic groups is called the **Human Genome Diversity Project** (HGDP). It aims to understand the degree of diversity amongst individuals within the entire human species. It is still in its planning stages, seeking the best way to achieve its goals.

Gene Mapping

This process involves determining the precise position of a gene on a chromosome. Once the position is known, it can be shown on a diagram.

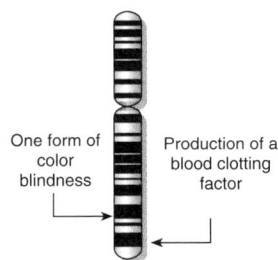

One form of color blindness

Production of a blood clotting factor

X Chromosome

Equipment used for DNA Sequencing

Banks of PCR machines are used to prepare DNA for the sequencing gel stage. This involves amplification of the DNA and chemical reactions to tag it (make the DNA fluorescent to enable visualization on a gel).

Banks of DNA sequencing gels and powerful computers are used to determine the order of bases in DNA samples.

Count of Mapped Genes

The length and number of mapped genes to date for each chromosome are tabulated below. The entire human genome contains approximately 30 000 genes. By early 2003, almost half these genes had been mapped.

Chromosome	Length (Mb)	No. of Mapped Genes
1	263	1261
2	255	845
3	214	609
4	203	460
5	194	605
6	183	799
7	171	801
8	155	437
9	145	491
10	144	395
11	144	950
12	143	678
13	114	192
14	109	698
15	106	371
16	98	502
17	92	817
18	85	185
19	67	750
20	72	575
21	50	295
22	56	439
X	164	770
Y	59	89
Total:		**14 014**

As at: 29 Dec 2002 For an update see:
http://gdbwww.gdb.org/gdbreports/ CountGeneByChromosome.html

Examples of Mapped Genes

The positions of an increasing number of genes have been mapped onto human chromosomes (see below). Sequence variations can cause or contribute to identifiable disorders. Note that chromosome 21 (the smallest human chromosome) has a relatively low gene density, while others are gene rich. This is possibly why trisomy 21 (Down syndrome) is one of the few viable human autosomal trisomies.

Key

☐ Variable regions (heterochromatin)

■ Regions reflecting the unique patterns of light and dark bands seen on stained chromosomes

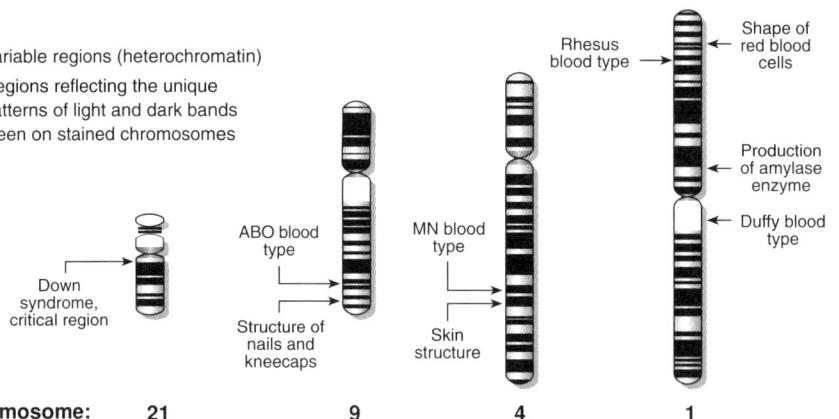

Down syndrome, critical region

ABO blood type

Structure of nails and kneecaps

MN blood type

Skin structure

Rhesus blood type

Shape of red blood cells

Production of amylase enzyme

Duffy blood type

Chromosome: 21   9   4   1

Qualities of DNA Sequence Data

The aim of the HGP is to produce a continuous block of sequence information for each chromosome. Sequence information is first obtained to draft quality. Golden standard sequence is higher quality and is obtained following more work (see below). By early 2003, four chromosomes had been sequenced to golden standard quality. A coverage of x5 means that most regions have been sequenced five times.

Quality	Error rate	Features	Coverage	Chromosomes completed
Draft	1 in 1000 bases	Significant gaps in the sequence exist. The location of some DNA sequences on chromosomes is only approximately known.	x 5	All (2000)
Golden Standard	1 in 10 000 bases	90% of the DNA is sequenced to high quality with gaps closed.	x 8-9	22, 21, 20, 14 (in order of completion date)

Benefits and ethical issues arising from the Human Genome Project

Medical benefits

- Improved **diagnosis** of disease and predisposition to disease by genetic testing.
- Better identification of disease carriers, through genetic testing.
- Better **drugs** can be designed using knowledge of protein structure (from gene sequence information) rather than by trial and error.
- Greater possibility of successfully using **gene therapy** to correct genetic disorders.

Non-medical benefits

- Greater knowledge of **family relationships** through genetic testing, e.g., paternity testing in family courts.
- Advances **forensic science** through analysis of DNA at crime scenes.
- Improved knowledge of the evolutionary relationships between humans and other organisms, which will help to develop better, more accurate classification systems.

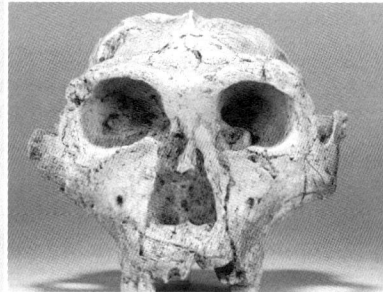

Possible ethical issues

- It is unclear whether third parties, e.g., health insurers, have rights to genetic test results.
- If treatment is unavailable for a disease, genetic knowledge about it may have no use.
- Genetic tests are costly, and there is no easy answer as to who should pay for them.
- Genetic information is hereditary so knowledge of an individual's own genome has implications for members of their family.

Couples can already have a limited range of genetic tests to determine the risk of having offspring with some disease-causing mutations.

When DNA sequences are available for humans and their ancestors, comparative analysis may provide clues about human evolution.

Legislation is needed to ensure that there is no discrimination on the basis of genetic information, e.g., at work or for health insurance.

1. Briefly describe the objectives of the Human Genome Project (HGP): _____

2. Describe two possible **benefits** of Human Genome Project (HGP):

    (a) Medical: _____

    (b) Non-medical: _____

3. Describe two possible **ethical issues** concerning the Human Genome Project (HGP):

    (a) _____

    (b) _____

4. Define the term **proteomics** and explain its significance to the HGP and the ongoing benefits arising from it: _____

5. (a) Describe the objective of the **Human Genome Diversity Project** (HGDP): _____

    (b) Suggest a reason why indigenous peoples around the world are reluctant to provide DNA samples for the HGDP: _____

The Ethics of GMO Technology

The risks of using **genetically modified organisms** (GMOs) have been the subject of considerable debate in recent times. Most experts agree that, provided GMOs are tested properly, the health risks to individuals should be minimal from plant products, although minor problems will occur. Health risks from animal GMOs are potentially more serious, especially when the animals are for human consumption. The potentially huge benefits to be gained from the use of GMOs creates enormous pressure to apply the existing technology. However, there are many concerns, including the environmental and socio-economic effects, and problems of unregulated use. There is also concern about the environmental and economic costs of possible GMO accidents. GMO research is being driven by heavy investment on the part of biotechnology companies seeking new applications for GMOs. Currently a matter of great concern to consumers is the adequacy of government regulations for the labeling of food products with GMO content. This may have important trade implications for countries exporting and importing GMO produce.

Some important points about GMOs

1. The foreign or altered DNA is in every cell of the genetically modified animal or plant.

2. The mRNA is only expressed in specific tissues.

3. The foreign protein is only expressed in those tissues but it may circulate (e.g. hormone in the bloodstream) or be secreted (e.g. milk).

4. In animals, the transgene is only likely to be transmitted from parent to offspring (but the use of viral vectors may provide a mechanism for accidental transfer of the transgene between unrelated animals).

5. In plants, transmission of the transgene in GMOs is possible by pollen, cuttings, and seeds (even between species).

6. If we eat the animal or plant proper, we will also be eating DNA. The DNA will remain 'intact' if raw, but "degraded" if cooked (remember that we eat DNA in our regular food every day).

7. Non-transgenic food products may be processed using genetically modified bacteria or yeast, and cells containing their DNA may be in the food product.

8. A transgenic product (e.g. a protein, polypeptide or a carbohydrate) may be in the GMO, but not in the portions sold to the consumer.

Potential effects of GMOs on the world

1. Increase food production.

2. Decrease use of pesticides, herbicides and animal remedies.

3. Improve the health of the human population and the medicines used to achieve it.

4. May result in transgenic products which may be harmful to some (e.g. new proteins causing allergies).

5. May have little real economic benefit to farmers (and the consumer) when increased production (as little as 10%) is weighed against cost, capital, competition.

6. May result in transgenes spreading uncontrollably into other species: plants, indigenous species, animals, and humans.

7. Concerns that the release of GMOs into the environment may be irreversible.

8. Release of GMOs into the environment may create an evolutionary or ecological "timebomb".

9. Crippling economic sanctions resulting from a consumer backlash against GMO foods and products.

10. May make the animals that are genetically modified unhealthy (animal welfare and ethical issues).

11. May cause the emergence of pest, insect, or microbial resistance to traditional control methods.

12. May create a monopoly and dependence of developing countries on companies who are seeking to control the world's commercial seed supply with "terminator seeds" (that produce plants that cannot themselves seed).

The use of GMOs: some potential problems, safeguards, and solutions

Issue	Problem	Safeguard or solution
Accidental release of GMOs into the environment	Recombinant DNA may be taken up by non-target, organisms. e.g. *weeds may take up a gene for herbicide resistance*. These unintended GMOs may have the potential to become pests or cause disease.	Legislation to control the production and release of GMOs varies in different countries. These controls are usually rigorous and strictly enforced. GMOs may have specific genes deleted so that their growth requirements can only be met under particular laboratory environments.
A new gene or genes may disrupt normal gene function	In humans, gene disruption may trigger cancer. In animals, successful transformation and expression of the desired gene is frequently very low.	Future developments in producing transgenic livestock involve the combination of genetic engineering, cloning, and screening so that only successfully transformed cells are used to produce organisms.
Targeted use of transgenic organisms in the environment	Once their desired function in the environment, e.g. environmental clean-up, has been completed, they may be undesirable invaders in the ecosystem	Organisms can be engineered to contain "suicide genes" or inherent metabolic deficiencies so that they do not survive for long in the new environment after completion of their task.
Use of antibiotic resistant genes as markers to identify transgenic organisms in culture	Spread of antibiotic resistance amongst non-target organisms. It has been shown that gut bacteria can take up genes for antibiotic resistance from ingested food products (e.g. wheat and soy products).	None, although alternative methods, such as gene probes, can be used to identify transformed cells. Better food labelling helps consumers identify foods made from GMOs but, even with this precaution, the problem has not been adequately addressed.

1. Suggest why genetically modified (GM) plants are thought to pose a greater environmental threat than GM animals:

_____

_____

_____

2. Describe an advantage and a problem with the use of genetically engineered herbicide resistant crop plants:

    (a) Advantage: _____

    _____

    (b) Problem: _____

    _____

3. Describe an advantage and a problem with using tropical crops genetically engineered to grow in cold regions:

    (a) Advantage: _____

    _____

    (b) Problem: _____

    _____

4. Describe an advantage and a problem with using crops that are genetically engineered to grow in marginal habitats (for example, in very saline or poorly aerated soils):

    (a) Advantage: _____

    _____

    (b) Problem: _____

    _____

5. Describe two uses of transgenic animals within the livestock industry:

    (a) _____

    (b) _____

6. Recently, Britain banned the import of a genetically engineered, pest resistant corn variety containing marker genes for ampicillin antibiotic resistance. Suggest why there was concern over using such marker genes:

    _____

    _____

7. Many agricultural applications of DNA technology make use of transgenic bacteria which infect plants and express a foreign gene. Explain one advantage of each of the following applications of genetic engineering to crop biology:

    (a) Development of nitrogen-fixing *Rhizobium* bacteria that can colonize non-legumes such as corn and wheat:

    _____

    (b) Addition of transgenic *Pseudomonas fluorescens* bacteria into seeds (bacterium produces a pathogen-killing toxin):

    _____

8. Some of the public's fears and concerns about genetically modified food stem from moral or religious convictions, while others have a biological basis and are related to the potential biological threat posed by GMOs.
    (a) Conduct a class discussion or debate to identify these fears and concerns, and list them below:

    _____

    _____

    _____

    _____

    (b) Identify which of those you have listed above pose a real biological threat: _____

    _____

    _____

    _____

Cloning by Nuclear Transfer

Clones are genetically identical individuals produced from one parent. Cloning is not new; it has been used in plant breeding for years. The early methods of animal cloning involved **embryo splitting**; a process that mimics the natural process of producing identical twins. In recent years clones have been produced from both embryonic and non-embryonic cells using **nuclear transfer**

techniques (below). In animal reproductive technology, cloning has facilitated the rapid production of genetically superior stock. These animals may then be dispersed among commercial herds. The **primary focus** of the new cloning technologies is to provide an economically viable way to rapidly produce transgenic animals with very precise genetic modifications.

Creating Dolly Using Nuclear Transfer

Dolly, the Finn Dorset lamb born at the Roslin Institute (near Edinburgh) in July 1996, was the first mammal to be cloned from **non-embryonic cells**. Nuclear transfer has been used successfully to clone cells from embryonic tissue, but Dolly was created from a fully differentiated udder cell from a six year old ewe. This cell was made quiescent and then 'tricked' into re-entering an embryonic state. Dolly's birth was a breakthrough, because it showed that the processes leading to cell specialization are not irreversible; even specialized cells can be 'reprogrammed' into an embryonic state. The steps involved in creating Dolly are outlined below. While cloning seems relatively easy to achieve using this method, Dolly's early death (right) has raised concerns that the techniques could have caused premature aging. Although there is, as yet, no evidence for this, the long term viability of animals cloned from non-embryonic cells has still to be established.

Dolly Dies

Dolly the sheep was euthanased (put to sleep) on **February 14th, 2003** after examinations showed she had developed progressive lung disease. Dolly was six years old; half the normal life expectancy of sheep. Post mortem examinations showed that her demise was due to a viral infection, not uncommon in older sheep, especially those housed inside. Despite the concerns of some scientists, there is no evidence that cloning was a factor in Dolly contracting the disease.

1 **Donor cells taken from udder:** Cells from the udder of a Finn Dorset ewe were cultured in low nutrient medium for a week. The nutrient deprived cells stopped dividing, switched off their active genes, and became dormant.

2 **Unfertilized egg has nucleus removed:** In preparation for the nuclear transfer, an **unfertilized** egg cell was taken from a Scottish blackface ewe. Using micromanipulation techniques, the nucleus containing the DNA, was removed. This left a recipient egg cell with no nucleus, but an intact cytoplasm and the cellular machinery for producing an embryo.

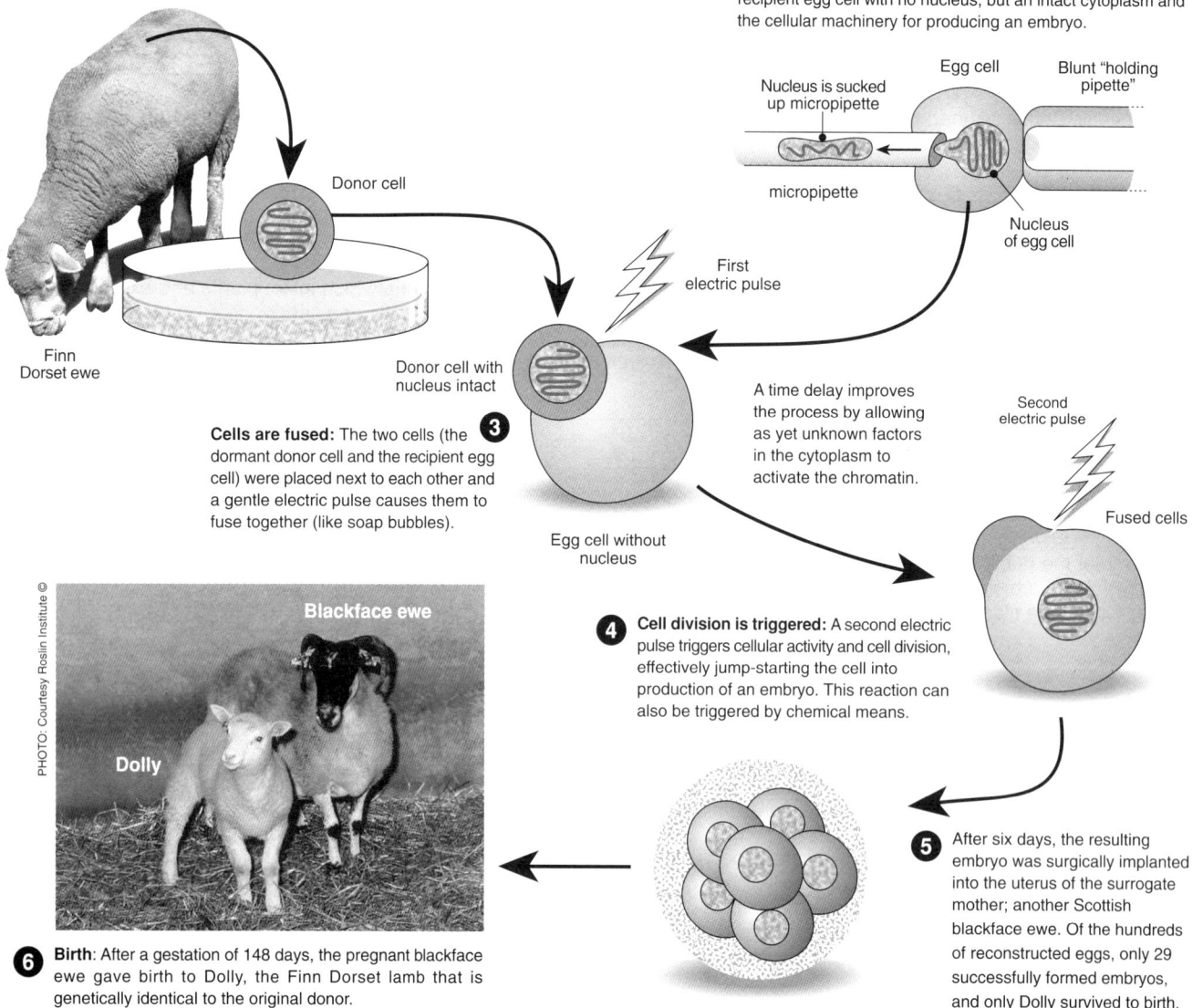

Nucleus is sucked up micropipette
Egg cell
Blunt "holding pipette"
micropipette
Nucleus of egg cell

Donor cell
Finn Dorset ewe
Donor cell with nucleus intact
First electric pulse

Cells are fused: The two cells (the dormant donor cell and the recipient egg cell) were placed next to each other and a gentle electric pulse causes them to fuse together (like soap bubbles). **3**

Egg cell without nucleus

A time delay improves the process by allowing as yet unknown factors in the cytoplasm to activate the chromatin.

Second electric pulse
Fused cells

4 **Cell division is triggered:** A second electric pulse triggers cellular activity and cell division, effectively jump-starting the cell into production of an embryo. This reaction can also be triggered by chemical means.

Blackface ewe
Dolly

6 **Birth**: After a gestation of 148 days, the pregnant blackface ewe gave birth to Dolly, the Finn Dorset lamb that is genetically identical to the original donor.

5 After six days, the resulting embryo was surgically implanted into the uterus of the surrogate mother; another Scottish blackface ewe. Of the hundreds of reconstructed eggs, only 29 successfully formed embryos, and only Dolly survived to birth.

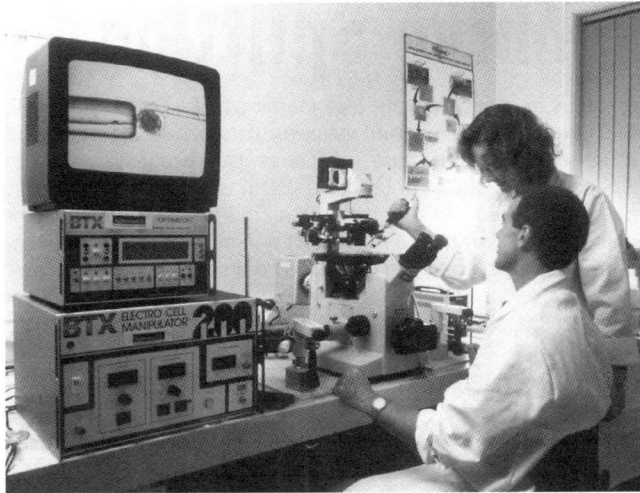

Embryo micromanipulation laboratory in Hamilton, New Zealand. Such labs use sophisticated equipment to manipulate ova (monitor's image is enlarged, right).

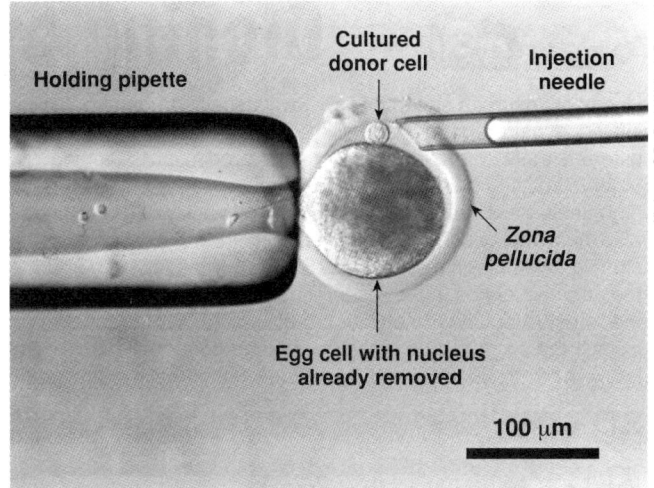

A single cultured cell is injected underneath the *zona pellucida* (the outer membrane) and positioned next to the egg cell (step 3 of diagram on the left).

Adult cloning heralds a new chapter in the breeding of livestock. Traditional breeding methods are slow, unpredictable, and suffer from a time delay in waiting to see what the phenotype is like before breeding the next generation. Adult cloning methods now allow a rapid spread of valuable livestock into commercial use among farmers. It will also allow the livestock industry to respond rapidly to market changes in the demand for certain traits in livestock products. In New Zealand, 10 healthy clones were produced from a single cow (the differences in coat color patterns arise from the random migration of pigment cells in early embryonic development).

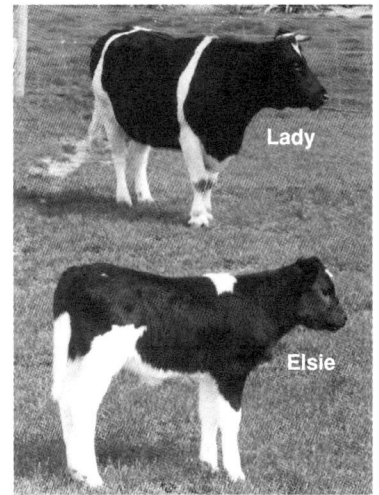

Lady is the last surviving cow of the rare Enderby Island (south of NZ) cattle breed. Adult cloning was used to produce her genetic duplicate, Elsie (born 31 July 1998). This result represents the first demonstration of the use of adult cloning in animal conservation.

1. Define the term **adult cloning** (as it relates to nuclear transfer techniques involving adult animals):

_____

_____

2. Explain how adult cloning differs from **embryo splitting**: _____

_____

3. Explain how each of the following events is controlled in the **nuclear transfer** process:

    (a) The switching off of all genes in the donor cell: _____

    _____

    (b) The fusion (combining) of the donor cell with the enucleated egg cell: _____

    _____

    (c) The activation of the cloned cell into producing an embryo: _____

    _____

4. Identify three potential applications of nuclear transfer technology for the cloning of animals: _____

_____

_____

Cloning by Embryo Splitting

Livestock, such as sheep or cows, will usually produce only one individual per pregnancy and all the individuals in a herd will have different traits (e.g. wool growth, milk production). Cloning (by embryo splitting or by other means) makes it possible to produce high value herds with identical traits very quickly. This technique also has applications in the medical field, for example, in the cloning of embryonic stem cells. Such applications demonstrate the huge advances made recently in cloning technology. Some of the most ambitious medical projects now being considered involve the production of universal human donor cells. Scientists know how to isolate undifferentiated stem cells from early embryos in mice. They are also learning how to force stem cells to differentiate into different tissues. Such techniques may make it possible to manufacture cells or replace tissue damaged by illness (e.g. diabetes, AIDS, Parkinson's, and muscular dystrophy). Stem cells matched to an individual patient could be made by transferring the nucleus of one of the patient's cells into a human egg to create an embryo. The embryo would be allowed to develop only to a stage needed to separate and culture undifferentiated stem cells from it. The embryo would consist of a few hundred cells and would therefore have no nervous system with which to sense the environment or feel pain.

Livestock are selected for cloning on the basis of desirable qualities such as wool, meat, or milk productivity.

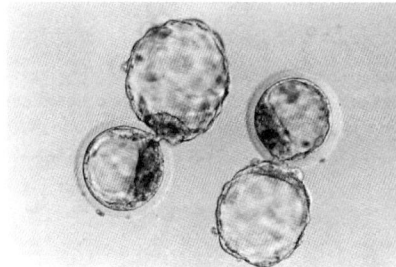

Cloned embryos immediately prior to implantation into a surrogate. These are at the blastocyst stage (a mass of cells that have begun to differentiate).

The individuals produced by embryo splitting have the same characteristics as the parents.

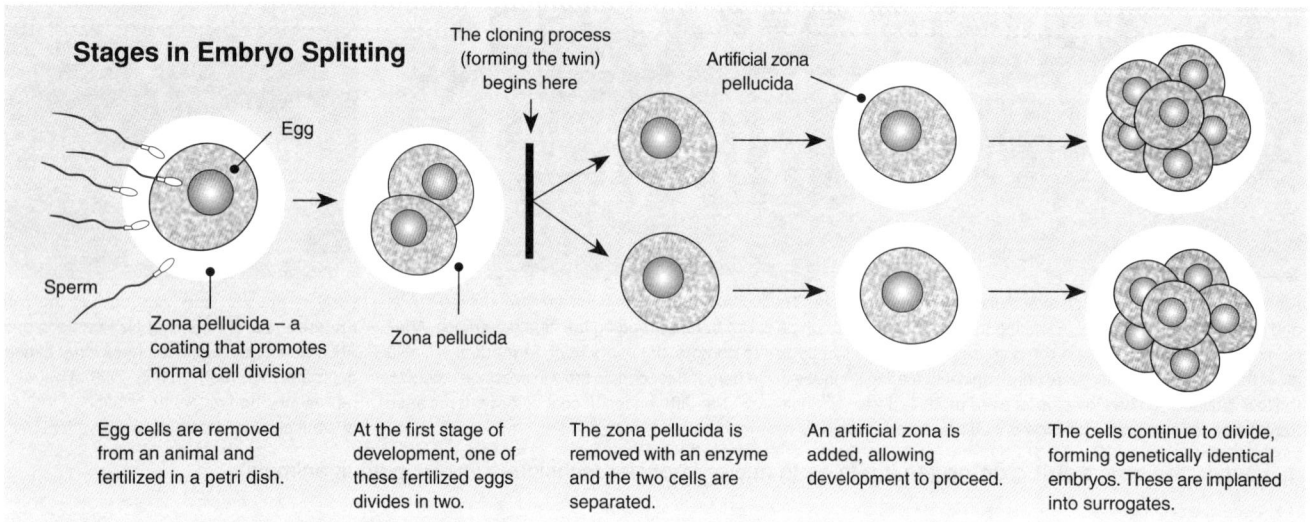

Stages in Embryo Splitting

Egg cells are removed from an animal and fertilized in a petri dish.

At the first stage of development, one of these fertilized eggs divides in two.

The zona pellucida is removed with an enzyme and the two cells are separated.

An artificial zona is added, allowing development to proceed.

The cells continue to divide, forming genetically identical embryos. These are implanted into surrogates.

1. With respect to animals, define the term **cloning**: _____

_____

2. Briefly list the possible benefits to be gained from cloning the following:

(a) Stem cells for medical use: _____

_____

_____

_____

(b) High milk yielding cows: _____

_____

_____

_____

3. Suggest one reason why it would undesirable to produce all livestock using embryo splitting: _____

_____

The Human Cloning Debate

The most controversial aspect of cloning is the potential to clone humans. In situations where couples cannot have children or where one prospective parent has a heritable genetic disease, cloning could produce a healthy child that is genetically the couple's own. However, the issue of human cloning raises concerns that clones may be generated out of vanity or that couples may want 'designer' clones e.g. of celebrities. One of the most promising applications of cloning is in the production of **stem cells**. Stem cells have the ability to generate a variety of cell types. This makes them potentially very useful for the treatment of a number of diseases. In many cases of traditional tissue transplantation, the patient's immune system rejects the donated cells. Cloning could solve this problem; if a patient's own cells could be used to generate stem cells, there would be no risk of rejection. Similarly, cloned stem cells could generate organs for transplantation. This would prevent immune rejection problems and alleviate the problem of organ shortages. Despite the potential benefits of cloning, there are enormous moral and ethical concerns surrounding its use. Before cloning can become a viable technology, these concerns need to be addressed.

Arguments Used **Against** Human Cloning	Arguments Used **For** Human Cloning
• Cloning might lead to the creation of genetically engineered groups of people for specific purposes, such as for warfare or slavery.	• Cloning would enable infertile couples to have children of their own.
• Cloning might lead to an attempt to improve the human race according to an arbitrary standard.	• Cloning would give couples at risk of producing a child with a genetic defect the chance to produce a healthy child.
• Cloning could result in the introduction of additional defects in the human gene pool.	• Cloning could shed light on how genes work and could lead to the discovery of new treatments for genetic diseases.
• Cloning is unsafe. There are too many unknown factors that could adversely affect the offspring.	• A ban on cloning may be unconstitutional. It would deprive people of the right to reproduce and restrict scientific freedom.
• A clone may have a diminished sense of individuality.	• A clone would not really be a duplicate, because environmental factors would mould him or her into a unique individual.
• A clone may have fewer rights than other people.	
• Clones may be created with the sole intention of using them as a source of organs and tissues for transplantation.	• A clone would have as much of a sense of individuality as do twins.
• Cloning is at odds with the traditional concept of family.	• A clone would have the same rights as do all other people.
• Cloning is against God's will.	• Cloning is comparable in safety to a number of other medical procedures.
• Some aspects of human life should be off limits to science.	• The current objections to cloning are similar to objections raised against scientific procedures developed earlier that are now largely accepted. Examples include heart transplants and some of the standard reproductive technologies (IVF).
• The cloning technique has not been perfected. Scientists expect that any attempt to clone a human would, as in the work that led to Dolly, result in the death of many embryos and newborns before success was achieved.	

Source: www.worldbook.com

1. Conduct a **survey** of your class, or perhaps even a wider sample of part of your school, to determine whether people approve or disapprove of the cloning of human embryos for the following purposes. Convert your results into percentages approving or disapproving of the use and enter them in the spaces below:

(a) To provide infertile couples using test tube *in vitro* fertilization with more embryos to increase their chances of conceiving.

Approve: _____ Disapprove: _____

(b) To make it easier for scientists to screen embryos for inherited abnormalities (such as cystic fibrosis and Huntington's disease).

Approve: _____ Disapprove: _____

(c) To produce babies whose vital organs can be used to save the life of others, such as a sibling requiring a bone marrow transplant.

Approve: _____ Disapprove: _____

(d) To make it possible for parents to have a twin at a later date.

Approve: _____ Disapprove: _____

(e) To establish 'embryo banks' from which prospective parent could select a child with genetic desirable traits.

Approve: _____ Disapprove: _____

(f) To make it possible for societies to clone and reproduce a number of individuals with genetically desirable traits for specific purposes (e.g. academics, soldiers, basketball players, or musicians).

Approve: _____ Disapprove: _____

(g) Your 2 month old baby is about to be taken off life support. You and your partner can no longer bear children. Would you clone the child if it were an option?

Approve: _____ Disapprove: _____

(h) Do you consider rejecting an 8-cell embryo produced in a lab to be an abortion?

Yes: _____ No: _____

(i) If scientist were able to produce new organs using your cells and cloning technology, would you consider receiving them:

Yes: _____ No: _____

(Source: questions (a) - (f) CNN/TIME Magazine survey, 8 Nov 1993, p53)

Ecosystems

IB SL
Complete nos:
1-4, 7

Extension: 5-6

IB HL
Complete nos:
1-4, 7

Extension: 5-6

IB Options
Complete nos:
Option G: 7, 9-10,
13-14, 16-24, 26
Extension: 8, 11-
12, 25, 27

AP Biology
Complete nos:
1-27
Some numbers
extension as
appropriate

Learning Objectives

□ 1. Compile your own glossary from the **KEY WORDS** displayed in **bold type** in the learning objectives below.

Biomes and ecosystems *(pages 250-252)*

□ 2. Define the terms: **ecology**, **ecosystem**, **community**, **population**, **species**, and **environment**, and provide examples of each. Distinguish between **biotic factors** and **abiotic factors** in terms of your definition of an ecosystem. Recognize that ecosystems are dynamic entities and are subject to change.

□ 3. Identify the different components of a named ecosystem - the living and non-living things that make up the ecosystem. In a general way, explain how the different parts of an ecosystem influence each other.

□ 4. Explain how the **biosphere** consists of interdependent and interrelated ecosystems. Appreciate the implications of this with respect to the impact that humans have on their environment.

□ 5. Recognize major **biomes** on Earth and explain how they are classified according to major vegetation type. Appreciate the influence of latitude and local climate in determining the distribution of world biomes.

□ 6. Describe an example of an ecosystem with which you are familiar. Include reference to the community (including the predominant **vegetation** type) and the abiotic factors that determine the characteristics of the ecosystem.

Habitat and niche

Habitats and microclimates *(pages 253-259, 291)*

□ 7. Define the term **habitat** and provide an example. List the factors used to describe a habitat. Recognize the habitat as part of the described niche of a **species**. Describe how variation in abiotic factors in a habitat may produce **microclimates** and that these influence species distribution and diversity in a general area.

□ 8. Understand the concept of **limiting factor** and explain how limiting factors restrict species distribution.

□ 9. Describe the factors (especially abiotic factors) that affect the distribution of plant species within an environment, including temperature, availability of water and light, soil pH, salinity, and mineral nutrients.

□ 10. Describe the biotic and abiotic factors that affect the distribution of animal species within an environment, including temperature, availability of water and breeding sites, food supply, and territory.

Environmental gradients *(pages 256-260)*

□ 11. Describe how abiotic factors may interact so that one factor changes another. Describe how gradients in physical factors can occur over a relatively short distance, e.g. on a rocky shore, in a forest, in a lake. Explain the cause of these gradients in each case.

□ 12. With reference to specific examples, describe the main features of the two most common types of distributional variation within a community: **zonation** and **stratification**. Explain how these patterns arise and how they increase the amount of community diversity. Identify the factors that determine the distribution of species within these communities.

The ecological niche *(pages 261-265)*

□ 13. Define the term '**ecological niche**' (niche), and describe examples for a variety of species. List the factors that are used to describe the niche.

□ 14. Recognize the constraints that are normally placed on the actual niche occupied by an organism. Distinguish between the **fundamental** and the **realized niche**. Demonstrate an understanding of Gause's **competitive exclusion** principle with respect to niche overlap between species. Understand the effects of competition on niche breadth.

□ 15. Explain what is meant by the term **adaptation** and describe examples. Recognize that organisms show **physiological**, **structural**, and **behavioral adaptations** for survival in a given niche and that these are the result of changes that occur to the species as a whole, but not to individuals within their own lifetimes.

The diversity and stability of ecosystems

Appreciation of diversity

□ 16. Recognize that the collection of quantitative population data provides the means by which to study ecosystems in a meaningful way. Identify the types of data that may be collected from communities.
NOTE: The techniques used for the sampling and analysis of populations and ecosystems are described in *Practical Ecology*, later in this manual.

Ecosystem diversity *(pages 266-267)*

□ 17. Explain what is meant by the stability of an ecosystem and identify its components. Explain the relationship between ecosystem stability and diversity.

□ 18. Explain the basis for the following relationships:
- The usually low stability and low diversity of extreme environments where abiotic factors predominate in determining population distribution and abundance.
- The usually high stability and high diversity of more moderate environments where biotic factors predominate in determining population distribution and abundance.

□ 19. Calculate and interpret an **index of diversity**. Appreciate the applications and disadvantages of diversity indices in natural ecosystems and in those modified by human activity.

Ecological succession *(pages 268-269)*

□ 20. Explain what is meant by the term **ecological succession**. Recognize succession as a community pattern in time that is the result of the interaction of species with their environment.

□ 21. Describe primary succession from **pioneer species** to a **climax community**. Identify the species typical of each **seral stage**, distinguishing between the features of the pioneer species and those species typical of the climax community.

□ 22. Explain how each seral stage (change in the biotic community) alters the physical environment such that conditions are made more favorable for the establishment of the next seral stage.

□ 23. Distinguish clearly between **primary** and **secondary succession**, outlining the features of each type. Include reference to the time scale over which these successions take place.

□ 24. Appreciate how the **climax** vegetation varies according to local climate, latitude, and altitude.

□ 25. Explain what is meant by a **deflected succession** and describe how such a succession arises. Explain the nature of the **plagioclimax** that develops as a result of a deflected succession.

□ 26. **Describe** one example of succession, identifying the effects of named organisms on the succession:
   (a) *Primary succession*: For example, the development of a climax community after volcanic activity or following glacial retreat.
   (b) *Secondary succession*: For example, the change occurring in abandoned agricultural land to established climax woodland.
   (c) *Deflected succession*: As when a particular community composition is maintained through human intervention (e.g. mowing or grazing).

□ 27. Describe how community diversity changes during the course of a succession (or **sere**). Comment on the stability of the pioneer and climax communities and relate this to the relative importance of abiotic and biotic factors at each stage.

Textbooks

See the 'Textbook Reference Grid' on pages 8-9 for textbook page references relating to material in this topic.

Supplementary Texts

See pages 5-6 for additional details of these texts:

■ Adds, J., *et al.,* 2001. **Genetics, Evolution and Biodiversity**, (NelsonThornes), pp. 28-35, 40-45, 61.

■ Allen *et al.*, 2001. **Applied Ecology** (Collins), pp. 13-19, 22-25, 34-44.

■ Chenn, P., 1999. **Ecology** (John Murray), pp. 1-6, 95-112.

Periodicals

See page 6 for details of publishers of periodicals:

STUDENT'S REFERENCE

Ecosystems and physical factors

■ **Climate Now** New Scientist, 16 March 1991 (Inside Science). *The reasons for different global weather patterns in space and time.*

■ **The Other Side of Eden** Biol. Sci. Rev., 15(3) February 2003, pp. 2-7. *An account of the Eden Project – the collection of artificial ecosystems in Cornwall. Its aims, future directions, and its role in the study of natural ecosystems and ecosystem modeling are discussed.*

■ **Extreme Olympics** New Scientist, 30 March 2002 (Inside Science). *Extreme ecosystems and the adaptations of the organisms that live in them.*

■ **How Climate Affects Plant Distribution** Biol. Sci. Rev., 7(5) May 1995, pp. 34-37. *The effects of climate on plant distribution. Good maps to indicate how abiotic factors affect distributions.*

■ **Biodiversity and Ecosystems** Biol. Sci. Rev., 11(4) March 1999, pp. 18-23. *Ecosystem diversity and its relationship to ecosystem stability.*

■ **All Life is Here** New Scientist, 15 March 1997, pp. 24-26. *Small, stagnant water bodies provide ideal models for studying biodiversity and ecosystem function.*

■ **Secrets from Another Earth** New Scientist, 18 May 1996, pp. 31-35. *Creation of an artificial ecological system - an enclosed biosphere.*

■ **Big Weather** New Scientist, 22 May 1999 (Inside Science). *Global weather patterns and their role in shaping the ecology of the planet.*

■ **Plants on the Move** New Scientist, 20 March 1999 (Inside Science). *Understanding how plants have coped with past climates could help us to predict how distributions will change in the future.*

Adaptation, habitat, and niche

■ **The Ecological Niche** Biol. Sci. Rev., 12(4), March 2000, pp. 31-35. *An excellent account of the niche - an often misunderstood concept that is never-the-less central to ecological theory.*

■ **The European Swift** Biol. Sci. Rev., 10(5) May 1998, pp. 23-25. *The niche of the European swift: includes detail of the anatomy, physiology, and behavior of this well known bird species.*

■ **Woodlice** Biol. Sci. Rev., 9(3) January 1997, pp. 39-41. *The biology and ecology of woodlice, including their adaptations to their terrestrial niche.*

Ecosystem patterns in space and time

■ **Birth of an Island** New Scientist, 25 Nov. 1995, pp. 36-39. *The development of an island provides the perfect chance to observe the colonization of a new and barren environment.*

■ **Plant Succession** Biol. Sci. Rev., 14 (2) November 2001, pp. 2-6. *Thorough coverage of primary and secondary succession, including the causes of different types of succession.*

TEACHER'S REFERENCE

■ **Life on the Edge** New Scientist, 20 November 1999, pp. 46-49. *If a new niche is all it takes for a new species to develop, then the space to find them is at the boundaries of rainforest: a place where new niches are available for exploitation.*

■ **Life Support** New Scientist, 15 August 1998, pp. 30-34. *What is the true cost of losing species diversity in ecosystems? The importance of biodiversity in the stability of ecosystems and their ability to recover from human impacts.*

■ **Learning Ecology by Doing Ecology** The American Biology Teacher, 61(3), March,1999, pp. 217-222. *Methods for developing long term field experiments to better teach ecology. A specific field experiment on mowing treatments over a time frame of a year is discussed.*

■ **The Flora of North America Project** The American Biology Teacher, 59(6), June,1997, pp. 338-343. *Studying the ecology and distribution of North American floral types.*

■ **Trenoids: An Ecological Simulation** The American Biology Teacher, 65(2), Feb. 2003, pp. 122-127. *How-to-do-it lab investigating the nature of taxa that fill a variety of habitats and niches*

■ **Ecology and Evolution of Wall-Dwelling Organisms** The American Biology Teacher, 62(6), June, 2000, pp. 429-435. *How-to-do-it ecology for improving understanding of habitat and niche, and basic community structure.*

■ **Textbook Misconceptions - the Climax Concept of Succession** The American Biology Teacher, 58(3), March, 1996, pp.135-140. *Community, succession and a discussion of the viability of the 'climax community' concept. Such communities are believed to be rare in nature.*

Internet

See pages 10-11 for details of how to access **Bio Links** from our web site: **www.thebiozone.com**. From Bio Links, access sites under the topics:

GENERAL BIOLOGY ONLINE RESOURCES > Online Textbooks and Lecture Notes • An on-line biology book • Learn.co.uk • Mark Rothery's biology web site ... *and others*

ECOLOGY: • EarthTrends: Information portal • eNature • Introduction to biogeography and ecology • Ken's bioweb referencing • NatureWorks

> Ecosystems: • Bright edges of the world • Canada's aquatic environment • Coral reef ecology • Desert biome • Freshwater ecosystems • Marine science • The rocky intertidal zone • Vegetation map checklist • What are ecosystems? ... *and others*

Biomes

A 2

Global patterns of vegetation distribution are closely related to climate. Although complex, major vegetation **biomes** can be recognized. These are large areas where the vegetation type shares a particular suite of physical requirements.

Biomes have characteristic features, but the boundaries between them are not distinct. The same biome may occur in widely separated regions of the world wherever the climatic and soil conditions are similar.

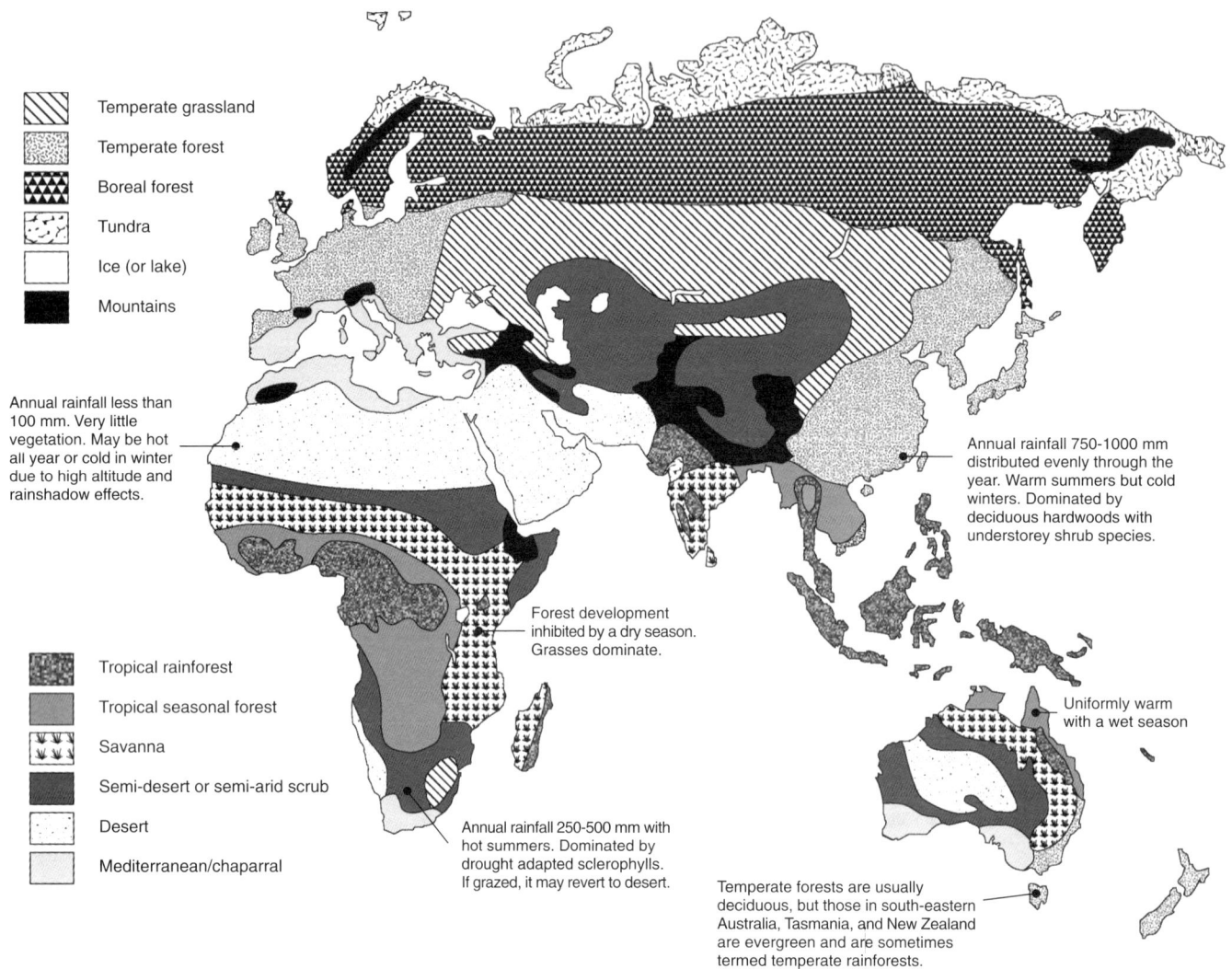

Temperate grassland

Temperate forest

Boreal forest

Tundra

Ice (or lake)

Mountains

Annual rainfall less than 100 mm. Very little vegetation. May be hot all year or cold in winter due to high altitude and rainshadow effects.

Annual rainfall 750-1000 mm distributed evenly through the year. Warm summers but cold winters. Dominated by deciduous hardwoods with understorey shrub species.

Tropical rainforest

Tropical seasonal forest

Savanna

Semi-desert or semi-arid scrub

Desert

Mediterranean/chaparral

Forest development inhibited by a dry season. Grasses dominate.

Uniformly warm with a wet season

Annual rainfall 250-500 mm with hot summers. Dominated by drought adapted sclerophylls. If grazed, it may revert to desert.

Temperate forests are usually deciduous, but those in south-eastern Australia, Tasmania, and New Zealand are evergreen and are sometimes termed temperate rainforests.

Tundra

Semi-arid scrub

Mediterranean/chaparral

Desert

1. Suggest what abiotic factor(s) limit the northern extent of boreal forest:

_____

2. Grasslands have about half the productivity of tropical rainforests, yet this is achieved with less than a tenth of the biomass – i.e. grasslands are more productive per unit of biomass. Suggest how this greater efficiency is achieved:

_____

_____

_____

Vegetation patterns are determined largely by climate but can be modified markedly by human activity. Semi-arid areas that are overgrazed will revert to desert and have little ability to recover. Similarly, many chaparral regions no longer support their original vegetation, but are managed for vineyards and olive groves. Wherever they occur, mountainous regions are associated with their own altitude adapted vegetation. The rainshadow effect of mountains governs the distribution of deserts in some areas too, as in Chile and the Gobi desert in Asia. The classification of biomes may vary slightly; some sources distinguish hot deserts (such as the Sahara) from cold deserts and semi-deserts (such as the Gobi). However, most classifications recognize desert, tundra, grassland and forest types and differentiate them on the basis of latitude.

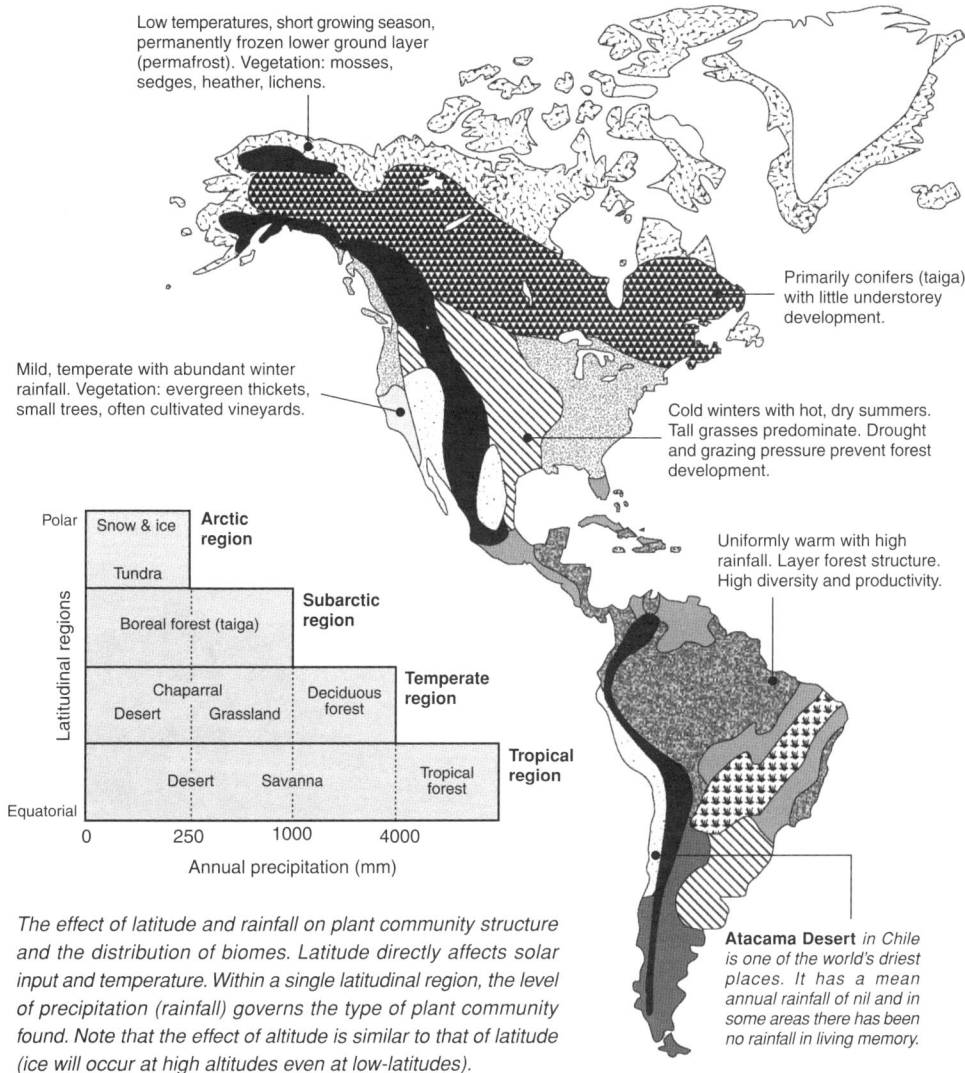

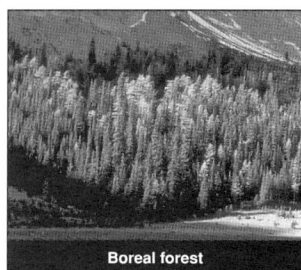

Low temperatures, short growing season, permanently frozen lower ground layer (permafrost). Vegetation: mosses, sedges, heather, lichens.

Primarily conifers (taiga) with little understorey development.

Mild, temperate with abundant winter rainfall. Vegetation: evergreen thickets, small trees, often cultivated vineyards.

Cold winters with hot, dry summers. Tall grasses predominate. Drought and grazing pressure prevent forest development.

Uniformly warm with high rainfall. Layer forest structure. High diversity and productivity.

Tropical rainforest

Tropical seasonal forest

Savanna

Temperate forest

Polar	Snow & ice	**Arctic region**
	Tundra	
	Boreal forest (taiga)	**Subarctic region**
	Chaparral / Desert / Grassland	Deciduous forest	**Temperate region**
	Desert / Savanna	Tropical forest	**Tropical region**
Equatorial		

Latitudinal regions

0   250   1000   4000

Annual precipitation (mm)

The effect of latitude and rainfall on plant community structure and the distribution of biomes. Latitude directly affects solar input and temperature. Within a single latitudinal region, the level of precipitation (rainfall) governs the type of plant community found. Note that the effect of altitude is similar to that of latitude (ice will occur at high altitudes even at low-latitudes).

Atacama Desert in Chile is one of the world's driest places. It has a mean annual rainfall of nil and in some areas there has been no rainfall in living memory.

Temperate grassland

Ice

Mountains

Boreal forest

3. Suggest a reason for the occurrence of deserts and semi-desert areas in northern parts of Asia and in the west of North and South America (away from equatorial regions):

_____

4. Compared with its natural extent (on the map), little unaltered temperate forest now exists. Explain why this is the case:

_____

_____

_____

Components of an Ecosystem

The concept of the ecosystem was developed to describe the way groups of organisms are predictably found together in their physical environment. A community comprises all the organisms within an ecosystem. Both physical (abiotic) and biotic factors affect the organisms in a community, influencing their distribution and their survival, growth, and reproduction.

The Biosphere

The **biosphere** containing all the Earth's living organisms amounts to a narrow belt around the Earth extending from the bottom of the oceans to the upper atmosphere. Broad scale life-zones or **biomes** are evident within the biosphere, characterized according to the predominant vegetation. Within these biomes, **ecosystems** form natural units comprising the non-living, physical environment (the air, soil, and water) and the **community** (all the populations of different species living and interacting in a particular area).

Physical Environment

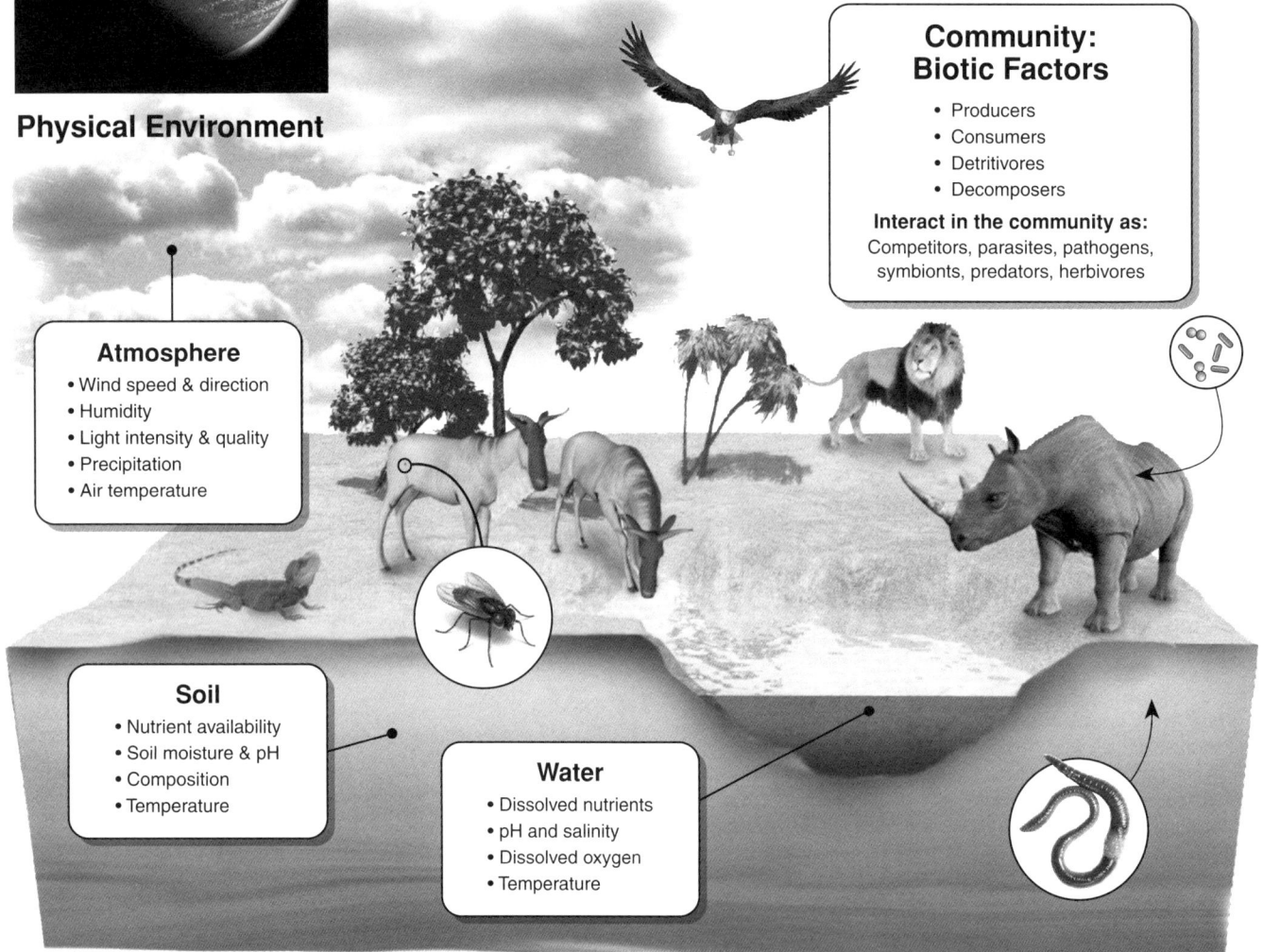

Community: Biotic Factors

- Producers
- Consumers
- Detritivores
- Decomposers

Interact in the community as:
Competitors, parasites, pathogens, symbionts, predators, herbivores

Atmosphere
- Wind speed & direction
- Humidity
- Light intensity & quality
- Precipitation
- Air temperature

Soil
- Nutrient availability
- Soil moisture & pH
- Composition
- Temperature

Water
- Dissolved nutrients
- pH and salinity
- Dissolved oxygen
- Temperature

1. Distinguish clearly between a community and an ecosystem: _____

_____

_____

2. Define the term: physical environment: _____

_____

3. Distinguish between biotic and abiotic factors: _____

_____

4. Use one or more of the following terms to describe each of the features of a rainforest listed below:
   Terms: *population, community, ecosystem, physical factor.*

   (a) All the howler monkeys present: _____ (c) All the organisms present: _____

   (b) The entire forest: _____ (d) The humidity: _____

RA②

Habitats

The environment in which an organism lives (including all the physical and biotic factors) is termed its **habitat**. For each of the organisms below, briefly describe their habitat (an example is provided). As well as describing the general environment (e.g. river, swamp), include detail about the biotic and abiotic factors in the habitat which enable the organism to thrive.

Jew's ear fungus: *Auricularia auricula*

Herring gull: *Larus argentatus*

Coyote: *Canis latrans*

White-tailed deer: *Odocoileus virginianus*

Common barn owl: *Tyto alba*

Oak: *Quercus virginiana*

1. General habitat of the Jew's ear fungus: Woodland, especially on elder.

   (a) Biotic factors: Source of live and/or dead wood (usually elder) from which to obtain its nutrition.

   (b) Abiotic factors: Autumnal: needs cooler temperatures, high moisture levels in the soil and high humidity.

2. General habitat of the herring gull: _____

   (a) Biotic factors: _____

   (b) Abiotic factors: _____

3. General habitat of a coyote: _____

   (a) Biotic factors: _____

   (b) Abiotic factors: _____

4. General habitat of white-tailed deer: _____

   (a) Biotic factors: _____

   (b) Abiotic factors: _____

5. General habitat of the common barn owl: _____

   (a) Biotic factors: _____

   (b) Abiotic factors: _____

6. General habitat of an oak tree: _____

   (a) Biotic factors: _____

   (b) Abiotic factors: _____

Dingo Habitats

An organism's habitat is not always of a single type. Some animals range over a variety of habitats, partly in order to obtain different resources from different habitats, and sometimes simply because they are forced into marginal habitats by competition. Dingoes are found throughout Australia, in ecosystems as diverse as the tropical rainforests of the north to the arid deserts of the Centre. Within each of these ecosystems, they may frequent several habitats or microhabitats. The information below shows how five dingo packs exploit a variety of habitats at one location in Australia. The table on the facing page shows how dingoes are widespread in their distribution and are found living in a variety of ecosystems.

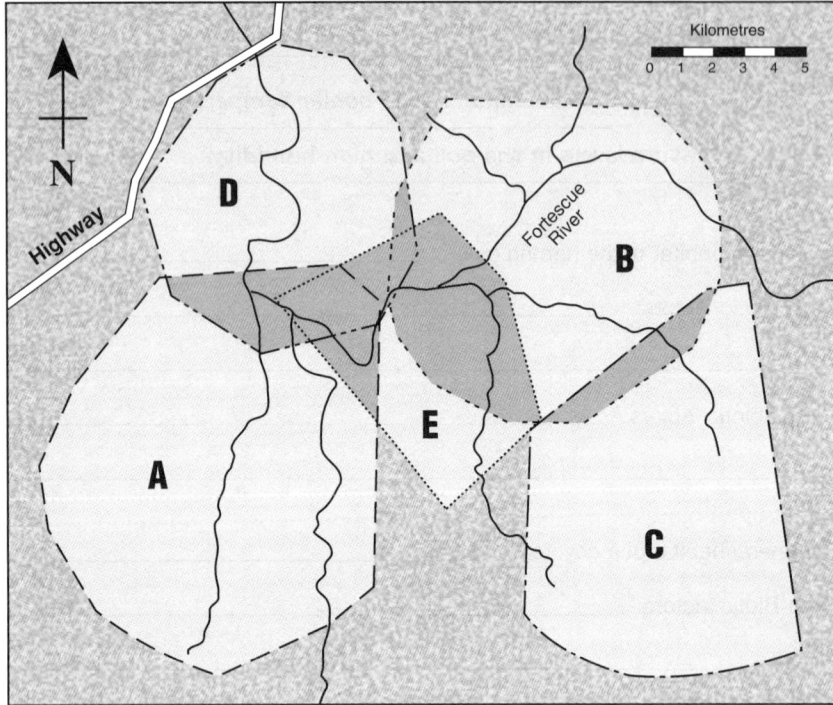

The map on the left shows the territories of five stable dingo packs (A to E) in the Fortescue River region in north-west Australia. The territories were determined by 4194 independent radio-tracking locations over 4 years. The size and nature of each territory, together with the makeup of each pack is given in the table below. The major prey of the dingoes in this region are large kangaroos (red kangaroos and euros).

Adapted from: Corbett, L. *The dingo in Australia and Asia*, 1995. University of NSW Press, after (original source) Thomson, P.C. 1992. *The behavioural ecology of dingoes in north-west Australia. IV. Social and spatial organisation, and movements. Wildlife Research* 19: 543-563.

Dingo pack name	Territory area (km²)	Pack size	Dingo density	Index of kangaroo abundance	Habitat types and usage in each territory (%)							
					Riverine		Stony		Floodplain		Hills	
Pack A	113	12	10.6	15.9%	10%	(49%)	1%	(2%)	21%	(6%)	69%	(44%)
Pack B	94	12		8.5%	14%	(43%)	9%	(10%)	38%	(25%)	39%	(23%)
Pack C	86	3		3.9%	2%	(3%)	0%	(0%)	63%	(94%)	35%	(3%)
Pack D	63	6		12.3%	12%	(35%)	5%	(8%)	46%	(20%)	37%	(37%
Pack E	45	10	22.2	8.4%	14%	(31%)	6%	(4%)	39%	(18%)	42%	(47%)

mean number of dingoes per 100 km² (calculated by you)

Percentage of observations of kangaroos per observations of dingoes

Portion of the territory with this kind of habitat

Percentage of time spent by the pack in this habitat

1. Calculate the density of each of the dingo packs at the Fortescue River site above (two have been done for you). Remember that to determine the density, you carry out the following calculation:

   Density = Pack size ÷ Territory area x 100   (to give the mean number per 100 km²)

2. Name the dominant habitat (or habitats) for each territory in the table above (eg. riverine, stony, floodplain, hills):

   (a) Pack A: _____

   (b) Pack B: _____

   (c) Pack C: _____

   (d) Pack D: _____

   (e) Pack E: _____

Dingo home range size in contrasting ecosystems

Location (study site)	Ecosystem	Range (km²)
3 Fortescue River, North-west Australia	Semi-arid, coastal plains and hills	77
6 Simpson Desert, Central Australia	Arid, gibber (stony) and sandy desert	67
1 Kapalga, Kakadu N.P., North Australia	Tropical, coastal wetlands and forests	39
4 Harts Ranges, Central Australia	Semi-arid, river catchment and hills	25
9 Kosciusko N.P., South-east Australia	Moist, cool forested mountains	21
8 Georges Creek N.R., East Australia	Moist, cool forested tablelands	18
11 Nadgee N.R., South-east Australia	Moist, cool coastal forests	10

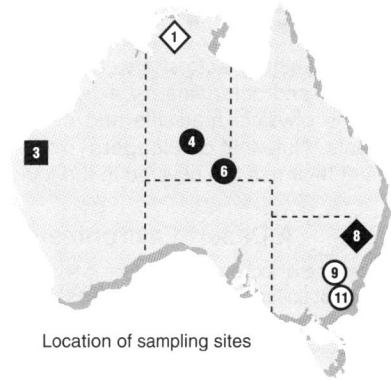

Location of sampling sites

The **home ranges** of neighboring dingo individuals and pack **territories** sometimes overlap to some degree, but individuals or packs avoid being in these communal areas (of overlap) at the same time. This overlap occurs especially during the breeding season or in areas where resources are shared (e.g. hunting grounds, water holes). Different ecosystem types appear to affect the extent of the home ranges for dingoes living in them.

3. Study the table on the previous page and determine which (if any) was the preferred habitat for dingoes (give a reason for your answer):

_____

_____

4. The dingoes at this site were studied using radio-tracking methods.

(a) Explain how radio-tracking can be used to determine the movements of dingoes: _____

_____

_____

(b) State how many independent tracking locations were recorded during this study: _____

(c) State how long a period of time the study was run for: _____

(d) Explain why so many records were needed over such a long period of time: _____

_____

_____

5. From the table on the previous page, state whether the relative kangaroo abundance (the major prey of the dingo) affects the density that a given territory can support:

_____

_____

6. Study the table at the top of this page which shows the results of an investigation into the sizes of home ranges in dingo populations from different ecosystems.

(a) Describe the feature of the ecosystems that appears to affect the size of home ranges: _____

_____

(b) Explain how this feature might affect how diverse (varied) the habitats are within the ecosystem:

_____

_____

_____

🖐 DA② Physical Factors and Gradients

Gradients in abiotic factors are found in almost every environment; they influence habitats and microclimates, and determine patterns of species distribution. This activity, covering the next four pages, examines the physical gradients and microclimates that might typically be found in four, very different environments. Note that **dataloggers** (pictured right), are being increasingly used to gather such data. The principles of their use are covered in the topic 'Practical Ecology".

A Desert Environment

Desert environments experience extremes in temperature and humidity, but they are not uniform with respect to these factors. This diagram illustrates hypothetical values for temperature and humidity for some of the microclimates found in a desert environment at midday.

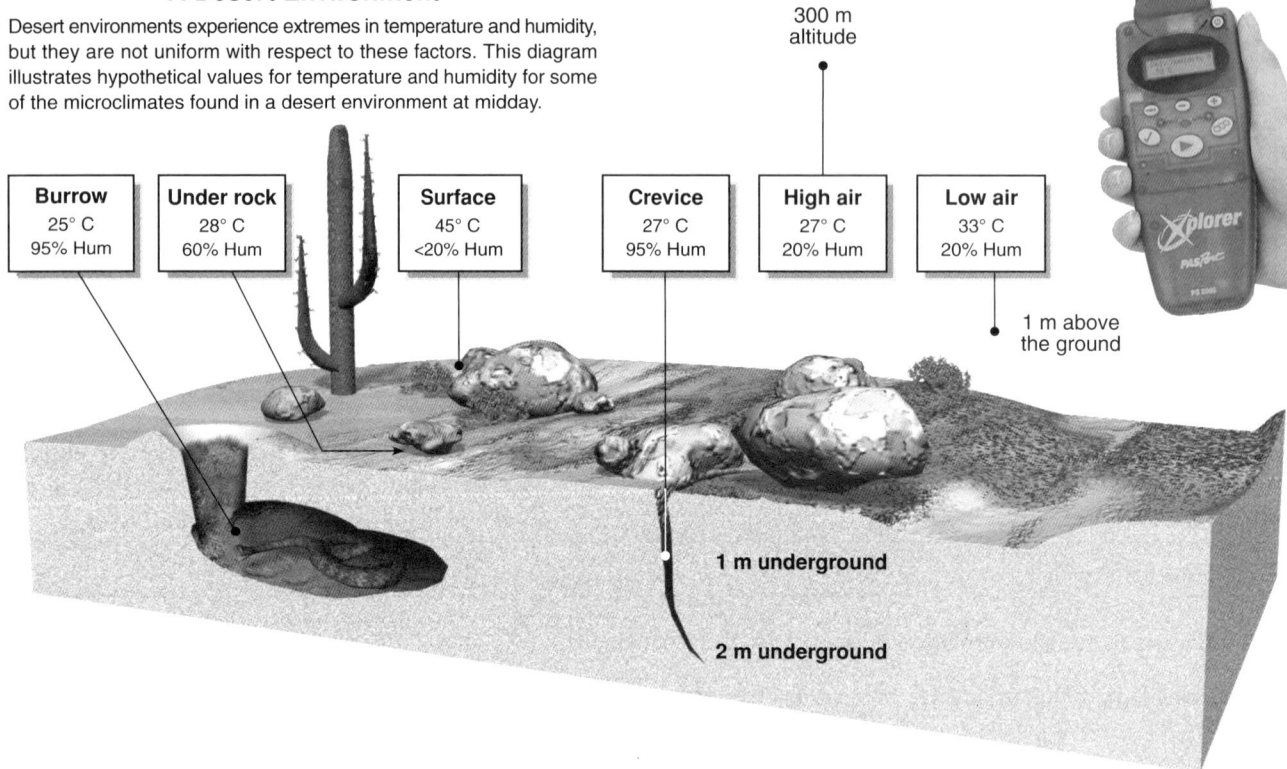

300 m altitude

Burrow	Under rock	Surface	Crevice	High air	Low air
25° C	28° C	45° C	27° C	27° C	33° C
95% Hum	60% Hum	<20% Hum	95% Hum	20% Hum	20% Hum

1 m above the ground

1 m underground

2 m underground

1. Explain the term **microclimate**: _____

2. Study the diagram above and describe the general conditions where high humidity is found: _____

3. Name the three microclimates that a land animal might exploit to avoid the extreme high temperatures of midday:

4. Describe the likely consequences for an animal that was unable to find a suitable microclimate to escape midday sun:

5. Describe the advantage of high humidity to the survival of most land animals: _____

6. Describe the likely changes to the temperature and relative humidity that occur during the night: _____

Physical Factors at Low Tide on a Rock Platform

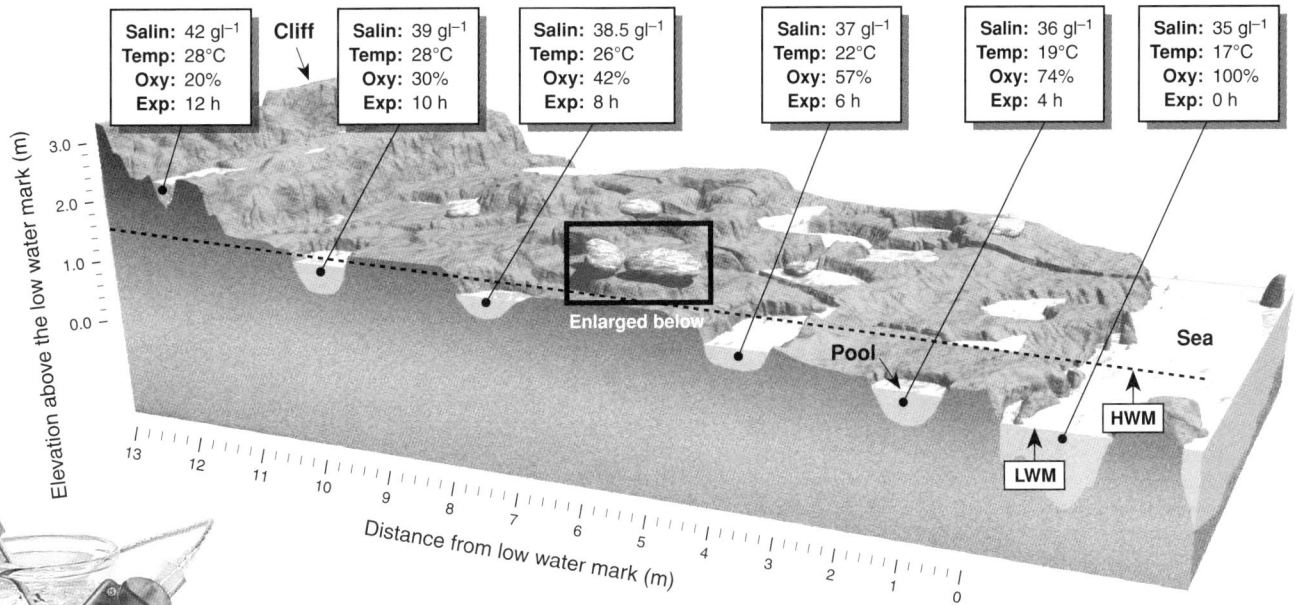

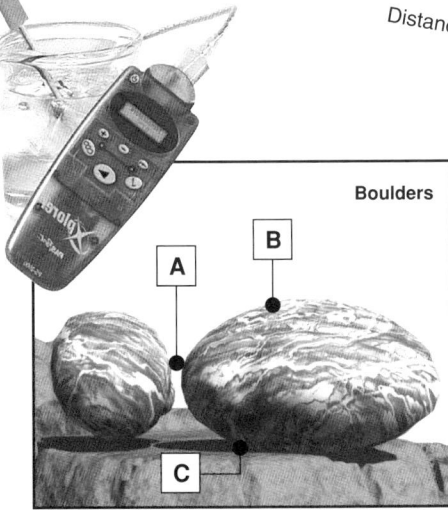

Salin: 42 gl⁻¹	Cliff

Salin: 42 gl^{-1} **Cliff**
Temp: 28°C
Oxy: 20%
Exp: 12 h

Salin: 39 gl^{-1}
Temp: 28°C
Oxy: 30%
Exp: 10 h

Salin: 38.5 gl^{-1}
Temp: 26°C
Oxy: 42%
Exp: 8 h

Salin: 37 gl^{-1}
Temp: 22°C
Oxy: 57%
Exp: 6 h

Salin: 36 gl^{-1}
Temp: 19°C
Oxy: 74%
Exp: 4 h

Salin: 35 gl^{-1}
Temp: 17°C
Oxy: 100%
Exp: 0 h

Elevation above the low water mark (m)

Enlarged below

Pool

Sea

HWM

LWM

Distance from low water mark (m)

Boulders

A   B   C

The diagram above shows a profile of a rock platform at low tide. The **high water mark** (HWM) shown here is the average height the spring tide rises to. In reality, the high tide level will vary with the phases of the moon (i.e. spring tides and neap tides). The **low water mark** (LWM) is an average level subject to the same variations due to the lunar cycle. The rock pools vary in size, depth, and position on the platform. They are isolated at different elevations, trapping water from the ocean for time periods that may be brief or up to 10 –

12 hours duration. Pools near the HWM are exposed for longer periods of time than those near the LWM. The difference in exposure times results in some of the physical factors exhibiting a **gradient**; the factor's value gradually changes over distance. Physical factors sampled in the pools include salinity, or the amount of dissolved salts (g) per liter (**Salin**), temperature (**Temp**), dissolved oxygen compared to that of open ocean water (**Oxy**), and exposure, or the amount of time isolated from the ocean water (**Exp**).

7. Describe the environmental gradient (general trend) from the low water mark (LWM) to the high water mark (HWM) for:

(a) Salinity: _____

(b) Temperature: _____

(c) Dissolved oxygen: _____

(d) Exposure: _____

8. Rock pools above the normal high water mark (HWM), such as the uppermost pool in the diagram above, can have wide extremes of salinity. Explain why these pools, under different conditions, may have either:

(a) Very low salinity: _____

_____

(b) Very high salinity: _____

_____

9. In the inset diagram (above, right) is an enlarged view of two boulders on the rock platform. The points labeled A, B and C experience physical conditions that differ from each other, even though they are on the same rock. Describe how the physical factors listed below may differ at each of the labeled points:

(a) Mechanical force of wave action: _____

_____

(b) Surface temperature when exposed: _____

_____

Physical Factors in a Tropical Rainforest

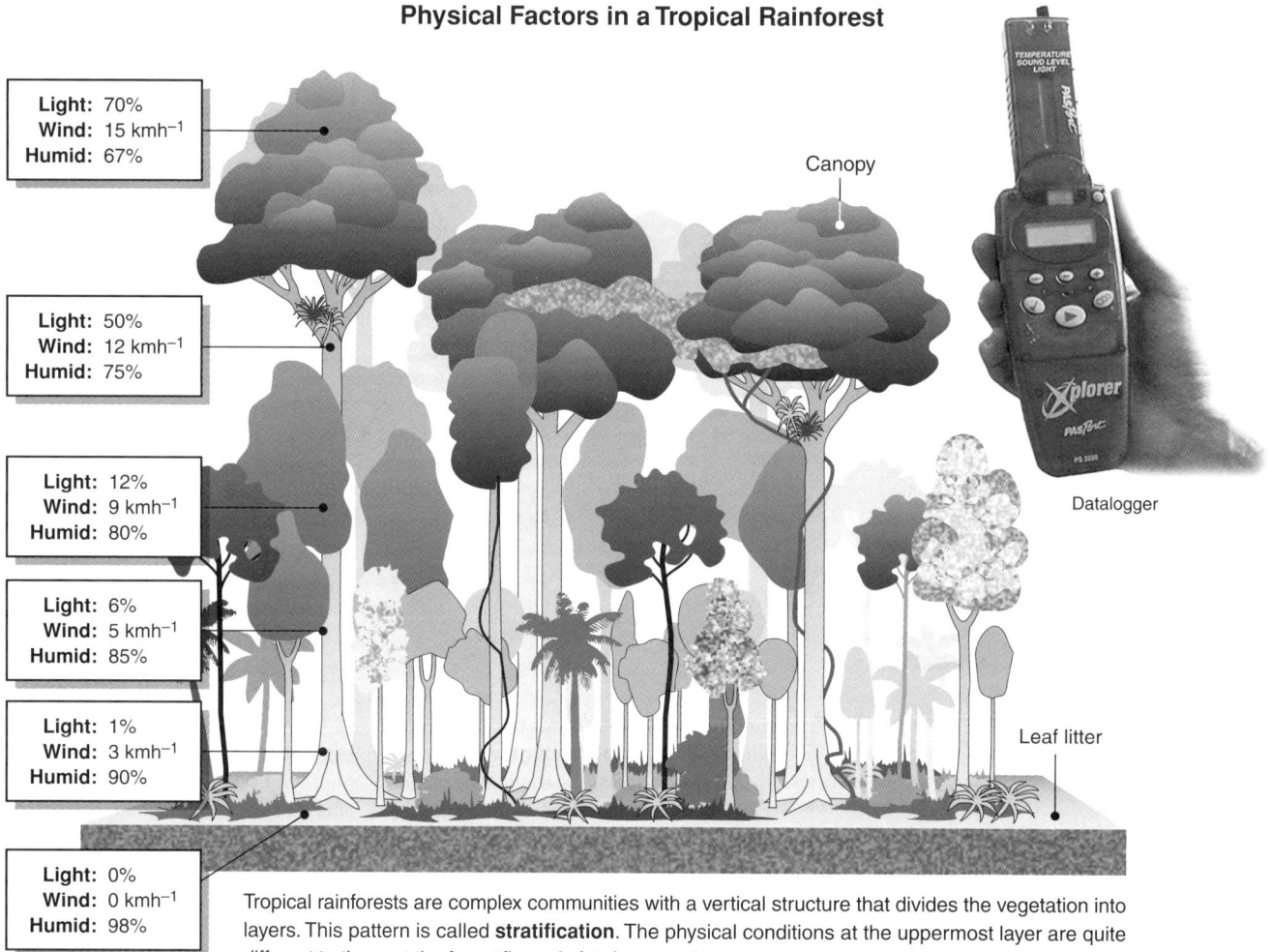

Light: 70%
Wind: 15 kmh⁻¹
Humid: 67%

Light: 50%
Wind: 12 kmh⁻¹
Humid: 75%

Light: 12%
Wind: 9 kmh⁻¹
Humid: 80%

Light: 6%
Wind: 5 kmh⁻¹
Humid: 85%

Light: 1%
Wind: 3 kmh⁻¹
Humid: 90%

Light: 0%
Wind: 0 kmh⁻¹
Humid: 98%

Canopy

Datalogger

Leaf litter

Tropical rainforests are complex communities with a vertical structure that divides the vegetation into layers. This pattern is called **stratification**. The physical conditions at the uppermost layer are quite different to those at the forest floor. A **datalogger** with suitable probes was used to gather data about three factors: *light intensity* (**Light**), *wind speed* (**Wind**), and *humidity* (**Humid**). These data are provided above for each layer. Note that light intensity is given here as a percentage of full sunlight.

10. Describe the environmental gradient (general trend) from the canopy to the leaf litter for:

(a) Light intensity: _____

(b) Wind speed: _____

(c) Humidity: _____

11. Explain why each of these factors changes as the distance from the canopy increases:

(a) Light intensity: _____

_____

(b) Wind speed: _____

_____

(c) Humidity: _____

_____

12. Apart from the intensity of light penetrating the forest foliage, what other feature of the light will change with distance:

_____

_____

13. Plants growing on the forest floor have some advantages and disadvantages with respect to the physical factors.

(a) Name one advantage: _____

(b) Name one disadvantage: _____

Physical Factors in an Oxbow Lake in Summer

Oxbow lakes are formed from old river meanders that have been cut off and become isolated from the main channel following the change of the river's course. Commonly, they are very shallow (about 2-4 meters deep) but occasionally they may be deep enough to develop temporary, but relatively stable, temperature gradients from top to bottom (below). Small lakes are relatively closed systems and events in them are independent of those in other nearby lakes, where quite different water quality may be found. The physical factors are not constant throughout the water in the lake. Surface water and water near the lake margins can have quite different values for such factors as water temperature (**Temp**), dissolved oxygen (**Oxygen**) measured in milligrams per liter (mg l^{-1}), and light penetration (**Light**) indicated here as a percentage of the light striking the surface.

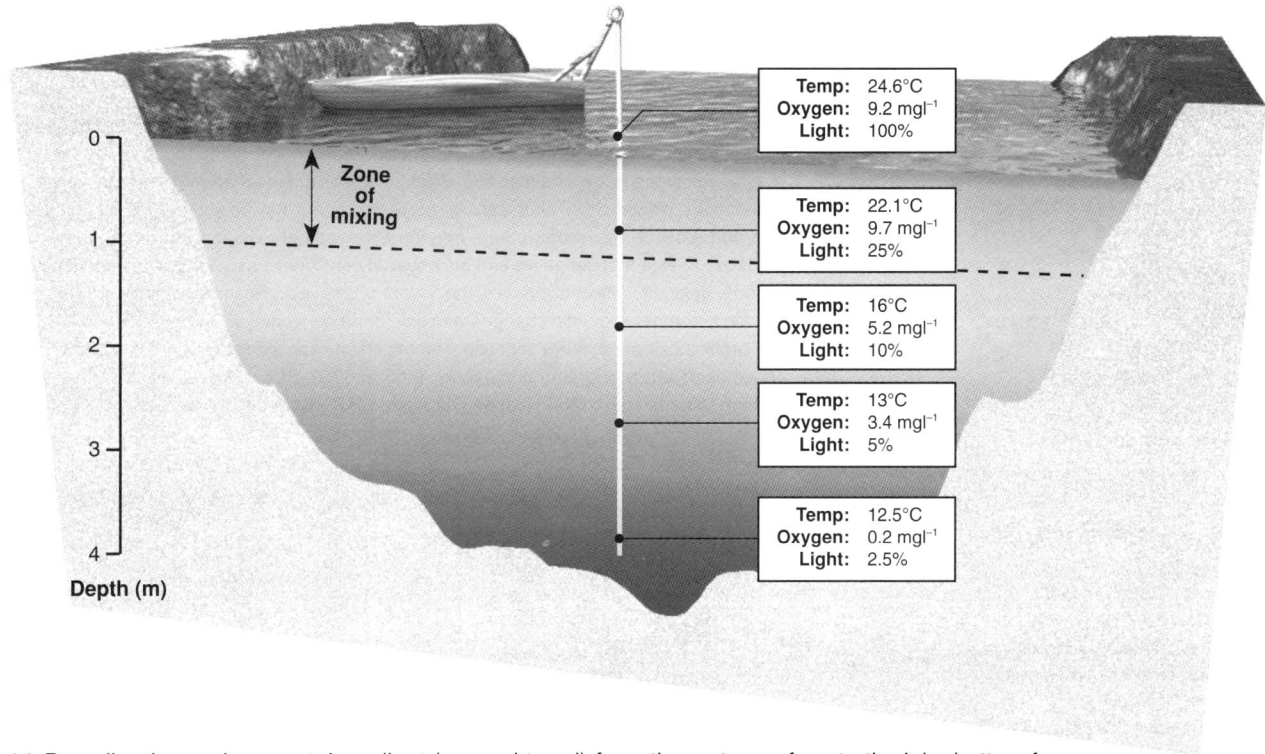

Temp:	24.6°C
Oxygen:	9.2 mgl⁻¹
Light:	100%

Temp:	22.1°C
Oxygen:	9.7 mgl⁻¹
Light:	25%

Temp:	16°C
Oxygen:	5.2 mgl⁻¹
Light:	10%

Temp:	13°C
Oxygen:	3.4 mgl⁻¹
Light:	5%

Temp:	12.5°C
Oxygen:	0.2 mgl⁻¹
Light:	2.5%

Zone of mixing

Depth (m)

14. Describe the environmental gradient (general trend) from the water surface to the lake bottom for:

(a) Water temperature: _____

(b) Dissolved oxygen: _____

(c) Light penetration: _____

15. During the summer months, the warm surface waters are mixed by gentle wind action. Deeper cool waters are isolated from this surface water. This sudden change in the temperature profile is called a **thermocline** which itself is a further barrier to the mixing of shallow and deeper water.

(a) Explain the effect of the presence of the thermocline on the dissolved oxygen at the bottom of the lake:

_____

_____

(b) Describe what causes the oxygen level to drop to the low level: _____

_____

_____

16. Many of these shallow lakes can undergo great changes in their conductivity (dissolved ions):

(a) Describe an event that could suddenly reduce the conductivity of small lake: _____

_____

_____

(b) Describe a process that can gradually increase the conductivity of a small lake: _____

_____

_____

Shoreline Zonation

A 2

Zonation refers to the division of an ecosystem into distinct zones that experience similar abiotic conditions. In a more global sense, differences in latitude and altitude create distinctive zones of vegetation type, or **biomes**. Ecosystem zonation is particularly clear on a rocky seashore, where assemblages of different species form a banding pattern approximately parallel to the waterline. This effect is marked in temperate regions where the prevailing weather comes from the same general direction.

Exposed shores show the clearest zonation. On sheltered rocky shores there is considerable species overlap and it is only on the upper shore that distinct zones are evident. Rocky shores exist where wave action prevents the deposition of much sediment. The rock forms a stable platform for the secure attachment of organisms such as large seaweeds and barnacles. Sandy shores are less stable than rocky shores and the organisms found there are adapted to the more mobile substrate (see below).

Rocky shore at Sleahead, Ireland.

Seashore Zonation Patterns

The zonation of species distribution according to an environmental gradient is well shown on rocky shorelines. In Britain, exposed rocky shores occur along much of the western coasts. Variations in low and high tide affect zonation, and in areas with little tidal variation, zonation is restricted. High on the shore, some organisms may be submerged only at spring high tide. Low on the shore, others may be exposed only at spring low tide. There is a gradation in extent of exposure and the physical conditions associated with this. Zonation patterns generally reflect the vertical movement of seawater. Sheer rocks can show marked zonation as a result of tidal changes with little or no horizontal shift in species distribution. The profiles below left, show zonation patterns on an exposed rocky shore (left profile) with an exposed sandy shore for comparison (right profile). **SLT** = Spring low tide mark, **MLT** = Mean low tide mark, **MHT** = Mean tide mark, **SHT** = Spring high tide mark.

Key to species

1. Lichen: sea ivory
2. Small periwinkle *Littorina neritoides*
3. Lichen *Verrucaria maura*
4. Rough periwinkle *Littorina saxatilis*
5. Common limpet *Patella vulgaris*
6. Laver *Porphyra*
7. Spiral wrack *Fucus spiralis*
8. Australian barnacle
9. Common mussel *Mytilus edulis*
10. Common whelk *Buccinum undatum*
11. Grey topshell *Gibbula cineraria*
12. Carrageen (Irish moss) *Chondrus crispus*
13. Thongweed *Himanthalia elongata*
14. Toothed wrack *Fucus serratus*
15. Dabberlocks *Alaria esculenta*
16. Common sandhopper
17. Sandhopper *Bathyporeia pelagica*
18. Common cockle *Cerastoderma edule*
19. Lugworm *Arenicola marina*
20. Sting winkle *Ocinebra erinacea*
21. Common necklace shell *Natica alderi*
22. Rayed trough shell *Mactra corallina*
23. Sand mason worm *Lanice conchilega*
24. Sea anemone *Halcampa*
25. Pod razor shell *Ensis siliqua*
26. Sea potato *Echinocardium* (a heart urchin)

Note: Where several species are indicated within a single zonal band, they occupy the entire zone, not just the position where their number appears.

Exposed Rocky Shore

Exposed Sandy Shore

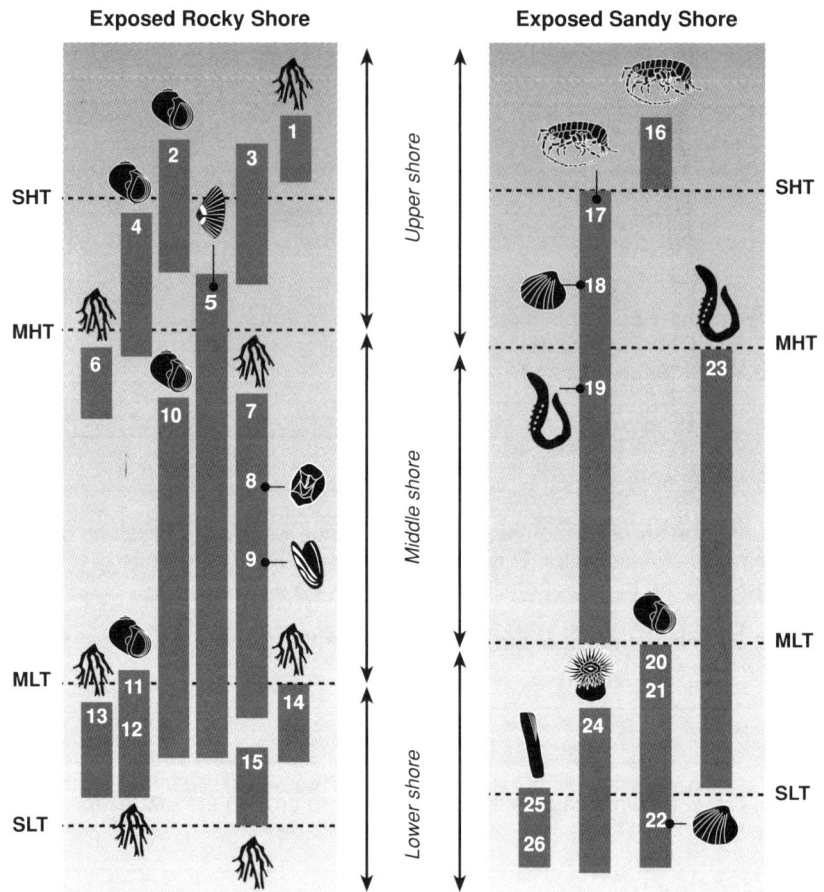

1. (a) Suggest why the time of exposure above water is a major factor controlling species distribution on a rocky shore: _____

_____

(b) List two other abiotic factors that might influence species distribution on a rocky shore: _____

_____

(c) List two biotic factors that might influence species distribution on a rocky shore: _____

_____

2. Describe the zonation pattern on a rocky shore: _____

Ecological Niche

A 2

The concept of the ecological niche has been variously described as an organism's 'job' or 'profession'. This is rather too simplistic for senior biology level. The **ecological niche** is better described as the functional position of an organism in its environment, comprising its habitat and the resources it obtains there, and the periods of time during which it is active. The diagram below illustrates the components that together define the niche of any organism. The full range of environmental conditions (biological and physical) under which an organism can exist describes its **fundamental niche**. As a result of pressure from, and interactions with, other organisms (e.g. superior competitors) species are usually forced to occupy a niche that is narrower than this and to which they are most highly adapted. This is termed the **realized niche**.

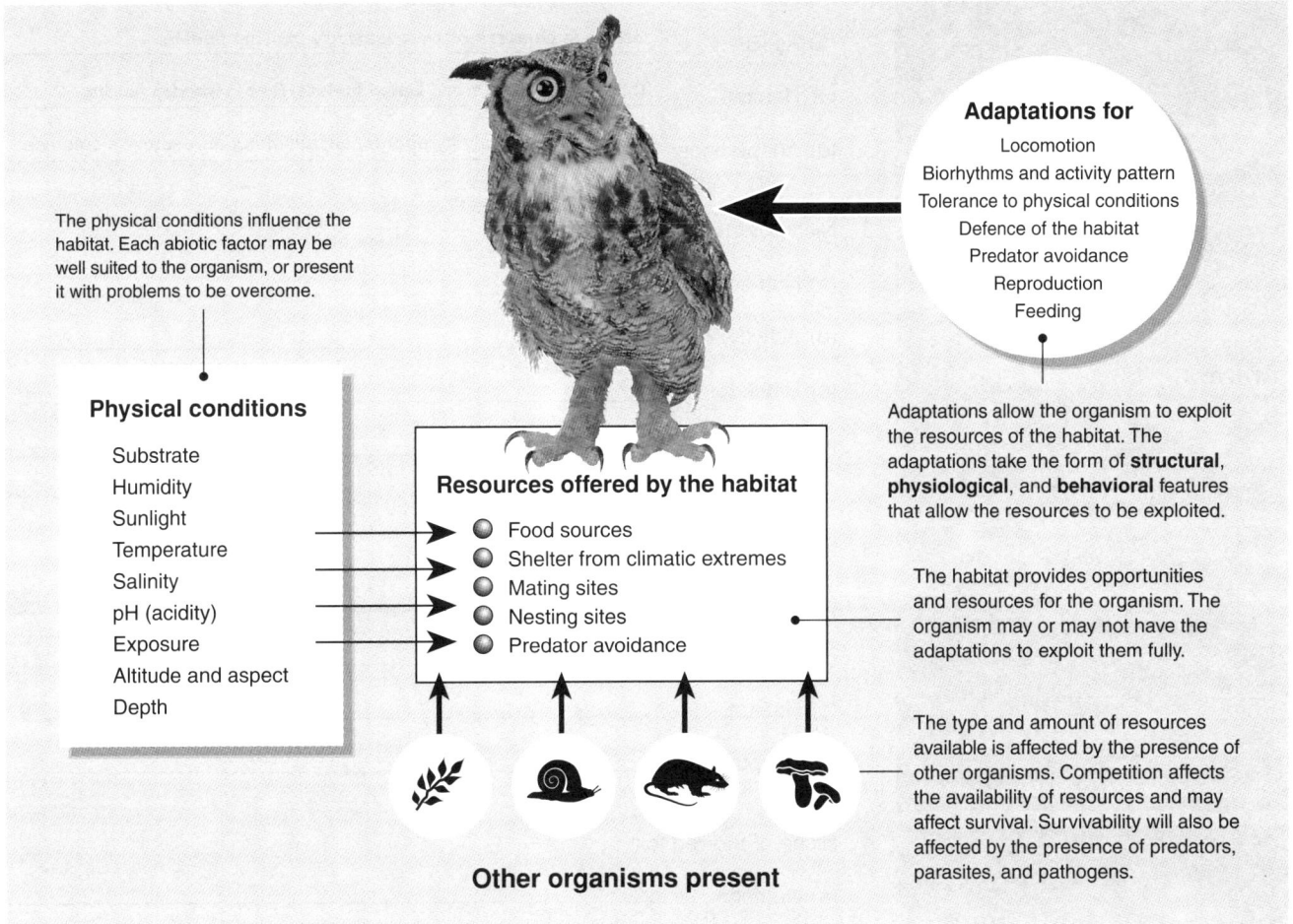

Adaptations for

Locomotion
Biorhythms and activity pattern
Tolerance to physical conditions
Defence of the habitat
Predator avoidance
Reproduction
Feeding

The physical conditions influence the habitat. Each abiotic factor may be well suited to the organism, or present it with problems to be overcome.

Physical conditions

Substrate
Humidity
Sunlight
Temperature
Salinity
pH (acidity)
Exposure
Altitude and aspect
Depth

Resources offered by the habitat

Food sources
Shelter from climatic extremes
Mating sites
Nesting sites
Predator avoidance

Adaptations allow the organism to exploit the resources of the habitat. The adaptations take the form of **structural**, **physiological**, and **behavioral** features that allow the resources to be exploited.

The habitat provides opportunities and resources for the organism. The organism may or may not have the adaptations to exploit them fully.

The type and amount of resources available is affected by the presence of other organisms. Competition affects the availability of resources and may affect survival. Survivability will also be affected by the presence of predators, parasites, and pathogens.

Other organisms present

1. Use the diagram above to develop your own definition of an **ecological niche**:

2. Explain why the niche actually occupied by an organism is narrower than the niche it could potentially occupy:

3. Gause's *Competitive Exclusion Principle* states that organisms occupying exactly the same niche cannot coexist because they will compete for the same resources. Using an example, explain how organisms with very similar habitat and feeding requirements can minimize niche overlap i.e. how do they differentiate their niches to avoid competition:

Ecological Niches

RA②

The concept of an organism's **ecological niche** is fundamental to understanding ecology. To fully describe a niche, take note of an organism's: trophic level, mode of feeding, activity periods, habitat and the resources exploited within it, as well as the adaptive features they possess to exploit them. Describe the **niche** for each of the following organisms:

White rot bracket fungus: *Coriolus*

1. Niche of the white rot bracket fungus:

   (a) Nutrition: Parasite of broadleaved trees using extracellular digestion.

   (b) Activity: Grows in clusters of thin, leathery fruiting bodies.

   (c) Habitat: Throughout most broad leaved forests. Pest in wooden fencing.

   (d) Adaptations: Spreads vigorously by spores, establishing as separate colonies.

Sea star: *Astropecten*

2. Niche of the sea star:

   (a) Nutrition: _____

   (b) Activity: _____

   (c) Habitat: _____

   (d) Adaptations: _____

Bluebottle blowfly: *Calliphora vomitoria*

3. Niche of the bluebottle blowfly:

   (a) Nutrition: _____

   (b) Activity: _____

   (c) Habitat: _____

   (d) Adaptations: _____

Red fox: *Vulpes vulpes*

4. Niche of the red fox:

   (a) Nutrition: _____

   (b) Activity: _____

   (c) Habitat: _____

   (d) Adaptations: _____

Pheasant: *Phasianus colchicus*

5. Niche of the pheasant:

   (a) Nutrition: _____

   (b) Activity: _____

   (c) Habitat: _____

   (d) Adaptations: _____

Gray squirrel: *Sciurus carolinensis*

6. Niche of the gray squirrel:

   (a) Nutrition: _____

   (b) Activity: _____

   (c) Habitat: _____

   (d) Adaptations: _____

Competition and Niche Size

DA ②

Niche size is affected by competition. The magnitude of the effect will vary depending on whether the competition is weak, moderate, or intense, and whether it is **intraspecific** or **interspecific**. The theoretical effects of competition on niche size are outlined in the diagram below. Further coverage of this topic is provided in '*The Dynamics of Populations*'.

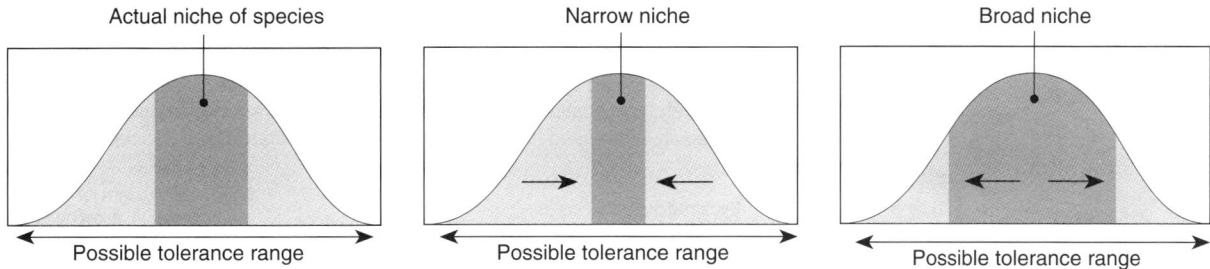

Actual niche of species — Possible tolerance range

Narrow niche — Possible tolerance range

Broad niche — Possible tolerance range

Moderate interspecific competition

The tolerance range represents the potential (**fundamental**) niche a species could exploit. The actual or **realized** niche a species occupies is smaller than its potential niche because of competition. Niches of closely related species may overlap at the extremes, resulting in competition for resources in the zones of overlap.

Intense interspecific competition

When the competition from one or more closely related species becomes intense, there is selection for a more limited niche. This severe competition prevents a species from exploiting potential resources in the more extreme parts of its tolerance range. As a result, niche breadth decreases (the niche becomes narrower).

Intense intraspecific competition

Competition is most severe between individuals of the same species, because their resource requirements are usually identical. When intraspecific competition is intense, individuals are forced to exploit resources in the extremes of their tolerance range. This leads to expansion of the realized niche to less preferred areas.

Overlap in resource use between competing species

From the concept of the niche arose the idea that two species with the same niche requirements could not coexist, because they would compete for the same resources, and one would exclude the other. This is known as Gause's "***competitive exclusion principle***". If two species compete for some of the same resources (e.g. food items of a particular size), their resource use curves will overlap. Within the zone of overlap competition between the two species will be intense.

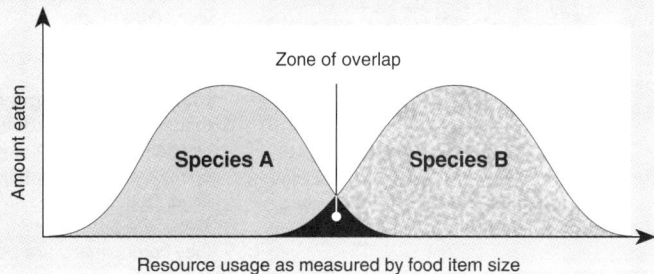

1. Define the following terms:

   (a) Interspecific competition: _____

   _____

   (b) Intraspecific competition: _____

   _____

2. Study the diagram above illustrating niche overlap between competing species and then answer the following questions:
   (a) Explain what you would expect to happen if the overlap in resource use of species A and B was to become very large (i.e. they utilized almost the same sized food item):

   _____

   (b) Describe how the degree of resource overlap might change seasonally: _____

   _____

   (c) If the zone of overlap between the resource use of the two species increased a little more from what is shown on the diagram, explain what is likely to happen to the breadth of the **actual** niche of each species:

   _____

3. Niche breadth can become broader in the presence of intense competition between members of the same species (top diagram). Describe one other reason why niche breadth could be very wide:

   _____

   _____

Adaptations to Niche

RA②

The adaptive features that evolve in species are the result of selection pressures on them through the course of their evolution. These features enable an organism to function most effectively in its niche, enhancing its exploitation of its environment and therefore its survival. The examples below illustrate some of the adaptations of two species: a British placental mammal and a migratory Arctic bird. Note that adaptations may be associated with an animal's structure (morphology), its internal physiology, or its behavior.

Northern or Common Mole
(Talpa europaea)

Head-body length: 113-159 mm, tail length: 25-40 mm, weight range: 70-130 g.

Mole hill

Lining of dry grass

Adult

Young

Moles (photos above) spend most of the time underground and are rarely seen at the surface. Mole hills are the piles of soil excavated from the tunnels and pushed to the surface. The cutaway view above shows a section of tunnels and a nest chamber. Nests are used for sleeping and raising young. They are dug out within the tunnel system and lined with dry plant material.

The northern (common) mole is a widespread insectivore found throughout most of Britain and Europe, apart from Ireland. They are found in most habitats but are less common in coniferous forest, moorland, and sand dunes, where their prey (earthworms and insect larvae) are rare. They are well adapted to life underground and burrow extensively, using enlarged forefeet for digging. Their small size, tubular body shape, and heavily buttressed head and neck are typical of burrowing species.

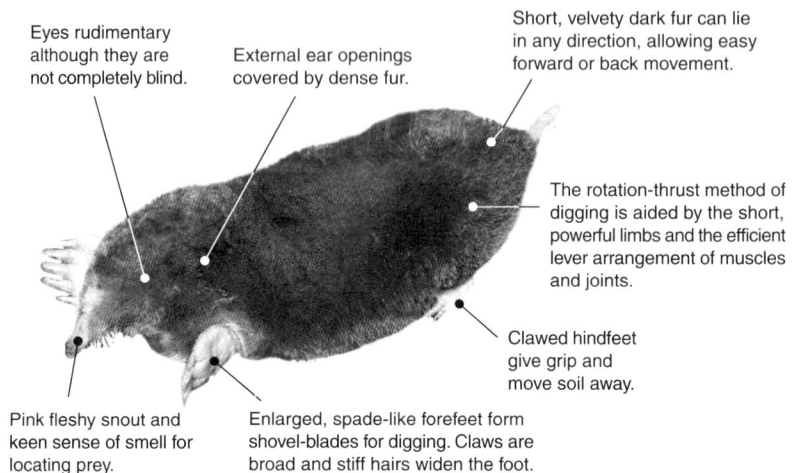

Eyes rudimentary although they are not completely blind.

External ear openings covered by dense fur.

Short, velvety dark fur can lie in any direction, allowing easy forward or back movement.

The rotation-thrust method of digging is aided by the short, powerful limbs and the efficient lever arrangement of muscles and joints.

Clawed hindfeet give grip and move soil away.

Pink fleshy snout and keen sense of smell for locating prey.

Enlarged, spade-like forefeet form shovel-blades for digging. Claws are broad and stiff hairs widen the foot.

Habitat and ecology: Moles spend most of their lives in underground tunnels. Surface tunnels occur where their prey is concentrated at the surface (e.g., land under cultivation). Deeper, permanent tunnels form a complex network used repeatedly for feeding and nesting, sometimes for several generations. **Senses and behavior**: Keen sense of smell but almost blind. Both sexes are solitary and territorial except during breeding. Life span about 3 years. Moles are prey for owls, buzzards, stoats, cats, and dogs. Their activities aerate the soil and they control many soil pests. Despite this, they are regularly trapped and poisoned as pests.

Snow Bunting
(Plectrophenax nivalis)

The snow bunting is a small ground feeding bird that lives and breeds in the Arctic and sub-Arctic islands. Although migratory, snow buntings do not move to traditional winter homes but prefer winter habitats that resemble their Arctic breeding grounds, such as bleak shores or open fields of northern Britain and the eastern United States.

Snow buntings have the unique ability to molt very rapidly after breeding. During the warmer months, the buntings are a brown color, changing to white in winter (right). They must complete this color change quickly, so that they have a new set of feathers before the onset of winter and before migration. In order to achieve this, snow buntings lose as many as four or five of their main flight wing feathers at once, as opposed to most birds, which lose only one or two.

Very few small birds breed in the Arctic, because most small birds lose more heat than larger ones. In addition, birds that breed in the brief Arctic summer must migrate before the onset of winter, often traveling over large expanses of water. Large, long winged birds are better able to do this. However, the snow bunting is superbly adapted to survive in the extreme cold of the Arctic region.

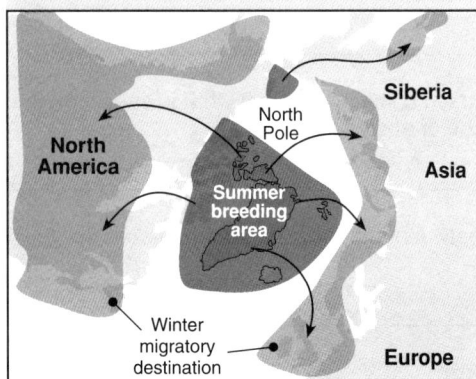

Less heat is lost from white plumage compared to dark plumage.

White feathers are hollow and filled with air, which acts as an insulator. In the dark colored feathers the internal spaces are filled with pigmented cells.

Snow buntings, on average, lay one or two more eggs than equivalent species further south. They are able to rear more young because the continuous daylight and the abundance of insects at high latitudes enables them to feed their chicks around the clock.

During snow storms or periods of high wind, snow buntings will burrow into snowdrifts for shelter.

North Pole

Siberia

North America

Summer breeding area

Asia

Winter migratory destination

Europe

Habitat and ecology: Widespread throughout Arctic and sub-Arctic Islands. Active throughout the day and night, resting for only 2-3 hours in any 24 hour period. Snow buntings may migrate up to 6000 km but are always found at high latitudes. **Reproduction and behavior**: The nest, which is concealed amongst stones, is made from dead grass, moss, and lichen. The male bird feeds his mate during the incubation period and helps to feed the young.

1. Describe a structural, physiological, and behavioral adaptation of the **common mole**, explaining how each adaptation assists survival:

   (a) Structural adaptation: _____

   _____

   (b) Physiological adaptation: _____

   _____

   (c) Behavioral adaptation: _____

   _____

2. Describe a structural, physiological, and behavioral adaptation of the **snow bunting**, explaining how each adaptation assists survival:

   (a) Structural adaptation: _____

   _____

   (b) Physiological adaptation: _____

   _____

   (c) Behavioral adaptation: _____

   _____

3. The rabbit is a colonial mammal which lives underground in warrens (burrow systems) and feeds on grasses, cereal crops, roots, and young trees. Rabbits are a hugely successful species worldwide and often reach plague proportions. Through discussion, or your own knowledge and research, describe **six adaptations** of rabbits, identifying them as structural, physiological, or behavioral. The examples below are typical:

   Structural: Widely spaced eyes gives wide field of vision for surveillance and detection of danger.

   Physiological: High reproductive rate - short gestation and high fertility aids rapid population increases when food is available.

   Behavioral: Freeze behavior when startled reduces the possibility of detection by wandering predators.

   (a) Structural adaptations: _____

   _____

   _____

   (b) Physiological adaptations: _____

   _____

   _____

   (c) Behavioral adaptations: _____

   _____

   _____

4. Examples of adaptations are listed below. Identify them as predominantly structural, physiological, and/or behavioral:

   (a) Relationship of body size and shape to latitude (tropical or arctic): _____

   (b) The production of concentrated urine in desert dwelling mammals: _____

   (c) The summer and winter migratory patterns in birds and mammals: _____

   (d) The C4 photosynthetic pathway and CAM metabolism of plants: _____

   (e) The thick leaves and sunken stomata of desert plants: _____

   (f) Hibernation or torpor in small mammals over winter: _____

![DA2]

Ecosystem Stability

Ecological theory suggests that all species in an ecosystem contribute in some way to ecosystem function. Therefore, species loss past a certain point is likely to have a detrimental effect on the functioning of the ecosystem and on its ability to resist change (its stability). Although many species still await discovery, we do know that the rate of species extinction is increasing. Scientists estimate that human destruction of natural habitat is driving up to 100,000 species to extinction every year. Every day on Earth 100 - 300 species disappear forever. This has serious implications for the long term stability of many ecosystems.

The Concept of Ecosystem Stability

The stability of an ecosystem refers to its apparently unchanging nature over time. Ecosystem stability has various components, including **inertia** (the ability to resist disturbance) and **resilience** (ability to recover from external disturbances). Ecosystem stability is closely linked to the biodiversity of the system, although it is difficult to predict which factors will stress an ecosystem beyond its range of tolerance. It was once thought that the most stable ecosystems were those with the greatest number of species, since these systems had the greatest number of biotic interactions operating to buffer them against change. This assumption is supported by experimental evidence but there is uncertainty over what level of biodiversity provides an insurance against catastrophe.

Monoculture

Natural grassland

Rainforest

Deforestation

Single species crops (monocultures), such as the soy bean crop above left, represent low diversity systems that can be vulnerable to disease, pests, and disturbance. In contrast, natural grasslands (above, right) may appear homogeneous, but contain many species which vary in their predominance seasonally. Although they may be easily disturbed (e.g. by burning) they are very resilient and usually recover quickly.

Tropical rainforests (above, left) represent the highest diversity systems on Earth. Whilst these ecosystems are generally resistant to disturbance, once degraded, (above, right) they have little ability to recover. The biodiversity of ecosystems at low latitudes is generally higher than that at high latitudes, where climates are harsher, niches are broader, and systems may be dependent on a small number of key species.

Community Response to Environmental Change

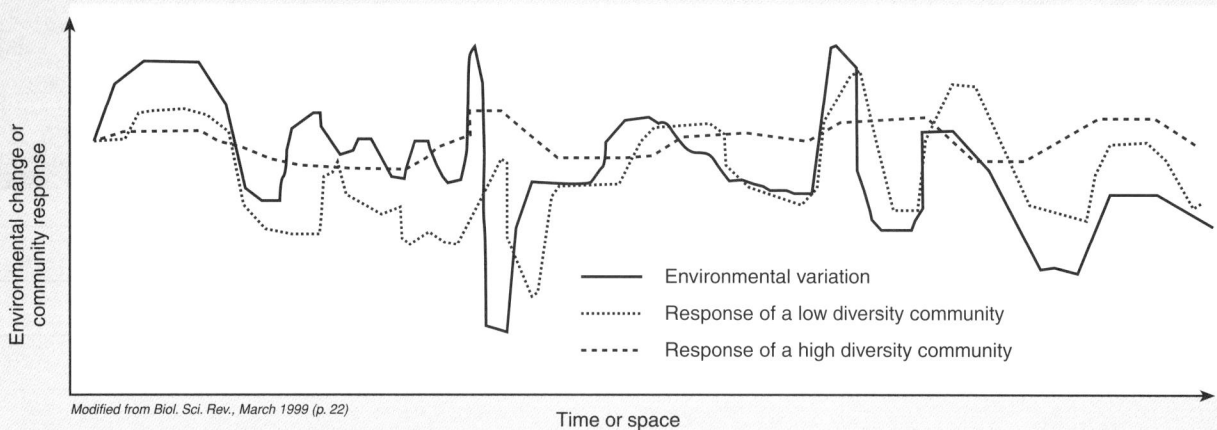

Modified from Biol. Sci. Rev., March 1999 (p. 22)

Time or space

— Environmental variation
·········· Response of a low diversity community
- - - - - Response of a high diversity community

In models of ecosystem function, higher species diversity increases the stability of ecosystem functions such as productivity and nutrient cycling. In the graph above, note how the low diversity system varies more consistently with the environmental variation, whereas the high diversity system is buffered against major fluctuations. In any one ecosystem, some species may be more influential than others in the stability of the system. Such **keystone (key) species** have a disproportionate effect on ecosystem function due to their pivotal role in some ecosystem function such as nutrient recycling or production of plant biomass.

Elephants can change the entire vegetation structure of areas into which they migrate. Their pattern of grazing on taller plant species promotes a predominance of lower growing grasses with small leaves.

Termites are amongst the few larger soil organisms able to break down plant cellulose. They shift large quantities of soil and plant matter and have a profound effect on the rates of nutrient processing in tropical environments.

The starfish *Pisaster* is found along the coasts of North America where it feeds on mussels. If it is removed, the mussels dominate, crowding out most algae and leading to a decrease in the number of herbivore species.

Calculation and use of diversity indices

One of the best ways to determine the health of an ecosystem is to measure the variety of organisms living in it. **Diversity indices** attempt to quantify the degree of diversity and identify indicators for environmental stress or degradation. They are widely used in ecological work, particularly for monitoring ecosystem change or pollution. Most indices of diversity are easy to use and widely applied in ecological studies. Two examples, both of which are derivations of Simpson's index, are described below.

Simpson's Index for finite populations

This diversity index (DI) is a commonly used inversion of Simpson's index, suitable for finite populations.

$$DI = \frac{N(N-1)}{\Sigma n(n-1)}$$

After Smith and Smith as per IOB.

Where:

DI = Diversity index

N = Total number of individuals (of all species) in the sample

n = Number of individuals of each species in the sample

This index ranges between 1 (low diversity) and infinity. The higher the value, the greater the variety of living organisms. It can be difficult to evaluate objectively without reference to some standard ecosystem measure because the values calculated can, in theory, go to infinity.

Complement of Simpson's Index

This diversity index (DI) is the complement of Simpson's original index. It is widely used, although it is based on an infinite population.

$$DI = 1 - \Sigma\, p_i^2$$

after Krebs: Ecological Methodology 1989

Where:

p_i^2 = N_i/N (the proportion of species i in the community)

N_i = Number of individuals of each species in the sample

N = Total number of individuals (of all species) in the sample

This index ranges between 0 and almost 1. The index is independent of sample distribution and, because of the more limited range of values, is easily interpreted. No single index offers the "best" measure of diversity: they are chosen on their suitability to different situations.

Example of species diversity in a stream

The table below shows the results from a survey of invertebrates living in a stream. Although the species have been identified, this is not necessary in order to calculate diversity as long as the different species can be distinguished from each other. Calculation of the diversity index using Simpson's index for finite populations is as follows:

Species	No. of individuals
A (Common backswimmer)	12
B (Stonefly larva)	7
C (Silver water beetle)	2
D (Caddis fly larva)	6
E (Water spider)	5
Total number of individuals = 32	

$$DI = \frac{32 \times 31}{(12 \times 11) + (7 \times 6) + (2 \times 1) + (6 \times 5) + (5 \times 4)} = \frac{992}{226}$$

$DI = 4.39$

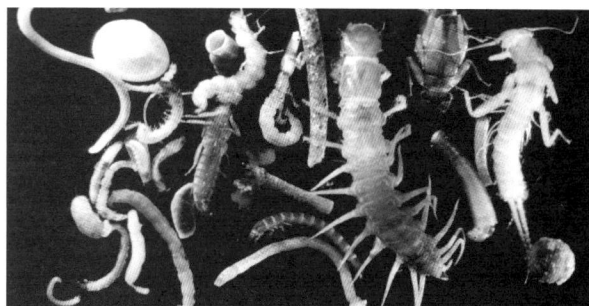

A stream community with a high diversity of macroinvertebrates (above) in contrast to a low diversity stream community (below).

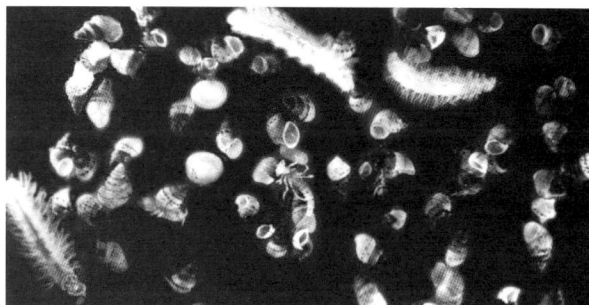

Photos: Stephen Moore

---

1. Explain what you understand by the term **ecosystem stability**: _____

_____

2. Suggest one probable reason why high biodiversity provides greater ecosystem stability: _____

_____

3. Name a situation where a species diversity index may provide useful information: _____

_____

4. An area of forest floor was sampled and six invertebrate species were recorded, with counts of 7, 10, 11, 2, 4, and 3 individuals. Using Simpson's index for finite populations, calculate DI for this community:

   (a) DI= _____   DI = _____

   (b) Comment on the diversity of this community: _____

   _____

5. Explain why **keystone species** are so important to ecosystem function: _____

_____

Ecological Succession

RA③

Ecological succession is the process by which communities in a particular area change over time. Succession takes place as a result of complex interactions of biotic and abiotic factors. Early communities modify the physical environment causing it to change. This in turn alters the biotic community, which further alters the physical environment and so on. Each successive community makes the environment more favorable for the establishment of new species. A succession (or **sere**) proceeds in **seral stages**, until the formation of a **climax community**, which is stable until further disturbance. Early successional communities are characterized by a low species diversity, a simple structure, and broad niches. In contrast, climax communities are complex, with a large number of species interactions, narrow niches, and high species diversity.

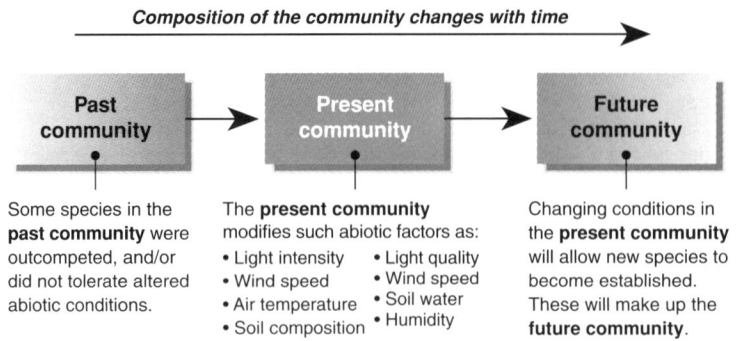

Composition of the community changes with time ➡

Past community	Present community	Future community

Some species in the **past community** were outcompeted, and/or did not tolerate altered abiotic conditions.

The **present community** modifies such abiotic factors as:
• Light intensity • Light quality
• Wind speed • Wind speed
• Air temperature • Soil water
• Soil composition • Humidity

Changing conditions in the **present community** will allow new species to become established. These will make up the **future community**.

Primary Succession

Primary succession refers to colonization of regions where there is no preexisting community. Examples include regions where the previous community has been extinguished by a volcanic eruption (such as the Indonesian island of Krakatau (Krakatoa), which erupted in 1883), newly formed glacial moraines, or newly formed volcanic islands (as when Surtsey appeared off Iceland in 1963). The sequence of colonization described below is typical of a Northern hemisphere lithosere; a succession on bare rock. This sequence is not necessarily the same as that occurring on another substrate, such as volcanic ash, which allows the earlier establishment of grasses.

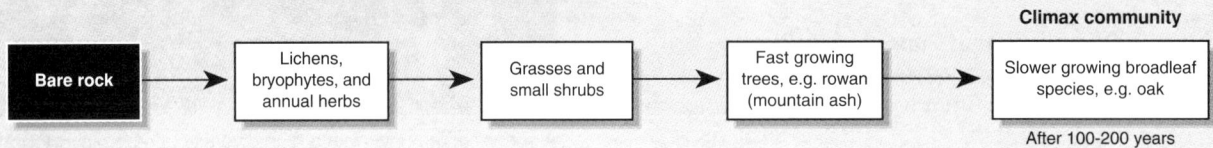

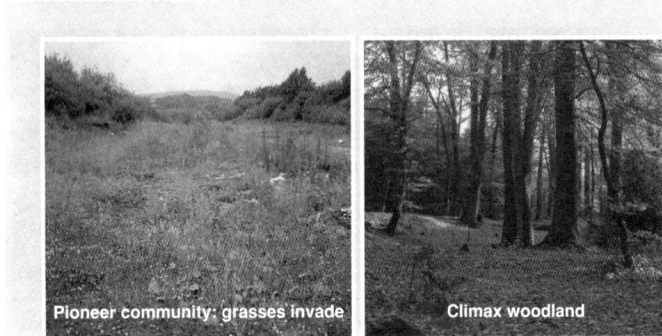

Climax community

| Bare rock | → | Lichens, bryophytes, and annual herbs | → | Grasses and small shrubs | → | Fast growing trees, e.g. rowan (mountain ash) | → | Slower growing broadleaf species, e.g. oak |

After 100-200 years

Secondary Succession in Cleared Land
(150+ years for mature woodland to develop again)

A secondary succession takes place after a land clearance (e.g., from fire or landslide). Such events do not involve loss of the soil and so tend to be more rapid than primary succession, although the time scale depends on the species involved and on climatic and edaphic (soil) factors. Humans may deflect the natural course of succession (e.g. by mowing) and the climax community that results will differ from the natural community. A climax community arising from a **deflected succession** is called a **plagioclimax**.

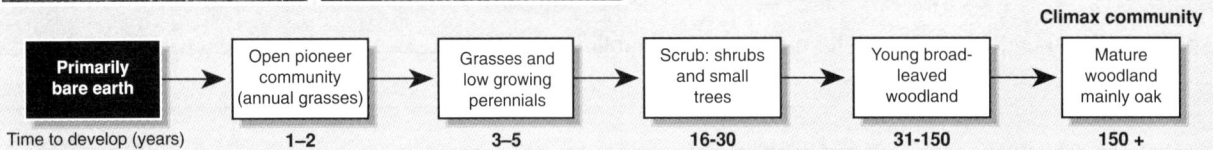

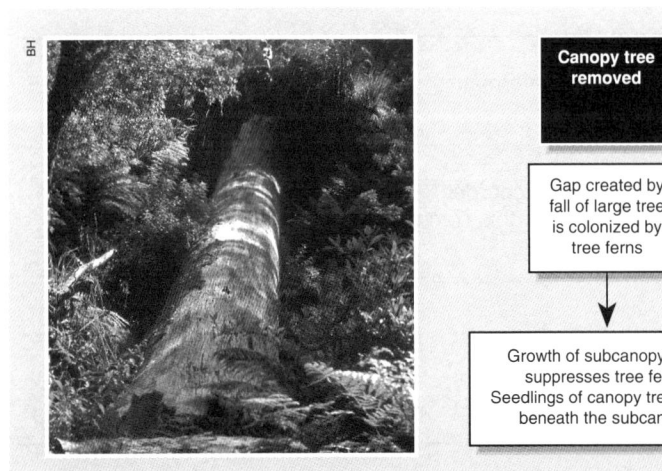

Pioneer community: grasses invade | **Climax woodland**

Climax community

| Primarily bare earth | → | Open pioneer community (annual grasses) | → | Grasses and low growing perennials | → | Scrub: shrubs and small trees | → | Young broad-leaved woodland | → | Mature woodland mainly oak |

| Time to develop (years) | 1–2 | 3–5 | 16-30 | 31-150 | 150 + |

Gap Regeneration Cycle in a Rainforest
(500-700 years)

Canopy tree removed

Large canopy trees have a profound effect on the make-up of a rainforest community, reducing light penetration and impeding the growth of saplings. When a large tree falls, it opens a hole in the canopy that lets in sunlight. Saplings then compete to fill the gap. The photograph on the left shows a large canopy tree in temperate rainforest that has recently fallen, leaving a gap in the canopy through which light can penetrate.

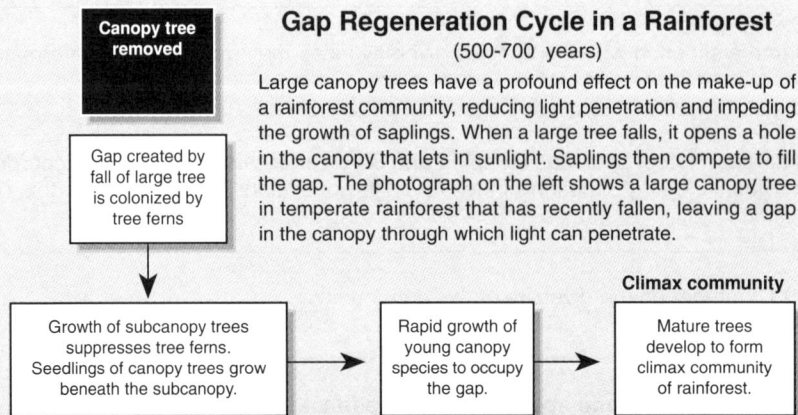

Gap created by fall of large tree is colonized by tree ferns

Climax community

| Growth of subcanopy trees suppresses tree ferns. Seedlings of canopy trees grow beneath the subcanopy. | → | Rapid growth of young canopy species to occupy the gap. | → | Mature trees develop to form climax community of rainforest. |

Wetland areas present a special case of ecological succession. Wetlands are constantly changing as plant invasion of open water leads to siltation and infilling. This process is accelerated by **eutrophication**. In well drained areas, pasture or **heath** may develop as a result of succession from freshwater to dry land. When the soil conditions remain non-acid and poorly drained, a swamp will eventually develop into a seasonally dry **fen**. In special circumstances (see below) an acid **peat bog** may develop. The domes of peat that develop produce a hummocky landscape with a unique biota. Wetland peat ecosystems may take more than 5,000 years to form but are easily destroyed by excavation and lowering of the water table.

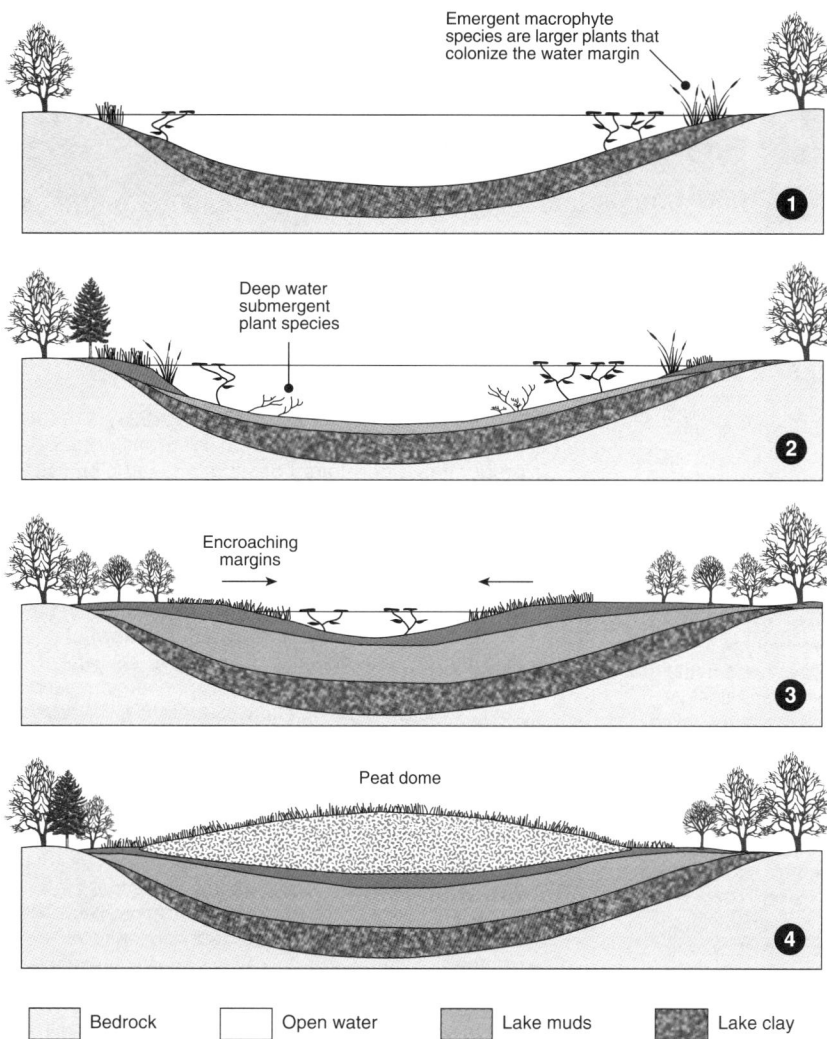

Emergent macrophyte species are larger plants that colonize the water margin

Deep water submergent plant species

Encroaching margins

Peat dome

| Bedrock | Open water | Lake muds | Lake clay | Swamp peat | Bog peat |

Wetland Succession

An open body of water, with time, becomes silted up and is invaded by aquatic plants. Emergent macrophyte species colonize the accumulating sediments, driving floating plants towards the remaining deeper water.

The increasing density of rooted emergent, submerged, and floating macrophytes encourages further sedimentation by slowing water flows and adding organic matter to the accumulating silt.

The resulting **swamp** is characterized by dense growths of emergent macrophytes and permanent (although not necessarily deep) standing water. As sediment continues to accumulate the swamp surface may, in some cases, dry off in summer.

In colder climates, low evaporation rates, high rainfall, and invasion by *Sphagnum* moss leads to development of a peat **bog**; a low pH, nutrient poor environment where acid-tolerant plants such as sundew replace swamp species.

1. (a) Explain what is meant by primary succession: _____

_____

(b) Explain how secondary succession differs from primary succession: _____

_____

2 (a) Explain what is meant by a deflected succession: _____

_____

(b) Explain the role that deflected succession may have in maintaining managed habitats: _____

_____

_____

_____

3. (a) In bog development, suggest how *Sphagnum* alters the environment to favor the establishment other bog species:

_____

(b) Name the two most important abiotic factors in determining whether or not a wetland will develop into bog:

_____

Energy Flow and Nutrient Cycles

IB SL
Complete nos:
1, 3-6, 8-9, 13-15, 17-20

Extension: 2

IB HL
Complete nos:
1, 3-6, 8-9, 13-15, 17-20

Extension: 2

IB Options
Complete nos:
Option G:
SL/HL: 5, 7, 10, 12, 16(a)
HL only: 4, 21

AP Biology
Complete nos:
1-23
Some numbers
extension as
appropriate

Learning Objectives

☐ 1. Compile your own glossary from the **KEY WORDS** displayed in **bold type** in the learning objectives below.

Energy in ecosystems

Background to the laws of energy *(page 272)*

☐ 2. Recognize that the first and second laws of thermodynamics govern energy flow in ecosystems. In practical terms, explain what the energy laws mean with respect to energy conversions in ecosystems.

☐ 3. Appreciate that light is the initial energy source for almost all ecosystems and that photosynthesis is the main route by which energy enters most food chains. Recognize that energy is dissipated as it is transferred through trophic levels.

☐ 4. Understand the interrelationship between nutrient cycling and energy flow in ecosystems:
   • Energy flows through ecosystems in the high energy chemical bonds within **organic matter**.
   • Nutrients move within and between ecosystems in **biogeochemical cycles** involving exchanges between the atmosphere, the Earth's crust, water, and living organisms.

Trophic relationships *(pages 273-279)*

☐ 5. Describe how the energy flow in ecosystems is described using **trophic levels**. Distinguish between **producers**, **primary and secondary consumers**, **detritivores**, and **saprotrophs (decomposers)**, identifying the relationship between them. Describe the role of each of these in energy transfer.

☐ 6. Describe how energy is transferred between different trophic levels in **food chains** and **food webs**. Compare the amount of energy available to each trophic level and recognize that the **efficiency** of this energy transfer is only 10-20%. Explain what happens to the remaining energy and why energy cannot be recycled.

☐ 7. With respect to the **efficiency** of energy transfer in food chains, explain the small biomass and low numbers of organisms at higher trophic levels.

☐ 8. Provide three examples of food chains, each with at least three linkages. Show how the (named) organisms are interconnected through their feeding relationships. Assign trophic levels to the organisms in a food chain.

☐ 9. Construct a food web for a named community, containing up to 10 organisms, showing how the (named) organisms are interconnected through their feeding relationships. Assign trophic levels to the organisms in the food web.

☐ 10. Recognize and discuss the difficulties of classifying organisms into trophic levels.

☐ 11. Appreciate what is meant **bioaccumulation**, with reference to the nature and function of trophic relationships *(see Senior Biology 2 page 371)*.

Measuring Energy Flow *(pages 280-281)*

☐ 12. Understand the terms: **productivity**, **gross primary production**, **net primary production**, and **biomass**. Recognize how these relate to the transfer of energy to the next trophic level. Calculate values for gross (primary) production, net production, and biomass for provided data *(also see Senior Biology 2, page 362)*.

☐ 13. Explain how the energy flow in an ecosystem can be described quantitatively using an **energy flow diagram**. Include reference to: *trophic levels* (scaled boxes to illustrate relative amounts of energy at each level), *direction of energy flow*, *processes involved in energy transfer*, *energy sources*, and *energy sinks*.

Ecological Pyramids *(pages 282-283)*

☐ 14. Describe food chains quantitatively using **ecological pyramids**. Explain how these may be based on **numbers** (numbers of organisms), **biomass** (weight of organisms), or **energy** (total energy content of organisms) at each trophic level. Identify problems with the use of number pyramids, and understand why pyramids of biomass or energy are usually preferable.

☐ 15. Interpret pyramids of energy for different communities. Express the energy available at each trophic level in appropriate units and explain the reasons for the pyramid's shape.

☐ 16. Given appropriate information, construct and interpret pyramids of:
(a) Energy   (b) Numbers   (c) Biomass
for different communities. Express the energy available at each trophic level in appropriate units. Identify the relationship between each of these types of pyramids and their corresponding food chains and webs. Explain why the shape of each graph is a pyramid (or sometimes an inverse pyramid).

Biogeochemical Cycles *(pages 284-288)*

☐ 17. Explain the terms: **nutrient cycle** and **environmental reservoir**. Draw and interpret a generalized model of a nutrient cycle, identifying the roles of **primary productivity** and **decomposition** in nutrient cycling.

☐ 18. Using named examples, describe the general role of **saprotrophs** and **detritivores** in nutrient cycling.

☐ 19. Using a diagram, describe the stages in the **carbon cycle**, identifying the form of carbon at the different stages, and using arrows to show the direction of nutrient flow and labels to identify the processes involved. Identify the role of microorganisms, carbon sinks, and carbonates in the cycle.

☐ 20. Identify factors influencing the rate of carbon cycling. Recognize the role of respiration and photosynthesis in the short-term fluctuations and in the long-term global balance of oxygen and carbon dioxide.

☐ 21. Using a diagram, describe the stages in the **nitrogen cycle**, identifying the form of nitrogen at the different stages, and using arrows to show the direction of nutrient flow and labels to identify the processes involved. Identify and explain the role of microorganisms in the cycle, as illustrated by:
(a) **Nitrifying bacteria** (*Nitrosomonas*, *Nitrobacter*).
(b) **Nitrogen-fixing bacteria** (*Rhizobium*, *Azotobacter*).
(c) **Denitrifying bacteria** (*Pseudomonas*, *Thiobacillus*).

☐ 22. Describe the features of the **water cycle**. Understand the ways in which water is cycled between various reservoirs and describe the major processes, including: **evaporation**, **condensation**, **precipitation**, **runoff**. Appreciate how humans intervene in the water cycle.

☐ 23. Using diagrams, describe the **phosphorus cycle**, using arrows to show the direction of nutrient flow and labels to identify the processes involved. Identify the role of microorganisms in the cycle and contrast the phosphorus cycle with other nutrient cycles.

Textbooks

See the 'Textbook Reference Grid' on pages 8-9 for textbook page references relating to material in this topic.

Supplementary Texts
See pages 4-6 for additional details of these texts:

■ Adds, J. *et al.*, 2000. **Exchange & Transport, Energy & Ecosystems** (NelsonThornes), pp. 122-32.

■ Chenn, P., 1999. **Ecology** (John Murray), pp. 1-32.

Internet

See pages 10-11 for details of how to access **Bio Links** from our web site: **www.thebiozone.com**. From Bio Links, access sites under the topics:

GENERAL BIOLOGY ONLINE RESOURCES > Online Textbooks and Lecture Notes: • An on-line biology book • Biology online.org • Kimball's biology pages • Learn.co.uk • Gondar design sciences • MIT biology hypertextbook - home • Mark Rothery's biology web site • Mr Biology's biology web site • S-cool! A level biology revision guide ... *and others*

ECOLOGY: • Introduction to biogeography and ecology • Ken's bioweb referencing • NatureWorks
> **Energy Flows and Nutrient Cycles:** • A marine food web • Bioaccumulation • Human alteration of the global nitrogen cycle • Nitrogen: The essential element • The carbon cycle • The nitrogen cycle • The water cycle (for revision) • Trophic pyramids and food webs ... *and others*

For the topic: The Dynamics of Populations, also see the following sites:
ECOLOGY > Populations and Communities: • Anemone fishes and their host sea anemones • Bull Shoals Lake 1995 report • Competition • Intraspecific relations: Cooperation and competition • Population ecology • Quantitative population ecology • Species interactions • Death squared

For the topic: Practical Ecology, also see:
ECOLOGY > Environmental Monitoring: • Amphibian monitoring program • Environmental Protection Agency • Remote sensing and monitoring > **Populations and Communities:** • Quantitative population ecology • Sirtracking for wildlife research

STUDENT PROJECTS: • A scientific report • Chi-square lesson • Scientific investigation • Study skills: biology • The scientific method • Tree lupins • Woodlice online ...*and others*

Periodicals

See page 6 for details of publishers of periodicals:

STUDENT'S REFERENCE
Energy flow: food chains and webs

■ **Ecosystems** Biol. Sci. Rev., 9(4) March 1997, pp. 9-14. *Ecosystem structure including food chains and webs, nutrient cycles and energy flows, and ecological pyramids.*

■ **The Other Side of Eden** Biol. Sci. Rev., 15(3) February 2003, pp. 2-7. *An account of the Eden Project – the collection of artificial ecosystems in Cornwall. Its aims, future directions, and its role in the study of natural ecosystems and ecosystem modeling are discussed.*

■ **Fish Predation** Biol. Sci. Rev., 14(1) September 2001, pp. 10-14. *Some fish species in freshwater systems in the UK are important top predators and can heavily influence the dynamics of the entire ecosystem.*

Nutrient cycles and soil organisms

General articles
■ **Ultimate interface** New Scientist, 14 November 1998 (Inside Science). *An excellent account of the cycling of chemicals in the biosphere, with particular emphasis on the role of the soil in nutrient cycling processes.*

■ **Microorganisms in Agriculture** Biol. Sci. Rev., 11(5) May 1999, pp. 2-4. *The vital role of microorganisms in the ecology of communities is discussed (includes a discussion of N-fixation and the role of micoorganisms in this process).*

■ **Dung Beetles: Nature's Recyclers** Biol. Sci. Rev., 14(4) April 2002, pp. 31-33. *The ecological role of dung beetles in the recycling of nutrients.*

■ **Gardeners of the Underworld** New Scientist, 4 August 1990, p. 34-37. *Burrowing animals play a vital role in cycling and recycling soil and sediment.*

Carbon cycle
■ **The Carbon Cycle** New Scientist, 2 Nov. 1991 (Inside Science). *Carbon is a vital element; its role in the world's ecosystems is explored in this four page, easy-to-read article.*

■ **Plants in the Greenhouse World** New Scientist, 6 May 1989 (Inside Science). *Plants and their pivotal role in the carbon cycle.*

Nitrogen cycle
■ **The Nitrogen Cycle** Biol. Sci. Rev., 13(2) November 2000, pp. 25-27. *An excellent account of the the nitrogen cycle: conversions, role in ecosystems, and the influence of human activity.*

■ **Microorganisms in Agriculture** Biol. Sci. Rev., 11(5) May 1999, pp. 2-4. *The vital role of microorganisms in the ecology of communities. Includes a discussion of N-fixation and the role of micoorganisms in this process.*

■ **The Little Nitrogen Factories** Biol. Sci. Rev., 10(2) November 1997, pp. 2-6. *Symbiosis between a fern (Azolla) and a bacterium which results in the fixation of nitrogen and improves crop yields.*

■ **Let's make Nodules** New Scientist, 11 Jan. 1997, pp. 22-25. *An account of the physiology of the mutualistic relationship between bacteria (Rhizobium) and plants (legumes).*

■ **Nitrates in Soil and Water** New Scientist, 15 Sept. 1990 (Inside Science). *Nitrates and their role in the nitrogen cycle.*

TEACHER'S REFERENCE
■ **Whale of an Appetite** New Scientist, 24 October 1998, p. 25. *A crash in seal populations in the Alaskan region has had serious ramifications to food web stability: the orcas have prey switched from seals to sea otters, the otters have declined as a consequence, and the sea urchin populations have exploded.*

■ **Kingdom of the Krill** New Scientist, 17 April 1999, pp. 36-41. *The details of the role of this marine organism in ocean food chains.*

■ **Waste Not** New Scientist, 29 August 1998, pp. 26-30. *Human sewage is often spread on land as fertilizer, but this carries the risk of passing pathogens through the food chain.*

■ **Ultimate Sacrifice** New Scientist, 6 September 1997, pp. 39-41. *The Alaskan salmon plays an important part in fuelling lake food webs. These salmon pass on vital nutrients obtained from the sea back into the food chain of the high latitude freshwater environments.*

■ **Terraria and Aquaria as Models for Teaching Relationships between Ecosystem Structure and Function** The Am. Biology Teacher, 59(1), January,1997, pp. 52-53. *Using classroom set-ups as models for examining ecosystem function: photosynthesis, respiration, and nutrient cycling.*

■ **The Ocean's Invisible Forest** Scientific American, August 2002, pp. 38-45. *The role of marine plankton in the global carbon cycle: ocean productivity and its influence on global climate.*

■ **Capturing Greenhouse Gases** Scientific American, February 2000, pp. 54-61. *New approaches to human interference in the carbon cycle: storing excess gases underground or in the oceans. Includes a useful synopsis of carbon transfers and how humans could intervene to alleviate the build-up of greenhouse gases.*

■ **A Demonstration of Nitrogen Dynamics in Oxic and Hypoxic Soils and Sediments** The American Biology Teacher, 63(3), March, 2001, pp. 199-206. *A practical scheme aimed at improving student understanding of the nitrogen cycle.*

■ **Global Population and the Nitrogen Cycle** Sci. American, July 1997, pp. 58-63. *The over use of nitrogen fertilizers is disturbing the nutrient balance in ecosystems and leading to pollution.*

Software and video resources are now provided in the Teacher Resource Handbook

Energy in Ecosystems

A 2

An ecosystem is a natural unit of living (biotic) components, together with all the non-living (abiotic) components with which they interact. Two processes central to ecosystem function are **energy flow** and **chemical cycling**. The mitochondria of eukaryotic cells use the organic products of photosynthesis as fuel for cellular respiration. Respiration generates ATP; an energy currency for cellular work. Cellular work generates heat which is lost from the system. The waste products of cellular respiration are used as the raw materials for photosynthesis (see diagram below). Chemical elements such as nitrogen, phosphorus, and carbon are cycled between the biotic and abiotic components of the ecosystem. Energy, unlike matter, cannot be recycled. Ecosystems must receive a constant input of new energy from an outside source. In most cases, this is the sun.

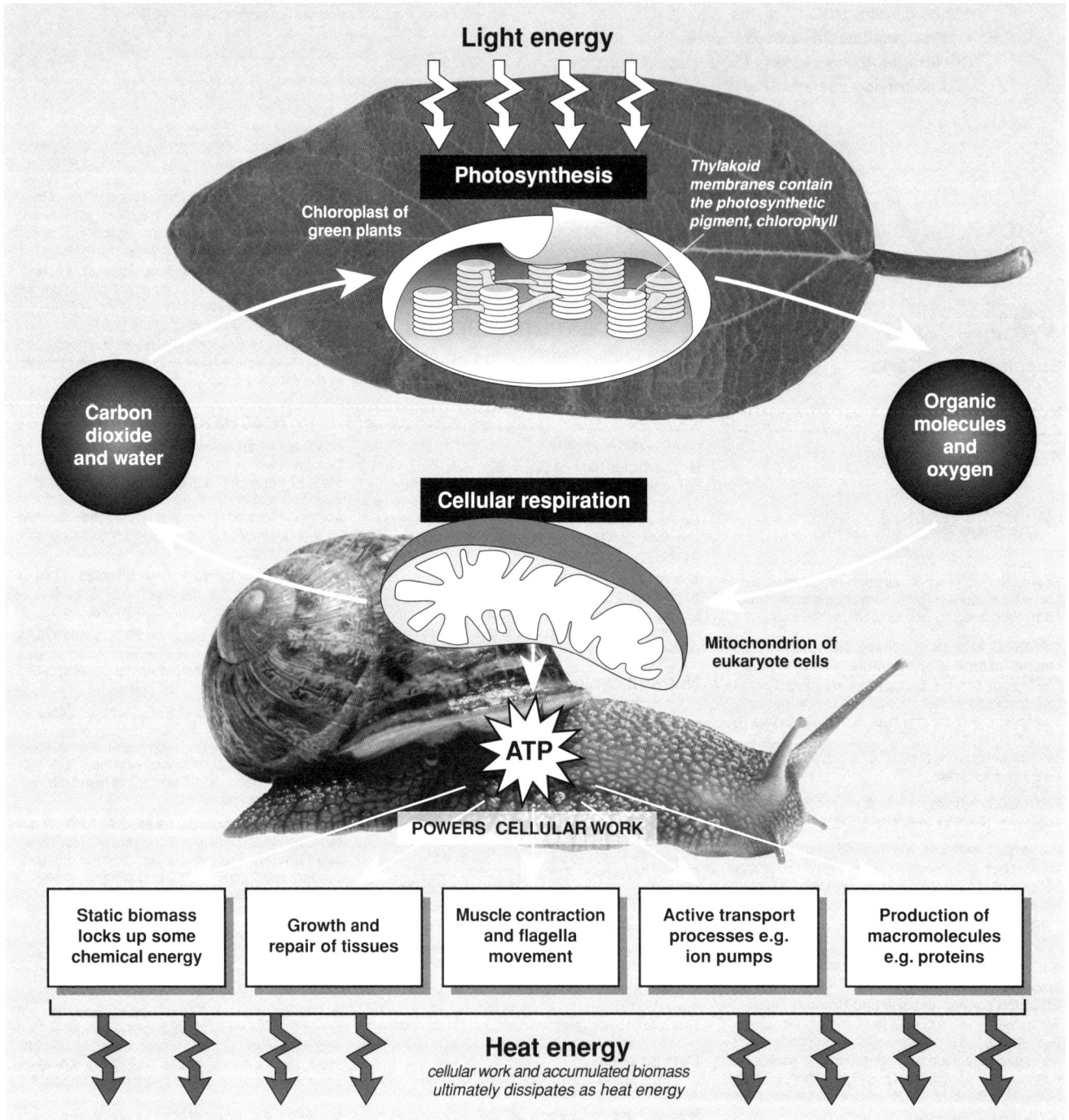

Light energy

Photosynthesis

Chloroplast of green plants

Thylakoid membranes contain the photosynthetic pigment, chlorophyll

Carbon dioxide and water

Organic molecules and oxygen

Cellular respiration

Mitochondrion of eukaryote cells

ATP

POWERS CELLULAR WORK

| Static biomass locks up some chemical energy | Growth and repair of tissues | Muscle contraction and flagella movement | Active transport processes e.g. ion pumps | Production of macromolecules e.g. proteins |

Heat energy
cellular work and accumulated biomass ultimately dissipates as heat energy

1. Write a word equation for each of the following processes. Include the energy source, raw materials, and waste products:

   (a) Photosynthesis: _____

   (b) Respiration: _____

2. Explain why ecosystems require a constant input of energy from an external source: _____

   _____

3. With respect to cycling of matter, explain the relationship between photosynthesis and respiration: _____

   _____

Food Chains

A 2

Every ecosystem has a trophic structure: a hierarchy of feeding relationships that determines the pathways for energy flow and nutrient cycling. Species are divided into trophic levels on the basis of their sources of nutrition. The first trophic level (**producers**), ultimately supports all other levels. The consumers are those that rely on producers for their energy. Consumers are ranked according to the trophic level they occupy (first order, second order, etc.). The sequence of organisms, each of which is a source of food for the next, is called a **food chain**. Food chains commonly have four links but seldom more than six. Those organisms whose food is obtained through the same number of links belong to the same trophic level. Note that some consumers (particularly "top" carnivores and omnivores) may feed at several different trophic levels, and many primary consumers eat many plant species. The different food chains in an ecosystem therefore tend to form complex webs of interactions (food webs).

Respiration

Producers
Trophic level: 1

Herbivores
Trophic level: 2

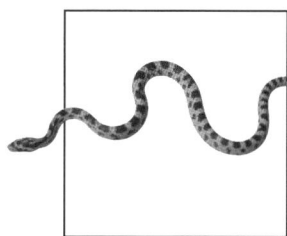

Carnivores
Trophic level: 3

Carnivores
Trophic level: 4

Detritivores and decomposers

The diagram above represents the basic elements of a food chain. In the questions below, you are asked to add to the diagram the features that indicate the flow of energy through the community of organisms.

1. (a) State the original energy source for this food chain: _____
    (b) Draw arrows on the diagram above to show how the energy flows through the organisms in the food chain.
    (c) Label each of the arrows with the process that carries out this transfer of energy.
    (d) Draw arrows on the diagram to show how the energy is lost by way of respiration.

2. (a) Describe what happens to the **amount** of energy available to each successive trophic level in a food chain:

    _____

    (b) Explain why this is the case: _____

    _____

3. Define the following terms:

    (a) Food chain: _____

    _____

    (b) Trophic level: _____

    _____

    (c) First order consumer: _____

    _____

    (d) Second order consumer: _____

    _____

4. If the eagle (above) was found to eat both snakes and mice, explain what you would infer about the tropic level(s) it occupied:

    _____

Constructing a Food Web

The actual species inhabiting any particular lake may vary depending on locality, but certain types of organisms (as shown below) are typically represented. For the sake of simplicity, only fifteen organisms are represented here. Real lake communities may have hundreds of different species interacting together. The bulk of this species diversity is in the lower trophic levels (producers and invertebrate grazers). Your task is to assemble the organisms below into a food web, in a way that illustrates their trophic status and their relative trophic position(s). The food resource represented by **detritus** is not shown here. Detritus comprises the accumulated debris of dead organisms in varying stages of decay. This debris may arise from within the lake itself or it may be washed in from the surrounding lake margins and streams. The detritus settles through the water column and eventually forms a layer on the lake bottom. It provides a rich food source for any organism that can exploit it.

Pond Organisms and their Feeding Requirements

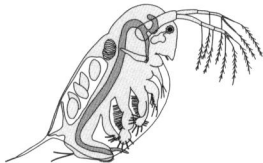

Zooplankton (*e.g., Daphnia*)
Small freshwater crustacean that forms part of the zooplankton. It feeds on planktonic algae by filtering them from the water with its limbs.

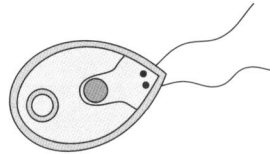

Planktonic algae (*e.g., Chlamydomonas*)
A microscopic freshwater alga with flagella enabling it to move. One of many species that forms the phytoplankton.

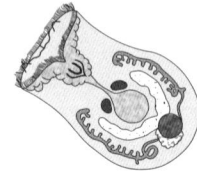

Asplanchna (Planktonic rotifer)
A large, carnivorous rotifer that feeds on protozoa and young zooplankton (e.g., *Daphnia*). Note that most rotifers are small herbivores.

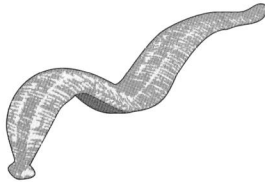

Leech (*Glossiphonia*)
Leeches are fluid feeding predators of smaller invertebrates, including rotifers, small pond snails and worms.

Macrophytes (large water plants)
A variety of flowering plants (e.g. *Elodea* and *Potamogeton*) are adapted for being submerged, free-floating or growing at the lake margin.

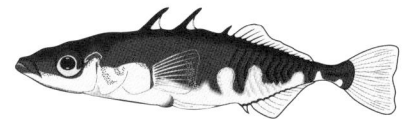

Three-spined stickleback (*Gasterosteus*)
A common fish of freshwater ponds and lakes. It feeds mainly on small invertebrates such as *Daphnia* and insect larvae.

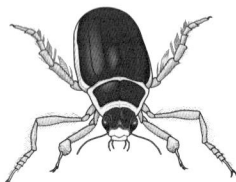

Great diving beetle (*Dytiscus*)
Feeds on small insects, insect larvae, and zooplankton, but will also eat organic detritus collected from the bottom mud.

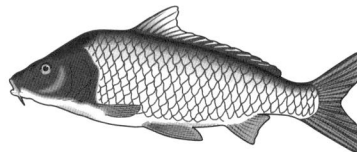

Carp (*Cyprinus*)
A heavy bodied freshwater fish that feeds mainly on bottom living insect larvae and snails, but will also take some plant material (not algae).

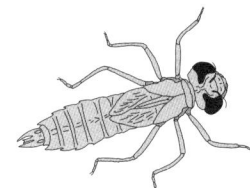

Dragonfly larvae
Large aquatic insect larvae that are voracious predators of small invertebrates including *Hydra*, *Daphnia*, other insect larvae, and leeches.

Great pond snail (*Limnaea*)
Omnivorous pond snail, eating both plant and animal material, living or dead, although the main diet is aquatic macrophytes.

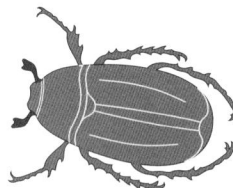

Herbivorous water beetles (*e.g., Hydrophilus*)
Feed on water plants, although the young beetle larvae are carnivorous, feeding primarily on small pond snails.

Protozan (*e.g., Paramecium*)
Ciliated protozoa such as *Paramecium* feed primarily on bacteria and microscopic green algae such as *Chlamydomonas*.

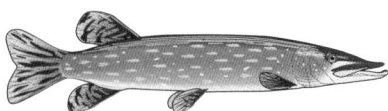

Pike (*Esox lucius*)
A top ambush predator of all smaller fish and amphibians, although they are also opportunistic predators of rodents and small birds.

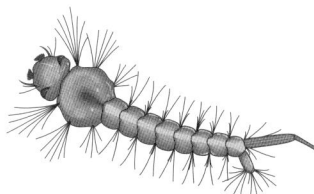

Mosquito larva
The larvae of most mosquito species feed on algae and plant and animal particles although some are predatory, feeding on protozoa.

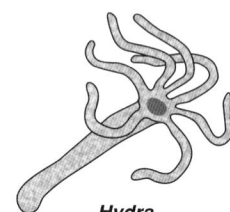

Hydra
A small carnivorous cnidarian that captures small prey items such as small *Daphnia* and insect larvae using its stinging cells on the tentacles.

1. Read the information provided for each lake community species on the previous page, taking note of what it feeds on.

2. Identify the **producer** species present, as well as herbivores, carnivores, and omnivores.

3. Starting with **producer** species, construct **four** different **food chains** (using their names only) to show the feeding relationships between the organisms (NOTE: some food chains may be shorter than others; some species will be repeated in one or more subsequent food chains). An example of a food chain has already been completed for you.

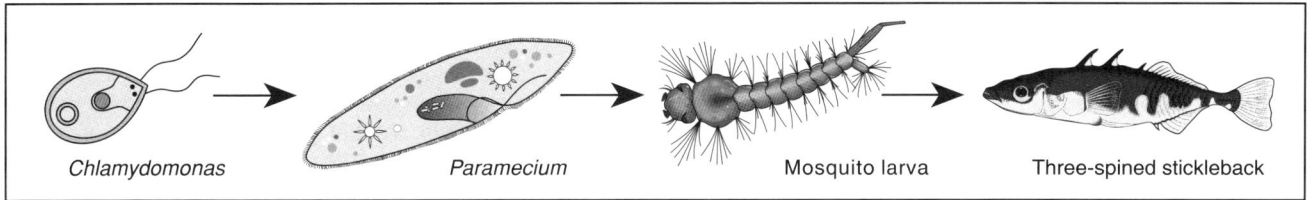

Chlamydomonas → Paramecium → Mosquito larva → Three-spined stickleback

Food chain 1:

Food chain 2:

Food chain 3:

Food chain 4:

4. (a) Use the food chains created above to help you to draw up a **food web** for this community. Use the information supplied to draw arrows showing the flow of **energy** between species (Only energy **from** the detritus is required).

   (b) Label each species to indicate its position in the food web i.e. its trophic level (**T1, T2, T3, T4, T5**). Where a species occupies more than one trophic level, indicate this e.g. **T2/3**:

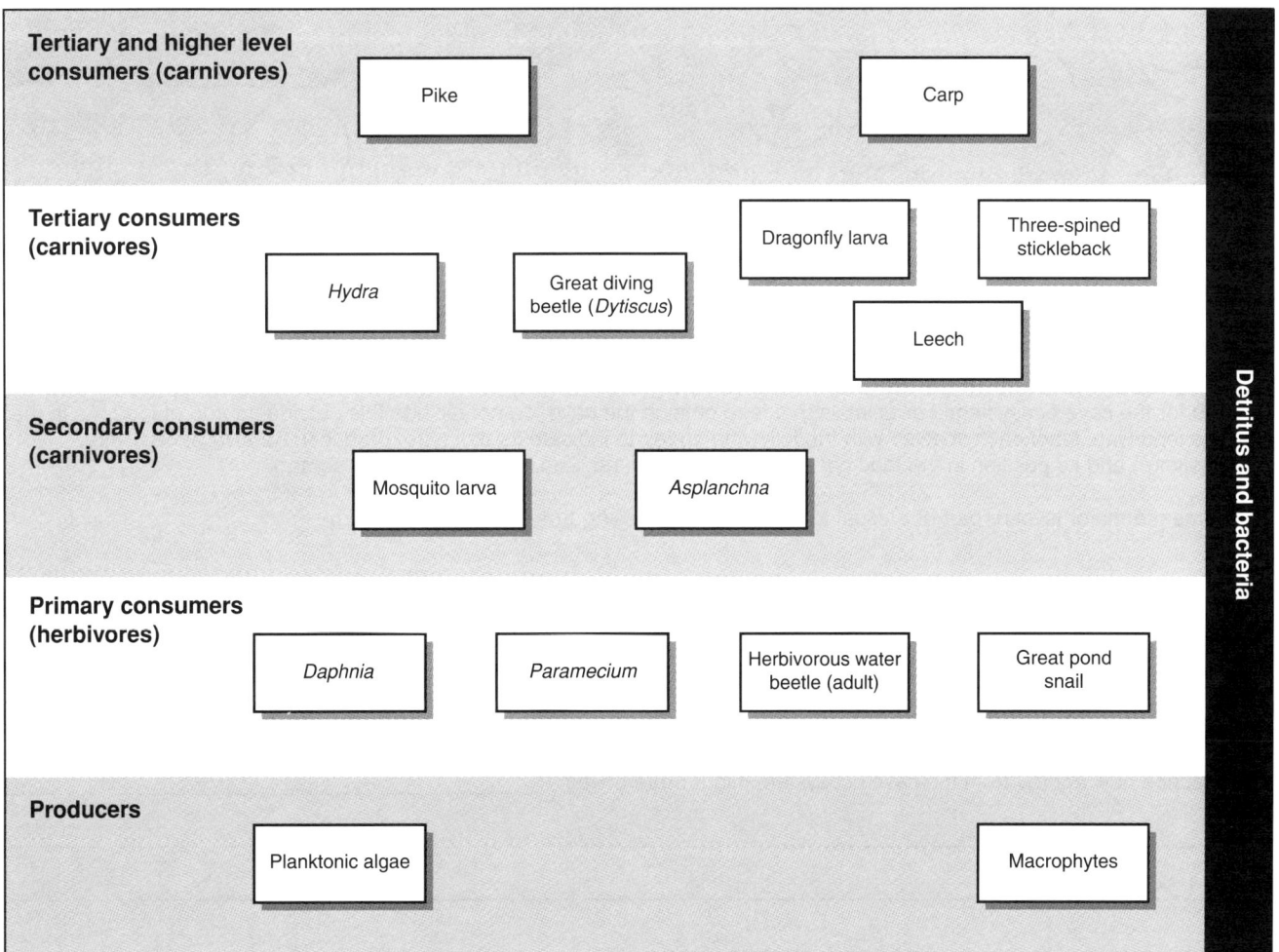

Tertiary and higher level consumers (carnivores)

Pike   Carp

Tertiary consumers (carnivores)

Hydra   Great diving beetle (*Dytiscus*)   Dragonfly larva   Three-spined stickleback

Leech

Secondary consumers (carnivores)

Mosquito larva   *Asplanchna*

Primary consumers (herbivores)

Daphnia   Paramecium   Herbivorous water beetle (adult)   Great pond snail

Producers

Planktonic algae   Macrophytes

Detritus and bacteria

A 3

Cave Food Webs

A cave is a barren environment, without the light that normally sustains most ecosystems. Despite this, a wide range of animals inhabit caves and are specially adapted to that particular environment. Other animals, such as bats, do not live permanently in the cave but use it as a roosting or resting and breeding area, safe from many predators and other dangers. The food webs of caves are very fragile and based on few resources. **Around the entrance** of the cave, the owl (**1**) preys on the mouse (**2**) which itself feeds on the vegetation outside the cave. The owl and the mouse leave droppings that support the cave dung beetle (**3**) and the millipede (**4**). The cave cricket (**5**) scavenges dead birds and mammals near the cave entrance. The harvestman (**6**) is a

predator of the dung beetle, the millipede, and the cricket. **Inside the cave**, the horseshoe bat (**7**) roosts and breeds in safety, leaving the cave to feed outside on slow flying insects. The bats produce vast quantities of guano (droppings). The guano is eaten by the blind cave beetle (**8**), the millipede (**4**) and the springtail (**9**). These invertebrates are hunted by the predatory cave spider (**10**). Occasionally, in tropical caves, snakes (not shown) may enter the cave and feed on bats. **In underground pools**, the bat guano supports the growth of bacteria (**11**). Flatworms (**12**) and isopods (**13**) feed on the bacteria and themselves are eaten by the blind cave shrimp (**14**). The blind cave fish (**15**) is the top predator, feeding on isopods and the blind cave shrimps.

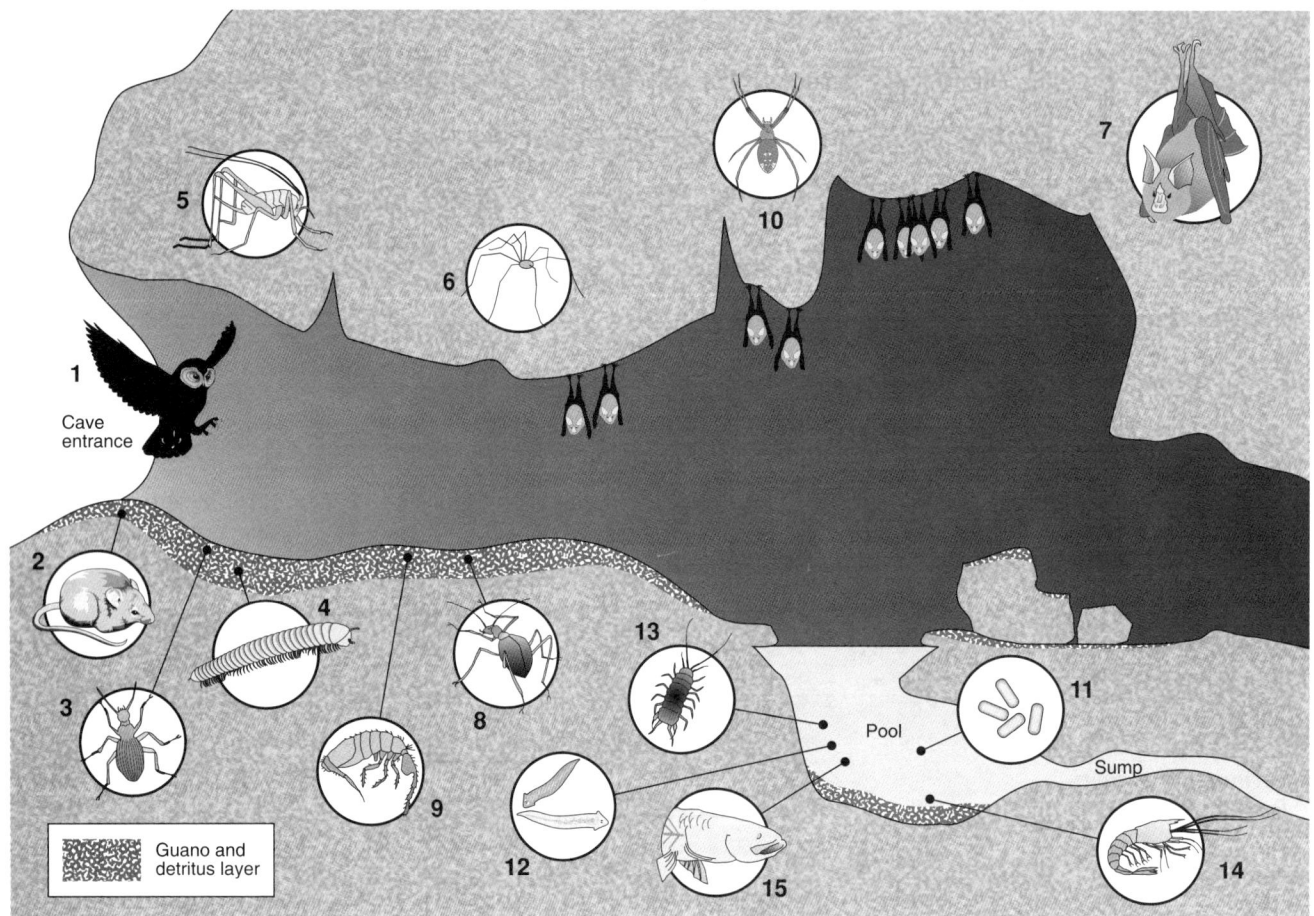

1. Using the lake foodweb on the previous two pages as a guide, in the space provided on the next page construct a food web for the cave ecosystem. For animals that feed outside the cave, do not include this outside source of food. As in the lake food web, label each species with the following codes to indicate its diet type (producer, herbivore, carnivore, omnivore) and its position in the food chain as a consumer (1st, 2nd, 3rd, 4th order consumer).

2. Name the major level or part of a usual food web that is missing from the cave food web:

_____

3. Explain how energy is imported into the cave's food web: _____

_____

_____

4. Describe how energy from the cave ecosystem might be removed: _____

_____

_____

_____

5. In many parts of the world, cave-dwelling bat species are endangered, often taken as food by humans or killed as pests. If bat numbers were to fall substantially, explain how this would affect the food web of the cave ecosystem:

A 1 # Energy Inputs and Outputs

The way living things obtain their energy can be classified into two categories. The group upon which all others depend is called **producers** or **autotrophs**. They are organisms able to manufacture their food from simple inorganic substances. The **consumers** or **heterotrophs** (comprising the herbivores, carnivores, omnivores, decomposers, and detritivores), feed on the autotrophs or other heterotrophs to obtain their energy. The energy flow into and out of each trophic level in a food chain can be identified and represented diagrammatically using arrows of different sizes. The sizes of the arrows (see the diagrams below and on the next page) represent different amounts of energy lost from that particular trophic level.

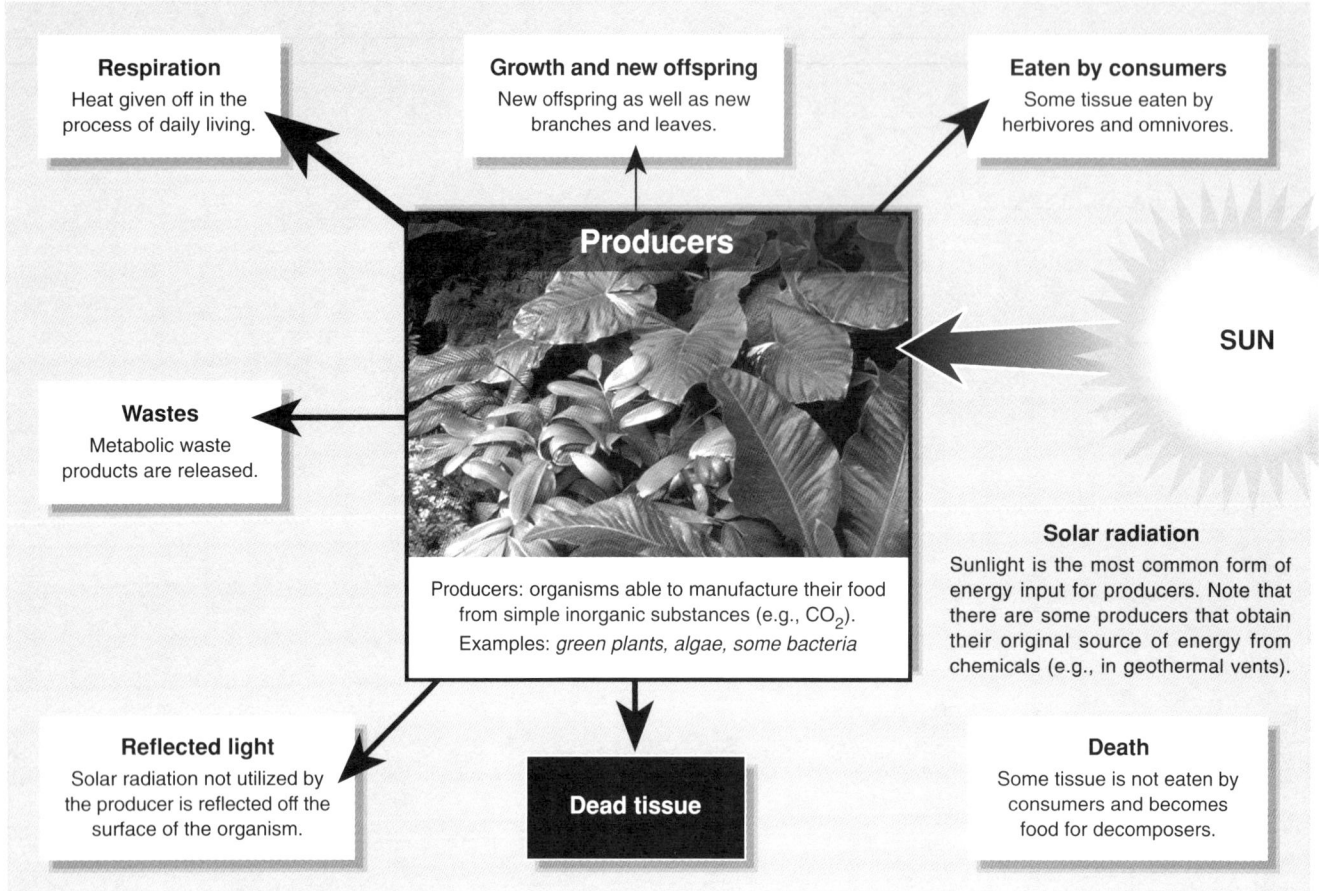

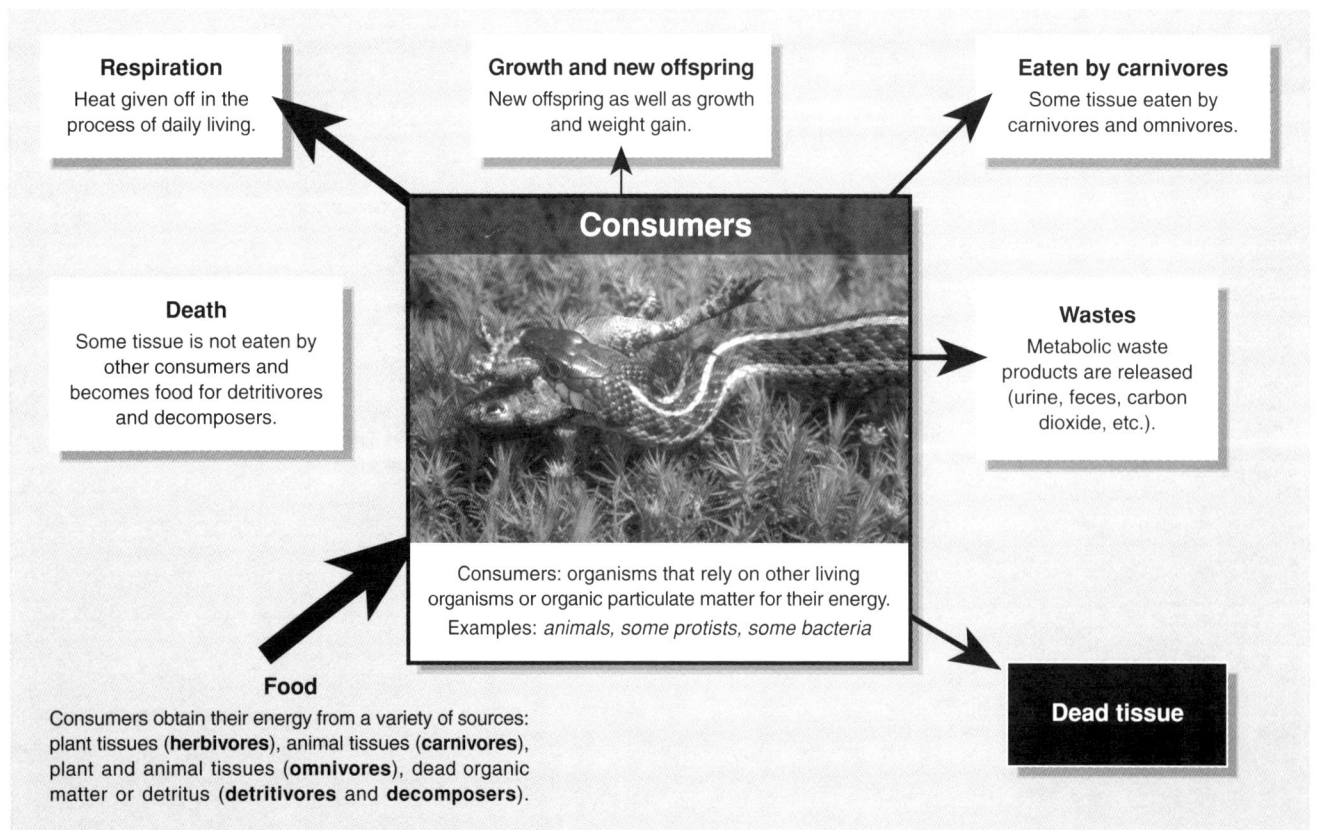

Respiration
Heat given off in the process of daily living.

Growth and new offspring
New offspring as well as new branches and leaves.

Eaten by consumers
Some tissue eaten by herbivores and omnivores.

Producers

SUN

Wastes
Metabolic waste products are released.

Solar radiation
Sunlight is the most common form of energy input for producers. Note that there are some producers that obtain their original source of energy from chemicals (e.g., in geothermal vents).

Producers: organisms able to manufacture their food from simple inorganic substances (e.g., CO_2).
Examples: *green plants, algae, some bacteria*

Reflected light
Solar radiation not utilized by the producer is reflected off the surface of the organism.

Dead tissue

Death
Some tissue is not eaten by consumers and becomes food for decomposers.

Respiration
Heat given off in the process of daily living.

Growth and new offspring
New offspring as well as growth and weight gain.

Eaten by carnivores
Some tissue eaten by carnivores and omnivores.

Consumers

Death
Some tissue is not eaten by other consumers and becomes food for detritivores and decomposers.

Wastes
Metabolic waste products are released (urine, feces, carbon dioxide, etc.).

Consumers: organisms that rely on other living organisms or organic particulate matter for their energy.
Examples: *animals, some protists, some bacteria*

Food
Consumers obtain their energy from a variety of sources: plant tissues (**herbivores**), animal tissues (**carnivores**), plant and animal tissues (**omnivores**), dead organic matter or detritus (**detritivores** and **decomposers**).

Dead tissue

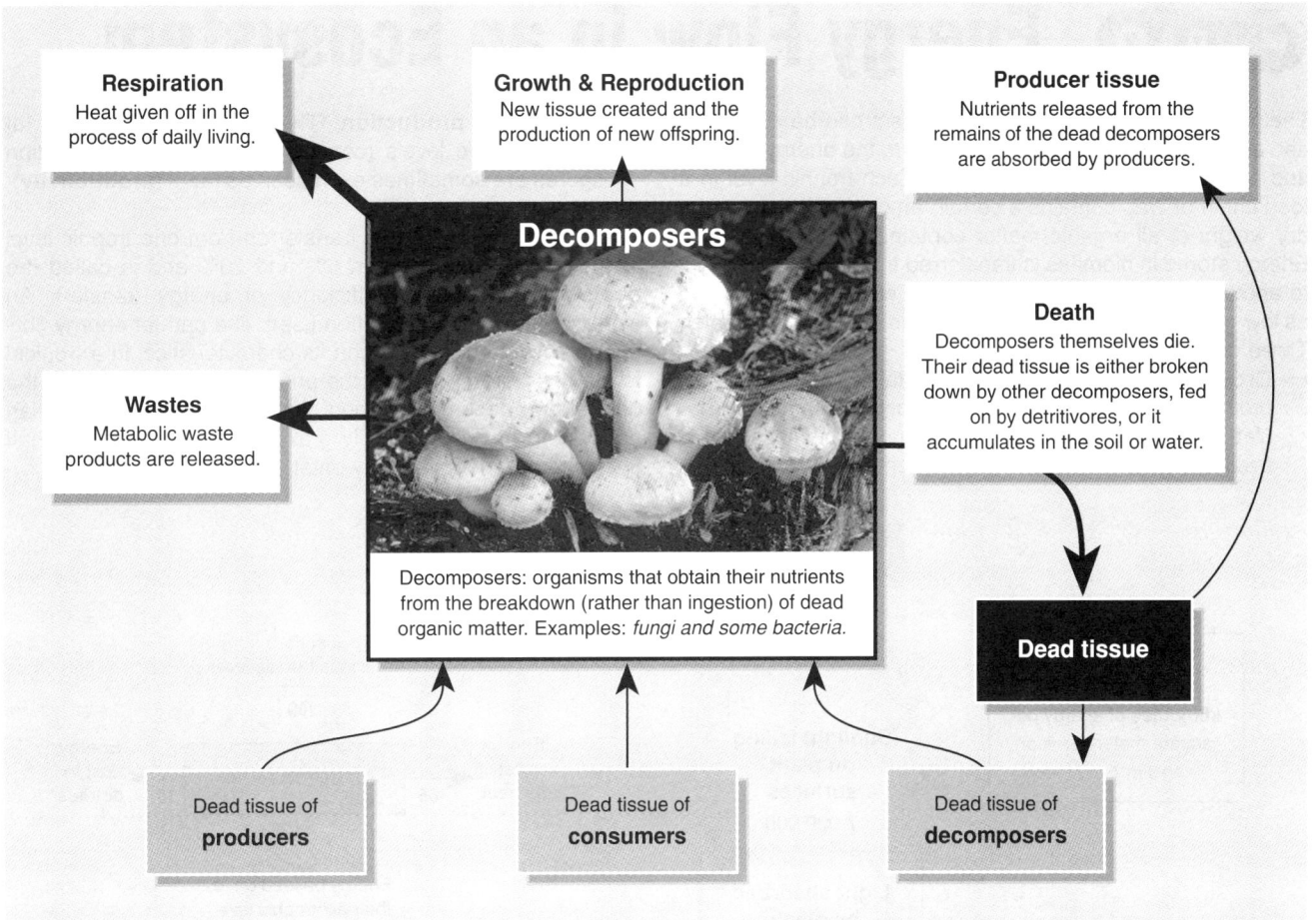

Respiration
Heat given off in the process of daily living.

Growth & Reproduction
New tissue created and the production of new offspring.

Producer tissue
Nutrients released from the remains of the dead decomposers are absorbed by producers.

Decomposers

Death
Decomposers themselves die. Their dead tissue is either broken down by other decomposers, fed on by detritivores, or it accumulates in the soil or water.

Wastes
Metabolic waste products are released.

Decomposers: organisms that obtain their nutrients from the breakdown (rather than ingestion) of dead organic matter. Examples: *fungi and some bacteria.*

Dead tissue

Dead tissue of **producers**

Dead tissue of **consumers**

Dead tissue of **decomposers**

1. Study the diagrams on energy flow relating to producers, consumers and decomposers. Define the following categories of organism with respect to how they obtain their energy:

(a) Autotroph: _____

_____

(b) Heterotroph: _____

_____

(c) Saprotroph: _____

_____

2. Compost heaps can generate a great deal of heat. Explain where this heat comes from:

_____

3. Describe the ecological importance of decomposer organisms:

_____

4. Decomposers and detritivores have similar ecological roles in that they both obtain nutriment from dead organic matter.

(a) Distinguish between decomposers and detritivores: _____

_____

(b) Suggest how the activity of detritivores might speed up the breakdown of dead organic matter by decomposers:

_____

_____

5. Explain how energy may be lost from organisms in the form of:

(a) Wastes: _____

(b) Respiration: _____

DA 2 Energy Flow in an Ecosystem

The flow of energy through an ecosystem can be measured and analyzed. It provides some idea as to the energy trapped and passed on at each trophic level. Each trophic level in a food chain or web contains a certain amount of biomass: the dry weight of all organic matter contained in its organisms. Energy stored in biomass is transferred from one trophic level to another (by eating, defecation etc.), with some being lost as low-grade heat energy to the environment in each transfer. Three definitions are useful:

- **Gross primary production**: The total of organic material produced by plants (including that lost to respiration).
- **Net primary production**: The amount of biomass that is available to consumers at subsequent trophic levels.

- **Secondary production**: The amount of biomass at higher trophic levels (consumer production). Production figures are sometimes expressed as rates (**productivity**).

The percentage of energy transferred from one trophic level to the next varies between 5% and 20% and is called the **ecological efficiency** (efficiency of energy transfer). An average figure of 10% is often used. The path of energy flow in an ecosystem depends on its characteristics. In a tropical forest ecosystem, most of the primary production enters the detrital and decomposer food chains. However, in an ocean ecosystem or an intensively grazed pasture more than half the primary production may enter the grazing food chain.

Energy Flow Through an Ecosystem

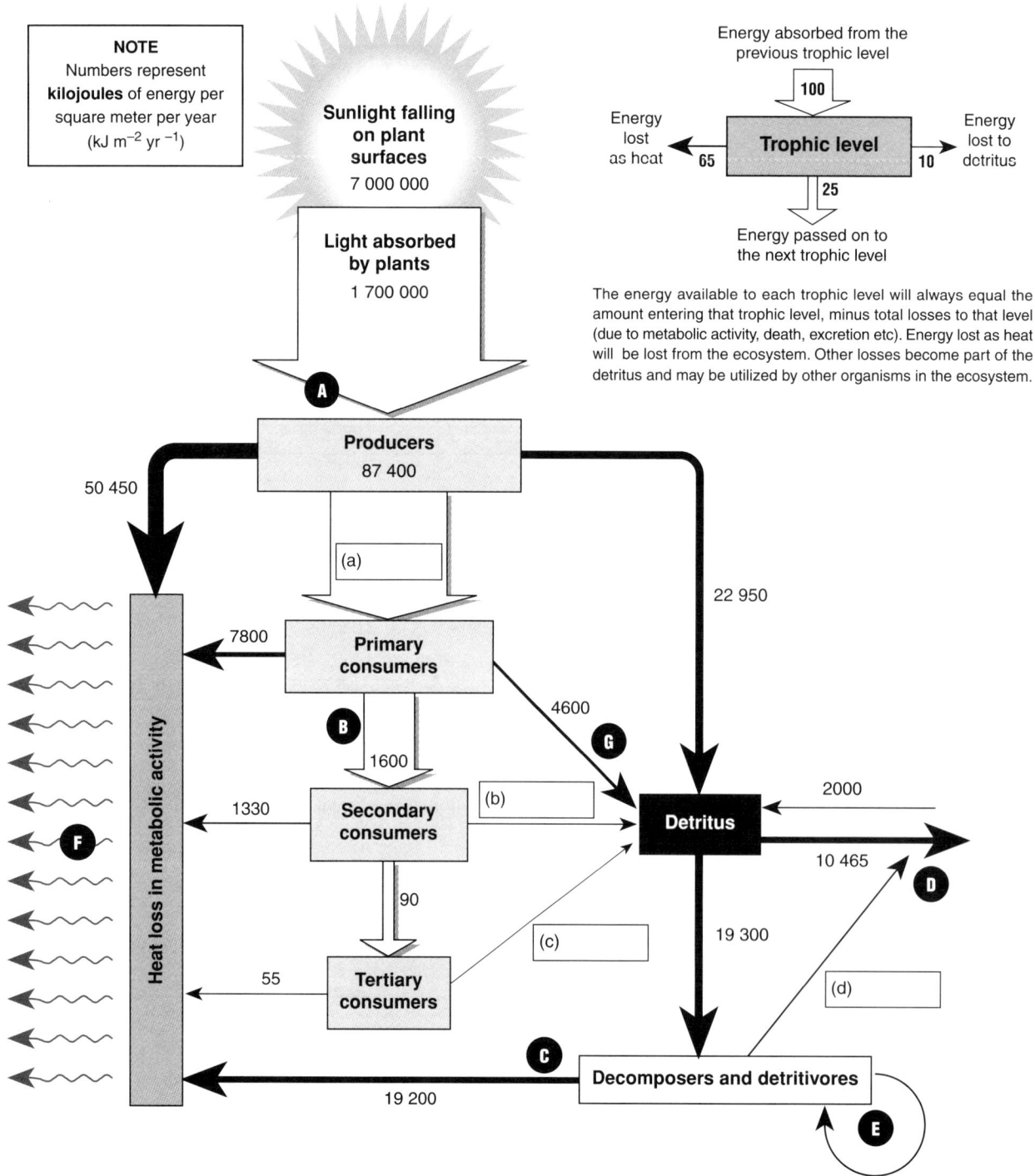

NOTE
Numbers represent **kilojoules** of energy per square meter per year
$(kJ\ m^{-2}\ yr^{-1})$

Sunlight falling on plant surfaces
7 000 000

Light absorbed by plants
1 700 000

Energy absorbed from the previous trophic level
100

Energy lost as heat   65   **Trophic level**   10   Energy lost to detritus

25

Energy passed on to the next trophic level

The energy available to each trophic level will always equal the amount entering that trophic level, minus total losses to that level (due to metabolic activity, death, excretion etc). Energy lost as heat will be lost from the ecosystem. Other losses become part of the detritus and may be utilized by other organisms in the ecosystem.

A

Producers
87 400

50 450

(a)

22 950

7800

Primary consumers

B

1600

4600

G

Heat loss in metabolic activity

1330

Secondary consumers

(b)

Detritus

2000

10 465

D

90

F

55

(c)

19 300

Tertiary consumers

(d)

C

Decomposers and detritivores

19 200

E

1. Study the diagram on the previous page illustrating energy flow through a hypothetical ecosystem. Use the example at the top of the page as a guide to calculate the missing values (a)–(d) in the diagram. Note that the sum of the energy inputs always equals the sum of the energy outputs. Place your answers in the spaces provided on the diagram.

2. State the original source of energy that powers this ecosystem: _____

3. Name the processes that are occurring at the points labeled **A – G** on the diagram:

   A. _____

   B. _____

   C. _____

   D. _____

   E. _____

   F. _____

   G. _____

4. Calculate the percentage of light energy falling on the plants that is absorbed at point A:

   Light absorbed by plants ÷ sunlight falling on plant surfaces x 100 = _____

5. Describe what happens to the light energy that is not absorbed: _____

   _____

   _____

6. Calculate the percentage of light energy absorbed that is actually converted into producer energy:

   Producers ÷ light absorbed by plants x 100 = _____

7. Of the total amount of energy absorbed by producers in this ecosystem (at point **A**) calculate:

   (a) The total amount that ended up as metabolic waste heat (in kJ): _____

   (b) The percentage of the total amount of energy entering the system that ended up as waste heat: _____

8. (a) State the groups for which detritus is an energy source: _____

   (b) Describe by what means detritus could be removed or added to an ecosystem: _____

   _____

9. In certain conditions, detritus will build up in an environment where few (or no) decomposers can exist.
   (a) Describe the consequences of this lack of decomposer activity to the energy flow:

   _____

   _____

   (b) Add additional arrow(s) to the diagram on the previous page to illustrate your answer.

   (c) Name **three** examples of materials that have resulted from a lack of decomposer activity on detritus material:

   _____

   _____

   _____

10. The **ten percent law** states that the total energy content of a trophic level in an ecosystem is only about one-tenth (or 10%) that of the preceding level. For each of the trophic levels in the diagram on the preceding page, determine the amount of energy passed on to the next trophic level as a percentage:

   (a) Producer to primary consumer: _____

   (b) Primary consumer to secondary consumer: _____

   (c) Secondary consumer to tertiary consumer: _____

Ecological Pyramids

The trophic levels of any ecosystem can be arranged in a pyramid shape. The first trophic level is placed at the bottom and subsequent trophic levels are stacked on top in their 'feeding sequence'. Ecological pyramids can illustrate changes in the **numbers**, **biomass** (weight), or content of organisms at each level. Each of these three kinds of pyramids tell us something different about the flow of energy and materials between one trophic level and the next. The type of pyramid you choose in order to express information about the ecosystem will depend on what particular features of the ecosystem you are interested in and, of course, the type of data you have collected.

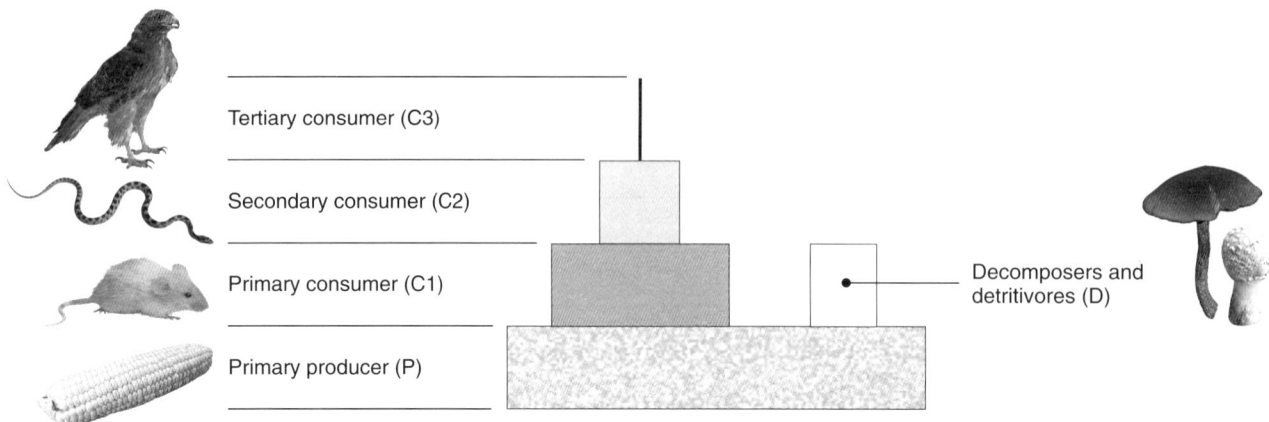

Tertiary consumer (C3)

Secondary consumer (C2)

Primary consumer (C1)

Primary producer (P)

Decomposers and detritivores (D)

The generalized ecological pyramid pictured above shows a conventional pyramid shape, with a large number (or biomass) of producers forming the base for an increasingly small number (or biomass) of consumers. Decomposers are placed at the level of the primary consumers and off to the side. They may obtain energy from many different trophic levels and so do not fit into the conventional pyramid structure. For any particular ecosystem at any one time (e.g. the forest ecosystem below), the shape of this typical pyramid can vary greatly depending on whether the trophic relationships are expressed as numbers, biomass or energy.

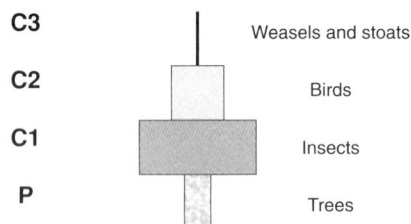

C3
C2
C1
P

Weasels and stoats
Birds
Insects
Trees

Numbers in a forest community

Pyramids of numbers display the number of individual organisms at each trophic level. The pyramid above has few producers, but they may be of a very large size (e.g. trees). This gives an 'inverted pyramid' although not all pyramids of numbers are like this.

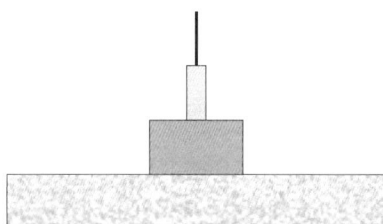

Biomass in a forest community

Biomass pyramids measure the 'weight' of biological material at each trophic level. Water content of organisms varies, so 'dry weight' is often used. Organism size is taken into account, so meaningful comparisons of different trophic levels are possible.

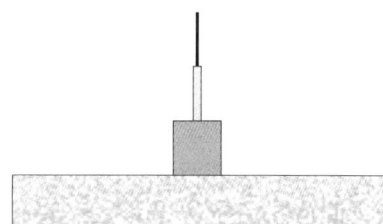

Energy in a forest community

Pyramids of energy are often very similar to biomass pyramids. The energy content at each trophic level is generally comparable to the biomass (i.e. similar amounts of dry biomass tend to have about the same energy content).

1. Describe what the three types of ecological pyramids measure:

   (a) Number pyramid: _____

   (b) Biomass pyramid: _____

   (c) Energy pyramid: _____

2. Explain the advantage of using a biomass or energy pyramid rather than a pyramid of numbers to express the relationship between different trophic levels:

   _____
   _____
   _____

3. Explain why it is possible for the forest ecosystem (on the next page) to have very few producers supporting a large number of consumers:

   _____
   _____

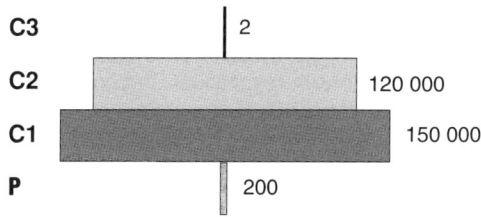

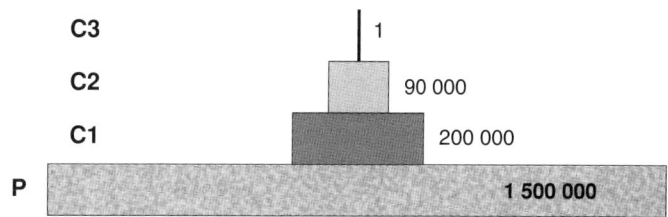

Pyramid of numbers: forest community

In a forest community a few producers may support a large number of consumers. This is due to the large size of the producers; large trees can support many individual consumer organisms. The example above shows the numbers at each trophic level for an oak forest in England, in an area of 10 m^2.

Pyramid of numbers: grassland community

In a grassland community a large number of producers are required to support a much smaller number of consumers. This is due to the small size of the producers. Grass plants can support only a few individual consumer organisms and take time to recover from grazing pressure. The example above shows the numbers at each trophic level for a derelict grassland area (10 m^2) in Michigan, United States.

Pyramids for a Plankton Community

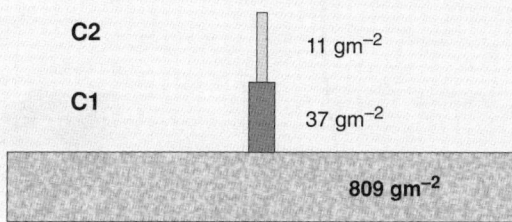

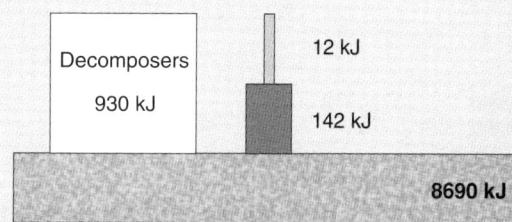

Biomass

The pyramids of biomass and energy are virtually identical. The two pyramids illustrated here relate to the same hypothetical plankton community. A large biomass of producers supports a smaller biomass of consumers. The energy at each trophic level is reduced with each

Energy

progressive stage in the food chain. As a general rule, a maximum of 10% of the energy is passed on to the next level in the food chain. The remaining energy is lost due to respiration, waste, and heat.

4. Determine the **energy loss** between trophic levels in the plankton community example in the above diagram:

(a) Between producers and the primary consumers: _____

(b) Between the primary consumers and the secondary consumers: _____

(c) Explain why the energy passed on from the producer to primary consumers is considerably less than the normally expected 10% occurring in most other communities (describe where the rest of the energy was lost to):

_____

_____

(d) After the producers, which trophic group has the greatest energy content: _____

(e) Give a likely explanation why this is the case: _____

_____

_____

An unusual biomass pyramid

The biomass pyramids of some ecosystems appear rather unusual with an inverted shape. The first trophic level has a lower biomass than the second level. What this pyramid does not show is the rate at which the producers (algae) are reproducing in order to support the larger biomass of consumers.

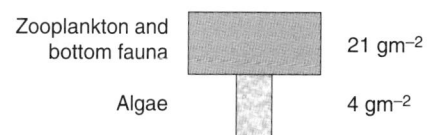

Biomass

5. Give a possible explanation of how a small biomass of producers(algae) can support a larger biomass of consumers (zooplankton):

_____

_____

_____

The Carbon Cycle

Carbon is an essential element in living systems, providing the chemical framework to form the molecules that make up living organisms (e.g. proteins, carbohydrates, fats, and nucleic acids). Carbon also makes up approximately 0.03% of the atmosphere as the gas carbon dioxide (CO_2), and it is present in the ocean as carbonate and bicarbonate, and in rocks such as limestone. Carbon cycles between the living (biotic) and non-living (abiotic)

environment: it is fixed in the process of photosynthesis and returned to the atmosphere in respiration. Carbon may remain locked up in biotic or abiotic systems for long periods of time as, for example, in the wood of trees or in fossil fuels such as coal or oil. Human activity has disturbed the balance of the carbon cycle (the global carbon budget) through activities such as combustion (e.g. the burning of wood and **fossil fuels**) and deforestation.

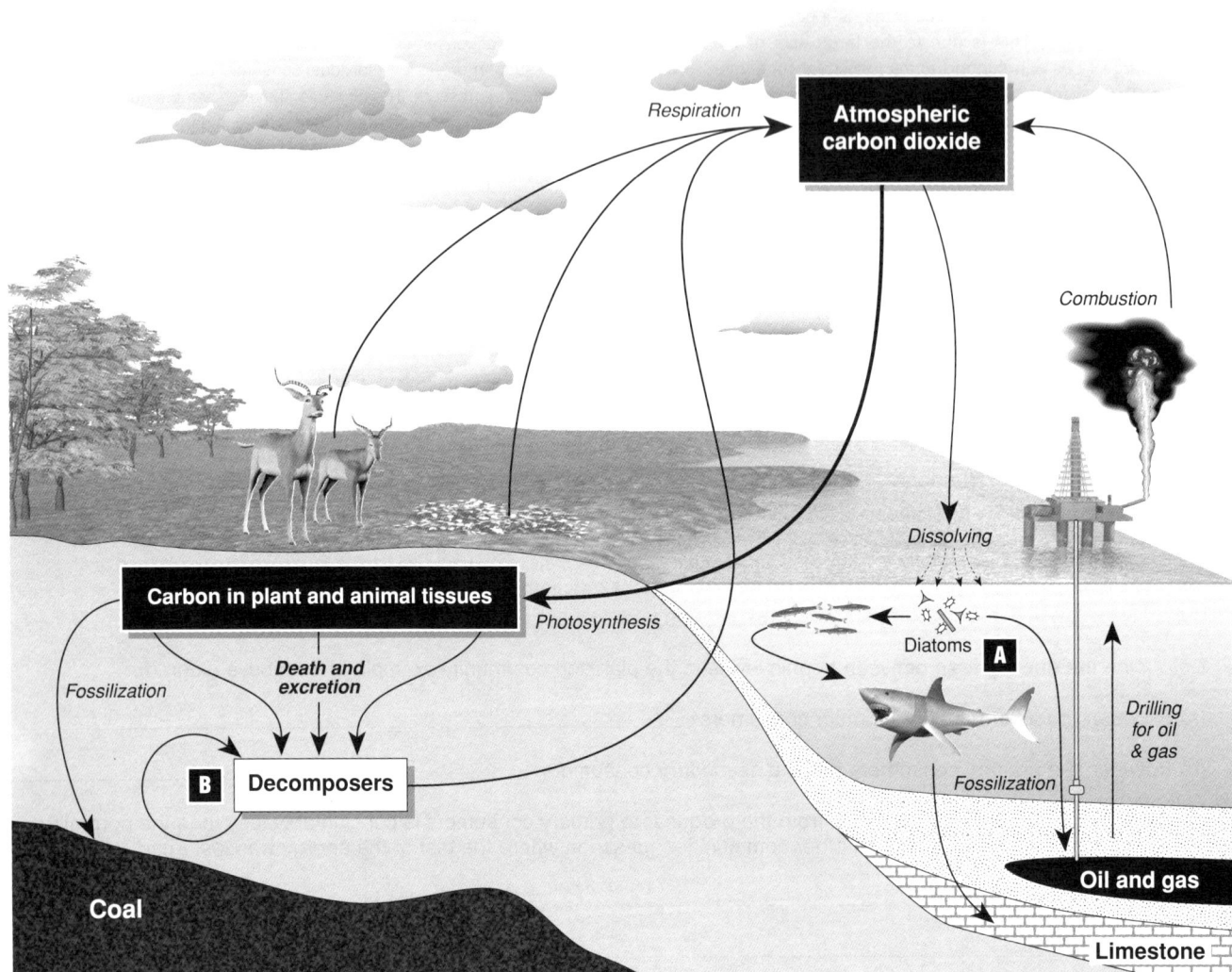

1. In the diagram above, add **arrows** and **labels** to show the following activities:

   (a) Dissolving of limestone by acid rain   (c) Mining and burning of coal
   (b) Release of carbon from the marine food chain (d) Burning of plant material.

2. Describe the **biological origin** of the following geological deposits:

   (a) Coal: _____

   (b) Oil: _____

   (c) Limestone: _____

3. Describe the two processes that **release** carbon into the atmosphere: _____

   _____

   _____

4. Name the **four** geological reservoirs (sinks), in the diagram above, that can act as a source of carbon:

   (a) _____ (c) _____

   (b) _____ (d) _____

Termite mound in rainforest

Dung beetle on cow pat

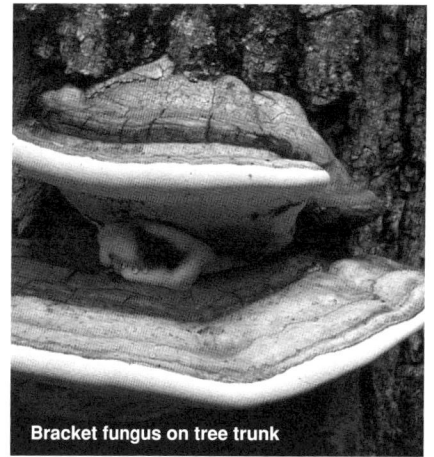

Bracket fungus on tree trunk

Termites: These insects play an important role in nutrient recycling. With the aid of symbiotic protozoans and bacteria in their guts, they can digest the tough cellulose of woody tissues in trees. Termites fulfill a vital function in breaking down the endless rain of debris in tropical rainforests.

Dung beetles: Beetles play a major role in the decomposition of animal dung. Some beetles merely eat the dung, but true dung beetles, such as the scarabs and *Geotrupes*, bury the dung and lay their eggs in it to provide food for the beetle grubs during their development.

Fungi: Together with decomposing bacteria, fungi perform an important role in breaking down dead plant matter in the leaf litter of forests. Some mycorrhizal fungi have been found to link up to the root systems of trees where an exchange of nutrients occurs (a mutualistic relationship).

5. Explain what would happen to the carbon cycle if there were no decomposers present in an ecosystem:

_____

_____

6. Study the diagram on the previous page and identify the processes represented at the points labeled [A] and [B]:

(a) Process carried out by the diatoms at label **A**: _____

(b) Process carried out by the decomposers at label **B**: _____

7. Explain how each of the three organisms listed below has a role to play in the carbon cycle:

(a) Dung beetles: _____

_____

_____

(b) Termites: _____

_____

_____

(c) Fungi: _____

_____

_____

8. In natural circumstances, accumulated reserves of carbon such as peat, coal and oil represent a **sink** or natural diversion from the cycle. Eventually the carbon in these sinks returns to the cycle through the action of geological processes which return deposits to the surface for oxidation.

(a) Describe what effect human activity is having on the **amount** of carbon stored in sinks: _____

_____

(b) Explain **two global effects** arising from this activity: _____

_____

_____

(c) Suggest what could be done to prevent or alleviate these effects: _____

_____

_____

The Nitrogen Cycle

A 2

Nitrogen is a crucial element for living things, forming an essential part of protein and nucleic acid structure. The Earth's atmosphere is about 80% nitrogen gas (N_2), but molecular nitrogen is so stable that it is only rarely available directly to organisms, and is often in short supply in biological systems. Bacteria are important in transferring nitrogen between the biotic and abiotic environments. Some bacteria fix atmospheric nitrogen, while others convert ammonia to nitrate, enabling it to be incorporated into plant and animal tissues. Nitrogen-fixing bacteria are found living freely in the soil (Azotobacter) and in

symbioses with some plants in root nodules (Rhizobium). Lightning discharges also oxidise nitrogen gas to nitrate, which ends up in the soil. Denitrifying bacteria reverse this activity and return fixed nitrogen to the atmosphere. Humans intervene in the cycle by producing and applying nitrogen fertilizers. Some of this is from organic sources (e.g. green crops and manures), but much is inorganic, produced from atmospheric nitrogen using an energy-expensive, industrial process. Excessive nitrogen use may pollute water supplies, particularly where land clearance increases the amount of leaching and runoff .

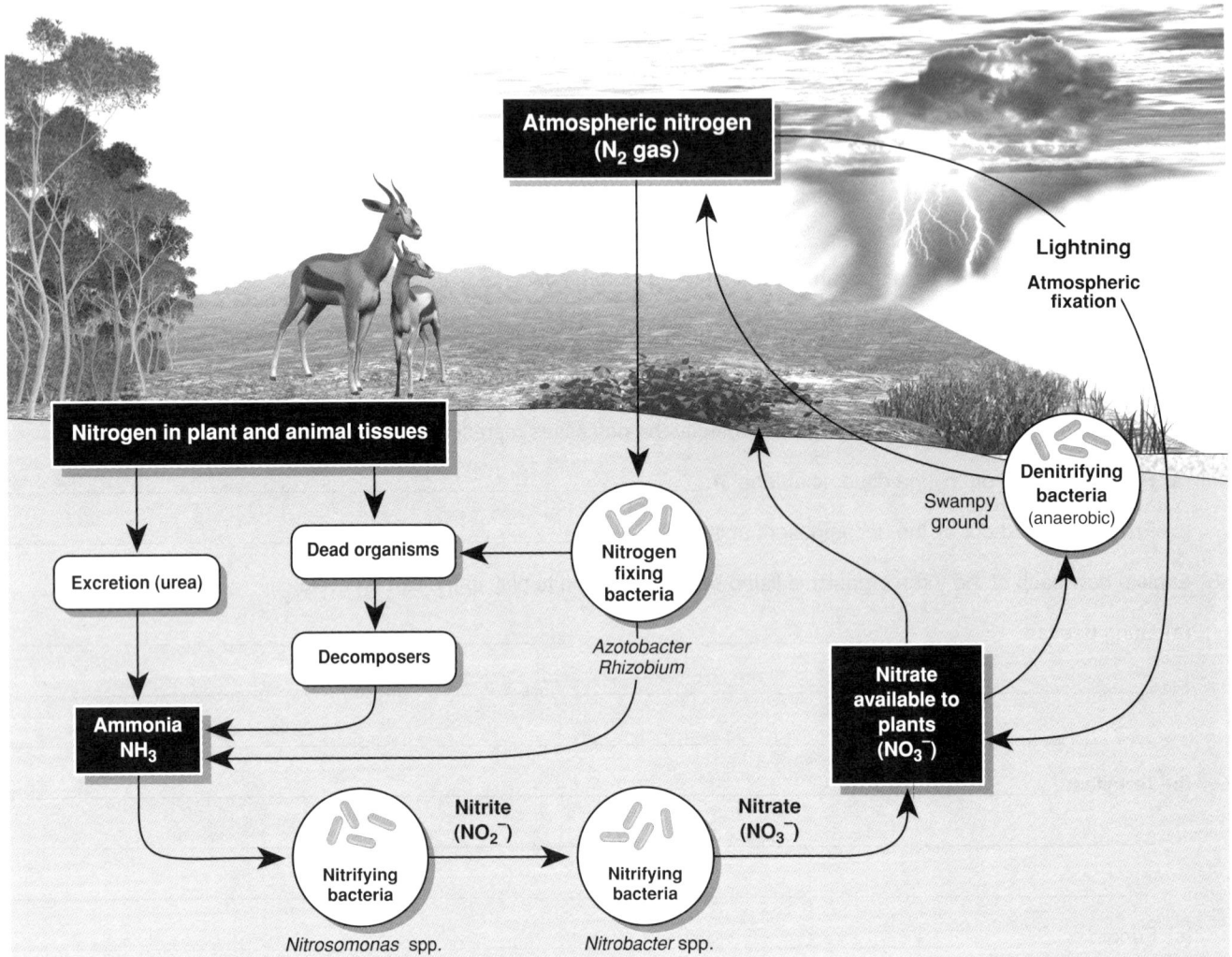

1. Describe **five** instances in the nitrogen cycle where **bacterial** action is important:

    (a) _____

    (b) _____

    (c) _____

    (d) _____

    (e) _____

2. List **three** processes that **fix** atmospheric nitrogen:

    (a) _____ (b) _____ (c) _____

3. Name the main geological reservoir that provides a source of nitrogen: _____

4. State the form in which nitrogen is available to most plants: _____

5. Briefly describe one way in which humans can intervene in the nitrogen cycle: _____

The Phosphorus Cycle

Phosphorus is an essential component of nucleic acids and ATP. Unlike carbon, phosphorus has no atmospheric component; cycling of phosphorus is very slow and tends to be local. Small losses from terrestrial systems by leaching are generally balanced by gains from weathering. In aquatic and terrestrial ecosystems, phosphorus is cycled through food webs. Bacterial decomposition breaks down the remains of dead organisms and excreted products. Phosphatizing bacteria further break down these products and return phosphates to the soil. Phosphorus is lost from ecosystems through run-off, precipitation, and sedimentation. Sedimentation may lock phosphorus away but, in the much longer term, it can become available again through processes such as geological uplift. Some phosphorus returns to the land as **guano**; phosphate-rich manure (typically of fish eating birds). This return is small though compared with the phosphate transferred to the oceans each year by natural processes and human activity. Excess phosphorus entering water bodies through runoff is a major contributor to **eutrophication** and excessive algal and weed growth, primarily because phosphorus is often limiting in aquatic systems.

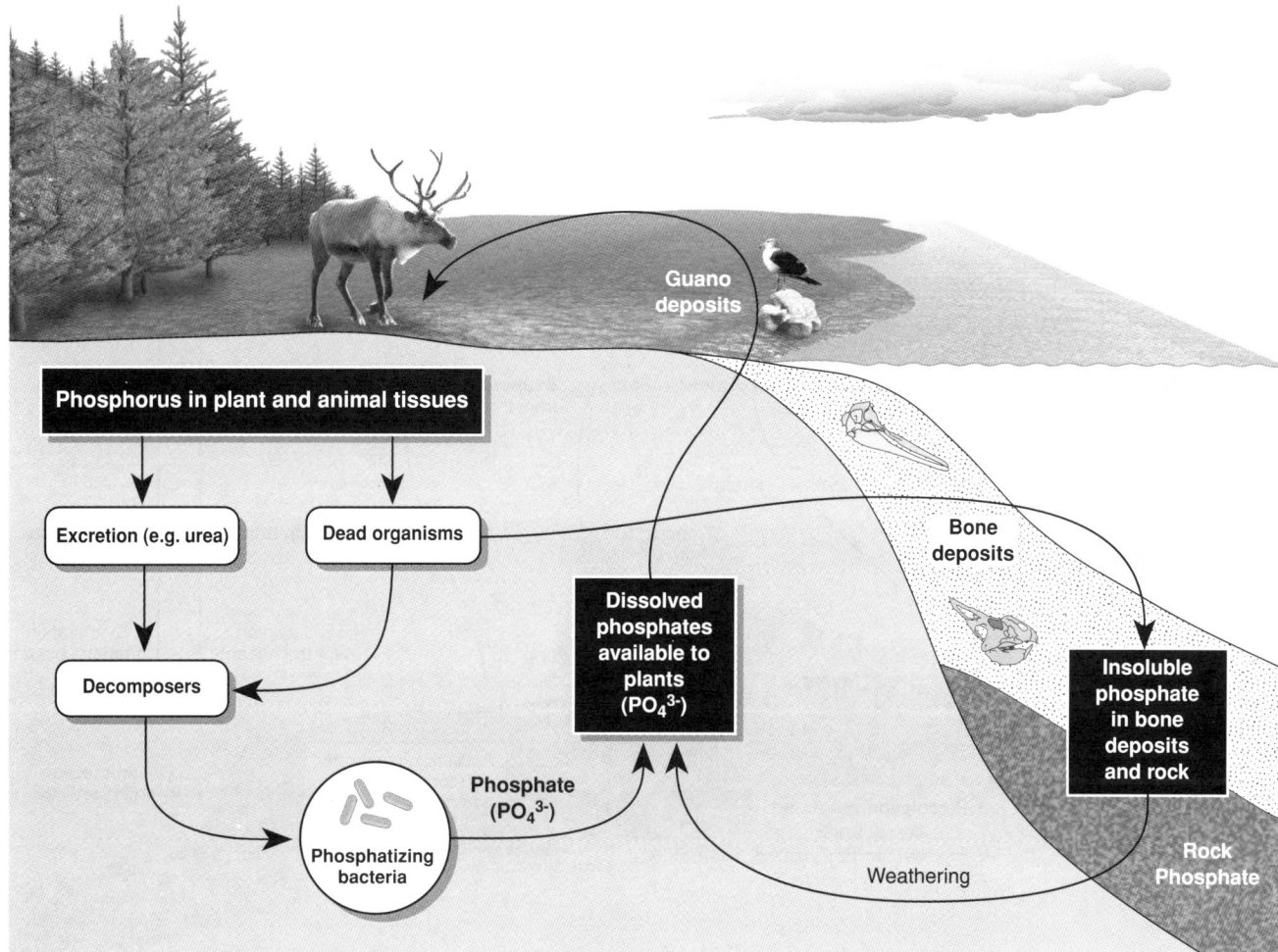

Diagram labels: Guano deposits; Phosphorus in plant and animal tissues; Excretion (e.g. urea); Dead organisms; Decomposers; Phosphatizing bacteria; Phosphate (PO_4^{3-}); Dissolved phosphates available to plants (PO_4^{3-}); Bone deposits; Insoluble phosphate in bone deposits and rock; Weathering; Rock Phosphate

1. In the diagram, add an arrow and label to show where ONE human activity might intervene in the phosphorus cycle.

2. Describe TWO instances in the phosphorus cycle where bacterial action is important:

   (a) _____

   (b) _____

3. Name TWO types of molecules found in living organisms which include phosphorus as a part of their structure:

   (a) _____ (b) _____

4. Name and describe the origin of THREE forms of inorganic phosphate that make up the geological reservoir:

   (a) _____

   (b) _____

   (c) _____

5. Name the processes that must occur in order to make rock phosphate available to plants again: _____

   _____

6. State one major difference between the phosphorus and carbon cycles: _____

The Water Cycle

The hydrologic cycle (water cycle), collects, purifies, and distributes the earth's fixed supply of water. The main processes in this water recycling are described below. Besides replenishing inland water supplies, rainwater causes erosion and is a major medium for transporting dissolved nutrients within and among ecosystems. On a global scale, evaporation (conversion of water to gaseous water vapor) exceeds precipitation (rain, snow etc.) over the oceans. This results in a net movement of water vapor (carried by winds) over the land. On land, precipitation exceeds evaporation. Some of this precipitation becomes locked up in snow and ice, for varying lengths of time. Most forms surface and groundwater systems that flow back to the sea, completing the major part of the cycle. Living organisms, particularly plants, participate to varying degrees in the water cycle. Over the sea, most of the water vapor is due to evaporation alone. However on land, about 90% of the vapor results from plant transpiration. Animals (particularly humans) intervene in the cycle by utilizing the resource for their own needs.

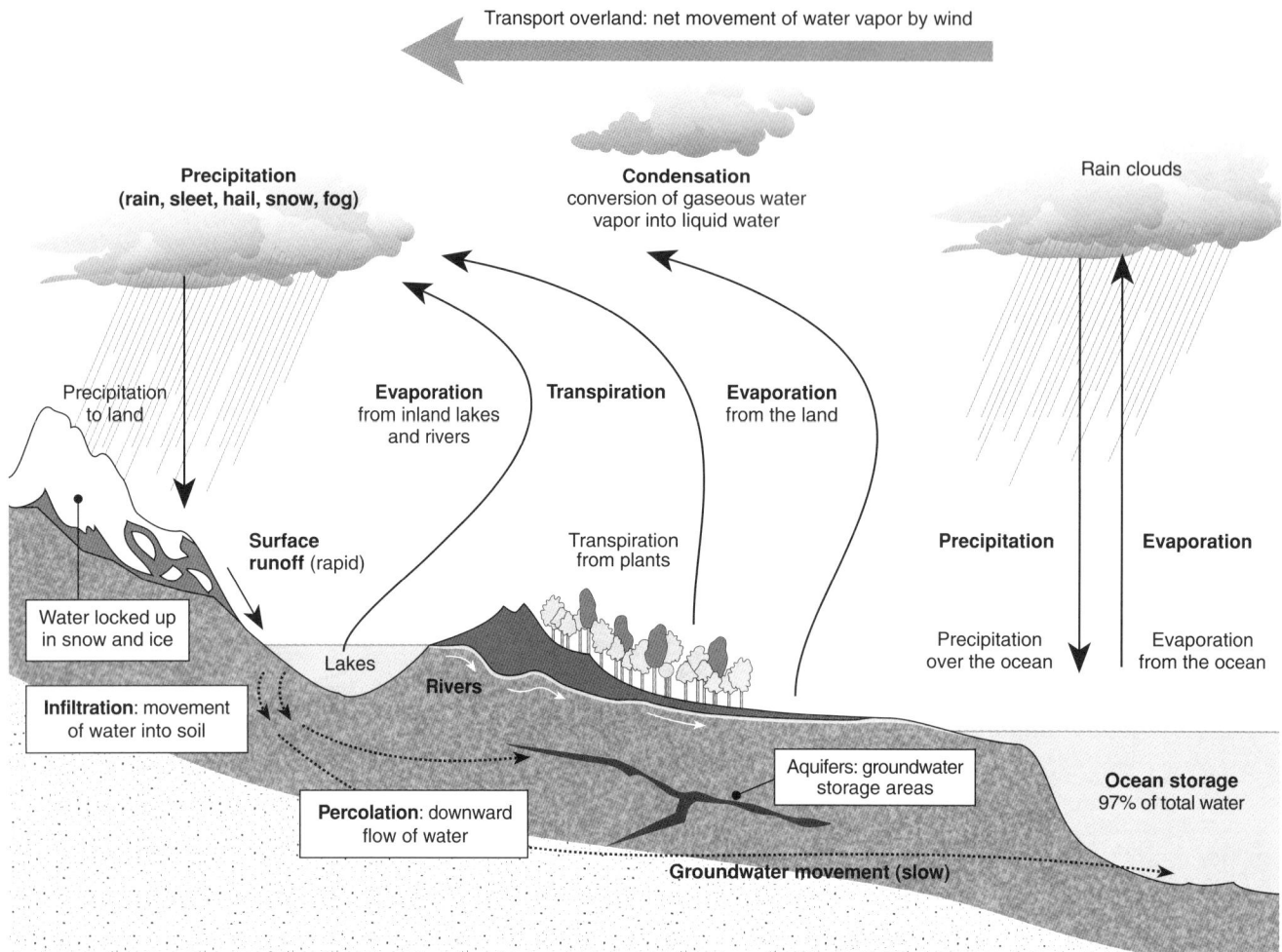

Transport overland: net movement of water vapor by wind

Precipitation (rain, sleet, hail, snow, fog)

Condensation conversion of gaseous water vapor into liquid water

Rain clouds

Precipitation to land

Evaporation from inland lakes and rivers

Transpiration

Evaporation from the land

Transpiration from plants

Precipitation

Evaporation

Water locked up in snow and ice

Lakes

Surface runoff (rapid)

Precipitation over the ocean

Evaporation from the ocean

Infiltration: movement of water into soil

Rivers

Percolation: downward flow of water

Aquifers: groundwater storage areas

Ocean storage 97% of total water

Groundwater movement (slow)

1. Name two ways in which water returns to the oceans from the land:

   (a) _____ (b) _____

2. Briefly describe three ways in which humans may intervene in the water cycle, and the effects of these interventions:

   (a) _____

   _____

   (b) _____

   _____

   (c) _____

   _____

3. Name the main reservoir for water on Earth: _____

4. Name the main reservoirs for fresh water: _____

5. Describe the important role of plants in the cycling of water through ecosystems:

   _____

The Dynamics of Populations

IB SL
Complete nos:
1-5, 7-9

Extension: 6, 10

IB HL
Complete nos:
1-5, 7-9

Extension: 6, 10

IB Options
Complete nos:
Option G:
SL/HL: 11-13

AP Biology
Complete nos:
1-13
Some numbers
extension as
appropriate

Learning Objectives

☐ 1. Compile your own glossary from the **KEY WORDS** displayed in **bold type** in the learning objectives below.

Features of populations *(pages 290-291, 297)*

☐ 2. Recall the difference between a **population** and a **community**. Explain what is meant by **population density** and distinguish it from **population size**.

☐ 3. Understand that populations are dynamic and that they exhibit attributes not shown by individuals themselves. Recognize the following attributes of populations: **population density**, **population distribution**, birth rate (**natality**), mean (average) age, death rate (**mortality**), **survivorship** (age specific survival), migration rate, average brood size, proportion of females breeding, **age structure**. Understand that these attributes are population specific.

☐ 4. Describe, with examples, the distribution patterns of organisms within their range: *uniform distribution*, *random distribution*, *clumped distribution*. Suggest which factors govern each type of distribution.

Population growth and size *(pages 292-296)*

☐ 5. Recall that populations are dynamic. Outline how population size can be affected by **births**, **deaths**, and **migration** and express the relationship in an equation.

☐ 6. Recognize the value of **life tables** in providing information of patterns of population birth and mortality. Explain the role of **survivorship curve** in analyzing populations. Providing examples, describe the features of a type I, II, and III survivorship curve.

☐ 7. Describe how the trends in population change can be shown in a **population growth curve** of population numbers (Y axis) against time (X axis).

☐ 8. Understand the factors that affect final population size, explaining clearly how they operate and providing examples where necessary. Include reference to:
   (a) **Carrying capacity** of the environment.
   (b) **Environmental resistance**.
   (c) **Density dependent factors**, e.g. intraspecific competition, interspecific competition, predation.
   (d) **Density independent factors**, e.g. climatic events.
   (e) **Limiting factors**, e.g. soil nutrient.

☐ 9. Distinguish between **exponential** and **sigmoidal growth curves**. Create labeled diagrams of these curves, indicating the different phases of growth and the factors regulating population growth at each stage.

☐ 10. Recognize patterns of population growth in colonizing, stable, declining, and oscillating populations.

Species interactions *(pages 298-304)*

☐ 11. Explain the nature of the **interspecific interactions** occurring in communities. Recognize: **competition**, **mutualism**, **commensalism**, **exploitation** (parasitism, predation, herbivory), **amensalism**, and **allelopathy**.

☐ 12. Describing at least one example, explain the possible effects of predator-prey interactions on the **population sizes** of both predator and prey.

☐ 13. Describe, and give examples of, **interspecific** and **intraspecific competition**. Explain the effects of **interspecific** and/or **intraspecific competition** on the distribution and/or population size of two species.

Textbooks

See the 'Textbook Reference Grid' on pages 8-9 for textbook page references relating to material in this topic.

Supplementary Texts

See pages 5-6 for additional details of these texts:

■ Allen *et al.*, 2001. **Applied Ecology** (Collins), pp. 15-17 (popn dynamics), 46-52 (productivity).
■ Chenn, P., 1999. **Ecology** (John Murray), pp. 72-94.

Software and video resources are now provided in the Teacher Resource Handbook

Periodicals

See page 6 for details of publishers of periodicals:

STUDENT'S REFERENCE

■ **The Other Side of Eden** Biol. Sci. Rev., 15(3) Feb. 2003, pp. 2-7. *An account of the Eden Project; its role in modeling ecosystem dynamics, including the interactions between species, is discussed.*

■ **Symbiosis: Mutual Benefit or Exploitation?** Biol. Sci. Rev., 7(4) March 1995, pp. 8-11. *Symbioses are poorly understood. This article explains them and provides illustrative examples.*

■ **Inside Story** New Scientist, 29 April 2000, pp. 36-39. *Ecological interactions between fungi and plants and animals: what are the benefits?*

■ **Logarithms and Life** Biol. Sci. Rev., 13(4) March 2001, pp. 13-15. *The basics of logarithmic growth and its application to real populations.*

■ **Predator-Prey Relationships** Biol. Sci. Rev., 10(5) May 1998, pp. 31-35. *Predator-prey relationships, and the defense strategies of prey.*

■ **Reds vs Grays: Squirrel Competition** Biol. Sci. Rev., 10(4) March 1998, pp. 30-31. *The nature of the competition between red and gray squirrels in the UK; an example of competitive exclusion?*

TEACHER'S REFERENCE

■ **Small Enclosures for Aquatic Ecology Experiments** The American Biology Teacher, 62 (6), June, 2000, pp. 424-428. *Using small aquatic populations to investigate life cycles, population dynamics, and community interactions.*

■ **Killer Pigments in Bacteria** The American Biology Teacher, 62(9), Nov. 2000, pp. 649-651. *Investigating interspecific competition using bacteria as the exemplar species.*

■ **Using Spreadsheets to Model Population Growth, Competition, and Predation in Nature** The American Biology Teacher, 61(4), April, 1999, pp. 294-296. *Using spreadsheets to improve understanding of models of population growth.*

Features of Populations

Populations have a number of attributes that may be of interest. Usually, biologists wish to determine **population size** (the total number of organisms in the population). It is also useful to know the **population density** (the number of organisms per unit area). The density of a population is often a reflection of the carrying capacity of the environment - how many organisms a particular environment can support. Populations also have structure; particular ratios of different ages and sexes. These data enable us to determine whether the population is declining or increasing in size. We can also look at the **distribution** of organisms within their environment and so determine what particular aspects of the habitat are favored over others. One way to retrieve information from populations is to **sample** them. Sampling involves collecting data about features of the population from samples of that population (since populations are usually too large to examine in total). Sampling can be done directly through a number of sampling methods or indirectly (e.g. monitoring calls, looking for droppings or other signs). Some of the population attributes that we can measure or calculate are illustrated on the diagram below.

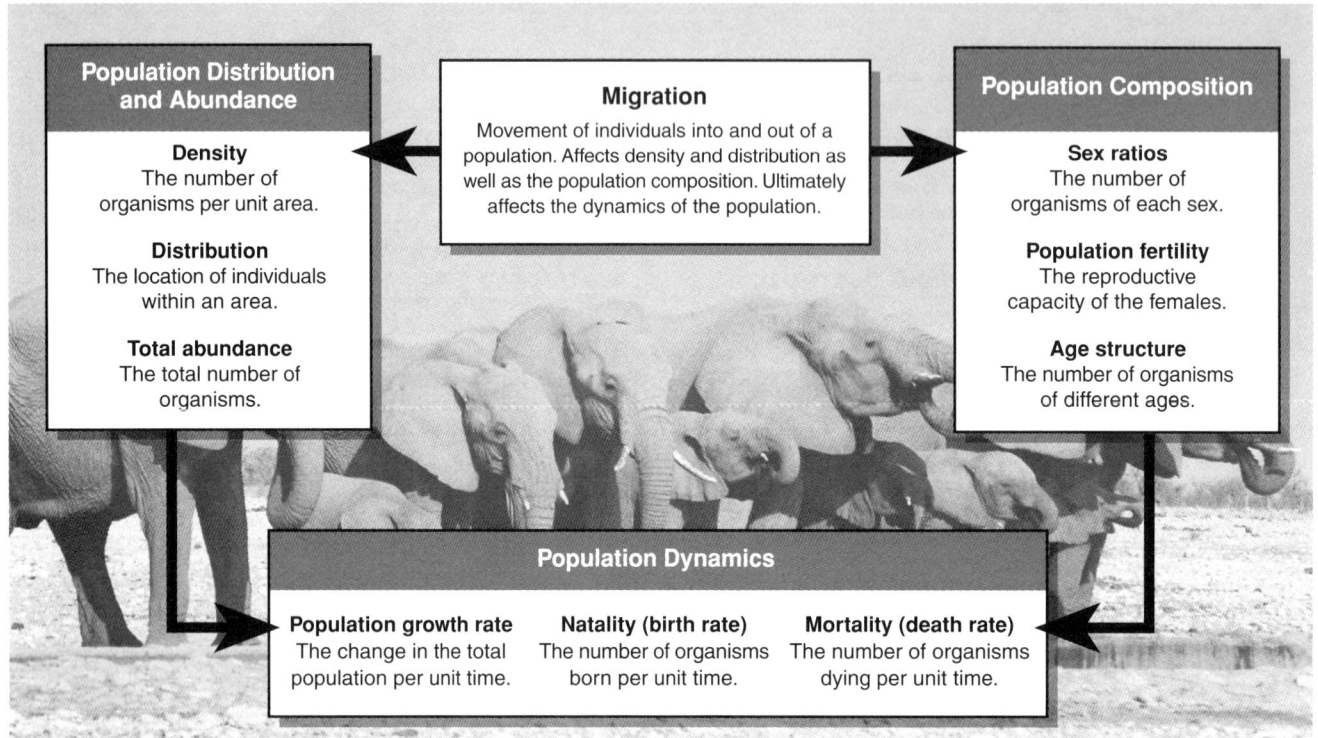

Population Distribution and Abundance

Density
The number of organisms per unit area.

Distribution
The location of individuals within an area.

Total abundance
The total number of organisms.

Migration
Movement of individuals into and out of a population. Affects density and distribution as well as the population composition. Ultimately affects the dynamics of the population.

Population Composition

Sex ratios
The number of organisms of each sex.

Population fertility
The reproductive capacity of the females.

Age structure
The number of organisms of different ages.

Population Dynamics

Population growth rate
The change in the total population per unit time.

Natality (birth rate)
The number of organisms born per unit time.

Mortality (death rate)
The number of organisms dying per unit time.

1. Give **one** example of a population attribute that would be a good indicator of each of the following (explain your answer):

   (a) Whether the population is increasing or decreasing: _____

   _____

   (b) The ability of the environment to support the population: _____

   _____

2. (a) List the population attributes that can be measured directly from the population: _____

   _____

   (b) List the population attributes that must be calculated from the data collected: _____

   _____

3. Describe the value of population sampling for each of the following situations:

   (a) Conservation of a population of an endangered species: _____

   _____

   _____

   (b) Management of a fisheries resource: _____

   _____

   _____

Density and Distribution

A 1

Distribution and density are two interrelated properties of populations. Population density is the number of individuals per unit area (for land organisms) or volume (for aquatic organisms). Careful observation and precise mapping can determine the distribution patterns for a species. The three basic distribution patterns are: random, clumped and uniform. In the diagram below, the circles represent individuals of the same species. It can also represent populations of different species.

Low Density

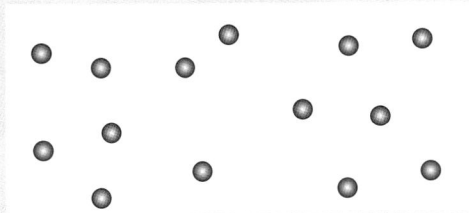

In low density populations, individuals are spaced well apart. There are only a few individuals per unit area or volume (e.g. highly territorial, solitary mammal species).

High Density

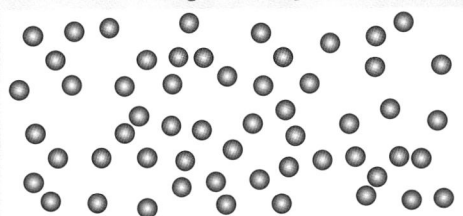

In high density populations, individuals are crowded together. There are many individuals per unit area or volume (e.g. colonial organisms, such as many corals).

Tigers are solitary animals, found at low densities.

Termites form well organized, high density colonies.

Random Distribution

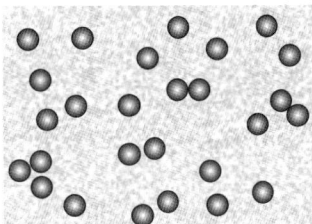

Random distributions occur when the spacing between individuals is irregular. The presence of one individual does not directly affect the location of any other individual. Random distributions are uncommon in animals but are often seen in plants.

Clumped Distribution

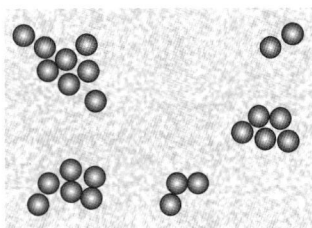

Clumped distributions occur when individuals are grouped in patches (sometimes around a resource). The presence of one individual increases the probability of finding another close by. Such distributions occur in herding and highly social species.

Uniform Distribution

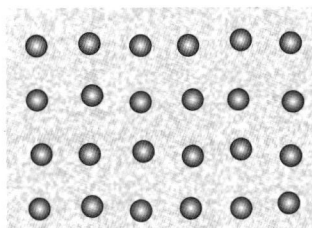

Regular distribution patterns occur when individuals are evenly spaced within the area. The presence of one individual decreases the probability of finding another individual very close by. The penguins illustrated above are also at a high density.

1. Describe why some organisms may exhibit a clumped distribution pattern because of:

   (a) Resources in the environment: _____

   (b) A group social behavior: _____

2. Name a social behavior found in some animals that may encourage a uniform distribution: _____

3. Describe the type of environment that would encourage uniform distribution: _____

4. Name an organism that exhibits the following type of distribution pattern:

   (a) Clumped: _____

   (b) Random (more or less): _____

   (c) Uniform (more or less): _____

Population Regulation

Very few species show continued exponential growth. Population size is regulated by factors that limit population growth. The diagram below illustrates how population size can be regulated by environmental factors. **Density independent factors** may affect all individuals in a population equally. Some, however, may be better able to adjust to them. **Density dependent factors** have a greater affect when the population density is higher. They become less important when the population density is low.

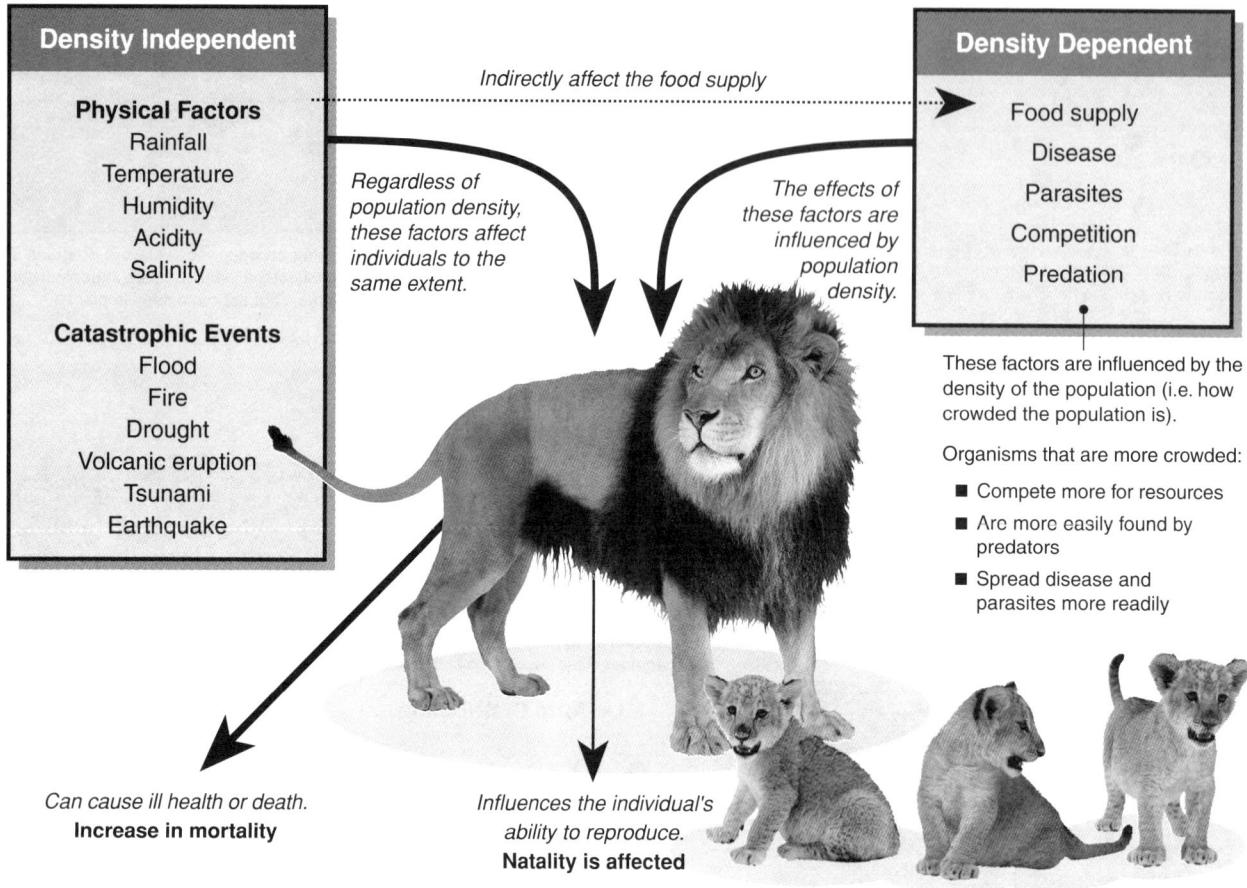

Density Independent

Physical Factors
Rainfall
Temperature
Humidity
Acidity
Salinity

Catastrophic Events
Flood
Fire
Drought
Volcanic eruption
Tsunami
Earthquake

Indirectly affect the food supply

Regardless of population density, these factors affect individuals to the same extent.

The effects of these factors are influenced by population density.

Density Dependent

Food supply
Disease
Parasites
Competition
Predation

These factors are influenced by the density of the population (i.e. how crowded the population is).

Organisms that are more crowded:

■ Compete more for resources
■ Are more easily found by predators
■ Spread disease and parasites more readily

Can cause ill health or death.
Increase in mortality

Influences the individual's ability to reproduce.
Natality is affected

1. Define the following terms as they relate to population regulation:

   (a) Density dependent factor: _____

   _____

   _____

   (b) Density independent factor: _____

   _____

   _____

2. Explain how an increase in population density allows disease to have a greater influence in regulating population size:

   _____

   _____

   _____

   _____

3. In cooler climates, aphids go through a huge population increase during the summer months. In autumn, the population 'crashes' to much lower numbers. Name a density dependent and a density independent factor regulating the population:

   (a) Density dependent: _____

   (b) Density independent: _____

Population Growth

A 1

Organisms do not generally live alone. A **population** is a group of organisms of the same species living together in one geographical area. This area may be difficult to define as populations may comprise widely dispersed individuals that come together only infrequently (e.g. for mating). The number of individuals comprising a population may also fluctuate considerably over time. These changes make populations dynamic: populations gain individuals through births or immigration, and lose individuals through deaths and emigration. For a population in **equilibrium**, these factors balance out and there is no net change in the population abundance. When losses exceed gains, the population declines.

Births, *deaths*, *immigrations* (movements into the population) and *emigrations* (movements out of the population) are events that determine the numbers of individuals in a population. Population growth depends on the number of individuals added to the population from births and immigration, minus the number lost through deaths and emigration. This is expressed as:

Calculating change in population numbers

> **Population growth =**
> **Births – Deaths + Immigration – Emigration**
> **(B) (D) (I) (E)**

The difference between immigration and emigration gives *net migration*. Ecologists usually measure the **rate** of these events. These rates are influenced by environmental factors and by the characteristics of the organisms themselves. Rates in population studies are commonly expressed in one of two ways:

- Numbers per unit time e.g. 20 150 live births per year.
- Per capita rate (number per head of population) e.g. 122 live births per 1000 individuals per year (12.2%).

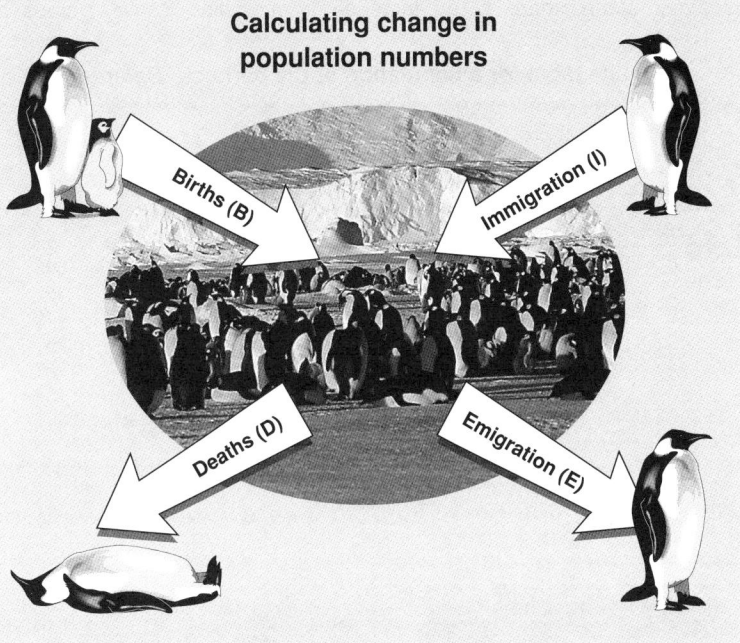

1. Define the following terms used to describe changes in population numbers:

   (a) Death rate (mortality): _____

   (b) Birth rate (natality): _____

   (c) Immigration: _____

   (d) Emigration: _____

   (e) Net migration rate: _____

2. Using the terms, B, D, I, and E (above), construct equations to express the following (the first is completed for you):

   (a) A population in equilibrium: ___B + I = D + E___

   (b) A declining population: _____

   (c) An increasing population: _____

3. The rate of population change can be expressed as the interaction of all these factors:

   > Rate of population change = Birth rate – Death rate + Net migration rate (positive or negative)

   Using the formula above, determine the annual rate of population change for Mexico and the United States in 1972:

	USA	Mexico
Birth rate	1.73%	4.3%
Death rate	0.93%	1.0%
Net migration rate	+0.20%	0.0%

   Rate of population change for USA = _____

   Rate of population change for Mexico = _____

4. A population started with a total number of 100 individuals. Over the following year, population data were collected. Calculate birth rates, death rates, net migration rate, and rate of population change for the data below (as percentages):

   (a) Births = 14: Birth rate = _____ (b) Net migration = +2: Net migration rate = _____

   (c) Deaths = 20: Death rate = _____ (d) Rate of population change = _____

   (e) State whether the population is increasing or declining: _____

Life Tables and Survivorship

DA②

The numerical data collected during a population study can be presented as a table of figures called a **life table** or graphically as a **survivorship curve**. These alternative presentations are shown below. Survivorship curves start at 1,000 and, as the population ages, the number of survivors progressively declines. The shape of a survivorship curve shows graphically at which life stages the highest mortality occurs. Wherever the curve becomes steep, there is an increase in mortality. Some

organisms suffer high losses of early life stages and compensate by producing vast numbers of offspring. Populations with higher survival rates for juveniles usually produce fewer young and have some degree of parental care. Note that many species exhibit a mix of two of the three basic types. Some birds have a high chick mortality (Type III) but adult mortality is fairly constant (Type II). Some invertebrates have high mortality only when moulting (e.g. crabs) and show a stepped curve.

Life table for a population of the barnacle *Balanus*

Age (yr)	No. alive at the start of the age interval	Proportion of original no. surviving at the start of the age interval	No. dying during the age interval	Mortality (d)
0	142	1.000	80	0.563
1	62	0.437	28	0.452
2	34	0.239	14	0.412
3	20	0.141	5	0.250
4	15	0.106	4	0.267
5	11	0.078	5	0.454
6	6	0.042	4	0.667
7	2	0.014	0	0.000
8	2	0.014	2	1.000
9	0	0.0	–	–

Life tables, such as that shown left, provide a summary of mortality for a population (usually for a group of individuals of the same age). The basic data are just the number of individuals remaining alive at successive sampling times. Life table data can tell us the ages at which most mortality occurs in a population. They can also provide information about life span and population age structure.

Life table data can be presented graphically as a **survivorship curve** (see below). Survivorship curves use a semi-log plot of the number of individuals surviving per thousand in the population against age. They are standardized as the number of survivors per 1000 individuals so that populations of different types can be easily compared.

Large mammals: Type I   **Rodents: Type II**   ***Hydra*: Type II**   **Barnacles: Type III**

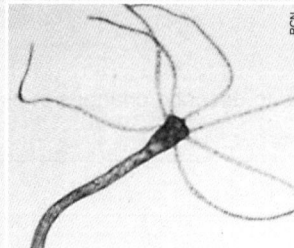

Type I survivorship curve
Mortality (death rate) is very low in the infant and juvenile years, and throughout most of adult life. Mortality increases rapidly in old age. **Examples:** humans (in developed countries) and many other large mammals (e.g. big cats, elephants).

Type II survivorship curve
Mortality is relatively constant through all life stages (no one age is more susceptible than another). **Examples:** some invertebrates such as *Hydra*, some birds, some annual plants, some lizards, and many rodents.

Type III survivorship curve
Mortality is very high during early life stages, followed by a very low death rate for the few individuals reaching adulthood. **Examples:** many fish (not mouth brooders) and most marine invertebrates (e.g. oysters, barnacles).

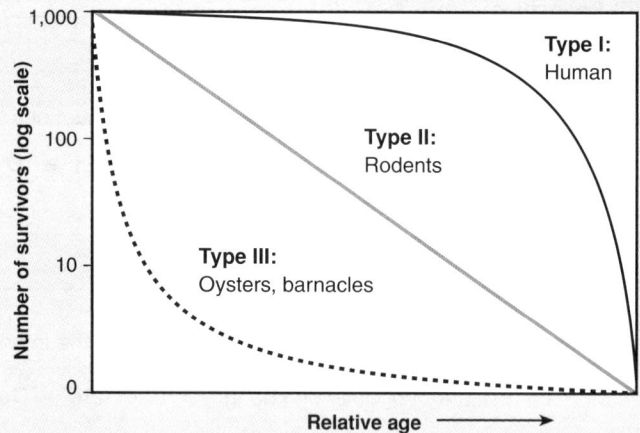

1. Suggest why human populations might not necessarily show a Type I curve: _____

_____

2. Explain how populations with a Type III survivorship compensate for the high mortality during early life stages: _____

_____

3. Describe the features of a species with a Type I survivorship that aid in high juvenile survival: _____

_____

4. In the *Balanus* example above, state when most of the group die: _____

DA 2 Population Growth Curves

Populations becoming established in a new area for the first time are often termed **colonizing populations** (below, left). They may undergo a rapid **exponential** (logarithmic) increase in numbers as there are plenty of resources to allow a high birth rate, while the death rate is often low. Exponential growth produces a J-shaped growth curve that rises steeply as more and more individuals contribute to the population increase. If the resources of the new habitat were endless (inexhaustible) then the population would continue to increase at an **exponential** rate.

However, this rarely happens in natural populations. Initially, growth may be exponential (or nearly so), but as the population grows, its increase will slow and it will stabilize at a level that can be supported by the environment (called the carrying capacity or K). This type of growth is called sigmoidal and produces the **logistic growth curve** (below, right). **Established populations** will fluctuate about K, often in a regular way (gray area on the graph below, right). Some species will have populations that vary little from this stable condition, while others may oscillate wildly.

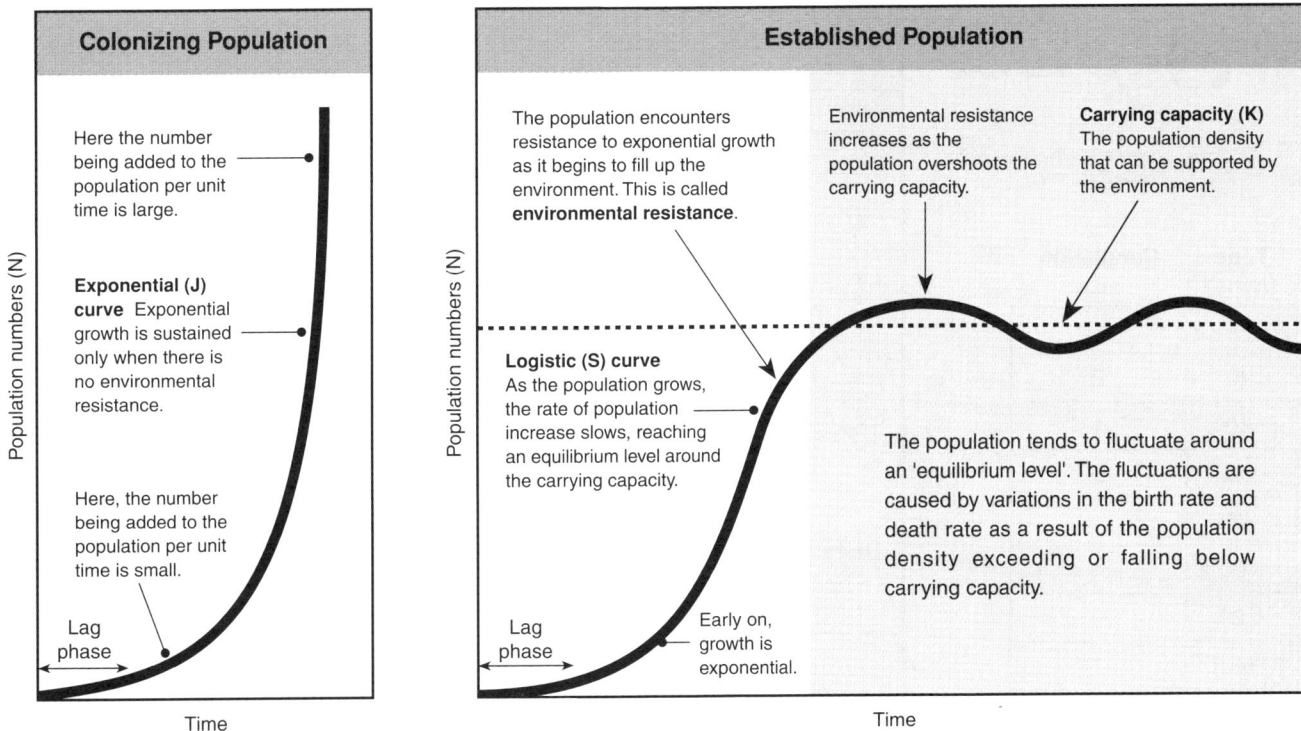

Colonizing Population

Here the number being added to the population per unit time is large.

Exponential (J) curve Exponential growth is sustained only when there is no environmental resistance.

Here, the number being added to the population per unit time is small.

Lag phase

Population numbers (N)

Time

Established Population

The population encounters resistance to exponential growth as it begins to fill up the environment. This is called **environmental resistance**.

Environmental resistance increases as the population overshoots the carrying capacity.

Carrying capacity (K) The population density that can be supported by the environment.

Logistic (S) curve As the population grows, the rate of population increase slows, reaching an equilibrium level around the carrying capacity.

The population tends to fluctuate around an 'equilibrium level'. The fluctuations are caused by variations in the birth rate and death rate as a result of the population density exceeding or falling below carrying capacity.

Lag phase

Early on, growth is exponential.

Population numbers (N)

Time

1. Explain why populations tend not to continue to increase exponentially in an environment: _____

_____

2. Explain what is meant by environmental resistance: _____

_____

3. (a) Explain what is meant by carrying capacity: _____

_____

(b) Explain the importance of **carrying capacity** to the growth and maintenance of population numbers: _____

_____

4. Species that expand into a new area, such as rabbits did in areas of Australia, typically show a period of rapid population growth followed by a slowing of population growth as density dependent factors become more important and the population settles around a level that can be supported by the carrying capacity of the environment.
   (a) Explain why a newly introduced consumer (e.g. rabbit) would initially exhibit a period of exponential population growth:

_____

_____

(b) Describe a likely outcome for a rabbit population after the initial rapid increase had slowed: _____

_____

5. Describe the effect that introduced grazing species might have on the carrying capacity of the environment:

_____

_____

DA② Growth in a Bacterial Population

Bacteria and protistans are able to reproduce by a process called **binary fission**: a simple mitotic cell division that involves a single cell dividing into two. In this activity, you will simulate the growth of a hypothetical bacterial population. Under suitable growing conditions, the bacteria divide every 20 minutes (**doubling time**). Starting with one cell, the population can increase very rapidly. A classic experiment along similar lines was conducted by the biologist Gause with species of *Paramecium*. Gause found that when a single species was grown in a test-tube culture and supplied regularly with fresh medium, its growth continued unchecked for the first few days, before levelling out (as the population reached the test-tube carrying capacity).

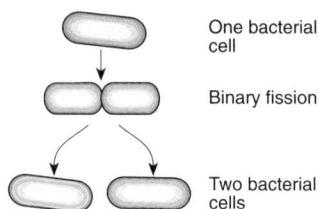

One bacterial cell

Binary fission

Two bacterial cells

Time (mins)	Population size
0	1
20	2
40	4
60	8
80	
100	
120	
140	
160	
180	
200	
220	
240	
260	
280	
300	
320	
340	
360	

1. Complete the table (above) by doubling the number of bacteria for every 20 minute interval.

2. Graph the results on the graph grid above. Make sure that you choose suitable scales for each axis. Label the axes and mark out (number) the scale for each axis.

3. State how many bacteria were present after: 1 hour: _____   3 hours: _____   6 hours: _____

4. Describe the shape of the curve you have plotted: _____

5. Explain why this hypothetical bacterial population's growth could not go on for ever in the real world: _____

_____

_____

Population Age Structure

DA②

Analyses of the age structure of populations can assist in their management because it can indicate where most population mortality occurs and whether or not reproductive individuals are being replaced. The age structure of both plant and animal populations can be examined; a common method is through an analysis of size which is often related to age in a predictable way.

Managed Fisheries
The graphs below illustrate the age structure of a hypothetical fish population under different fishing pressures. The age structure of the population is determined by analyzing the fish catch to determine the frequency of fish in each size (age) class.

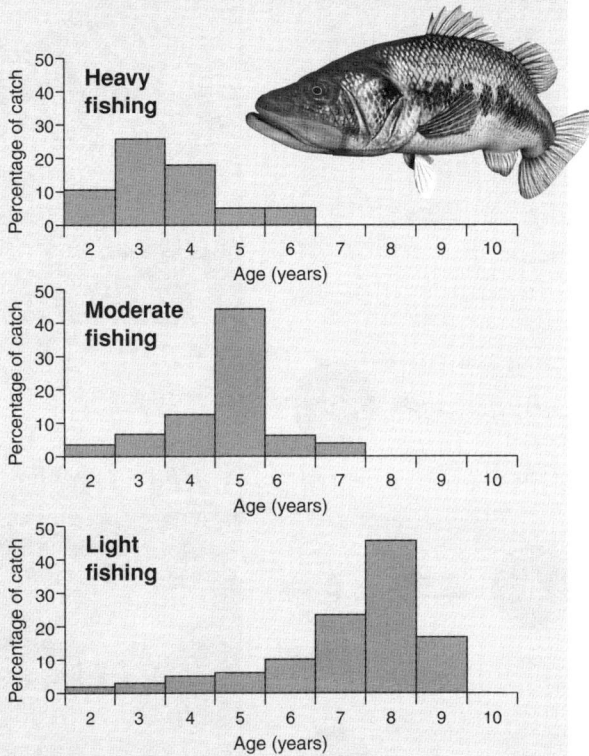

Thatch Palm Populations on Lord Howe Island
Lord Howe Island is a narrow sliver of land approximately 770 km northeast of Sydney. The age structure of populations of the thatch palm *Howea forsteriana* was determined at three locations on the island: the golf course, Gray Face and Far Flats. The height of the stem was used as an indication of age. The differences in age structure between the three sites are mainly due to the extent of grazing at each site.

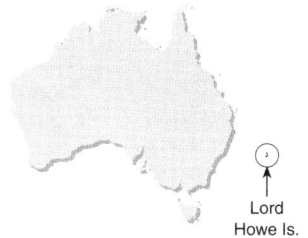

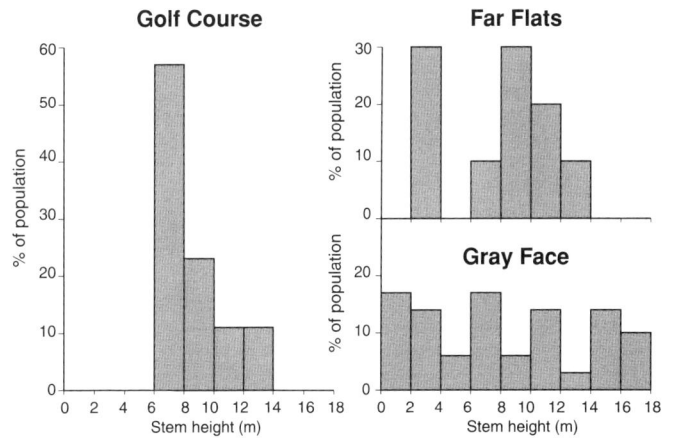

1. For the managed fish population above left:
   (a) Name the general factor that changes the age structure of this fish population: _____

   (b) Describe how the age structure changes when the fishing pressure increases from light to heavy levels:

   _____

2. State the most common age class for each of the above fish populations with different fishing pressures:

   (a) Heavy: _____   (b) Moderate: _____   (c) Light: _____

3. Determine which of the three sites sampled on Lord Howe Island (above, right), best reflects the age structure of:

   (a) An ungrazed population: _____

   Reason for your answer: _____

   (b) A heavily grazed and mown population: _____

   Reason for your answer: _____

4. Describe the likely long term prospects for the population at the golf course: _____

   _____

5. Suggest a potential problem with using size to estimate age: _____

   _____

6. Give one reason why a knowledge of age structure could be important in managing a resource: _____

   _____

Species Interactions

A 2

No organism exists in isolation. Each takes part in many interactions, both with other organisms and with the non-living components of the environment. Species interactions may involve only occasional or indirect contact (predation or competition) or they may involve close association or **symbiosis**. Symbiosis is a term that encompasses a variety of interactions involving close species contact. There are three types of symbiosis: parasitism (a form of exploitation), mutualism, and commensalism. Species interactions affect population densities and are important in determining community structure and composition. Some interactions, such as allelopathy, may even determine species presence or absence in an area.

Type of Interaction	Species A	Species B	Example
Mutualism Both species benefit from the association. In some texts, mutualism is used as a synonym for symbiosis. **Example:** Tick bird on a zebra removes parasites and alerts the zebra to danger, while the tick bird gains access to food.	A Benefits	B Benefits	
Commensalism The presence of one species has a beneficial effect on the other, but is not itself affected by the association (i.e. it is not harmed or benefiting). **Example:** Many perching plants (epiphytes) gain access to better light for photosynthesis without harming the host tree.	A Not affected	B Benefits	
Amensalism The presence of one species has a harmful effect on the other, but is not affected by the association itself. **Example:** Grazing mammals trample plants around waterholes, creating bare zones. The mammals are unaffected by the loss.	A Not affected	B Harmed	
Exploitation One species benefits at the expense of the other. Includes: 1. Predation: predator kills the prey outright. 2. Herbivory: herbivore usually does not kill the plant. 3. Parasitism: parasite usually does not kill its host. **Example:** Parasitic wasp laying eggs in a caterpillar.	A Harmed	B Benefits	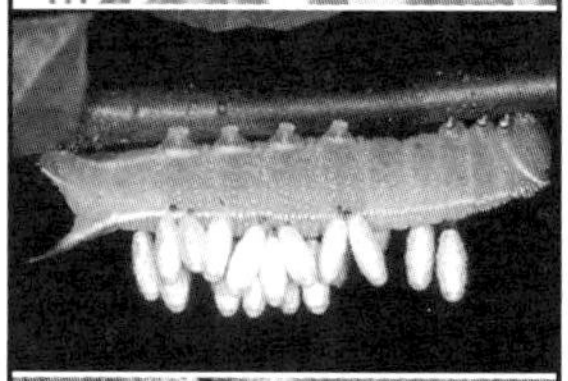
Antibiosis One species benefits by producing a compound (e.g., alkaloid, phenol, antibiotic) which inhibits the growth of another organism. **Example:** Allelopathy: a plant releases toxic compounds into the soil which prevent nearby plants growing. The allelopathic plant benefits by reduced competition.	A Benefits	B Harmed	
Competition Species, or individuals, compete for the same resources, with both parties suffering, especially when resources are limited. **Example:** Plants growing close to each other are competing for light and soil nutrients.	A Harmed	B Harmed	

For the purposes of this exercise, assume that species A in the diagram represents humans. Briefly describe an example of our interaction with another species (B in the diagram above) that matches each of the following interaction types:

1. Mutualism: _____

_____

2. Commensalism: _____

_____

3. Amensalism: _____

_____

4. Exploitation: _____

_____

5. Competition: _____

_____

Examples of interactions between different species are illustrated below. For each example, identify the type of interaction, and explain how each species in the relationship is affected in terms of its survival and the food resources that are available to it.

6. Clown fish spend much of the time taking refuge among the tentacles of this large sea anemone. They may discard food scraps to the anemone and gain significant protection from predators.

   (a) Name this type of interaction: _____

   (b) Describe how each species is affected (benefits/harmed/no effect):

   _____

   _____

7. This tiny shrimp might receive some leftover food from its host sea anemone (tentacles shown), but primarily, it is given protection from predators. Probably, the anemone is neither harmed nor benefitted.

   (a) Name this type of interaction: _____

   (b) Describe how each species is affected (benefits/harmed/no effect):

   _____

   _____

8. Many insects eat leaves from plants as a source of food. This provides the insect with nutrients and energy.

   (a) Name this type of interaction: _____

   (b) Describe how each species is affected (benefits/harmed/no effect):

   _____

   _____

9. Oxpecker or tick birds feed on skin parasites of large herbivores, such as Cape buffalo, zebra and rhinoceros. These birds will act as an early warning system by calling when predators approach.

   (a) Name this type of interaction: _____

   (b) Describe how each species is affected (benefits/harmed/no effect):

   _____

   _____

10. Ticks are small insect-like animals that are found living in the coats of many grazing mammals. They bite into the skin and feed on blood.

   (a) Name this type of interaction: _____

   (b) Describe how each species is affected (benefits/harmed/no effect):

   _____

   _____

11. In East African open grasslands, scavengers such as hyenas, vultures, and maribou storks try to get their share of the meat remaining on the carcass of a lion kill. For the interaction between hyenas and vultures:

   (a) Name the type of interaction: _____

   (b) Describe how each species is affected (benefits/harmed/no effect):

   _____

   _____

Niche Differentiation

Competition is most intense between members of the same species because their habitat and resource requirements are identical. In naturally occurring populations, **interspecific competition** (between different species) is usually less intense than intraspecific competition because coexisting species have developed (through evolution) slight differences in their realized niches. In fact, when the niches of naturally coexisting species are described, there is seldom much overlap. Species with similar ecological requirements may reduce competition by exploiting microhabitats within the ecosystem. In the eucalypt forest below, different bird species exploit tree trunks, leaf litter, different levels within the canopy, and air space. Competition may also be reduced by exploiting the same resources at a different time of the day or year.

Reducing competition in a eucalypt forest

The diagram on the left shows the foraging heights of birds in an eastern Australian eucalypt forest. A wide variety of food resources are offered by the structure of the forest. Different layers of the forest allow birds to specialize in foraging at different heights. The ground-dwelling yellow-throated scrubwren and ground thrush have robust legs and feet, while the white-throated treecreeper has long toes and large curved claws and the swifts are extremely agile fliers capable of catching insects on the wing.

Key to bird species

Ys	Yellow-throated scrubwren	Lf	Leaden flycatcher
Bt	Brown thornbill	Gt	Ground thrush
Sw	Spine-tailed swift	Rf	Rufous fantail
St	Striated thornbill	Wt	White-throated treecreeper

Adapted from: Recher, Lunney & Dunn (1986): *A Natural Legacy. Ecology in Australia.* Maxwell Macmillan Publishing Australia.

Distribution of ecologically similar fish

The diagram below shows the distribution of ecologically similar damsel fish over a coral reef at Heron Island, Queensland. The habitat and resource requirements of these species overlap considerably.

Key to fish species

Pw *Pomacentrus wardi*
Pf *Pomacentrus flavicauda*
Pb *Pomacentrus bankanensis*
Sa *Stegastes apicalis*
Pl *Plectroglyphidodon lacrymatus*
Ef *Eupomacentrus fasciolatus*
Eg *Eupomacentrus gascoynei*
Gb *Glyphidodontops biocellatus*

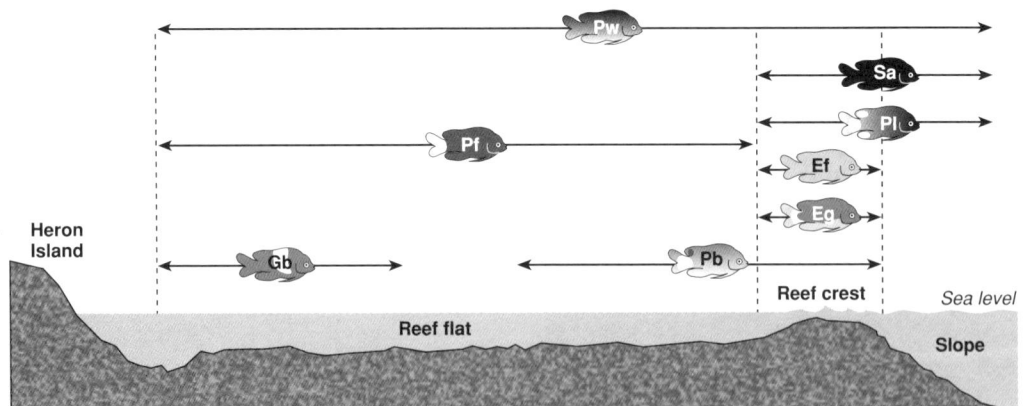

1. Name two ways in which species can avoid directly competing for the same resources in their habitat:

   (a) _____

   (b) _____

2. Suggest how the damsel fish on the reef at Heron Island (above) might reduce competition: _____

   _____

   _____

   _____

Interspecific Competition

When two species with very similar niche requirements are brought into direct competition through the introduction of a foreign species, one usually benefits at the expense of the other. The inability of two species with the same described niche to coexist (and the exclusion of one of those species) is often referred to as the **competitive exclusion principle**. In Britain, introduction of the larger, more aggressive, gray squirrel in 1846

has contributed to a contraction in range of the native red squirrel. Today, healthy populations of red squirrels exist only in the forests of north-east and north-west England, and in Ireland and Scotland. Although there is a marked relationship between the decline of the red squirrels and the invasion of the gray squirrels, other factors, such as habitat fragmentation and disease may also be implicated.

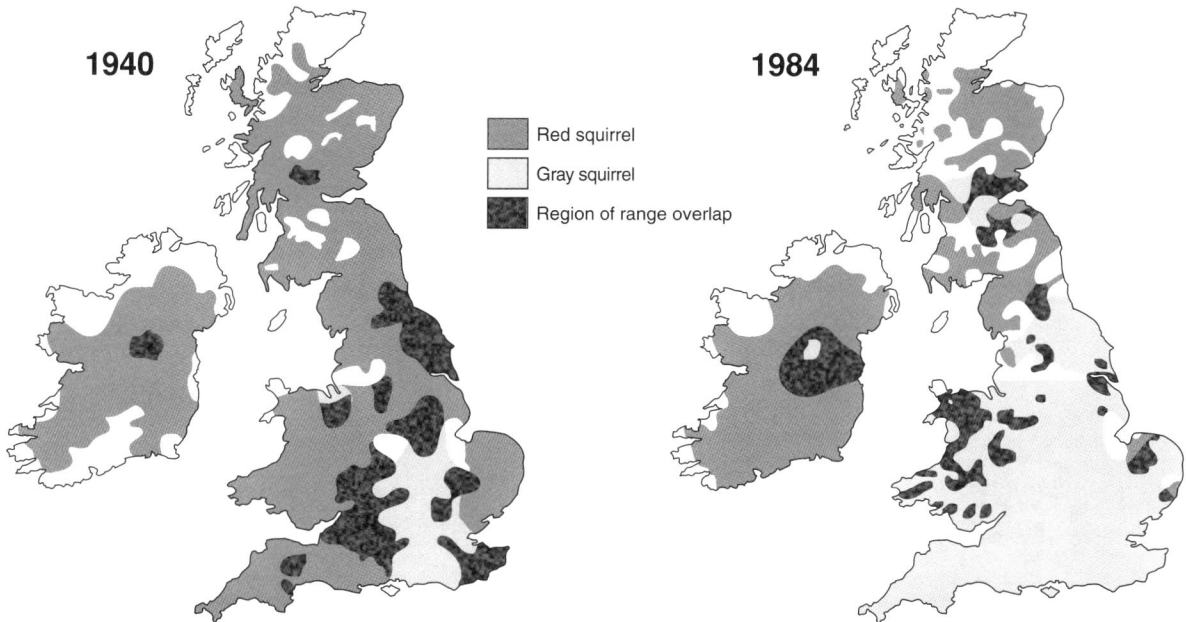

1940

1984

- Red squirrel
- Gray squirrel
- Region of range overlap

The **European red squirrel**, *Sciurus vulgaris*, was the only squirrel species in Britain until the introduction of the **American gray squirrel**, *Sciurus carolinesis*, in 1876. In 44 years since the 1940 distribution survey (above left), the more adaptable gray squirrel has displaced populations of the native red squirrels over much of the British Isles, particularly in the south (above right). Whereas the red squirrels once occupied both coniferous and broad leafed woodland, they are now almost solely restricted to coniferous forest and are completely absent from much of their former range.

Red squirrel

Gray squirrel

1. Describe the evidence to support the view that the red-gray squirrel distributions in Britain are an example of the competitive exclusion principle:

2. Some biologists believe that competition with gray squirrels is only one of the factors contributing to the decline in the red squirrels in Britain. Explain the evidence from the 1984 distribution map that might support this view:

3. The ability of red and gray squirrels to coexist appears to depend on the diversity of habitat type and availability of food sources (reds appear to be more successful in regions of coniferous forest). Suggest why careful habitat management is thought to offer the best hope for the long term survival of red squirrel populations in Britain:

Intraspecific Competition

Competition between individuals of the same species is known as **intraspecific competition**. Most populations have the capacity to grow rapidly, but their numbers cannot increase indefinitely because environmental resources are finite. Every ecosystem has a **carrying capacity** (K); defined as the number of individuals in a population that the environment can support. Intraspecific competition for resources increases with increasing population size and, at carrying capacity, it reduces the per capita growth rate to zero. When the demand for a particular resource (e.g. food, water, nesting sites, nutrients, or light)

exceeds supply, that particular resource becomes a **limiting factor**. *Populations* respond to resource limitation by reducing their population growth rate (e.g. through lower birth rates or higher mortality). The response of *individuals* to limited resources varies depending on the organism. In many invertebrates and some vertebrates such as frogs, individuals reduce their growth rate and mature at a smaller size. In some vertebrates, territoriality spaces individuals within a habitat so that only those with access to adequate resources can breed. When resources are very limited the number of available territories will decline.

Golden eagle breeding territories in Northern Scotland, 1967

- ● Single site
- ⊶ Group of sites belonging to one pair
- ⊶ Marginal site, not regularly occupied
- ● Breeding, year of survey 1967
- ▨ Low ground unsuitable for breeding eagles.

Territoriality in birds and other animals is usually a result of intraspecific competition, and often produces a pattern of uniform distribution over an area of suitable habitat. The diagram above shows the territories of golden eagles (*Aquila chrysaetos*) in Scotland. Note the relatively uniform distribution of the breeding sites.

Competition between tadpoles of *Rana tigrina*

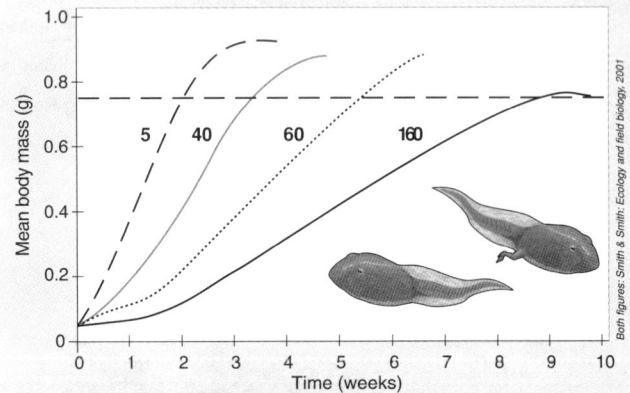

Both figures: Smith & Smith: Ecology and field biology, 2001

Food is a common limiting factor within populations. The graph above shows how growth rate of tadpoles of *Rana tigrina* declines as the density increases from 5 to 160 individuals (in the same sized space). Those at high densities grow more slowly, taking longer to reach the minimum size for metamorphosis (0.75 g), and decreasing their chances of successfully metamorphosing from tadpoles into frogs. Tadpoles held at lower densities grow faster, to a larger size, transforming at an average size of 0.889 g.

1. Define **intraspecific competition**: _____

   _____

2. Explain the effect of intraspecific competition on each of the following:

   (a) Population growth rate: _____

   _____

   (b) Final population size: _____

   _____

3. (a) Suggest why carrying capacity might decline: _____

   _____

   (b) State how a decline in carrying capacity would affect final population size: _____

4. Suggest how territoriality helps to determine final population size in golden eagles: _____

   _____

5. In the tank experiment with *Rana* (above, right), the tadpoles were contained in a fixed volume with a set amount of food:

   (a) State how *Rana* tadpoles respond to resource limitation: _____

   (b) Categorize the effect on the tadpoles as density-dependent or density-independent: _____

   (c) Comment on how much the results of this experiment are likely to represent what happens in a natural population:

   _____

   _____

Predator-Prey Strategies

A 2

A predator eating its prey is one of the most conspicuous species interactions. In most cases, the predator and prey are different species, though cannibalism occurs in many animals. Predators have acute senses that locate and identify potential prey. Many also have structures such as teeth, claws, stingers, fangs and poison to catch and subdue their prey. Animals can avoid being eaten by using passive defenses, such as hiding, or active ones, such as escaping or defending themselves against predators.

Predator Avoidance Strategies

Mimicry
Harmless prey gain immunity from attack by mimicking harmful animals (called *Batesian mimicry*).

Poisonous
Poisonous animals often advertise the fact that they are unpalatable by using brightly colored and gaudy markings.

Visual deception
Deceptive markings such as large, fake eyes can apparently deceive predators, allowing the prey to escape.

Chemical defense
Some animals can produce offensive smelling chemicals. American skunks squirt a nauseous fluid at attackers.

Offensive weapons
Offensive weapons are essential if prey are to actively fend off an attack by a predator.

Camouflage
Cryptic shape and coloration allows some animals to blend into their background, like this insect above.

Prey Capturing Strategies

Concealment
Some animals camouflage themselves in their surroundings, striking when the prey comes within reach.

Filter feeding
Many marine animals (e.g. barnacles, baleen whales, sponges, manta rays) filter the water to extract tiny plankton.

Tool use
Some animals are gifted tool users. Chimpanzees use carefully prepared twigs to extract termites from mounds.

Stealth
The night hunting ability of some poisonous snakes is greatly helped by the presence of infrared senses.

Lures
This angler fish, glow worms, and a type of spider all use lures to attract prey within striking range.

Traps
Spiders have developed a unique method of trapping their prey. Strong, sticky silk threads trap flying insects.

1. For each of the animals listed below, state a feature of its strategy for avoiding or repelling a predator:

    (a) Spiny lobster (crayfish): _____

    (b) German wasp: _____

    (c) American skunk: _____

2. Explain why poisonous (unpalatable) animals are often brightly colored so that they are easily seen: _____

3. Describe the purpose of large, fake eyes on some butterflies and fish: _____

4. Explain how Batesian mimicry **benefits** the mimic (the one that is actually edible): _____

5. Describe a **behavior** typical of a (named) prey species that makes them difficult to detect by a predator:

DA② Predator-Prey Interactions

Some mammals, particularly in highly seasonal environments, exhibit regular cycles in their population numbers. Snowshoe hares in Canada exhibit such a cycle of population fluctuation that has a periodicity of 9–11 years. Populations of lynx in the area show a similar periodicity. Contrary to early suggestions that the lynx controlled the size of the hare population, it is now known that the fluctuations in the hare population are governed by other factors - probably the availability of palatable grasses. The fluctuations in the lynx numbers however, do appear to be the result of fluctuations in the numbers of hares (their principal food item). This is true of most **vertebrate** predator-prey systems: predators do not usually control prey populations, which tend to be regulated by other factors such as food availability and climatic factors. Most predators have more than one prey species, although one species may be preferred. Characteristically, when one prey species becomes scarce, a predator will "switch" to another available prey item. Where one prey species is the principal food item and there is limited opportunity for prey switching, fluctuations in the prey population may closely govern predator cycles.

Oscillations in snowshoe hare and Canadian lynx populations

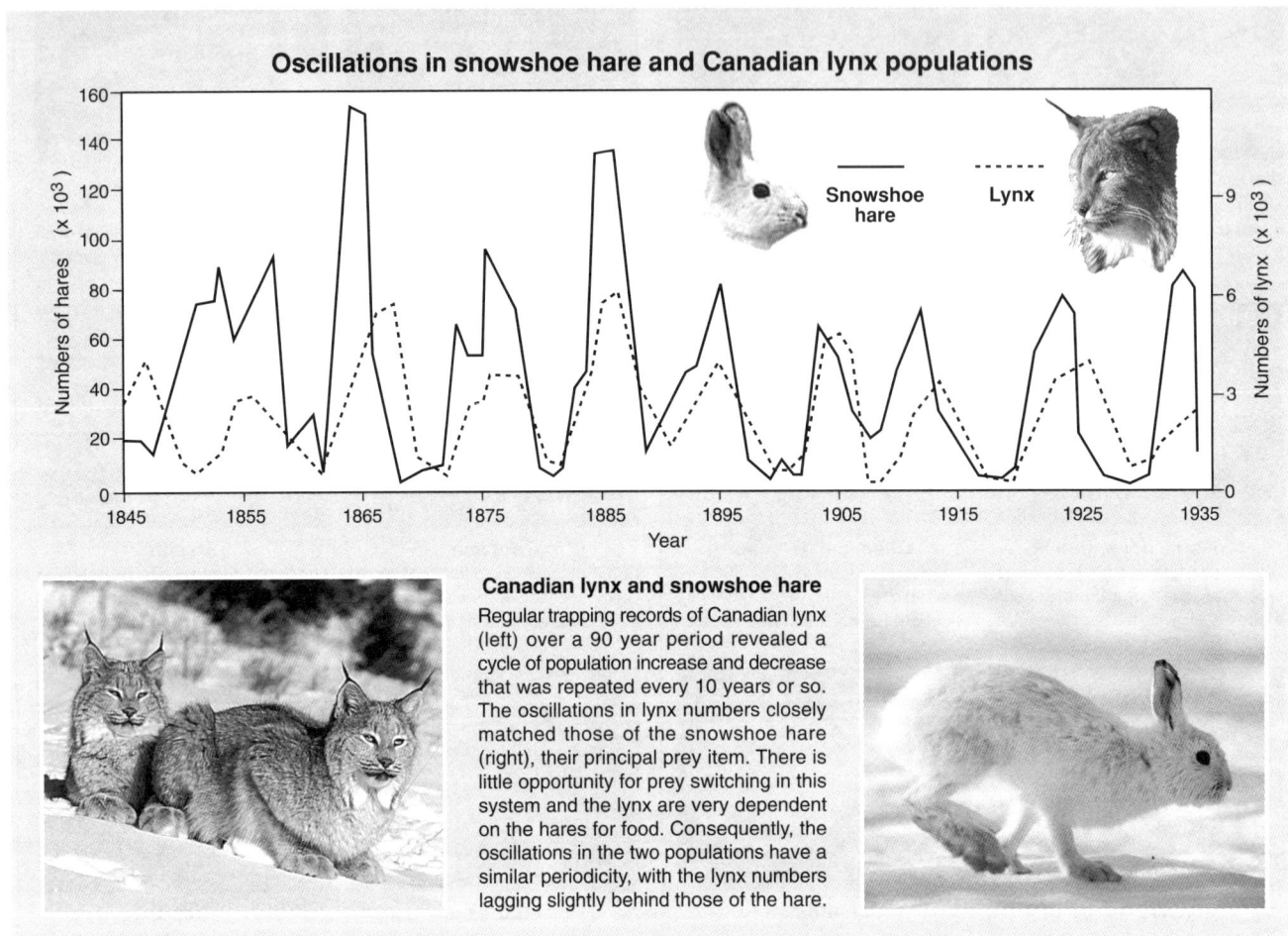

Canadian lynx and snowshoe hare

Regular trapping records of Canadian lynx (left) over a 90 year period revealed a cycle of population increase and decrease that was repeated every 10 years or so. The oscillations in lynx numbers closely matched those of the snowshoe hare (right), their principal prey item. There is little opportunity for prey switching in this system and the lynx are very dependent on the hares for food. Consequently, the oscillations in the two populations have a similar periodicity, with the lynx numbers lagging slightly behind those of the hare.

1. (a) From the graph above, determine the lag time between the population peaks of the hares and the lynx:

   _____

   (b) Explain why there is this time lag between the increase in the hare population and the response of the lynx:

   _____

2. Suggest why the lynx populations appear to be so dependent on the fluctuations on the hare: _____

   _____

   _____

3. (a) In terms of birth and death rates, explain how the availability of palatable food might regulate the numbers of hares:

   _____

   _____

   (b) Explain how a decline in available palatable food might affect their ability to withstand predation pressure:

   _____

   _____

Practical Ecology

IB SL	IB HL	IB Options	AP Biology
Complete nos: 1-4, 6 (b), (d), 7, 9-10, 13 *Extension: 5, 6(c), 8, 12*	**Complete nos:** 1-4, 6 (b), (d), 7, 9-10, 13 *Extension: 5, 6(c), 8, 12*	**Complete nos:** *Option G: SL/HL: 11*	**Complete nos:** *1-13 Some numbers extension as appropriate*

Learning Objectives

☐ 1. Compile your own glossary from the **KEY WORDS** displayed in **bold type** in the learning objectives below.

Sampling populations *(pages 306-307, 310-321)*

☐ 2. Ecosystems comprise different groups, or **populations**, of species. Recall the sort of information that is gained from population studies (e.g. **abundance**, **density**, **age structure**, **distribution**).

☐ 3. Explain why we **sample** populations. Appreciate that population sampling allows us to study particular aspects of large populations (e.g. **distribution**, **abundance**, **density**, **age structure**).

☐ 4. A field study should enable you to test a hypothesis about a certain aspect of a population. You should provide a clear outline of your study with attention to: *the methods you will use to collect **data**, the type of data you are collecting (relevance to the hypothesis), the number of recordings you will make, the size of your sampling unit (e.g. quadrat size) and the number of **samples** you will take, the assumptions that you are making in the investigation, and appropriate **controls**.*

☐ 5. Explain how and why sample size affects the accuracy of population estimates. Explain how you would decide on a suitable sample size. Discuss the compromise between sampling accuracy and sampling effort.

☐ 6. Demonstrate an understanding of **random sampling** using one or more of the following techniques. Identify the advantages and limitations of each method with respect to sampling time, cost, and the suitability to the organism and specific habitat type:
(a) **Direct counts**
(b) **Frame** and/or **point quadrats**
(c) **Belt** and/or **line transects**
(d) **Mark and recapture** and the **Lincoln index**
(e) **Netting** and **trapping**

☐ 7. Describe the methods used to ensure **random sampling**, and appreciate why this is important.

☐ 8. Describe **qualitative methods** for investigating the distribution of organisms in specific habitats.

☐ 9. Recognize appropriate ways in which different types of data may be recorded, analyzed, and presented.

☐ 10. Demonstrate an ability to calculate and use simple statistics (**mean** and **standard deviation**) for the analysis and comparison of population data.

☐ 11. Calculate simple statistical tests, such as the chi-square and student's *t* test, and apply them *appropriately* to the analysis and comparison of population data. Recognize that the design of any field study will determine how the data can be analyzed.

Measuring abiotic factors *(pages 308-309)*

☐ 12. Describe methods to measure abiotic factors in a habitat. Include reference to the following (as appropriate): pH, light, temperature, dissolved oxygen, current speed, total dissolved solids, and conductivity.

☐ 13. Appreciate the influence of abiotic factors on the distribution and abundance of organisms in a habitat.

Textbooks

See the 'Textbook Reference Grid' on pages 8-9 for textbook page references relating to material in this topic.

Supplementary Texts

See pages 5-6 for additional details of these texts:

■ Adds, J., *et al.*, 2001. **Genetics, Evolution and Biodiversity**, (NelsonThornes), pp. 36-40, 46, 59-60.

■ Allen *et al.*, 2001. **Applied Ecology** (Collins), pp. 6-14 (includes diversity indices).

■ Cadogan, A. and Sutton, R., 2002. **Maths for Advanced Biology** (NelsonThornes), as required.

■ Chenn, P., 1999. **Ecology** (JM), pp. 184-205.

■ Jones, A., *et al.*, 1994. **Practical Skills in Biology** (Addison-Wesley).

> Software and video resources are now provided in the Teacher Resource Handbook

Periodicals

See page 6 for details of publishers of periodicals:

STUDENT'S REFERENCE

■ **Ecological Projects** Biol. Sci. Rev., 8(5) May 1996, pp. 24-26. *Planning and carrying out a field-based project: from choosing the topic to data analysis and reporting.*

■ **Fieldwork - Sampling Animals** Biol. Sci. Rev., 10(4) March 1998, pp. 23-25. *Appropriate methods for collecting different animals in the field. Includes a synopsis of the mark and recapture technique.*

■ **Fieldwork Sampling - Plants** Biol. Sci. Rev., 10(5) May 1998, pp. 6-8. *The methodology for sampling plant communities (transects & quadrats).*

■ **Bird Ringing** Biol. Sci. Rev., 14(3) Feb. 2002, pp. 14-19. *The practical investigation of populations of highly mobile organisms. Includes discussion of mark and recapture, and ringing methods.*

■ **British Butterflies in Decline** Biol. Sci. Rev., 14(4) April 2002, pp. 10-13. *Documented changes in the distribution of British butterfly species. This account includes a description of the techniques used to monitor changes in butterfly numbers in different regions of the UK. How this information is used to indicate patterns of population abundance in relation to habitat change is also discussed.*

TEACHER'S REFERENCE

■ **Ecology Fieldwork in 16 to 19 Biology** SSR, 84(307) December 2002, pp. 87. *Fieldwork is recognized as an important element of education in biology, yet the anecdotal evidence suggests that it is declining. This article examines the fieldwork opportunities provided to 16-19 students and suggests how these could be enhanced and firmly established for all students studying biology.*

■ **Enhancing Student Understanding of Environmental Sciences Research** The American Biology Teacher, 63 (4), April, 2001, pp. 236-241. *Ideas for improving understanding in practical ecology: sampling, field study design, and data analysis and interpretation.*

■ **Effective Population Size: Biological Duality, Field and Molecular Approaches** The American Biology Teacher, 62 (1), January 2000, pp. 51-57. *Investigating attributes of populations using mark and recapture techniques and DNA analyses.*

References to web site resources are provided in the topic "Energy Flow and Nutrient Cycles".

Designing your Field Study

The example below provides some ideas for designing a field study. It gives a working framework, which can be modified for most simple comparative field studies. For reasons of space, the full methodology is not included.

Pill millipede
Glomeris marginata

Oak woodland

Coniferous woodland

Observation

A student read that a particular species of pill millipede (left) is extremely abundant in forest leaf litter, but a search in the litter of a conifer-dominated woodland near his home revealed only very low numbers of this millipede species.

Hypothesis

This millipede species is adapted to a niche in the leaf litter of oak woodlands and is abundant there. However, it is rare in the litter of coniferous woodland. The **null hypothesis** is that there is no difference between the abundance of this millipede species in oak and coniferous woodland litter.

Oak or coniferous woodland

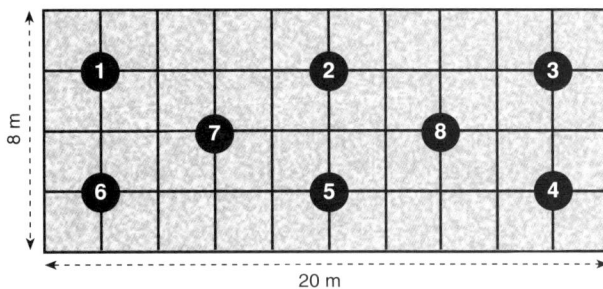

8 m

1   2   3

7   8

6   5   4

20 m

1   Sampling sites numbered 1-8 at evenly spaced intervals on a 2 x 2 m grid within an area of 20 m x 8 m.

Sampling equipment: Leaf litter light trap

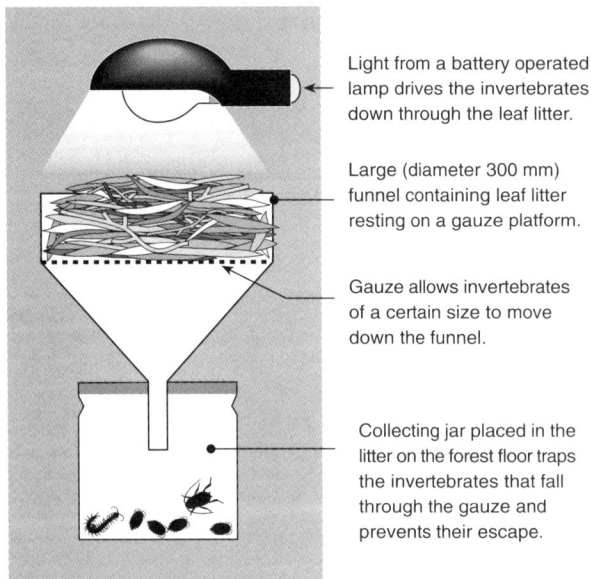

Light from a battery operated lamp drives the invertebrates down through the leaf litter.

Large (diameter 300 mm) funnel containing leaf litter resting on a gauze platform.

Gauze allows invertebrates of a certain size to move down the funnel.

Collecting jar placed in the litter on the forest floor traps the invertebrates that fall through the gauze and prevents their escape.

Sampling Program

A sampling program was designed to test the prediction that the millipedes are more abundant in the leaf litter of oak woodlands than in coniferous woodlands.

Equipment and Procedure

Sites: For each of the two woodland types, an area 20 x 8 m was chosen and marked out in a 2 x 2 m grid. Eight sampling sites were selected, evenly spaced along the grid as shown left.

- The general area for the study chosen was selected on the basis of the large amounts of leaf litter present.
- Eight sites were chosen as the largest number feasible to collect and analyze in the time available.
- The two woodlands were sampled on sequential days.

Capture of millipedes: At each site, a 0.4 x 0.4 m quadrat was placed on the forest floor and the leaf litter within the quadrat was collected. Millipedes and other leaf litter invertebrates were captured using a simple gauze lined funnel containing the leaf litter from within the quadrat. A lamp was positioned over each funnel for 2 hours and the invertebrates in the litter moved down and were trapped in the collecting jar.

- After 2 hours each jar was labelled with the site number and returned to the lab for analysis.
- The litter in each funnel was bagged, labelled with the site number and returned to the lab for weighing.
- The number of millipedes at each site was recorded.
- The numbers of other invertebrates (classified into major taxa) were also noted for reference.

Assumptions

- The areas chosen in each woodland were representative of the woodland types in terms of millipede abundance.
- Eight sites were sufficient to adequately sample the millipede populations in each forest.
- A quadrat size of 0.4 x 0.4 m contained enough leaf litter to adequately sample the millipedes at each site.
- The millipedes were not preyed on by any of the other invertebrates captured in the collecting jar.
- All the invertebrates within the quadrat were captured.
- Millipedes move away from the light, are effectively captured by the funnel apparatus and cannot escape.
- Two hours was long enough for the millipedes to move down through the litter and fall into the trap.

  Note that these last two assumptions could be tested by examining the bagged leaf litter for millipedes after returning to the lab.

Notes on collection and analysis

- Mean millipede abundance was calculated from the counts from the eight sites. The difference in abundance at the sites was tested using a Student's *t* test.
- After counting and analysis of the samples, all the collected invertebrates were returned to the sites.

A note about sample size

When designing a field study, the size of your sampling unit (e.g., quadrat size) and the sample size (the number of samples you will take) should be major considerations. There are various ways to determine the best quadrat size. Usually, these involve increasing the quadrat size until you stop finding new species. For simple field studies, the number of samples you take (the sample size or *n* value) will be determined largely by the resources and time that you have available to collect and analyze your data. It is usually best to take as many samples as you can, as this helps to account for any natural variability present and will give you greater confidence in your data. For a summary of these aspects of study design as well as coverage of collecting methods see: *Jones, A. et al. (1994) Practical Skills in Biology.*

1. Explain the importance of recognizing any assumptions that you are making in your study:

_____

_____

2. Describe how you would test whether the quadrat size of 0.4 x 0.4m was adequate to effectively sample the millipedes:

_____

_____

3. Suggest why the litter was bagged, returned to the lab and then weighed properly for the analysis:

_____

_____

4. Suggest why the numbers of other invertebrates were also recorded even though it was only millipede abundance that was being investigated:

_____

_____

_____

_____

YOUR CHECKLIST FOR FIELD STUDY DESIGN

The following provides a checklist for a field study. Check off the points when you are confident that you have satisfied the requirements in each case:

1. **Preliminary:**

   ☐ (a) Makes a hypothesis based on observation(s).

   ☐ (b) The hypothesis (and its predictions) are testable using the resources you have available (the study is feasible).

   ☐ (c) The organism you have chosen is suitable for the study and you have considered the ethics involved.

2. **Assumptions and site selection:**

   ☐ (a) You are aware of any assumptions that you are making in your study.

   ☐ (b) You have identified aspects of your field design that could present problems (such as time of year, biological rhythms of your test organism, difficulty in identifying suitable habitats etc.).

   ☐ (c) The study sites you have selected have the features necessary in order for you to answer the questions you have asked in your hypothesis.

3. **Data collection:**

   ☐ (a) You are happy with the way in which you are going to take your measurements or samples.

   ☐ (b) You have considered the size of your sampling unit and the number of samples you are going to take (and tested for these if necessary).

   ☐ (c) You have given consideration to how you will analyze the data you collect and made sure that your study design allows you to answer the questions you wish to answer

Monitoring Physical Factors

Most ecological studies require us to measure the physical factors (parameters) in the environment that may influence the abundance and distribution of organisms. In recent years there have been substantial advances in the development of portable, light-weight meters and dataloggers. These enable easy collection of storage of data in the field.

Quantum light meter: Measures light intensity levels. It is not capable of measuring light quality (wavelength).

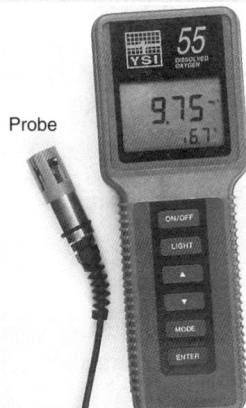

Dissolved oxygen meter: Measures the amount of oxygen dissolved in water (expressed as mgl⁻¹).

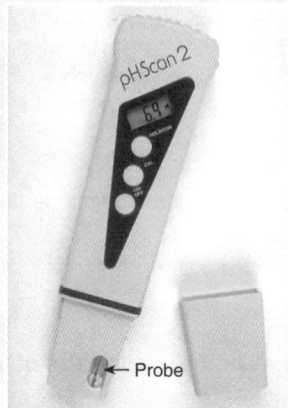

pH meter: Measures the acidity of water or soil, if it is first dissolved in pure water (pH scale 0 to 14).

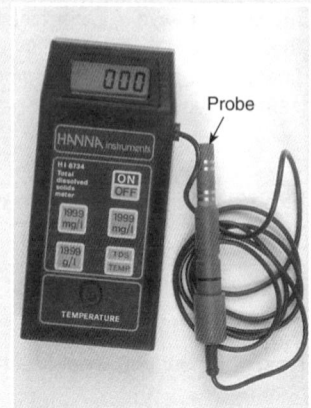

Total dissolved solids (TDS) meter: Measures content of dissolved solids (as ions) in water in mgl⁻¹.

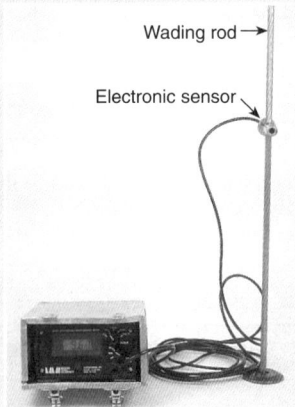

Current meter: The electronic sensor is positioned at set depths in a stream or river on the calibrated wading rod as current readings are taken.

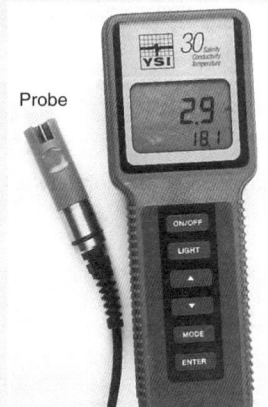

Multipurpose meter: This multipurpose meter can measure *salinity*, *conductivity* and *temperature*, simply by pushing the MODE button.

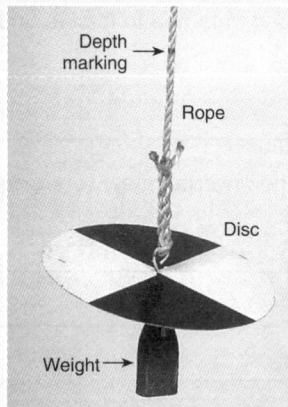

Secchi disc: This simple device is used to provide a crude measure water clarity (the maximum depth at which the disc can just be seen).

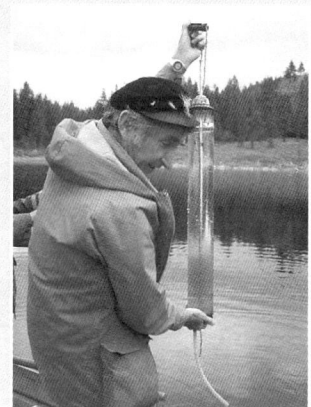

Collecting a water sample: A Nansen bottle is used to collect water samples from a lake for lab analysis, testing for nutrients, oxygen and pH.

Dataloggers and Environmental Sensors

Dataloggers are electronic instruments that record measurements over time. They are equipped with a microprocessor, data storage facility, and sensor. Different sensors are employed to measure a range of variables in water (photos A and B) or air (photos C and D), as well as make physiological measurements. The datalogger is connected to a computer, and software is used to set the logging parameters (e.g. sampling interval) and initiate the logger. The logger is then disconnected and used remotely to record and store data. When reconnected to the computer, the data are downloaded, viewed, and plotted. Dataloggers, such as those pictured here from PASCO, are being increasingly used in professional and school research. They make data collection quick and accurate, and they enable prompt data analysis.

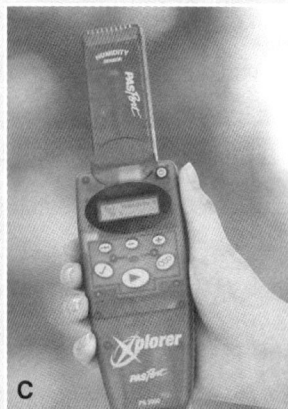

Dataloggers are now widely used to monitor conditions in aquatic environments. Different variables such as pH, temperature, conductivity, and dissolved oxygen can be measured by changing the sensor attached to the logger.

Dataloggers fitted with sensors are portable and easy to use in a wide range of terrestrial environments. They are used to measure variables such as air temperature and pressure, relative humidity, light, and carbon dioxide gas.

1. The table below lists a variety of ecosystems and physical parameters that may influence the abundance and distribution of organisms within them. For each ecosystem, identify which environmental measurements would be most useful in a study of the ecosystems listed (the first one has been completed for you):

Ecosystem	Temperature	Wind velocity	Light intensity	pH	Dissolved oxygen	Specific ions	Humidity
Freshwater stream	✓		✓	✓	✓	✓	
Polluted stream							
Ocean waters							
Estuarine mudflat							
Woodland leaf litter							
Open field							
Small pond (diurnal changes)							
Soil							
Peat bog							

2. The physical parameters of an exposed rocky shore and a sheltered estuarine mudflat differ markedly. For each of the parameters listed below, briefly describe how they may differ (if at all):

Environmental parameter	Exposed rocky coastline	Estuarine mudflat
Severity of wave action		
Light intensity and quality		
Salinity/ conductivity		
Temperature change (diurnal)		
Substrate/ sediment type		
Oxygen concentration		
Exposure time to air (tide out)		

Sampling Populations

Information about the populations of rare organisms in isolated populations may, in some instances, be collected by direct measure (direct counts and measurements of all the individuals in the population). However, in most cases, populations are too large to be examined directly and they must be sampled in a way that still provides information about them. Most practical exercises in population ecology involve the collection or census of living organisms, with a view to identifying the species and quantifying their abundance and other population features of interest. Sampling techniques must be appropriate to the

community being studied and the information you wish to obtain. Some of the common strategies used in ecological sampling, and the situations for which they are best suited, are outlined in the table below. It provides an overview of points to consider when choosing a sampling regime. One must always consider the time and equipment available, the organisms involved, and the impact of the sampling method on the environment. For example, if the organisms involved are very mobile, sampling frames are not appropriate. If it is important not to disturb the organisms, observation alone must be used to gain information.

Method	Equipment and procedure	Information provided and considerations for use
Point sampling Random Systematic (grid)	Individual points are chosen on a map (using a grid reference or random numbers applied to a map grid) and the organisms are sampled at those points. Mobile organisms may be sampled using traps, nets etc.	**Useful for**: Determining species abundance and community composition. If samples are large enough, population characteristics (e.g. age structure, reproductive parameters) can be determined. **Considerations**: Time efficient. Suitable for most organisms. Depending on methods used, disturbance to the environment can be minimized. Species occurring in low abundance may be missed.
Transect sampling	Lines are drawn across a map and organisms occurring along the line are sampled. **Line transects**: Tape or rope marks the line. The species occurring on the line are recorded (all along the line or, more usually, at regular intervals). Lines can be chosen randomly (left) or may follow an environmental gradient.	**Useful for**: Well suited to determining changes in community composition along an environmental gradient. When placed randomly, they provide a quick measure of species occurrence. **Considerations for line transects**: Time efficient. Most suitable for plants and immobile or easily caught animals. Disturbance to the environment can be minimized. Species occurring in low abundance may be missed.
0.5 m *Environmental gradient*	**Belt transects**: A measured strip is located across the study area to highlight any transitions. Quadrats are used to sample the plants and animals at regular intervals along the belt. Plants and immobile animals are easily recorded. Mobile or cryptic animals need to be trapped or recorded using appropriate methods.	**Considerations for belt transects**: Time consuming to do well. Most suitable for plants and immobile or easily caught animals. Good chance of recording most or all species. Efforts should be made to minimize disturbance to the environment.
Quadrat sampling	Sampling units or quadrats are placed randomly or in a grid pattern on the sample area. The occurrence of organisms in these squares is noted. Plants and slow moving animals are easily recorded. Rapidly moving or cryptic animals need to be trapped or recorded using appropriate methods.	**Useful for**: Well suited to determining community composition and features of population abundance: species density, frequency of occurrence, percentage cover, and biomass (if harvested). **Considerations**: Time consuming to do well. Most suitable for plants and immobile or easily caught animals. Quadrat size must be appropriate for the organisms being sampled and the information required. Some disturbance if organisms are removed.
Mark and recapture (capture-recapture) First sample: marked Second sample: proportion recaptured	Animals are captured, marked, and then released. After a suitable time period, the population is resampled. The number of marked animals recaptured in a second sample is recorded as a proportion of the total.	**Useful for**: Determining total population density for highly mobile species in a certain area (e.g. butterflies). Movements of individuals in the population can be tracked (especially when used in conjunction with electronic tracking devices). **Considerations**: Time consuming to do well. Not suitable for immobile species. Population should have a finite boundary. Period between samplings must allow for redistribution of marked animals in the population. Marking should present little disturbance and should not affect behavior.

1. Briefly explain why we **sample** populations: _____

_____

2. Suggest what sampling technique would be appropriate for determining the following:

(a) The percentage cover of a plant species in pasture: _____

(b) The density and age structure of a plankton population: _____

(c) Change in community composition from low to high altitude on a mountain: _____

Quadrat Sampling

DA 2

Quadrat sampling is a method by which organisms in a certain proportion (sample) of the habitat are counted directly. As with all sampling methods, it is used to estimate population parameters when the organisms present are too numerous to count in total. It can be used to estimate population **abundance** (number), **density**, **frequency of occurrence**, and **distribution**. Quadrats may be used without a transect when studying a relatively uniform habitat. In this case, the quadrat positions are chosen randomly using a random number table.

The general procedure is to count all the individuals (or estimate their percentage cover) in a number of quadrats of known size and to use this information to work out the abundance or percentage cover value for the whole area. The number of quadrats used and their size should be appropriate to the type of organism involved (e.g. grass vs tree).

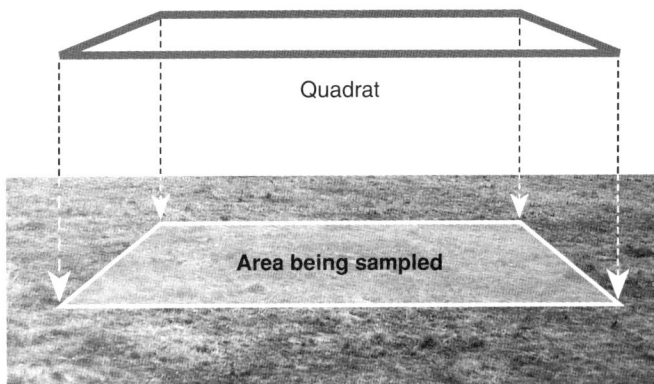

Quadrat

Area being sampled

$$\text{Estimated average density} = \frac{\text{Total number of individuals counted}}{\text{Number of quadrats X area of each quadrat}}$$

Guidelines for Quadrat Use:

1. The **area of each quadrat** must be known exactly and ideally quadrats should be the same shape. The quadrat does not have to be square (it may be rectangular, hexagonal etc.).

2. **Enough quadrat samples** must be taken to provide results that are representative of the total population.

3. The **population of each quadrat** must be known exactly. Species must be distinguishable from each other, even if they have to be identified at a later date. It has to be decided beforehand what the count procedure will be and how organisms over the quadrat boundary will be counted.

4. The size of the quadrat should be appropriate to the organisms and habitat, e.g., a large size quadrat for trees.

5. The quadrats must be **representative of the whole area**. This is usually achieved by **random sampling** (right).

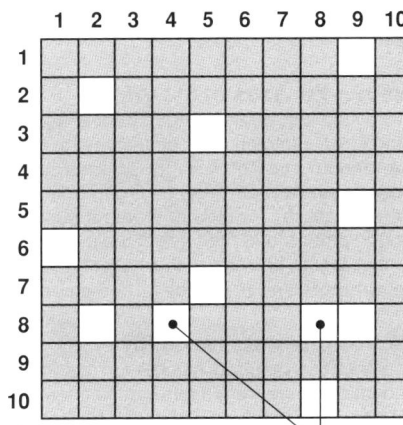

The area to be sampled is divided up into a grid pattern with indexed coordinates

Quadrats are applied to the predetermined grid on a random basis. This can be achieved by using a random number table.

Sampling a centipede population

A researcher by the name of Lloyd (1967) carried out a sampling of centipedes in Wytham Woods, near Oxford in England. A total of 37 hexagon–shaped quadrats were used, with a diameter of 30 cm (see diagram on right). These were arranged in a pattern so that they were all touching each other. Use the data in the diagram to answer the following:

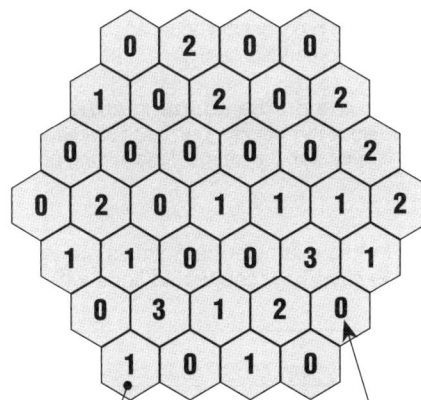

1. Determine the average number of centipedes captured per quadrat:

2. Calculate the estimated average density of centipedes per square meter (remember that each quadrat is 0.08 square meters in area):

3. Looking at the data for individual quadrats, describe in general terms the distribution of the centipedes in the sample area:

4. Describe one factor that might account for the distribution pattern:

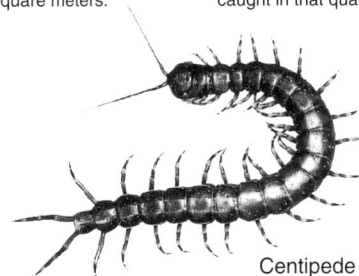

Each quadrat was a hexagon with a diameter of 30 cm and an area of 0.08 square meters.

The number in each hexagon indicates how many centipedes were caught in that quadrat.

Centipede

PDA2 Sampling a Leaf Litter Population

The diagram on the facing page represents an area of leaf litter from a forest floor with a resident population of organisms. The distribution of four animal species as well as the arrangement of leaf litter is illustrated. Leaf litter comprises leaves and debris that have dropped off trees to form a layer of detritus. This exercise is designed to practice the steps required in planning and carrying out a sampling of a natural population. It is desirable, but not essential, that students work in groups of 2–4.

1. Decide on the sampling method
For the purpose of this exercise, it has been decided that the populations to be investigated are too large to be counted directly and a quadrat sampling method is to be used to estimate the average density of the four animal species as well as that of the leaf litter.

2. Mark out a grid pattern
Use a ruler to mark out 3 cm intervals along each side of the sampling area (area of quadrat = 0.03 x 0.03 m). **Draw lines** between these marks to create a 6 x 6 grid pattern (total area = 0.18 x 0.18 m). This will provide a total of 36 quadrats that can be investigated.

3. Number the axes of the grid
Only a small proportion of the possible quadrat positions are going to be sampled. It is necessary to select the quadrats in a random manner. It is not sufficient to simply guess or choose your own on a 'gut feeling'. The best way to choose the quadrats randomly is to create a numbering system for the grid pattern and then select the quadrats from a random number table. Starting at the *top left hand corner*, **number the columns** and **rows** from 1 to 6 on each axis.

4. Choose quadrats randomly
To select the required number of quadrats randomly, use random numbers from a random number table. The random numbers are used as an index to the grid coordinates. Choose 6 quadrats from the total of 36 using table of random numbers provided for you at the bottom of the facing page. Make a note of which column of random numbers you choose. Each member of your group should choose a different set of random numbers (i.e., different column: A–D) so that you can compare the effectiveness of the sampling method.

Column of random numbers chosen: _____

NOTE: Highlight the boundary of each selected quadrat with colored pen/highlighter.

5. Decide on the counting criteria
Before the counting of the individuals for each species is carried out, the criteria for counting need to be established.

There may be some problems here. You must decide before sampling begins as to what to do about individuals that are only partly inside the quadrat. Possible answers include:

(a) Only counting individuals if they are completely inside the quadrat.
(b) Only counting individuals that have a clearly defined part of their body inside the quadrat (such as the head).
(c) Allowing for 'half individuals' in the data (e.g., 3.5 snails).
(d) Counting an individual that is inside the quadrat by half or more as one complete individual.

Discuss the merits and problems of the suggestions above with other members of the class (or group). You may even have counting criteria of your own. Think about other factors that could cause problems with your counting.

6. Carry out the sampling
Carefully examine each selected quadrat and **count the number of individuals** of each species present. Record your data in the spaces provided on the facing page.

7. Calculate the population density
Use the combined data TOTALS for the sampled quadrats to estimate the average density for each species by using the formula:

$$\text{Density} = \frac{\text{Total number in all quadrats sampled}}{\text{Number of quadrats sampled} \times \text{area of a quadrat}}$$

Remember that a total of 6 quadrats are sampled and each has an area of 0.0009 m². The density should be expressed as the number of individuals *per square metre (no. m^{-2})*.

Woodlouse: [   ]   False scorpion: [   ]

Centipede: [   ]   Leaf: [   ]

Springtail: [   ]

8. (a) In this example the animals are not moving. Describe the problems associated with sampling moving organisms. Explain how you would cope with sampling these same animals if they were really alive and very active:

_____

_____

_____

(b) Carry out a direct count of all 4 animal species and the leaf litter for the whole sample area (all 36 quadrats). Apply the data from your direct count to the equation given in (7) above to calculate the actual population density (remember that the number of quadrats in this case = 36):

Woodlouse: [   ]   Centipede: [   ]   False scorpion: [   ]   Springtail: [   ]   Leaf: [   ]

Compare your estimated population density to the actual population density for each species:

_____

_____

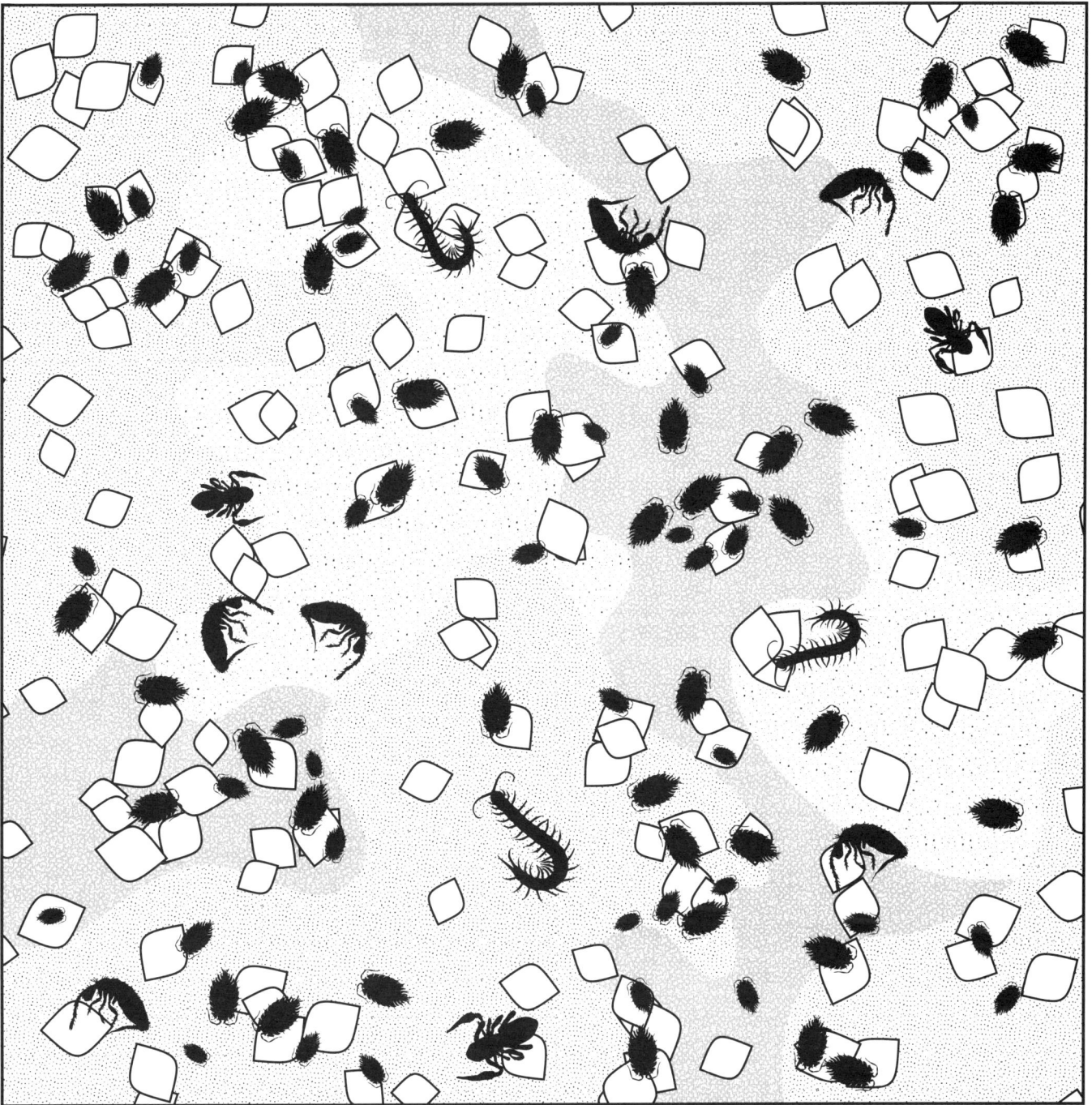

Coordinates for each quadrat	Woodlouse	Centipede	False scorpion	Springtail	Leaf
1:					
2:					
3:					
4:					
5:					
6:					
TOTAL					

Table of random numbers

A	B	C	D
2 2	3 1	6 2	2 2
3 2	1 5	6 3	4 3
3 1	5 6	3 6	6 4
4 6	3 6	1 3	4 5
4 3	4 2	4 5	3 5
5 6	1 4	3 1	1 4

The table above has been adapted from a table of random numbers from a statistics book. Use this table to select quadrats randomly from the grid above. Choose one of the columns (A to D) and use the numbers in that column as an index to the grid. The first digit refers to the row number and the second digit refers to the column number. To locate each of the 6 quadrats, find where the row and column intersect, as shown below:

Example: | 5 2 | refers to the 5th row and the 2nd column

Transect Sampling

DA ②

A **transect** is a line placed across a community of organisms. Transects are usually carried out to provide information on the **distribution** of species in the community. This is of particular value in situations where environmental factors that change over the sampled distance. This change is called an **environmental gradient** (e.g. up a mountain or across a seashore). The usual practice for small transects is to stretch a string between two markers. The string is marked off in measured distance intervals, and the species at each marked point are noted. The sampling points along the transect may also be used for the siting of quadrats, so that changes in density and community composition can be recorded. Belt transects are essentially a form of continuous quadrat sampling. They provide more information on community composition but can be difficult to carry out. Some transects provide information on the vertical, as well as horizontal, distribution of species (e.g. tree canopies in a forest).

Point sampling

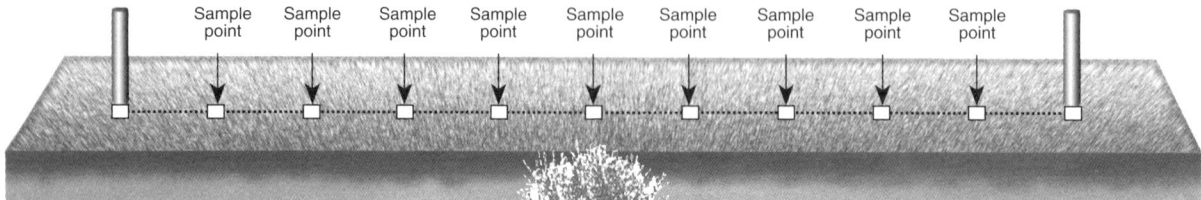

Sample point Sample point Sample point Sample point Sample point Sample point Sample point Sample point Sample point

Continuous belt transect

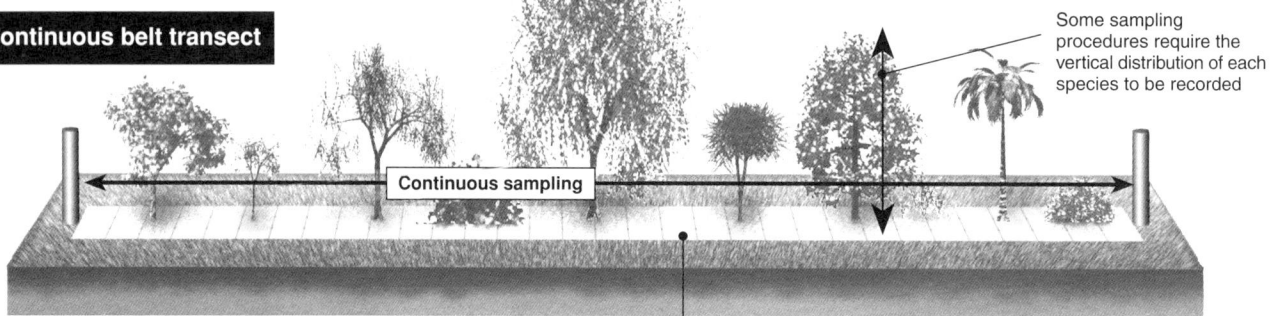

Some sampling procedures require the vertical distribution of each species to be recorded

Continuous sampling

Quadrats are placed adjacent to each other in a continuous belt

Interrupted belt transect

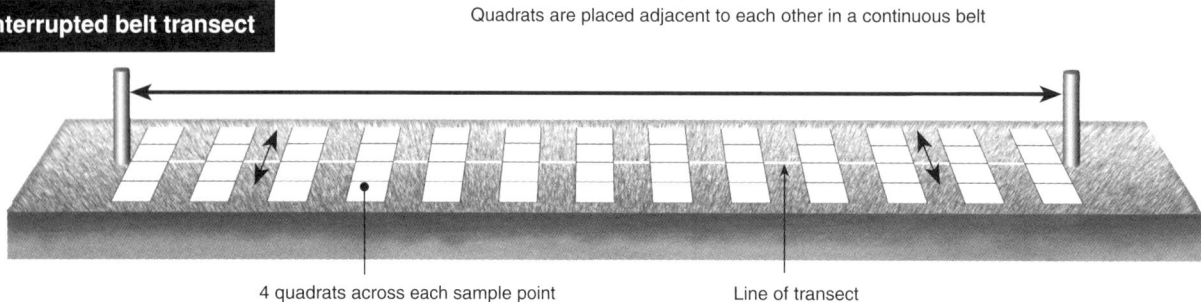

4 quadrats across each sample point   Line of transect

1. Belt transect sampling uses quadrats placed along a line at marked intervals. In contrast, point sampling transects record only the species that are touched or covered by the line at the marked points.

    (a) Describe one disadvantage of belt transects: _____

    _____

    (b) Explain why line transects may give an unrealistic sample of the community in question: _____

    _____

    _____

    (c) Explain how belt transects overcome this problem: _____

    _____

    (d) Describe a situation where the use of transects to sample the community would be inappropriate: _____

    _____

2. Explain how you could test whether or not a transect sampling interval was sufficient to accurately sample a community:

    _____

    _____

    _____

Kite graphs are an ideal way in which to present distributional data from a belt transect (e.g. abundance or percentage cover along an environmental gradient). Usually, they involve plots for more than one species. This makes them good for highlighting probable differences in habitat preference between species. Kite graphs may also be used to show changes in distribution with time (e.g. with daily or seasonal cycles).

3. The data on the right were collected from a rocky shore field trip. Periwinkles from four common species of the genus *Littorina* were sampled in a continuous belt transect from the low water mark, to a height of 10 m above that level. The number of each of the four species in a 1 m² quadrat was recorded.

   Plot a **kite graph** of the data for all four species on the grid provided below. Do not forget to include a scale so that the number at each point on the kite can be calculated.

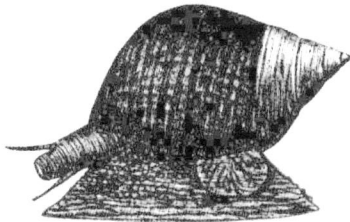

Field data notebook
Numbers of periwinkles (4 common species) showing vertical distribution on a rocky shore

Periwinkle species:

Height above low water (m)	L. littorea	L. saxatalis	L. neritoides	L. littoralis
0-1	0	0	0	0
1-2	1	0	0	3
2-3	3	0	0	17
3-4	9	3	0	12
4-5	15	12	0	1
5-6	5	24	0	0
6-7	2	9	2	0
7-8	0	2	11	0
8-9	0	0	47	0
9-10	0	0	59	0

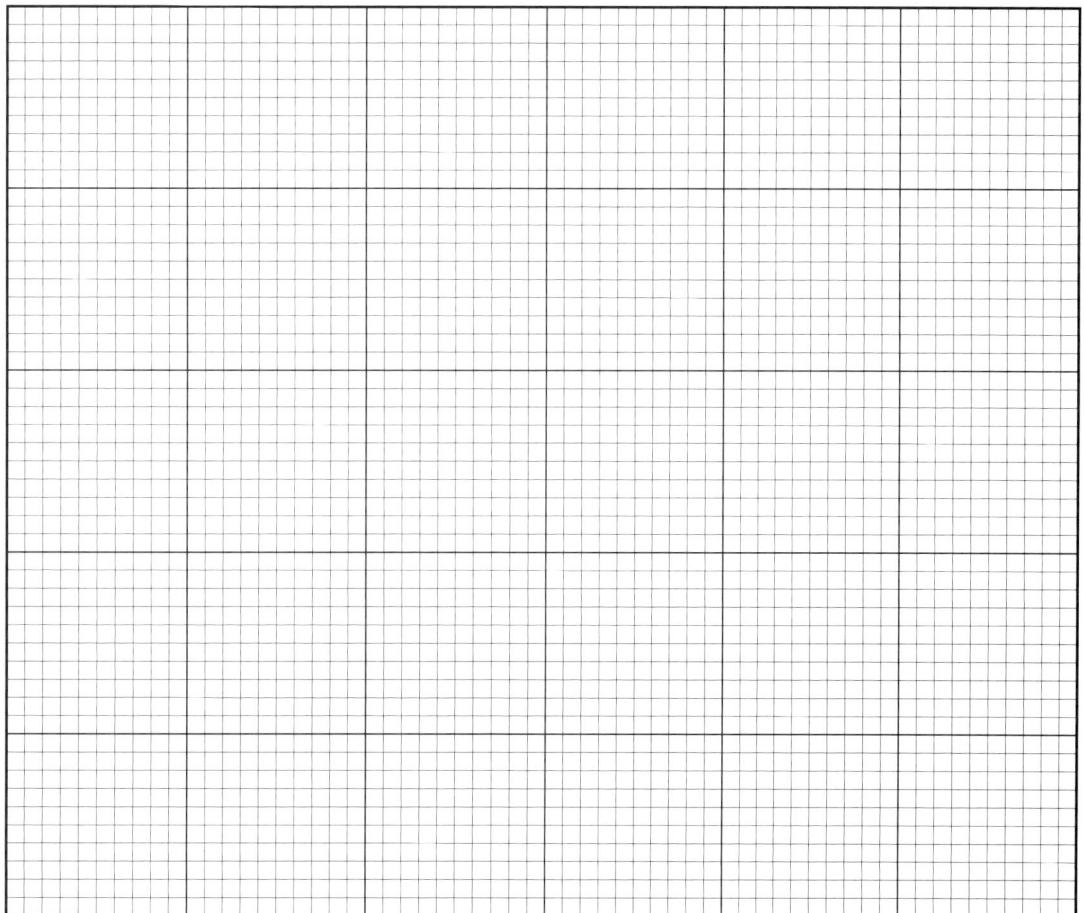

Mark and Recapture Sampling

PDA❷

The mark and recapture method of estimating population size is used in the study of animal populations where individuals are highly mobile. It is of no value where animals do not move or move very little. The number of animals caught in each sample must be large enough to be valid. The technique is outlined in the diagram below.

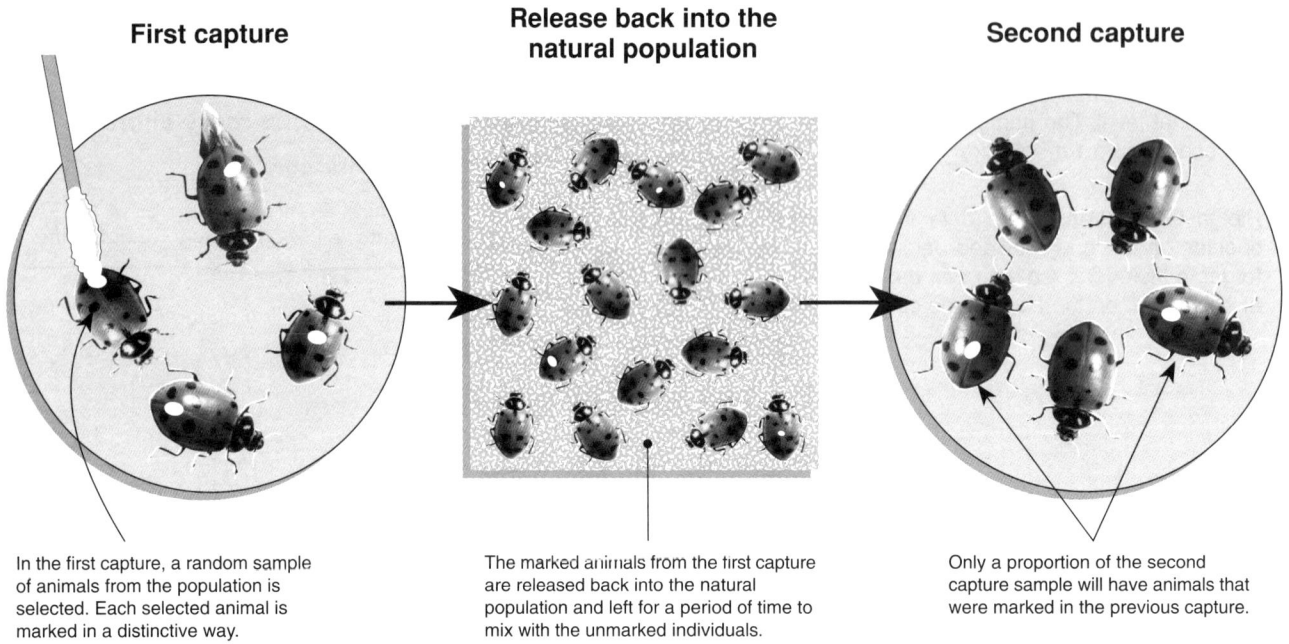

First capture	Release back into the natural population	Second capture

In the first capture, a random sample of animals from the population is selected. Each selected animal is marked in a distinctive way.

The marked animals from the first capture are released back into the natural population and left for a period of time to mix with the unmarked individuals.

Only a proportion of the second capture sample will have animals that were marked in the previous capture.

The Lincoln Index

$$\text{Total population} = \frac{\text{No. of animals in 1st sample (all marked)} \quad X \quad \text{Total no. of animals in 2nd sample}}{\text{Number of marked animals in the second sample (recaptured)}}$$

The mark and recapture technique comprises a number of simple steps:

1. The population is sampled by capturing as many of the individuals as possible and practical.

2. Each animal is marked in a way to distinguish it from unmarked animals (unique mark for each individual not required).

3. Return the animals to their habitat and leave them for a long enough period for complete mixing with the rest of the population to take place.

4. Take another sample of the population (this does not need to be the same sample size as the first sample, but it does have to be large enough to be valid).

5. Determine the numbers of marked to unmarked animals in this second sample. Use the equation above to estimate the size of the overall population.

---

1. For this exercise you will need several boxes of matches and a pen. Work in a group of 2-3 students to 'sample' the population of matches in the full box by using the Mark and Recapture method. Each match will represent one animal.

   (a) Take out 10 matches from the box and mark them on 4 sides with a pen so that you will be able to recognize them from the other unmarked matches later.
   (b) Return the marked matches to the box and shake the box to mix the matches.
   (c) Take a sample of 20 matches from the same box and record the number of marked matches and unmarked matches.
   (d) Determine the total population size by using the equation above.
   (e) Repeat the sampling 4 more times (steps 2–4 above) and record your results:

	Sample 1	Sample 2	Sample 3	Sample 4	Sample 5
Estimated Population					

   (f) Count the actual number of matches in the matchbox : _____

   (g) Compare the actual number to your estimates. By how much does it differ: _____

2. In 1919 a researcher by the name of Dahl wanted to estimate the number of trout in a Norwegian lake. The trout were subject to fishing so it was important to know how big the population was in order to manage the fish stock. He captured and marked 109 trout in his first sample. A few days later, he caught 177 trout in his second sample, of which 57 were marked. Use the **Lincoln index** (on the previous page) to estimate the total population size:

Size of 1st sample: _____

Size of 2nd sample: _____

No. marked in 2nd sample: _____

Estimated total population: _____

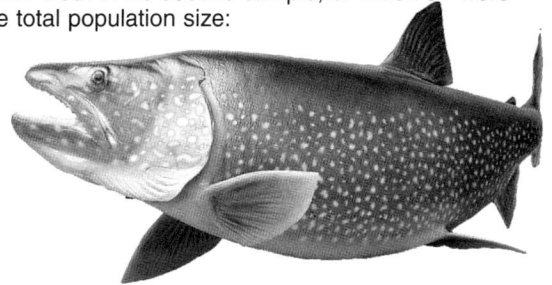

3. Describe some of the problems with the mark and recapture method if the second sampling is:

(a) Left too long a time before being repeated: _____

_____

_____

(b) Too soon after the first sampling: _____

_____

_____

4. Describe two important assumptions being made in this method of sampling, that would cause the method to fail if they were not true:

(a) _____

_____

_____

(b) _____

_____

_____

5. Some types of animal would be **unsuitable** for this method of population estimation (i.e. would not work).

(a) Name an animal for which this method of sampling would not be effective: _____

(b) Give a reason for your answer above: _____

_____

_____

6. Name 3 methods for marking animals for mark and recapture sampling. Take into account the possibility of animals shedding their skin, or being difficult to get close to again:

(a) _____

(b) _____

(c) _____

7. Scientists in Australia are involved in a computerized tagging program for southern bluefin tuna (a species also found in New Zealand waters). Describe the type of information that could be obtained through this tagging program:

_____

_____

_____

_____

Sampling Animal Populations

RA②

Unlike plants, most animals are highly mobile and present special challenges in terms of sampling them **quantitatively** to estimate their distribution and abundance. The equipment available for sampling animals ranges from various types of nets and traps (below), to more complex electronic devices, such as those used for radio-tracking large mobile species.

Plankton net

Tow rope
Bridle
Metal hoop
Canvas sleeve
Cone of bolting silk
Plastic container for collecting plankton sample
Tie cord
Direction of current →

Beating tray

Tree branch is shaken or beaten with a stick
Insects and other invertebrates fall
Canvas stretched over frame

Kick sampling

Direction of current
Rocks upstream of the net are disturbed
Small aquatic invertebrates are dislodged and collect in the net

Longworth small mammal trap

Nestbox containing bedding
Tunnel
Entrance to trap (door closed)
Nestbox is supported at an angle so that urine and rain water can drain out

Pooter or aspirator

Glass collecting tube that sucks up small animals
Specimen tube
Clear plastic tube
Rubber or cork bung
Gauze covering opening of tube
Glass mouthpiece through which operator sucks

Pitfall trap

Flat rock
Ground slopes away from trap to assist drainage
Jam jar sunk into ground
Support made of small stones or sticks
3 cm of water or 50% ethanol may be added as immobilizer

1. Describe what each the following types of sampling equipment is used for in a sampling context:

    (a) Kick sampling technique: _Provides a semi-quantitative sample of substrate-dwelling stream invertebrates_

    (b) Beating tray: _____

    _____

    (c) Pooter or aspirator: _____

    _____

2. Suggest why pitfall traps are not recommended for estimates of population density: _____

    _____

3. (a) Suggest what influence mesh size might have on the sampling efficiency of a plankton net: _____

    _____

    (b) Explain how this would affect your choice of mesh size when sampling animals in a pond: _____

    _____

DA❸ Using Chi-Square in Ecology

The following exercise illustrates the use of chi-square (χ^2) in ecological studies of habitat preference. In the first example, it is used for determining if the flat periwinkle *(Littorina littoralis)* shows significant preference for any of the four species of seaweeds with which it is found. Using quadrats, the numbers of periwinkles associated with each seaweed species were recorded. The data from this investigation are provided for you in Table 1. In the second example, the results of an investigation into habitat preference in woodlice (also called pillbugs, sowbugs, or slaters) are presented for analysis (Table 2).

1. (a) State your null hypothesis for this investigation (H0):

    _____

    _____

    _____

    (b) State the alternative hypothesis (HA): _____

    _____

    _____

Table 1: Number of periwinkles associated with different seaweed species

Seaweed species	Number of periwinkles
Spiral wrack	9
Bladder wrack	28
Toothed wrack	19
Knotted wrack	64

2. Use the chi-square test to determine if the differences observed between the samples are significant or if they can be attributed to chance alone. The table of critical values of χ^2 is provided in "The Chi-Square Test" in *Skills in Biology*.

    (a) Enter the observed values (no. of periwinkles) and complete the table to calculate the χ^2 value:

    (b) Calculate χ^2 value using the equation:

    $$\chi^2 = \sum \frac{(O - E)^2}{E} \qquad \chi^2 = \text{_____}$$

    (c) Calculate the degrees of freedom: _____

    (d) Using the χ^2 table, state the *P* value corresponding to your calculated χ^2 value:

    _____

    (e) State whether you accept or reject your null hypothesis:

    reject H0 / accept H0   *(circle one)*

Category	O	E	O – E	$(O - E)^2$	$\frac{(O - E)^2}{E}$
Spiral wrack					
Bladder wrack					
Toothed wrack					
Knotted wrack					
Σ					Σ

3. Students carried out an investigation into habitat preference in woodlice. In particular, they were wanting to know if the woodlice preferred a humid atmosphere to a dry one, as this may play a part in their choice of habitat. They designed a simple investigation to test this idea. The woodlice were randomly placed into a choice chamber for 5 minutes where they could choose between dry and humid conditions (atmosphere). The investigation consisted of five trials with ten woodlice used in each trial. Their results are shown on Table 2 (right):

    (a) State the null and alternative hypotheses (H0 and HA):

    _____

    _____

Table 2: Habitat preference in woodlice

Trial	Atmosphere	
	Dry	Humid
1	2	8
2	3	7
3	4	6
4	1	9
5	5	5

Use a separate piece of paper (or a spreadsheet) to calculate the chi-square value and summarize your answers below:

(b) Calculate the χ^2 value: _____

(c) Calculate the degrees of freedom and state the P value corresponding to your calculated χ^2 value:_____

(d) State whether you accept or reject your null hypothesis: reject H0 / accept H0   *(circle one)*

DA③ Student's *t* Test Exercise

Provided below are data from two flour beetle populations. Ten samples were taken from each population and the number of beetles in each sample were counted. The experimenter wanted to test if the densities of the two populations were significantly different. The exercise below involves manual computation to

determine a *t* value. Follow the steps to complete the test. If you do not have access to a statistical program, you will be able to use the steps outlined here to analyze your results (if the *t* test is appropriate). The calculations are very simply done using a spreadsheet if you wish (see opposite).

1. (a) Complete the table to calculate the sum of squares (see Step 4a below right). Some calculations are provided for you.

x (counts)		$x - \bar{x}$ (deviation from the mean)		$(x - \bar{x})^2$ (deviation from mean)^2	
Popn A	Popn B	Popn A	Popn B	Popn A	Popn B
465	310	9.3	−10.6	86.5	112.4
475	310	19.3	−10.6	372.5	112.4
415	290				
480	355				
436	350				
435	335				
445	295				
460	315				
471	316				
475	330				

$n_A = 10$ $n_B - 10$
The number of samples in each data set

The sum of each column is called the sum of squares

$\sum(x - \bar{x})^2$ $\sum(x - \bar{x})^2$

(b) The variance for population A: $s^2_A =$

The variance for population B: $s^2_B =$

(c) The difference between the population means

$(\bar{x}_A - \bar{x}_B) =$

(d) t (calculated) $=$

(e) Determine degrees of freedom (d.f.)

d.f. $(n_A + n_B - 2) =$

(f) $P =$

t (critical value) $=$

(g) Your decision is:

Step 1: Summary statistics

Tabulate the data as shown in the first 2 columns of the table (left). Calculate the mean and give the *n* value for each data set. Compute the standard deviation if you wish.

Popn A $\bar{x}_A = 455.7$ Popn B $\bar{x}_B = 320.6$
        $n_A = 10$ $n_B = 10$
        $s_A = 21.76$ $s_B = 21.64$

Step 2: State your null hypothesis

Step 3: Decide if your test is one or two-tailed

Calculating the t value

Step 4a: Calculate sums of squares

Complete the computations outlined in the table left. The sum of each of the final two columns (left) is called the sum of squares.

Step 4b: Calculate the variances

Calculate the variance (s^2) for each set of data. This is the sum of squares divided by $n - 1$ (number of samples in each data set − 1). In this case the *n* values are the same, but they need not be.

$$s^2_A = \frac{\sum(x - \bar{x})^2}{n_A - 1}_{(A)} \qquad s^2_B = \frac{\sum(x - \bar{x})^2}{n_B - 1}_{(B)}$$

Step 4c: Difference between means

Calculate the *actual* difference between the means

$$(\bar{x}_A - \bar{x}_B)$$

Step 4d: Calculate t

Calculate the *t* value. Ask for assistance if you find interpreting the lower part of the equation difficult

$$t = \frac{(\bar{x}_A - \bar{x}_B)}{\sqrt{\dfrac{s^2_A}{n_A} + \dfrac{s^2_B}{n_B}}}$$

Step 4e: Determine degrees of freedom

Degrees of freedom (d.f.) are defined by the number of samples (e.g., counts) taken: d.f. $= n_A + n_B - 2$ where n_A and n_B are the number of counts in each of populations A and B.

Step 5: Consult the t table

Consult the *t*-tables (opposite page) for the critical *t* value at the appropriate degrees of freedom and the acceptable probability level (e.g., $P = 0.05$).

Step 5a: Make your decision

Make your decision to reject or accept H_0. If your *t* value is large enough you may be able to reject H_0 at a lower *P* value (e.g., 0.001), increasing your confidence in the alternative hypothesis.

2. The previous example (manual calculation for two beetle populations) is outlined below in a spreadsheet (created in *Microsoft* Excel). The spreadsheet has been shown in a special mode with the formulae displayed. Normally, when using a spreadsheet, the calculated values will appear as the calculation is completed (entered) and a formula is visible only when you click into an individual cell. When setting up a spreadsheet, you can arrange your calculating cells wherever you wish. What is important is that you accurately identify the cells being used for each calculation. Also provided below is a summary of the spreadsheet notations used and a table of critical values of *t* at different levels of *P*. Note that, for brevity, only some probability values have been shown. To be significant at the appropriate level of probability, calculated values must be greater than those in the table for the appropriate degrees of freedom.

(a) Using the data in question 1, set up a spreadsheet as indicated below to calculate *t*. Save your spreadsheet. Print it out and staple the print-out into your manual.

Data values

$x_A - \bar{x}_A$ $x_B - \bar{x}_B$ $(x_A - \bar{x}_A)^2$ $(x_B - \bar{x}_B)^2$

Population A Population B

SS for t test formula

	A	B	C	D	E	F	G
1		XA	XB	Deviation of XA	Deviation of XB	(Deviation of XA	(Deviation of XB
2				from mean A	from mean B	from mean A)^2	from mean B)^2
3		465	310	=(B3-B16)	=(C3-C16)	=(D3^2)	=(E3^2)
4		475	310	=(B4-B16)	=(C4-C16)	=(D4^2)	=(E4^2)
5		415	290	=(B5-B16)	=(C5-C16)	=(D5^2)	=(E5^2)
6		480	355	=(B6-B16)	=(C6-C16)	=(D6^2)	=(E6^2)
7		436	350	=(B7-B16)	=(C7-C16)	=(D7^2)	=(E7^2)
8		435	335	=(B8-B16)	=(C8-C16)	=(D8^2)	=(E8^2)
9		445	295	=(B9-B16)	=(C9-C16)	=(D9^2)	=(E9^2)
10		460	315	=(B10-B16)	=(C10-C16)	=(D10^2)	=(E10^2)
11		471	316	=(B11-B16)	=(C11-C16)	=(D11^2)	=(E11^2)
12		475	330	=(B12-B16)	=(C12-C16)	=(D12^2)	=(E12^2)
13							
14	Totals	=SUM(B3:B12)	=SUM(C3:C12)				
15	Count	=COUNT(B3:B12)	=COUNT(C3:C12)		Sum of squares	=SUM(F3:F12)	=SUM(G3:G12)
16	Mean	=(B14/B15)	=(C14/C15)				
17					Variance	=(F15/(B15-1))	=(G15/(C15-1))
18		Difference					
19		between means	=(B16-C16)				
20							
21		t value	=C19/SQRT((F17/B15)+(G17/C15))				
22							

Take the value in cell B16 away from the value in cell B12

$$\frac{(\bar{x}_A - \bar{x}_B)}{\sqrt{\frac{s^2_A}{n_A} + \frac{s^2_B}{n_B}}}$$

$(\bar{x}_A - \bar{x}_B)$

$\sum(x - \bar{x})^2$ $s^2 = \dfrac{\sum(x - \bar{x})^2}{n - 1}$

Table of critical values of *t* at different levels of *P*.

Notation	Meaning
Columns and rows	Columns are denoted A, B, C ... at the top of the spreadsheet, rows are 1, 2, 3, ... on the left. Using this notation a cell can be located e.g. C3
=	An "equals" sign *before* other entries in a cell denotes a formula follows.
( )	Parentheses are used to group together terms for a single calculation. This is important for larger calculations (see cell C21 above)
C3:C12	Cell locations are separated by a colon. C3:C12 means "every cell between and including C3 and C12"
SUM	Denotes that what follows is added up. =SUM(C3:C12) means "add up the values in cells C3 down to C12"
COUNT	Denotes that the number of values is counted =COUNT(C3:C12) means "count up the number of values in cells C3 down to C12"
SQRT	Denotes "take the square root of what follows"
^2	Denotes an exponent e.g. x^2 means that value x is squared.

Degrees of freedom	Level of Probability		
	0.05	0.01	0.001
1	12.71	63.66	636.6
2	4.303	9.925	31.60
3	3.182	5.841	12.92
4	2.776	4.604	8.610
5	2.571	4.032	6.869
6	2.447	3.707	5.959
7	2.365	3.499	5.408
8	2.306	3.355	5.041
9	2.262	3.250	4.781
10	2.228	3.169	4.587
11	2.201	3.106	4.437
12	2.179	3.055	4.318
13	2.160	3.012	4.221
14	2.145	2.977	4.140
15	2.131	2.947	4.073
16	2.120	2.921	4.015
17	2.110	2.898	3.965
18	2.101	2.878	3.922
19	2.093	2.861	3.883
20	2.086	2.845	3.850

Above is a table explaining some of the spreadsheet notations used for the calculation of the t value for the exercise on the previous page. It is not meant to be an exhaustive list for all spreadsheet work, but it should help you to become familiar with some of the terms and how they are used. This list applies to *Microsoft* Excel. Different spreadsheets may use different notations. These will be described in the spreadsheet manual.

(b) Save your spreadsheet under a different name and enter the following new data values for population B: **425, 478, 428, 465, 439, 475, 469, 445, 421, 438**. Notice that, as you enter the new values, the calculations are updated over the entire spreadsheet. Re-run the *t*-test using the new *t* value. State your decision for the two populations now:

New *t* value: _____ Decision on null hypothesis (delete one): Accept / Reject

Classification

IB SL
Complete nos:
1-12

IB HL
Complete nos:
1-12

IB Options
Not applicable
to options

AP Biology
Complete nos:
1-12

Learning Objectives

☐ 1. Compile your own glossary from the **KEY WORDS** displayed in **bold type** in the learning objectives below.

Biodiversity *(pages 324-325)*

☐ 2. Understand what is meant by **biodiversity** and explain the importance of accurate classification in recognizing, appreciating, and conserving the biodiversity on Earth.

☐ 3. Understand the concept of a **species** in terms of their reproductive isolation and potential for breeding.

Classification systems

The five kingdoms *(pages 323, 326-333)*

☐ 4. Explain what is meant by classification. Recognize **taxonomy** as the study of the theory and practice of classification. Describe the principles and importance of scientific classification.

☐ 5. Explain what is meant by the **five kingdom classification system**. Describe the **distinguishing features** of each of the five kingdoms:
   • **Prokaryotae** (Monera): bacteria and cyanobacteria.
   • **Protista**: includes the algae and protozoans.
   • **Fungi**: includes yeasts, moulds, and mushrooms.
   • **Plantae**: includes mosses, liverworts, tracheophytes.
   • **Animalia**: all invertebrate phyla and the chordates.

☐ 6. Demonstrate a working knowledge of taxonomy by classifying familiar organisms. Recognize at least seven major **taxonomic categories**: **kingdom**, **phylum**, **class**, **order**, **family**, **genus**, and **species**.

☐ 7. Appreciate that taxonomic categories should not be confused with **taxa** (sing. **taxon**), which are groups of real organisms: "genus" is a taxonomic category, whereas the genus *Drosophila* is a taxon.

☐ 8. Understand the basis for assigning organisms into different taxonomic categories. Recall what is meant by a **distinguishing feature**. Explain that species are usually classified on the basis of **shared derived characters** rather than primitive (ancestral) characters. *For example, within the subphylum Vertebrata, the presence of a backbone is a derived, therefore a distinguishing, feature. However, within the class Mammalia, the backbone is an ancestral feature and is not distinguishing, whereas mammary glands (a distinguishing feature) are derived.*

☐ 9. Explain how **binomial nomenclature** is used to classify organisms and understand the rules of presentation for these names. Explain the limitations of using **common names** to identify organisms.

☐ 10. Recognize the relationship between classification and **phylogeny**. Appreciate that newer classification schemes (such as the reclassification of organisms into three domains) attempt to better reflect the true phylogeny of organisms.

Use of taxonomic keys *(pages 334-335)*

☐ 11. Demonstrate an understanding of the proper use of **classification keys**. Describe the essential features of any classification key.

☐ 12. Apply and/or design a simple taxonomic key to identify and classify a group of up to eight organisms.

Textbooks

See the 'Textbook Reference Grid' on pages 8-9 for textbook page references relating to material in this topic.

Internet

See pages 10-11 for details of how to access **Bio Links** from our web site: **www.thebiozone.com**. From Bio Links, access sites under the topics:
GENERAL BIOLOGY ONLINE RESOURCES: See sites under **Online Textbooks and Lecture Notes**.

BIODIVERSITY > Taxonomy and Classification: • Birds and DNA • Taxonomy: Classifying life • The phylogeny of life... *and others*

MICROBIOLOGY > General Microbiology: • Biological identity of the prokaryotes • British Mycological Society • Major groups of prokaryotes • The microbial world ... *and others*

PLANT BIOLOGY: • Kimball's plant biology lecture notes • Plant biology for non-science majors > **Classification and Diversity**: • Flowering plant diversity • Natural perspective: Plant Kingdom • Introduction to the Plantae • Vascular plant families

Periodicals

See page 6 for details of publishers of periodicals:

STUDENT'S REFERENCE

■ **The Species Enigma** New Scientist, 13 June 1998 (Inside Science). *An account of the nature of species, ring species, and the status of hybrids.*

■ **Taxonomy: The Naming Game Revisited** Biol. Sci. Rev., 9(5) May 1997, pp. 31-35. *New tools for taxonomy and how they are used (includes the exemplar of the reclassification of the kingdoms).*

TEACHER'S REFERENCE

■ **Family Feuds** New Scientist, 24 January 1998, pp. 36-40. *Molecular and morphological analysis used for determining species inter-relatedness.*

■ **The Problematic Red Wolf** Scientific American, July 1995, pp. 26-31. *Is the red wolf a species or a long-established hybrid? Correctly naming and recognising species can affect conservation efforts.*

■ **The Loves of the Plants** Scientific American, February 1996, pp. 98-103. *The classification of plants and the development of effective keys to plant identification.*

■ **A Universal Phylogenetic Tree** The American Biology Teacher, 63(3), March 2001, pp.164-170. *A comparison of the three domains versus five kingdoms systems, with an examination of the features of the Archaea and the Eubacteria.*

■ **Bats in the Classroom** The American Biology Teacher, 64(6), August 2002, pp. 415-421. *This account explains how to use one animal, the bat, to introduce a variety of biological concepts, including classification, phylogeny, speciation, coevolution, and adaptation.*

Software and video resources are now provided in the **Teacher Resource Handbook**

The New Tree of Life

With the advent of more efficient genetic (DNA) sequencing technology, the genomes of many bacteria began to be sequenced. In 1996, the results of a scientific collaboration examining DNA evidence confirmed the proposal that life comprises three major evolutionary lineages (domains) and not two as was the convention. The recognized lineages were the **Eubacteria**, the **Eukarya** and the **Archaea** (formerly the Archaebacteria). The new classification reflects the fact that there are very large differences between the archaea and the eubacteria. All three domains probably had a distant common ancestor.

A Five Kingdom World (right)

The diagram on the right represents the five kingdom system of classification. It recognizes two basic cell types: prokaryote and eukaryote. The domain Prokaryota includes the prokaryotes: all bacteria and cyanobacteria. Domain Eukaryota includes protists, fungi, plants, and animals. This is the system most commonly represented in modern biology textbooks.

A New View of the World (below)

In 1996 a large collaboration of scientists deciphered the full DNA sequence of every gene of a strange type of bacteria called *Methanococcus jannaschii*. Termed an extremophile, this methane-producing archaebacterium lives at 85°C; a temperature lethal for regular bacteria as well as multicellular plants and animals. The DNA sequence confirmed that life consists of three major evolutionary lineages, not the two that have been routinely described in textbooks. Only 44% of this archaebacterium's genes resemble those in bacteria or eukaryotes, or both.

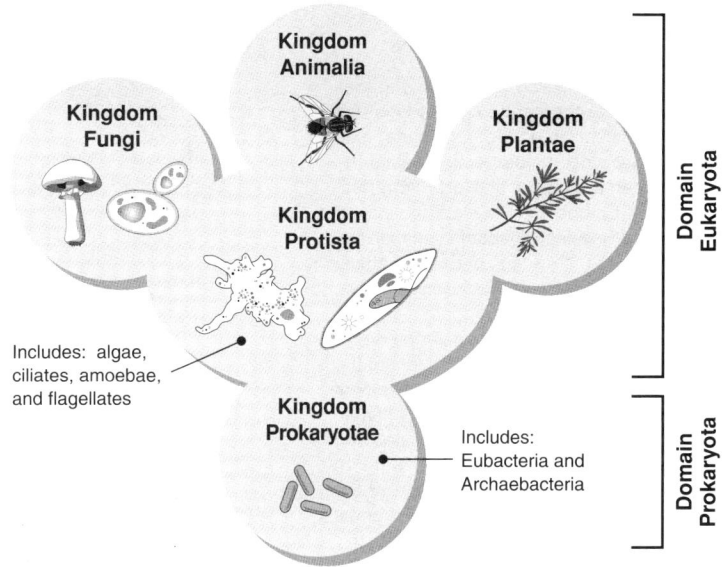

Kingdom Animalia

Kingdom Fungi

Kingdom Plantae

Kingdom Protista

Includes: algae, ciliates, amoebae, and flagellates

Kingdom Prokaryotae

Includes: Eubacteria and Archaebacteria

Domain Eukaryota

Domain Prokaryota

Domain Eubacteria

Lack a distinct nucleus and cell organelles. Generally prefer less extreme environments than Archaea. Includes well-known pathogens, many harmless and beneficial species, and the cyanobacteria (photosynthetic bacteria containing the pigments chlorophyll a and phycocyanin).

Domain Archaea

Closely resemble eubacteria in many ways but cell wall composition and aspects of metabolism are very different. Live in extreme environments similar to those on primeval Earth. They may utilize sulfur, methane, or halogens (chlorine, fluorine), and many tolerate extremes of temperature, salinity, or pH.

Domain Eukarya

Complex cell structure with organelles and nucleus. This group contains four of the kingdoms classified under the more traditional system. Note that Kingdom Protista is separated into distinct groups: e.g. amoebae, ciliates, flagellates.

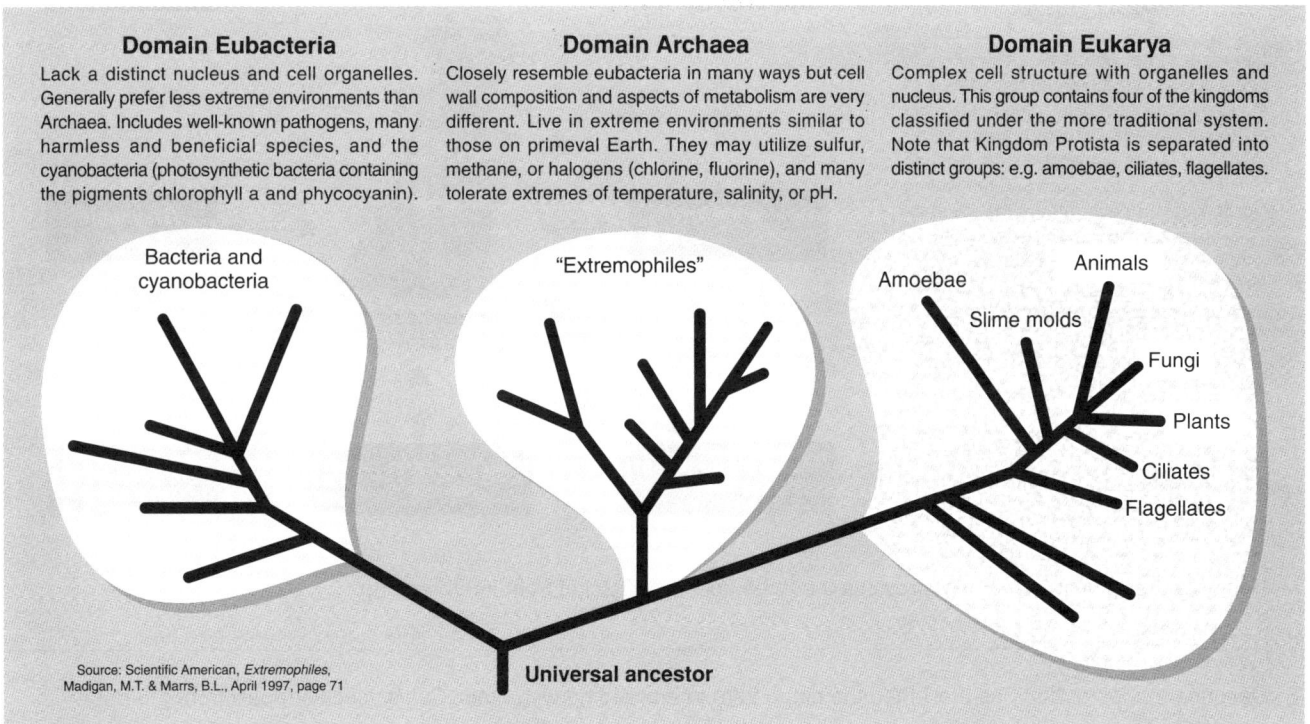

Bacteria and cyanobacteria

"Extremophiles"

Amoebae

Slime molds

Animals

Fungi

Plants

Ciliates

Flagellates

Source: Scientific American, *Extremophiles*, Madigan, M.T. & Marrs, B.L., April 1997, page 71

Universal ancestor

1. Explain why some scientists have recommended that the conventional classification of life be revised so that the Archaea, Eubacteria and Eukarya are three separate domains:

_____

_____

2. Describe two features of the new classification scheme that are very different from the five kingdom classification:

(a) _____

_____

(b) _____

_____

The Species Concept

The concept of a species is not as simple as it may first appear. Interbreeding between closely related species, such as the dog family below and 'ring species' on the facing page, suggest that the boundaries of a species gene pool can be somewhat unclear. One of the best recognized definitions for a species has been proposed by the respected zoologist, Ernst Mayr: "*A species is a group of actually or potentially interbreeding natural populations that is reproductively isolated from other such groups*". Each species is provided with a unique classification name to assist with future identification.

Geographical distribution of selected *Canis* species

The global distribution of most of the species belonging to the genus *Canis* (dogs and wolves) is shown on the map to the right. The **gray wolf** (timber wolf) inhabits the cold, damp forests of North America, northern Europe and Siberia. The range of the three species of **jackal** overlap in the dry, hot, open savannah of Eastern Africa. The now-rare **red wolf** is found only in Texas, while the **coyote** is found inhabiting the open grasslands of the prairies. The **dingo** is found widely distributed throughout the Australian continent inhabiting a variety of habitats. As a result of the spread of human culture, distribution of the domesticated **dog** is global. The dog has been able to interbreed with all other members of the genus listed here, to form fertile hybrids.

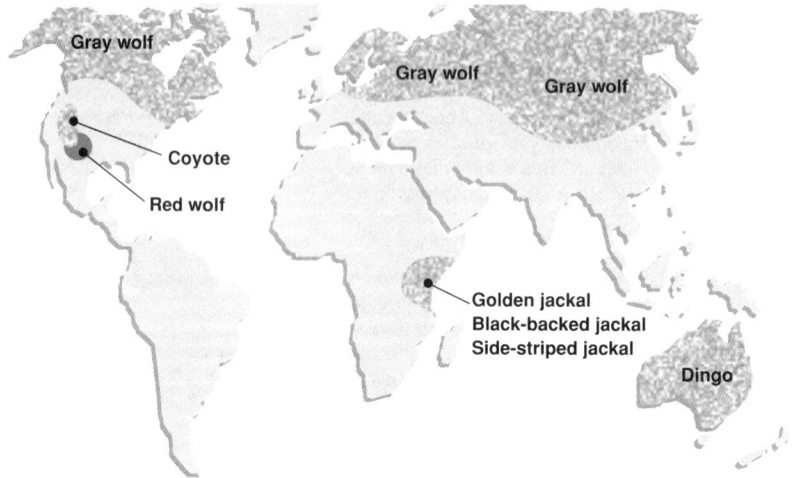

Interbreeding between *Canis* species

Members of the genus to which all dogs and wolves belong present problems with the species concept. The domesticated dog is able to breed with numerous other members of the same genus to produce fertile hybrids. The coyote and red wolf in North America have ranges that overlap. They are also able to produce fertile hybrids, although these are rare. By contrast, the ranges of the three distinct species of jackal overlap in the Serengeti of Eastern Africa. These animals are highly territorial, but simply ignore members of the other jackal species and no interbreeding takes place.

For an excellent discussion of species definition among dogs see the article "The Problematic Red Wolf" in Scientific American, July 1995, pp. 26-31. This discusses whether or not the red wolf is a species or a long established hybrid of the gray wolf and coyote.

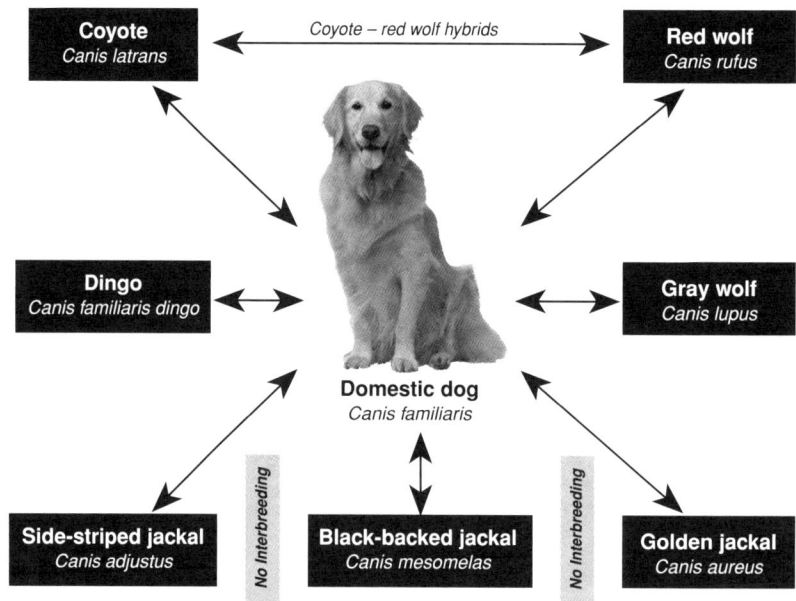

Map labels: Gray wolf, Gray wolf, Gray wolf, Coyote, Red wolf, Golden jackal, Black-backed jackal, Side-striped jackal, Dingo

Diagram labels:
- **Coyote** *Canis latrans*
- Coyote – red wolf hybrids
- **Red wolf** *Canis rufus*
- **Dingo** *Canis familiaris dingo*
- **Gray wolf** *Canis lupus*
- **Domestic dog** *Canis familiaris*
- **Side-striped jackal** *Canis adjustus*
- No Interbreeding
- **Black-backed jackal** *Canis mesomelas*
- No Interbreeding
- **Golden jackal** *Canis aureus*

1. Describe the type of barrier that prevents the three species of jackal from interbreeding:

_____

2. Describe the factor that has prevented the dingo from interbreeding with other *Canis* species (apart from the dog):

_____

_____

3. Suggest a possible contributing factor to the occurrence of interbreeding between the coyote and red wolf:

_____

_____

4. The gray wolf is a widely distributed species. Give a reason why the North American population is considered to be part of the same species as the northern European and Siberian populations:

_____

_____

Gene Pool of the Lesser Black-Backed Gull and the Herring Gull

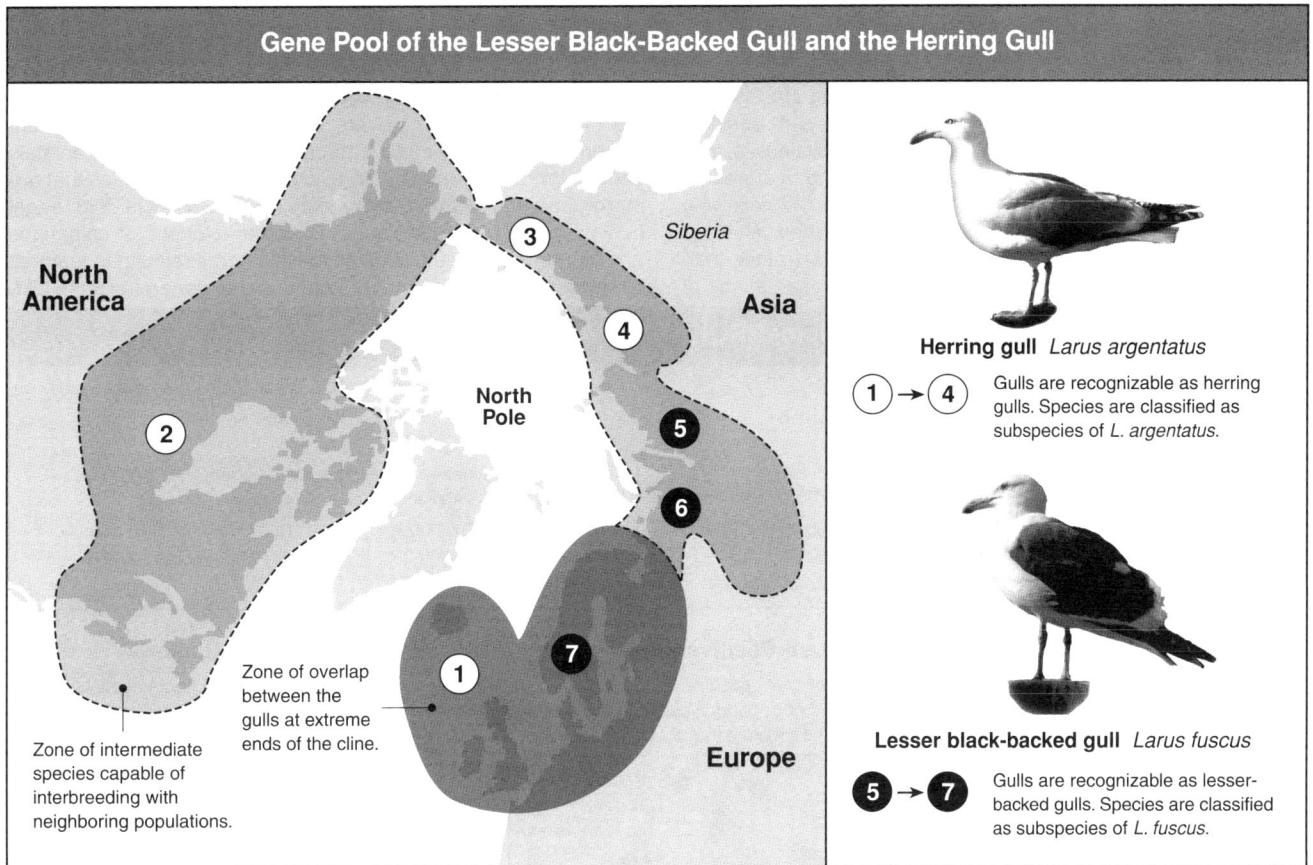

Herring gull *Larus argentatus*

1 → 4   Gulls are recognizable as herring gulls. Species are classified as subspecies of *L. argentatus*.

Lesser black-backed gull *Larus fuscus*

5 → 7   Gulls are recognizable as lesser-backed gulls. Species are classified as subspecies of *L. fuscus*.

Zone of overlap between the gulls at extreme ends of the cline.

Zone of intermediate species capable of interbreeding with neighboring populations.

Species may show a gradual change in phenotype over a geographical area. Such a continuous gradual change is called a **cline**, and often occurs along the length of a country or continent. All the populations are of the same species as long as interbreeding populations link them together. **Ring species** are a special type of cline that has a circular or looped geographical distribution, resulting in the two ends of the cline overlapping. Adjacent populations can interbreed but not where the arms of the loop overlap. In the example above, four subspecies of the herring gull, and three of the lesser black-backed gull are currently recognized, forming a chain that circles the North Pole. The evidence suggests that all subspecies were derived from a single ancestral population that originated in Siberia. Members of this ancestral population migrated in opposite directions, and at the same time evolved so that, at various stages, new subspecies could be identified. Each subspecies can breed with those on either side of it. For instance, subspecies 2 can breed with subspecies 1 and 3, subspecies 3 can breed with subspecies 4 and 2, and so on. The two populations at the ends of the cline, which overlaps in northern Europe, rarely interbreed (i.e. subspecies 1 and 7 behave as two distinct species) even though they are connected by a series of intermediate interbreeding populations.

5. Give a clear and concise definition of species: _____

_____

_____

_____

6. The **ring species** illustrated above do not fit comfortably with the standard definition of a species. Describe the aspects of the populations of gulls that:

(a) Supports the idea that they are a single species: _____

_____

_____

_____

(b) Contradicts the standard definition of a species: _____

_____

_____

7. Explain what a 'ring species' is: _____

_____

_____

Features of Taxonomic Groups

In order to distinguish organisms, it is desirable to classify and name them (a science known as **taxonomy**). An effective classification system requires features that are distinctive to a particular group of organisms. The distinguishing features of some major taxonomic groups are provided in the following pages by means of diagrams and brief summaries. Revised classification systems, recognizing three domains (rather than five kingdoms) are now recognized as better representations of

the true diversity of life. However, for the purposes of describing the groups with which we are most familiar, the five kingdom system (used here) is still appropriate. Note that most animals show **bilateral symmetry** (body divisible into two halves that are mirror images). **Radial symmetry** (body divisible into equal halves through various planes) is a characteristic of cnidarians and ctenophores. Definitions of specific terms relating to features of structure or function can be found in any general biology text.

Kingdom: PROKARYOTAE (Bacteria)

- Also known as monerans or prokaryotes.
- Two major bacterial lineages are recognized: the primitive **Archaebacteria** and the more advanced **Eubacteria**.
- All have a prokaryotic cell structure: they lack the nuclei and chromosomes of eukaryotic cells, and have smaller (70S) ribosomes.
- Have a tendency to spread genetic elements across species barriers by sexual conjugation, viral transduction and other processes.
- Can reproduce rapidly by binary fission in the absence of sex.

- Have evolved a wider variety of metabolism types than eukaryotes.
- Bacteria grow and divide or aggregate into filaments or colonies of various shapes.
- They are taxonomically identified by their appearance (form) and through biochemical differences.

Species diversity: 10 000 + Bacteria are rather difficult to classify to the species level because of their relatively rampant genetic exchange, and because their reproduction is usually asexual.

Eubacteria

- Also known as 'true bacteria', they probably evolved from the more ancient Archaebacteria.
- Distinguished from Archaebacteria by differences in cell wall composition, nucleotide structure, and ribosome shape.
- Very diverse group comprises most bacteria.
- The **gram stain** provides the basis for distinguishing two broad groups of bacteria. It relies on the presence of peptidoglycan (unique to bacteria) in the cell wall. The stain is easily washed from the thin peptidoglycan layer of gram negative walls but is retained by the thick peptidoglycan layer of gram positive cells, staining them a dark violet color.

Gram-Positive Bacteria

The walls of gram positive bacteria consist of many layers of peptidoglycan forming a thick, single-layered structure that holds the gram stain.

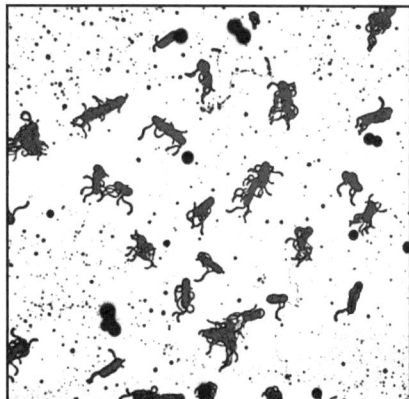

Bacillus alvei: a gram positive, flagellated bacterium. Note how the cells appear dark.

Gram-Negative Bacteria

The cell walls of gram negative bacteria contain only a small proportion of peptidoglycan, so the dark violet stain is not retained by the organisms.

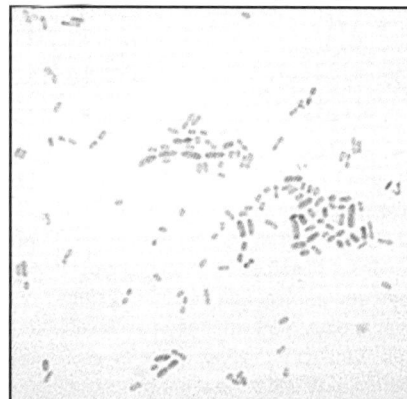

Alcaligenes odorans: a gram negative bacterium. Note how the cells appear pale.

Photos: CDC

Kingdom: FUNGI

- Heterotrophic.
- Rigid cell wall made of chitin.
- Vary from single celled to large multicellular organisms.
- Mostly saprotrophic (i.e. feeding on dead or decaying material).
- Terrestrial and immobile.

Examples:
Mushrooms/toadstools, yeasts, truffles, morels, molds, and lichens.

Species diversity: 80 000 +

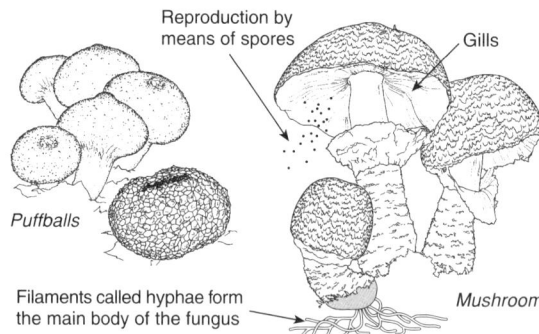

Reproduction by means of spores
Gills
Puffballs
Filaments called hyphae form the main body of the fungus
Mushrooms
Lichens

- **Lichens** are symbiotic associations of a fungus (provides protection) and an alga (provides the food).

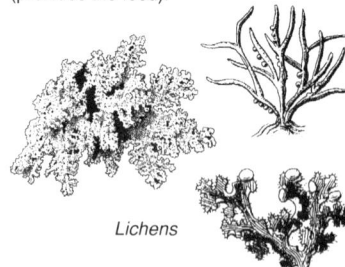

Kingdom: PROTISTA

- A diverse group of organisms that do not fit easily into other taxonomic groups.
- Unicellular or simple multicellular.
- Widespread in moist or aquatic environments.

Examples of algae: green, brown, and red algae, dinoflagellates, diatoms.

Examples of protozoa: amoebas, foraminiferans, radiolarians, ciliates.

Species diversity: 55 000 +

Algae 'plant-like' protists

- Autotrophic (photosynthesis)
- Characterized by the type of chlorophyll present

Cell walls of cellulose, sometimes with silica
Diatom

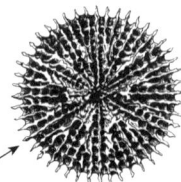

Protozoa 'animal-like' protists

- Heterotrophic nutrition and feed via ingestion
- Most are microscopic (5 μm-250 μm)

Move via projections called pseudopodia
Amoeba
Lack cell walls

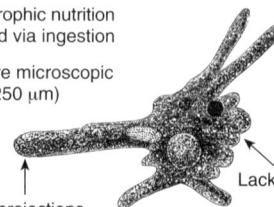

Kingdom: PLANTAE

- Multicellular organisms (the majority are photosynthetic and contain chlorophyll).
- Cell walls made of cellulose; Food is stored as starch.
- Subdivided into two major divisions based on tissue structure: **Bryophytes** (non-vascular) and **Tracheophytes** (vascular) plants.

Non-Vascular Plants:

- Non vascular, lacking transport tissues (no xylem or phloem).
- They are small and restricted to moist, terrestrial environments.
- Do not possess 'true' roots, stems or leaves

Phylum Bryophyta: Mosses, liverworts, and hornworts.
Species diversity: 18 600 +

Phylum: Bryophyta

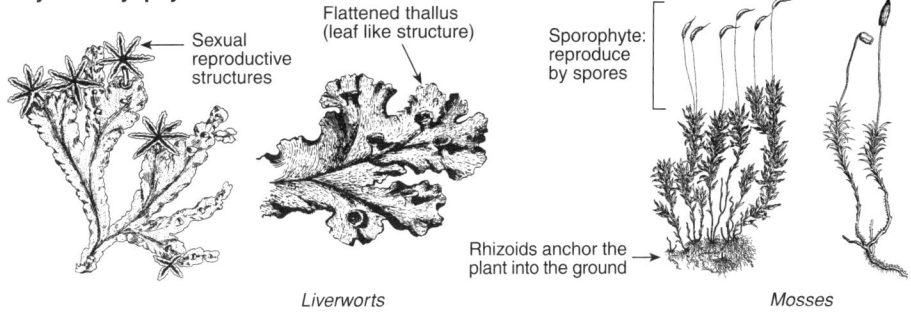

Sexual reproductive structures

Flattened thallus (leaf like structure)

Sporophyte: reproduce by spores

Rhizoids anchor the plant into the ground

Liverworts

Mosses

Vascular Plants:

- Vascular: possess transport tissues.
- Possess true roots, stems, and leaves, as well as stomata.
- Reproduce via spores, not seeds.
- Clearly defined *alternation of sporophyte and gametophyte generations*.

Seedless Plants:

Spore producing plants, includes:
Phylum Filicinophyta: Ferns
Phylum Sphenophyta: Horsetails
Phylum Lycophyta: Club mosses
Species diversity: 13 000 +

Phylum: Lycophyta

Leaves

Club moss

Phylum: Sphenophyta

Leaves

Horsetail

Phylum: Filicinophyta

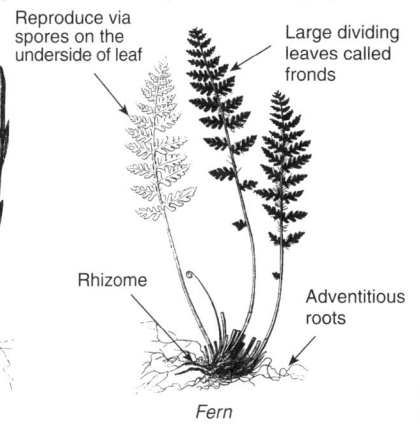

Reproduce via spores on the underside of leaf

Large dividing leaves called fronds

Rhizome

Adventitious roots

Fern

Seed Plants:

Also called Spermatophyta. Produce seeds housing an embryo. Includes:

Gymnosperms

- Lack enclosed chambers in which seeds develop.
- Produce seeds in cones which are exposed to the environment.

Phylum Cycadophyta: Cycads
Phylum Ginkgophyta: Ginkgoes
Phylum Coniferophyta: Conifers
Species diversity: 730 +

Phylum: Cycadophyta

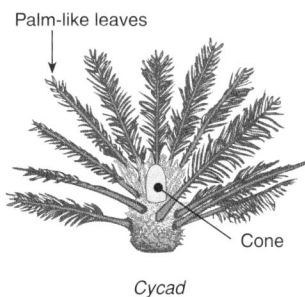

Palm-like leaves

Cone

Cycad

Phylum: Ginkophyta

Flat leaves

Ginkgo

Phylum: Coniferophyta

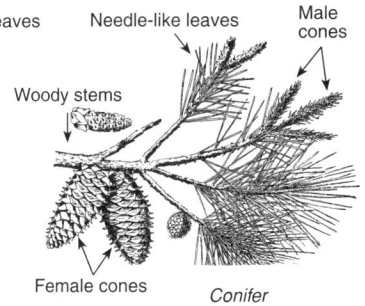

Needle-like leaves

Male cones

Woody stems

Female cones

Conifer

Angiosperms
Phylum: Angiospermophyta

- Seeds in specialized reproductive structures called flowers.
- Female reproductive ovary develops into a fruit.
- Pollination usually via wind or animals.

Species diversity: 260 000 +

The phylum Angiospermophyta may be subdivided into two classes:

Class *Monocotyledoneae* (Monocots)
Class *Dicotyledoneae* (Dicots)

Angiosperms: **Monocotyledons**

Flower parts occur in multiples of 3

Leaves have parallel veins

- Only have one cotyledon (food storage organ)
- Normally herbaceous (non-woody) with no secondary growth

Examples: cereals, lilies, daffodils, palms, grasses.

Angiosperms: **Dicotyledons**

Leaves have branching veins

- Flower parts occur in multiples of 4 or 5
- Possible to have secondary growth (either herbaceous or woody)

Have two cotyledons inside the seed (acorn)

Oak

Examples: many annual plants, trees and shrubs.

Kingdom: ANIMALIA

- Over 800 000 species described in 33 existing phyla.
- Multicellular, heterotrophic organisms.
- Animal cells lack cell walls.

- Further subdivided into various major phyla on the basis of body symmetry, type of body cavity, and external and internal structures.

Phylum: Rotifera

- A diverse group of small organisms with sessile, colonial, and planktonic forms.
- Most freshwater, a few marine.
- Typically reproduce via cyclic parthenogenesis.
- Characterized by a wheel of cilia on the head used for feeding and locomotion, a large muscular pharynx (mastax) with jaw like trophi, and a foot with sticky toes.

Species diversity: 1500+

Cilia
Head
Mastax
Foot
Toes

Bdelloid: non planktonic, creeping form

Spines for protection against predators
Lorica
Ovary
Eggs

Planktonic forms swim using their crown of cilia

Phylum: Porifera

- Lack organs.
- All are aquatic (mostly marine).
- Asexual reproduction by budding.
- Lack a nervous system.

Examples: sponges.
Species diversity: 8000 +

Body wall perforated by pores through which water enters
Water leaves by a larger opening - the osculum
Sponge

- Capable of regeneration (the replacement of lost parts)
- Possess spicules (needle-like internal structures) for support and protection

Tube sponge
Sessile (attach to ocean floor)

Phylum: Cnidaria

- Two basic body forms:

  Medusa: umbrella shaped and free swimming by pulsating bell.

  Polyp: cylindrical, some are sedentary, others can glide, or somersault or use tentacles as legs.

- Some species have a life cycle that alternates between a polyp stage and a medusa stage.
- All are aquatic (most are marine).

Examples: Jellyfish, sea anemones, hydras, and corals.

Species diversity: 11 000 +

Some have air-filled floats
Nematocysts (stinging cells)
Jellyfish (Portuguese man-o-war)
Single opening acts as mouth and anus
Polyps may aggregate in colonies
Polyps stick to seabed
Sea anemone
Brain coral
Contraction of the bell propels the free swimming medusa
Colonial polyps

Phylum: Platyhelminthes

- Unsegmented body.
- Flattened body shape.
- Mouth, but no anus.
- Many are parasitic.

Examples: Tapeworms, planarians, flukes.

Species diversity: 20 000+

Hooks
Detail of head (scolex)
Liver fluke
Tapeworm
Planarian

Phylum: Nematoda

- Tiny, unsegmented round worms.
- Many are plant/animal parasites

Examples: Hookworms, stomach worms, lung worms, filarial worms

Species diversity: 80 000 - 1 million

Muscular pharynx
Ovary
Anus
Mouth
Intestine
A general nematode body plan
A roundworm parasite

Phylum: Annelida

- Cylindrical, segmented body with chaetae (bristles).
- Move using hydrostatic skeleton and/or parapodia (appendages).

Examples: Earthworms, leeches, polychaetes (including tubeworms).

Species diversity: 15 000 +

Mouth
Clitellum
Segments with parapodia (fleshy projections)
Anterior sucker
Posterior sucker
Anus
Earthworm
Polychaete
Leech

Kingdom: ANIMALIA *(continued)*

Phylum: Mollusca

- Soft bodied and unsegmented.
- Body comprises head, muscular foot, and visceral mass (organs).
- Most have radula (rasping tongue).
- Aquatic and terrestrial species.
- Aquatic species possess gills.

Examples: Snails, mussels, squid.
Species diversity: 110 000 +

Class: Bivalvia

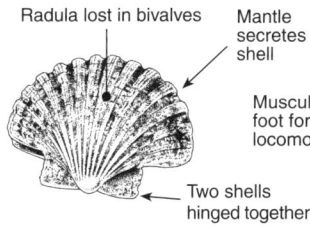

Radula lost in bivalves
Mantle secretes shell
Muscular foot for locomotion
Two shells hinged together

Class: Gastropoda

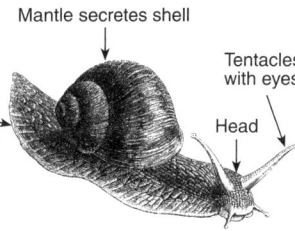

Mantle secretes shell
Head

Class: Cephalopoda

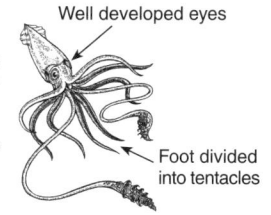

Well developed eyes
Tentacles with eyes
Foot divided into tentacles

Phylum: Arthropoda

- Exoskeleton made of chitin.
- Grow in stages after moulting.
- Jointed appendages.
- Segmented bodies.
- Heart found on dorsal side of body.
- Open circulation system.
- Most have compound eyes.

Species diversity: 1 million +
Make up 75% of all living animals.

Arthropods are subdivided into the following classes:

Class: Crustacea (crustaceans)
- Mainly marine.
- Exoskeleton impregnated with mineral salts.
- Gills often present.
- Includes: Lobsters, crabs, barnacles, prawns, shrimps, isopods, amphipods
- **Species diversity**: 35 000 +

Class: Arachnida (chelicerates)
- Almost all are terrestrial.
- 2 body parts: cephalothorax and abdomen (except horseshoe crabs).
- Includes: spiders, scorpions, ticks, mites, horseshoe crabs.
- **Species diversity**: 57 000 +

Class: Insecta (insects)
- Mostly terrestrial.
- Most are capable of flight.
- 3 body parts: head, thorax, abdomen.
- Include: Locusts, dragonflies, cockroaches, butterflies, bees, ants, beetles, bugs, flies, and more
- **Species diversity**: 800 000 +

Class: Myriapoda (=many legs)
Diplopods (millipedes)
- Terrestrial.
- Have a rounded body.
- Eat dead or living plants.
- **Species diversity**: 2000 +

Chilopods (centipedes)
- Terrestrial.
- Have a flattened body.
- Poison claws for catching prey.
- Feed on insects, worms, and snails.
- **Species diversity**: 7000 +

Class: Crustacea

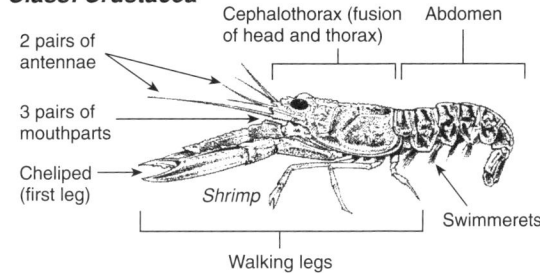

2 pairs of antennae
Cephalothorax (fusion of head and thorax)
Abdomen
3 pairs of mouthparts
Cheliped (first leg)
Shrimp
Swimmerets
Walking legs

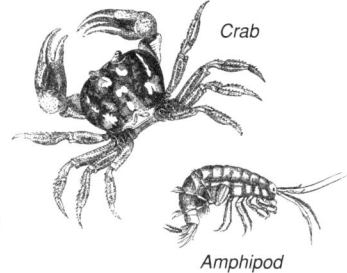

Crab
Amphipod

Class: Arachnida

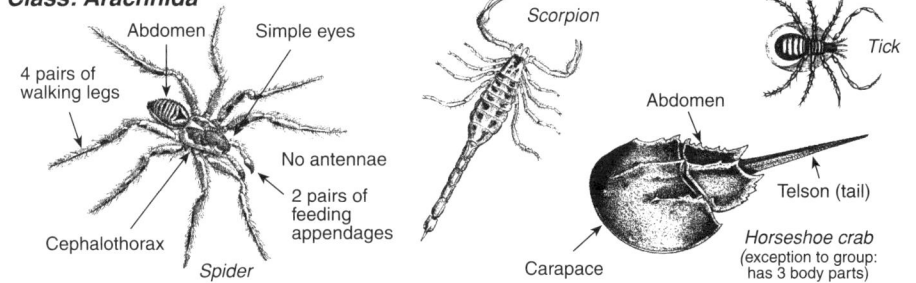

Abdomen
Simple eyes
4 pairs of walking legs
No antennae
2 pairs of feeding appendages
Cephalothorax
Spider
Scorpion
Tick
Abdomen
Telson (tail)
Carapace
Horseshoe crab (exception to group: has 3 body parts)

Class: Insecta

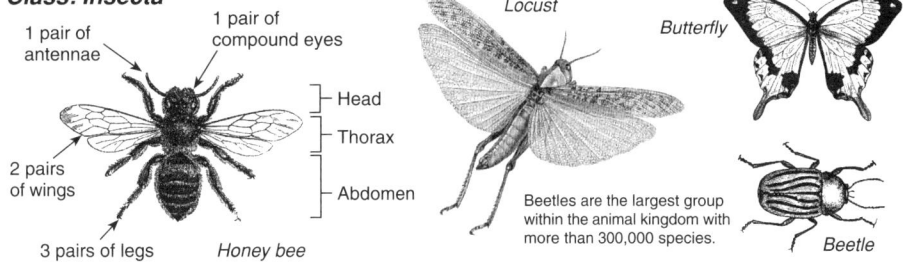

1 pair of antennae
1 pair of compound eyes
Head
Thorax
Abdomen
2 pairs of wings
3 pairs of legs
Honey bee
Locust
Butterfly
Beetles are the largest group within the animal kingdom with more than 300,000 species.
Beetle

Class: Myriapoda

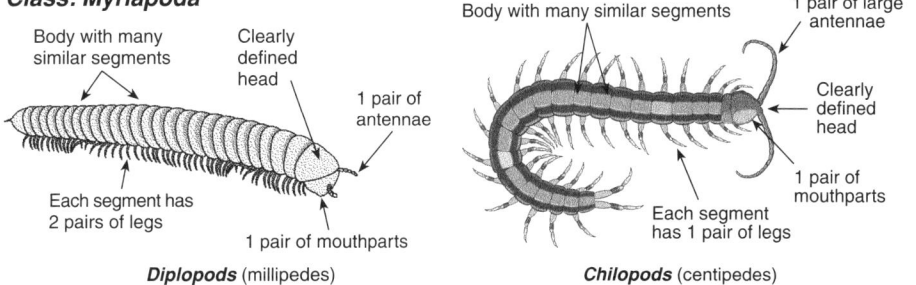

Body with many similar segments
Clearly defined head
1 pair of antennae
Each segment has 2 pairs of legs
1 pair of mouthparts
Diplopods (millipedes)

Body with many similar segments
1 pair of large antennae
Clearly defined head
1 pair of mouthparts
Each segment has 1 pair of legs
Chilopods (centipedes)

Phylum: Echinodermata

- Rigid body wall, internal skeleton made of calcareous plates.
- Many possess spines.
- Ventral mouth, dorsal anus.
- External fertilization.
- Unsegmented, marine organisms.
- Tube feet for locomotion.
- Water vascular system.

Examples: Starfish, brittlestars, feather stars, sea urchins, sea lilies.
Species diversity: 6000 +

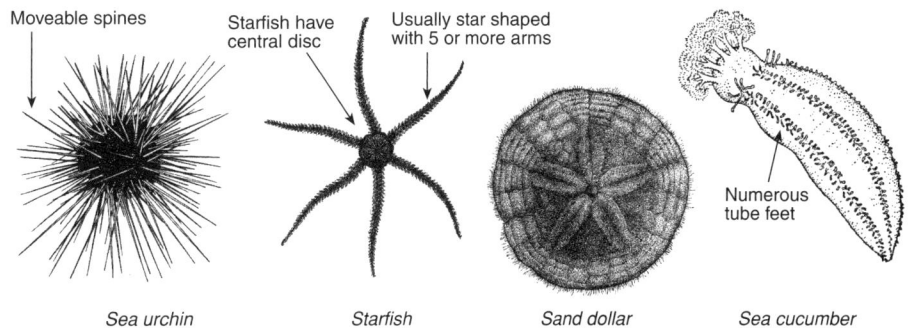

Moveable spines
Starfish have central disc
Usually star shaped with 5 or more arms
Numerous tube feet
Sea urchin
Starfish
Sand dollar
Sea cucumber

Kingdom: ANIMALIA (continued)

Phylum: Chordata

- Dorsal notochord (flexible, supporting rod) present at some stage in the life history.
- Post-anal tail present at some stage in their development.
- Dorsal, tubular nerve cord.
- Pharyngeal slits present.
- Circulation system closed in most.
- Heart positioned on ventral side.

Species diversity: 48 000 +

- A very diverse group with several sub-phyla:
  - Urochordata (sea squirts, salps)
  - Cephalochordata (lancelet)
  - Craniata (vertebrates)

Sub-Phylum Craniata (vertebrates)
- Internal skeleton of cartilage or bone.
- Well developed nervous system.
- Vertebral column replaces notochord.
- Two pairs of appendages (fins or limbs) attached to girdles.

Further subdivided into:

Class: Chondrichthyes
(cartilaginous fish)
- Skeleton of cartilage (not bone).
- No swim bladder.
- All aquatic (mostly marine).
- Include: Sharks, rays, and skates.

Species diversity: 850 +

Class: Osteichthyes (bony fish)
- Swim bladder present.
- All aquatic (marine and fresh water).

Species diversity: 21 000 +

Class: Amphibia (amphibians)
- Lungs in adult, juveniles may have gills (retained in some adults).
- Gas exchange also through skin.
- Aquatic and terrestrial (limited to damp environments).
- Include: Frogs, toads, salamanders, and newts.

Species diversity: 3900 +

Class Reptilia (reptiles)
- Ectotherms with no larval stages.
- Teeth are all the same type.
- Eggs with soft leathery shell.
- Mostly terrestrial.
- Include: Snakes, lizards, crocodiles, turtles, and tortoises.

Species diversity: 7000 +

Class: Aves (birds)
- Terrestrial endotherms.
- Eggs with hard, calcareous shell.
- Strong, light skeleton.
- High metabolic rate.
- Gas exchange assisted by air sacs.

Species diversity: 8600 +

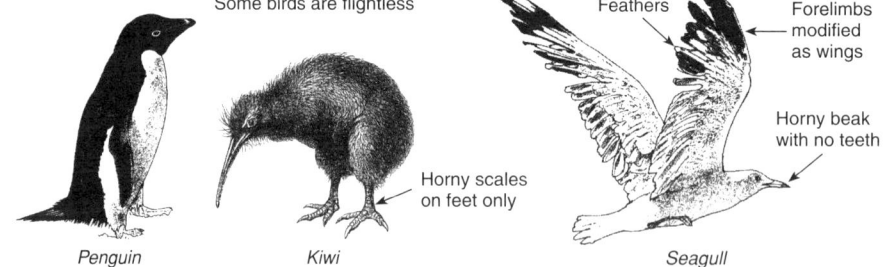

Class: Mammalia (mammals)
- Endotherms with hair or fur.
- Mammary glands produce milk.
- Glandular skin with hair or fur.
- External ear present.
- Teeth are of different types.
- Diaphragm between thorax/abdomen.

Species diversity: 4500 +
Subdivided into 3 groups:
Monotremes, marsupials, placentals.

Class: Chondrichthyes (cartilaginous fish)

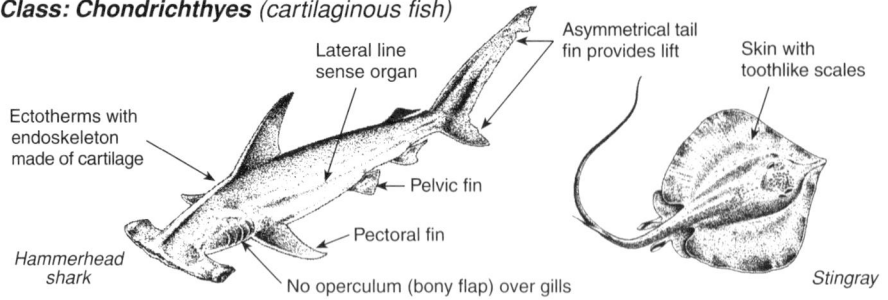

Ectotherms with endoskeleton made of cartilage
Lateral line sense organ
Asymmetrical tail fin provides lift
Skin with toothlike scales
Pelvic fin
Pectoral fin
No operculum (bony flap) over gills
Hammerhead shark
Stingray

Class: Osteichthyes (bony fish)

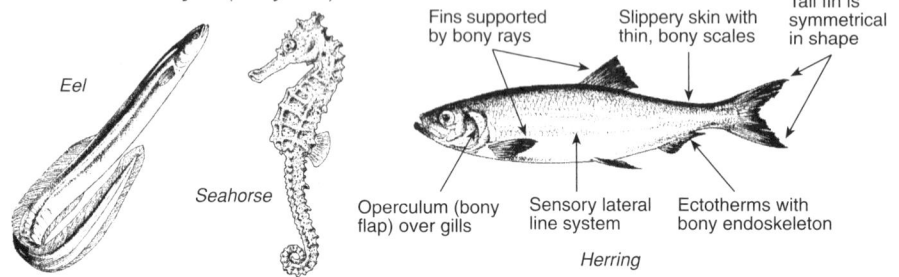

Eel
Seahorse
Fins supported by bony rays
Slippery skin with thin, bony scales
Tail fin is symmetrical in shape
Operculum (bony flap) over gills
Sensory lateral line system
Ectotherms with bony endoskeleton
Herring

Class: Amphibia

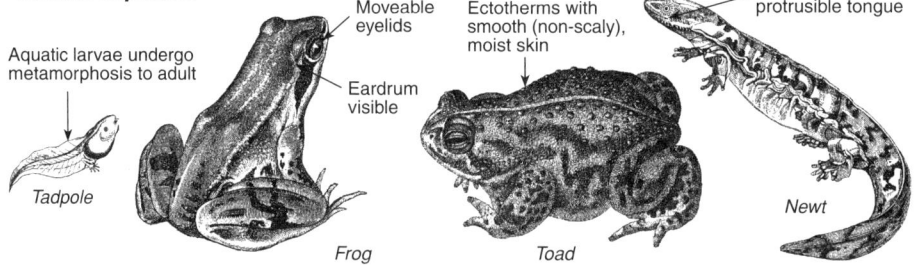

Aquatic larvae undergo metamorphosis to adult
Moveable eyelids
Ectotherms with smooth (non-scaly), moist skin
Well developed protrusible tongue
Eardrum visible
Tadpole
Frog
Toad
Newt

Class: Reptilia

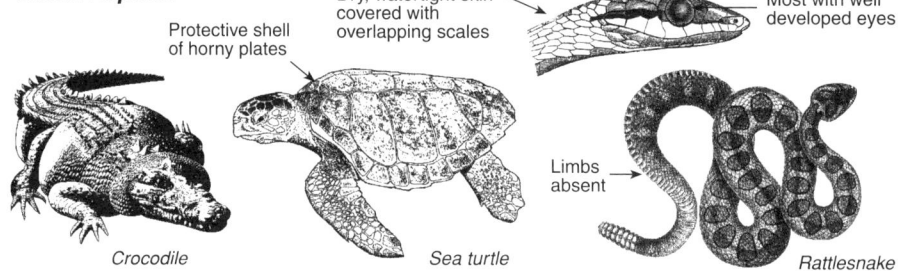

Protective shell of horny plates
Dry, watertight skin covered with overlapping scales
Most with well developed eyes
Limbs absent
Crocodile
Sea turtle
Rattlesnake

Class: Aves

Some birds are flightless
Feathers
Forelimbs modified as wings
Horny scales on feet only
Horny beak with no teeth
Penguin
Kiwi
Seagull

Class: Mammalia

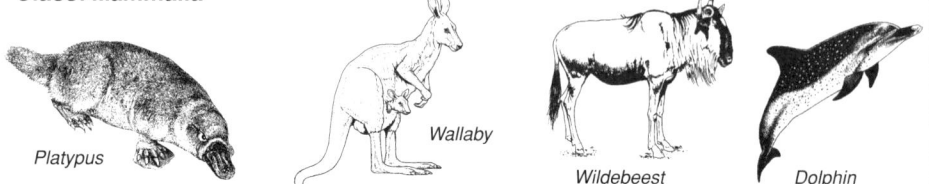

Platypus
Wallaby
Wildebeest
Dolphin

Monotremes
Egg laying mammals

Marsupials
Give birth to live, very immature young which then develop in a pouch

Placentals
Have a placenta and give birth to live, well developed young

Features of the Five Kingdoms

RA1

The classification of living things into taxonomic groups is based on how biologists believe they are related in an evolutionary sense. Organisms in a taxonomic group share some common features that set the group apart from others.

By identifying these features, it is possible to gain an understanding of the evolutionary development of the group. The focus of this activity is to summarize the characteristic features of each of the five kingdoms.

1. Distinguishing features of Kingdom **Prokaryotae**:

_____

_____

_____

_____

_____

2. Distinguishing features of Kingdom **Protista**:

_____

_____

_____

_____

3. Distinguishing features of Kingdom **Fungi**:

_____

_____

_____

_____

4. Distinguishing features of Kingdom **Plantae**:

_____

_____

_____

_____

_____

5. Distinguishing features of Kingdom **Animalia**:

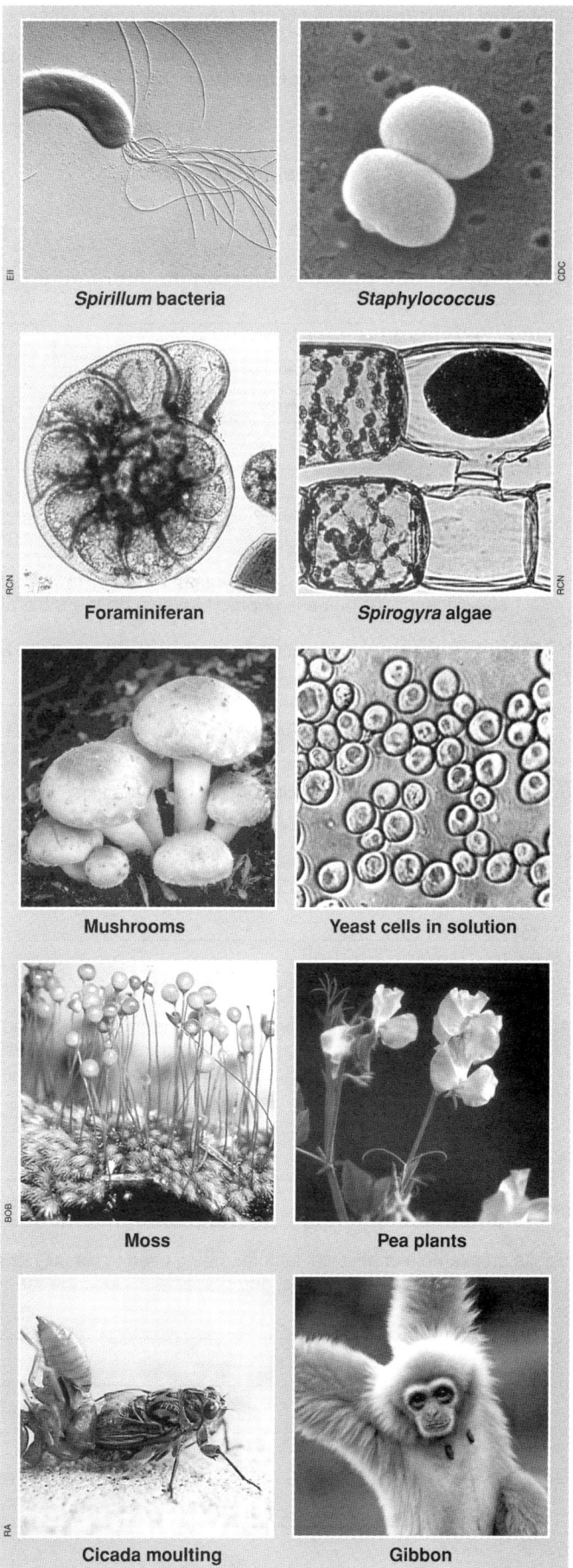

_____

_____

_____

_____

_____

Spirillum bacteria

Staphylococcus

Foraminiferan

Spirogyra algae

Mushrooms

Yeast cells in solution

Moss

Pea plants

Cicada moulting

Gibbon

RA② Classification System

The classification of organisms is designed to reflect how they are related to each other. The fundamental unit of classification of living things is the **species**. Its members are so alike genetically that they can interbreed. This genetic similarity also means that they are almost identical in their physical and other characteristics. Species are classified further into larger, more comprehensive categories (higher taxa). It must be emphasized that all such higher classifications are human inventions to suit a particular purpose.

1. The table below shows part of the classification for humans using the seven major levels of classification. For this question, use the example of the classification of the Ethiopian hedgehog, on the facing page, as a guide.

   (a) Complete the list of the classification levels on the left hand side of the table below:

	Classification Level	Human Classification
1.	_____	_____
2.	_____	_____
3.	_____	_____
4.	_____	_____
5.	Family	Hominidae
6.	_____	_____
7.	_____	_____

   (b) The name of the Family that humans belong to has already been entered into the space provided. Complete the classification for humans (*Homo sapiens*) on the table above.

2. Describe the two-part scientific naming system (called the **binomial system**) which is used to name organisms:

   _____

   _____

3. Give **two** reasons why the classification of organisms is important:

   (a) _____

   _____

   (b) _____

   _____

4. Traditionally, the classification of organisms has been based largely on similarities in physical appearance. More recently, new methods involving biochemical comparisons have been used to provide new insights into how species are related. Describe an example of a biochemical method for comparing how species are related:

   _____

   _____

   _____

5. As an example of physical features being used to classify organisms, mammals have been divided into three major groups: the monotremes, marsupials, and placentals. Describe the main physical feature that distinguishes each of these groups:

   (a) Monotreme: _____

   _____

   (b) Marsupial: _____

   _____

   (c) Placental: _____

   _____

Classification of the Ethiopian Hedgehog

Below is the classification for the **Ethiopian hedgehog**. Only one of each group is subdivided in this chart showing the levels that can be used in classifying an organism. Not all possible subdivisions have been shown here. For example, it is possible to indicate such categories as **super-class** and **sub-family**. The only natural category is the **species**, often separated into geographical **races**, or **sub-species**, which generally differ in appearance.

Kingdom:
Animalia
Animals – one of 5 kingdoms

Phylum:
Chordata
Animals with a notochord (supporting rod of cells along the upper surface)
Tunicates, salps, lancelets, and vertebrates

23 other phyla

Sub-phylum:
Vertebrata
Animals with backbones
fish, amphibians, reptiles, birds, mammals

Class:
Mammalia
Animals that suckle their young on milk from mammary glands
placentals, marsupials, monotremes

Sub-class:
Eutheria or Placentals
Mammals whose young develop for some time in the female's reproductive tract gaining nourishment from a placenta
placental mammals

Order:
Insectivora
Insect eating mammals
An order of over 300 species of primitive, small mammals that feed mainly on insects and other small invertebrates.

17 other orders

Sub-order:
Erinaceomorpha
The hedgehog-type insectivores. One of the three suborders of insectivores. The other suborders include the tenrec-like insectivores (*tenrecs and golden moles*) and the shrew-like insectivores (*shrews, moles, desmans, and solenodons*).

Family:
Erinaceidae
The only family within this suborder. Comprises two subfamilies: the true or spiny hedgehogs and the moonrats (gymnures). Representatives in the family include the common European hedgehog, desert hedgehog, and the moonrats.

Genus:
Paraechinus
One of eight genera in this family. The genus *Paraechinus* includes three species which are distinguishable by a wide and prominent naked area on the scalp.

7 other genera

Species:
aethiopicus
The Ethiopian hedgehog inhabits arid coastal areas. Their diet consists mainly of insects, but includes small vertebrates and the eggs of ground nesting birds.

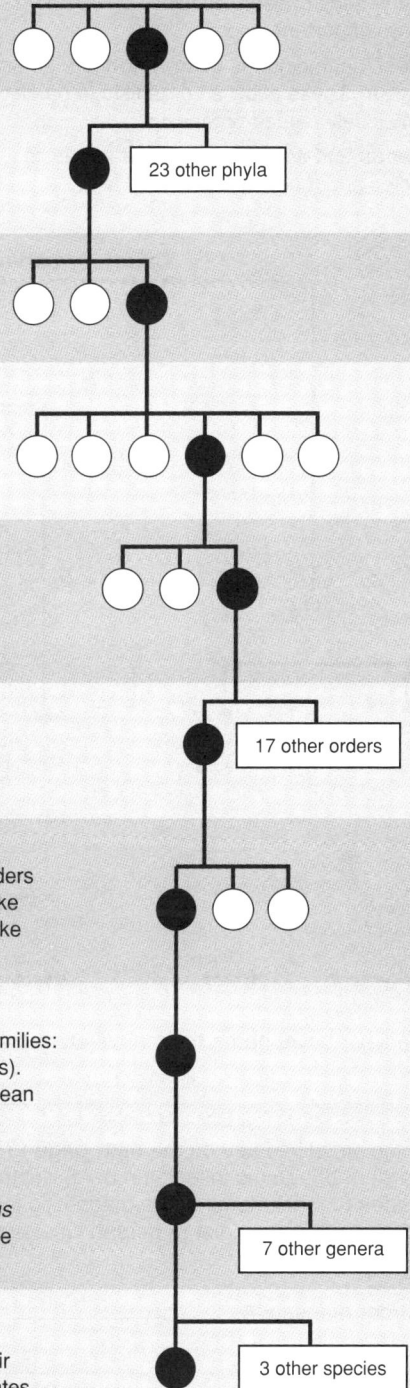

3 other species

The order *Insectivora* was first introduced to group together shrews, moles, and hedgehogs. It was later extended to include tenrecs, golden moles, desmans, tree shrews, and elephant shrews and the taxonomy of the group became very confused. Recent reclassification of the elephant shrews and tree shrews into their own separate orders has made the Insectivora a more cohesive group taxonomically.

Ethiopian hedgehog
Paraechinus aethiopicus

Classification Keys

The classification of organisms into groupings with similar form is important to biology. Classification systems provide biologists with a way in which to identify different but similar species. This avoids confusion over which particular species is being referred to. Classification systems also indicate how closely related, in an evolutionary sense, each species is to others. Classification requires two important steps:

1. A clear, unambiguous **description** and an accurate **diagram**. These allow an organism to be distinguished from closely related organisms.

2. A **genus** and **species** name that are assigned to a species and together are unique to it.

Using classification keys: Keys are used to identify an unknown organism and assign it to a genus and species. Providing that the unknown organism has been previously classified by someone else, it is possible to use these keys to identify it. Typically, keys use a series of linked questions highlighting contrasting characters. The key is followed until an identification is made. If the organism cannot be identified with the established key, it may be a newly discovered species and the key may need to be altered. Two examples of classification keys are provided on these two facing pages. The key for caddisfly larvae identification (below) is a diagrammatic one, while the key on the facing page for identification of aquatic insect orders is a text-based example.

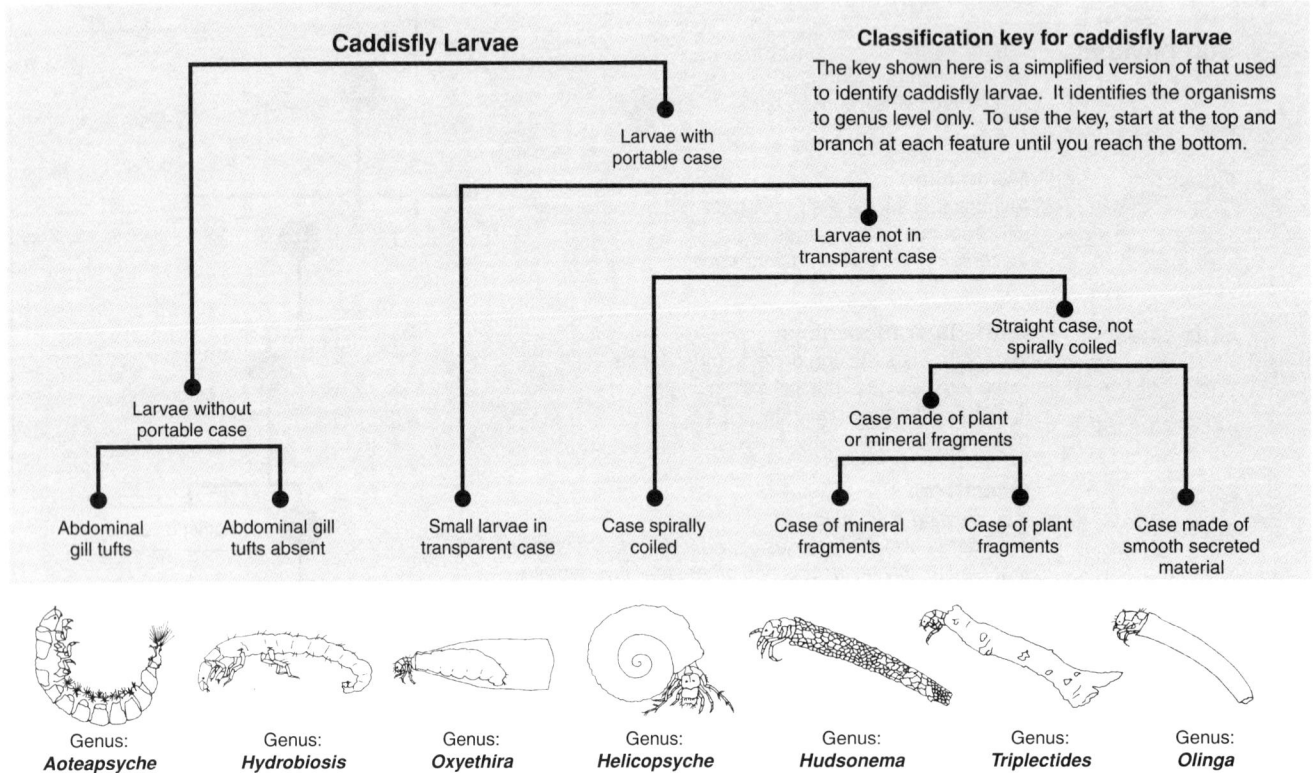

Caddisfly Larvae

Classification key for caddisfly larvae
The key shown here is a simplified version of that used to identify caddisfly larvae. It identifies the organisms to genus level only. To use the key, start at the top and branch at each feature until you reach the bottom.

Larvae with portable case

Larvae not in transparent case

Straight case, not spirally coiled

Larvae without portable case

Case made of plant or mineral fragments

| Abdominal gill tufts | Abdominal gill tufts absent | Small larvae in transparent case | Case spirally coiled | Case of mineral fragments | Case of plant fragments | Case made of smooth secreted material |

| Genus: *Aoteapsyche* | Genus: *Hydrobiosis* | Genus: *Oxyethira* | Genus: *Helicopsyche* | Genus: *Hudsonema* | Genus: *Triplectides* | Genus: *Olinga* |

1. In the key above, name the main feature that has been used to distinguish the different genera of caddis larvae:

_____

2. Use the simplified key on the **next page** to identify each of the orders of aquatic insects (in bold) illustrated below. The key does not include all of the diagnostic features normally used by an entomologist (a person who studies insects):

(a) Order of insect A: _____

   Common name: _____

(b) Order of insect B: _____

   Common name: _____

(c) Order of insect C: _____

   Common name: _____

(d) Order of insect D: _____

   Common name: _____

(e) Order of insect E: _____

   Common name: _____

(f) Order of insect F: _____

   Common name: _____

(g) Order of insect G: _____

   Common name: _____

(h) Order of insect H: _____

   Common name: _____

(i) Order of insect I: _____

   Common name: _____

Key to Orders of Aquatic Insects

1	Insects with chewing mouthparts; forewings are hardened and meet along the midline of the body when at rest (they may cover the entire abdomen or be variably reduced in length)	**Coleoptera**	Beetles
	Mouthparts are of the piercing and/or sucking type and form a pointed cone	*Go to 2*	
2	Mouthparts form a short, pointed beak; legs may be fringed for swimming or long and well-spaced apart for suspension on water	**Hemiptera**	Bugs
	Mouthparts do not form a beak; legs (if present) not fringed or long, spaced apart	*Go to 3*	
3	Prominent upper lip (labium) extendable, forming a food capturing structure longer than the head	**Odonata**	Dragonflies and damselflies
	Without a prominent, extendable labium	*Go to 4*	
4	Abdomen terminating in 3 tail filaments which may be long and thin, or with fringes of hairs	**Ephemeroptera**	Mayflies
	Without 3 tail filaments	*Go to 5*	
5	Abdomen terminating in 2 tail filaments	**Plecoptera**	Stoneflies
	Without long tail filaments	*Go to 6*	
6	With 3 pairs of jointed legs on thorax	*Go to 7*	
	Without jointed, thoracic legs (although non-segmented prolegs or false legs may be present)	**Diptera**	True flies
7	Abdomen with pairs of non-segmented prolegs bearing rows of fine hooks	**Lepidoptera**	Moths and butterflies
	Without pairs of abdominal prolegs	*Go to 8*	
8	With 8 pairs of finger-like abdominal gills; abdomen with 2 pairs of posterior claws	**Megaloptera**	Dobsonflies (toebiter)
	Either, without paired, abdominal gills, or, if such gills are present, without posterior claws	*Go to 9*	
9	Abdomen with a pair of short or long posterior prolegs bearing claws with subsidiary hooks; sometimes a portable case	**Trichoptera**	Caddisflies

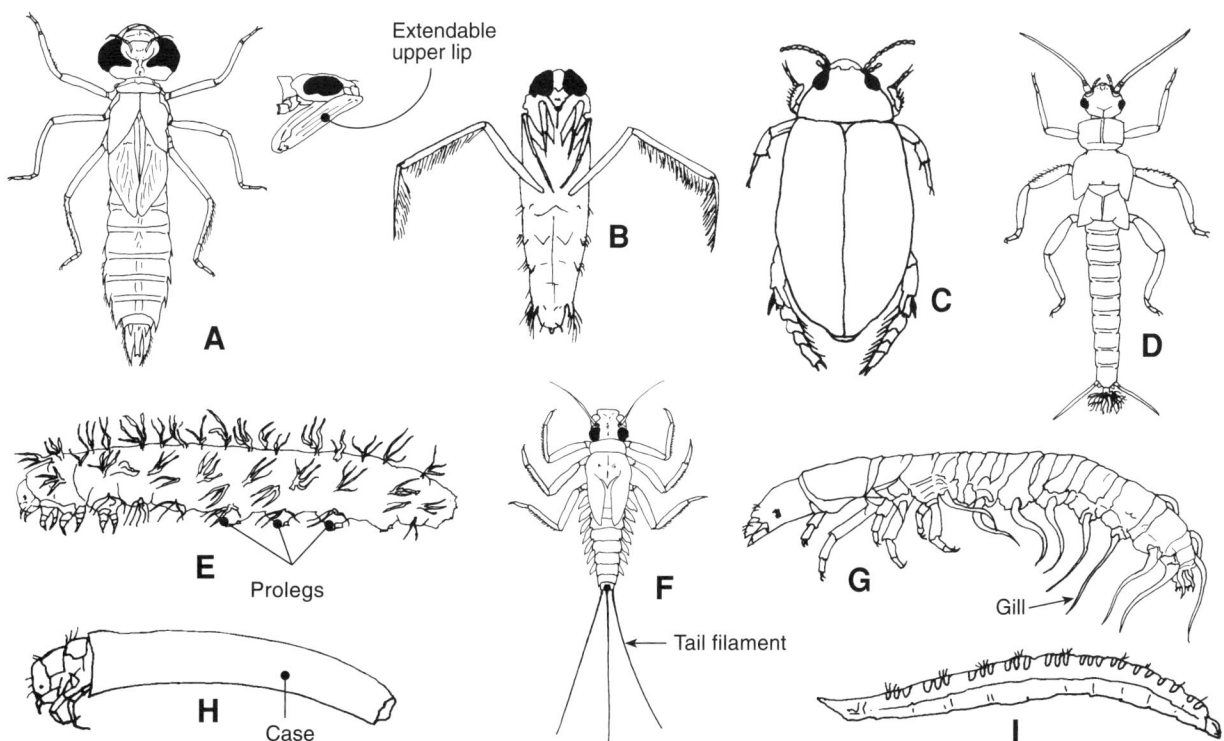

Extendable upper lip

A

B

C

D

E — Prolegs

F — Tail filament

G — Gill

H — Case

I

Human Impact and Conservation

Learning Objectives

☐ 1. Compile your own glossary from the **KEY WORDS** displayed in **bold type** in the learning objectives below.

Human impact & resource use *(pages 338-339)*

☐ 2. *Background:* Appreciate that the impact of humans on the global environment is the result of resource use, rapid population growth, large population size, and disproportionate distribution of resources.

Case studies in human impact *(see page 267)*

☐ 3. Outline two local or global examples of human impact causing damage to an ecosystem (see # 8-31). One example should be increased greenhouse effect. In your examples, you should:
  • Discuss the causes and biological effects of the human impact.
  • Examine measures for preventing or reducing the effects of the impact (with reference to the functioning of the ecosystem).

☐ 4. With reference to appropriate examples, explain the use of **biotic indices** and **indicator species** in monitoring environmental change.

Atmospheric pollution *(pages 344-345)*

☐ 5. Explain the term **atmospheric pollution**. Describe different causes of air pollutants and, for each, identify its effect on the environment. Recognize **acid rain**, the **greenhouse effect**, and stratospheric **ozone depletion** as consequences of atmospheric pollution.

Global warming *(pages 346-347)*

☐ 6. Explain what is meant by the terms **greenhouse effect** and **global warming**. Outline the main causes of the increase in greenhouse gases. Describe what countries are doing to reduce outputs of these gases.

☐ 7. Discuss measures that could be taken to reduce global warming or its impact. Consider both short and long term measures and comment on the feasibility of these.

Acid rain *(pages 344, 350)*

☐ 8. Describe the origin, causes (formation), and biological consequences of **acid rain**. Explain the global distribution of the acid rain problem in terms of the original source of the pollution.

☐ 9. Discuss measures for the reduction and mitigation of acid rain, and comment on the feasibility of these.

☐ 10. Explain how air quality is monitored and appreciate that air quality standards regulate air emissions. Describe, with an example, the role of **indicator organisms** in the assessment of air quality.

Stratospheric ozone depletion *(pages 348-349)*

☐ 11. Describe the role of the atmospheric (strictly stratospheric) ozone in absorbing ultraviolet (UV) radiation. Outline the effects of UV radiation on living tissues and biological productivity.

☐ 12. Explain what is meant by the term **stratospheric ozone depletion**. Identify some of the agents that are implicated in its destruction, including reference to the chemical effect of **chlorine** on the ozone layer. Describe the probable long term environmental effects of stratospheric depletion.

☐ 13. Discuss measures to reduce the rate of ozone depletion. Emphasize methods for reducing the manufacture and release of ozone-depleting chemicals.

☐ 14. Distinguish between stratospheric ozone and localized ozone pollution in the lower atmosphere.

Water pollution *(pages 340-343)*

☐ 15. Explain what is meant by the term **water pollution**. Briefly describe different causes of water pollution and describe their effects. Distinguish between point and diffuse sources for water pollutants.

☐ 16. Describe the effects of **organic effluent** (e.g. sewage or milk) and **fertilizer run-off** (nitrates and phosphates) on aquatic ecosystems. Include reference to: *water quality, biochemical oxygen demand, effects on biodiversity, eutrophication and algal blooms, spread of pathogens, and (toxic) nitrate load in the groundwater.*

☐ 17. Recognize the link between soil degradation, fertilizer and pesticide misuse, and subsequent pollution of water sources and **eutrophication**.

☐ 18. Discuss measures for the prevention, reduction, or mitigation of water pollution, e.g. sewage treatment. If required, describe an example of recovery of a formerly polluted water body following removal of the pollutant.

☐ 19. Appreciate that country-specific legislation provides water quality standards for different water uses. Describe the role of **indicator organisms** in the assessment of water quality. Identify some common indicator organisms for freshwater systems and explain what their presence indicates.

Rainforests and biodiversity *(page 357)*

☐ 20. Define the term **biodiversity**. Identify some of the regions of naturally-occurring high biodiversity and describe the importance of these regions to global ecology. Using **rainforests** as an example, discuss the ethical, ecological, economic, and aesthetic reasons for the conservation of biodiversity.

☐ 21. Discuss the causes and effects of **deforestation**, emphasizing the impact on the **biodiversity** and stability of forest ecosystems, and on carbon and nitrogen cycling. Identify regions (globally or locally) where deforestation is a major problem.

☐ 22. Identify forests as a potentially sustainable resource and appreciate differences in the sustainability of different forest types. Discuss methods for the sustainable management of the forestry resource.

Managing resources (pages 343, 351-353, 358-360)

☐ 23. Explain the importance of **conserving resources** and appreciate the impact of humans on the Earth's resources. Using one or more examples, describe how resources can be managed for long term sustainability with minimal impact on natural ecosystems:

(a) **Energy resources**: Distinguish between **renewable** and **non-renewable** energy resources. With reference to coal and oil, describe how **fossil fuels** are used and comment on our dependence on these fuels given their long term sustainability. Describe the use of **renewable** energy resources with reference to: *energy from fast growing biomass, fuel alcohol used to produce gasohol, biogas from waste*. For each example, describe its method of production, and advantages and drawbacks with its use as a fuel.

(b) **Fisheries**: Discuss fishing as an example of harvesting from a natural ecosystem. Describing an appropriate example, identify key aspects of fisheries management, including the significance of quotas, closed seasons, and exclusion zones. Explain the terms: maximum sustainable yield and by-catch, and explain their significance to fisheries management and to the ecology of marine ecosystems.

(c) **Waste water management**: Describe the treatment of waste water (sewage) and explain the role of physical (mechanical), chemical, and biological processes in this. Comment on the importance of the water resource and the need for its effective use and reuse.

(d) **Solid waste management**: Discuss the view of solid waste as a potential resource (in part) and describe methods for waste management, including reducing waste and recycling organic waste and valuable commodities such as paper and glass.

Endangered species (pages 354-356)

☐ 24. Explain what is meant by an **endangered species** and identify factors that might cause species to become endangered. Using an example of a locally or globally endangered species (e.g. African elephant), describe its conservation status, management, and potential for recovery. You could include reference to one or more of the management strategies outlined in #25.

☐ 25. Using appropriate examples, discuss the advantages and application of the following conservation measures:
- *In-situ* conservation methods such as protection of terrestrial or aquatic nature reserves.
- Management programs for nature reserves, including control of alien species, **habitat restoration**, control of human exploitation, and **species recovery plans**.
- *Ex-situ* conservation methods such as **captive breeding** (and release) of animals, **botanic gardens**, and **seed** and sperm (gene) **banks**.
- International agencies (CITES, WWF) and, where applicable, their legislation.

Textbooks

See the 'Textbook Reference Grid' on pages 8-9 for textbook page references relating to material in this topic.

Supplementary Texts

See pages 4-6 for additional details of these texts:

■ Adds, J. *et al.*, 2000. **Exchange & Transport, Energy & Ecosystems** (NelsonThornes), pp. 143-76.

■ Adds, J., *et al.*, 2001. **Genetics, Evolution and Biodiversity**, (NelsonThornes), pp. 51-58, 61-71.

■ Allen *et al.*, 2001. **Applied Ecology** (Collins), pp. 49-99 as required.

■ Chenn, P., 1999. **Ecology** (JM), pp. 113-178.

Periodicals

See page 6 for details of publishers of periodicals:

STUDENT'S REFERENCE

Biodiversity & endangered species

■ **Biodiversity and Ecosystems** Biol. Sci. Rev., 11(4) March 1999 pp. 18-21. *The importance of biodiversity to ecosystem stability and sustainability.*

■ **Hot Spots** New Scientist, 4 April 1998, pp. 32-36. *An examination of the reasons for the very high biodiversity observed in the tropics.*

■ **Biodiversity: Taking Stock of Life** National Geographic, 195(2) February 1999 (entire issue). *Special issue exploring the Earth's biodiversity and what we can do to preserve it.*

Pollution and global warming

■ **Unlocking the Climate Puzzle** National Geographic, 193(5) May 1998, pp. 38-71. *Earth's climate, including global warming & desertification.*

■ **The Greenhouse Effect** New Scientist, 13 July 1996 (Inside Science). *An excellent summary of*

the causes and effects of greenhouse gases.

■ **The Forest Decline Mystery: Is Acid Rain the Killer?** Biol. Sci. Rev., 13(2) Nov. 2000, pp. 10-14. *Acid rain in Europe: how it is formed and its impact.*

■ **Nitrates in Soil and Water** New Scientist, 15 Sept. 1990, (Inside Science). *Nitrogen fertilizers as a cause of disease and environmental pollution.*

Resource management issues

■ **In Search of Solutions** National Geographic, Feb. 1999, pp. 72-87. *The impact of deforestation and measures possible to restore the damage.*

■ **Blue Revolutionaries** New Scientist, 7 Dec. 1996, pp. 32-35. *Depletion of fish stocks worldwide and the benefits and drawbacks of aquaculture.*

■ **Watery Wastelands** New Scientist, 16 May 1998, pp. 40-44. *Marine ecology and conservation, and the effects of fishing techniques and take.*

■ **Ethanol: Brazil's Green Fuel** Biol. Sci. Rev., 13(1) Sept. 2000, pp. 27-29. *Alternative fuels: the production of gasohol from waste carbohydrates.*

TEACHER'S REFERENCE

■ **All Wrapped Up in Kudzu and Other Ecological Disasters** The American Biology Teacher, 61(1), Jan., 1999, pp.42-46. *The impact of alien species: 7 scenarios for students to analyze.*

■ **The Case of the Missing Anurans** The Am. Biology Teacher, 63(9), Nov. 2001, pp. 670-676. *The threat to the world's frog populations; an article investigating threatened species decline.*

■ **Can Sustainable Management Save Tropical Rainforests?** Scientific American, April 1997, pp. 34-39. *The difficulties of sustainable management of rainforests and the implications for conservation.*

■ **Tropical Forests for Sale!** The American Biology Teacher, 60(9), Nov. 1998, pp. 677-680. *A simulation to increase awareness of the difficulties of tropical rainforest conservation.*

■ **The Impact of Habitat Fragmentation on Arthropod Biodiversity** The American Biology Teacher, 62(6), June 2000, pp. 414-420. *An account of experimental work to investigate the impact of human activity on arthropod populations.*

■ **Seven Guideposts for Tropical Rain Forest Education** The American Biology Teacher, 61(1), January, 1999, pp. 24-30. *Improving understanding of rainforest ecology and conservation.*

■ **A Standardized Ecotoxicological Test Using Redworms** The American Biology Teacher, 63(9) Nov. 2001, pp. 662-668. *An account of how to use red worms as indicators of soil contamination.*

■ **Atmospheric Dust and Acid Rain** Scientific American, Dec. 1996, pp. 56-60. *A look at why acid rain is still a problem, despite tighter controls.*

■ **Global Population and the Nitrogen Cycle** Scientific American, July 1997, pp. 58-63. *Nitrogen based fertilizers are widely used but have a detrimental effect on aquatic environments.*

■ **The World's Imperiled Fish** Sci. American, Nov. 1995, pp. 30-37. *The collapse of the world's fisheries and its wide-reaching implications.*

■ **Kicking the Habit** New Scientist, 25 Nov. 2000, pp. 34-42. *The pressing need for alternative fuels.*

Internet

See pages 10-11 for details of how to access **Bio Links** from our web site: **www.thebiozone.com**. From Bio Links, access sites under the topics:

CONSERVATION: see the sites listed under the sub-topics: *Endangered Species, Habitat Loss*, and *Conservation Issues*

HUMAN IMPACT: see the general sites and those sites listed under: *Pollution, Global Warming*, and *Ozone Depletion*

RESOURCE MANAGEMENT & AGRICULTURE: see sites under: *Resource Management - General, Land Management, Fisheries and Aquaculture, Forestry*, and *Agriculture*.

Software and video resources are now provided in the Teacher Resource Handbook

Human Impact on Resources

During the past 100 years, human impact on the natural world has increased dramatically as the scope and intensity of human activities have increased. Although there has been recent progress in solving air and water pollution problems in some countries, many negative trends continue unabated. Unresolved problems include the loss of tropical forests, the buildup of greenhouse gases, and the loss of biodiversity. The world population, now at 6 billion, is growing at the rate of about 80 million per year. This growth is slower than predicted just a few years ago but the world population is still expected to increase substantially before stabilizing. Projections put world population at between 8 and 12 billion in 2050, with nearly all of this growth expected in the developing world. The figures below show the trends and projections for population growth from 1950-2050.

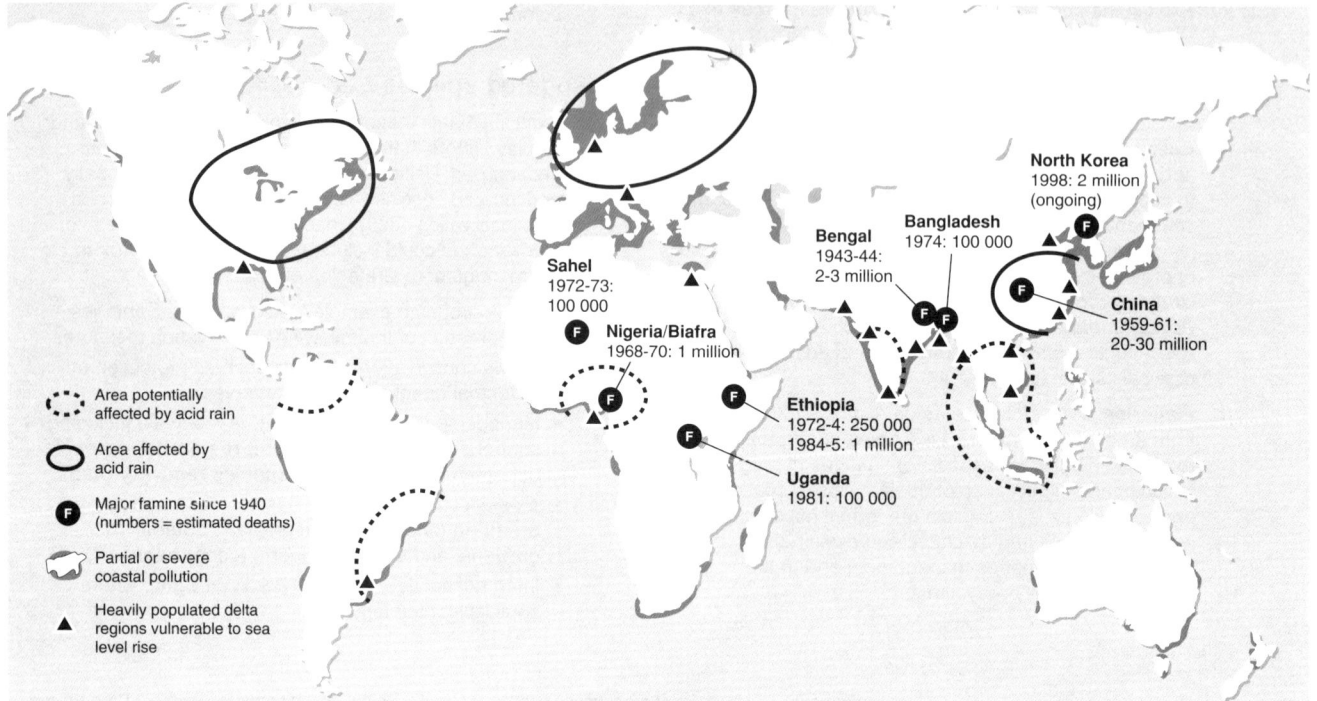

North Korea
1998: 2 million
(ongoing)

Bengal
1943-44:
2-3 million

Bangladesh
1974: 100 000

China
1959-61:
20-30 million

Sahel
1972-73:
100 000

Nigeria/Biafra
1968-70: 1 million

Ethiopia
1972-4: 250 000
1984-5: 1 million

Uganda
1981: 100 000

Area potentially affected by acid rain

Area affected by acid rain

Major famine since 1940 (numbers = estimated deaths)

Partial or severe coastal pollution

Heavily populated delta regions vulnerable to sea level rise

Figure 1: Progress towards population stabilization

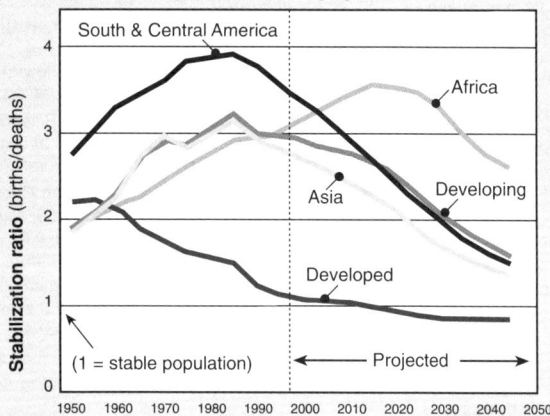

South & Central America

Africa

Asia

Developing

Developed

Stabilization ratio (births/deaths)

(1 = stable population)

← Projected →

1950 1960 1970 1980 1990 2000 2010 2020 2030 2040 2050

Figure 2: Trends in fertility rates

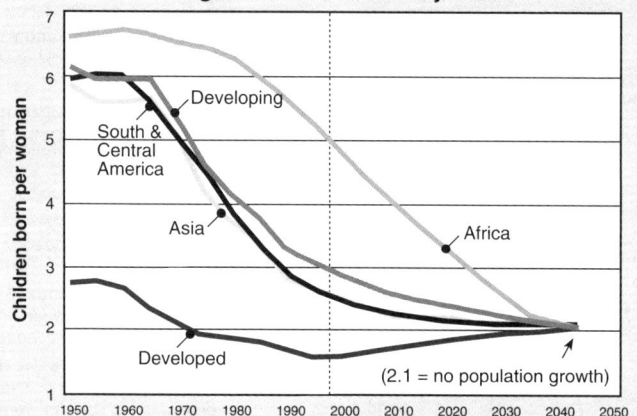

Developing

South & Central America

Asia

Africa

Developed

Children born per woman

(2.1 = no population growth)

1950 1960 1970 1980 1990 2000 2010 2020 2030 2040 2050

Figure 3: Global population growth

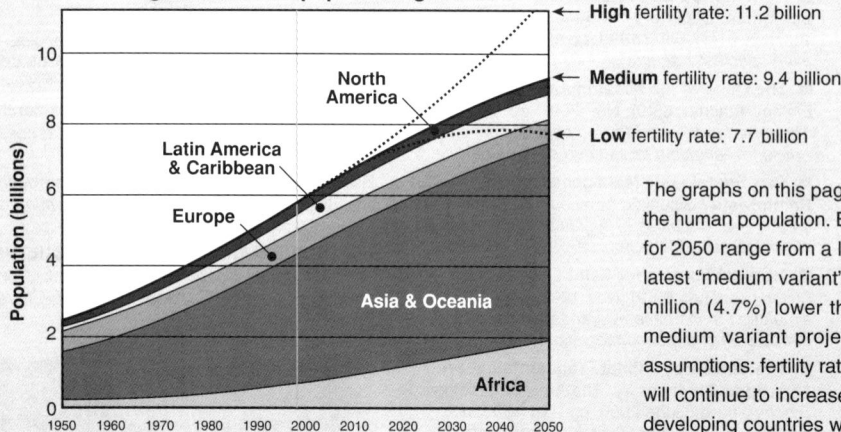

← High fertility rate: 11.2 billion

← Medium fertility rate: 9.4 billion

← Low fertility rate: 7.7 billion

North America

Latin America & Caribbean

Europe

Asia & Oceania

Africa

Population (billions)

1950 1960 1970 1980 1990 2000 2010 2020 2030 2040 2050

Source for graphs: United Nations Population Division, World Population Prospects 1950-2050 (The 1996 Revision), U.N., New York, 1996.

The graphs on this page attempt to show the likely future growth of the human population. Estimates are highly uncertain and projections for 2050 range from a low of 7.7 billion to a high of 11.2 billion. The latest "medium variant" U.N. projection of 9.37 billion is nearly 500 million (4.7%) lower than the 9.83 billion projected in 1994. The medium variant projection depends on a number of important assumptions: fertility rates will continue to decline and life expectancy will continue to increase (as in the industrialized countries), and that developing countries will broadly follow these demographic trends.

Air pollution contributes to global warming, ozone depletion and acid rain, and is set to increase markedly in some third world countries in the next 30 years.

Global water consumption is rising rapidly. The availability of water is likely to become one of the most pressing resource issues of the 21st Century.

Combustion engine emissions, plaguing the West with pollution, are increasing rapidly in Asia as their economies develop and become more affluent.

Global energy use has increased by 70% since 1970 and will increase 2% annually over the next 15 years. Using fossil fuels will raise greenhouse gases by 50%.

Global climate change due to the greenhouse effect will cause a rise in sea level and threaten coastal populations such as those in Bangladesh (above).

In industrialized societies, a person consumes many tonnes of raw materials each year, which must be extracted, processed and disposed of as waste.

Aquatic environments such as coral reefs and freshwater habitats in lakes, rivers and wetlands are at risk (58% of the worlds reefs and 34% of all fish species).

Threats to biodiversity from all sources are quickly reaching a critical level. Current extinction rates are 100 to 1000 times higher than prehuman levels.

Consumption of natural resources by modern industrial economies remains very high, in the range of 45 to 85 tonnes per person annually.

Forest fires and logging continue to shrink world forests. Deforestation in the Amazon doubled from 1994 to 1995 before declining in 1996.

Overfishing of fish stocks to levels where they may not recover for many decades has occurred in many fishing grounds (e.g. cod fishing in the North Atlantic).

Although food production is generally adequate to meet human needs there are problems with distribution. Some 800 million people remain undernourished.

1. The future growth of world population is highly uncertain. State the estimated population levels for the year 2050, based on low, medium and high fertility rates:

(a) Low: _____ (b) Medium: _____ (c) High: _____

2. Fertility rates of populations for all geographic regions are predicted to decline in the next 50 years.
(a) State which continent is predicted to have the highest fertility rate at the beginning of next century: _____

(b) Suggest a reason why the population of this region is slower to achieve a low fertility rate than other regions:

3. List three major unresolved problems associated with human impact on the planet: _____

4. Name the three regions most affected by acid rain: _____

5. State the location, date and number of deaths for the largest famine since 1950: _____

6. Identify the one of the most pressing resource issues for the 21st Century: _____

7. State the range of consumption per person annually, of natural resources by modern industrial economies: _____

8. Biodiversity is threatened worldwide. State how many times higher the extinction rates are over prehuman levels:

9. Make a general assessment about how human population levels have an impact on the natural world:

 RA②

Water Pollution

Pollution of water can occur as a result of contamination from sources that range from urban and industrial to agricultural. Pollutants may first enter the groundwater where they are difficult to detect and manage. Some enter surface waterways directly through runoff from the land, but most are deliberately discharged at single or 'point' sources. Some forms of pollution simply alter the physical state of the body of water, such as its temperature, acidity (pH), or its turbidity (how dirty it looks). Other forms of pollution involve the addition of potentially harmful substances. Even substances that are beneficial at a low concentration may cause problems when their concentration increases. One such form of pollution involves excessive nutrient loading of waterways by organic effluent. This causes accelerated **eutrophication** (enrichment) or water bodies and results in excessive weed and algal growth. It also increases the

uptake of dissolved oxygen by microorganisms that are busy decomposing organic matter in the effluent. This reduces the amount of dissolved oxygen available to other organisms living in the water and may cause the deaths of many aquatic organisms. An indicator of the polluting capacity of an effluent is known as the **biochemical** (or biological) **oxygen demand** or **B.O.D**. This is measured as the weight (mg) of oxygen used by one liter of sample effluent stored in darkness at 20°C for five days. The development of global and national initiatives to control water pollution is important because many forms of water pollution cross legislative boundaries. The US is the world's largest user of water but loses about 50% of the water it withdraws. Water conservation is required to enable more effective use of water, reduce the burden on wastewater systems, decrease pollution of surface and groundwater, and slow the depletion of aquifers.

Sources of Water Pollution

Sediment pollution: Soil erosion causes soil particles to be carried into waterways. The increased sediment load may cause choking of waterways, buildup behind dams, and the destruction of aquatic habitats.

Sewage: Water containing human wastes, soaps and detergents from toilets, washing machines, and showers are discharged into waterways such as rivers, lakes and the sea. Most communities apply some treatment.

Disease-causing agents: Disease-causing microbes from infected animals and humans can be discharged into waterways. This is particularly a problem during floods when human waste may mix with drinking water.

Inorganic plant nutrients: Fertilizer runoff from farmland adds large quantities of nitrogen and phosphorus to waterways. This nutrient enrichment accelerates the natural process of **eutrophication**, causing algal blooms and prolific aquatic weed growth.

Organic compounds: Synthetic, often toxic, compounds, may be released into waterways from oil spills (see above), the application of agrochemicals, and as the waste products of manufacturing processes (e.g. dioxin, PCBs, dieldrin, phenols, and DDT).

Thermal pollution: Many industrial processes, including thermal power generation (above), release heated water into river systems. The increase in water temperature reduces oxygen levels and may harm the survival of river species.

Radioactive substances: Mining and refinement of radioactive metals may discharge radioactive materials. Accidental spillages from atomic power stations, such as the Chornobyl nuclear accident of 1986, (pictured above) may contaminate waterways.

Kurchatov Inst.

Inorganic chemicals: Acid drainage from mines and acid rain can severely alter the pH of waterways. The runoff from open-caste mining operations can be loaded with poisonous heavy metals such as mercury, cadmium, and arsenic.

Detecting Pollution

Water pollution can be monitored in several ways. The nutrient loading can be assessed by measuring the **BOD**. **Electronic probes** and **chemical tests** can identify the absolute levels of various inorganic pollutants (e.g. nitrates, phosphates, and heavy metals). The presence of **indicator species** can give an indication of the pollution status for a waterway. This method relies on an understanding of the *tolerance levels* to pollution of different species that should be living in the waterway (e.g. worms, insect larvae, snails, and crustaceans).

1. Explain the term **accelerated eutrophication** and its primary cause: _____

   _____

2. Name **three** uses of water for each of the following areas of human activity:

   (a) Domestic use: _____

   _____

   (b) Industrial use: _____

   _____

   (c) Agricultural use: _____

   _____

3. (a) Explain what is meant by the term **biochemical oxygen demand** (B.O.D.) as it is related to water pollution:

   _____

   _____

   _____

   (b) Describe how a very high B.O.D. in a body of water such as a lake or river may be created by human activity:

   _____

   (c) Describe the likely effect of a very high B.O.D. on the invertebrates and fish living in a small lake:

   _____

   _____

   (d) Explain why, when measuring B.O.D., that the sample is kept in darkness: _____

   _____

4. Sewage effluent may be sprayed onto agricultural land to irrigate crops and plantations of trees:

   (a) Describe an advantage of utilizing sewage in this way: _____

   _____

   (b) Describe a major drawback of using sewage effluent in this way: _____

   _____

   (c) Suggest an alternative treatment or use of the effluent: _____

5. When studying aquatic ecosystems, the species composition of the community (its biodiversity) in different *regions* of a water body or *over time* is often recorded. In general terms, describe how a change in species composition of an aquatic community could be used to indicate water pollution:

   _____

   _____

   _____

   _____

   _____

   _____

   _____

   _____

Monitoring Water Quality

There is no single measure to objectively describe the quality of a stream, river, or lake. Rather it is defined in terms of various *chemical*, *physical*, and *biological* characteristics. Together, these factors define the 'health' of the aquatic ecosystem and its suitability for various desirable uses. It is normally not feasible to monitor for all contaminants potentially in water. For example, analysis for pesticides, dioxins, and other trace 'organics' can be a costly, ongoing expense. Water quality is determined by making measurements on site or by taking samples back to a laboratory for physical, chemical, or microbiological analysis. The measurements listed below are routinely made by agencies involved in water quality monitoring.

Some aspects of water quality, such as black disk clarity measurements (above), must be made in the field.

The collection of water samples allows many quality measurements to be carried out in the laboratory.

Telemetry stations transmit continuous measurements of the water level of a lake or river to a central control office.

Temperature and dissolved oxygen measurements must be carried out directly in the flowing water.

Water quality variable	Reason for monitoring	Where monitored	Guideline & standards	
Dissolved oxygen	• Requirement for most aquatic life • Indicator of organic pollution • Indicator of photosynthesis (plant growth)	Field	More than 80% saturation More than 5 gm^{-3}	*(F, FS, SG)* *(WS)*
Temperature	• Organisms have specific temperature requirements • Indicator of mixing processes • Computer modelling examining the movement (uptake and release) of nutrients through the ecosystem	Field	Less than 25°C Less than 3°C change along a stretch of river	*(F)* *(AE, F, FS, SG)*
Conductivity	• Indicator of total salts dissolved in water • Indicator for geothermal input	Laboratory		
pH (acidity)	• Aquatic life protection • Indicator of industrial discharges, mining	Laboratory	Between pH 6 - 9	*(WS)*
Clarity - turbidity - black disk	• Aesthetic appearance • Aquatic life protection • Indicator of catchment condition, land use	Laboratory or field	Turbidity: 2 NTU Black disk: more than 1.6 m *(AE, CR, A)*	
Colour - light absorption	• Aesthetic appearance • Light availability for excessive plant growth • Indicator of presence of organic matter	Laboratory		
Nutrients (Nitrogen and phosphorus)	• Enrichment, excessive plant growth • Limiting factor for plant and algal growth	Laboratory	DIN: less than 0.100 gm^{-3} DRP: less than 0.030 gm^{-3} NO$_3$: less than 10 gm^{-3}	*(AE, A)* *(WS)*
Major ions (Mg^{2+}, Ca^{2+}, Na$^+$, K$^+$, Cl$^-$, HCO$_3^-$, SO$_4^{2-}$)	• Baseline water quality characteristics • Indicator for catchment soil types, geology • Water hardness (magnesium/calcium) • Buffering capacity for pH change (HCO$_3$)	Laboratory		
Organic carbon	• Indicator of organic pollution • Catchment characteristics	Laboratory	BOD: less than 5 gm^{-3}	*(AE, CR, A)*
Fecal bacteria	• Indicator of pollution with fecal matter • Disease risk for swimming etc.	Laboratory	ENT: less than 33 cm^{-3} FC: less than 200 cm^{-3}	*(CR)*

Guidelines and **standards** refer to the following specified water uses and values: *AE* = aquatic ecosystem protection, *CR* = contact recreation, *A* = aesthetic, *SG* = shellfish gathering, *WS* = water supply (drinking), *F* = fishery, *FS* = fish spawning, *SW* = stock watering.

Key to abbreviations: NTU = a unit of measurement for turbidity, DIN = dissolved inorganic nitrogen, DRP = dissolved reactive phosphorus, BOD = biochemical oxygen demand, ENT = enterococci, FC = fecal coliform.

1. Explain why *dissolved oxygen, temperature,* and *clarity* measurements are made in the field rather than in the laboratory:

_____

_____

2. Name a human activity that could increase the amount of siltation in a river or lake: _____

3. Virtually all water pollution originates on land. Explain why the link between water quality and land use is important:

_____

_____

Sewage Treatment

Once water has been used by household or industry, it becomes sewage. Sewage includes toilet wastes and all household water, but excludes storm water, which is usually diverted directly into waterways. In some cities, the sewerage and stormwater systems may be partly combined, and sewage can overflow into surface water during high rainfall. When sewage reaches a treatment plant, it can undergo up to three levels of processing (purification). Primary treatment is little more than a mechanical screening process, followed by settling of the solids into a sludge. Secondary sewage treatment is primarily a biological process in which aerobic and anaerobic microorganisms are used to remove the organic wastes. Advanced secondary treatment targets specific pollutants, particularly nitrates, phosphates, and heavy metals. Before water is discharged after treatment, it is always disinfected (usually by chlorination) to kill bacteria and other potential pathogens.

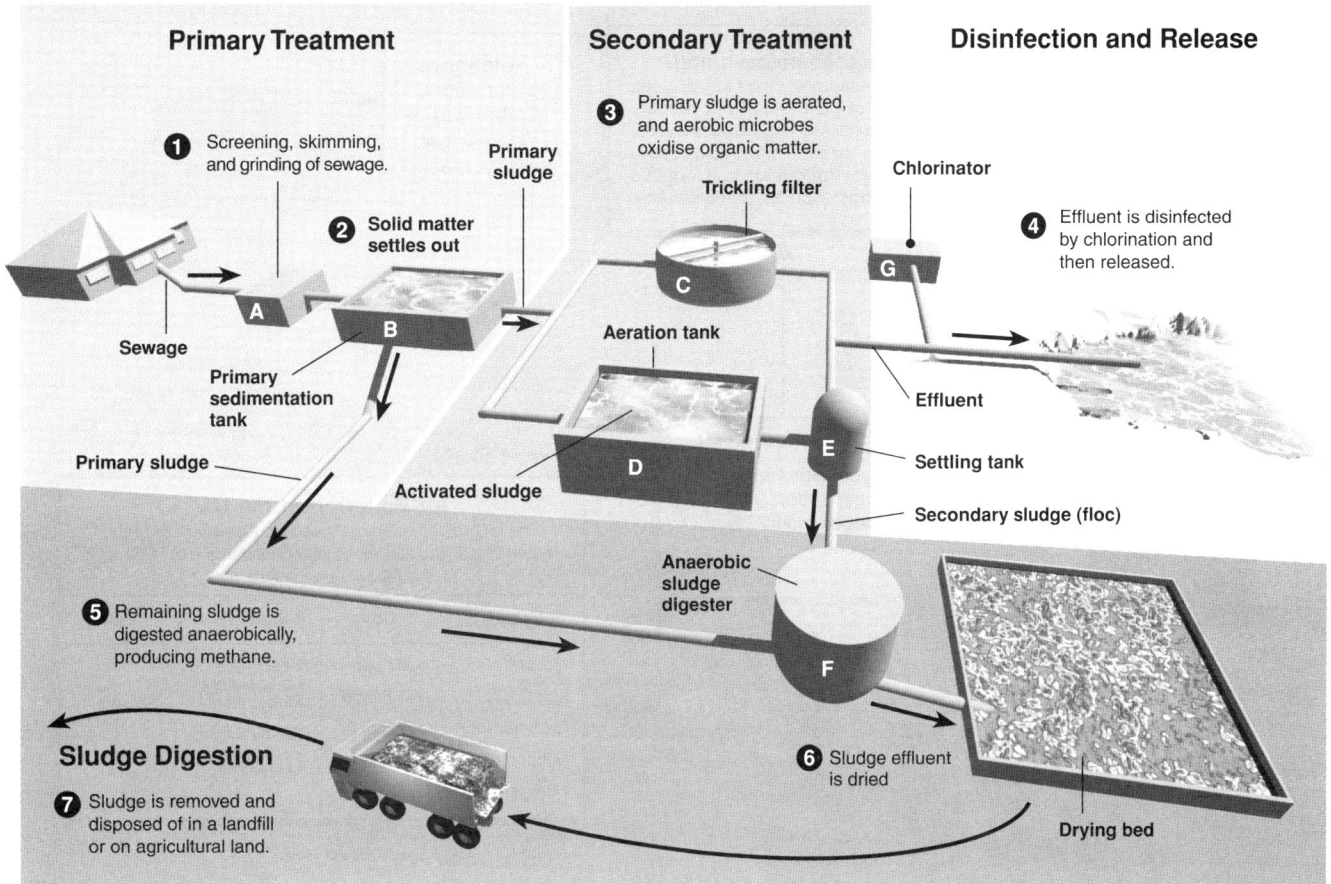

1. Using the information provided in the diagram and text above, classify each of the processes indicated A-G as either mechanical, biological, or chemical. If you wish, color code these on the diagram for easy reference:

A: _____   D: _____   G: _____

B: _____   E: _____

C: _____   F: _____

2. Using the diagram above for reference, investigate the sewage treatment process in your own town or city, identifying the specific techniques and problems of waste water management in your area. Make a note of the main points to cover in the space provided below, and develop your discussion as a separate report. Identify:

(a) Your urban area and treatment station: _____

(b) The volume of sewage processed: _____

(c) The degree of purification: _____

(d) The treatment processes used (list): _____

(e) The discharge point(s): _____

(f) Problems of waste water management: _____

(g) Future options or plans: _____

Atmospheric Pollution

Air pollution consists of gases, liquids, or solids present in the atmosphere at levels high enough to harm living things (or cause damage to materials). Human activities make a major contribution to global air pollution, although natural processes can also be responsible. Lightning causes forest fires, oxidizes nitrogen and creates ozone, while erupting volcanoes give off toxic and corrosive gases. Air pollution tends to be concentrated around areas of high population density, particularly in Western industrial and post-industrial societies. In the last few decades there has been a massive increase in air pollution in parts of the world that previously had little, such as Mexico city and some of the large Asian cities. Air pollution does not just exist outdoors. The air enclosed in spaces such as cars, homes, schools, and offices may have significantly higher levels of harmful air pollutants than the air outdoors.

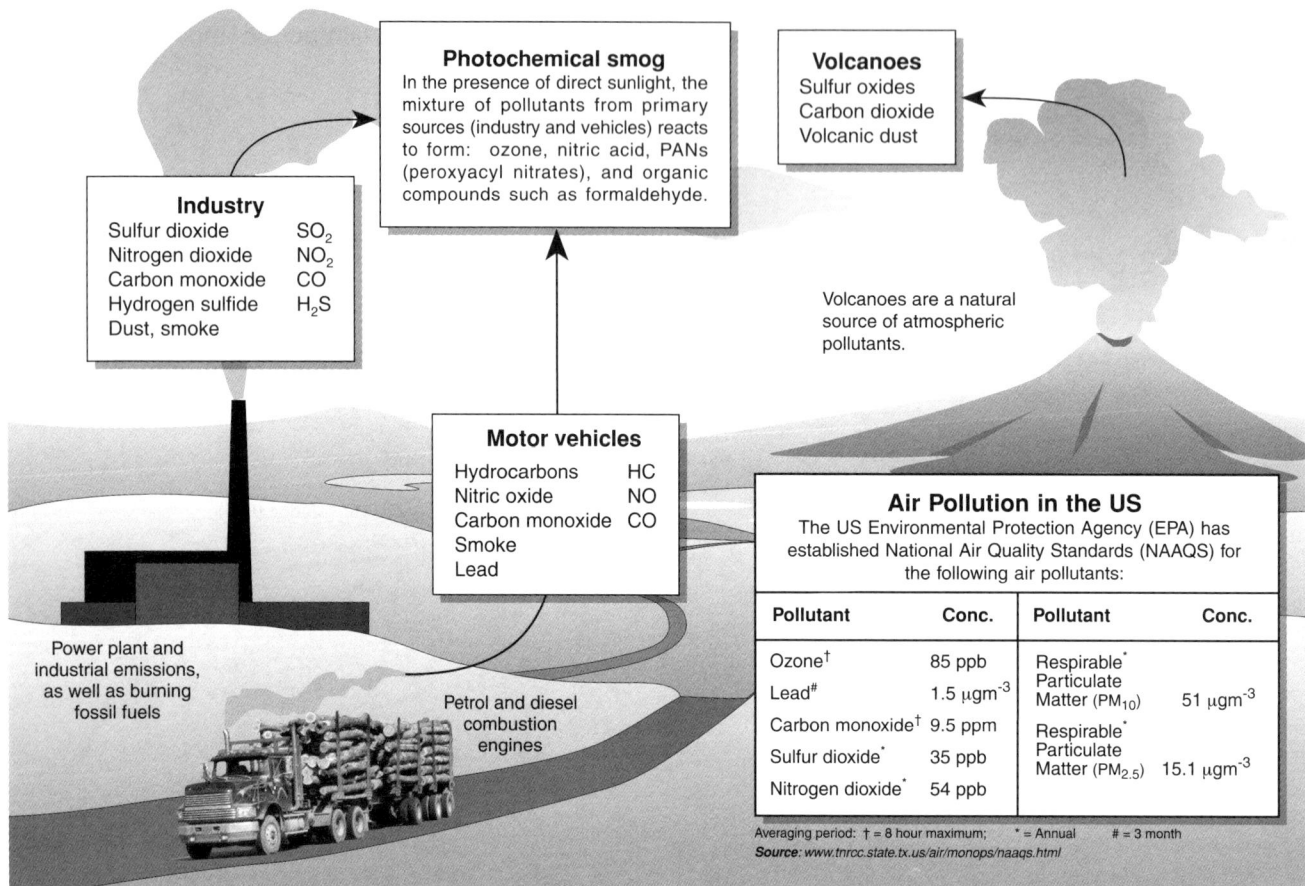

Photochemical smog
In the presence of direct sunlight, the mixture of pollutants from primary sources (industry and vehicles) reacts to form: ozone, nitric acid, PANs (peroxyacyl nitrates), and organic compounds such as formaldehyde.

Volcanoes
Sulfur oxides
Carbon dioxide
Volcanic dust

Industry
Sulfur dioxide	SO_2
Nitrogen dioxide	NO_2
Carbon monoxide	CO
Hydrogen sulfide	H_2S
Dust, smoke	

Volcanoes are a natural source of atmospheric pollutants.

Motor vehicles
Hydrocarbons	HC
Nitric oxide	NO
Carbon monoxide	CO
Smoke	
Lead	

Power plant and industrial emissions, as well as burning fossil fuels

Petrol and diesel combustion engines

Air Pollution in the US
The US Environmental Protection Agency (EPA) has established National Air Quality Standards (NAAQS) for the following air pollutants:

Pollutant	Conc.	Pollutant	Conc.
Ozone[†]	85 ppb	Respirable[*] Particulate Matter (PM$_{10}$)	51 µgm^{-3}
Lead[#]	1.5 µgm^{-3}		
Carbon monoxide[†]	9.5 ppm	Respirable[*] Particulate Matter (PM$_{2.5}$)	15.1 µgm^{-3}
Sulfur dioxide[*]	35 ppb		
Nitrogen dioxide[*]	54 ppb		

Averaging period: † = 8 hour maximum;   * = Annual   # = 3 month
Source: www.tnrcc.state.tx.us/air/monops/naaqs.html

1. Name a primary source of air pollution in large cities: _____

2. A major cause of air pollution is the burning of fossil fuels to supply energy for domestic or industrial purposes. List four fossil fuels and a typical application that their energy is required for:

   (a) Name of fossil fuel: _____   Application: _____

   (b) Name of fossil fuel: _____   Application: _____

   (c) Name of fossil fuel: _____   Application: _____

   (d) Name of fossil fuel: _____   Application: _____

3. One way of monitoring the level of air pollution is to make regular inspections of what are called 'biological indicators', such as lichen, in the environment.

   (a) Explain what a **biological indicator** is: _____

   _____

   _____

   (b) Explain how **lichen** could be used in this way: _____

   _____

   _____

   _____

Health officials are paying increasing attention to the *sick building syndrome*. This air pollution inside office buildings can cause eye irritations, nausea, headaches, respiratory infections, depression and fatigue. Gases, ozone and microbes are implicated.

Aircraft contribute to atmospheric pollution with their jet exhaust at high altitude (at 10 000 m). The cabin environment of aircraft is also often polluted. Some passengers may spread infections (e.g. TB and SARS) through the recirculated cabin air.

Automobiles are the single most important contributor of air pollutants in large cities, producing large amounts of carbon monoxide, hydrocarbons, and nitrous oxides. Some countries require cars to have **catalytic converters** fitted to their exhausts.

4. Complete the table below that summarizes the main types of air pollutants:

Pollutant	Major sources	Harmful effects	Prevention or control
Carbon monoxide			Fit cars with catalytic converters and keep well tuned.
Hydrogen sulfides	Burning fuels, oil refineries, wood pulp processing.		
Sulfur oxides			Use alternative, sulfur free fuels such as natural gas and LPG (liquid petroleum gas).
Nitrogen oxides		Forms photochemical smog which irritates the eyes and nose. Retards plant growth.	
Smoke			
Lead		Causes convulsions, coma and damage to the nervous system.	
Ozone			Fit cars with catalytic converters to reduce the amount of nitrogen oxides and volatile hydrocarbons emitted.
Hydrocarbons	Incomplete combustion		

5. **Sick building syndrome** affects large office buildings where the workers are breathing in an air conditioned atmosphere. The pollutant gases are released from the materials and equipment in the office, while disease-causing microbes may live in the heating, air conditioning and ventilation ducts.

(a) Explain what **sick building syndrome** is: _____

(b) Suggest a way of reducing this form of indoor pollution: _____

(c) A more extreme example of indoor pollution has been recently diagnosed on long distance flights in modern passenger jets with their pressurized cabin atmospheres. Explain why this situation is potentially more threatening than sick building syndrome, particularly when taking into account that most modern jets recirculate most cabin air:

Global Warming

DA②

The Earth's atmosphere comprises a mixture of gases including nitrogen, oxygen, and water vapor. Also present are small quantities of carbon dioxide, methane, and a number of other "trace" gases. In the past, our climate has shifted between periods of stable warm conditions to cycles of ice ages and 'interglacials'. The current period of warming climate is partly explained by the recovery after the most recent ice age that finished 10 000 years ago. Eight of the ten warmest years on record (records kept since the mid-1800s) were in the 1980s and 1990s. Global surface temperatures in 1998 set a new record by a wide margin, exceeding those of the previous record year, 1995. Many researchers believe the current warming trend has been compounded by human activity, in particular, the release of certain gases into the atmosphere. The term '**greenhouse effect**' describes a process of global climate warming caused by the release of 'greenhouse gases', which act as a thermal blanket in the atmosphere, letting in sunlight, but trapping the heat that would normally radiate back into space. About 75% of the natural greenhouse effect is due to water vapor. The next most significant is carbon dioxide. Since the industrial revolution and expansion of agriculture about 200 years ago, additional carbon dioxide gas has been pumped into the atmosphere. The effect of global warming on agriculture, other human activities, and the biosphere in general, is likely to be considerable.

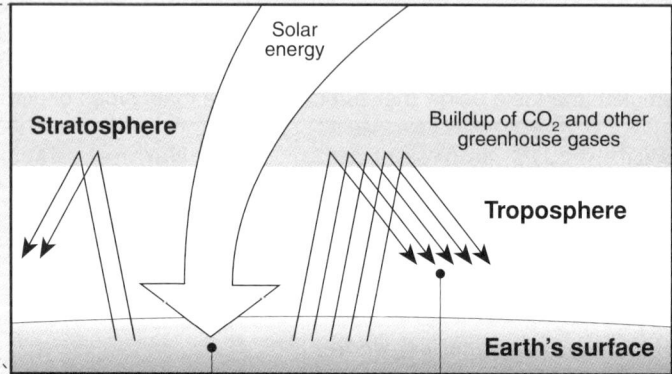

Solar energy is absorbed as heat by Earth, where it is radiated back into the atmosphere

Most heat is absorbed by CO_2 in the stratosphere and radiated back to Earth

Sources of 'Greenhouse Gases'

Carbon dioxide
- Exhaust from cars
- Combustion of coal, wood, oil
- Burning rainforests

Methane
- Belching and flatus of cows

Chloro-fluoro-carbons (CFCs)
- Leaking coolant from refrigerators
- Leaking coolant from air conditioners

Nitrous oxide
- Car exhaust

Tropospheric ozone*
- Triggered by car exhaust (smog)

*Tropospheric ozone is found in the lower atmosphere (not to be confused with ozone in the stratosphere)

Greenhouse gas	Tropospheric conc.		Global warming potential *(compared to CO_2)*¶	Atmospheric lifetime *(years)*§
	Pre-industrial 1860	Present day (2002)		
Carbon dioxide	288 ppm	370 ppm	1	120
Methane	848 ppb	1785 ppb	21	12
Nitrous oxide	285 ppb	316 ppb	310	120
CFCs	0 ppb	0.89 ppb	4000+	50-100
Tropospheric ozone	25 ppb	34 ppb	17	hours

ppm = parts per million; **ppb** = parts per billion;
¶ Figures contrast the radiative effect of different greenhouse gases relative to CO_2, e.g., methane is 21 times more potent as a greenhouse gas than CO_2 § How long the gas persists in the atmosphere *Source: Carbon Dioxide Information Analysis Center, Oak Ridge National Laboratory, USA.*

The graph on the right shows how the mean temperature for each year from 1860 until 2003 (gray bars) compared with the average temperature between 1961 and 1990. The black fitted line represents the mathematically smoothed curve and shows the general trend indicated by the annual data. Most anomalies since 1977 have been above normal; warmer than the long term mean, indicating that global temperatures are tracking upwards. In 1998 the global temperature exceeded that of the previous record year, 1995, by about 0.2°C.

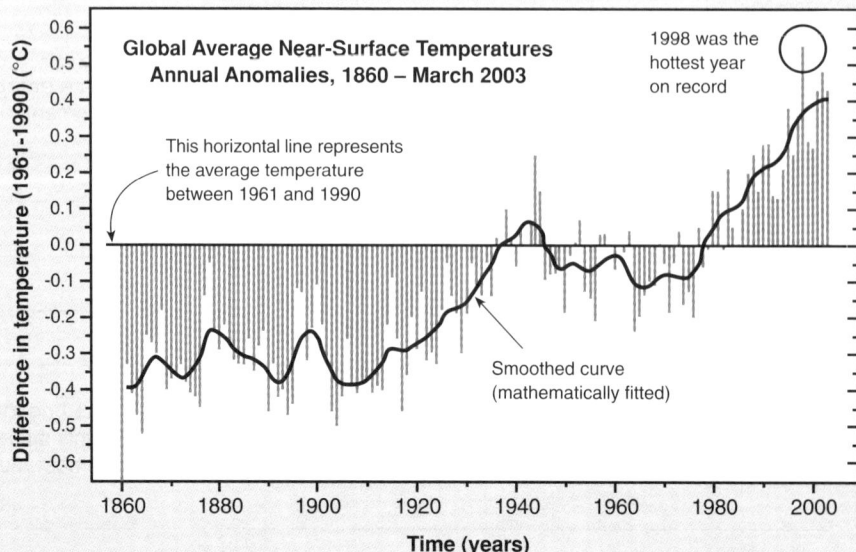

Source: Hadley Center for Prediction and Research

Changes in atmospheric CO$_2$ since 1000 AD

Expanded in detail on the next graph (note the different vertical scale)

Year

Changes in atmospheric CO$_2$ since 1955

Year

Sources: NASA Goddard Space Flight Center; NOAA / CMDL

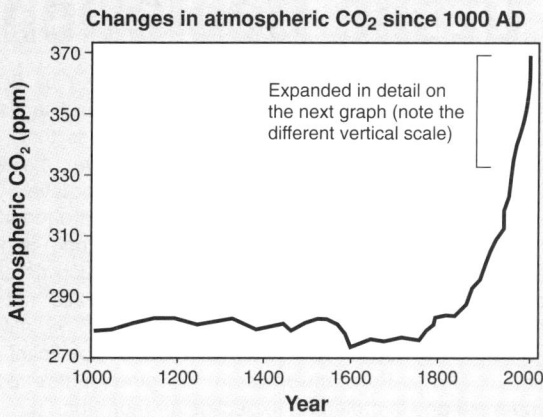

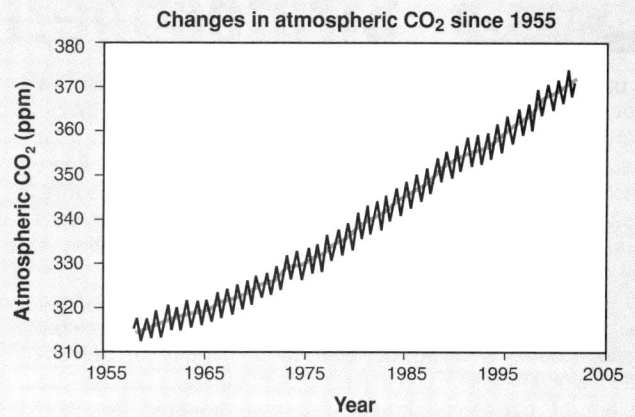

Potential Effects of Global Warming

Coastal resources: The sea level is expected to rise by 50 cm by the year 2100. This is the result of ocean water expanding as it warms and by some melting of non-polar ice.

Forests: Higher temperatures and precipitation changes could increase forest susceptibility to fire, disease, and insect damage. A richer CO$_2$ atmosphere will reduce transpiration in plants.

Weather patterns: Global warming may cause regional changes in weather patterns such as El Niño and La Nina, as well as affecting the intensity and frequency of storms (hurricanes).

Water resources: Changes in precipitation and increased evaporation will affect water availability for irrigation, industrial use, drinking, and electricity generation.

Agriculture: Impacts of climate change in developing countries could be significant. Changes in climate may affect the viability of staple crops in some regions.

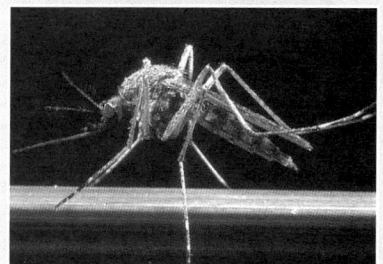

Health: Higher temperatures over longer periods may increase heat-stress mortality. Climate changes may produce new breeding sites for pests, shifting the range of infectious diseases.

1. Calculate the increase (as a %) in the 'greenhouse gases' between the pre-industrial era and the 2002 measurements (use the data from the table, see facing page). **HINT**: The calculation for carbon dioxide is: (370 - 288) ÷ 288 x 100 =

(a) Carbon dioxide: _____ (b) Methane: _____ (c) Nitrous oxide: _____

2. Describe the probable effect the 'greenhouse effect' will have on:

(a) Sea levels: _____

(b) Regional climates: _____

(c) Distribution and extent of habitats in different parts of the world: _____

(d) Survival of the various species of plant and animals (natural populations as well as agricultural):

RA② Stratospheric Ozone Depletion

In a band of the upper stratosphere, 17-26 km above the Earth's surface, exists a thin veil of renewable **ozone** (O₃). This ozone absorbs about 99% of the harmful incoming UV radiation from the sun and prevents it from reaching the Earth's surface. Apart from health problems, such as increasingly severe sunburns, increase in skin cancers, and more cataracts of the eye (in both humans and other animals), an increase in UV-B radiation is likely to cause immune system suppression in animals, lower crop yields, a decline in the productivity of forests and surface dwelling plankton, more smog, and changes in the global climate. Ozone is being depleted by a handful of human-produced chemicals (ozone depleting compounds or ODCs). The problem of **ozone depletion** was first detected in 1984. Researchers discovered that ozone in the upper stratosphere over Antarctica is destroyed during the Antarctic spring and early summer (September–December). Rather than a "hole", it is more

a thinning, where ozone levels typically decrease by 50% to 100%. In 2000, the extent of the hole above Antarctica was the largest ever, but depletion levels were slightly less than 1999. Severe ozone loss has also been observed over the Arctic. During the winter of 1999-2000, Arctic ozone levels were depleted by 60% at an altitude of 18 km, up from around 45% in the previous winter. The primary cause for ozone depletion appears to be the increased use of chemicals such as chloro-fluoro-carbons (**CFCs**). Since 1987, nations have cut their consumption of ozone-depleting substances by 70%, although the phaseout is not complete and there is a significant black market in CFCs. **Free chlorine** in the stratosphere peaked around 1999 and is projected to decline for more than a century. Ozone loss is projected to diminish gradually until around 2050 when the polar ozone holes will return to 1975 levels. It will take another 100-200 years for full recovery to pre-1950 levels.

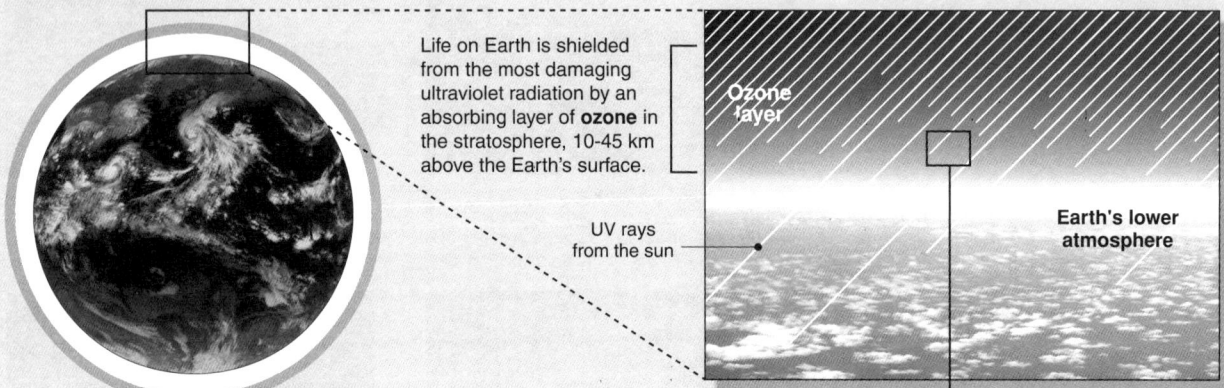

Life on Earth is shielded from the most damaging ultraviolet radiation by an absorbing layer of **ozone** in the stratosphere, 10-45 km above the Earth's surface.

UV rays from the sun

Ozone layer

Earth's lower atmosphere

Sources of ozone depleting chemicals

The chemicals below drift up to the stratosphere, where ultraviolet radiation causes release of free chlorine, a highly reactive chemical.

Chloro-fluoro-carbons (CFCs)
• Propellants for aerosol cans
• Coolants in air-conditioners
• Coolants (freon) in refrigerators
• Styrofoam insulation/packaging
• Medical sterilizers

Halons
• Used in many fire extinguishers

Methyl bromide
• Used as a fumigant in agriculture

Methyl chloroform
• Used to degrease metals

Carbon tetrachloride
• Used in many industrial processes

UV light hits a CFC molecule and releases a chlorine atom

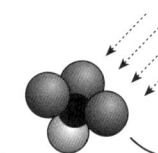

C.Cl₃F
Chlorofluorocarbon
(CFC)

The destruction of ozone by free chlorine

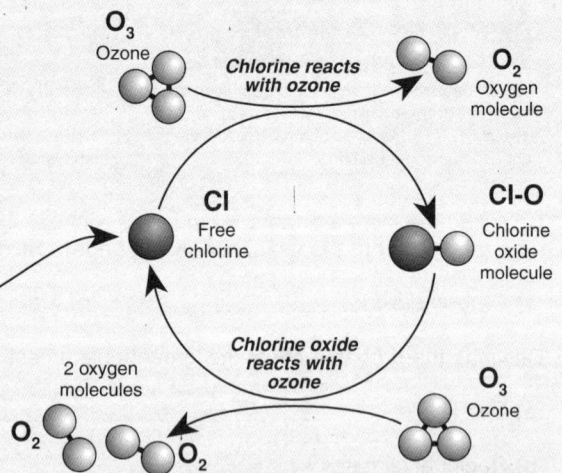

O₃
Ozone

Chlorine reacts with ozone

O₂
Oxygen molecule

Cl
Free chlorine

Cl-O
Chlorine oxide molecule

2 oxygen molecules

Chlorine oxide reacts with ozone

O₃
Ozone

O₂   O₂

A large 'hole' in the ozone layer develops over Antarctica each summer, dropping the ozone well below its normal level. The size and intensity of the hole is growing each year, as can be seen in the satellite photos on the right. In recent years, a similar hole has developed over the Arctic.

Dobson Unit (DU): A measurement of **column ozone** levels (the ozone between the Earth's surface and outer space). In the tropics, ozone levels are typically between 250 and 300 DU year-round. In temperate regions, seasonal variations can produce large swings in ozone levels. These variations occur even in the absence of ozone depletion. **Ozone depletion** refers to reductions in ozone below normal levels after accounting for seasonal cycles and other natural effects. For a graphical explanation, see NASA's TOMS site: ***http://toms.gsfc.nasa.gov/teacher/basics/dobson.html***

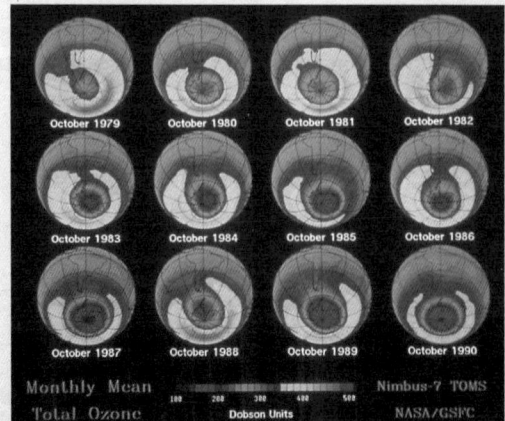

October 1979   October 1980   October 1981   October 1982
October 1983   October 1984   October 1985   October 1986
October 1987   October 1988   October 1989   October 1990

Monthly Mean
Total Ozone   Dobson Units   Nimbus-7 TOMS
                                            NASA/GSFC

Photos: NASA/Goddard Space Flight Center

Characteristics of the ozone 'hole'

The ozone 'hole' (depletion of ozone in the stratosphere) can be characterized using several measures. The five graphs on this page are derived from data supplied by NASA's Goddard Space Flight Center and the National Oceanic and Atmospheric Administration (NOAA) in the United States. They show how the size and intensity of the hole varies through the course of a year, as well as how the phenomenon has progressed over the last two decades. An explanation of the unit used to measure ozone concentration (Dobson units) is given on the previous page. Graphs 2 and 5 illustrate readings taken between the South Pole (90° south) and 40° latitude.

Graph 1: Ozone hole altitude profile

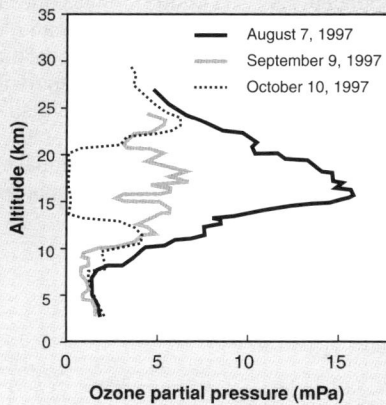

Legend:
- August 7, 1997
- September 9, 1997
- October 10, 1997

Y-axis: Altitude (km); X-axis: Ozone partial pressure (mPa)

Graph 2: Antarctic ozone hole area (<220 DU, 40° – 90° South)

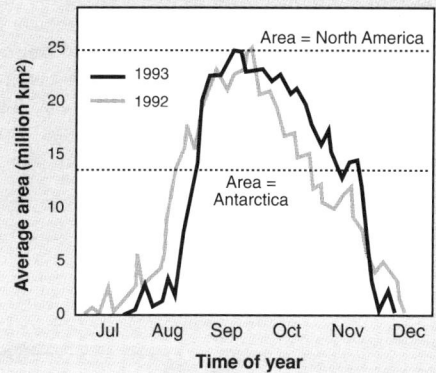

Legend:
- 1993
- 1992

Area = North America
Area = Antarctica

Y-axis: Average area (million km²); X-axis: Time of year (Jul–Dec)

Graph 3: Change in area of the Antarctic ozone hole*

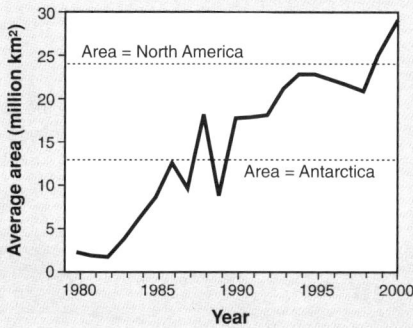

Area = North America
Area = Antarctica

Y-axis: Average area (million km²); X-axis: Year (1980–2000)

Graph 4: Antarctic ozone hole minimum values* (60° – 90° S)

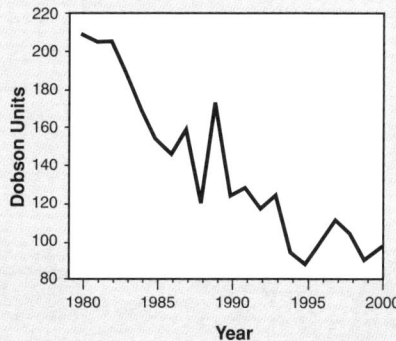

Y-axis: Dobson Units; X-axis: Year (1980–2000)

Graph 5: Antarctic ozone hole minimum values (40° – 90° South)

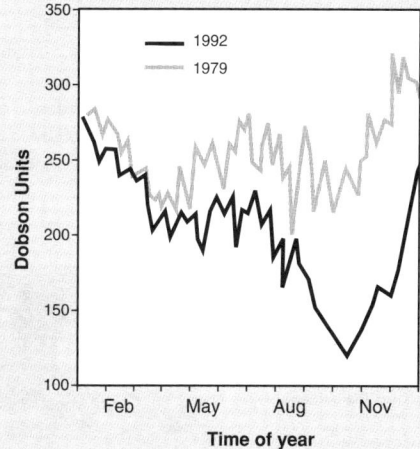

Legend:
- 1992
- 1979

Y-axis: Dobson Units; X-axis: Time of year (Feb–Nov)

* Date range in which samples were collected in each year: 7 Sep–13 Oct
The ozone 'hole' is defined as region with less than 220 Dobson units

Sources: NASA Goddard Space Flight Center; NOAA / CMDL

1. List some of the damaging effects of excessive amounts of ultraviolet radiation on living organisms:

_____

_____

2. Explain how the atmospheric release of CFCs has increased the penetration of UV radiation reaching the Earth's surface:

_____

_____

3. List some of the political and commercial problems associated with reducing the use of ozone depleting chemicals:

_____

_____

4. With reference to the graphs (1-5 above) illustrating the characteristics of the stratospheric ozone depletion problem:

(a) State the time of year when the ozone 'hole' is at its greatest geographic extent: _____

(b) Determine the time of the year when the 'hole' is at its most depleted (thinnest): _____

(c) Describe the trend over the last 2 decades of changes to the abundance of stratospheric ozone over Antarctica:

_____

_____

(d) Describe the changes in stratospheric ozone with altitude between August and October 1997 in Graph 1 (above):

_____

Acid Rain

DA 2

Acid rain is not a new phenomenon. It was first noticed last century in regions where the industrial revolution began. Buildings in areas with heavy industrial activity were being worn away by rain. More correctly termed **acid deposition**, it can fall to the Earth as rain, snow or sleet, as well as dry, sulfate-containing particles that settle out of the air. It is a problem that crosses international boundaries. Gases from coal-burning power stations in England fall as acid rain in Norway and Sweden, emissions from the United States produce acid deposition in Canada, while Japan receives acid rain from China. The effect of this fallout is to produce lakes that are so acid that they cannot support fish, and forests with sickly, stunted tree growth. Acid rain also causes the release of heavy metals (e.g. cadmium and mercury) into the food chain. Changes in species composition of aquatic communities may be used as **biological indicators** measuring the severity of acid deposition.

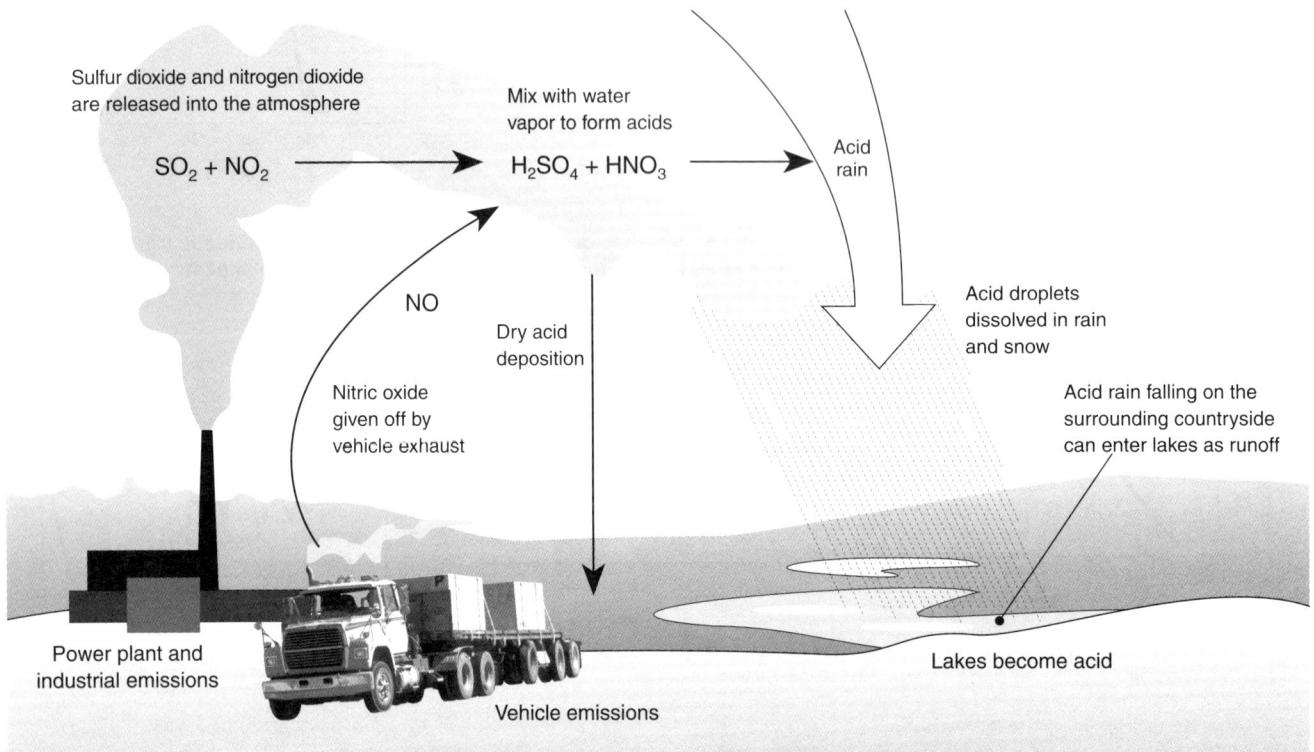

Sulfur dioxide and nitrogen dioxide are released into the atmosphere

$$SO_2 + NO_2 \longrightarrow H_2SO_4 + HNO_3 \longrightarrow$$

Mix with water vapor to form acids

Acid rain

NO

Dry acid deposition

Nitric oxide given off by vehicle exhaust

Acid droplets dissolved in rain and snow

Acid rain falling on the surrounding countryside can enter lakes as runoff

Power plant and industrial emissions

Vehicle emissions

Lakes become acid

Acidity Tolerance in Lake Organisms

Different aquatic organisms have varying sensitivities to higher acidity (lower pH). The graph on the right shows how much acidity certain species can tolerate. The absence of certain indicator species from a waterway can provide evidence of pollution in the recent past as well as the present.

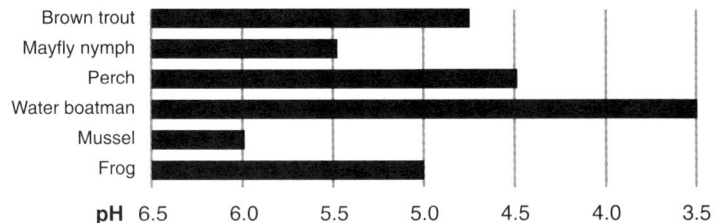

Species	
Brown trout	
Mayfly nymph	
Perch	
Water boatman	
Mussel	
Frog	

pH 6.5　6.0　5.5　5.0　4.5　4.0　3.5

---

1. Describe the effect of acid deposition on communities of living organisms:

_____

_____

2. Study the graph of 'Acidity Tolerance in Lake Organisms' above.
   (a) State which species is the most **sensitive** to acid conditions: _____

   (b) State which species is the most **tolerant** of acid conditions: _____

   (c) Explain how you could use these kinds of measurements as an indicator of the 'health' of a lake:

   _____

   _____

3. Describe some of the measures that could be taken to reduce acid emissions: _____

_____

4. Explain why these measures are slow to be implemented: _____

_____

DA ② Energy Resources

There is a global energy crisis looming. The combined effect of the dwindling reserves of fossil fuels, combined with their rather catastrophic long term effect on the world's climate, make the search for renewable energy sources imperative. Alternative energy sources such as solar power and the requisite high efficiency batteries have yet to become efficient enough and cheap enough to be serious replacements for fossil fuels.

Renewable biomass energy resources may provide a useful supplement to traditional fuels such as **coal**, **gas**, and **oil** (including its refined products of diesel, petrol, and kerosene). **Biofuels** include ethanol, **gasohol** (a blend of petrol and ethanol), methanol, and diesel made from a blend of plant oils and traditional diesel oil. **Biogas** (methane) is an important renewable gas fuel made by fermenting wastes in a digester.

Gasohol

Gasohol is a blend of finished motor gasoline containing alcohol (generally ethanol but sometimes methanol). In Brazil, gasohol consists of 24% ethanol mixed with petrol.

Advantages	Disadvantages
• Cleaner fuel than petrol	• Ethanol burns hotter than petrol so petrol engines tend to overheat and they need to be modified
• Renewable resource	
• Creates many jobs in rural areas	• Fuel tank and pipes need coating to prevent corrosion by ethanol
	• Fuel consumption 20% greater compared with petrol

Sources of biomass for ethanol production

• *Sugar cane* (ethanol is produced in this way in Brazil).

• *Corn starch* (in the USA).

• Grass, certain waste materials (paper, cardboard), and from wood. Fast-growing hardwood trees can be treated to release *cellulose*. Once released, it may be converted to simple glucose by hydrolytic enzymes and then fermented to produce ethanol.

Biogas

Methane gas is produced by anaerobic fermentation of organic wastes such as sewage sludge at sewage waste treatment stations, animal dung, agricultural wastes, or by the rotting contents of landfill sites.

Stages in methane production

Saprophytic bacteria (facultative anaerobes) break down fats, proteins, and polysaccharides.

↓

Acid-forming bacteria break down these monomers to short-chain organic acids.

↓

Methanogen bacteria (strict anaerobes) produce methane gas.

Biogas

Biogas	
Methane:	50-80%
CO_2:	15-45%
Water:	5%

Digester

Small scale fermenter

Sources: *Biological Sciences Review*, Sep 2000, pp.27-29; *Biologist*, Feb 1998, pp. 17-21; Microorganism & Biotechnology, 1997, Chenn, P. (John Murray Publishers).

Traditional sources of renewable energy include animal dung, which is collected and then dried in the sun and used as fuel.

Fuels such as petrol, diesel, LPG, and CNG are derived from oil and natural gas extracted from non-renewable geological deposits.

Coal provided the energy for the industrial revolution. It is now regarded as a dirty fuel with many health hazards associated with its use.

1. Explain the nature of the following renewable fuels:

   (a) Biogas: _____

   _____

   (b) Gasohol: _____

   _____

2. Name the sources of biomass that are commonly used for the production of ethanol fuel: _____

   _____

3. List two disadvantages of using pure ethanol as a motor fuel: _____

   _____

4. Suggest how a small biogas fermenter may be used on a farm to reduce waste and provide a fuel source:

   _____

   _____

   _____

Waste Management

RA 3

The disposal of solid and hazardous waste is one of the most urgent problems of today's industrialized societies. Traditionally, solid waste has been disposed of in open dumps and, more recently, in sanitary, scientifically designed landfills. Even with modern designs and better waste processing, landfills still have the potential to contaminate soil and groundwater. In addition, they occupy valuable land, and their siting is often a matter of local controversy. More and more today, city councils and local authorities support the initiatives for the reduction, reuse, and recycling of solid wastes. At the same time, they must develop strategies for the safe disposal of hazardous wastes, which pose an immediate or potential threat to environmental and human health. A program of integrated waste management (below) combines features of traditional waste management with new techniques to reduce and incinerate wastes. Such schemes will form the basis of effective waste management in the future.

Components of Integrated Waste Management

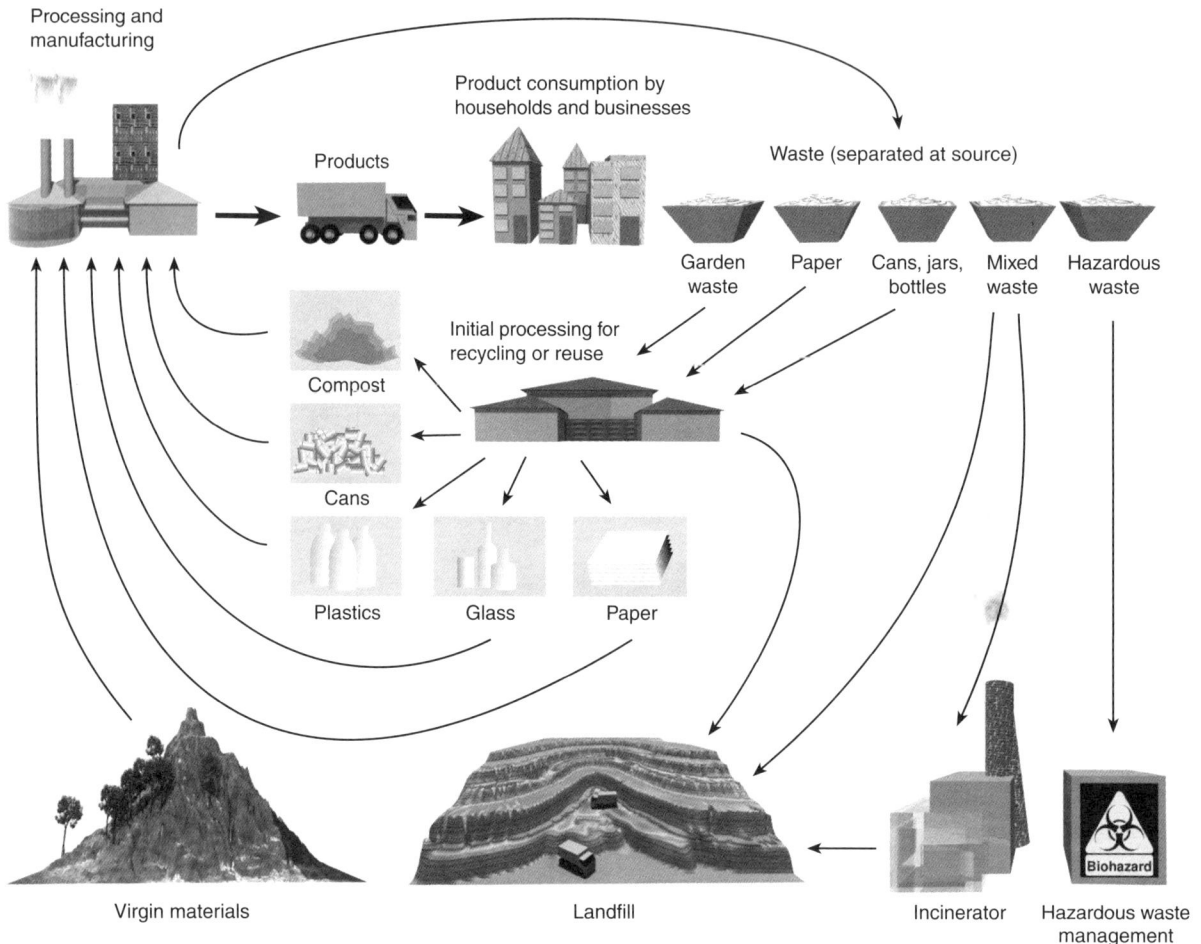

Processing and manufacturing

Product consumption by households and businesses

Products

Waste (separated at source)

Garden waste   Paper   Cans, jars, bottles   Mixed waste   Hazardous waste

Initial processing for recycling or reuse

Compost

Cans

Plastics   Glass   Paper

Virgin materials   Landfill   Incinerator   Hazardous waste management

Household wastes for recycling, e.g., plastic and glass, may be collected in bins at the kerbside of many houses.

Community recycling centers provide a centralized place for people to recycle household items for reuse.

Portable bins are frequently used for collecting rubbish from apartment blocks, businesses, and institutions.

Plastic containers for recycling are sorted according to the type of material they are made from.

A lot of household waste ends up in landfills where it is eventually buried – a legacy for future generations.

This person in Manila (Philippines) is collecting items from other people's rubbish – a crude form of recycling.

Car scrap yards are a dumping ground for cars that are past their useful life. The metal components are recycled.

With the increasing use of electronic and electrical technology, disposing of these items is becoming harder.

1. The diagram opposite provides an overview of an **idealized management system** for waste materials from households and industries. It provides a starting point for comparing how different waste products *could be* disposed of or processed. Using the information provided for guidance, investigate the disposal, recycling, and post-waste processing options for each of the waste products listed below. **Summarize** the important points in the spaces provided, including reference to disposal methods and particular problems associated with these, processing or recycling (if relevant), and useful end-products (if relevant). If required, develop this summary, or part of it, as a separate report:

(a) Glass waste: _____

_____

(b) Paper: _____

_____

(c) Aluminum: _____

_____

(d) Steel: _____

_____

(e) Organic waste: _____

_____

(f) Hazardous waste (including medical): _____

_____

2. Compare and contrast two different options for waste disposal as indicated below. Summarize the important points in the spaces provided. If required, develop this summary, or part of it, as a separate report:

WASTE DISPOSAL IN LANDFILLS:

(a) Problems (list): _____

_____

(b) Advantages (list): _____

_____

(c) Basic design and operation: _____

_____

(d) Suitability for all waste types: _____

(e) Viability as a sustainable option for the future: _____

_____

INCINERATION OF WASTE:

(a) Problems (list): _____

_____

(b) Advantages (list): _____

_____

(c) Basic design and operation: _____

_____

(d) Suitability for all waste types: _____

(e) Viability as a sustainable option for the future: _____

_____

Endangered Species

Extinctions are a natural process that are part of the life cycle of a species. Many species last only 2 to 10 million years before they become extinct. What is of concern today is the rapid increase in extinction rates as a result of human activity. Various management strategies are proving successful in protecting species already at risk, and helping those on the verge of extinction to return to sustainable population sizes. Internationally, there are a number of agencies concerned with monitoring and managing the loss of

biodiversity. **The Nature Conservancy** is one such organization. The mission of the Conservancy is to preserve the plants, animals, and natural communities that represent the diversity of life on Earth, by protecting the lands and waters they need to survive. With donations from over a million members, the Conservancy has purchased 12 621 000 acres in the USA and a further 96 386 000 acres outside the USA (an area greater than the combined size of Costa Rica, Honduras and Panama).

Causes of Species Decline

Commercial and "scientific" whaling

Clear felling of native rainforest

Habitat Destruction
Loss of habitat can occur through clearance for agriculture, urban development and land reclamation, or trampling and vegetation destruction by introduced pest plants and animals. Habitats potentially suitable for a threatened species may be too small and isolated to support a viable population.

Commercial Hunting and Collecting
Animals and plants may be hunted or collected legally for commercial gain. This may be due to a lack of adequate controls over the rate and scale of hunting. Some protected marine species (e.g. dolphin, sealion, and albatross) are at risk because they are caught as by-catch by trawlers. Some commercial marine species (e.g. cod) are at risk through overfishing.

Sport Hunting, Poaching, and Collection
Some species are hunted to the verge of extinction because they interfere with human use of an area. Illegal trade in some species (especially reptiles and parrots) threatens population viability. The taking of specimens by collectors has been instrumental in the decline of some species.

Introduced Exotic Species
Introduced animal predators prey on endangered species. On remote islands, rats, mustelids, and feral cats are major predators of birds and invertebrates. Introduced grazing animals (e.g. deer, goats, pigs) may damage sensitive plants, decimate populations of invertebrates, and trample vegetation. Introduced weeds may smother and out-compete endemic species.

Pollution
Toxic substances released by humans into the environment are passed along the food chain or cause harm directly. Estuaries, wetlands, river systems and coastal ecosystems near urban areas are particularly vulnerable.

Management Strategies

Bat with radio tracker

Color banding of birds

Captive Breeding, Relocation and Monitoring
Individuals are captured and bred under protected and 'ideal' conditions. If breeding programs are successful and there is suitable habitat available, captive individuals may be relocated to the wild where they can establish natural populations.

Restoring Habitats and use of Protected Areas
Control of weeds and animal pests combined with replanting to restore habitat. A *"research by management"* approach links this with careful population monitoring and management to return species to viable levels. Small, managed reserves are well suited to this approach.

Zoos, Botanical Gardens, and Gene Banks
Many zoos specialize in captive breeding programs. Universities and government agencies participate by providing practical help and expertise. Seed and sperm collections (**gene banks**) can preserve the genetic diversity of threatened species.

Habitat Protection
Most countries have a system of National Parks, National Wildlife Refuges or Nature Reserves that are designed to identify and protect important habitats. Such protected areas aim to preserve remnants of habitat that are typical of the region or have special significance.

Public Education and Corporate Sponsorship
Improving public awareness of the plight of threatened species is an important part of a management plan. Species recovery is expensive and many of the plans now involve sponsorship. Sponsorship provides the funding for species restoration and increasing public awareness.

Ban on Trade in Endangered Species
CITES (the Convention on International Trade in Endangered Species of Wild Fauna and Flora) is an international agreement between governments. Its aim is to ensure that international trade in species of wild animals and plants does not threaten their survival.

Black rhinoceros (*Diceros bicornis*)

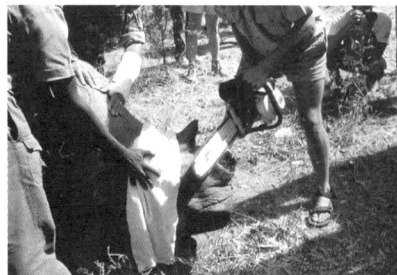

Game wardens dehorning a rhinoceros with a chainsaw to make it an unworthy target for poachers.

A collection of rhinoceros horns removed as part of a dehorning program.

Black rhinoceros were once plentiful throughout sub-Saharan, southern, and eastern Africa. Remnant populations are now found only in Kenya, Tanzania, the Central African Republic, and Zimbabwe. In Kenya, numbers of black rhino fell from a total of 19 000 in 1970 to less than 400 in 1987; a loss of 98% of the

population in 17 years. The dehorning programs carried out in Zimbabwe in 1991 have not halted the slaughter. Large numbers of dehorned rhinos were still being shot; conservationists suspect that a trader with a large stockpile of horn is trying to cause their extinction to increase the horn's value.

1. Distinguish between the following terms that describe the conservation status of a species:

   (a) Vulnerable: _____

   _____

   (b) Endangered: _____

   _____

   (c) Extinct: _____

   _____

2. Describe two good reasons why any species should be preserved from extinction:

   (a) Reason 1: _____

   _____

   _____

   (b) Reason 2: _____

   _____

   _____

3. Explain the role of the following in preserving species diversity:

   (a) CITES: _____

   _____

   _____

   (b) Gene banks: _____

   _____

   _____

   (c) Habitat restoration: _____

   _____

   _____

   (d) Habitat protection: _____

   _____

   _____

   (e) Captive breeding and release programs: _____

   _____

   _____

4. (a) Name an **endangered species** from your own country: _____

   (b) Describe the probable **cause** of its decline: _____

   _____

   _____

   (c) Describe any **management strategy** that is already being carried out (if none, then suggest one):

   _____

   _____

   _____

Conservation of African Elephants

Both African and Asian elephant species are under threat of extinction. The International Union for the Conservation of Nature (**IUCN**) has rated the Asian elephant as endangered and the African elephant as vulnerable. In India, the human pressure on wild habitat has increased by 40% in the last 20 years. Where elephants live in close proximity to agricultural areas they raid crops and come into conflict with humans. The ivory trade represents the greatest threat to the African elephant. Elephant tusks have been sought after for centuries as a material for jewelry and artworks. In Africa, elephant numbers declined from 1.3 million to 600 000 during the 1980s. At this time, as many as 2000 elephants were killed for their tusks every week. By the late 1980s, elephant populations continued to fall in many countries, despite the investment of large amounts of money in fighting poaching. From 1975 to 1989 the ivory trade was regulated under CITES, and permits were required for international trading. Additional protection came in 1989, when the African elephant was placed on *Appendix I* of CITES, which imposed a ban on trade in elephant produce. In 1997 Botswana, Namibia, and Zimbabwe, together with South Africa in 2000, were allowed to transfer their elephant populations from Appendix I to Appendix II, allowing limited commercial trade in raw ivory. In 2002, CITES then approved the sale, to Japan, of legally stockpiled ivory by Namibia, South Africa, and Botswana. African countries have welcomed this decision, although there is still great concern that such a move may trigger the reemergence of a fashion for ivory goods and illegal trade.

Two subspecies of African elephant *Loxodonta africana* are currently recognized: the **savannah elephant** *(L. a. atricana)* and the less common **forest elephant** *(L. a. cyclotis)*. Recent evidence from mitochondrial DNA indicates that they may, in fact, be two distinct species.

In 1989 the Kenyan government publicly burned 12 tonnes of confiscated ivory. With the increased awareness, the United States and several European countries banned ivory imports. The photo above shows game wardens weighing confiscated ivory tusks and rhinoceros horns.

1960: From 1960 onwards, figures for African exports are unreliable because of political unrest.

1975: CITES intervention which regulated the trade in ivory

1989: World wide ban on trade in ivory

2002: Sale of stockpiled ivory by Botswana, Namibia, and South Africa approved by CITES.

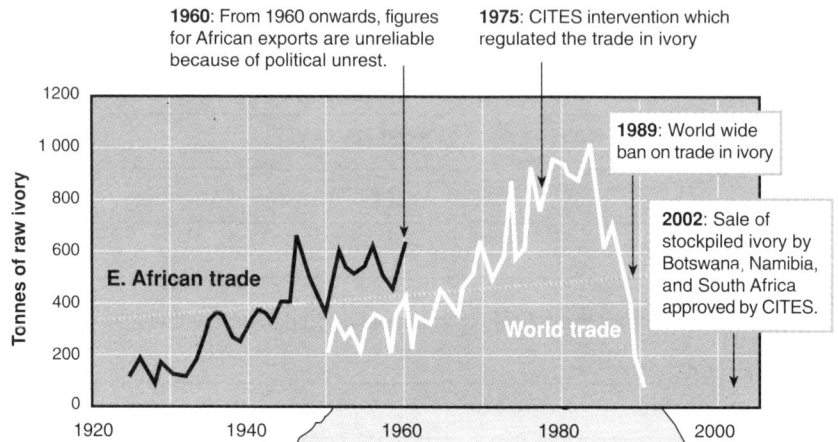

E. African trade

World trade

Distribution

Present

Former

African Elephant Census

	1995	1998
Definite:	286 234	301 773
Probable:	101 297	56 196
Possible:	155 944	60 780
Speculative:	36 057	68 596
Total:	**579 532**	**487 345**

These categories relate to the confidence limits of the various sampling methods used: aerial total counts, aerial sample counts, dung counts, informed guesses, and other guesses.

Source: **African Elephant Database (IUCN)**: (1995/1998) The website can be accessed via *Bio Links* from Biozone's website.

1. Outline the action taken in 1989 to try and stop the decline of the elephant populations in Africa: _____

_____

_____

2. In early 1999, Zimbabwe, Botswana and Namibia were allowed a one-off, CITES-approved, experimental sale of ivory to Japan. This involved the sale of 5,446 tusks (50 tonnes) and earned the governments approximately US$5 million.

   (a) Suggest why these countries are keen to resume ivory exports: _____

   _____

   (b) Suggest two reasons why the legal trade in ivory is thought by some to put the remaining elephants at risk:

   _____

   _____

Tropical Deforestation

Tropical rainforests prevail in places where the climate is very moist throughout the year (200 to 450 cm of rainfall per year). Almost half of the world's rainforests are in just 3 countries: **Brazil** in South America, **Zaire** in Africa, and **Indonesia** in Southeast Asia. Much of the world's biodiversity resides in rainforests. Destruction of the forests will contribute towards global warming through a large reduction in photosynthesis. In the Amazon, 75% of deforestation has occurred within 50 km of Brazil's roads. Many potential drugs could still be discovered in rainforest plants, and loss of species through deforestation may mean they will never be found. Rainforests can provide economically sustainable crops (rubber, coffee, nuts, fruits, and oils) for local people.

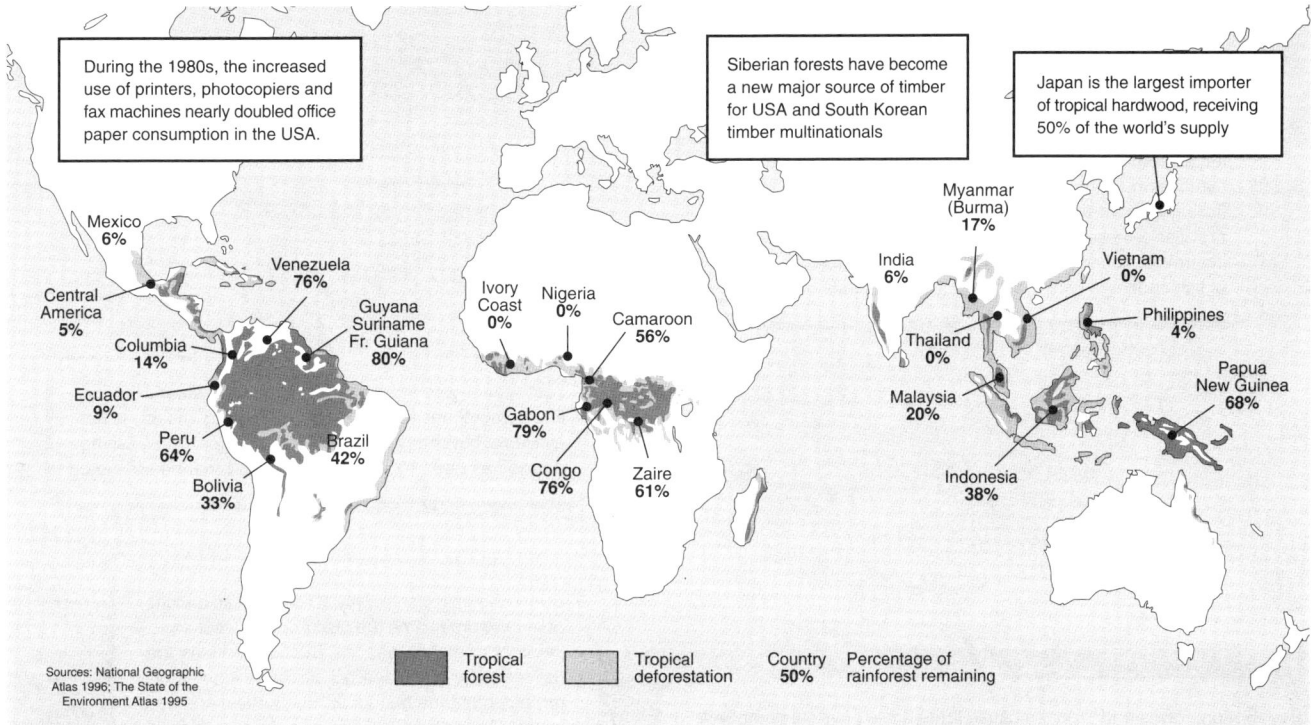

During the 1980s, the increased use of printers, photocopiers and fax machines nearly doubled office paper consumption in the USA.

Siberian forests have become a new major source of timber for USA and South Korean timber multinationals

Japan is the largest importer of tropical hardwood, receiving 50% of the world's supply

Mexico 6%

Central America 5%

Venezuela 76%

Guyana Suriname Fr. Guiana 80%

Columbia 14%

Ecuador 9%

Peru 64%

Bolivia 33%

Brazil 42%

Ivory Coast 0%

Nigeria 0%

Camaroon 56%

Gabon 79%

Congo 76%

Zaire 61%

Myanmar (Burma) 17%

India 6%

Vietnam 0%

Thailand 0%

Philippines 4%

Malaysia 20%

Papua New Guinea 68%

Indonesia 38%

Sources: National Geographic Atlas 1996; The State of the Environment Atlas 1995

Tropical forest | Tropical deforestation | Country 50% | Percentage of rainforest remaining

The felling of rainforest trees is taking place at an alarming rate as world demand for tropical hardwoods increases and land is cleared for the establishment of agriculture. The resulting farms and plantations often have shortlived productivity.

Huge forest fires have devastated large amounts of tropical rainforest in Indonesia and Brazil in 1997/98. The fires in Indonesia were started by people attempting to clear the forest areas for farming in a year of particularly low rainfall.

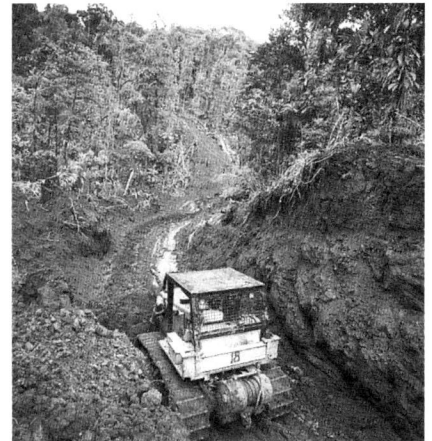

The building of new road networks into regions with tropical rainforests causes considerable environmental damage. In areas with very high rainfall there is an increased risk of erosion and loss of topsoil.

1. Describe three good reasons why tropical rainforests should be conserved:

   (a) _____

   (b) _____

   (c) _____

2. List the three main human activities that cause tropical deforestation: _____

   _____

3. Name the three countries that collectively contain almost half of the tropical rainforests in the world:

   _____

RA 2 Ecological Impacts of Fishing

Fishing is an ancient human tradition that not only satisfies our need for food, but is economically, socially, and culturally important. Today, however, tradition has been transformed in a worldwide resource extraction industry. Several decades of overfishing in all of the world's oceans has pushed commercially important species (such as cod) into steep decline. The United Nation's Food and Agriculture Organization (FAO) reports that almost seven out of ten of the ocean's commercially targeted marine fish stocks are either fully or heavily exploited (44%), over-exploited (16%), depleted (6%), or very slowly recovering from previous overfishing (3%). The **maximum sustainable yield** has been exceeded by too many fishing vessels catching too many fish, often using wasteful and destructive methods.

Over-capitalization of the fishing industry has led to the build up of excessive fishing fleets, particularly of the large scale vessels. This has led to widespread overfishing (with many fish stocks at historic lows and fishing effort at unprecedented highs). Not only are the activities of these large vessels ecologically unsustainable in terms of fish stocks but, on average, for every calorie of fish caught, a fishing vessel uses 15 calories of fuel.

Lost fishing gear (particularly drift nets) threatens marine life. Comprehensive data on **ghost fishing** impacts is not available, but entanglement in, and or ingestion of, fishing debris has been reported for over 250 marine species.

Bottom trawls and dredges cause large scale physical damage to the seafloor. Non-commercial, bottom-dwelling species in the path of the net can be uprooted, damaged, or killed, turning the seafloor into a barren, unproductive wasteland unable to sustain marine life. An area equal to half the world's continental shelves is now trawled every year. In other words, the world's seabed is being scraped 150 times faster than the world's forests are being clear-cut.

Due to the limited selectivity of fishing gear, millions of marine organisms are discarded for economic, legal, or personal reasons. Such organisms are defined as **by-catch** and include fish, invertebrates, protected marine mammals, sea turtles, and sea birds. Depending on the gear and handling techniques, some or all of the discarded animals die. A recent estimation of the worldwide by-catch is approximately 30 million tons per year, which is about one third of the estimated 85 million tons of catch that is retained each year.

Photo: Jane Ussher

NOAA

Longline fishing (mainly for tuna) results in the death of 100 000 albatrosses and petrels every year in the southern Pacific alone. Six of the world's twenty albatross species are in serious decline and longline fishing is implicated in each case.

Over-harvesting of abundant species, or removal of too many reproductive individuals from a population, can have far reaching ecological effects. Modern boats, with their sophisticated fish-finding equipment, have the ability to catch entire schools of fish.

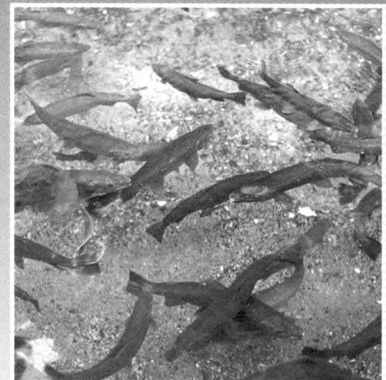

Fish farming, once thought to be the solution to the world's overfishing problems, actually accelerates the decline of wild fish stocks. Many farmed fish are fed meal made from wild fish, but it takes about one kilo of wild fish to grow 300 g of farmed fish. Some forms of fish farming destroy natural fish habitat and produce large scale effluent flows.

1. Explain the term **over-exploitation** in relation to commercial fisheries management: _____

_____

2. Define the term **by-catch**: _____

_____

The Peruvian Anchovy Fishery: An Example of Over-Exploitation

Before 1950, fish in Peru were harvested mainly for human consumption. The total annual catch was 86 000 tonnes. In 1953, the first fish meal plants were developed. Within nine years, Peru became the number one fishing nation in the world by volume; 1700 purse seiners exploited a seven month fishing season and Peru's economy was buoyant.

In 1970, fearing a crash, a group of scientists in the Peruvian government issued a warning. They estimated that the sustainable yield was around 9.5 million tonnes, a number that was being surpassed. The government decided to ignore this; due to the collapse of the Norwegian and Icelandic herring fisheries the previous year, Peru was the dominant player in the lucrative anchovy market. In 1970, the government allowed a harvest of 12.4 million tonnes. In 1971, 10.5 million tonnes were harvested. In 1972, the combination of environmental changes (El Niño) and prolonged overfishing led to a complete collapse of the fishery, which has never recovered.

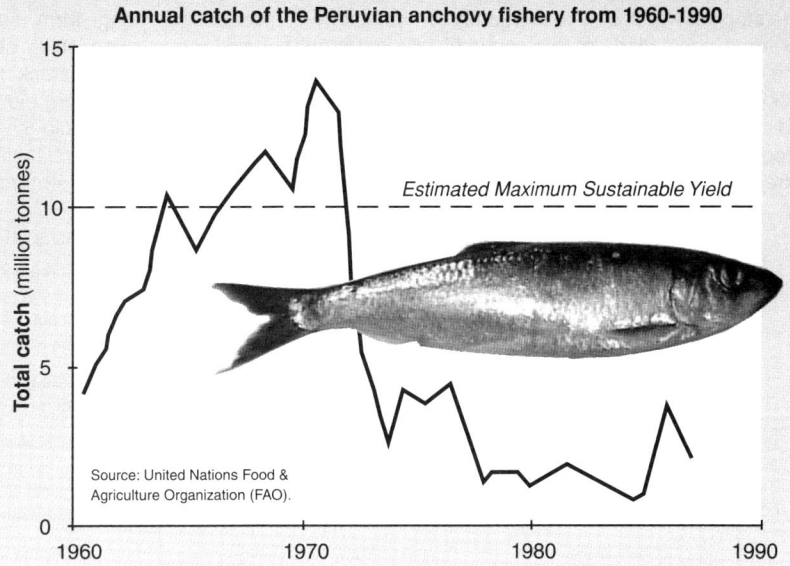

Annual catch of the Peruvian anchovy fishery from 1960-1990

Estimated Maximum Sustainable Yield

Source: United Nations Food & Agriculture Organization (FAO).

3. (a) Define the term **maximum sustainable yield (MSY)**: _____

_____

(b) Outline one major ecological impact of the collapse of the Peruvian anchovy fishery: _____

_____

4. Use the graph showing the relationship between age, biomass, and stock numbers in a commercially harvested fish population (below, right) to answer the following questions:

(a) State the optimum age at which the animals should be harvested:

_____

(b) Identify the age range during which the greatest increase in biomass occurs:

_____

(c) Suggest what other life history data would be required by fisheries scientists when deciding on the management plan for this population:

_____

_____

_____

The relationship between age, biomass and stock numbers in a commercially harvested fish population

Stock number

Biomass

Average mass (kg)

Number of individuals

Increase in biomass

Age in years

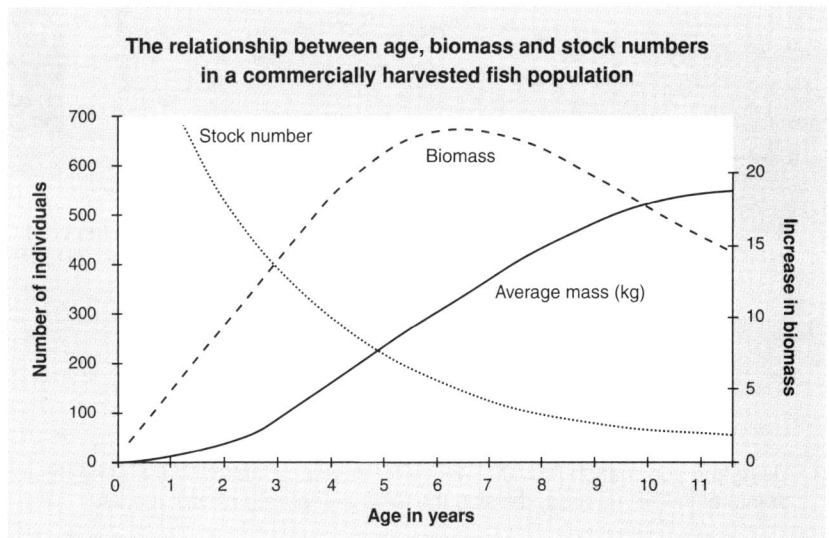

5. Suggest three methods by which fish populations can be conserved: _____

_____

_____

6. (a) Outline two advantages of marine fish farming: _____

_____

_____

(b) Outline two disadvantages of marine fish farming: _____

_____

Fisheries Management

A 2

The stock of North Sea cod (*Gadus morhua*) is one of the world's six large populations of this economically important species. As one of the most intensively studied, monitored, and exploited fish stocks in the North Sea, it is considered a highly relevant indicator of how well sustainable fisheries policies are operating. Stocks of commercially fished species must be managed carefully to ensure that the catch (take) does not undermine the long term sustainability of the fishery. This requires close attention to **stock indicators**, such as catch per unit of fishing effort, stock recruitment rates, population age structure, and spawning biomass. Currently, the North Sea cod stock is below safe biological limits and stocks are also depleted in all waters adjacent to the North Sea, where the species is distributed. Recent emergency measures plan to arrest this decline.

Total international landings of North Sea cod

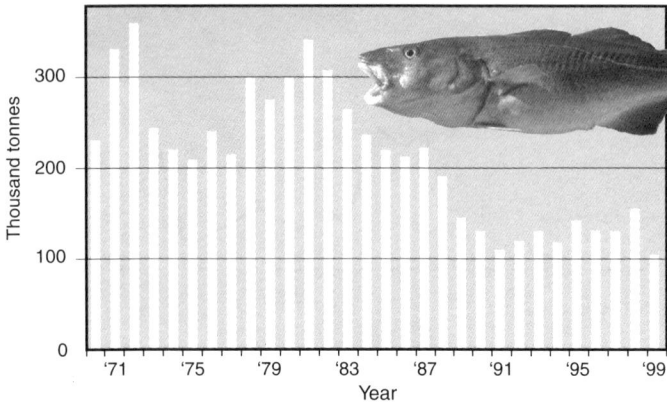

Recruitment and spawning stock biomass of North Sea cod

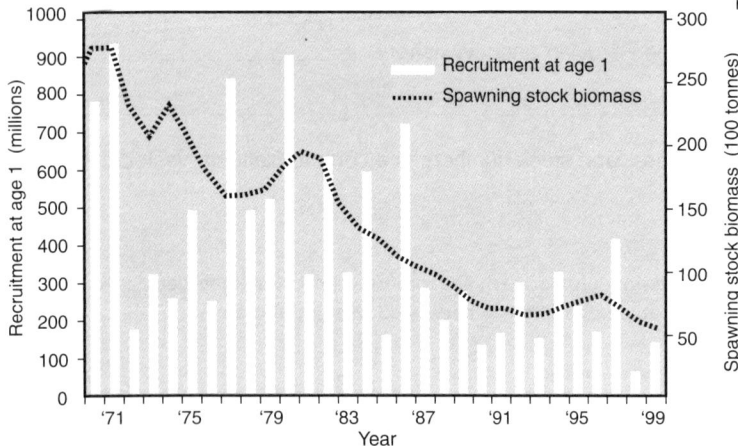

The state of the fishery

- Fishing mortality has increased gradually, and has been above the precautionary limit (that considered to be a safe take) since 1980 (left).

- Recruitment has been generally poor since 1987 (below, left).

- The number of spawning adults has fallen to levels below those required to recruit new individuals into the stock (below, left).

- ICES (the International Council for the Exploration of the Sea) advised that the spawning stock biomass (an indicator of the number of breeding adults) reached a new historic low in 2001, and that the risk of stock collapse is high.

What has been done?

- A large part of the North Sea was closed for cod fishing between February and April 2001, to protect juvenile cod .

- The TAC has been set at approximately half that set for the year 2000. Further regulations, such as increasing net mesh size and reducing the volume of fish discarded, are planned, and will further restrict the effort of fishing fleets until (if) the stock recovers.

- The ICES has recommended a recovery plan that will ensure recovery of the spawning stock to a level of more than 150 000 t. Reductions in TAC alone are insufficient to stop the declines.

Some important definitions

Stock: The part of the population from which catches are taken in a fishery

Stock recruitment: The entry of juvenile fish into the fish stock

Total Allowable Catch (TAC): The catch that can be legally taken from the stock

Stock collapse: Population level at which the fish stock cannot recover

Sources: European Environmental Agency (EEA), CEFAS (The Centre for Environment, Fisheries, and Aquaculture Science), and the ICES.

1. It has been known for more than a decade that the stock of cod in the North Sea has been declining drastically and that fishing takes were not sustainable. With reference to the data above, discuss the evidence to support this statement:

_____

_____

_____

2. Using the information provided above for guidance, describe the state the North Sea cod fishery, summarizing the main points below. If required, develop these as a separate report. Identify:

(a) The location of the fishery: _____

(b) The current state of the fishery (including stock status, catch rates, TAC, and quota): _____

_____

(c) Features of the biology of cod that are important in the management of the fishery (list): _____

_____

(d) Methods used to assess sustainability (list): _____

(e) Management options for the fishery (list): _____

_____

_____

Index